SMALL-TOWN DREAMS

Small-Town Dreams

STORIES OF MIDWESTERN

BOYS WHO SHAPED AMERICA

John E. Miller

University Press of Kansas

Published by the University Press of Kansas (Lawrence, Kansas
66045), which was organized by the Kansas Board of Regents and is
operated and funded by Emporia State University, Fort Hays State
University, Kansas State University, Pittsburg State University,
the University of Kansas, and Wichita State University

Library of Congress Cataloging-in-Publication Data

Miller, John E., 1945–
Small-town dreams : stories of Midwestern boys who shaped America /
John E. Miller.
pages cm.
Includes bibliographical references and index.
ISBN 978-0-7006-1949-8
1. Middle West—Biography. I. Title.
F350.5.M55 2014
977—dc23
2013041646

British Library Cataloguing-in-Publication Data is available.

Printed in the United States of America

10 9 8 7 6 5 4 3 2 1

The paper used in this publication is recycled and contains 30
percent postconsumer waste. It is acid free and meets the minimum
requirements of the American National Standard for Permanence of
Paper for Printed Library Materials z39.48-1992.

To Tom Miller—a small-town boy from the Midwest

Contents

vii

Acknowledgments and Note on Sources

A book of this sort depends upon the support and generous assistance of many people, and this one particularly so. Having thought about writing it for years beforehand, I began seriously researching the subject of small-town boys from the Midwest in 1999 when, during the summer, I visited Norfolk, Nebraska, Johnny Carson's hometown, and then, in the fall, drove my daughter, Ann, to graduate school at Yale and stayed for a week to work on Sinclair Lewis at the Beinecke Library and to study Charles Lindbergh at the Sterling Library. The following week, spent researching Bob Feller and Mickey Mantle at the National Baseball Hall of Fame in Cooperstown, New York, was a glorious interlude for one who became a historian because he was a baseball fan first. Naturally, I had to spend some of that time perusing files pertaining to my hero, Stan Musial; the St. Louis Cardinals were my team in the beginning and remain so today. Although I made significant progress that first year, while on sabbatical leave from South Dakota State University, the time it took to complete the book extended far longer than I had anticipated at the outset.

In the whittling down of my original cast of characters to twenty-two, chapters on Charles Lindbergh and Mickey Mantle got chopped, new names appeared and others were dropped, and much else was revised and rearranged. I began to tell people who inquired about my progress that I had taken John Wooden's advice to heart, quoting from Miguel de Cervantes: "The journey is more important than the destination." As the summers rolled by, I visited the hometowns of each of my subjects and traveled to dozens of libraries, archives, museums, historical sites, and other places where they had lived and worked. Two of the three men who were still living when the project commenced—John Wooden and Bob Feller—graciously agreed to interviews. Two letters to Johnny Carson failed to elicit a response. But I was able to talk to several of his schoolmates (Chuck Howser, Marilee Thorburn, Bob Bottorff, Bob Sewell, and Jerry Huse) and to his teacher and football coach, Fred Egley. I would also like to thank Fletcher Jennings, Bobby Burgess, Paul Samuelson, Hank Hansen, Harley Ransom, Art Fishbeck, and a number of others who were willing to discuss their friendship with or knowledge about the men I was studying and the towns with which they were associated.

The dozens of city libraries and ones located on college and university campuses, historical societies, archival sources, photographic collections, newspaper offices, and other sources of information that graciously assisted me are too numerous to mention, but I extend my thanks to everyone who responded to my inquiries and requests. I am particularly grateful for being allowed access to a variety of personal papers and other historical collections, including the following: Frederick Jackson Turner Papers, Huntington Library, San Marino, California; William Jennings Bryan Papers, Nebraska State Historical Society, Lincoln; Henry Ford Papers, Benson Ford Research Center, Dearborn, Michigan; Sinclair Lewis Papers, Beinecke Library, Yale University, New Haven, Connecticut; Sinclair Lewis Papers, St. Cloud State University Archives, St. Cloud, Minnesota; Carl Sandburg Papers, University of Illinois Archives, Urbana; Thomas Hart Benton Files, Nelson-Atkins Museum of Art, Kansas City, Missouri; Ernie Pyle Papers, Lilly Library, Indiana University, Bloomington; Bob Feller Museum, Van Meter, Iowa; Bob Feller Files, National Baseball Hall of Fame and Museum, Cooperstown, New York; Alvin Hansen Papers, Pusey Library, Harvard University, Cambridge, Massachusetts; James Dean Collection, Fairmount Historical Museum, Fairmount, Indiana; Sports Information Files, UCLA Athletic Department; Lawrence Welk Scrapbooks, North Dakota Institute for Regional Studies, North Dakota State University, Fargo; Ronald Reagan Papers, Reagan Presidential Library, Simi Valley, California; and Sam Walton and Wal-Mart Collections, University of Arkansas Archives, Fayetteville.

Photographs appearing in the chapter openers are courtesy of the following institutions: Wisconsin Historical Society, page 26; Nebraska State Historical Society (Bryan), page 47; Ohio Historical Society (McKinley), page 47; the Collections of the Henry Ford (THF97264), page 73; Library of Congress (Carver), page 92; South Dakota State Historical Society (Micheaux), page 92; Carl Van Vechten Trust, page 132; Rare Book and Manuscript Library, University of Illinois at Urbana-Champaign, page 150; State Historical Society of Missouri, page 171; Lilly Library, Indiana University, page 199; Harvard University Archives, HUP Hansen, Alvin (7), page 243; Bob Feller Museum, Van Meter, Iowa, page 257; Fairmount, Indiana, Historical Museum, page 274; Mason City Public Library Archives, page 293; Disney Enterprises, Inc., page 310; Welk Archives, Los Angeles (Welk), page 335; Elkhorn Valley Museum and Research Center, Norfolk, Nebraska (Carson), page 335; UCLA Athletics, page 367; Ronald Reagan Library, page 388; Special Collections, University of Arkansas Libraries, Fayetteville, page 410.

I wish to extend special thanks to a number of scholars and associates who generously lent their time to read and comment on one or more chapters and, in a couple of cases, the entire manuscript: Joseph A. Amato, Andrew R. L. Cayton, David B. Danbom, Richard Fried, Joshua C. Hall, Jon K. Lauck, Susan J. Matt, Thomas K. McCraw, Gary D. Olson, Jon H. Roberts, Michael E. Stevens, and Charles L. Woodard. Their advice did much to reduce errors and infelicities and to enhance the quality of the book, but I take full responsibility for any factual errors or mistaken interpretations that inevitably creep into works of this sort.

My life has been hugely enhanced by the love and support of our daughter, Ann, who observed how attractive a scholar's life could be and decided to become one herself, and our son, Tom, another small-town boy from the Midwest and to whom this book is dedicated. My wife, Kathy, deserves a badge of honor for listening to most of these stories multiple times, which is only one of the many excellent qualities that make her so lovable.

All writing boils down in large part to the question of what to put in and what to leave out. What an author knows of his or her subject, in turn, derives from the amount and richness of the sources that are available, the amount of time that can be had to study them, and one's ability to assimilate and interpret the information. For a number of my subjects, for example, Henry Ford, Sinclair Lewis, Walt Disney, Ronald Reagan, and Sam Walton, the sources were so extensive that a great deal simply had to be set aside in attempting to take a fair measure of the man within the framework of my inquiry. On the other hand, for one man, Alvin Hansen, there has as yet been no proper biography, and for another, Meredith Willson, biographies (two, in fact) began to appear only after I had done most of my research and had started to write. With regard to Frederick Jackson Turner, I enjoyed the luxury of investigating his papers while attending a five-week seminar sponsored by the National Endowment for the Humanities at the Huntington Library, which houses the collection. Personal papers were crucial for my investigations in several other instances, but for a number of my subjects, books and other printed sources constituted the bulk of my research material. Each essay posed its own special requirements, and thus the nature of the discussion varies from chapter to chapter. Throughout, however, the focus has been on the ways in which the small-town or farm origins of the men on whom I have chosen to concentrate affected their later lives, attitudes, and behaviors.

The Boys' Hometowns

North Dakota
Lawrence Welk

Minnesota

South Dakota

Sinclair Lewis

Wisconsin

Frederick Jackson Turner

Michigan

Alvin Hansen

Johnny Carson

Nebraska

Meredith Willson

Iowa

Grant Wood

Ronald Reagan

James Dean

Henry Ford

William McKinley

Ohio

Bob Feller

Carl Sandburg

Indiana

Walt Disney

Illinois

Ernie Pyle

John Steuart Curry

Kansas

Missouri

William Jennings Bryan

John Wooden

Sam Walton

Oscar Micheaux

George Washington Carver

Thomas Hart Benton

Scale in Miles

0   200

North Dakota
Lawrence Welk - *Strasburg*

South Dakota
Alvin Hansen - *Viborg*

Nebraska
Johnny Carson - *Norfolk*

Kansas
John Steuart Curry - *Dunavant*

Minnesota
Sinclair Lewis - *Sauk Centre*

Iowa
Meredith Willson - *Mason City*
Bob Feller - *Van Meter*
Grant Wood - *Anamosa*

Missouri
Walt Disney - *Marceline*
Sam Walton - *Columbia*
George Washington Carver - *Diamond*
Thomas Hart Benton - *Neosho*

Wisconsin
Frederick Jackson Turner - *Portage*

Illinois
Ronald Reagan - *Dixon*
Carl Sandburg - *Galesburg*
William Jennings Bryan - *Salem*
Oscar Micheaux – *Metropolis*

Michigan
Henry Ford – *Dearborn*

Indiana
James Dean – *Fairmount*
Ernie Pyle – *Dana*
John Wooden - *Martinsville*

Ohio
William McKinley – *Canton*

George Skoch

Midwestern Small Towns and the Experience of Place

The country town is one of the great American institutions; perhaps the greatest, in the sense that it has had and continues to have a greater part than any other in shaping public sentiment and giving character to American culture.

—Thorstein Veblen

I wrote this book because I believe that small towns have garnered less attention from journalists and scholars, including my own fraternity of historians, than they deserve.[1] Writing in 1947, the literary critic Granville Hicks observed that "it was not so long ago that the United States was a nation of small towns, and we have not outgrown our small-town heritage." Several years later, the historian Lewis Atherton noted that the history of the Middle West "has been largely the history of its towns."[2] The United States today has become a nation largely dominated by its cities and metropolitan complexes, but by definition, all cities, large and small, wherever they exist, had their origins as small towns.

History, it has been said, is written by and for the winners, and for nearly a century small towns have not generally been on the winning side. Rural towns and their surrounding hinterlands were home to about seven of every ten Americans in 1900. By 2000, that figure had dropped to only two in ten.[3] From being located at the center of the action for much of American history, extending all the way back to the earliest colonial settlements, small towns have devolved, in the eyes of many observers, into cultural backwaters, and today they fail to register very highly on the public's attention meter.

Public opinion polls show Americans in large numbers professing a desire to live in small-town atmospheres and preferring to move to non-

1

metropolitan areas. Yet they often scorn and denigrate people who actually reside there. Too often, their knowledge of such places and their understanding of the people who inhabit them is wanting. Few of them ever actually move to rural environments or even seriously consider the possibility. The small town has become a vague concept in many people's minds of an alternative way of life, an escape from the city and the suburbs, a nostalgic return to a place that never was—in a word, a myth.[4]

This book, then, seeks to enhance our understanding of the importance of the small town in American life and the influence it has exerted across time. Telling the entire story would require a shelf of books, because for most of U.S. history this was a nation largely composed of small towns and their rural environs. But inevitably change has come, and in recent years with a rush. In the memorable words of the historian Richard Hofstadter, "The United States was born in the country and has moved to the city."[5] In the span of a generation or two after the Civil War, a people that had historically been to a large degree characterized and defined by its towns and farms was transformed into one dominated and given meaning by its cities and industries.

In the process, much was gained, but much was also lost. Having passed through the take-off stage of economic growth during the years before the Civil War, the United States rapidly proceeded during the late nineteenth century through a tumultuous phase of industrialization, urbanization, and bureaucratization that produced stunning increases in economic output, income, and wealth, accompanied by massive social change and dislocation. By the time the United States entered World War I, it was becoming increasingly difficult to remember that only a relatively short time earlier the nation had consisted of, in the words of the historian Robert Wiebe, a conglomeration of "island communities" in which people's lives and thoughts revolved around local concerns and happenings and for whom events in distant places were, by and large, of small import.[6]

Yet if in retrospect it seems obvious that small towns would necessarily give way to the metropolis in terms of power, influence, and sheer numbers of residents, millions of people still resided in those towns and in the countryside, and many new urban dwellers remained in the thrall of small-town habits, values, and ways of thinking. The lingering presence of the small town in the American psyche continued far into the twentieth century and, to a significant degree, remains a powerful presence today. Call it nostalgia, call it cultural lag, call it what you will—Americans have yet to rid themselves of their deeply felt, emotional ties to their small-town origins.

A nerve was struck during the 2008 election when Republican presidential candidate John McCain chose as his running mate Alaska governor Sarah Palin, who hailed from Wasilla, a town of 7,000. For much of the Republican base, this was an energizing moment, as millions of conservative voters who lived in small towns or who identified with small-town values and folkways recognized in the forty-four-year-old self-styled maverick one of their own. In her acceptance speech at the convention, Palin sought to fire up delegate enthusiasm with a quotation from 1930s right-wing newspaper columnist Westbrook Pegler: "We grow good people in our small towns, with honesty and sincerity and dignity," adding in her own words that small-town people are "the ones who do some of the hardest work in America, who grow our food and run our factories and fight our wars."[7] Liberal pundits and critics, meanwhile, were quick to counter with the observation that small towns are not the exclusive preserve of conservatives and that being mayor of a small town and governor of a sparsely populated state hardly constitute sufficient qualification for being a heartbeat away from the presidency. Putting aside the merits of the debate, what is striking about the episode is the emotional energy and contentiousness unleashed by McCain's decision. He clearly understood the symbolism involved in his choice, as was evidenced by his own immediate postconvention itinerary, which launched the Republicans' general election campaign by taking him and Palin to stops in the small-town Midwest, where the surrounding atmospherics of Main Street America were on prominent display.

By 2008, these kinds of efforts at media symbolism had become little more than political spin and appeals to a bygone way of life. The actual impact of small-town America in the exercise of power and in the broader decision-making process of the nation was meager at best. Demography, it has been said, is destiny, and the story told by the census over the decades has been stark. An early tipping point occurred in 1920, when for the first time urban Americans (arbitrarily defined as people living in places of 2,500 or more) outnumbered their rural cousins, 51.2 percent to 48.8 percent. By 1950, the urban percentage had risen to 64.0 percent, and in 2000 the urban percentage stood at 79.0. By then, more than half of all Americans lived in metropolitan areas of at least 1 million people, and nearly one-third of the total population lived in ones containing at least 5 million people.

But demographics do not constitute the entire story. Even as most of the smallest towns began to lose population absolutely and even as rural America as a whole declined in relative political and cultural clout, they retained an influence disproportionate to their declining numbers. In a *Time* magazine column written in 1976, when Jimmy Carter—"the man from Plains"—was running for the presidency, political commentator Hugh Sidey noted that, with the exception of John F. Kennedy, every twentieth-century president after William Howard Taft had been born or raised in a small town. He quoted Bill Moyers, a small-town boy from Texas, who observed, "I think a person gets a better grip on himself and the world when he spends these early years in a smaller place," and he cited favorably the New York intellectual Irving Kristol's contention that the citification of the United States had been exaggerated: "We do have an urbanized culture, but we are not a city people."[8]

Thirty-two years later, however, after Ronald Reagan, who hailed from small-town northern Illinois; Bill Clinton, "the man from Hope"; and George H. W. and George W. Bush, deriving from Connecticut and Texas, had completed their turns in the White House, Peggy Noonan, a former Reagan speechwriter, bemoaned in the pages of the *Wall Street Journal* "the end of placeness" as one of the identifying features of the 2008 campaign. Barack Obama? "He's from Young. He's from the town of Smooth in the state of Well Educated. He's from TV," she commented. And John McCain? "He's from Military. He's from Vietnam Township in the Sunbelt State." Neither candidate, to Noonan's way of thinking, "has or gives a strong sense of place in the sense that American politicians almost always have, since Mr. Jefferson of Virginia, and Abe Lincoln of Illinois, and FDR of New York, and JFK of Massachusetts."[9]

And so with the rest of us. It is not so much that place has lost all significance in our lives, but rather that the terms in which we think about it have been transformed in ways we seldom stop to consider. Having removed ourselves from small towns, where people often knew each other personally and interacted face-to-face, to larger towns, cities, and metropolitan areas, where most of the people we meet on the street are unfamiliar to us and where human interactions are increasingly anonymous, we have become, in large measure, a people for whom place is more and more abstract, artificial, and ephemeral—in a word, unreal.

This book thus is also an effort to comment on and reassert the importance of place in people's lives, with a specific emphasis on the small-town experience, which, after all, for most of American history provided the locus, along with rural farmsteads, where most people lived out their daily lives. The cultural geographer Yi-Fu Tuan has eloquently described the emotional attachments people carry to the landscapes in which they grew up. He uses the term "topophilia" to refer to the affective bonds that tie individuals to the settings in which they live. The literary scholar Stephen C. Behrendt writes, "People tend to identify with their earliest experiences and the places in which those experiences transpired, perhaps because those residual places and experiences provide a security that rootless adulthood usually denies us." Or, in the words of the homely aphorism, "Tell me where you come from and I will tell you who you are."[10]

The power of place in influencing human lives has been recognized throughout the course of human history. Our thoughts, our emotions, and our behavior all derive to a significant degree from our surroundings, as well as from our genetic makeup and neurochemistry, family background, education, social situation, and personal relationships.[11] But people are not merely passive receptors of environmental signals; from early on, they actively help create the contexts in which they live. In the words of author Becky Bradway, "We create place and are shaped by it."[12] It is a dialectical process. For the young boys growing up in the Midwest who are the subjects of this book, the impact of the social environment on them admittedly was greater than their reciprocal impact on that environment, but the experiences, memories, attitudes, hopes, and dreams they carried with them into adulthood all emerged out of a dynamic dialectic that occurred between themselves and the places in which they were born and grew up. U.S. senator and 1996 Republican presidential candidate Bob Dole, who grew up in Russell, Kansas, spoke for countless others like him when he said, "I long ago outgrew my boyhood house. But I have never outgrown my boyhood home, and I hope I never will. A house, after all, is a roof over your head. A home is a classroom of character, usually a classroom without walls. In this case, home was a small town whose sense of community was as vast as the Kansas prairie."[13]

It is not my intention, however, to argue for "home" as a universal ideal or as an unqualified good. The idea of home, as the novelist Marilynne Robinson tells us, is always complicated by feelings of ambivalence and ambiguity.[14] Not everyone remembers their home or homes with affection or enthusiasm. And even for those who retain warm feelings for and positive memories of their childhood homes, the opportunity to leave home and to pursue new adventures and make successes of themselves is a liberating force that drives them on to new achievements and more expansive goals. Many of the young men described in this book departed their hometowns at the first opportunity without looking back, while most of them nurtured positive memories of those towns that provided emotional ballast and support.

My purpose thus is somewhat different from that of the historian Susan J. Matt in her excellent book *Homesickness: An American History*. Longing for a lost home, which is the essence of homesickness, traces back to ancient times. Matt takes note of the appearance of the term in colonial America during the years preceding the Revolution and traces its evolution across the decades right up to the present. She distinguishes it from "nostalgia," or a yearning for a lost time, observing that while nostalgia admits the ultimate impossibility of either literally going back to the home of one's childhood or figuratively returning to the time in which it took place, it allows for a sense of comfort and stability that many people deem mentally beneficial. Both "homesickness" and "nostalgia" have taken on negative connotations to one degree or other in the minds of many observers. My focus in these pages is simply to describe how the conscious memories of and sometimes the unconscious feelings associated with my subjects' places of their childhood resonated with them in later life and made an impact on their thoughts and behavior. At least for these individuals, they served as crucial factors in formulating a stable notion of self and in establishing patterns of thought and behavior that would be important to them, to one degree or other, in later life.[15]

Ironically, in the past, although people generally enjoyed less choice than they do today over where they would live, they more closely identified with those places than people usually do now. All around us lies evidence of an attenuated sense of place in a society in which every locale has begun to look alike: huge, faceless, national and international corporations now dominate the marketplace; supercharged and constantly evolving forms of electronic media bombard people with overloads of information and visual and auditory stimuli; and old habits, patterns, and traditions rapidly fall by the wayside in the wake of new technologies, industrial change, and cultural transformation. Social critics and commentators speak now not merely of a *loss* of place but of a *crisis* of place. The latter phrase implies that we suffer from a crisis of *community* as well. "We have become accustomed to living in places where nothing relates to anything else, where disorder, unconsciousness, and the absence of respect reign unchecked," writes author and cultural critic James Howard Kunstler. "The small town life that Americans long for when they are depressed by their city apartments or their suburban bunkers is really a conceptual substitute for the idea of community."[16]

It was not always thus. "The American country town," William Allen White asserted in 1912, "preserves better than the crowded city and better than the lonely ranch and isolated farm life the things that make America great." The Emporia, Kansas, newspaper editor, a product of the small town and an impassioned defender of it, was certainly biased in its defense, but he also knew whereof he spoke. He remained confident regarding the small town's future and was committed to its preservation. With its "broad circle of friendships," the "close homely simple relations" among its residents, its "spirit of co-operation," and a general level of equality that permitted the emergence of "no immensely rich and no abjectly poor," the country town, he believed, was "the most hopeful of our American institutions."[17] A century later, I believe, he would be astonished and perplexed by what he would see.

The same social forces that have contributed to the withering away of place have helped undermine the notion of community from the second half of the twentieth century right up to the present: the impact of the electronic media, especially television; increasing dependency on the automobile, particularly with the building of the Interstate Highway System; the growing ubiquity of air-conditioning; the expansion of malls and big-box discount stores; the proliferation of franchised fast-food eateries, filling stations, motels, and stores of all kinds; and the standardization of newspapers, school curriculums, popular music. All these tendencies contribute to the balkanization of society, to the fragmentation of lives and identities, to the loss of a sense of place, and to the notion that we exist "elsewhere."[18] Wendell Berry, the Kentucky poet, essayist, and eloquent spokesman for localism, laments, "Increasingly, Americans—including, notoriously, their politicians—are not *from* anywhere."[19]

What author Harry Crews observed about southern writing in 1986—that the region's dream of neighborhood, including its distinctive speech patterns, music, food, and even worship practices, had all disappeared—could apply to every region of the country. "Now our manners are gone and our idiom turns up in the *Journal of Popular Culture*," Crews complained. "The food we eat comes from McDonald's and our preachers are more interested in sociology than theology. There is just enough of the dream of neighborhood left to caricature all that it once was."[20]

If regional distinctiveness is in decline in the United States, the trend is doubly evident with regard to the Middle West, which has generally projected a vaguer and more elusive image than its counterparts.[21] Although this study only obliquely addresses the theme of midwestern regionalism, that phenomenon provides some of the context for the biographical essays that make it up. I am heartened by the reviving interest in regionalism as a general phenomenon and in the midwestern variant in particular. A major impulse behind writing this book has been to make a contribution to our understanding of midwestern history and culture.

Exactly what comprises the Midwest poses an interesting question, and notions about the geographic limits of the region have evolved over time. Here, I simply follow the standard definition currently accepted by most historians, geographers, journalists, and government agencies, which includes the twelve states running west and north from Ohio to the Dakotas: Ohio, Michigan, Indiana, Wisconsin, Illinois, Minnesota, Iowa, Missouri, North Dakota, South Dakota, Nebraska, and Kansas.[22] The region has typically been defined as much by absence as by the presence of certain distinctive elements or characteristics. Whatever is peculiar about the Midwest, it sometimes seems, is what is left over after considering New England and the Northeast, with their Puritan heritage, industrial development, and centers of politics and culture; the South, home of slaves and plantations and inheritor of the legacy of the Civil War; and the West, with its majestic scenery, exploitable natural resources, and images of cowboys, Indians, and gunfights in the O.K. Corral. All of these are caricatures, of course, but the Midwest seems less amenable to caricature than does any other region. How do you exaggerate "normalcy"? Midwestern historian Andrew Cayton contends that people generally do not feel passionate about the region; that journalists, novelists, and filmmakers have projected a midwestern image of "normalcy and niceness"; that when it comes to history, not much seems to have happened; and that the area's outstanding military and political figures—from Abraham Lincoln and Ulysses S. Grant to Herbert Hoover and Dwight D. Eisenhower—have by and large been ordinary and uncharismatic figures. "The Midwest, it would seem," he observes, "is a place where, to paraphrase Gertrude Stein's famous line, there is no there there."[23]

Be that as it may, there was a time, between the Civil War and World

War I, when the Middle West was the ascendant region of the country and when outsiders looked to it for leadership, energy, and creativity. Containing 28.9 percent of the nation's population in 1860, the Midwest saw its share steadily rise to a peak of 35.6 percent in 1890 and then gradually decline to 29.5 percent in 1950 and 22.9 percent in 2000. One of the Civil War's many unanticipated consequences was to lift up the Middle West to a place of preeminence within the sectional scheme. Historians Cayton and Susan E. Gray have observed that "in the second half of the nineteenth century there was no more dynamic or powerful regional story in the United States than the one that Midwesterners told about themselves."[24] The region, in its very tendency toward the mean and the middle ground, seemed in the minds of many observers to embody the broader aspirations and values of the entire American public. "The 'Middle West,' the prairie country, has been the center of active social philosophies and political progressivism," John Dewey wrote in 1922. In his view, it had "formed the solid element in our diffuse national life and heterogeneous populations. . . . Like every mean it has held things together and given unity and stability of movement."[25] But broad historical forces were operating by the middle of the twentieth century to deflect attention away from the Middle West. Whereas from 1861 to 1961, eleven of eighteen occupants of the White House had grown up in the Midwest, during the half-century after 1961 only two of ten presidents did.

So long as agriculture remained a sizable and powerful economic force, the midwestern breadbasket was the pride of the country. The premier industry in the United States, the manufacture of automobiles, was concentrated around Detroit in Michigan, Ohio, and Indiana. Chicago, the nation's second-largest city, had emerged by the time of the Civil War as the railroad—and thus the transportation—hub of the nation. During the postbellum period, Chicago's steel industry, stockyards, lumber mills, grain elevators, newspapers, and architectural innovations were at or near the top in the nation. In the twentieth century, Chicago writers from Carl Sandburg, Harriet Monroe, and Sherwood Anderson to James T. Farrell, Ernest Hemingway, and Saul Bellow stood in the forefront of American l etters. The University of Chicago and a bevy of midwestern state universities vied for influence with Harvard, Yale, Princeton, and other higher-educational institutions.

Once, the *Chicago Tribune, Cleveland Plain Dealer,* and *St. Louis Post-Dispatch* stood toe to toe with the *New York Times, Boston Globe,* and

Los Angeles Times as sources of news and political commentary. Midwestern professional sports teams in baseball, football, and basketball ranked with their rivals from the Northeast. Not till the 1950s did such sports franchises begin to spread south of the Ohio and west of the Mississippi. Until 1953, the Midwest was home to seven of the sixteen major-league baseball clubs; the Northeast claimed the other nine. The Big Ten athletic conference ranked supreme in college football, and although considerable competition existed elsewhere, Indiana reigned as the basketball capital of the nation.

During the latter decades of the twentieth century, with proliferating references to the region as the "Rust Belt" and the "forgotten quarter," the Midwest found itself readjusting its ambitions and images of itself. The so-called heartland appeared no longer to spell dominance and pride of place. Despite its relative loss of status and influence and its smaller share of population, with a resultant reduction of representation in the House of Representatives, the Midwest continued to play important roles in agriculture, manufacturing, politics, scientific research, education, and cultural creativity. Signs of the region's renewed vitality can be found in books like Robert Wuthnow's *Remaking the Heartland: Middle America since the 1950s*.[26]

The stories told here begin in the 1890s and continue right up to the present; I present them in an effort to comprehend both the continuity of small-town influence and the changes that have occurred over time. Putting the focus on the Midwest is partly accidental, partly intentional, and partly a matter of practicality. It quickly became apparent that trying to cover the entire United States would make the book much too long. Weighing breadth against depth, I opted for the latter, trusting that other writers could train their attention on other regions of the country, assuming that similar processes operated there to make one's place of origin highly influential on one's development in later life. Writing a book about small-town boys from the Midwest comes naturally to someone who fits into that category himself. I was born in a small town in north-central Kansas and grew up in four more of them in Missouri and one in Illinois. For the past thirty-nine years I have lived in Brookings, South Dakota, a university town of a little more than 20,000 people. It is no little Nirvana, but it has been an appealing place for me and my wife to live in and, as people say, a "great place to raise" our two children.

An additional reason to focus on the Midwest is that it has been the most neglected region of the country as a subject for scholarly research during recent decades. New England and the Northeast, the South, and the West all have their own historical societies, scholarly journals, conferences, college courses, textbooks, and other types of attention. The Midwest benefits from hardly any of these. Several historical journals that once focused on the region, such as *The Old Northwest, Upper Midwest History,* and *Mid-America: An Historical Review,* have disappeared. In Chicago, the demise after just several issues of *The Midwesterner,* which touted itself as a regional version of the *New Yorker,* was a telling indicator of the relative dearth of cultural supports that exist for a distinctive sense of midwestern regionalism. The twelve state historical societies in the region are quite active, and much good historical work gets accomplished, but a great deal remains to be done to promote a collective sense of midwesternness.

A parallel case exists for promoting the history of small towns. Evidence of interest in small-town history is extensive, and a number of excellent books on the subject have been written in recent years.[27] Yet in comparison to the books and articles that have appeared about the history of cities and suburbs, small-town history lags far behind. The "new urban history" that emerged during the 1960s, accompanied by its own college courses and programs, textbooks, scholarly conferences, and journals, devoted relatively little attention to the role of small towns. These historians spent far more time investigating large cities, the growth of suburbs, urban sprawl, the rise of edge cities, and the growing spread of megalopolis. The time has come to rectify this imbalance by reasserting the profound historical importance of small towns in American history.

Between the 1940s and the 1960s, Richard Hofstadter, brilliant and insightful historian as he was, contributed to the diminution of small towns as a legitimate subject of study. Earlier, in promulgating his frontier thesis of American history, Frederick Jackson Turner had placed rural society at the heart of his analysis, and his interpretation of the frontier derived primarily from his understanding of his own native Middle West. During the 1920s, a successor of his at Harvard, Arthur M. Schlesinger Sr., developed an urban interpretation of American history. For Schlesinger, small towns were something of an afterthought; in Hofstadter's hands, they all too often became objects of derision. Small towns had furnished the formative experiences for Turner and Schlesinger, as they did for many other historians of their generations. In contrast, Hofstadter, who grew up in Buffalo, New York, emerged as a quintessential New York intellectual after moving to the city in 1936, first to study law, then to enter graduate study in history at Columbia University. He later became a professor at the school, remaining until his death in 1970.[28]

Few American intellectuals of the 1950s and 1960s exerted more of an impact than Hofstadter. His perspective was urban through and through. "As a historian, he legitimized the city," wrote fellow historian Jack Pole in 2000.[29] His lack of firsthand knowledge of the Middle West or of its small towns made it easy for him to believe that Sinclair Lewis's narrow-minded village dwellers, eruptions of Ku Klux Klan activity, and enthusiasm for the rants of Senator Joseph McCarthy were all typical of the Middle West as a region.[30] Whereas Frederick Jackson Turner overemphasized the western frontier and scanted urban places, Hofstadter and historians of his inclination failed to give small towns and rural America their due. Small towns as a category and the Midwest as a region deserve a closer and more balanced look than he and some of his colleagues were willing to give them.

Readers may wonder why I have not been as interested in rectifying gender imbalance in this study. Needless to say, it is not because I bear any animus against women. I have written three books about a small-town girl from the Midwest, Laura Ingalls Wilder, with frequent references to her daughter and writing collaborator, Rose Wilder Lane. With more time, I would love to probe more deeply into the subject of small-town women but have chosen here to focus my resources.

A final note on methodology. One way of examining the impact of small-town backgrounds on a sample of about two dozen highly successful men would be to look for regularities in their ideas and behavior and to attempt to specify cause and effect in statistical terms. One might probe the connections that exist between farm backgrounds and self-reliance, entrepreneurialism, ingenuity, or conservative politics. Or one might delineate the relationships existing between small-town childhoods and traits of optimism, civic-mindedness, drive, and ambition. Such an investigation might be quite useful, but that is not my approach in this book. It would take a larger sample than I have assembled to arrive at any rigorous conclusions. There is a place and a use for such endeavors. Social scientists who extrapolate behavioral regularities from mounds of data have much to teach us. Equally impressive is the unpredictability of people's behavior in any particular instance.

I start from the premise that human beings are individuals—complex, ambivalent, and variable creatures who are difficult to fathom and pigeonhole. People exercise considerable freedom within the constraints and pressures imposed on them. Garrison Keillor, a small-town boy from Anoka, Minnesota, underlined this point in one of his radio monologues about the fictional Lake Wobegon. "This is a country that believes in openness—openness of human nature, whether it be Ray Charles or Ronald Reagan, or both of them together," he noted. "We believe in individuals. We believe that the crucial differences are between individuals, not between groups. . . . And that is freedom—not to be trapped within your category." True stories, to his way of thinking, are about individuals, not groups, such as womanhood, manhood, "westernness," or "easternness." People, he suggested, are too various in their attitudes, inclinations, habits, and ideas to make blanket generalizations about them as members of groups.[31]

People's thoughts and behavior are often highly unpredictable, varying with time, place, and circumstances. People frequently change considerably over time and behave differently when operating within different groups and in response to varying cues, pressures, and influences. We all have a variety of roles to play as context and circumstances change. All of this suggests that choice and unpredictability matter as much as necessity and patterned or regular behavior. Our hypotheses and generalizations about people thus must remain tentative and contingent.

This book illustrates the variety of ways in which the experience of growing up in small towns or on farms in the Middle West influenced young men who went on to distinction in a variety of fields. These highly accomplished individuals were hardly representative of midwesterners in general. But in heightened form these stories dramatically illustrate how place exerts profound effects on people's lives. For example, Meredith Willson was so fond of telling stories about his childhood days in Mason City, Iowa, that he finally took up the challenge of a show-business friend of his to write a musical play about the town. Henry Ford was so in thrall to rural nostalgia that he built a historical reconstruction of small-town America, calling it Greenfield Village, and he later spent millions of dollars relocating some of his industrial facilities to small-town settings. John Wooden imbibed values and teachings learned at home and on the playing fields and basketball courts of Martinsville, Indiana, to such a degree that he later incorporated them in his famous Pyramid of Success, which he continued to use as a teaching tool into his late nineties and which inspired numerous books, videos, and seminars developed by other teachers of character education. Bob Feller was universally identified in the public mind with his hometown of Van Meter as the "Iowa Farm Boy" in a way that current ballplayers seldom are. Sinclair Lewis felt the sting of students' taunts and suffered from feelings of being stifled in the social environment of Sauk Centre, Minnesota, so keenly that when he was thirty-five he wrote an acerbic novel based on the town, but a decade later he admitted that it had been a good time as well as a good place for him to grow up. William Jennings Bryan's famous "Cross of Gold" speech, enshrined in American history textbooks, derived directly from attitudes and ideas that took root in him during his boyhood days in small-town Illinois. All the figures discussed in this book were affected in one way or another by their small-town or rural childhoods.

The stories told in this book are additive, cumulative, and mutually re-inforcing. I cannot *prove* that the imprint of one's time and place in child-hood deeply influences one's later behavior and thought processes. Nor could a thousand quantitative studies make an irrefutable case for the proposition. Ten examples might have sufficed as well as twenty-two to make a prima facie case, and thirty-five or ninety-five would probably have been even more persuasive. But twenty-two seems to be about the right number to illustrate the variety of experiences of growing up in small mid-western towns. I include at least one person from each of the twelve states in the region in order to provide a variety of examples from a number of walks of life, and to trace historical change and continuity I cover a time span extending over the course of a century.

I believe that the cases described here are sufficient to establish the plau-sibility of my thesis and to suggest that parallel processes were operating in the lives of many other midwestern boys, including those who stayed in the towns or regions in which they were born. "We are all regionalists in our origins, however 'universal' our themes and characters," the novelist and short-story writer Joyce Carol Oates has written, "and without our cher-ished hometowns and childhood landscapes to nourish us, we would be like plants set in shallow soil. Our souls must take root—almost liter-ally."[32] The stories contained in this volume demonstrate that the phenom-enon of roots applies not only to writers such as Oates but to a wide variety of people, including many who have grown up in the Middle West.

■

Small Towns in the Crucible of Change, 1890–1920

Introduction to Section I

For its first three centuries of development, two of them under colonial rule by Great Britain and the third as a rising nation, the United States remained heavily influenced by its village and small-town origins. At George Washington's inauguration in 1789, more than 90 percent of the population still made its living from farming, and more than 95 percent of the people lived in places defined as rural (fewer than 2,500 population). During the decades after the Civil War, accelerating trends of industrialization and urbanization worked a profound transformation in the American economy and society, and by the turn of the century great and rapidly expanding cities such as New York (population: 3,437,202), Philadelphia (1,293,697), Boston (560,892), Baltimore (508,957), Cleveland (381,768), Detroit (285,704), Chicago (1,698,575), St. Louis (575,238), New Orleans (287,104), and San Francisco (342,782) had begun to dominate American life and culture.

As modernizing trends spread their impact through every sector of the society, residents of small towns perceived that their way of life was losing ground to urban forces and influences. In 1900, the 6.3 million people who lived in 8,931 places with less than 2,500 population constituted 8.3 percent of the population, numbering slightly fewer than the 6.4 million who lived in the three cities of more than a million, which made up 8.5 percent of the population. Another 2.9 million people lived in the 832 towns of between 2,500 and 4,999 population (3.8 percent of the total); 3.2 million resided in 465 towns numbering between 5,000 and 9,999 (4.2 percent of the total); and 4.4 million lived in 280 towns of more than 10,000 and fewer than 25,000 (5.7 percent of the total). Most people living at the time would have considered the last number to be the upper limit of a small town. Meanwhile, 45.8 million people (52.0 percent of the population) lived on farms and in other rural areas outside of towns having less than 2,500 people. Thus, the total rural population still constituted 60.3 percent of the total and was half again as large as the urban population.

Although urban numbers and population trends clearly had put small towns in a defensive position by 1900, there were still many of them, and most of them continued to grow in absolute numbers until the 1920s and 1930s, when the populations of many, especially the smaller ones, started to trend downward. Nevertheless, the central importance of small towns and their surrounding rural hinterlands remained deeply embedded in the American psyche, and many aspects of U.S. economy, politics, society, and culture remained strongly influenced by the nation's rural, small-town traditions. Cultural lag may help explain why it was not until the 1920s that a full-scale assault was launched on the traditional dominance of small-town folkways and culture in America.

One of the key developments in the transformation that occurred in American society during the late 1800s and early 1900s was a rising tide of professionalism. Prominently situated within the new professions were social scientists, including historians, who saw their prestige and influence growing among the general public. Colleges and universities such as Harvard, Yale, Johns Hopkins, Chicago, Stanford, Michigan, and Wisconsin began to play prominent roles in developing and disseminating theoretical and practical knowledge that made a major impact on industry, politics, and society in general. Emerging as the most prominent historian in the United States during the early 1900s was Frederick Jackson Turner of the University of Wisconsin and later Harvard. He was a small-town boy from Portage, Wisconsin, a county-seat town, which expanded from about 3,000 to around 4,000 residents while he was growing up there during the 1860s and 1870s. His coming-of-age in the household of a prominent newspaper publisher and politician in south-central Wisconsin had profound consequences for his choice of a profession to follow and later for the scholarly work he engaged in.

He originally intended to follow in the journalistic footsteps of his father. While engaged in his studies at the University of Wisconsin, he changed his mind and switched to history after taking a course in the subject from a charismatic professor. As an undergraduate student he was assigned to do some historical research on the fur trade in the area surrounding his hometown; he built on that experience and made the fur trade in the state the topic of his master's thesis at Wisconsin. Later, he expanded that work into a Ph.D. dissertation at Johns Hopkins University in Baltimore. There and at other schools in the East, the reigning interpretation of American history centered on European influences in a new continent (the "germ theory" of development), but the young scholar recoiled against what he perceived to be too narrow a point of view and opted instead to focus on the impact made by the kind of frontier conditions in which he had grown up in Wisconsin. He developed an entire scholarly career researching the influence of the frontier and the American "West," which in his mind was, in large part, an expanded version of his own Middle West.

Interestingly, he trained his attention neither on the kinds of small towns in which he had grown up nor on rising metropolitan America, although by the time urban interpretations of American history began to appear during the 1920s, he expressed an interest in wanting to learn about them, too. But by then he was in his sixties and probably felt it was too late to drastically redirect his research agenda (he continued his investigations and writing after his retirement in 1924 up until his death in 1932). In a real sense, however, throughout a career that brought him prominent mention in history textbooks, Turner projected on the broad canvas of American historical development the remembered events and transformations characterizing his own small-town beginnings in Portage. In that light, he may have regretted leaving the University of Wisconsin for Harvard and might have better enjoyed staying in Madison his entire career, despite the greater prestige that came to him as a professor in Cambridge after 1910. Although the Turner thesis (or frontier thesis) is largely passé among American historical interpretations today, for several decades it remained the reigning paradigm in the profession, and it made the Wisconsinite one of the most influential American historians of all time.

Meanwhile, the dramatic election of 1896 went down not only as one of the most exciting but also as one of the most bitter and contentious in

American history. The two major candidates—the eventual winner, William McKinley, for the Republicans and his opponent, William Jennings Bryan, for the Democrats and Populists—possessed similar midwestern small-town backgrounds. Bryan, whose father was a local judge, was born into a family of higher social standing and obtained a college education. McKinley managed only to accumulate a semester of college plus a small amount of formal training in the law. Both became lawyers and then quickly gravitated toward careers in politics during their early thirties.

Like most of their contemporaries, they had assimilated the rudiments of the region's dominant bourgeois culture and accepted the traditional Protestant beliefs and commitments of their families. Both men displayed ambition, rectitude, love for family, and conventional morality as well as allegiance to capitalistic institutions and a desire for social and economic progress; however, they ended up on opposite sides in the political realm. McKinley, a Civil War veteran, fell easily into the patterns of midwestern Republican politics, deifying Abraham Lincoln, identifying strongly with the victorious North, assigning to government a major role in enhancing economic growth, and supporting policies that favored business, both at the national level and back home on Main Street. Bryan, as a Democrat, identified instinctively with small-town dwellers as well as with agrarians in the South, the West, and his own native Midwest while also maintaining a special place in his thinking for the working classes in all sections.

McKinley characterized himself as a simple country boy. Nevertheless, he emerged as an outspoken advocate for industrial progress and economic expansion. During the election of 1896, his backers came primarily from the highly populated, more heavily urbanized and industrialized northeastern quadrant of the nation that contained New England, the Mid-Atlantic states, and parts of the Midwest. Bryan, meanwhile, drew his electoral strength primarily from the South, the West, and other parts of the Midwest. Bryan, the "Boy Orator of the Platte," deliberately identified himself with evangelical religious elements and more generally with rural residents and traditional small-town dwellers—the kinds of people he had grown up with in central Illinois and had come to know well as an adult in Lincoln, Nebraska. His campaign in 1896 was the last great defense of the traditional rural agrarian order against irresistible modernizing trends that were transforming the United States at the time.

McKinley, whose victory in that contest established the Republicans as the majority party in the country for the next generation, sided with the forces of industrialization, urbanization, modernization, and empire. He did not live to see the United States emerge as a world power during the early 1900s, falling to an assassin's bullet in 1901, but his actions after the Spanish-American War, his modernization of the U.S. Army, his buildup of the executive bureaucracy, and his business-friendly economic policies all helped ensure that the kind of life he and Bryan had known as boys growing up in the Midwest would continue to fade away, giving way to new behaviors and conditions. Yet McKinley, much like his Democratic counterpart, retained huge affection for his hometown. Bryan visited Salem, Illinois, dozens of times after leaving home to attend college. McKinley, for his part, fervently longed to return to Canton, Ohio, after his time in the White House ended, a dream that was denied fulfillment when a crazed gunman shot him fatally in Buffalo, New York, in 1901. Recollections of childhood exerted a profound influence on both men.

More than Turner, Bryan, or McKinley, Henry Ford found himself in thrall to his boyhood origins. Despite this, no one did more to undermine the dominance of small-town ways and practices than Ford, whose Model T automobile became a revolutionary social force after he introduced it to the public in 1908. Having grown up on a farm near the village of Dearborn, Michigan, 10 miles west of Detroit, he did not manufacture cars in order to change people's lives nor, indeed, to transform society. He sold them to make money, but in the process he did more than perhaps any other single person to undermine the traditional rural way of life he had known and loved. The practical, affordable vehicles he manufactured, hugely popular in the countryside, also appealed to urbanites. By the time he entered his sixties, nostalgia for the familiar habits and practices he had known as a youth grew so strong in him that he devoted much of his time to historical preservation. His most spectacular project was Greenfield Village in Dearborn, a historical village that went up alongside a museum complex where he displayed many kinds of historical artifacts, from kettles and guns to automobiles and airplanes.

Ford was often portrayed in the press as the epitome of midwestern agrarian values, counting among them honesty, shrewdness, unpretentiousness, and dependability. The huge wealth he accumulated did not prevent him from being a genuine folk hero, and thousands of ordinary Americans wrote to him much as if he were a friend, a valued neighbor, or a member of their immediate family rather than being the powerful billionaire that he was. To many, he symbolized the America of an earlier, simpler time when society was less complex, individuals made more of a difference, and traditional folkways continued to prevail. But although in some ways he did seem the fulfillment of the expectations people had of him as a product of rural, small-town Michigan, his behavior, goals, and ambitions were far too expansive and mercurial to be easily explained by anything detectable in his parentage and background. His closest associates were quick to observe that he was a mystery even to them.

Even if Ford himself remained enigmatic, the impact his vehicles had on the rural countryside as well as on the towns that dotted it was plainly immense. The proliferating presence of the automobile helped restructure the geography of the rural community, gave a boost to the larger towns and cities where people increasingly drove to shop and entertain themselves, and altered in a variety of ways the daily habits and rituals of the populace. In acting out his enormous role in the creation of a new consumer culture in the United States, Ford inadvertently undermined the very traditional institutions and folkways he wished to preserve.

Besides attending to the development of Greenfield Village, the automaker pursued a variety of other projects intended to revivify as well as to derive lessons from the rural way of life that he had known as a youth. Chemurgy, the movement to exploit science for the development of new agricultural products, was one of his hobbyhorses. Another was the establishment of a number of village industries, mostly in southeastern Michigan, in which the production of parts for the manufacture of automobiles was farmed out to factories in rural settings rather than being concentrated around Detroit. The most dramatic of these efforts was the establishment of a rubber-producing facility in the jungles of Brazil along lines of small-town memories he retained from his childhood. The project was given the name Fordlandia. These kinds of activities had paradoxical results: Ford, a farm boy from rural Michigan, could not get over his love for his rural, small-town origins, and at the same time his business enterprises did more than anything else to transform and undermine that way of life.

The lot of African Americans during the decades after the Civil War was much more difficult than that of European Americans, regardless of their ethnic origins. Among those in the former group who made the largest marks were two midwestern youths born two decades apart—George Washington Carver, who began life on a farm in southwestern Missouri living with white surrogate parents, and Oscar Micheaux, who grew up in a family of eleven children on a farm near Metropolis, Illinois, on the Ohio River. The former left home around age eleven (many specifics about his early life are lost in the shadows of history) to get a better education for himself; the latter was sixteen when he journeyed north to Chicago to seek his fortune.

Carver's delight in the land and in nature accompanied him throughout his life as he carved out a career as an agricultural scientist and teacher. Micheaux tried his hand at farming in South Dakota as a young man and did fairly well at it until a severe drought put him out of business. Clever and creative as he was, he drew on his experience as a Dakota homesteader to launch a new career as a novelist and, later, to produce movies, becoming in the process the first great black filmmaker in American history. Both men were hugely resourceful and successful in their own, but very different, ways, and they were in agreement that Booker T. Washington's philosophy for achieving progress for the black race was the correct approach to follow.

Born into slavery and left an orphan as an infant when his mother disappeared after being kidnapped by white night riders, Carver demonstrated remarkable resilience and an exceptional ability to adapt to circumstances while moving about from a very young age from family to family—some white and some black—in a series of Missouri, Kansas, and Iowa towns. Always, his sweet disposition, religious faith, positive outlook, and drive to improve himself landed him on his feet and placed him in positions where good-hearted and benevolent adults could perceive his potential and help set him in the right direction. His winding up at Tuskegee Institute in Alabama under the famed leadership of Washington was a fortunate piece of luck. The Tuskegee director was looking for young men like Carver to beef up the academic status of the school, and Carver, who by then had a master's degree in horticulture from Iowa State College, felt a calling to improve his race and at the same time to make his own life worthwhile and successful.

He spent most of his life in the Deep South in the heart of the Black Belt and Jim Crow racism, far from his origins in the Midwest. But he retained affection for his roots, returned several times to visit the area around his birthplace in Diamond, Missouri, and maintained a sporadic correspondence over the years with several acquaintances he had made along the way. Having grown up in the rural Midwest, he made it his life's mission to improve the lot of rural dwellers everywhere, both among his own people and with regard to all races. Tuskegee, with a population of around 2,000, was a small town that, although differing in many respects from the ones he had known as a youth, also had many things that were familiar about it, which made it a comfortable fit for him as he proceeded through maturity into old age.

Oscar Micheaux, whose artistic achievements took much longer for white Americans to learn about (he was widely known in the black community during his heyday in the 1920s and 1930s), had in some ways a career much more varied and exciting than Carver's. In the course of writing seven novels and writing, producing, directing, and distributing approximately forty-five movies, he traveled all over the United States, developed a flamboyant personality, and lived through a long series of dramatic ups and downs in his career and private life. There is no record that he ever returned to visit his early home ground in the Little Egypt region of southern Illinois, and he probably did not get back much or at all to the place where he homesteaded in southern South Dakota. He would spend most of his time as a novelist and filmmaker in Sioux City, Iowa; Chicago; and the New York City area.

He maintained a special place in his heart for the "great Northwest," the region surrounding the Dakotas where the homesteading frontier was coming to a close and where he had gambled on his future during the early 1900s. He continued to believe that African Americans possessed exceptional opportunities to better themselves by taking out homesteads and making a living on the land, his own experience notwithstanding. In three novels describing his homesteading saga in South Dakota, he devoted several chapters to life in the small towns that catered to homesteaders like himself, and he was pleased to have earned the respect and even the admiration of most of the white people among whom he had been either the only one or one of the few black people living in the area.

Thus, although in much different ways and with varied consequences, Carver and Micheaux were heavily influenced by their boyhoods on the farm and by their experiences of growing up in small midwestern towns, and they drew lessons from those experiences that they believed were relevant to others, especially people of their own race.

Taken together, the youthful experiences of Turner, Bryan, McKinley, Ford, Carver, and Micheaux illustrate the huge variety of tendencies and outcomes that characterized the lives of Americans during the decades after the Civil War, but they also provide evidence of the channelizing forces that were operating to transform the day-to-day circumstances of people everywhere. Economic growth, industrial expansion, and transportation improvements were bettering people's lives, rendering them more mobile, and expanding their options. Although factors of class, race, education, and social background considerably constrained people's life chances and actions, opportunities were increasing for many individuals, at least, to move, grow, and improve themselves. The tug of tradition and memories of the past, however, remained strong, and small-town mores and values retained a special power to influence attitudes and behavior.

CHAPTER ONE

Frederick Jackson Turner: Frontier Historian

I spent my youth in a newspaper office in contact with practical politics, and in a little town at "The Portage," Wis. over which Marquette had passed. There were still Indian (Winnebago) teepees where I hunted and fished, and Indians came into the stores to buy paints and trinkets and sell furs. . . . Is it strange that I saw the frontier as a real thing and experienced its changes? My people were pioneers from the beginning of the seventeenth century. . . . My mother's ancestors were preachers! Is it strange that I preached of the frontier?

—Turner to Constance Lindsay Skinner, March 15, 1922

Frederick Jackson Turner, who grew up on the edge of the post–Civil War Wisconsin frontier, became a historian, inspired by a class he took at the state university during the early 1880s. Being an unusually bright, creative, and ambitious young man, he emerged not only as one of the first professional historians in the United States but also as one of its best. He ensconced the remembered frontier of his boyhood at the center of his interpretation of American historical development. The Turner thesis (or frontier thesis) reigned supreme in the United States during the years of his professional eminence—first at the University of Wisconsin, where he taught from 1889 to 1910, and later at Harvard, until his retirement in 1924. It became the interpretation of choice in grade school, high school, and college history textbooks. Turner's graduate students fanned out across the country to spread their master's viewpoint in universities from Stanford and the University of Kansas to the University of Chicago and Yale. He was showered with accolades and prizes, from honorary doctorates to the Pulitzer Prize.[1]

Strangely enough, significantly enough, although he projected his own childhood experience of living on the frontier onto his own understanding and interpretation of American history, it was only late in his career that he began to appreciate the importance of urban history. His hometown of Portage was one of thousands of similar bustling, aspiring communities during the years between his birth there in 1861 and his heading off to college seventeen years later at Madison, 30 miles to the south. The very ubiquity of small towns like these invited him and his colleagues to take them for granted, considering them unworthy of special attention. Although a handful of historians started writing books and articles about the history of various American cities around the turn of the twentieth century, it was not until the early 1920s, just about the time Turner retired from teaching, that they began to formulate an explicit agenda for investigating urban history. Characteristically, the Wisconsinite took note of these early soundings, registering his endorsement of the project and agreeing to the importance of urbanism in the life of the nation. Although he continued his historical researches right up until the time of his death in 1932, it was too late for him to reorient his attention and methods, which had been focused on the study of what had become by then a declining rural America.[2] It is ironic that Turner, who lived almost all of the first forty-nine years of his life in the towns of Portage and Madison, later making his home in Boston and Los Angeles, paid only passing attention either to small towns or to cities in his writing.

Turner rocketed to the top of the historical profession within a decade of entering it. Rising to a privileged position within an inner circle that controlled the major professional organizations, he was, in modern parlance, connected. Able to attract a steady stream of job offers from schools like Stanford, Princeton, Pennsylvania, Chicago, Harvard, California, and Johns Hopkins, he capitalized on the leverage such invitations brought him to improve his salary and working conditions in Madison. He practiced what his biographer Allan Bogue terms "aggressive professionalism" at the University of Wisconsin, building up a little empire for himself there and utilizing his stature as a researcher and his agreeable personality to make an impact on institutional policy, including the choice of the university's president.[3]

As one of the first of the "progressive historians" who dominated the field during the early 1900s, he enhanced his status by being associated with the likes of Charles A. Beard, Vernon L. Parrington, Carl Becker, and James Harvey Robinson. All the major progressive historians came from small-town backgrounds in the Middle West, were born within a decade and a half of each other around the time of the Civil War, and went east for their education.[4] According to Richard Hofstadter, who has written the best book on the progressive historians, progressive history did for history what pragmatism did for philosophy, what muckraking did for journalism, what critical realism did for literature, and what sociological jurisprudence did for the law: it transformed the field into something new.[5]

Despite Turner's unsurpassed stature in the field, his scholarly output remained surprisingly meager, emerging only with the greatest and most reluctant effort on his part. Words could flow effortlessly from his pen when he was writing letters or taking voluminous notes on books and documents he was reading, as those jottings accumulated relentlessly in file drawers and boxes. As time went by, writing for publication became an increasingly onerous chore for him, often necessitating steady prodding from impatient editors. Book publishers never stopped asking him to write textbooks or monographs for them, however, despite his dismal record at producing publishable manuscripts. At one time in 1901, he had signed contracts to write nine different books, never delivering on a single one of them. He had to turn down frequent invitations for speeches, articles, and public appearances, while keeping busy enough working on the ones he did accept.[6]

A perfectionist as well as a perpetual procrastinator, Turner was a supremely curious person, almost pathologically unwilling to bring a halt to his accumulation of notes and reference materials. There was always one more fact to gather, one more source to consult. It therefore came as no surprise to his associates on Wednesday, July 12, 1893, the day he was scheduled to present the final paper at the evening session of a special meeting of the American Historical Association, that he was holed up in his hotel room putting the finishing touches on his talk. Many of them were out enjoying the sights of the Chicago World's Fair, including a performance of Buffalo Bill's Wild West show. Turner, not yet thirty-two, missed seeing the cowboy hero that afternoon, but the paper he delivered, "The Significance of the Frontier in American History," launched him on the path to success.[7]

The document ran to over thirty printed pages. Taking his cue from a recent bulletin of the superintendent of the 1890 census, which indicated that it was no longer possible to identify a clear frontier line of settlement in the West, Turner addressed the question of the frontier's long-term significance in the life of the nation. "Up to our own day American history has been in a large degree the history of the colonization of the Great West," he asserted in soon-to-become famous words. "The existence of an area of free land, its continuous recession, and the advance of American settlement westward, explain American development."[8] Stated in clear, forceful, unqualified language, the Turner thesis quickly helped make him the most famous historian in the United States.

As the line of settlement pushed constantly westward, Turner argued, American society frequently reconstituted itself along the frontier. "This perennial rebirth, this fluidity of American life, this expansion westward with its new opportunities, its continuous touch with the simplicity of primitive society, furnish the forces dominating American character," he contended. The central dynamic force of American history had lain not along the Atlantic coast but in the "Great West." The qualities of frontier populations that set them apart from their counterparts back east were nationalism, individualism, freedom, and, above all, democracy. Specific character traits included practicality, inventiveness, energy, and exuberance.[9] Over time, as Turner extended and revised his ideas in numerous classroom lectures, speeches, presentations, essays, and articles in scholarly journals and popular publications, he added other qualities to the list, including egalitarianism, optimism, idealism, industry, ambition, and courage.[10]

In Turner's view, previous historians had overemphasized "[the] European germs developing in an American environment."[11] They had devoted too much attention to the Germanic origins of American culture, too little to peculiarly American factors. He proposed to substitute a developmental model identifying several stages through which frontiers passed as the line of settlement moved in successive waves across the continent—traders, ranchers, miners, farmers, merchants, and capitalists.

Turner's implicit question for his listeners was, Now, with the frontier gone, closing the first period of American history, what does the future hold?[12] That query held tremendous resonance for thoughtful observers in a year in which the national economy plunged into its worst depression up until that time, striking laborers raised the specter of class warfare, hoboes and unemployed workers rode the rails, agricultural protesters ramped up their demonstrations, and social observers worriedly pondered the future.

Considering the huge impact that the young professor's paper eventually exerted on the historical profession in particular and American thought in general, the piece stimulated very little initial response. U.S. Civil Service Commissioner Theodore Roosevelt, whose first two volumes of *The Winning of the West* Turner had earlier reviewed, noted that the Wisconsin historian's paper contained "some first class ideas" and that it put "into shape a good deal of thought that has been floating around rather loosely."[13] As Roosevelt suggested, Turner had drawn on a wide variety of sources in writing his paper. It succeeded so well in later years in large part because it embodied many of the attitudes and assumptions prevailing in the culture at the time. Thinkers and writers ranging from Europeans Alexis de Tocqueville, Friedrich List, and Thomas Babington Macaulay to homegrown intellectuals Thomas Jefferson, Ralph Waldo Emerson, and Henry David Thoreau had previously noted the central importance of westward expansion in the life of the nation. In 1865, *Nation* magazine editor E. L. Godkin anticipated Turner in arguing that frontier conditions bore responsibility for most of the unique traits separating Americans from Europeans.[14]

The idea of the moving frontier, conceived of as a place of bountiful nature and republican virtue where hardworking agrarians enjoyed a superior mode of living in what Henry Nash Smith called the "Garden of the World," enjoyed virtually universal popularity among nineteenth-century Americans. This "agrarian myth," which was only beginning to lose force by the 1890s, heavily influenced Turner's way of thinking, and he never quite managed to transcend it. With the rise of industry, the expansion of cities, the spread of bureaucracy, the emergence of labor unrest, and the growth of agrarian protest during the 1890s, Turner's reason told him that the mythical "Garden" was gone forever, but his heart told him that rural life and small-town ways had been good. Turner's West (or, more accurately, his Middle West) was a positive, appealing place, closely identifiable with the Wisconsin surroundings in which he had grown up and the romantic aura he attached to them. The historian David S. Brown has observed, "Like Henry Ford's Greenfield Village, the Rockefellers' restoration of Colonial Williamsburg, and Walt Disney's famous 'Main Street' theme parks, Turner selectively commemorated those characteristics of American life he found appealing and ossified them in a dream world of virtuous pioneers and brave frontiersmen."[15]

As all this might suggest, psychological factors figured along with intellectual ones in inspiring Turner's emerging interpretation of American history. In later years, he often noted that his boyhood on the edge of the Wisconsin frontier had been a significant factor in turning his scholarly attention to the forces and developments operating within that environment, whose lessons were later projected onto the broader canvas of all American history. Portage, named for the confluence of the Fox and Wisconsin Rivers where Indians had crossed over long before Europeans arrived on the scene, was a bustling new community, full of energy and high aspirations. It was only a year old when upstate New Yorker Andrew Jackson Turner and his wife, Mary, who came from the western part of the state, arrived in 1855. The town had grown to 2,870 inhabitants (one-third of them born abroad) by the 1860 census, a year before the birth of their first child, Frederick Jackson, on November 14, 1861.

With two younger siblings, Fred, as he was called as a child, watched Portage expand to more than 4,000 inhabitants by the time he left for college at the nearby state university in 1878. The frontier, already pushing westward toward the Mississippi River by the time he was born, left many reminders for the boy to observe while he was growing up. Able to watch Indians still pitching their tepees when he went out hunting and fishing, the youth listened to countless stories of Indians, fur traders, and loggers who had once roamed the area. Portage consisted of an immigrant stew. Children of Yankee background like Fred mingled freely with German, Irish, Norwegian, Scottish, Swiss, English, and Italian immigrants, as well as with a few southerners who had migrated north. He and his younger sister and brother enjoyed doing the kinds of things children everywhere did— skating and sledding on the Wisconsin River when it froze over in winter, swimming in it when warm weather arrived, enjoying weekly band concerts in the park, waxing patriotic on the Fourth of July, engaging in pranks on Halloween, and participating in spelling bees, oratorical contests, parties, and dances. As a high school student, Fred earned notice as a budding orator, a talent later honed in college and useful to him as an adult.[16]

Social relations in Portage remained more fluid and democratic than in more-established places further east, but some families and groups obviously possessed greater wealth and power than others. Elitism and egalitarianism coexisted somewhat uneasily. During Frederick's youth, his father, who was comfortably situated but not especially wealthy by the standards of the time, was part of the town's social and political elite. He acted in a variety of roles as newspaper editor, political operative, local historian, and town booster. As a Republican Party stalwart, he served four terms in the state legislature, two on the state railroad commission, nine as clerk of the state senate, and three as mayor of Portage. He also attended four Republican National Conventions as a delegate.[17] Turner later identified his family and the quasi-frontier atmosphere surrounding Portage as the two most significant shaping influences on his career.[18]

As an undergraduate student at the University of Wisconsin he was drawn to the study of his own native region, partly by accident, partly by instinct. In the late 1870s, with fewer than 500 undergraduate students, all of whom enjoyed free tuition, the nascent institution was hardly more than a glorified high school. It was still far from the vibrant, respected institution of higher education that it was destined to become during the time that he was a professor there. The best that can be said of it during the 1880s is that it nurtured and did not stand in the way of bright, curious, and hardworking students. Classes in Greek and Latin, oratorical competitions, special researches, and standard course work posed worthy challenges. Turner's commonplace books, in which he jotted down thoughts and notes from books he was reading, testified to his thirst for learning, catholic taste, and seriousness of purpose. Emerson, especially, appealed to him. But he also filled page after page with quotations from Horace, Dante, Francis Bacon, Henry Wadsworth Longfellow, William Shakespeare, Charles Dickens, William Makepeace Thackeray, Nathaniel Hawthorne, Walter Scott, Thomas Babington Macaulay, John Milton, Thomas Carlyle, John Ruskin, Washington Irving, and other writers and thinkers. Beyond the knowledge and stimulus to the imagination that reading provided, his reading also prompted him to make many connections among ideas, which in turn sparked his creative instincts. These activities fostered habits that continued throughout his life. A major part of his genius was his ability to draw ideas, insights, and facts from a wide array of sources and his talent for linking thinkers, fields, and realms of knowledge, thereby generating new insights and new questions.[19]

Anyone inclined to think of Turner simply as a provincial intellect, drawn to study his own limited locale and narrowly focused in his historical thinking, needs only to peruse his commonplace books to realize how mistaken such a view is. Throughout his life Turner emphasized that his frontier concept was only one aspect of a much broader conception of historical change and development that took into account all geographic areas and every aspect of human activity.[20] At the start of his career, however, practicality led him to choose a subject closer to home, one he was more familiar with, and one for which primary sources were close at hand—the western frontier.

Ironically, the man who became America's most highly regarded historian took only minimal course work in the subject as a student. At Wisconsin he had only one class in American history.[21] The course's teacher, however, changed his life. William Francis Allen was a professor of Latin and history, having emerged from a background in classical studies. He inspired the young student with his vision of scholarly inquiry and dogged industry in the search for historical facts and the generation of reasoned interpretations. Until his introduction to Professor Allen, Turner had assumed that he would follow his father into the field of journalism. Now he began to waver. In retrospect, he would say that no other person had influenced him so much as Allen, whose unique teaching style jettisoned rote learning. Instead, Allen used a topical method in which students worked with primary sources and formulated plausible explanations for historical actions and developments. A Harvard graduate, he had done graduate studies in Berlin and Göttingen. He frequently brought historical charts and maps into his classes, just as Turner would later on. Further imitating his mentor, Turner largely abandoned narrative history for an interpretive model that identified important topics and analyzed subjects from every angle. He asked probing questions and sought plausible explanations for the "whys" of history, going far beyond simple description.[22]

Allen, the university's sole historian at the time, was primarily interested in medieval history. Turner adapted the lessons he took from his medieval studies and later applied them to the study of American history. Allen, who impressed associates and colleagues as a "wise friend," "well beloved teacher," and "noble soul," was a Renaissance man in the range of his interests and talents. Influenced by him, Turner became a social evolutionist and learned the importance of community life.[23] His commitment to doing research in primary sources, his devotion to historical truth, his penchant for institutional analysis, and his interest in comparative studies all rubbed off on his young follower. Turner would never be satisfied to follow the easy path or to take shortcuts. His interests and methods were wide-ranging and eclectic. "He made me realize what scholarship meant; what loyalty to truth demanded," Turner later told his own student Carl Becker.[24]

Turner's mentor and future colleague on the Wisconsin faculty also facilitated and indirectly guided his pupil toward serious study of the frontier. Responding to a request from Professor Herbert Baxter Adams of Johns Hopkins University for information on early land holdings in Wisconsin, Allen invited six of his best students to examine land records of early French settlers in the surrounding region. Turner's assignment, appropriately enough, was the Grignon Tract at Portage. Fascinated by the exercise, the young man later followed up on it, picking the early French fur trade in Wisconsin as the subject for his master's thesis several years later. Recalling bundles of letters written by French fur traders that he had stumbled on while working on the earlier project, he obtained Allen's approval to tackle the larger subject for his thesis. Hours of energetic labor spent in the Draper Collection at the State Historical Society of Wisconsin, working with manuscripts, government documents, newspaper files, and other sources, hooked him on the attractions of research.[25]

In the process, the notion emerged that he might be able to carve out a field of specialization for himself in western history. "The more I dip into American history the more I can see what a great field there is here for a life study," Turner wrote his fiancée, Mae Sherwood, the daughter of a Chicago businessman, in September 1887. "One must even specialize here. I think I shall spend my study chiefly upon the Northwest and more generally on the Mississippi Valley. The history of this great country remains to be written. I shall add my mite in the way of studying it."[26]

At a time when virtually no one else thought of western history as a legitimate subject of research, this was an unusual and bold decision. From the beginning, too, it is evident that when Turner talked about "the West," he was thinking primarily of his own Middle West, called the Northwest or Old Northwest in the terminology of the time.[27] Reinforcement for his choice of specialization came when an ill Professor Allen asked him to take over an assignment to compile a study guide for women's clubs on the history of the Northwest. Stealing time from an already busy schedule of studies and teaching, the young scholar was able to turn out the first published outline of frontier history.[28]

By the time he finished his studies in Madison, Turner had acquired many of the skills and scholarly habits of mind that would make him an outstanding researcher and teacher. Master's degree in hand, he moved on to Johns Hopkins University in Baltimore during the 1888–1889 academic year to work on a Ph.D. degree. Hopkins, only a dozen years old at the time, already stood at the forefront of graduate research in the United States. It was popularizing Germanic methods of scholarship and providing a home for teachers and students who would become leaders in their fields of study during the next several decades. Turner was already indirectly acquainted with his adviser there, Herbert Baxter Adams, one of the founders five years earlier of the American Historical Association. Adams was the best-known history professor in the United States.[29] Turner also benefited from his association with Professors Albion W. Small, a pioneer in the nascent field of sociology; Richard T. Ely, a rising economist; and Woodrow Wilson, a Hopkins graduate on leave from Wesleyan College during the spring semester to teach a course in administration, which Turner took.

Wilson, only five years older than Turner, immediately liked the Wisconsinite, and the two engaged in many long conversations, finding themselves in fundamental agreement on most issues. On one thing, especially, they were passionate. They believed that Wilson's South (he had been born in Virginia and had grown up in Georgia and South Carolina) and Turner's West and Midwest had been treated shabbily by previous historians and that the situation needed rectifying.[30] Adams, widely known as the leading purveyor of the "germ theory" of American development, was part of the problem. He traced American character and institutions back to their alleged Teutonic origins in the forests of Germany, as modified when carried through England on their way to the American colonies. With their focus on the East and on Anglo-Saxon culture, most American historians remained unaware of and uninterested in western American history. "Not a man that I know here," Turner wrote Allen in Madison, "is either studying, or is hardly aware of the country beyond the Alleghenies."[31] A number of years later, he acknowledged that personal resentment and a sense of wounded sectional pride had influenced his thinking: "The Frontier paper [of 1893] was a programme, and in some degree a protest against eastern neglect, at the time, of institutional study of the West, and against Western antiquarian spirit in dealing with their own history."[32]

Returning to Madison in the fall of 1889 after his year in Baltimore (he finished the requirements for the Ph.D. degree the following spring), Turner quickly rose to take over his mentor's duties as head of the History Department when Allen contracted pneumonia and suddenly died in December. During the following three years, Turner's growing interest in frontier history found several outlets. A paper for the Madison Literary Club in February 1891 anticipated a number of ideas he later made famous in his 1893 essay. An article published in the campus's student newspaper in 1892 accused historians of neglecting "the fundamental dominating fact in United States history"—the expansion of its population from coast to coast. "In a sense American history up to our own day has been colonial history, the colonization of the Great West," he wrote. "The ever retreating frontier of free land is the key to American development." As had become his practice, Turner sent out copies of the article to a number of friends and scholars, including Adams. The latter was so impressed by it that he invited his former student to present a paper at the American Historical Association meeting scheduled for the following year in conjunction with the Chicago World's Fair. Ironically, therefore, the person against whom much of Turner's animus was directed in formulating his frontier thesis was also the one responsible for providing the platform that initially enabled him to broadcast his views to a wider public.[33]

Turner was not alone in championing the cause of his section of the country during the 1890s, a decade of growing unrest and agrarian protest, especially on the western plains. His 1893 essay constituted, according to historian Michael Steiner, "the historiographic counterpart of the farmer's revolt, the Populist campaign, the rise of literary regionalism, and the development of skyscrapers and prairie houses at the heart of the continent in the last years of the nineteenth century."[34] No one was more in tune with Turner's mood and way of thinking than his fellow Wisconsinite Hamlin Garland, only a year older than Turner, who envisioned the future of American literature taking place in the same western prairies and forests where Turner saw American history being made. "The mighty West, with its swarming millions, remains undelineated in the novel, the drama, and the poem," Garland observed in his book *Crumbling Idols*. Not eastern models and experiences but western ones were the wave of the future, he believed: "Our task is not to imitate but to create."[35]

Turner's frontier thesis emerged as the dominant explanatory paradigm in American history around the turn of the century. One of his critics, historian Louis Hacker, complained in 1933 that for forty years Turner had "so completely dominated American historical writing that hardly a single production of that time has failed to show the marks of his influence."[36] By 1910, the year he moved to Harvard and rose to the presidency of the American Historical Association, his prestige was unmatched. The frontier thesis governed textbook treatments of American history until almost mid-century and became a part of the climate of opinion, insinuating itself into movies, novels, comic books, and other forms of popular culture. A collection of Turner's essays published in 1920 as *The Frontier in American History* finished second in a 1952 poll, behind Vernon L. Parrington's *Main Currents in American Thought,* on a list of American historians' favorite books. A second compendium, *The Significance of Sections in American History,* captured the Pulitzer Prize for history in 1932. A group of nearly 300 members of the profession surveyed in 1964 deemed his ideas "still dominant."[37]

Just as Turner's theory had displaced his mentor Adams's interpretation of American history, his own formulations came under increasing fire as time went on. Slowly during the 1920s, more loudly during the 1930s and '40s, and rising to a crescendo after midcentury, critics attacked his ideas, prompting vigorous and often emotional defenses from his disciples and admirers. Turner himself expressed some surprise that more opposition to his views had not surfaced earlier.[38] In the 1920s, prominent scholars such as Benjamin F. Wright, Charles A. Beard, and Carl O. Sauer called into question his linking of democracy and the frontier; argued for the importance of slavery, labor, class, and capitalism as alternative explanations for American historical development; and began undermining many of the details of Turner's interpretive scheme.[39] After his death in 1932, many felt less constrained in aiming their barbs against a scholar who had been universally admired as a person and teacher, even by his staunchest critics, while he was living.[40]

With regard to his rhetoric and methods, Turner was accused during succeeding decades of using fuzzy language, exaggerating his findings, employing vague concepts, and reasoning imprecisely. Empirically, he came under fire for a whole host of misstatements, overstatements, unsupported assertions, contradictions, and gaps in analysis. His notion that the frontier had served as a "safety valve" for eastern discontent, draining off excess population and providing new opportunities for the unemployed, came under especially heavy criticism.[41] His emphasis on the frontier to the exclusion of other factors, such as industrialism, urbanization, corporate expansion, politics, religion, economic growth, class divisions, slavery, and cultural carryovers from Europe, also drew sustained opposition.

The 1960s, a decade that witnessed the growth of a variety of liberation movements, antiwar protests, and cultural criticism of all kinds, unleashed major changes in the historical profession, including heightened criticism of the Turnerian legacy. The seeds of the "new western history" were planted during this period, at a time when some practitioners in the discipline began to question whether western history itself would survive as a subdiscipline in the field.[42] The new western historians, led by Patricia Limerick, Richard White, Donald Worster, and others, trained their guns especially on Turner's obvious omissions from the canvas of the West: Indians; blacks, Chicanos, Asian Americans, and other minority groups; women (almost completely absent); and the environment (strange, from someone so attracted to environmental interpretations). More, they demanded an entire reconceptualization of the frontier process, insisting that rather than being heroic and progressive, it could better be described in terms of "conquest," "invasion," and "triumphalism." In their effort to demythologize the subject, they largely rejected models of progress, more often turning their attention to the brutalities, inequities, shameful conduct, environmental degradation, and political shenanigans associated with the conquest of the West. They did not hesitate to call Turner and Turnerians nostalgic, racist, ethnocentric, sexist, imperialist, and worse.

The new western historians were present-minded in approach, just as Turner himself had been, but the conclusions they reached were radically different, reflecting the conditions of their own time, just as he reflected those of his. They rejected the idea that the frontier came to an end during the 1890s and insisted that historians ought properly to turn their attention toward the West as a place rather than focus on the frontier as a process. (Turner's emphasis on the movement and fluidity of the frontier, as it progressed continually westward across the continent, downplayed its connection with any particular place, although he tended to think of his own Middle West as the section best epitomizing the process.) Above all, they insisted upon the complexity of the subject, rejecting simple, linear explanations, and they generally surrendered claims of objectivity, neutrality, and omniscience in favor of engagement and enthusiastic caring about their subject.[43]

Despite the barrage of criticism ranged against Turner's views in recent years, his image still seems firmly lodged in the historical imagination, even if often as a target for attack by his many critics. William Cronon, a successor of his and the Frederick Jackson Turner Professor of American History at the University of Wisconsin, has been counted among the leading lights of new western history, although he quickly rejected the label. In an article published in 1987, he noted "[the] remarkable persistence of the Turner thesis in the face of so much criticism," observing, "We have not yet figured out a way to escape him. His work remains the foundation not only for the history of the West, but also for much of the rest of American history as well. Textbooks still follow the basic outline which he and his students established in their lecture courses." Despite all the criticism that has been directed at Turner, Cronon suggests, no satisfactory paradigm for understanding western history has emerged to replace his work.[44]

If, like a pesky fly that refuses to leave, Turner and his legacy remain with us, it should not surprise us. The historian's hold on the American imagination derives from many sources. Primarily, it is a result of the intuition many people hold to, just as Turner did himself, that the process of movement across the land from the Atlantic to the Pacific was one of the most important developments in American history. People will continue to disagree over what to call it—progress or conquest—but the significance of what happened is widely agreed on. Turner had either the good sense or the good luck to be the first to elaborate the thesis in detail. His restatement of it in a variety of forms and often in less-than-precise language invited considerable criticism from scholars, but it also allowed him and his defenders considerable room to maneuver in trying to explain what he meant or to reposition him in the critical debate. Turner's greatest distinction as a high school student and as an undergraduate at the University of Wisconsin had been as an orator. He parlayed that skill into a job as a teaching assistant in graduate school before switching over full time to historical studies.[45] That rhetorical mastery shone through in all his writing.

Added to it were a love for poetry and a penchant for poetic expression. Turner liked to clip verses or copy them in his commonplace books, store them away in his files, read them to his classes, and insert them in his essays. One that he copied and saved was *Song of the English* by Rudyard Kipling, one of his favorite authors:

> We were dreamers, dreaming greatly, in the man-stifled town;
> We yearned beyond the sky-line where the strange roads go down.
> Came the Whisper, came the Vision, came the Power with the Need.
> Till the Soul that is not man's soul was lent us to lead.[46]

Dreaming, yearning, pursuing visions, drawing on soul power—these were all attributes of Turner, who was not, it should be said, a conventionally religious person. His passion for discovery, his drive to learn and understand, and his love for things intellectual were closely related to his expressive turn of mind. As many observers—both critics and followers—have commented, he was as much literary artist as historian.[47] Turner certainly recognized this quality in himself: "I always wanted to be an artist—tho' a truthful one!"[48]

Like many others, Richard Hofstadter recognized Turner's poetic proclivities, which, he observed, existed side by side with his critical inclinations. Poet and positivist coincided in uneasy tension.[49] In public venues, Turner often stated his points in grand, vague, and exaggerated language. In the classroom and in private conversation, on the other hand, he was generally careful to stick close to facts, eschew easy generalizations, and insist on the complexity and contradictoriness of historical experience.[50] This is what made him an exemplary teacher, especially of graduate students, who almost unanimously testified to his open-mindedness, his stress on objectivity, and his insistence on following what he called the "multiple hypothesis" rather than relying on single-factor interpretations.[51] His mind was anything but simple. The relentless posing of questions and unrestricted immersion in primary sources were his watchwords as a researcher.

Turner denied that he possessed any explicit methodology or that he had formulated a well-thought-out philosophy of history or even of historical research. To a Columbia University sociologist who suggested that he sounded like a sociologist, not a historian, Turner replied that he did not care what people called him so long as he "was left to ascertain the truth, and the relation of the facts to cause and effect in [his] own way."[52] Turner's dual roles—as hardheaded empiricist and as poetic romantic—underlay both his greatest strengths as a scholar and his greatest weaknesses.

CHAPTER ONE

Turner's reputation as a scholar derived mainly from his identification with the frontier thesis, which he continued to defend vigorously, even though he recognized many of its flaws and gaps and realized that some of the language he used in supporting it tended toward exaggeration and lacked nuance. "The truth is," he wrote in 1922 to Arthur M. Schlesinger Sr., who would follow in his footsteps as a professor at Harvard, "that I found it necessary to hammer pretty hard and pretty steadily on the frontier idea to 'get it in,' as a corrective to the kind of thinking I found some thirty years ago and less."[53]

In truth, although Turner never repudiated his frontier thesis, he quickly moved beyond it to concentrate his attention on regions—the sections, as he called them, that had been present from the beginning of colonial America and that had spun off from the frontier during the course of its three-century progress across the continent to the Pacific. To Turner, sectionalism offered far more intellectual excitement and provided a much more complex and satisfying explanation for American historical development than did the frontier, partly because the latter was subsumed within the former. His goal became the formulation of a "total" regional history into which he could fit every section from coast to coast and north to south.

Sectionalism was valuable as a working model, he believed, because of its comprehensiveness and potential for encompassing every aspect of the American experience. It illuminated conflicts that emerged out of economic and cultural interests rooted in geography. Sectional divisions had led to the Civil War, and they helped explain a wide variety of other developments.

Turner thus developed two big ideas during his career—the frontier and sectionalism. The first brought him lasting fame and influence, although he himself rather quickly moved beyond it, and many historians eventually deemed much of his frontier interpretation to be untenable. The only book-length publication to emerge from his work on the subject was the collection of essays put together in 1920, *The Frontier in American History*. Turner had written or presented ten of the thirteen essays contained in the collection before his move to Harvard in 1910, so it was already dated by the time it was published.[54] By 1920 he had already spent the better part of two decades concentrating on sectionalism, a subject that would occupy him until his death twelve years later. The topic generated the only real book he ever completed during his lifetime, *The Rise of the New West, 1819–1829*, which appeared in 1906 as one of twenty-eight volumes in the American Nation series published by Harper and Brothers. Invited by series editor Albert Bushnell Hart of Harvard to write on virtually any subject he wished, Turner chose to investigate the decade of the 1820s as a case study illustrating his contention about the central importance of sectionalism in American life. Only as a result of Hart's persistent encouragement, cajoling, and badgering did the book finally emerge in print. Turner gratefully acknowledged that Hart had accomplished what nobody else could. "It ought to be carved on my tombstone," commented Hart, who later would be a colleague of Turner's at Harvard. "I was the only man in the world that secured what might be called an adequate volume from Turner."[55]

During his final years, Turner worked on a large volume carrying his sectional themes forward into the 1830s and 1840s. Despite laboring on it for almost a quarter of a century, "the Book," as the coterie around him referred to it, remained unfinished when he died. It appeared three years later with editing by his personal secretary and two of his former colleagues. How devoted he was to this work and how frustrating it was for him not to publish more shone through in the final words he ever uttered: "I know this is the end. Tell Max [Farrand] I am sorry that I haven't finished my book."[56] In addition to finishing his big book, Turner's former students and friends also put together a series of his essays on sectionalism, which came out in late 1932 as *The Significance of Sections in American History*. He received the Pulitzer Prize for it posthumously the following year.[57]

Historians found much that was praiseworthy in Turner's three volumes on sectionalism and admitted that the topic was worth investigating. But most of them were moving in other directions and certainly did not deem the topic useful as a central organizing theme for interpreting the American past. Turner's continued insistence throughout the 1920s that the concept of sectionalism was growing in importance seemed not very convincing to them, and the challenges facing the United States during the Depression 1930s and war-torn 1940s only reinforced nationalistic tendencies in the culture. Ironically, the frontier thesis, which Turner researched much less rigorously than sectionalism and which he veered away from as an all-purpose explanation, continued to be the major basis for his vaunted historical reputation. Sectionalism, to which he devoted the better part of his career and to which he actually made his most important contribution, was perceived as a dead end by most of his colleagues.[58] Regionalism as a theme, however, did enjoy considerable currency, especially in the art world, during the 1930s and subsequently engaged the attention of a number of interdisciplinary researchers. Regionalism, as developed by art critics, geographers, cultural historians, and other social scientists and humanities scholars, tended to be more wide-ranging in its subject matter and more eclectic in its methods than the kind of sectionalism practiced by Turner, who focused more on economic and political themes in his research.[59]

Whether Turner was talking about the frontier or about the workings of sectionalism, he always concentrated his attention, first and foremost, on his own native section—the Middle West. People often remain loyal to the place of their birth and view the world through lenses that reflect the region in which they grew up. As a student at the University of Wisconsin, he was already thinking about making his own section his major subject of investigation.[60] During his year of study at Johns Hopkins, he planned to offer a seminar on the history of the Northwest when he returned to Madison. Once back home, as he launched his career as a professor, he channeled most of his energy into his midwestern researches. Many of his papers and essays focused explicitly on his native section, including "The Democratic Education of the Middle West" (1903), "The Ohio Valley in American History" (1909), "Middle Western Pioneer Democracy" (1918), "The Children of the Pioneers" (1926), and "The Significance of the Mississippi Valley in American History" (delivered in 1910 at Iowa City at a meeting of the fledgling Mississippi Valley Historical Association).[61] Most of the proof Turner advanced for his frontier thesis derived from the nineteenth-century Midwest, and his books on sectionalism reflected a similar midwestern bias.[62] *The Rise of the New West, 1819–1829,* and *The United States, 1830–1850,* followed similar formats. The first part of each book sketched the characteristics of each section of the country, and the second part chronicled historical events during the period under discussion as sectional forces impinged on them. Most obviously, the latter, his major opus, devoted ninety-nine pages to the Middle West, whereas the South Atlantic states received only sixty-six pages and no other section received more than fifty-three.

In his 1901 essay "The Middle West," referring to the twelve states from Ohio to Kansas, Nebraska, and the Dakotas, Turner identified the region as "the economic and political center of the Republic" and concluded that the future of the nation lay with it.[63] Hofstadter saw Turner's overemphasis on his native section as a case of "arrested development."[64] But even if the Wisconsinite was perhaps too attached to his own Middle West and generalized too much from it, as many scholars think,[65] he was not alone. Many Americans during the early 1900s agreed with him that the Midwest was the coming region—the center of growth, innovation, and influence in the United States.

Turner was not only describing home territory when he wrote; he was personally identifying with it and arguing for its worth. He had enjoyed life in Madison and never quite felt at home in Boston. Though he was warmly welcomed by the Harvard community and involved himself in many clubs and organizations there, he never developed the close personal friendships that had enveloped him in Madison. He sensed a chill in the social atmosphere in Cambridge, which sometimes made it seem like purgatory. "I love my Middle West," he wrote Carl Becker several years after leaving Madison, and he sometimes wondered why he had ever moved away. "I am," he admitted, "still a western man in all but my residence."[66]

Clearly, Turner was a bifurcated man. He was attracted to the adventure and excitement of movement and change, as embodied in his notion of the frontier, on the one hand. Meanwhile, he remained attached to a romantic vision of home, implicit in his concept of sectionalism, with a specific focus on his native Midwest. A wide range of thinkers have commented on this general phenomenon. "Human life," according to Lewis Mumford, "swings between two poles: movement and settlement," notions embodied in Turner's concepts of frontier and section.[67] Communities, Robert Bellah and his associates have written, have a history and are constituted by their past in the form of a "community of memory," which does not forget its past.[68] Turner partook of this process and did as much as anyone to promote it during the early 1900s. His attachment to the Midwest and his desire to defend it and to burnish its image may have led him at points to exaggerate its importance. Then again, his predecessors in the historical profession had overstated the relative importance of Puritan New England, so there was some kind of rough justice there.

Even if Turner accomplished something to redress regional imbalances in American historiography, he failed to advance understanding in another area: urban history, including the study of small towns. He was not unaware of the increasing importance of cities in American life, and he did pay some attention to towns and cities in his writings and in the classroom, but they always remained peripheral in his accounts.[69] In some versions of his presentation of the stages of frontier development, he threw in the rise of towns and cities along with industrialism during the final stage, but he never developed his analysis of urbanism in any detail. The sociologist C. Wright Mills and others have noted that many early twentieth-century so-

CHAPTER ONE

cial theorists, like Turner, derived from similar small-town and rural roots.[70] Even if his background in Portage and Madison helps explain his failure to discuss the role of larger cities in American development, it does not explain why he failed to say much about small towns.

To some degree, Turner shared the antiurban bias of many of his contemporaries, such as Theodore Dreiser, John Dewey, and Frank Lloyd Wright.[71] His aversion to an urban interpretation might better be explained, however, by the lack of much in the way of models for such discussion and by his inability to formulate a conceptual framework to encompass the subject. Before the 1920s and 1930s, when such historians as Arthur Schlesinger Sr., and Carl Bridenbaugh began urging the importance of urban history, studies of towns and cities by historians and other scholars, though not entirely lacking, remained infrequent and underdeveloped. Turner, closely in tune with prevailing intellectual currents, seems to have been intrigued by an urban interpretation, even if he never pursued the idea himself. He wrote Schlesinger in 1925, "There seems likely to be an urban reinterpretation of our history."[72] Earlier, he had jotted down some notes for a possible paper, "The Significance of the City in American History," which would examine the relationship among frontier, section, and city. In different times and circumstances Turner might have become the advocate of an urban thesis of American history. "Use data on city growth in relation to developing section and extension of frontier," he wrote in a note to himself during the 1920s. "Show how sectional rivalry for extending frontier, new settled regions & new resources affected urban society. When & how & why did cities become densely populated and why? How did urban (including alien) ideas, interests, and ideals react on frontier and sectional items?"[73] Although intellectually Turner was prepared to grant the importance of cities in American life, he felt more comfortable contemplating a future following upon lines of the nation's more rural past.

This from a man who lived a decade and a half in Boston and the last five years of his life in the Los Angeles suburb of Pasadena (where he continued his historical researches at the Huntington Library). His ideal place to live remained Madison, which, with a population of 57,899 in 1930, ranked somewhere between a large town and a small city. Although Turner retained some nostalgia for his boyhood home, his reactions on returning to Portage from a year spent in Baltimore as a graduate student had been decidedly negative. Writing his fiancée in June 1889, he had said he was "stagnating" there. "What an awful life." After having resided in Madison and Baltimore, Portage had seemed like a "terrible" place to live. "Even home is a little changed. I have grown away from my native place. How could I live elsewhere than in a university town."[74] As he grew older, however, a nostalgic tone crept into his recollections of the town, and he grew much more affectionate toward it, speaking glowingly of its attractions.

It would take at least another generation before historians paid much serious attention to small towns. Studies like Lewis Atherton's 1954 book, *Main Street on the Middle Border,* about midwestern small towns remained the exception rather than the rule. Stanley Elkins and Eric McKitrick published an article that year suggesting that Turner's frontier thesis could be rescued as a useful guide for research if scholars would investigate the development of community ties in small midwestern towns, for it "was unquestionably the town from which the tone of life in Ohio, Indiana and Illinois came to be taken, rather than from the agriculture in which an undoubted majority of the population was engaged." Richard C. Wade, meanwhile, deftly described the importance of larger cities operating as "spearheads of the frontier" in the pre–Civil War Midwest, a theme picked up by other scholars.[75] It took some time for momentum to build. During the 1960s and '70s, social historians in search of community development expanded our knowledge of small-town and rural community. Histories of colonial towns written from a social history perspective proliferated, and eventually researchers began paying more attention to small towns in the Midwest and other sections of the country. In recent years, small-town history has begun to establish itself as a respectable part of urban history.[76]

Unfortunately, much less has been accomplished in the way of writing midwestern history. As noted in the introduction to this book, the Middle West remains a poor cousin compared to the other sections in American historiography. The Northeast, the South, and the West all have vigorous historical associations, journals, conferences, and networks devoted to their study. The Midwest has been gaining ground during the last decade or two, but it remains to be seen how much it will be able to close the huge gap that continues to exist between it and the other regions in the historical imagination. Were Frederick Jackson Turner still with us today, it is likely that he would be in the vanguard of scholars calling for a renewed interest in the history of the section.

CHAPTER TWO

William McKinley and
William Jennings Bryan: Battling for
the Soul of America

You know, I was a simple country boy.

—William McKinley

*For Bryan was the last great spokesman of the America of the
nineteenth century—of the America of the Middle West and the
South, the America of the farm and the country town, the
America that read its Bible and went to Chautauqua, distrusted
the big city and Wall Street, believed in God and the
Declaration of Independence.*

—Henry Steele Commager

By the time they finish high school, American schoolchildren have probably encountered the storied election of 1896 more than once in their history textbooks. They learn that former Ohio governor William McKinley's modest—but decisive—victory over former Nebraska congressman William Jennings Bryan ranks with the election of Thomas Jefferson in 1800, Andrew Jackson in 1828, Abraham Lincoln in 1860, Franklin Roosevelt in 1932, and Ronald Reagan in 1980 as one of the significant turning points in American political history. After decades of stalemate in national politics, the United States entered into a generation of Republican rule. In a broader sense, a country till then largely dominated by small-town and rural influences increasingly came under the sway of modernizing forces associated with urban-industrial America. During the 1890s, the rise of Populism, a primarily agrarian protest movement, facilitated the eloquent Bryan's dramatic emergence on the political scene. After 1896, the Republican Party led by McKinley promoted a vision of urbanization and industrialization that helped transform society and the economy. In the early 1900s, the development of political progressivism, which was more of an urban than a rural phenomenon, dominated American politics until the nation entered World War I, decisively altering the tenor of American life. Good reasons exist, therefore, to take a closer look at the election of 1896, one that pitted two small-town boys from the Midwest against each other. In a real sense, the election became a battle for the soul of America.

Bryan's dramatic nomination, seemingly out of the blue, at the Democratic National Convention in Chicago in July and his later selection by the People's Party, or "Populists," as their nominee also guaranteed that this would be an unusually momentous and hard-fought election. At thirty-six, he was only one year beyond the constitutionally mandated minimum age for running and the youngest candidate ever to capture a presidential nomination, prompting the label "Boy Orator of the Platte." The premier platform performer in a period noted for political oratory, he relied on his sparkling elocutionary talent, first to capture the nomination, then to wage the campaign, and later to sustain his career in politics for another three decades. The Republicans respected his speaking prowess enough to launch an unprecedented solicitation of funds, which were spent to send out tens of millions of pieces of campaign literature and hundreds of speakers in a blitz that established a model for all future presidential campaigns.

Bryan's message, as much as his mode of campaigning, stimulated consternation in the opposition as well as interest in the public. Adopting a number of the issues contained in the Populist platform as his own, he concentrated most of his energies on one, "free silver," which was designed as a mechanism to address the agricultural population's greatest concern at the time: a shortage of currency in the economy. Scarcity of money resulted in depressed farm prices and reduced farm incomes. ("Free silver" was a shorthand term for the free and unlimited coinage of silver by the federal government at a ratio of sixteen parts of silver to one part of gold.) Congressional passage of free silver legislation would have resulted in a substantial expansion of the currency through the minting of silver coins from bullion brought to the U.S. Treasury out of the ever-expanding production of silver mines in the West. Billed by Democratic "silverbugs," who had captured control of the Democratic Party, as a panacea for the farmers' predicament as well as a benefit for urban workers and for all Americans, free silver struck fear in the bosoms of most Republicans and substantial numbers of disaffected Democrats, who deemed it to be too radical and destructive of property rights. Republicans contended that Bryan and his cohorts represented the forces of "socialism," "communism," "anarchy," and worse.

Besides the unusual drama surrounding Bryan's candidacy, several other factors stimulated heightened interest in the election. The country had entered the fourth year of the most severe economic depression it had yet undergone. The debacle closed the doors of hundreds of banks and thousands of businesses, leaving as much as one-fifth of the workforce unemployed and precipitating bloody strikes and labor violence, most notably the 1894 Pullman Strike on the south side of Chicago. It also generated a number of "industrial armies," including one led by Ohioan Jacob Coxey, which marched on Washington to "petition Congress with their boots on."[1] In 1892, when the Populists launched their first national campaign, their platform described a nation "brought to the verge of moral, political, and material ruin." Four years later, their voices and those of political rebels of every stripe joined in clamorous cacophony. After deposing their own party's leader, President Grover Cleveland, and wresting control away from his conservative backers, the insurgent, mostly agrarian, predominantly southern and western, silver-minded wing of the Democratic Party allied with the Populists to launch one of the most rancorous election campaigns in U.S. history. The Bryanites' penchant for demonizing their opponents as "cukoos," "gold bugs," "yellow bellies," "eastern elitists," "city slickers," "plutocrats," "corporate moguls," and "Wall Street manipulators" only reinforced their opponents' inclination to picture Bryan and his followers as "demagogues," "repudiationists," "blatherskites," "rabble rousers," "windbags," "country hicks," "Jacobins," "Popocrats," "nihilists," and "revolutionaries."[2] Theodore Roosevelt termed Bryanism "criminal" and "vicious" and believed it reflected "a genuine and dangerous fanaticism." In the opinion of soon-to-be secretary of state John Hay, the Democratic candidate was no more than "a half-baked glib little briefless jack-leg lawyer" whose only concern was to collect the office's $50,000 salary by "promising the millennium to everybody with a hole in his pants and destruction to everybody with a clean shirt."[3] But to his rabid supporters, Bryan represented "the new Messiah" and "a man raised up by God."[4] The press reinforced and multiplied the politicos' tendencies to denigrate and exaggerate. Normally partisan and biased in their reporting and editorializing, newspaper editors carried these tendencies to an extreme during this contest. Press support for Bryan, even among normally Democratic publications, withered away.

The deep sense of unrest and dissatisfaction blanketing the country helped make this not only the most eventful and exciting but also the most historically significant election since Lincoln's transformative victory in 1860.[5] Occurring in an atmosphere of national crisis, it caused many people to seriously doubt whether social order could be maintained and even whether democracy would survive in the United States. It also raised the question of the future direction of the country. Would it go the traditional route, dominated by rural, small-town mores and emphasizing producer values and small-scale organization, or would it take the United States down the path of urban industrialism, in which large organizations and business values predominated? Bryan's insistence that industrial prosperity rested on the nation's agricultural base was countered by McKinley's conviction that the health of agriculture and every other aspect of the American economy ultimately rested on the growth of industry. Bryan is remembered primarily for his defiant demand at the Democratic convention not to "press down upon labor this crown of thorns" or to "crucify mankind upon a cross of gold." But he also memorably argued for the primacy of rural America, asserting, "The great cities rest upon our broad and fertile prairies. Burn down your cities and leave our farms, and your cities will spring up again as if by magic; but destroy our farms and the grass will grow in the streets of every city in the country."[6] The election of 1896 thus constituted, in the words of the historian J. Rogers Hollingsworth, "the last great protest of the agrarian order against urban domination."[7]

At first glance, the two candidates could hardly have seemed more different. Fifty-three-year-old former Ohio congressman and two-term governor William McKinley had risen steadily through the ranks of the Grand Old Party (GOP). With Cleveland industrialist and future U.S. senator Mark Hanna advising him and championing his cause after 1888, he handily locked up the Republican nomination in 1896 on the first ballot. After growing up in Niles and Poland, small villages near Youngstown, and serving with distinction in the Civil War, McKinley had read law privately and briefly attended law school in Albany, New York, before starting up a practice in 1867 in Canton, Ohio, a bustling, growing town of about 6,000 population.[8] Nine years later, still only thirty-three, he first won election to Congress. Solid, trustworthy, and reliable, McKinley gained a reputation as the House of Representatives' foremost champion of the protective tariff, becoming known otherwise for his caution and inscrutability. He possessed an elusive personal attraction that was the opposite of charisma but that bound men closely to him. More than most politicians, who tend toward loquacity, he was a good listener, giving all he met a sense that he was genuinely interested in what they had to say.[9] McKinley was a valued friend of President Rutherford B. Hayes, who had been one of his commanding officers during the Civil War and who had just moved into the Executive Mansion when he first arrived in Washington in 1877. He also was close to James Garfield, whose friendship helped obtain for him a slot on the powerful House Ways and Means Committee at the start of his third term in office. Throughout his career, he benefited heavily from the friendships and alliances he so easily made, quite apart from the positions he took on the issues of the day.

Intelligent, conscientious, and hardworking, McKinley could hardly be described as brilliant, but few of his associates in Congress merited that description either. Timing, luck, and resourcefulness played important roles in his rise to prominence, and he enjoyed the useful quality of being able to land on his feet after a defeat, always a helpful attribute for an ambitious politician. Having lost his bid for the speakership in 1889 by a single vote and having then had his name attached to a major tariff bill the following year, he was swept out of office in the fall of 1890 in one of the most thorough congressional housecleanings in American history. A 166–159 Republican majority turned overnight into a 235–88 Democratic advantage. Being out of office and thus available to run for the Ohio governorship, however, immediately made him the front-runner for his party's nomination for that position in 1891, and he swept back into office, handily winning reelection two years later. Taking leave of the governor's chair in 1895 enabled him to devote full time to running for the presidency the following year with the help of Mark Hanna, whose organizational genius and fundraising skills proved crucial to his success, first in obtaining the nomination and then in proceeding to victory in November.

William Jennings Bryan was born in 1860 in Salem, a county-seat town of about 1,500 people in southern Illinois. He grew up in the nurturing confines of a genteel family presided over by circuit court judge Silas Bryan. The judge had served eight years in the Illinois state senate and had also run unsuccessfully for a seat in Congress in 1872, when his son Will was twelve years old. The boy went on to obtain four years of collegiate education (compared to McKinley's single semester) at a small sectarian school in Jacksonville, a larger county-seat town of approximately 10,000 in the central part of the state.[10] He followed that with two years of legal training in Chicago at Union Law College, one of the most distinguished institutions in the state. "I was born in the greatest of all ages," Bryan wrote in his memoirs, proud of his family upbringing and grateful for the chances he had received to better himself. "The story of my life is but an account of opportunities improved and of circumstances of which I have taken advantage."[11] Looking for better chances to advance himself and his young family, he moved to Lincoln, Nebraska, in 1887, after four years of practicing law in Jacksonville. Having quickly doubled its population during the previous several years to about 40,000, Nebraska's capital city was the political, educational, and cultural center of the state.

Bryan's political rise was more meteoric than McKinley's, elevating him to a seat in Congress just three years after arriving in Nebraska. Then, after two terms in the House of Representatives and a failed bid for a U.S. Senate seat in 1894 (as a Democrat in heavily Republican Nebraska, despite his having obtained 75 percent of the vote in a senatorial preference primary), he captured the Democratic presidential nomination at thirty-six. Bryan's attractive personal qualities, similar to McKinley's, stood him in good stead in the political environment of eastern Nebraska, where Republicans almost always won elections. Like his Ohio counterpart, the Nebraskan won people over by his honesty, integrity, and hard work, as well as by his approachableness, kindliness, and good humor. Male compatriots often used the word "love" to describe their attachment to McKinley; Bryan's devoted followers virtually elevated him to sainthood. His devotion to principle and his constant evocation of "democracy" as his guiding dictum rendered him, in the eyes of his adherents, "the Great Commoner." Warm, expressive, and heartily enthusiastic in his dealings with people, he possessed a knack for seducing even his staunchest enemies when he got the chance to engage with them personally. Even more than McKinley, who could appear remote on first meeting, Bryan behaved democratically with everyone, from powerful prince to lowliest servant.

Unlike McKinley, who developed a reputation for being a man of many masks, Bryan seemed to harbor no secret places in his personality. With him, everything appeared to rest on the surface. "His life is an open book," wrote one observer; "there are no revelations to be made, no surprises to be sprung, no scandals to be feared."[12] Bryan in his thirties and forties cut a striking figure, often commented on in the press. Standing 5'10" and weighing about 200 pounds, erect of bearing, and with warm brown eyes and flowing dark mane, he commanded people's attention with his dramatic appearance. Although later he would grow a paunch, his hair would thin and he would go bald, his eyes would lose their luster, and his skin would wrinkle early, Bryan as a young man was dashing and magnetic, "beautiful as Apollo," a Missouri politician was quoted as saying.[13] Never careful about clothes, Bryan typically wore black alpaca coats—the better to hide dirt, stains, and wrinkles—and baggy trousers. A friend of his doubted whether he had ever owned evening dress.[14] McKinley, in contrast, although not a flashy dresser, was meticulous about his attire. At 5'6" and tending toward portliness, he used clothes as a way to make himself appear taller and to reinforce his natural dignity. Naturally reticent and inclined to listen more than to talk, McKinley tended to keep his counsel; Bryan, much more extroverted, hearty, and unguarded in his words, found it difficult to conceal his emotions.

Although both men were highly ambitious, Bryan's drive for political advancement shone through more obviously. The mere idea that he could, and would, run for the nation's highest office in 1896 astounded many political insiders, but no more than had his run for Congress in 1890, at age thirty, after having lived in Nebraska for less than three years. Bryan's boldness in striving was matched by his success in capturing the prizes he went after. Known later primarily for having lost three bids for the presidency (in 1896, 1900, and 1908), he should be remembered as much for having been able to capture those nominations in the first place and for remaining a vital force within the Democratic Party for three decades, longer than either Theodore Roosevelt or Woodrow Wilson were active in their respective parties. He finished his political career in Wilson's cabinet as secretary of state and retained the respect and affection of millions of devoted followers throughout his lifetime.

Only Bryan, and perhaps his wife, thought in early July 1896 that "the logic of the situation," as he put it, would dictate his choice as the Democratic nominee that year. It took a remarkable convergence of circumstances to make that happen, but in the end Bryan's strategy worked just as he had planned. He believed that if he could get a chance to address the convention, he would be able to stampede the delegates to his side. Afterward, it was said that his stem-winding "Cross of Gold" speech had brought him out of nowhere to victory, but the facts were somewhat more complicated.[15] For more than a year, Bryan had been communicating with various state Democratic leaders and delegates, preaching the cause of free silver and letting it be known that although he wanted individual delegations to go to the convention uncommitted, he was available for the nomination. Beyond that, he had energetically crisscrossed the country, mainly throughout the West and South, delivering speeches on the subject and trying out themes and phrases that he would later weave into his seemingly spontaneous oration at the national convention. By the time he arrived there, he had already tested the "crown of thorns" and "cross of gold" metaphors multiple times. At Chicago, he successfully maneuvered to be the last of five speakers in the platform debate on the money issue, so that when he bounded up the steps to the podium for his twenty minutes of fame, he was eminently ready.[16]

As he proceeded through his carefully rehearsed speech, he made a point of not criticizing people in the East. Rather, he expressed the wish that his counterparts along the Atlantic coast would take note of and be responsive to the needs and desires of residents in the interior. Just three years earlier and not far from the Chicago Coliseum where the convention was being held, Frederick Jackson Turner had urged his fellow historians to direct closer attention to the western frontier. Bryan now called on his fellow Democrats to pay heed to

> the hardy pioneers who have braved all the dangers of the wilderness, who have made the desert to blossom as the rose—the pioneers away out there (pointing to the West), who rear their children near to Nature's heart, where they can mingle their voices with the voices of

CHAPTER TWO

the birds—out there where they have erected schoolhouses for the education of their young, churches where they praise their Creator, and cemeteries where rest the ashes of their dead—these people, we say, are as deserving of the consideration of our party as any people in this country.[17]

This was a summons for sectional parity.

Bryan's speech also sounded the trumpet for remembering the vital place of small towns and farmsteads alongside the developing constellation of cities in America. Conservative spokesmen had fashioned their definition of the businessman too narrowly, he suggested: "The man who is employed for wages is as much a business man as his employer, the attorney in a *country town* is as much a business man as the corporation counsel in a great metropolis; the merchant at the *cross-roads store* is as much a business man as the merchant of New York; the *farmer* who goes forth in the morning and toils all day . . . is as much a business man as the man who goes upon the board of trade and bets upon the price of grain."[18]

The gallery, like a well-trained choir, was with Bryan from the beginning—now quiet, now cheering—punctuating the air with spontaneous shouts of "Give it to them, Bill," and "Go after them, Willie!" Hushed at the end, as Bryan stood transfixed for several seconds in a Christlike pose, it then joyously exploded in astonishment, people laughing, crying, and embracing each other in the wonder of the moment. "The floor of the convention seemed to heave up," a reporter for Joseph Pulitzer's *New York World* wrote. "Everybody seemed to go mad at once. . . . The whole face of the convention was broken by the tumult—hills and valleys of shrieking men and women."[19] During the ensuing demonstration, which lasted almost twice as long as the speech itself, stout men lifted Bryan on their shoulders and paraded him around the hall. The following day, aided by all his careful preparation and by the work of faithful lieutenants on the convention floor, Bryan amassed the two-thirds vote needed to obtain the nomination on the fifth ballot. The impact of his address reverberated across the nation, as wire services carried news of the proceedings to every corner of the land. The speech, according to William Allen White, "thrilled a continent, and for a day a nation was in a state of mental and moral catalepsy. If the election had been held that July day, Bryan would have been chosen President."[20] But his work had only begun.

Once Republicans realized they had a fight on their hands, they pulled out all the stops, raising an unprecedented campaign chest, estimated at anywhere from $3.5 million to $16 million,[21] enabling them to flood the country with campaign literature, speakers, posters, newspaper ready-prints (preprinted pages with national, regional, or state news and advertising), all under the watchful direction of campaign chairman Mark Hanna. Although Hanna urged his candidate to emulate Bryan and take to the hustings, McKinley insisted on staying home, as almost every previous candidate had done, to run a "front-porch campaign." For eight weeks in September and October, every day but Sunday, thousands of enthusiastic supporters and numbers of the merely curious traveled by train to Canton, where they were welcomed by military escorts and brass bands and taken in tow by loyal McKinley lieutenants. They trampled his lawn and flowerbeds, leaving them a sea of mud. They were pleased to meet and listen in person to their hero, who made it a point to shake the hand of everyone wanting to do so. The proceedings were all heavily scripted, with McKinley or one of his aides vetting and often revising the prepared statements of the visiting delegation leaders before they were delivered. The candidate tailored his own remarks in response, always aiming at shaping the stories that would be published in the next morning's newspapers. Some days, he met as many as a couple of dozen delegations and spoke to as many as 30,000 enthusiastic listeners. Altogether, an estimated 750,000 people came into personal contact with the Ohioan in this way.[22]

The Democratic financial team's inability to raise more than a tiny fraction of the Republicans' total (they obtained around $300,000 for the national campaign and a similar amount at the local level) largely dictated Bryan's strategy. Taking advantage of his oratorical ability and youthful energy, he undertook a virtually unprecedented national speaking tour. Only Stephen A. Douglas in 1860, Horace Greeley in 1872, and James G. Blaine in 1884 had violated the unwritten rule that major party candidates should let "the office seek the man" and toured to stump for votes. All of them had gone down to defeat in the process. With little help forthcoming from the Democratic National Committee, Bryan tried to make a virtue of necessity, taking to the rails during August, September, and October. He traveled more than 18,000 miles across twenty-six states, making approximately 250 major addresses, as well as hundreds of other brief whistle-stop speeches from the rear platform of the train, and talking to as many as 5 million people. The crowds, ranging from a few dozen at village depots to as many as 50,000 in Columbus, Ohio, and 75,000 on the Boston Common, were with few exceptions noisy, responsive, and enthusiastic. During the early weeks, until he was provided with a private car, Bryan often made his own travel arrangements, purchased his own tickets, and even carried his own luggage. Throughout his grueling travels, he displayed remarkable stamina, patience, and good humor.[23]

In retrospect, Democratic strategists made two major miscalculations. The more serious one was the decision to focus primarily on free silver. Although not entirely neglecting other points in the Democratic platform and although trying to encompass industrial laborers and other urban residents in his appeal, Bryan directed most of his energies at the money issue. Hanna gleefully observed, "He's talking silver all the time, and that's where we've got him."[24] Many observers also criticized Bryan's decision to follow the advice of party potentates essentially to write off the Northeast, including the crucial states of New Jersey and New York, in order to concentrate his attention during the latter weeks of the campaign on the Midwest. Focusing primarily on the heartland made a certain kind of sense, but since 1872 the Democrats had carried New Jersey, with its ten electoral votes, every time and New York, with its thirty-six votes, three of six times. Wins in those two states, which in retrospect were attainable, would have brought the Democrats within three electoral votes of victory in 1896.[25]

In the end, as Bryan noted in *The First Battle,* his postmortem book on the election, the margins in California, Oregon, North Dakota, Indiana, Kentucky, and West Virginia were so thin that fewer than 20,000 changed votes in those six states would have turned the election to him.[26] In a system governed by the Electoral College, Bryan, like everyone else, organized his thinking as much along geographic lines as in terms of interest groups, ethnicity, religion, or other breakdowns of the electorate. Both parties assumed that the Democrats would carry the Solid South and most of the West and that the Republicans would dominate the Northeast, with the possible exceptions of the swing states of New York and New Jersey.

McKinley and Bryan and their campaign managers operated on the correct assumption that the election would be largely decided in the Midwest.[27] Bryan, not surprisingly, spent most of his time campaigning there, especially during the final month, hoping that his midwestern origins, free silver's appeal, and his moralistic preachments would win over farmers and urban workers as well as middle-class voters there. McKinley, the best-known politician in the Midwest, had made himself a familiar figure with the electorate by his frequent travels in the region, and only Bryan managed to outdo him in that regard. In 1892 the governor had undertaken a major speaking tour from Iowa to Maine for the GOP, and two years later, during the off-year election campaign, he had traveled 16,000 miles and delivered 371 speeches in 300 cities to an estimated 2 million people.[28] McKinley loved touring. No president before him had traveled as extensively. Running for governor in 1891, he had visited eighty-six of Ohio's eighty-eight counties, speaking more than 130 times. Running for reelection two years later, he crossed eighty of those counties, speaking more than 300 times.[29] McKinley thus was no foreigner to the kind of full-bore traveling campaign that Bryan waged in 1896.

Bryan's touring and McKinley's front-porch politicking, however, required backup from effective campaign organizations, and this is where the Republicans pressed their advantage. With the midwestern vote likely to turn the election, both parties broke precedent to establish their headquarters in Chicago, with the Democrats opening an auxiliary office in Washington, D.C., and the Republicans also operating one in New York City, where Hanna spent most of his time.[30] As his chief aide and right-hand man in Chicago, the Cleveland industrialist chose Charles G. Dawes, a thirty-one-year-old businessman and former resident of Lincoln, who had lived near the Bryans and attended the same church, and who continued his friendship with them despite the nasty things Republicans were saying about the Nebraskan that year. From Chicago, the Republicans launched their educational campaign, pouring out 275 different pamphlets and pieces of literature in more than a dozen languages. They also sent out hundreds of campaign speakers to canvass the region. Altogether, the organization distributed some 250 million documents, or eighteen for every vote cast in November. Theodore Roosevelt joked that Hanna was advertising McKinley just like patent medicine. To finance these activities, millions of dollars flowed in, mainly from large corporations and from wealthy bankers and businessmen. On September 11, Dawes recorded in his diary that Hanna had handed him an envelope stuffed with fifty $1,000 bills from an unnamed railroad, and that he had deposited a check for a similar amount from another source that day.[31] Contributions of a quarter million dollars each from Standard Oil and J. P. Morgan helped underwrite the unprecedented blitz. The Republican message, coinciding with McKinley's homiletic speeches in Canton, emphasized three main themes: the inflationary dangers posed by free silver, not the least of which was the negative impact it would have on wage laborers; the prosperity that would derive from McKinley's tariff policies and steady leadership; and the class hatred unleashed by the Democratic platform.[32]

By the standards of the twentieth century, in which landslide victories of 60 percent or more occurred several times, McKinley's triumph on November 3, with 271 electoral votes to Bryan's 176, capturing 7,102,246 popular votes (51.1 percent) to Bryan's 6,492,559 (46.7 percent), was modest enough. Nevertheless, it turned out to be a decisive win in several ways. The 4.4 percentage points separating the candidates in the popular vote, in fact, constituted a sizable gap in comparison to the razor-thin differences characteristic of the previous two decades. McKinley established prosperity, as he had promised, and organized a practical and effective administration, and he later built on that foundation to perpetuate Republican rule for a generation.

Many reasons for the Republican victory were advanced: Bryan's faulty geographic strategy and his overemphasis on silver, McKinley's winning personality and extensive governmental experience, the defection of conservative—or gold—Democrats allied with outgoing President Grover Cleveland, the ten to one or greater spending advantage enjoyed by the Republicans, the effectiveness of the Republican advertising campaign, the lies and exaggerations spread about Bryan, and the fraud, intimidation, and bribery that had been so prevalent in the campaign. The last point, much touted by Bryan and his adherents and often emphasized in history textbooks, had some basis in fact to be sure, but recent historians have tended to downplay its importance.[33]

Bryan's natural constituency lay more among the poor sharecroppers of the South and the displaced wheat farmers on the edge of the Great Plains than in the relatively more prosperous agricultural regions of the Midwest. Of the twelve states from Ohio to the Dakotas, Kansas, and Nebraska, Bryan carried only Missouri, Kansas, Nebraska, and South Dakota. The first of these was as much southern in character as midwestern, and the others were all heavily caught up in the Populism associated with low wheat prices on the Plains. Most contemporary characterizations of Bryan, like those made by later historians, identified him as a champion of the West and South. Few associated him particularly with the Midwest, despite his Illinois origins and his residence in Lincoln, Nebraska, which straddles the Midwest and the Great Plains. This may help explain why the Midwest experienced especially marked shifts to the Republicans in the urban vote.[34]

Bryan failed to carry a single heavily industrialized state, and McKinley prevailed in virtually every large city. McKinley's business-friendly, economically expansionist orientation, in tune with the rise of cities and industry, had carried the day. Bryan, the spokesman for a more traditional, agriculturally oriented society, where small-town values and mind-sets prevailed, saw his cause go down to defeat.

The election, close as it was, was a historic one. Its most obvious effect was to engineer a major realignment in the political system, bringing to an end twenty years of stalemate and inaugurating a generation of Republican rule that would be broken only with the advent of Franklin D. Roosevelt in 1932. (Woodrow Wilson's election in 1912 was merely an aberration, made possible by the split in the Republican vote caused by Theodore Roosevelt's third-party revolt that year.) Political historians refer to the years between 1894 and 1896 as a realigning period. To perpetuate itself, the realignment that occurred would have to be followed by several more Republican victories, which is in fact what occurred. Along with the new Republican majority came a shift in the foundation that underlay it. The GOP had become the "party of prosperity," according to the political historian Paul Kleppner, rather than one sustained primarily by evangelical Protestantism or piety.[35]

In addition, although the rises of urbanization and of industrialization, which had been accelerating for several decades, were not direct outcomes of the election, they clearly were facilitated by McKinley's victory. He, more than Bryan, felt comfortable with the direction of change at the turn of the century. Nor was it accidental that American industry experienced a major phase of consolidation between 1897 and 1904. McKinley and Roosevelt expressed some concern about monopolistic tendencies but did relatively little to hinder them. More than the Democrats, the Republicans located America's future in the cities and the factory system.[36]

A third outcome of the 1896 election was a significant alteration in the political process, as a new style of politics came to the fore. The prevailing "army" or "military" mode of organization gave way to an "educational" or "merchandising" style of campaigning, which sought to market and advertise candidates much like soap or cornflakes. The millions of dollars raised by Hanna's organization that year carried this new style of politicking to levels earlier unimagined. Military language had continued to dominate General Benjamin Harrison's rhetoric in his runs for the presidency. William McKinley, who enjoyed being referred to as "Major" because of his Civil War experience, nevertheless discarded the kind of military language he had used earlier in his career and replaced it with a merchandising approach to run for office. The election of 1896 was precedent setting with regard to strategies for soliciting votes. Torchlight parades, bonfires, and mass meetings, which had been de rigueur for decades, gave way to other kinds of rallies, public speaking, and the increased distribution of campaign literature and advertising. Bryan's dramatic whistle-stop tour quickly became the accepted mode of presidential campaigning, whereas McKinley's front-porch approach became a virtual relic. But the Republicans' highly organized, lavishly funded, and expertly manned effort became the model that all subsequent efforts attempted to emulate as far as they were able to afford it.[37]

A fourth major effect of the election was to boost political progressivism, which had already begun to emerge fitfully at the state and local levels. The contest effectively dealt a death blow to the Populists, but, like many other soon-to-be progressives, Bryan picked avidly among the Populist bones, adopting many of their platform proposals as his own, from the direct election of U.S. senators and the initiative and referendum to progressive income taxes, increased regulation of corporations, and measures to boost farm prices. From 1896 until his death in 1925, Bryan, always in search of new and appealing issues, stood in the vanguard of those trying to push the Democratic Party away from its traditional small-government orientation and toward a more activist approach to governmental policy.[38]

McKinley, generally depicted as a standpat conservative, also deserves credit for smoothing the way toward a more progressive brand of politics. Although recognized primarily throughout his congressional career for his unbending advocacy of the protective tariff, he softened his position after 1890 and began preaching the virtues of trade reciprocity and the desirability of expanding foreign markets. On the money issue, although he pragmatically went along with Republican platform phraseology endorsing "the existing gold standard" in order to win the nomination in 1896, he had long been known as a friend of silver coinage. After 1897, the discovery of new gold deposits in Alaska, Australia, and South Africa and the development of new methods for processing the metal turned free silver into a moot issue. Although doing little in a practical way to address the trust question while in office, McKinley did make some rhetorical overtures in the direction of investigating them and might actually have done something effective about them had he served a full second term. He obtained a deserved reputation as a friend of labor and maintained fairly good relations with the unions. His man Hanna, hidebound on many issues and closely identified with corporate interests, was nevertheless known in Cleveland as an enlightened employer and one who sought to improve the welfare of labor in general. It is fair to say that McKinley served as an important transitional figure on the road to progressivism.[39]

A fifth major area transformed in the wake of the 1896 election was foreign affairs. McKinley's presidency was heavily weighted toward foreign policy, and by the end he had done more than anyone else to expand American horizons and to carve out a larger position for the United States in the world. Though reluctant to lead the United States into the Spanish-American War in 1898, he quickly became an enthusiastic expansionist, winning Senate approval for the peace treaty annexing the Philippines and subsequently moving forward on many foreign policy fronts. During and after the war, the United States annexed Hawaii and made Cuba a protectorate, paved the way for building an isthmian canal, converted the Caribbean into an American lake, proclaimed an "open door" in China (thereby establishing precedent for the economic penetration of other regions), and involved itself diplomatically in a variety of unprecedented ways. From the beginning, foreign affairs occupied the predominant place in cabinet discussions, and McKinley vigorously took the lead in formulating policy before, during, and after the war with Spain.[40]

New responsibilities demanded additional powers. Just as the president became more of a world leader, he also assumed a more expansive role in domestic policy making. A sixth and final result of the election of 1896 was McKinley's initiation of the first modern presidency in American history. That is the contention of McKinley biographer Lewis L. Gould. The Ohioan deserves credit for introducing a number of the changes for which Theodore Roosevelt and Woodrow Wilson later received credit. When McKinley entered the White House in 1897, the building itself was outmoded in many ways. It lacked electricity and modern plumbing and was falling apart. The tiny presidential staff, consisting of a private secretary and six clerks and typists (one of whom handled his wife's callers and mail), expanded sixfold by the beginning of his second term in order to cope with the additional duties, paperwork, and correspondence that came along with the new activities and responsibilities of the office. Quick to take advantage of emerging technologies, McKinley was the first president to talk on the telephone extensively, the first to use a dictating machine, and the first to ride in an automobile while in office. During the Spanish-American War, he converted one room of the White House into a war room, replete with up-to-date charts and maps of the battle zones, and in it he installed fifteen telephone lines linked to the eight executive departments as well as to leaders in the Senate and House.[41]

As the first twentieth-century president, and being more comfortable with modern communications than any of his predecessors, McKinley recognized the advantages for enhancing his own image and power that could result from establishing better relations with the press. Although generally unwilling to do interviews for the record, McKinley granted reporters considerably greater access than they had enjoyed in the past. He made an effort to get to know them, arranged accommodations for them on the second floor of the Executive Mansion, and had his personal secretary, John Addison Porter, meet twice daily with them to provide information they could use in their articles. The White House became a news center in a way it had never been before. George B. Cortelyou, on whom McKinley relied heavily to manage office affairs even before he formally took over Porter's job in 1900, emerged as a prototype of the modern White House press secretary. All of this worked to the advantage of McKinley, who can be seen as the initiator of news management in the executive branch. The president also drew on his extensive experience and numerous contacts on Capitol Hill to influence congressional actions and legislative programs in unprecedented ways. One of his favored tools was the special commission, set up to deal with specific problems by collecting facts and making reports and recommendations. The process was used to good effect on issues such as Hawaii, the Philippines, and monetary policy. The use of experts in government, which became a hallmark of progressivism, was experimented with earlier by McKinley.[42]

The presidential office, in effect, became institutionalized. McKinley and Cortelyou, who also became the prototype for the modern chief of staff, led the way in initiating the process. The president, being a man of routine, scheduled regular cabinet meetings on Tuesday and Friday mornings. Two members of his original cabinet, Secretary of State John B. Sherman and Secretary of War Russell B. Alger, proved to be weak links and became the victims of the necessity for modern, streamlined executive management, which had been imposed by the Spanish-American War. Their respective successors John Hay, who had served as Abraham Lincoln's secretary, and Elihu Root, a successful New York lawyer, emerged as dominant figures in McKinley's new cabinet, epitomizing the qualities demanded by a new, fast-paced, organizational society. Root's reorganization of the army during the early years of the new century was a largely unheralded but hugely important reform. It allowed a much quicker military mobilization than otherwise would have been possible later on when the country went to war in 1917.[43]

McKinley's penchant for travel, which brought the public into closer contact with him than with any previous chief executive, was a final factor in making him the first modern president. Although history remembers Bryan for his extensive touring of the country in 1896, McKinley, who stayed at home during that election, did not lag far behind the Democratic contender as an energetic traveler during the years before and after that contest. In office, he continued to travel widely, primarily to promote the Republican Party but also for relaxation and to expand his contacts with the voters. During the 1898 congressional elections, he undertook a two-week tour through six western states, making fifty-seven public appearances in Chicago, St. Louis, Omaha, and other places before enthusiastic crowds. The following October, he arranged another two-week political excursion, this time through nine states in the Middle West, making eighty speeches and talks along the way. GOP leaders welcomed him enthusiastically, hoping that some of his popularity would rub off on them. McKinley understood the benefits such junkets could confer on Republicans in outlying areas as well as the enhanced popularity they would bring him. His final journey ended tragically in Buffalo, New York, at the Pan-American Exposition on September 6, 1901, when he was fatally shot by anarchist gunman Leon Czolgosz. McKinley's appearance at Buffalo had originally been scheduled for June 13, at the culmination of a six-week swing through the Southwest to the West Coast and back again by a northern route—the most extensive tour he had ever undertaken. When his wife Ida fell ill in California, however, they cut short the excursion, returned to Washington, and rescheduled the Buffalo meeting.[44]

The journeys McKinley seemed to enjoy most were the ones he made each year back home to Canton, a place for which he retained deep affection and which, throughout his life, he longed to return to. At the depot there, as he and his wife departed for his first inauguration, he took leave of friends and neighbors, voice faltering as he told them that he would cherish in his heart "the sweetest memories and the tenderest thoughts of my old home—my home now, and, I trust, my home hereafter, so long as I live." While living in the White House, he enjoyed reminiscing about his barefoot days as a youth in Ohio driving the cows out to pasture. "You know, I was a simple country boy," he said in a reminiscent mood. In July 1899, anticipating retirement, the McKinleys bought back their old home in Canton, where they had lived before going to Congress and from which he had waged his front-porch campaign three years earlier. Theodore Roosevelt, much wealthier than he, was not much impressed with the house, but McKinley was rightfully proud of it and looked forward expectantly to returning to it. While in the White House, he continued to peruse his home-town newspaper to keep apprised of friends and local affairs there. In 1900, before deciding to run for reelection, he had hinted that he might opt to retire after a single term in order to get back all the sooner to his beloved Canton.[45]

Bryan was a capable and intelligent person who thought seriously about and possessed many useful ideas for addressing public issues and problems. Nevertheless, he appears to have been more suited for campaigning than for governing. However effective an executive he might or might not have made, we can be sure that a Bryan administration would have been a progressive one, geared to change and reform. Long before many of his contemporaries joined the movement and up until the end of his life, Bryan stood in the vanguard of reform-minded leadership in the Democratic Party. The historian Lawrence Levine identified his closeness to the people as the most salient feature of his career.[46] His democratic faith, summed up in the phrase "let the people rule," derived from his father's teaching, his reading of Jefferson and the inspiration he took from Jackson, and his own experience among ordinary people like himself, first in the Midwest and later all over the country. He believed, he wrote in his memoirs, in "the goodness of the American people, their patriotism, their moral courage, their high ideals, their willingness to sacrifice for their convictions—the virtues that not only make popular government possible but insure its success."[47]

His mind-set, typical among progressives, was dualistic, setting good against evil and morality against treachery. Progressive politicians typically branded their opponents as "enemies" and maintained a wide gulf between themselves and those who dared to contradict them. History for them was a story of continual conflict between rich and poor, dominators and dominated, the "interests" and the "people," society's oppressors and its saviors. Bryan's general inclination was to define issues in stark, black-and-white terms. He displayed an unfortunate tendency to demonize opponents, even within his own party, in a way that threatened or ended old friendships and alienated potential backers. He possessed a penchant for oversimplifying issues, and his rhetoric, though sometimes magnificent, tended to exaggeration and windiness. By nature, he was as much a moralist and a preacher as a politician—thus "the political evangelist" tag, which clung to him throughout his career.

Yet although he did not yield readily to accommodation and compromise solutions, Bryan was capable of working with those who were not entirely in accord with him. Like his contemporaries, he drank from the fount of pragmatism, which emerged as the dominant American philosophy during the heyday of progressivism in the early 1900s. That made him, in the words of biographer Louis Koenig, a "practical ideologue," one who sought workable solutions to problems while simultaneously maintaining high ideals. He also simply bowed to political expediency more often than he was willing to admit. Though a teetotaler himself and strongly opposed to intoxicating drink, he hesitated to ally with the temperance cause for twenty years because it would not have gone down well with most of his Nebraska constituents. The greatest blot on his career was his unwillingness to apply his democratic principles to African Americans as well as to the rest of the population by challenging racists within his own party and, more generally, in the public at large. His political courage possessed distinct limits.[48]

On many other issues, however, he was willing to stake out positions in advance of many of his contemporaries. Some of his prominent critics, such as the historian Richard Hofstadter, believed that Bryan's political career after 1896 could best be understood as "a long, persistent search for an issue comparable in effect to free silver, and an equally persistent campaign to keep himself in the public eye," but other observers discovered in his record far more consistency, integrity, and idealism.[49] His progressive views, like those of many of his contemporaries, evolved naturally, advancing beyond free silver and antimonopoly positions to include such measures as the progressive income tax, the initiative and referendum, stricter railroad regulation, municipal ownership of utilities, pure food and drug laws, a department of labor, a ban on corporate financing of campaigns, the popular election of U.S. senators, a one-term limit on the presidency, and a variety of other political and economic reforms. Earlier than most of his fellows, he advocated the vote for women. Although he always remained a *rural* progressive at heart, his work on behalf of issues like those mentioned above brought him into contact and sometimes into effective alliance with the larger and more powerful wing of urban progressives, including people such as Jane Addams, John Dewey, Theodore Roosevelt, and Woodrow Wilson. The Republican Roosevelt, though opposed to Bryan on many points, drew liberally on the Great Commoner's ideas in formulating his own programs.[50]

Bryan was a different type of political leader, one reliant on his own oratorical skills and power of personality to maintain a large and devoted following, holding office only for brief periods of time. With the help of his wife and his brother, Charles, he developed an extensive personal organization, maintaining card files containing as many as a half million names of friends and supporters. Between 1901 and 1923, his weekly newspaper, *The Commoner,* went out to as many as 150,000 subscribers.[51]

In the end, Bryan's most lasting political legacy lay in his success in helping transform the Democratic Party from a laissez-faire entity into one more in tune with progressive principles. During Bryan's day in the arena, it began to become a party of political reform, one that later transitioned through Woodrow Wilson's New Freedom into Franklin Roosevelt's New Deal. In the process, he exerted a greater impact on American politics during the quarter century after 1896 than any other political leader aside from Wilson and the first Roosevelt.[52] They, however, spoke for national constituencies, whereas Bryan, to a large degree, remained a sectional spokesman for the South and West as well as for his own native Midwest.

A distinction needs to be made between politics and culture, for with regard to the latter Bryan clung much more closely to the innate conservatism that was so much a part of his personality. The various impulses that so profoundly disrupted American life after the turn of the century— technological, economic, social, intellectual, and cultural, as well as political—were more disturbing to Bryan and his followers than they were to McKinley and his backers, although the latter were also affected by them. The pace of change in America picked up dramatically during the second decade of the twentieth century, a decade after McKinley's assassination, and Bryan increasingly found himself enmeshed in more emotional and more difficult challenges than McKinley had ever been required to confront. The American people, living in a world increasingly dominated by cities and factory production, felt keenly the effects of the new media and modes of communication; the adoption of the automobile; the rise of the New Woman; an influx of new immigrants from southern and eastern Europe; a proliferation of scientific discoveries, challenging new philosophies, and imported European ideas; growing secularism; and rising educational opportunities and expectations. These all tended to call into question long-held values and assumptions and to suggest new ways of thinking and living. Bryan and his admirers and followers were able to cope with and accommodate themselves to many of the new challenges and questions facing them, but at some point they began to feel uncomfortable with and to resist the changes they were being called on to make. During the last decade of his life, the Great Commoner, while still engaged in many of the battles he had been waging for years, found himself frequently entangled in issues and in alliances with people he had generally avoided earlier.

During the second decade of the twentieth century, he vigorously took up the prohibition cause, from which he had earlier distanced himself, and he championed world peace, calling for a popular referendum on war and seeing Henry Ford off on his Peace Ship mission in 1915, although he declined to join the auto magnate on the cruise. It was during the last five years of his life, when he became associated in the public mind with anti-Darwinism, the Ku Klux Klan, and the promotion of Florida real estate, that his good intentions and his reputation as a progressive reformer suffered the most. Bryan certainly harbored no sympathy for the Klan, but he argued at the 1924 Democratic National Convention that to condemn the organization by name would be politically counterproductive for the party. His real estate shilling, though out of character for him, was conducted with restraint and was hardly more egregious than some of the moneymaking schemes engaged in by many of his contemporaries. On the Chautauqua circuit, which brought educational and inspirational entertainments to rural Americans at the turn of the century, his theme increasingly became the dangers posed to the morals and ideals of the citizenry by deteriorating values and declining faith. In his famous "Prince of Peace" speech, delivered thousands of times over the years, Bryan revealed that although he was interested in the science of government, he remained even more interested in religion and that although he enjoyed making political speeches, he would rather talk about religion than politics.[53] In becoming the most visible leader during the early 1920s of the movement to ban the teaching of evolution in the public schools, Bryan reinforced his ties with millions of evangelical Christians who had long admired him, and he won the affection of countless others who sided with him on the issue. In so doing, however, he became a scapegoat for other millions of Americans whose values were more liberal on cultural and religious matters and who perceived him as a narrow-minded, provincial purveyor of retrograde ideas and values.[54]

In large part, the people for whom Bryan was speaking during the 1920s resided in rural and small-town America, and his antagonists were city dwellers and those with an increasingly urban mind-set. When Bryan died five days after the famous Scopes trial ended in the small town of Dayton, Tennessee, in July 1925 (twenty-nine years to the month after his famous "Cross of Gold" speech), H. L. Mencken, who had reported the trial for the *Baltimore Sun,* penned one of the most acerbic and memorable pieces ever written by one American about another. City-born and city-bred, the iconoclastic journalist lacked empathy for small-town types like Bryan, whose religious convictions and moral values impelled them to try to mold the beliefs and behaviors of their fellow citizens. The worst thing Mencken could conceive of to say about the former Populist idol was that he was a rural man. "He knew every country town in the South and West, and he could crowd the most remote of them to suffocation by simply winding his horn," Mencken sniffed.

> He liked country lawyers, country pastors, all country people. He liked the country sounds and country smells. . . . In the presence of city folks he was palpably uneasy. Their clothes, I suspect, annoyed him, and he was suspicious of their too delicate manners. He knew all the while that they were laughing at him—if not at his baroque theology, then at least at his alpaca pantaloons. But the yokels never laughed at him.[55]

Despite the patent unfairness of Mencken's words and the provincialism and narrowness he himself was subject to, his essay reflected the tremendous changes occurring in American culture by the mid-1920s. It spoke for an increasingly large segment of the population that looked to the cities for progress, perceiving only backwardness and parochialism in America's small towns and rural hinterlands. Bryan had not changed much since 1896, but the United States had undergone a profound transformation since the time when two small-town boys from the Middle West had dueled for the presidency. For all their differences in outlook and political platforms, McKinley and Bryan had both grown up in small towns in the heartland, and they had imbibed their values, assumptions, and dreams of the future there. Yet it is not particularly helpful and in fact can be counterproductive to attempt to explain people's adult attitudes and activities by simply pointing to their childhood backgrounds. Although their experiences growing up undoubtedly profoundly influenced their mature views and behavior, there is nothing inevitable or clearly predictable about what they eventually became.

To think that there is leads to what the historian Michael Kammen calls the "fallacy of retrospective determinism." One cannot look back at an individual's previous history and identify elements in it that predictably determine that person's later actions or achievements. Too many conflicting forces and contingencies intervene to make simple explanations valid. As the historian LeRoy Ashby notes, Bryan's "solidly Protestant, village background was virtually the same as McKinley's,"[56] but the two certainly did not turn out the same. Of course, one can point to more specific influences on each and suggest how those influences might have channeled them in certain directions. For example, having a father who had worked as an iron-maker and later living in Canton, with its growing industrial output of plows, reapers, axles, boilers, roller bearings, and bridges, might have predisposed McKinley to take a favorable view toward protective tariffs. He, however, explained to people that it was President Hayes who suggested he focus on the tariff issue when he arrived as a representative in Washington. In similar fashion, Bryan's father's Bible readings, hymn singing, and practice of praying thrice daily at stated hours may well have encouraged son William to become an especially pious young man.[57] But other boys rebelled from such an atmosphere and turned into skeptics.

Ultimately, what we can say with some confidence is that the boyhood experiences of Bryan and McKinley—and of millions of boys like them who grew up in small midwestern towns and rural areas during the nineteenth century—exerted a profound influence on them and were indelibly impressed on their thoughts and psyches. Bryan remained fond of his hometown and retained so many ties with friends, relatives, and acquaintances living there that he visited it more than thirty times after moving to Nebraska in 1887.[58] (Interestingly, Salem also was the home of John T. Scopes for part of his growing-up years.) After his family moved to a farm on the edge of town when he was six years old, he spent many hours pitching hay, shoveling manure, and doing all the other chores associated with farm life, something he continued to enjoy playing at as a gentlemen farmer later at his Fairview estate outside Lincoln.

As small-town boys from the Midwest, Bryan and McKinley displayed many similar traits and adhered to many of the same beliefs and values. Both grew up in highly religious families and emerged as men of generosity and rectitude. Both learned the lessons taught in Sunday school and in their McGuffey Readers, both underwent a religious awakening during their teens, and both made religion a central part of their adult lives. Both were heavily influenced by heartland myths. As the historian Paul W. Glad points out, Bryan was more closely associated with the agrarian myth, harkening back to Jefferson and his predecessors; McKinley connected more readily with the myth of the self-made man, undergirded by the writings of Horatio Alger, the teachings of William Graham Sumner, and the attitudes of much of the general public.[59] For both, their personalities were the pillars of their success. Both were instinctively democratic, and both were addicted to sentimental poetry, Protestant hymnody, and homiletic sayings. Both carried over the family values they had imbibed as youths into their relationships with their wives and their children. McKinley's two daughters, tragically, were cut down in infancy. That experience, in part, accounted for his wife Ida's chronic invalidism, a condition that the Ohioan responded to with admirable solicitude and devotion. Bryan's wife raised their three children, ran the household efficiently, and became his most trusted and useful political adviser, even acquiring a law degree to aid her in the task. The two men, despite the personas they acquired in the press and in the public mind during the 1896 election, constructed lives that were remarkably similar in many ways.

Yet they also displayed major differences. Bryan was exuberant and outgoing, generally transparent in displaying his emotions to the public; McKinley remained stoic and reserved, hiding his feelings more often than not. Bryan's speeches touched the heart and lifted up his audiences; McKinley's aimed at the intellect and persuaded listeners by appealing to their common sense and to predictable logic. Bryan was more devoted to words, McKinley to action. Bryan spent most of his career out of office concocting new issues, devising new programs, and making promises, trying to manufacture victories for the Democrats. McKinley spent almost a quarter century in office, one third of that time as governor and president, and was practiced in executive decision making and administration. Bryan was the more willing of the two to take political risks; McKinley remained inherently cautious. Bryan frequently insulted his political opponents; McKinley almost never did. The largest difference in their careers may have hinged on Bryan's almost complete reliance on his own powers of expression and appealing personality, while McKinley enjoyed the benefit of mentors and advisers such as Hayes, Garfield, and Hanna and, behind them, the coffers of the Republican Party. Nobody ever said politics was fair.

In the end, McKinley and Bryan were quintessential expressions of democratic politics in the United States. Although both of them showed how far individuals could rise in a fluid and open society, with plentiful opportunities, especially for white males with stellar family backgrounds and adequate educations, they also were committed, like their fellow countrymen, to the building up of community. Both joined almost every organization open to them in their hometowns and quickly became local boosters.[60] Both appealed to their fellow citizens, not by standing out in any conspicuous way above them (aside from their oratorical skills), but, rather, by embodying in themselves their viewpoints, ideals, hopes, dreams, and aspirations. Despite being associated with different political parties, they were both representative of midwesterners who had grown to maturity on the Midwest's farms and in its ubiquitous small towns, and they both remained loyal to and affectionately attached to them throughout their lives.[61]

CHAPTER THREE

Henry Ford:
The Revolutionary as Nostalgist

The old village sites are still the best. These little towns made America.

—Henry Ford

During a lifetime spanning the years from the Civil War to the Cold War, Henry Ford witnessed epochal social and economic changes, playing a pivotal role himself in some of them and a lesser one in a number of others.[1] Although not the inventor of the automobile, as many people believe, nor even the creator of the assembly line and mass production, he was the first to produce a cheap, reliable motor vehicle in large quantities for the masses. By the early 1920s, half the automobiles in the world were Model T Fords. During the Ford Motor Company's remarkable expansion, its major founder, chief stockholder, and driving force emerged as the most powerful industrialist in the world. In putting America on wheels, he did more than anyone else to transform the countryside, narrow the gap between rural and city life, and boost urban influence in the economy and in politics. In so doing, he helped place his cherished small towns in an increasingly vulnerable position, exposing them to intense economic competition from and cultural domination by their larger urban counterparts.

Ford incorporated the Ford Motor Company in 1903, just before turning forty. Immensely successful during the first two decades of his reign at the company, he turned increasingly rigid, sour, and despotic during the last two, as he aged and found himself unable to effectively meet the competition and challenges facing him. His influence peaked during the 1920s, and Ford strode the industrial world as the "Colossus of Roads"—praised, fawned over, and deferred to as perhaps no other businessman in American history. Relentlessly pursued by the press, he became the most quoted and most heavily publicized private citizen in the United States.[2]

A farm boy from Michigan, Ford was regarded by the general public as the embodiment of midwestern ordinariness, projecting an image as honest, shrewd, straightforward, unpretentious, genuine, and dependable.[3] Though one of the richest men in the world, he was not thought of by most people as a fat cat or robber baron. After 1919, the entire stock of the Ford Motor Company lay in his hands and those of his wife, Clara, and his son, Edsel (the shares divided among them 55.2, 3.1, and 41.7 percent, respectively).[4] Yet he remained a genuine folk hero, in the tradition of America's proverbial self-made men, individualistic to the core. Part of the public's fascination with him lay in the tension between his image as totally ordinary and commonplace, on the one hand, and his position as larger than life and colossally rich and successful, on the other.

An avalanche of mail descended on the company—1,000 to 1,500 letters a day by the early 1920s—often addressed directly to Henry Ford himself. A large proportion of the letters were personal rather than business related. Rural folk especially came to feel that they knew the man personally. A grateful Georgia farm woman wrote in 1918 to thank him: "You know, Henry, your car lifted us out of the mud. It brought joy to our lives. We loved every rattle in its bones."[5] At the time of his death in 1947, 100,000 mourners filed past his open casket to pay their respects, and 30,000 more stood outside St. Paul's Cathedral in Detroit during the funeral. The *Cleveland Press* editorialized, "He was a multimillionaire, but the ordinary folks who came from the farm on Saturday night rated him one of them. In many ways he was."[6]

CHAPTER THREE

Ford's popular standing invited political figures to think about him as a possible candidate for office. Spending no money and making no speeches in his own behalf, he lost a bid in 1918 for one of Michigan's two U.S. Senate seats by about 7,500 votes out of 430,000 cast. (President Woodrow Wilson had personally entreated him to enter the race.)[7] Five years later, public opinion polls showed him far out in front of every other presumptive candidate for the presidency, including incumbent Warren G. Harding. The president's numbers added up to little more than half of Ford's, despite uncertainty over whether Ford was a Republican or a Democrat. After Calvin Coolidge ascended to the presidency in August 1923, Ford, who had trouble speaking more than a few words in front of audiences and who possessed no talent for democratic decision making, made the sensible decision not to run against him.[8]

The man's fame and appeal were so enormous that they extended far beyond the borders of the United States. In western Europe, "Fordismus" stood for the assembly line and new methods of mass production, which promised growing abundance for all. Ford's name was magical in the Soviet Union. In voicing praise for his production techniques, Communists thought of the Detroit automobile manufacturer more as a revolutionary and modernizing force than as a capitalist.[9] In Germany during the 1920s, Adolf Hitler hung a large portrait of Ford on the wall behind his desk. Enthusiastic about the publication of the spurious "Protocols of the Learned Elders of Zion" and "The International Jew" in the Ford-owned *Dearborn Independent,* the Nazi leader told a *Chicago Tribune* reporter in March 1923, "We look to Heinrich Ford as the leader of the growing Fascist movement in America."[10]

As a folk hero who transcended political lines, Ford assumed mythical status in the minds of millions. Regarded as a kind of sorcerer, magician, or industrial superman, he promised hope and deliverance for common people, especially for the kind of rural folk from which he sprang. He seemed to epitomize an earlier, simpler era when individuals could make a difference, society was less complex, and traditional values held sway. At the same time, he represented the forces of modern technology, economic abundance, and scientific improvement. Starting out as a simple midwestern farm boy, Ford emerged as the "Sage of Dearborn," "Oracle of the Common Man," "New Messiah," and "Dictator of Detroit." He so dominated the 1920s that, as much as the Prosperity Decade, Jazz Decade, New Era, Age of the Flapper, or Age of Magnificent Nonsense, the decade could just as reasonably have been dubbed the Age of Ford. Halfway through it, the Detroit minister and social reformer Reinhold Niebuhr announced, "Henry Ford is America."[11] Having heard so many people tell him he was great, Ford began believing it himself. He told Ray Dahlinger, who superintended the Ford farms in Dearborn, "I invented the modern age."[12]

Reality did not quite match the image, however. For his considerable accomplishments as an inventor and business leader, Ford merited some of the adulation he received. But much of it also was attributable to the credulity of the public and to the systematic public relations efforts of Ford himself and of hired hands at the Ford Motor Company. Although to the public at large Ford's personality and character may have appeared simple and transparent, people who knew him and those who studied him seriously regarded him as an enigma. Almost unanimously, they noted his complex nature, contradictory qualities, and ultimate opaqueness. Even photographers claimed to be unable to adequately capture him on film.[13]

Some analysts located the source of his personality in his midwestern rural background. That accounted, they suggested, for his reliance on instinctive hunches, his restless curiosity, his practicality, his suspicion of theory and experts, his distrust of outsiders, and his combination of self-confidence and ignorance.[14] This kind of analysis, though not entirely without merit, strayed too far in the direction of overgeneralization about rural midwesterners. It did not go far enough in probing the contradictions within Ford's own psyche. "It was useless to try to understand Henry Ford," observed his production chief, Charles Sorensen, who worked with him for four decades. "One had to *sense* him." Rev. Samuel S. Marquis, for a time Ford's pastor and later head of the Ford Motor Company's Sociology Department, concluded, after twenty years of acquaintance, that Ford possessed "the most elusive personality of any man I have ever known." The Wisconsin novelist Hamlin Garland, a small-town boy himself, called Ford a psychological puzzle: "Those who know him best confess that they do not understand him."[15]

New York Herald reporter William C. Richards, who worked the Dearborn beat between World War I and the early 1930s, observed that Ford "was hard and gentle, straightforward and devious. Men who made any flat statement about him usually found they had to hedge." Ford was a man of many masks, the newspaperman concluded, and it was difficult to discern the real person behind them. Biographer Allan Nevins contended that interpretations imputing a Jekyll-and-Hyde dualism to Ford were actually too simple, because "he was not two men but a dozen."[16] He was kind at some times, cruel at others; genuinely modest in many ways, he loved to make headlines; soft-spoken most of the time, he could be belligerent at others; puritanical when it came to liquor, tobacco, and other habits, he felt unbound by conventional norms; a man of purportedly simple tastes, he lived in a costly mansion, bought a huge yacht, traveled in private rail cars, and owned land equivalent to the state of Connecticut; a hugely practical man, he was also an idealist and a visionary.[17]

Perhaps no single word captures Ford better than "dreamer."[18] Responding to intuitive hunches, he embarked on many productive ventures as well as many quixotic quests. "Life," he declared, was "not a location, but a journey."[19] "Mr. Ford," observed William J. Cameron, his ghostwriter and personal publicist, "had a twenty-five track mind and there were trains going out and coming in on all tracks at all times."[20] His favorite Bible verse was Hebrews 11:1: "Now faith is the substance of things hoped for, the evidence of things not seen."[21]

Obviously, Ford was a man of many ideas. The one that made him a fortune and landed him in the history books was the notion of building a sturdy, lightweight, reliable, and inexpensive motor vehicle for the masses. He was not the first person to conceive the idea, nor did he formulate and commit himself to it in one giant step. But once he made the decision, he pursued it to its utmost conclusion with ferocious tenacity and considerable creativity. In the process he left his competitors far behind and worked a modern miracle.

Stories like Ford's get reformulated in legend and myth, and his biography is no exception. Born on July 30, 1863, the eldest of six children of Irish immigrants William and Mary Ford, he grew up on a farm 10 miles west of the rapidly growing city of Detroit. He would live his entire life within a few miles of his birthplace. Like countless other self-made men, he embellished the narrative of his rise to success, depicting his family as poorer than it had been, his father as more demanding and restrictive, and his own uniqueness as more pronounced. On one point everyone agreed: young Henry hated the boredom and drudgery of farmwork and longed to escape from it as fast as he could. As a boy, he was the archetypical "tinkerer"—the child who loved to fiddle with tools, take apart machines, and examine how things work. His father indulged him in these activities, contrary to the son's later assertions. The boy received special treatment from family members, who recognized his gift for mechanics and released him from some of the chores and duties that otherwise would have fallen on him.[22]

In the oft-repeated story that Henry used later to explain how he became interested in motor vehicles, he and his father were riding to Detroit in the family buggy one afternoon in July 1876 when they spied a crude, self-propelled steam locomotive chugging down the road toward them. The thirteen-year-old boy jumped out of the buggy before his father realized what was happening and started shooting questions at the engineer, who was happy to answer them. "I remember that engine as though I had seen it only yesterday," he would say many decades later. "It was that engine which took me into automotive transportation."[23] Whatever the immediate impact of Ford's initial encounter with the steam locomotive, two decades would pass before he produced his first automobile in 1896. It took seven more years of experimentation and two failed manufacturing companies before the launching in 1903 of the Ford Motor Company. The road to success, in other words, was not at all straight or unmarked by ruts and obstacles.

At sixteen, Ford left home for Detroit to make a living and to learn mechanics as an apprentice, but within three years he was back home farming (and working with steam engines) in Dearborn. He remained there for nine more years before making the final break and moving again to Detroit in 1891, this time taking a job with the Edison Illuminating Company. In 1888 he had married a Dearborn neighbor, Clara Jane Bryant, three years younger than himself. Like Henry, Clara had grown up on a farm. She always fully supported his mechanical tinkering and the pursuit of his dream, leading him gratefully to refer to her as "the Believer."[24]

Having experimented in his spare time with tractors and steam engines while in his twenties and with internal combustion engines and primitive automobiles during his thirties, Ford was finally able to obtain financial backing to launch the Detroit Automobile Company in August 1899. His angels were his friend William Maybury, who was the new mayor of Detroit, and a trio of other businessmen. That first operation folded in less than a year and a half after producing fewer than two dozen cars. Ford's association with his second firm, the Henry Ford Company, ended even more quickly. He was forced out by his major financial backer, William H. Murphy, in March 1902, after just three months, when the company was reorganized under the Cadillac label. In neither instance had Ford come up with an acceptable production prototype, and he had spent too much time driving racing cars in an attempt to build up publicity for himself and the company.[25]

Twice a failure, Ford might have never received another chance had his third venture gone the same way as the first two. As before, the first step was to secure working capital in order to obtain factory space, purchase materials, and pay the workers. Without capital, nothing could be done. But Ford also desired complete freedom to build whatever kind of vehicle he wanted and complete personal control over the production process.

Luckily for him, after several months' start-up time, the Ford Motor Company turned into an impressive moneymaker. During its first fifteen months of operation it built 1,708 vehicles, and the original investors, who had put up $28,000 in cash, had already received 100 percent dividends on their money, returns that multiplied enormously later on. Within two years' time, Ford had bought out his original financial angel, coal distributor Alexander Malcolmson, allowing him to concentrate on developing the kind of lightweight, sturdy, inexpensive automobile for the masses that he by now had his sights set on. Malcolmson, like most automobile investors at the time, believed that more money could be made in larger, upscale models, so he and Ford came to a parting of ways. In mid-1905, a third 100 percent dividend was paid out to investors, and in early 1906 the unveiling of the new lightweight four-cylinder Model N proved to be a sensation. Selling at a base price of $500, when the average price of a car topped $2,000, the Model N generated more orders than the factory could supply. In its third year in business, the Ford Motor Company, with 8,500 cars sold, rose for the first time to the top of the industry.[26]

In 1907, the stage was set for developing one of the most successful consumer products in industrial history—the Model T. By the following year, when it went on sale, the Ford Motor Company had gone through eight different models—A, B, C, F, K, N, R, and S. By this time, Henry Ford, owning almost three-fifths of the stock in the company, had established himself as its dominant, even though not unchallenged, leader, and the Model T was basically his baby. Ford's success with this vehicle derived not from his own engineering genius, although he possessed considerable skill and knowledge in the area. Nor was it because he was the first to conceive the idea of a cheap, practical car for mass consumption. Many people had independently arrived at that concept, and Ransom E. Olds had shown how it could be done. Then Olds's original company shifted its focus to the higher-priced market.

What Ford alone possessed was the foresight, capacity, and sheer will to persist in designing an automobile that would win the public's favor and then to create an organization that could manufacture it extremely cheaply with increasing efficiency, thus allowing continual cutting of costs. His singular intuition told him that his goal should not be simply to manufacture a cheap car. Rather, it should be first to build a good, reliable car, after which he would be able to focus on continually improving the production process to enable reductions in prices. Whether Ford had this idea explicitly in mind when he started out is arguable. Practical tinkerer that he was—one who learned from experience through trial and error—his vision evolved over time, as he and his cohorts learned day by day about what worked and what did not.[27]

The Model T Ford, known affectionately as the "Tin Lizzie," quickly became a manufacturing phenomenon, its sales figures exploding geometrically throughout the decade and a half after it was introduced. Annual sales jumped from 10,660 cars in the twelve months ending in September 1909 to 523,000 in 1916 (32 percent of all the cars produced in the United States), peaking at 2.12 million in 1923 (57 percent of the market).[28] Profits between 1903 and 1919 amounted to $355 million and rose to $566 million from 1919 to 1926. By then, Ford's buyout of his minority stockholders in 1919 for $106 million looked like a pretty good bargain. It was lucrative for them, too. The original $10,000 investment by brothers Horace and John Dodge, for example, brought them $25 million, on top of millions of dollars in dividends they had already earned up until that time.[29]

Largely because of Ford's contributions, Detroit quickly became the automobile capital of America. Before the turn of the century, early manufacturers had spread out their operations from coast to coast. Steam and electric cars came primarily from New England and New York. Early internal combustion models emerged from Ohio, Indiana, and Michigan. Through what economists call the clustering phenomenon, a remarkable group of automakers, including Ransom E. Olds, William C. Durant, the Dodge brothers, and Ford himself, obtained their start in Detroit. With car and parts manufacturing spurring it on, the city's population burgeoned from 285,000 in 1900 to 466,000 in 1910 and 994,000 in 1920.[30]

As time went by, Ford often took personal credit for his company's success, implying that he alone had been responsible for creating and marketing the Ford automobile. Certainly, he played the central role in the script.

He inspired the Model T's creation, assembled the team that guided the company, and kept his cohorts focused on building a single, high-quality, low-priced car. Skeptics, such as the economist John Kenneth Galbraith, later minimized Ford's personal role in the process. Galbraith argued that Ford had contributed nothing really new and that men such as business manager James Couzens, who ran the business end of the company for the first dozen years, were actually more important in superintending the company's spectacular growth. Galbraith's argument can help us place Ford's contribution in perspective, so long as we do not deny Ford his status as the major force and prime visionary of the operation.[31]

Couzens, who went on to become the mayor of Detroit and then a U.S. senator from Michigan, was brilliant at introducing order and system to the company's business operations. He also put the marketing of the car on a solid footing. He was joined over the years by a cadre of other creative, efficient, and loyal executives, without whom the company could never have achieved as much as it did. Among these were the gifted engineer C. H. Wills, who played the major role in designing the Model T and earlier prototypes; Norval Hawkins, who steadily expanded the sales force; William Knudsen, who set up more than two dozen branch assembly plants; Charles "Engine Charlie" Sorensen, whose hard-driving plant management, first at the Highland Park factory after 1910 and later at the huge River Rouge complex from the 1920s through the early 1940s, squeezed the last ounce of energy from his workers, often at a high cost in morale.[32]

The appeal of the Model T itself must rank high on the list of explanations for the company's success. Powered by a reliable four-cylinder, 20-horsepower engine and featuring a justly famous planetary transmission, the vehicle was simply constructed, uncomplicated to drive, and easy to repair. It was large enough to hold five passengers but light in weight because of its innovative use of vanadium steel. It sat high off the ground, allowing it to more easily traverse unpaved rural roads—still by far the predominant type in the nation—which remained muddy in wet weather and became dusty and rutted in dry. Built for utility rather than looks, it was well suited to the needs of farmers while also appealing to town and city drivers.[33] The Model T perfectly mirrored Ford's own practical, egalitarian, and unostentatious personality. Automobiles, once a "rich man's toy," moved out of the luxury class and into the plain man's orbit.[34]

Utilitarian the Model T certainly was. With a belt attachment, farmers could use it as a power source to shell corn, grind grain, fill silos, saw wood, shear sheep, pump water, and wash clothes. In the fields, it was able to pull machinery such as mowers, binders, harrows, and hay rakes. It reduced women's isolation on the farm, enabling them to visit their neighbors and drive to town. The Model T, the in-house periodical *Ford Times* boasted, "remodeled the social life of the country."[35]

The phenomenon of small-town Saturday nights swelled in importance during the 1920s, just as automobiles were becoming commonplace in rural areas. Farm families would drive into town to market their cream and eggs, conduct the weekly shopping, and visit with neighbors or maybe take in a movie. After the first several years of car production during the early 1900s, when city people formed the primary market and farm folk remained skeptical, or even downright hostile to autos, the rural population became Detroit's most enthusiastic and reliable customers. States with the largest proportion of farmers in the population had the highest rates of car ownership. Farm-state editors and politicians, concerned by the steady drain of young people from the farms and small towns, thought they perceived a solution in the automobile. *Outing Magazine* forecast in 1902 that with increasing car ownership, "the millions of our rural population will be brought into closer relations with the towns and with neighbors, and the loneliness of farm life, which drives so many to the cities, with detriment to all, will no longer retard our agricultural growth, nor prevent a proper distribution of population for the national welfare." The automobile historian James J. Flink argues that with the mass production of the Model T, travel by car "became the most important force for change in American civilization."[36]

What made Ford's car such an unparalleled sales phenomenon was his unrelenting push to keep cutting prices. Every time sales faltered a bit, his inclination was to slash prices even further. Introduced at $850 in 1908, the price of the cheapest model dropped to $525 in 1912, $345 in 1916, and $290 in 1926. Meanwhile, the quality of the cars was constantly improving. First under James Couzens and then under sales manager Norval Hawkins, the company established an intricate web of 10,000 dealerships around the country, leaving few people in the midwestern states very far away from one. Company advertising, assisted by the huge press coverage accorded to Henry Ford and his organization as well as by word of mouth from hordes of satisfied customers, made the Model T an almost irresistible product. Until the early 1920s, when Chevrolet, under former Ford-man William Knudsen and General Motors chairman Alfred P. Sloan, began picking up momentum with sleeker styling, improved engineering, and more competitive pricing, the Model T virtually had the low-priced market to itself.[37]

The ability to reduce prices so drastically derived from the company's unceasing search for increased efficiency through improved production methods and better management of its labor force. Ford refused to make dramatic changes in the basic features or outward appearance of his automobile (minor improvements were constantly being made). But he was fanatical about refitting his factories, reorganizing the production process, and securing cheaper parts and materials in order to reduce further the cost of manufacturing the Model T. "Fordism," the relentless drive for continual improvement in production procedures and consequent cost-cutting, would sweep the industrialized world and subsequently become standard operating procedure in business. Seven principles—power, accuracy, economy, system, continuity, speed, and repetition—defined Ford's approach to mass production.[38]

The fifth of these, emphasizing continuous motion with no break in the production process, was especially important in switching over to a moving assembly line at the Highland Park facility starting in 1913. Not the first to conceive of or to implement the method, Ford was the first to install it with such scope and comprehensiveness. It became the standard for mass production in the automobile industry and in many others during the next several decades. Its development was a group effort, much trial and error being involved. Beginning with magneto coils and moving on to crankcases and other parts, moving assembly lines were applied during 1913 and 1914 to the production of a variety of components and ultimately to the chassis production and to the final assembly of finished vehicles.[39]

The moving assembly line brought with it huge gains in productivity, allowing further reductions in prices and undergirding expanding profits. But the improvement came at a human price. By breaking tasks involved in the production process into their smallest possible components, workers who formerly had prided themselves as craftsmen were deskilled and became, in effect, replaceable cogs in the machine. At the same time that work sped up, it became more monotonous and less meaningful to those on the line. As assembly lines went into operation, Ford officials confronted serious problems with a workforce increasingly alienated from the physically draining and emotionally deadening work. Employees reacted in predictable ways. Absenteeism at Highland Park jumped to 10 percent, and the annual turnover rate rose to an astonishing 370 percent. Apparently, it was Couzens who proposed doubling the base pay rate from around $2.35 a day to $5.00 a day as a way of motivating the workforce and cutting down on absenteeism and job changing. Ford at first was skeptical about the idea, but he quickly bought into it, believing that it would also provide a humane way of sharing some of the profits the company was accumulating. He later observed that the five-dollar day was the best cost-cutting measure he ever implemented. Employee turnover quickly dropped by 90 percent, and absenteeism declined from 10 percent to 0.3 percent. The company was able to have its pick of labor, and plant supervisors were able to speed up their assembly lines in the aftermath.[40]

In ways that people only later fully understood or appreciated, the philosophy implicit in the new wage policy contributed to a new consumer consciousness that had been developing since before the turn of the century. In reducing the prices of his automobiles, Ford urged his customers to spend the difference rather than save it. Acting out his role as prophet of a new gospel of consumption, he anticipated that his workers would spend their newly won wage increases, thereby increasing the circulation of money and spreading prosperity throughout the economy. In his path-breaking 1936 opus *The General Theory of Employment, Interest and Money,* British economist John Maynard Keynes assigned to the national government the key role in boosting spending when private investment and consumer spending lagged. Two decades earlier, Ford had perceived the need to get more money into workers' hands so that they could consume the rapidly expanding output of America's factories. United Auto Workers leader Walter Reuther later put it succinctly when he observed that "mass consumption makes mass production possible."[41]

The five-dollar day not only made for a revolutionary force in American society, but it also helped transform Ford's personal life, because it shone on him the blazing light of publicity. Too often, he seemed ready to believe his own publicity and the adulation showered upon him. No longer shy and retiring, Ford appeared to thrive in the limelight. Once open to suggestions for change in company policies, he increasingly insisted on imposing his will on every aspect of the business and became less interested in listening to other people's input.[42] After he bought out the minority stockholders in 1919, a string of top executives and assistants, including C. H. Wills, Samuel Marquis, Norval Hawkins, Frank Klingensmith, and William

Knudsen, made their sometimes forced exits, weakening the company. For the next quarter century, the most powerful Ford underlings would be men like Charles Sorensen and Harry Bennett. The former was a production genius but was seldom inclined to contradict his employer, and the latter was a ham-fisted thug who never questioned orders. During the 1920s and '30s, Ford's actions and public statements attracted a rapidly expanding volume of criticism. He grew more and more distant from his workforce and intransigently opposed their unionization. Meanwhile, he launched a widely publicized campaign of anti-Semitism, outspokenly opposed President Franklin Roosevelt and the New Deal, and joined the isolationist forces before Pearl Harbor, consorting with Charles Lindbergh and less savory advocates of accommodation with Hitler and the aggressors.[43]

People around him discerned significant personality changes in Ford as time went by. The ill-fated 1915 Peace Ship episode, in which he financed a quixotic sailing expedition to Europe in an attempt to head off American entry into World War I, stimulated considerable ridicule. The following year, his testimony in a libel suit he initiated against the *Chicago Tribune*, which had referred to him as an "anarchist" and an "ignorant idealist," made him look foolish and extremely ill-informed about history, politics, and everything else outside his own business. After being quoted in that case as saying, "History is the bunk," he resolved to present his own version of the past to the public for their edification. A fitness buff and food faddist, he remained physically active and youthful looking, but after turning sixty in 1923 he increasingly began to display signs of age. With the Ford Motor Company controlling half the automobile market, Ford's interest began to drift away from the day-to-day affairs of the company and toward memories of his childhood and reveries about history and tradition.

During the 1920s, Ford began to spend more and more of his time contemplating the past—his own and the country's—and the growing challenges facing rural and small-town America. That decade, one of accelerating modernization in the United States, also stimulated a revival of interest in America's history. As a youth, Ford had been repelled by the drudgery and boredom of farm labor, and the prospect of following in his father's agricultural footsteps had held no appeal for him. As the years passed, however, he found himself growing increasingly nostalgic for the place and time of his boyhood. He began to devote large amounts of time and resources to preserving the traditions, values, and artifacts of rural, small-town society. He was devoted to "the simple, homely, virtuous ways," in the words of Allan Nevins. "In some respects the cast of his mind resembled that of Bryan: the Bryan who crusaded against Wall Street, who fought war to the last, who at the Scopes trial championed the old religious outlooks." Ford, according to his ghost writer William J. Cameron, "was a product of an agrarian society with their basic thoughts. He never got out of it. The city was all on the edge of his life; the farm and the tool shed were always in the center of it. He always had the agrarian point of view."[44]

To countless contemporary journalists and commentators as well as to biographers and historians ever since, Ford's fixation on the past and his devotion to preserving rural values and folkways while simultaneously doing more than anyone else to undermine the old America posed a tremendous paradox.[45] But Ford viewed the matter differently. He saw himself as building a bridge between the past and future, providing a means of reconciling the best of tradition and modernity. His visionary ideal was not the Jeffersonian yeoman farmer, working a small acreage by the sweat of his brow, but rather a modern, efficient producer, using the best power-driven machinery and benefiting from the latest scientific improvements.

Much like a growing coterie of intellectuals and writers who had become increasingly disillusioned with the fruits of early twentieth-century urbanization, Ford looked for salvation in some sort of reconciliation between the country and the city. Convinced that "the modern city concentrates within its limits the essence of all that is wrong, artificial, wayward and unjust in our social life," Ford wanted to change life in the city and return part of the urban population back to the rural countryside.[46] But he also hoped to reform rural America, relieving it of its drudgery, poverty, and isolation. While automobiles could help close the gap between urban and rural America, power-driven machinery could lighten the burden of labor. In his autobiography, *My Life and Work*, Ford emphasized the need to replace human labor with machine power. "Power-farming is simply taking the burden from flesh and blood and putting it on steel," he reassured readers.[47] Retaining bad childhood memories of cows, horses, and pigs, he seriously proposed that they all be eliminated from farmsteads, because they were inefficient and unnecessary. Milk derived from soybeans, cloth made from fibers fabricated from soybean meal, and new food products as substitutes for hams and bacon would serve consumers better and more cheaply.[48]

CHAPTER THREE

During the 1920s and '30s Ford devoted considerable time and resources to attempting to translate several of these dreams into reality. Having worked on farm locomotion during the 1880s before he ever started thinking about a car, he began experimenting with gasoline-powered tractors as early as 1905 and started producing a lightweight Fordson tractor in 1917, spurred on by wartime demand for such machines. Though production ceased in 1928 after more than 700,000 had been manufactured, Ford returned his attention to the subject during the late 1930s, when he was able again to capture 20 percent of the market.[49]

Another effort to reform agriculture and rural life appealed to him because of the potential benefits it might have for the Ford Motor Company. Chemurgy, the name given to the growing scientific movement to develop new uses for agricultural products, captured Ford's attention after 1929, when he began financing experiments at Dearborn to develop new uses for farm crops, both as foods and for industrial applications. He especially saw possibilities in soybeans and soon had 8,000 acres on the Ford Farms around Dearborn planted in them. He envisioned all kinds of everyday products, from chairs and desks to doors and countertops, someday being made out of soybean-derived materials. The research also put him on the ground floor of a developing interest in plastics, and for several years the Ford Motor Company actually used soybean-derived enamels, gearshift knobs, door handles, horn buttons, and other materials and parts in its cars. Ford's dream of making an automobile body entirely out of plastic never saw fruition, but in a few years automakers would introduce bodies made out of fiberglass and other synthetic materials. In his work with soybeans, Ford became closely involved with George Washington Carver of Tuskegee Institute, promoting and funding the latter's research on the plant. Ford was also ahead of his time in his interest in ecology and in his efforts to discover alternate fuels in ethanol and other plant-based products during the 1930s.[50] Ford's general lack of prejudice toward blacks was one of the admirable sides of his character. Carver's esteem for Ford could be seen in the way he addressed letters to him: "My beloved friend, Mr. Ford," "My great inspiring friend, Mr. Ford," and "My great inspiring friend and prophet, Mr. Ford."[51]

In addition to his work with tractors and chemurgy, Ford's village industries became part of his continuing effort to assist farm and small-town people in making better lives for themselves. "The life of an American village is a pretty fine thing," Ford observed. "What the small industry can do is make it possible for people to continue to enjoy the wholesome life of the country and at the same time enjoy a city income."[52]

Ford expressed his antiurban leanings in a variety of ways, sometimes even calling for the cities to be abandoned. In his view, cities lacked soul and were artificial, overcompetitive, and inimical to community. Although generally granting the need for and benefits of cities, the auto magnate believed that they had grown too large and congested and that society would benefit from shifting some of its population back to small towns and rural areas. Country living was wholesome, close to nature, and removed from urban noise, confusion, violence, and extremes of wealth.[53] To a *Chicago Tribune* interviewer in 1935 he asserted that the great cities did not typify the United States. "Chicago and New York are not America. Neither is Washington. America is out there in the United States. That's the place to know." For those trying to restore village life and opportunity, he counseled, "The old village sites are still the best. These little towns made America."[54]

Starting in the late 1930s, he acquired close to two dozen manufacturing facilities and water-power sites on rivers and streams in southeastern Michigan. In these village (or rural) industries, Ford workers fabricated parts such as valves, springs, starters, and ignition coils for his automobiles. Working part-time in the plants allowed farmers to supplement their incomes while remaining on the land and at the same time providing needed labor for industry. As described by William J. Cameron on the *Ford Sunday Evening Hour* radio program, this arrangement provided an ideal way to integrate urban and rural living. With "one foot in industry and one foot on the land," workers could enjoy "country living with a city income."[55]

The concept of village industries proved more successful on paper than in practice. Never a moneymaker, the program quickly disappeared after Ford's death. The 3,500 or so workers operating in the facilities paled in comparison to the more than 100,000 employed at one time at the huge River Rouge complex at Dearborn. Ford's enthusiasm for the concept may have reflected his own subconscious regret that his success as a manufacturer had helped eradicate the kind of life he had known as a child. "Cities are all right for some," he informed Fred C. Kelly of the *New York Times*. "The great movement into the cities during the last thirty years had important results. But in cities it is winter all the time, humanly speaking. There is no neighborly acquaintance and little neighborly help."[56]

During the late 1920s, Ford also attempted to export his idealized vision of small-town America to jungles deep in Brazil on the banks of the Tapa-jos River, a tributary of the Amazon. Needing to find a ready source of rubber to fabricate tires, hoses, and other parts for his cars, he hoped si-multaneously to replicate the virtues of his remembered midwestern boy-hood. The project was given the pretentious name of Fordlandia. Major Lester Barker, the U.S. military attaché in Brazil, characterized Fordlandia as an oasis—a midwestern dream fitted out with telephones, electric lights, refrigerators, and washing machines. The two plantations that Ford's men carved out of the jungle failed economically, but the towns that he built in conjunction attracted considerable media attention. After Walt Disney's 1941 visit to Fordlandia under the auspices of the U.S. State Department, the Disney studio made a movie painting a picture of an ideal town worthy of inclusion among the Amazon's four greatest cities. (Disney's own ideal town, Disneyland, would go up in southern California a decade and a half later.) Fordlandia never proved as profitable as anticipated and did not outlive Ford's personal enthusiasm for the project. With the abandonment of the project in 1945, the land and the buildings were sold back to the Brazilian government for about 1 percent of the amount Ford had invested in the venture.[57]

Finding hope where little was warranted, Henry Ford thought he was witnessing a small-town revival during the 1920s. "The American village is regaining its importance in American life," asserted an editorial in his *Dearborn Independent* in November 1926. "More than twelve million per-sons—or about one in eight—live in villages or small towns at the present time. For a time the trend was away from the village toward the city; now it is reversed. Main Street is coming into its own. Not only is village life better industrially than it was twenty years ago; it is better socially."[58]

Ultimately, nostalgia and an effort to preserve memories of America's rural, small-town past constituted Ford's most distinctive response to the changes sweeping through American life after World War I—changes in which he played a primary role. Like many of his contemporaries, Ford clung to the populist-progressive ideal, which, in the words of the historian Richard Hofstadter, was one that advocated a life "close to nature and the soil," that esteemed "the primary contacts of country and village life," and that cherished "the image of the independent and self-reliant man." A fit-ness buff and a lover of old-time dances, Ford decided to launch a revival of traditional dancing and fiddling during the 1920s, hiring noted dancing master Benjamin B. Lovett of Worcester, Massachusetts, to be his full-time dance instructor in Dearborn. His motive was moral as well as preservationist. He opposed modern ballroom dancing and, even more so, jazz and the new dances associated with it. "I want to compliment you for the good work you are doing to bring back 'old time music,'" C. C. Bell, a Civil War veteran from Boonville, Missouri, wrote Ford, "especially in dancing, as I think it is high time to show our young people that Jazz is anything else but right."[59]

More conspicuously, Ford engaged in a mammoth project of collecting artifacts and buildings from the past as a means of informing the public about what he considered to be the true history of the country. This was not the kind of textbook history that he usually denigrated but rather the "real" story of technological innovation and improvements in day-to-day living. In the 1910s he had already started collecting old tools, utensils, furniture, and other items, storing them in empty buildings and warehouses. In 1919 the widening of the road in front of the old Ford family homestead had led him to move the house he had been born in and convert it into a shrine. Four years later, when a Boston group solicited a donation from him to save the historic Wayside Inn in Sudbury, Massachusetts, made famous by a poem by Henry Wadsworth Longfellow, he bought the property himself and restored it. He followed that with the purchase of another historic building, the Botsford Inn, 16 miles northwest of Detroit.

Now he began seriously thinking about building a museum and historical village in Dearborn that could tell the entire story of American historical development. Preserving his special version of history and thereby celebrating rural and small-town America became Ford's major hobby as he moved into his sixties and would remain his major interest to the end of his life.[60] The dedication in 1929 of the Edison Institute and Greenfield Village (named after his wife's girlhood home) was a grand occasion. The event was billed as "Light's Golden Jubilee" in honor of the fiftieth anniversary of Thomas Edison's invention of the electric light bulb. Edison, the "Wizard of Menlo Park," who had been Ford's boyhood hero, journeyed to Dearborn to add luster to the occasion, along with President Herbert Hoover, Marie Curie, Jane Addams, Orville Wright, Will Rogers, and several hundred other guests. Opened to the public in 1933, the museum that Ford referred to as "my Smithsonian Institution" contained an eclectic variety of almost every imaginable type of Americana, from spoons and fiddles to wrenches and harnesses. Eventually, he invested over $30 million in his collection and restoration projects.[61]

Greenfield Village embodied Ford's nostalgic effort to re-create the atmosphere of bygone village life. In addition to putting his own birthplace on display, he brought in part of Edison's research laboratory, Wilbur and Orville Wright's bicycle shop, William Holmes McGuffey's birthplace, the slave quarters in which George Washington Carver had lived, Luther Burbank's study, and the dwellings of Patrick Henry, Noah Webster, and Walt Whitman. "Of all Ford's outside activities," the historian David L. Lewis has written, "Greenfield Village was the closest to his heart. It memorialized his most treasured friend, Edison, and it symbolized much of what Ford valued in life."[62]

The historic village was Henry Ford's tribute to the American heritage and to his own remembered past. It constituted an idealized re-creation of a time and place rapidly receding from view, presented in a manner reminiscent of the poems of James Whitcomb Riley. In his decline, Ford spent less time at the company offices and more time puttering around in the Greenfield exhibits, listening to singing in the Martha-Mary Chapel and observing classes in the McGuffey School he had installed there. He commissioned Irving Bacon to paint a series of tableaux re-creating scenes from his childhood and put them on display. In 1935, while being given a personal tour of the village, a *New York Times* reporter detected a note of tenderness in the automaker's voice when he reminisced about the one-story red schoolhouse he had attended as a youth. "It was revealing to hear this man with a reputation for hardness become almost sentimental over these relics of the past," the newsman observed.[63]

One of the last things Ford did on the day he died in 1947 was to have his chauffeur take him over to Greenfield Village as they were driving around Dearborn viewing the effects of flooding caused by heavy rains. When he died later that evening in a house lighted by candles, because of a power outage caused by the storm, he was in close proximity, both physically and in spirit, to his rural roots, which he had done so much during his eighty-three years to render obsolete.[64]

George Washington Carver and Oscar Micheaux: African American Dreamers and Doers

[Providing biographical details about me for your book] will be very difficult indeed as there are so many things that naturally I erased from my mind. There are some things that an orphan child does not want to remember.

—George Washington Carver

While he found cities marvelous, in many ways Micheaux remained a small-town creature, a man of the soil who preferred travel and open land and untamed territory.

—Patrick McGilligan

While attending school in Mississippi during the 1930s, the historian David Donald recalled, the only black people he encountered in his American history textbooks were Booker T. Washington, the eminent founder and director of Tuskegee Institute in Alabama, and his protégé George Washington Carver, the famous "peanut scientist" and, in his later years, cultural icon.[1] Most white Americans of the time were not yet ready to acknowledge the seminal contributions of more assertive or controversial African Americans such as Nat Turner, Sojourner Truth, Frederick Douglass, W. E. B. Du Bois, Ida B. Wells, or Mary McLeod Bethune. It would take World War II, a rising civil rights movement, extensive cultural transformation, and the emergence of a new generation of historians to facilitate their entry into the broader American historical consciousness and to fashion a more balanced, realistic history of black people in the United States. The massive exodus of blacks out of the South and into the North and West, known as the Great Migration, demanded a new way of telling the story. The percentage of the group's population living in the old Confederacy declined from 85 percent in 1890 to 77 percent in 1940. Thirty years later, only half the African American population remained in the South, fewer than half of those being rural, and their people's whole way of life had been transformed.[2]

In some ways, however, precious little had changed. African Americans were able to obtain favorable legal decisions that formally, at least, eliminated segregation in public schools, guaranteed the right to vote, mandated equality in public accommodations, banned racially restrictive housing covenants, and improved conditions in other areas. However, they still found themselves searching for things they had long coveted: full social equality, significant economic opportunity, and, no less important, basic decency, humane treatment, and genuine respect from their fellow Americans. This last goal, for black men during the late 1800s and early 1900s, translated into a desire to achieve true manhood, following on several centuries of slave status in which a major part of the formula by which whites had kept them in chains was to emasculate them while simultaneously asserting their own right to violate black women.

Until World War I erupted in 1914, only a tiny fraction of the freedmen's population had moved out of the South to take up residence in the Midwest, joining the few from their race who were already there. Before the Civil War, many midwestern states had banned blacks from residing within their borders. Most African Americans living in the Midwest resided in larger towns and cities. Small towns sometimes harbored lone individuals and families, or perhaps even a few, but they were exceptional. So-called sundown towns became known for their formal or unwritten rules barring blacks and often other scorned groups from living or even staying overnight in them. Beginning in 1877, small colonies of black agriculturalists joined the Exoduster movement and settled in places like Kansas and Oklahoma, but black farmers north of the Ohio River generally remained isolated and lonely.[3]

The North had fought the Civil War in part, at least, to abolish slavery, but afterward it did little to welcome the freed slaves and by 1900 had largely abandoned efforts to guarantee even minimal rights for them. The condition of the black populace during the decades in which the United States metamorphosed from an essentially rural, agrarian society into an urban, industrial one confronted African Americans with almost impossible challenges and difficulties. Even had their white counterparts exhibited sympathy and good will during the transition—which, almost uniformly, they did not—the burdens would have been formidable. Southerners remained captive to the delusional Lost Cause and were committed to the maintenance of white supremacy. Northerners showed themselves unwilling to do much to effectively protect or assist the former slaves. Black Americans as a result watched helplessly as their condition steadily deteriorated.[4]

Historians consider the era between 1880 and 1920 to be the nadir in American race relations in post–Civil War America. With Jim Crow laws proliferating all across the South, massive disfranchisement of black voters, horrific increases in lynching and other forms of racial violence, a ghastly outbreak of race riots in the North as well as the South, and a general souring of relations between the races, black Americans lived in an environment increasingly dangerous, noxious, and oppressive. The political system proved unequal to the challenge, and progressive politicians, who after 1900 sought to address a variety of other social and economic problems, largely dodged the race issue, viewing it as an intractable morass.[5]

This was the historical context in which two black-skinned, small-town boys from the Midwest grew to adulthood during the late 1800s and early 1900s, full of ambition to improve themselves and to establish a place for themselves in American society. George Washington Carver and Oscar Micheaux, displaying highly different temperaments and dissimilar in many ways, shared a number of impulses and characteristics. Curious, artistic, creative, and attentive to the world around them, they each possessed keen social intelligence, an unusual thirst for knowledge, a desire to leave home and chart his own path, and an intense drive to compete and succeed.

The life trajectories and developing careers of these ambitious fellows, two decades apart in age, illustrated the challenges, limitations, and sometimes insuperable obstacles placed in the way of young black men during their era. Later, neither of them seemed able to remember or wanted to recall much about his childhood, and their earliest years remain vague to us more than a century later.[6] Micheaux used the events of his young adulthood as source materials for his novels and movies, and both men consciously and effectively fashioned durable myths of their rise and progress in ways that enhanced their reputations while obscuring the historical record.

Born into slavery in Newton County, Missouri, toward the end of the Civil War, George Washington Carver never knew his father, a slave on a nearby farm who was killed in a log-hauling accident around the time of the boy's birth. When George was an infant, he and his mother were kidnapped by a band of armed men and hustled across the border into Arkansas. Rescued by a Union scout who was stationed nearby, George was returned to his owner, Moses Carver, in return for a racehorse valued at $300. He never saw his mother again. Instead, he grew up in the household of Carver and his wife, Susan, pious German immigrants. The story of the $300 racehorse became a staple in the Carver legend, and a pattern emerged that carried on throughout his life: he would spend most of his time, establish his closest relationships, and feel most comfortable with white people.[7]

The southwest Missouri frontier, bordering on Unionist Kansas and Oklahoma Indian Territory on the west and Confederate Arkansas on the south, was an extremely dangerous place and the site of three major Civil War battles. Confederate and Union armies alternately controlled the seat of Newton County, Neosho, which basically was a Unionist town. Lingering animosities continued to divide residents in the area long after formal hostilities ended. But young George largely escaped these divisions as he grew up in the household of the childless Carvers, who showered love on him and his brother, Jim, treating them as if they were their own children. The Carvers were the only parents he ever remembered. The labor of Jim, a husky lad, contributed substantially to the economic welfare of the family, but George, possibly suffering from the results of his kidnapping, grew up frail and sickly, stunted in growth and susceptible to infection. The high pitch of his voice led some people to speculate that his kidnappers might have castrated him.[8] Withal, the boy grew up a happy and curious child enveloped within the comfortable cocoon of a loving and protective household.

Largely exempted from hard labor by dint of his fragile constitution, George remained a pampered child, free to roam the nearby fields and woods by the hour, collecting rocks, frogs, insects, and plants, which he carefully saved and hoarded away. Early on, he developed an active curiosity about the natural world surrounding him, a world that continued to inspire his scientific investigations as an adult. Spending much of his time with Susan doing household chores, he became adept at the "womanly" activities of cooking, cleaning, mending, sewing, and embroidering. Though tending to remain quiet and shy in the presence of other children, he enjoyed interacting with a variety of black and white playmates, some of whom stayed in touch with him for years after he left the area. The things that distinguished him from other children—frailty and sickliness, high intelligence, unlimited curiosity, musicality, and rapport with nature—marked him from an early age. His ability to grow plants and to nurse injured ones back to health got him labeled the "plant doctor." Whereas Jim seemed desirous of passing as white, the darker-hued George never evinced any such wish. Carver's lifelong ambivalence regarding race traced to his youngest days. In the words of his biographer Linda O. Mc-Murry, "On the one hand he rejected the validity of race as a category; on the other he expressed a solidarity with 'his people.'"[9]

The nearby village of Diamond Grove (later shortened to Diamond) offered no opportunity for black schooling. Therefore, at around age twelve, George adventurously headed off for Neosho, 8 miles away, where there was a freedmen's school. He was taken in by a childless black couple who, like the Carvers, treated George as if he were their own. This was his first time living in a predominantly black environment. Thus began a pattern of moving from place to place, establishing quick rapport with people, both black and white, who found him instantly likable and took him under their wings. Realizing that the teacher at the school was hardly more knowledgeable than he, George learned of an opportunity to go along with a family moving to Fort Scott, Kansas, and eagerly jumped at the chance. He lodged in the home of a blacksmith in return for assisting his wife with the cooking and other household chores, utilizing skills picked up from Susan. He supplemented that with a variety of odd jobs around town.

In March 1879, his world was violently shaken when he witnessed the brutal lynching, while hundreds of spectators enthusiastically looked on, of a black man accused of raping a twelve-year-old white girl. Terrified by the episode, he quickly fled the community and found a new home in Olathe, Kansas, where he found refuge with another black family, Ben and Lucy Seymour, whom he assisted with their laundry business. Again he was able to supplement his income with a variety of odd jobs. The next year, he followed the family west to the little town of Minneapolis, Kansas. In this predominantly white community, just as in everyplace else he went, he made many friends among his white neighbors and got actively involved in local religious life, in this instance with the Presbyterian church that the Seymours attended.[10]

In 1886, following a brief stay in Kansas City, Kansas, and after being rejected for admission to a small Presbyterian college in Highland, Kansas, because of his race, Carver wound up in the frontier settlement of Beeler, in the far western part of the state. Purchasing a relinquishment on a quarter section of land and playing the role of pioneer farmer for two years, Carver was among a handful of blacks living in the area. Seemingly destined to gravitate toward places predominantly inhabited by whites, he exhibited unusual skill in winning the respect and friendship of his neighbors, who were impressed by his intelligence and knowledge and were won over by his outgoing, modest personality.[11]

In 1888, the young black man's midwestern wanderings brought him to the small town of Winterset in south-central Iowa. As was his habit, he attended church services regularly. At one of them he made the acquaintance of a local doctor and his wife, John and Helen Milholland, who afterward frequently invited him into their home. Impressed by his wide-ranging intelligence and evident ambition, they urged him to enroll in Simpson College, a small Methodist school 20 miles away in Indianola, Iowa. Despite his bad experience in Highland, he followed the Milhollands' advice, beginning classes in the preparatory department in the fall of 1890. He was the only African American student enrolled in the college. In keeping with most of his previous interracial experiences, Carver, who was several years older than most of his classmates, quickly won many friends and admirers. "They made me believe I was a real human being," he later observed.[12] He dreamed of becoming an artist. Though Etta Budd, his art teacher, discerned genuine talent in the young man, she doubted the practicality of his ambition. Her father, Joseph L. Budd, was a professor of horticulture at Iowa State College. Aware of her talented student's love of plants, she encouraged him to pursue botanical research and enroll at the college in Ames. Carver took her advice. Calculating that he could be of better service to "his people" as a scientist than as a painter, he gave up his dream of becoming an artist and turned his attention to the other great passion in his life—plants.

Winding up at Ames was fortuitous, for by 1891 it was emerging as a leading center of agricultural research in the United States. In addition to Joseph L. Budd, its faculty included the estimable Louis Pammel, head of the horticulture department, and two future U.S. secretaries of agriculture, James Wilson and Henry C. Wallace. The latter's son, Henry A. Wallace, who would follow in his father's footsteps in the U.S. Department of Agriculture, was only six years old when he began to tag along with Carver on frequent rambles beyond the edge of the campus to observe and collect plant specimens. The younger Wallace would later recall Carver as the "kindliest, most patient teacher I ever knew."[13] The only black student on campus, Carver found his initial reception there less hospitable than it had been at Simpson, but he soon won over his fellow students with his genial modesty and enthusiastic participation in campus life, including membership in the YMCA and in debate, literary, religious, and other groups. Recognizing his obvious talents as a botanist, his classmates began referring to him as "Doctor" and the "green thumb boy."

Appointed as an assistant in botany and continuing on for postgraduate work after obtaining his bachelor's degree, Carver established a solid reputation for himself as a researcher and instructor at Iowa State, earning his master's degree in 1896. He could have remained on the staff at the college and built a solid career there. However, when Booker T. Washington learned about him and invited him to Tuskegee Institute to head up their new agricultural department, Carver believed that he had a responsibility to take the job as a means of improving the condition of his race. That decision effectively determined his career path over the next four decades. Tuskegee would be where Carver achieved fame, as he, in turn, bestowed some of his sparkling reputation on the institution.[14]

Arriving at Tuskegee with high hopes and expectations, fired with missionary zeal, and determined to use science to transform the lives of his people and his newly adopted region, Carver failed to anticipate many of the obstacles and frustrations he would encounter, especially during his early years in Alabama. Having departed the familiar terrain of the small towns of his native Midwest, he would spend most of his life in and become identified in the public mind with the rural South. Although the region was similar in some respects to the heartland in which he had matured, Carver, now in his early thirties, found himself forced to adjust to southern mores and folkways, to accommodate himself to much harsher forms of racial separation, and to notice explicit and implied warnings and sanctions that governed and limited every action he and his fellow blacks essayed and every word they uttered. Few allowances would be made by a governing white society that insisted on the complete subordination of the race to which he belonged. How Carver reacted to this situation, how he approached the most difficult and intractable social problem confronting the American people, would over time become a model both widely admired and frequently criticized.[15]

Carver admired and would entwine his social philosophy with that of Tuskegee's charismatic leader, Booker T. Washington. In advancing their careers and garnering national reputations for themselves, they fed on each other. But their relationship, though close, was never smooth. Washington, with minimal financial resources at first, had built Tuskegee from nothing into a nationally famous school, and he always seemed to be demanding more from his staff members, especially his director of the Agricultural Department. He grew especially frustrated with Carver's lack of skill at and seeming unconcern about administrative duties. Carver, in turn, often felt overwhelmed by the multiple tasks assigned him in the areas of teaching, research, extension education, supervision of students, public relations, and administration. The two often sparred over teaching loads, supervisory responsibilities, laboratory equipment deficiencies, research and publishing duties, and other matters. Nor did the new recruit always get along easily with his fellow black teachers and workers. Although many observers testified that Carver was warm and congenial once one got to know him, others noted his seeming aloofness and arrogance. Some of his colleagues remained suspicious of him and resented his $1,000-a-year salary, since they were averaging less than 40 percent of that. On the other hand, he quickly developed warm relationships with a number of white families in town, continuing his pattern of often feeling more comfortable among his white acquaintances than with his fellow African Americans.[16]

Being the only one on the faculty with an advanced degree from a white college when he arrived on campus in 1896, Carver discovered reinforcement for his long-held belief that he was special and that he had been chosen by God to fulfill a unique destiny—that of guiding and serving as a role model for his race. The town of Tuskegee, founded in 1832 and containing a population of approximately 2,000, resembled in many ways the small towns in which he had grown up in Missouri, Kansas, and Iowa. Located on a highway linking Montgomery, 40 miles to the west, and Atlanta, 140 miles to the northeast, the town was obviously different from the ones he had known in two ways: it was southern, not midwestern, and its population was half African American. Carver would have to learn how to cope with those facts.[17]

Carver's primary duty at Tuskegee was teaching, a task at which he won high marks. Even when Washington grew most frustrated with his rising star, he readily admitted that Carver was "a great teacher, a great lecturer, a great inspirer of young men and old men."[18] The problem was that teaching was only one of the many responsibilities loaded on him. Carver imaginatively developed an agricultural extension program for bringing education to the masses. Annual farmers' conferences attracted thousands of attendees. Other methods of disseminating advice and expertise included farmers' institutes, fairs, practical demonstrations, short courses, periodic bulletins, and research reports, all initiated to enlighten small farmers in Alabama and nearby states. Carver also headed up the state's black agricultural experiment station.

His true passion was researching new agricultural methods and plant varieties that could improve people's diets and lives and, ideally, jump-start economic development in the region. Carver's career at Tuskegee can be conveniently divided into two periods—pre– and post–Booker T. Washington. By the time of Washington's death in 1915, the great, and sometimes controversial, educational leader and spokesman for black self-improvement and advancement had long presided, along with the more militant W. E. B. Du Bois, as one of the African American community's two most prominent public spokesmen. The last two decades of his life, beginning with his famous speech at the Cotton States Exposition in Atlanta in 1895, coincided with Carver's first twenty years at Tuskegee. At the time of Washington's death, his protégé was already in his early fifties, and although highly successful at what he did, he remained mostly unknown beyond the borders of his adopted state. After Washington's demise, Carver, while working with the school's new principal, Robert Russa Moton, gradually gained new freedom to operate on his own. He was permitted to shed some of his previous duties and responsibilities, obtained more time for research, and began winning national recognition for his scientific discoveries. He also spent more of his time on the road, lecturing, giving demonstrations, and publicizing his work. "After years of relative obscurity," Linda O. McMurry notes, "he began to give the public what it wanted."[19]

World War I directed greater public attention to the work that Carver was doing in his laboratory. Afterward, he began shifting his focus from sweet potatoes to peanuts as a possible replacement for cotton as a major cash crop for southern farmers. Carver's memorable 1921 testimony in Washington, D.C., on a proposed tariff bill before the House Ways and Means Committee touted the many virtues of and uses for peanut products. It generated a huge amount of favorable publicity, making him something of a household name at the start of a decade noted for ballyhoo. Originally allotted ten minutes for his remarks, Carver heard the committee chairman extend his testimony several times, until he finally had spent more than an hour describing a variety of alternate uses for peanuts, ranging from dyes and stock feed to ice cream flavorings and instant coffee. That dramatic episode made him a national figure, earning a hallowed place in the Carver legend, which he continued to develop and elaborate on until his death in 1943.[20]

By then he had evolved into a kind of folk saint, establishing a reputation as a magician with plants and as a creative chemist who discovered hundreds of uses for cowpeas, sweet potatoes, peanuts, and other agricultural products. In the minds of the American public, he became the "Goober Wizard," the "Wizard of Tuskegee," the "Negro Burbank," and the "Columbus of the Soil."[21] Much of Carver's appeal to white America derived from the nonthreatening image he presented—courteous, kind, soft-spoken, and deferential. Congressman Dewey Short, who represented the southwestern Missouri district containing Carver's boyhood home, eulogized the peanut scientist at the time of his death, noting, "The meekness and humility of Dr. Carver, and his unassuming manner, his modesty, are things that went far in the affection of all who met him."[22] David Herbert Donald observed that, in addition to his genius for publicity, Carver served as a symbol—"a marvelously ambiguous symbol that could find acceptance by all groups in society."[23] Appealing equally to both whites and blacks, he illustrated for the former what his black compatriots might be able to achieve if they pursued an education, applied themselves diligently, accepted traditional ways of doing things, and remained patient. This was a prescription for carrying on with the status quo, another way of saying that traditional ways of white supremacy would continue to prevail. To his fellow African Americans, he stood out as a highly successful exemplar of their own race who strikingly demonstrated the kinds of capabilities and potential that they all possessed.

By the 1960s and '70s, however, a host of skeptics had begun to dampen the enthusiasm of the army of Carver celebrators, and his star went into decline. Although he remained a staple in elementary school textbooks and on lists of children's biographies, Carver became an anachronism among many academic historians and something of an embarrassment to large numbers of black activists, leading them to agree with David Herbert Donald that Carver was "no longer part of our usable past."[24] Critics of his accommodationist racial stance characterized him as an Uncle Tom who had failed to stand up uncompromisingly for full dignity, racial equality, and equal rights for blacks. In addition, much of the credit he had received for his discoveries, and the notion that he had almost single-handedly transformed economic conditions in the South, took on the status of myth. Essaying a balanced assessment, Linda O. McMurry, although agreeing that many of Carver's accomplishments were greatly exaggerated, notes the many complexities and contradictions in the man, granting him credit as a creative naturalist, an inspiring teacher, and a valuable role model and inspiration for those who followed him.[25]

If Carver stands out for his scientific and educational work, Oscar Micheaux, another small-town African American boy from the Midwest, shines in the cultural arena. His importance has long been recognized by black moviegoers and students of black filmmaking, but until recently he has been almost entirely unknown among the general white population. Biographies published in 1999 and 2007, along with a growing list of articles and books addressing his life, movie career, and novels, have finally begun to introduce him to a wider audience, who are struck by the remarkable nature of his achievement in the face of numerous obstacles.[26]

Although his route to success diverged significantly from Carver's, he also emerged from small towns and their rural environs in the Midwest. Both men encountered similar racial prejudice, discrimination, threats, and constraints, which were the lot of virtually every person of color at the time. Micheaux's parents both came from Kentucky, where they had been born into slavery. His father, Calvin Swan Michaux (Oscar added an *e* to the family name), was already a small landowner near Metropolis, Illinois, a town of about 3,500 people (approximately one-sixth of whom were African American) on the Ohio River, when he married Bell Gough in 1875. Oscar, born on January 2, 1884, was the fifth of the couple's eleven children. It was a hard life for small farmers in the Little Egypt area of southern Illinois, whose population was heavily black and whose culture in many ways resembled that of the South more than that of the North. Its fertile farmland supported a relatively prosperous agriculture, but the racial climate was forbidding. Among the resident German farmers, who formed one-third of the population, and southerners who had migrated across the Ohio River from Kentucky, Tennessee, Virginia, and the Carolinas, African Americans always had to be on guard. The Ku Klux Klan and other species of night riders patrolled the area after the Civil War, and even after such groups began to decline, the dominant white population always assumed that they had both the duty and the right to keep the former slaves living among them "in their place."[27]

Within these strictures and limitations, some leeway existed for ambitious and resourceful blacks to earn a modest living and to try to better their economic circumstances. Oscar's illiterate father, working from dawn to dusk, provided a model of industry and application for his children. His mother, though uneducated, greatly valued books and knowledge and tried to instill high ideals in her children. One of her heroes was Booker T. Washington, who served as a family role model and became an inspiration for Oscar. The woman's interest in religion rubbed off on the boy, too, although he never seems to have identified with any particular denomination. In the autobiographical second novel that he later wrote, he describes Sidney Wyeth, his alter ego, as a "hopeless believer." Micheaux developed a more complex, ambivalent attitude toward religion than his mother's, reacting strongly against her brand of "shouting Methodism" and taking offense at what he perceived to be the hypocrisy, money lust, and philandering of some of the preachers he witnessed during his youth and later in life. If we are to believe a story recounted in another novel, *The Homesteader,* he actually had an unpleasant confrontation as a child with his future wife's father, who was briefly the pastor of the African Methodist Episcopal (AME) congregation that the family attended in Metropolis and who later served as presiding elder for the southern Illinois district.[28]

Growing up in such an environment instilled in Micheaux a set of bourgeois values and aspirations that guided him throughout his life. The details of his boyhood remain even more obscure than those of George Washington Carver's. Most of what we know about his early years needs to be extrapolated from his three autobiographical novels, which were based on his childhood experiences and homesteading days on the Dakota frontier. It seems fair to say that the dominant characteristics of his personality—optimism, pride, ambition, resourcefulness, industry, competitiveness, tenacity, and sense of responsibility—emerged naturally out of his family environment. The youth's persistent aversion to farmwork may seem to contradict this, but when given a chance to prove himself in other ways, Oscar readily demonstrated his mettle. Frustrated by his fifth-born child's aversion to farm chores, Calvin Micheaux instructed him to haul the family's farm produce into town to sell at the local market. The boy turned out to be a born salesman, readily striking up conversations with customers, white and black alike. His easygoing banter, laced with humor and flattery, sold the goods, winning people over and bringing them back another time. The interpersonal skills he honed in Metropolis stood him in good stead later on when he began peddling his novels door to door and booking his movies.[29]

The family lived for a time in town, because Bell Micheaux believed the children would get a better education there. Jim Crow laws to separate the races were being enacted all over the South beginning in the 1890s, and the practice spread into southern Illinois. Metropolis was, in effect, a southern town tucked just across the river in a nominally northern state. White children attended a substantial school in the center of the community, while black students were relegated to a rickety wooden building in Colored Town on the burg's west side. Micheaux turned into a voracious reader and prolific writer, but the schooling offered in Metropolis sparked little enthusiasm in him. He later remembered his teachers criticizing him for talking too much and for asking too many questions. The experience did not endear the school, the town, his classmates, or his neighbors to him. Already apparent was a tendency to criticize his fellow blacks for their alleged backward ways and lack of ambition. He suggested in his first novel, *The Conquest*, that they were for the most part "wretchedly poor, ignorant and envious. They were set in the ways of their localisms, and it was quite useless to talk to them of anything that would better oneself."[30]

Metropolis, as described in that book, was an "old town" containing a marketplace, where Oscar sold his family's farm produce, along with "a few factories, two flour mills, two or three saw mills, box factories and another concern where veneering was peeled from wood blocks softened with steam." There was little in it to hold him. Neighbors resented his questioning their work ethic, and church elders deemed him too worldly, too free-thinking, and too dangerous for other young people to associate with. He was anxious to get away, and in 1900, at age sixteen, before graduating from high school, he made his escape.[31]

Having an older brother living in Chicago, he worked his way up the state to the big city, taking jobs in towns along the way. That rapidly growing metropolis was a "new and strange" place to him, what with its recently built skyscrapers, numerous factories and warehouses, streetcar lines, and a sprinkling of horseless carriages. The throngs of people filling the streets, the screeching noise, the rush of activity, the constant turmoil—all of these were stimulating, but also disorienting. Approximately 98 percent of the population was white, and nine-tenths of the city's 30,000 or so African Americans lived in the Black Belt on the south side, mainly between Twelfth and Thirty-First Streets. Oscar had no difficulty finding jobs, but he kept switching in search of better pay and opportunities.[32]

Eventually he managed to latch on as a sleeping-car porter, a position that, in addition to allowing him to accumulate a modest capital stake, afforded him a chance to see the country and further develop his interpersonal skills. The job also instructed him in how to invest in land and planted in him the idea of starting anew as a frontier farmer. The Pullman Company, headquartered in Chicago, was the largest employer of black men in the United States. The demands of the job bred a sort of double consciousness in its employees. On the one hand, their effectiveness as porters and the tips they earned depended upon their adopting a deferential—even obsequious—manner in dealing with their generally well-heeled white clients, putting down their beds, shining their shoes, and promptly answering their every beck and call. The more effectively porters played their "Uncle Tom" roles, the more highly they were regarded by their customers and employer. In the meantime, they were able to travel about the country; educate themselves regarding different regions and lifestyles; take in entertainments at vaudeville houses, movie theaters, and nightspots; and learn about business and investment opportunities. All this increased their knowledge, self-confidence, and understanding of the society in which they were operating.[33]

To while away the time when they were not on the job, porters tended to tell stories, affording Micheaux considerable opportunity to perfect his storytelling skills. Though demeaning in many ways, the position provided exposure to successful and powerful people, and porters often internalized the practices and habits of the customers they served, which, according to the historian Larry Tye, "helped shape today's black middle class and intelligentsia." Off the job, porters commanded respect, often becoming community leaders, and by the 1920s more than a third of them owned their own homes.[34] Micheaux's experiences riding the rails could only have reinforced his youthful attraction to bourgeois values and striving, and they increased his eagerness to leave behind his roots, travel about the country, and take the kinds of risks necessary to achieve success. The entrepreneurial spirit became an essential part of him.

So, too, did thrift. Somehow, in just several years' time as a porter, the young man managed to build a nest egg of several thousand dollars. He enjoyed the work and was fascinated by the scenery and the new places he encountered in his travels. Remaining ambivalent about his experience in large cities, he grew interested in the life of small towns. In chapter 4 of *The Conquest,* he cataloged the places he passed through on runs to Portland. Describing the countryside between Chicago and North Platte, Nebraska, he observed, "During the summer it is one large garden farm, dotted with numerous cities, thriving hamlets and towns, fine country homes so characteristic of the great middle west, and is always pleasing to the eye." Beyond North Platte, he ticked off the towns: Cheyenne, Rawlins, Medicine Bow, Rock Springs, and Green River, Wyoming; Minidoka, Idaho; Granger, Washington; and on to Portland, Oregon.[35]

Traveling from place to place, he became intrigued with the possibilities of homesteading, lured on by Horace Greeley's siren call, "Go West young man, and grow up with the country." He calculated that his savings would not extend very far in Iowa, the first place he considered settling. Land prices were skyrocketing there, so he turned his sights to the great Northwest when he learned that land was being opened up there for settlement on the Rosebud Indian Reservation in South Dakota. The federal government set up a lottery to distribute 2,400 available parcels of land; 107,000 people signed up. Micheaux drew number 6,504, affording him no real chance to buy a cheap government homestead. Nevertheless, he remained undiscouraged. In October 1904, he purchased a relinquishment on a homestead in Gregory County, just west of the Missouri River, on 160 acres quit by the original claimant. Most of what we know about his homesteading experience derives from his own fictionalized accounts of it in three of his novels—*The Conquest, The Wind from Nowhere,* and *The Homesteader,* which contain somewhat varying descriptions of the eight years he spent in South Dakota. Considering how much he had detested farmwork as a youth, it is ironic that he so enthusiastically embraced tilling the soil during his twenties and that he afterward held it up as an ideal way for his race to escape the corruptions of city life and make an independent life for themselves on the land.[36]

Homesteading appealed to him in part because it offered a new kind of freedom. Unlike railroading, which allowed extensive movement and escape from the close surveillance of watchful whites, agriculture on the plains of Dakota kept its practitioners in a fixed place, ensconcing them in community settings where people's neighbors heavily determined the satisfaction they derived from their lives. But being located far from oppressive social restrictions imposed by southern culture, blacks living in South Dakota were able to enjoy a much more open social environment. For one thing, there were not very many of them. Although Micheaux's assertion that he was the only black homesteader living in the area may have been slightly exaggerated, it was not far off the mark. Most of his white neighbors shared the kinds of prejudices, deficiencies, ignorance, and discriminatory tendencies prevailing in the country at large, but they were also more inclined than many others to judge black people on their merits and to establish friendly relations with them if they appeared congenial, industrious, and willing to cooperate. The young man from Chicago was all of these. Most of Micheaux's white neighbors and the people he did business with treated him amiably, and many came to admire and respect him.[37]

He quickly made friends with local power brokers, the Jackson brothers, whose wealthy father, a close friend of Chicago and Northwestern Railroad executive Marvin Hughitt, advanced the financial backing they needed to promote their business and real estate ventures. This relationship proved beneficial in Micheaux's business dealings and in making friends with other white people in the area. Willing to poke fun at himself for his ignorance about horses and agriculture in general, he quickly won people over with his easy affability and lack of pretense as well as with his hard work and willingness to experiment. In five years' time, he amassed 500 acres of land and seemed well on his way to accumulating even more before a hard drought set in during 1911 and 1912, wiping him out, along with most of his neighbors, and forcing him to seek out new opportunities.[38]

In the meantime, he had married a young black woman from Chicago, the daughter of Rev. Newton J. McCracken, the same AME minister he had encountered as a boy in southern Illinois. The preacher's domineering ways soon led his daughter to leave Micheaux and return to her family, a devastating blow to the young man's pride, added to his failure at farming. Undaunted, he decided that if he could not make a go of it as an agriculturalist, he would write a book about the experience and market it himself. The process worked so successfully that he wrote another book based on the same raw materials, and then another. When the third novel, *The Homesteader*, came to the attention of George P. Johnson, who with his brother Noble operated the most successful early black film company in the United States, he approached Micheaux about using the narrative as the basis for a movie. When negotiations broke down over the film's length, direction, and other details, Micheaux decided to produce the movie himself, although he had no experience whatsoever in the business. He had gone into novel writing with no background in the field and succeeded. Now he would reinvent himself a second time.[39]

Success in the movie business did not come easily, nor did it ever bring great financial reward to Micheaux. But the success he did achieve came startlingly quickly. Just three years after the release of D. W. Griffith's extremely racist and hugely successful epic of the post–Civil War South, *The Birth of a Nation*, the aspiring African American filmmaker incorporated the Micheaux Book and Film Company, sold stock in it to raise capital, recruited actors and technicians, and made his first moving picture, all while learning on the job. Remarkably, in little more than a year, *The Homesteader* premiered before an audience of 8,000 people in Chicago's Eighth Regiment Armory on February 20, 1919, just three months after the armistice ending the Great War. Costing only $15,000 to make (one-tenth Griffith's expenditure), the film electrified the mostly black audiences that attended it in Chicago. Micheaux had produced the longest, most technically proficient, and most impressive race movie ever made up until that time. Critics raved about it. In the estimation of the film historian and Micheaux biographer Patrick McGilligan, "It was a triumph on every level: artistic, commercial, and personal."[40]

Micheaux, among the first and certainly the most prolific of the early black film producers, eventually earned a reputation as the best and the most provocative practitioner of the art.[41] He produced around forty-five films during his career, almost two-thirds of them during the first decade, which coincided with the silent film era. We will probably never know exactly how many to credit him with, because most of them have been lost. Only three of his silent productions, which are generally considered to be superior to his sound movies, have been recovered: *Within Our Gates* and *The Symbol of the Unconquered,* both done in 1920, and *Body and Soul,* from 1925. All his releases were put together on shoestring budgets, with only three or four prints generally being made, and most of them underwent considerable censoring, leaving latter-day film historians uncertain about exactly what material was contained in the originals.[42]

Several of Micheaux's early films were autobiographical, based on the homesteading experience that inspired his first three novels. Other productions likewise drew on his life story. Always a businessman first and foremost, he wrote novels and produced films to sell and to attract an audience. He succeeded well enough to keep at it for three decades, but he never managed to capture many white readers or viewers for his films. This disappointed him, inasmuch as he had launched his artistic career by selling his early novels to white neighbors, friends, and others. Sometimes white theater owners allowed screenings of race movies during off hours or on slow days, but by and large, Micheaux failed to persuade them to book his films, and white moviegoers seldom ventured into black theaters. Estimates of the number of film venues catering to black audiences during the early 1920s vary from around 400 to about 800, few of them containing more than 250 seats. In contrast, approximately 22,000 white exhibition halls were in operation, some of them able to accommodate thousands of viewers.[43]

Unable to reach white audiences and almost entirely unknown to the white public, Micheaux built a considerable reputation for himself among people of color during the decade after the war. It was easier to book his movies into large cities like Chicago, Pittsburgh, and Atlanta, but he also wormed his way into smaller cities and towns, especially in the South, as he traveled extensively as his own booking and publicity agent. During the 1930s, with the shift to sound and as the technology of filmmaking advanced, Micheaux relied increasingly on scripts featuring bands and nightclub scenes, allowing him to utilize performers and acts straight off the stage. He was also trying to compete with Hollywood, whose much larger budgets made his efforts look relatively cheap and primitive in comparison. Until the late 1930s, however, as black moviemakers sensed their industry was about to go under, Micheaux retained the support of a substantial core audience within the black community for his films. For two decades he intuited what black filmgoers wanted to watch, and he fairly successfully supplied it. In the words of Patrick McGilligan, "The race-picture pioneer was always mindful about possible viewers' reactions; it was a cornerstone of his philosophy to be at one with his audience."[44]

What he provided them, however, often offended the sensibilities of white censors as well as black audiences. Ever the entrepreneur, he always tried to entertain people while at the same time attempting to enlighten them. His movies usually came with a message. His primary purpose as an artist, reflecting his personal drive to succeed, was to promote upward class mobility—the uplift of his race.[45] The kinds of themes he addressed, in addition to trying to educate people about the attractions of homesteading in the great Northwest, were among the most controversial of the day: racism, segregation, labor peonage, the Ku Klux Klan, lynching, passing for white, miscegenation, rape, religious hypocrisy, and gambling, among others. Many of his characters frequented gin joints and nightclubs. They gambled, drank, and took drugs. Women wore sexy clothes, or little at all, and men abused their wives and girlfriends. Gangsters and prize-fighters added color to the mix. Censors sometimes demanded that he cut a quarter or more of the footage out of his films. But Micheaux was not just a Hollywood-style titillater. While picturing successful black people in positions of wealth and power in some of his movies, he also depicted brutal violence and discrimination directed against them in others. Never placid, never complacent, he aimed to stir up viewers and often managed to do so.

During the 1940s, as audiences for race films rapidly dwindled, lured away by the appeal of Hollywood with its increasing use of African American actors, constant improvements in production values, and more realistic and appealing story lines, the black movie industry virtually disappeared, along with black professional baseball and other components of black culture. Micheaux returned to writing novels, turning out four more during the decade, before taking one last shot at making a movie blockbuster. In 1948, at age sixty-four, suffering from severe arthritis and sometimes confined to a wheelchair, he produced *The Betrayal*, which took him back one last time to his Dakota homestead years. The movie was a critical disaster. Referring to its "flimsy" and "purposeless" plot and to a script that it likened to that of a grade school play, the *New York Daily*

News casually dismissed the film. The *New York Herald Tribune* termed it a "preposterous, tasteless bore," and the *New York Times,* which had never bothered to review any of his previous pictures, called it "confusing," "gauche," and "consistently amateurish."[46] The kind of moviemaking that had been in the vanguard of race films a decade or two earlier had become passé by the late 1940s, as the culture began to consolidate, bringing the races together and forcing both to play by the same rules and to live by the standards of a new popular culture spawned during the Depression and World War II years. When Micheaux died in 1951, he remained almost entirely forgotten or overlooked in the white world, although many blacks recalled his work with admiration and affection.

The lives and careers of George Washington Carver and Oscar Micheaux, although never directly interconnecting, can help us understand the changes wrought in American society and within the black community from the late nineteenth through the first half of the twentieth century. They also have important things to say about the small-town, rural Midwest and the place of African Americans within it. We can learn much by comparing the challenges and obstacles the two men faced and the resiliency and creativity they applied in coping with them.

Carter's ingenious responses to adversity at Tuskegee Institute over the years resembled the ways blacks everywhere sought to deal with problems of discrimination, educational deprivation, limited occupational opportunities, and scarce resources. Although Carver's relatively large salary at Tuskegee occasioned considerable resentment among his peers there, money never enticed him. He habitually stashed paychecks away in a drawer, saving them for a rainy day, sometimes not cashing them for years. Of greater concern to him were the primitive conditions of the classrooms and labs at the school and the general paucity of resources for getting the job done. During his early years at the school, he constantly scratched for dollars to make minimal improvements. The white experiment station at Auburn University received between ten and forty times as much annual funding as did its black counterpart at Tuskegee Institute. Heavy teaching loads and multiple duties and responsibilities left Carver with little time to pursue his beloved research projects.[47]

He scavenged trash piles and appropriated materials anywhere he could find them. He utilized jars and bottles rescued from dumps to substitute for the flagons and beakers he would have purchased had he had more money. He became famous for practicing "cook stove chemistry," making scientific discoveries in primitive conditions that astonished his counterparts at other schools. His method of coping with pressures on his time was simply to devote most of his waking hours to his job and to religious work, leaving little time for leisure or hobbies other than his walks in the woods and reading. Possessing no family, he regarded his students and other young boys whom he mentored—the "Carver boys" as they came to be called—as his surrogate family. He regularly taught Bible classes, packing students in, and devoted much time talking to and counseling his young charges. He spent much of his energy early on at Tuskegee trying to persuade Booker T. Washington to lighten his workload to open up more time for work in the lab. After 1915, under Robert Moton, he was relieved of most of his classroom duties and was able to enjoy more time for research, outside lecturing, extension work, and travel.[48]

Micheaux proved no less ingenious in scrounging up resources for his many projects. Only a prodigious saver could have accumulated in a relatively few years' time the sum it took to buy land in South Dakota. Turning to writing books, he raised the money to self-publish his first volume by enlisting friends and neighbors to subscribe for it, and he then traveled around the region, selling it door-to-door. To raise the capital necessary for his first film, he sold stock in his newly formed corporation, accumulating $5,000 in a few weeks' time.[49]

But money—or more precisely the lack thereof—remained a constant problem throughout his career. Financial constraints could force black filmmakers to be especially creative in their techniques.[50] More often, however, such constraints led critics at the time and latter-day scholars to point out a variety of shoddy practices Micheaux was forced to put up with: incompetent camera work, poor lighting and sound setups, weak acting, bad or nonexistent editing (including shots showing microphone booms or passing bicyclists), and other deficiencies. Although much of his work was skillfully done and sometimes came close to measuring up to Hollywood standards, many criticisms of his work were on target. Micheaux became notorious for refusing to do second takes of scenes, not wishing to take the time or to use up precious film stock. His critics tended to overlook how little money he had available to make his pictures. Always short of cash, he frequently required his actors to provide their own costumes, usually paid them a pittance, and sometimes never got around to compensating them at all. Different sets were sometimes put together by simply rearranging the furniture and changing the pictures on the walls. If a woman wearing a fur coat happened to appear on location, Micheaux was capable of grabbing a camera and taking a shot of her, which he would incorporate later in another film. He did what was necessary to get the job done. Speed and frugality were essential just to survive. Black filmmakers like Micheaux, according to the film historian Thomas Cripps, "did not fail so much as they were overwhelmed by the impossible."[51] Continually flirting with financial disaster, Micheaux finally declared bankruptcy in 1928, afterward reorganizing his entire operation. Beginning in 1931, he benefited for several years from an infusion of white capital from New Yorkers Leo Brecher and Frank Schiffman, who owned and operated the four largest movie theaters in Harlem and invested in all-black stage shows. During this brief period, he had the opportunity to do some of the things he had not been able to do previously.[52]

For someone completely untutored in the business, Micheaux proved to be an enormously quick study. He relied heavily on actors recruited from existing theater companies, such as the well-known Lafayette Players of New York. Some of his stars, including Evelyn Preer, Shingzie Howard, Lorenzo Tucker, and Lawrence Chenault, were cast over and over again. Paul Robeson, already famous for his singing and theatrical performances, made his screen debut in Micheaux's 1925 production *Body and Soul.* Micheaux married one of his actresses, Alice Bertrand Russell, and as time went by she assumed most of the managerial responsibilities of the company (she also apparently edited his later books), leaving her husband to produce the films and to go on the road to market and advertise them. Micheaux, in truth, literally did it all when it came to filmmaking. He not only produced, directed, and distributed his own work, but he also conceived the projects and often wrote the scripts, several of which were adaptations of novels he had previously written. Beyond that, he repeatedly drew on his own life story for many of the plotlines.

Part of his marketing strategy was the attempt to inflate his own power and influence, realizing that the higher people estimated a producer, the more likely they were to attend his movies. He traveled around in chauffeured limousines and wore expensive clothing, relying on his impressive appearance to create a commotion when he arrived. His captivating visage and personality commanded attention whenever he entered a room, allowing him to dominate a discussion when he began talking. Film historians

Pearl Bowser and Louise Spence have documented the filmmaker's crafting of his own "biographical legend" in order to shape favorable public reception for his work. During the 1920s, "Micheaux developed the public persona of an aggressive and successful businessman and a controversial and confident maverick producer," they write, a persona that sustained him during the following two decades. Part of his intent in reconstructing history was to simplify his life story, making it seem like a seamless progression from penury to success, thereby enabling him to serve as a role model for people of his own race.[53]

From an early age, Micheaux learned from his parents to aim high and exert himself. He believed that his fellow African Americans bore responsibility for their own failures and lack of advancement and felt called on to rectify the situation. Not attracted to politics or social action to advance the cause of his race, he believed that by the example he set and through his writings and films he could pave the way for others to follow in his footsteps (and, not incidentally, earn money for himself). Though generally accurate in their depictions of the United States, these works never hesitated to alter the facts if in so doing it would advance the story line. It is ironic that Micheaux advised his fellow blacks to relocate to homesteads in the great Northwest, where they supposedly would be able to prosper and live freely and in friendly association with whites. In reality, of course, the reason that Micheaux began writing books and producing movies about his experiences in South Dakota was because he had ultimately been an economic failure there. This contradiction never dimmed his enthusiasm for telling and retelling the story.

In contrast to Oscar Micheaux's self-conscious fashioning of his biographical legend as an artistic and public relations ploy, George Washington Carver's role in crafting the widely accepted Carver myth was more passive and unplanned. This detracted in no way from its pervasiveness and influence. People were impressed by his humility and lack of pretense. Signature elements of Carver's public image were his shabby clothes, frugal habits, and quiet, unpretentious demeanor. All of these were unfeigned, to be sure, but we can assume that Carver took pleasure in the good will they generated.[54]

The Carver myth related, in the first place, to his personal qualities, including meekness, frugality, contentment, earnestness, religiousness, friendliness, and generosity. More important in the minds of many were the contributions he had presumably made to science, education, southern economic development, and improvements in race relations. Carver's congressional testimony in 1921 initiated him into the national spotlight. During the 1930s, as he proceeded into his seventies, a series of magazine articles and a spate of worshipful biographies helped transform him into something of a living saint. A 1936 article in *The Chemist* entitled "The Wizard of Tuskegee" was followed the next year by a *Reader's Digest* condensation of an earlier-published piece entitled "A Boy Who Was Traded for a Horse." Meanwhile, an academic historian writing a textbook on southern history asserted Carver's "leading rank as an industrial scientist," based on his having developed 165 products from the peanut and another 107 from the yellow yam. *Life* magazine, in a photo spread that identified him as "one of the great scientists of the U.S.," almost doubled the number of peanut products Carver allegedly discovered, indicating how arbitrary those kinds of estimates could be. Most of the early books about Carver both before and after his death in 1943 were adulatory and uncritical, and their readers could not have been blamed for placing him on a par with Alfred Einstein, Niels Bohr, and Ernest O. Lawrence.[55]

As time went by, however, skeptical journalists and writers began to question and debunk many of Carver's reputed achievements, noting that most of them lacked scientific proof, resulted from overzealous publicity agents and overenthusiastic hero-worshippers, or served the purposes of various interested parties dedicated to promoting their own particular causes.[56] The peanut industry was the most obvious group inclined to exaggerate Carver's achievements. Spokesmen for the New South and promoters of southern economic development also had it in their interest to advance inflated claims for Carver's contribution to their cause. Religious leaders warmed to Carver's frequently expressed faith in God, nostalgists appreciated his attempts to reconcile the old and the new, patriots and capitalists enjoyed quoting statements of his that resonated with them, and members of his race welcomed him to their bosom for his achievements as a black man, even as other black spokesmen condemned him for his evidently accommodationist stance on racial issues.

Carver, who from first to last allied himself closely with the social and educational views of his boss and mentor, Booker T. Washington, seemed a likely ally to many southern conservatives and white supremacists. In a letter written to George Foster Peabody in 1923, the pride of Tuskegee expressed his view that progress for his people would come primarily through the actions of individuals. "I believe," he wrote, "in the providence of God working in the hearts of men, and that the so-called Negro problem will be satisfactorily solved in His own good time, and in His own way."[57] Although Carver had many clashes with Booker T. Washington over workloads, funding, and research support, he never questioned the rightness of his superior's emphasis on self-help, gradual progress, and the need for patience in obtaining improvements in the lot of their race. His religious principles reinforced his inclination to rely on reason, discussion, and compromise rather than on confrontation, assertiveness, and threats. Furthermore, his personal experiences in Missouri, Kansas, Alabama, and elsewhere impressed on him the intransigence and dangerousness of white extremists, who would stop at nothing, including violence and murder, to maintain white supremacy. His personality, too, dictated a gradualist response to the situation. In only a few instances, such as when he was denied service at a New York hotel where he had a long-standing reservation, did Carver make a commotion and insist vocally on his rights as a black person.[58]

Micheaux, like Carver, became an outspoken disciple of the famous founder of Tuskegee. He dedicated his novel *The Conquest* "To the Honorable Booker T. Washington," and several of his movies had pictures of Washington hanging prominently on the walls of the sets. Micheaux's stance on racial matters, however, was much more complicated than Carver's. For one thing, he came from a younger generation and was in his prime during the 1920s and '30s, by which time Carver was already in his sixties and seventies, and it was becoming more common for black spokesmen to state their views more openly and even to demonstrate in favor of civil rights and equal treatment for blacks. On the one hand, Micheaux accepted Washington's urging of black people to adopt standard American bourgeois values—hard work, thrift, educational achievement, self-improvement and self-reliance, ambition, striving, and working within the system. Micheaux's favored approach for black empowerment and advancement was to have fellow members of his race follow his example by moving onto land in the Northwest and attempting to make a go of it in agriculture. This provoked skepticism from critics who accused him of being an apologist for the middle class and of remaining too complacent about a capitalist system that had little to offer but crumbs for those left behind.[59]

Micheaux, however, was no quietist, willing to wait patiently until things righted themselves in some distant future. His silent films made during the 1920s, especially, addressed problems of racial discrimination, violence, lynching, crime, and miscegenation. This was Micheaux as angry young man. His vivid description of a brutal lynching in *Within Our Gates,* released a year after the bloody 1919 Chicago race riots, which cost thirty-eight lives, was a throwing down of the gauntlet, in effect, to a system that systematically ground down African Americans and that was presided over by a white power structure little concerned about injustice and inequality. Micheaux complicated matters by frequently directing criticism against his fellow blacks for what he perceived as their all too frequent self-indulgence, corruption, bad habits, complacency, and lack of initiative. Like his description of the fictional book publisher and film producer Sidney Wyeth (who appears as Micheaux's alter ego in several of his novels) in his 1946 novel *The Story of Dorothy Stanfield,* Micheaux considered himself to be "an intense race man; and while he can and does criticize the Negro in his books . . . , he is for his people at all times, regardless of the circumstances."[60]

He presented himself and others like him as examples of imagination, initiative, application, and achievement. He endeavored to motivate his people toward greater striving and creativity in solving their own problems, rather than relying on whites to solve their problems for them. In his first novel, he has his alter ego Oscar Devereaux say, "One of the greatest tasks of my life has been to convince a certain class of my racial acquaintances that a colored man can be anything."[61] That imperative remained a constant theme in his art from beginning to end. Although some of his statements and artistic expressions reflected the kind of militancy W. E. B. Du Bois exemplified during the early 1900s, Micheaux's message more often coincided with that of Booker T. Washington, and that is where his heart lay.[62]

In addition, Micheaux can be viewed as a black Turnerian because of his attraction to and fascination with homesteading in the West. *The Conquest* was the first American novel in which a leading black character played the role of a pioneer.[63] Like Frederick Jackson Turner, Micheaux located economic opportunity for blacks and the possibility of a more ideal community in the West, in particular in what he referred to as "the great Northwest." In *The Wind from Nowhere* he described the sense of ease and inclusion he felt among his neighbors in South Dakota through the character of alter ego Martin Eden: "He knew of no place where he could have had better neighbors and lived so happily. Indeed, he was far more popular, on the whole, than any individual white man." According to Pearl Bowser and Louise Spence, "The frontier, for Micheaux, is the mythic space of moral drama and the site of opportunities seemingly free of the restrictive and discriminatory laws and social arrangements of the rural South and the urban metropolis, where the characteristic model of economic expansion is entrepreneurship."[64]

Micheaux and Carver found themselves confronting new kinds of challenges that stood in the way of all American men, regardless of race, during the decades around the turn of the century, as the United States underwent tremendous socioeconomic change associated with industrialization and urbanization. With the culture's center of gravity shifting from small towns to metropolitan areas, a solid sense of identity became increasingly difficult to maintain. The historian Joel Williamson persuasively argues that agricultural depression in the South during the 1880s and 1890s shocked many white men, who "found themselves disadvantaged and locked into a rapidly changing national and international economics that they were powerless to control." Added to this was the perception that black people were becoming increasingly competitive with them. One way in which white men could reassert their manhood in these circumstances was to demonstrate their racial dominance in the form of lynching, disfranchisement, and new forms of segregation.[65] On the receiving end of this assault, Carver, Micheaux, and their fellow blacks were forced to defend their own manhood. Booker T. Washington, in his famous Atlanta Exposition address of 1895, and W. E. B. Du Bois, in his Niagara address of 1906, both made mention of "manhood" and "manhood rights." George Washington Carver, whose high-pitched voice, soft-spoken manner of speaking, artistic tendencies, attraction to needlework, gentle nature, and religious activities might have inclined people to think of him as less than manly, never felt compelled to modify his behavior in order to impress people with evidence of his gender orientation. He was enough of an individualist to feel comfortable being himself, and the legendary status he achieved during his dotage left him free to behave pretty much as he pleased.[66]

For Micheaux, on the other hand, expressing one's manhood was very much a matter of conscious concern, affecting both his writing and his filmmaking. Literary critic Jayna Brown points to the link between national identity and black manhood in *The Conquest* and *The Homesteader*. Those narratives work, she writes, "to establish the young man (Devereaux/Baptiste) as the new secular example for the black working class.

Within these novels, the de-crowning of the old patriarch, the preacher-father figure, and the crowning of the son, the new, enterprising capitalist, is the fundamental process of a black man's transformation."[67] *The Homesteader* contains multiple references to manhood. Its plot could be interpreted as one involving the loss and regaining of manhood, with the culmination of the process occurring at the end, when protagonist Jean Baptiste discovers that his "dream girl," Agnes Stewart, has black blood in her, enabling him to marry her. "She did not resist as she saw his manly love and felt his body quiver," Micheaux writes.[68] Micheaux's films as well as his novels frequently take up the theme. Film historian Gerald Butters argues that in response to the challenge posed by D. W. Griffith's *The Birth of a Nation* and the phenomenal success it achieved, early black filmmakers made defense of black manhood their major theme. In his estimation, Micheaux's silent films "are the most provocative, confrontational, thought-provoking films regarding African-American men and their place in American society in the post–World War I era."[69]

The treatment accorded Carver and Micheaux by the dominant white society reflected the attitudes, assumptions, and values that held sway during the period. By the time of Carver's death, the United States was slowly beginning to move in the direction of egalitarianism and justice for its largest and most abused racial minority. In June 1941, President Franklin Roosevelt had issued Executive Order 8802 banning discrimination in government and defense industry jobs in order to head off a threatened march on Washington by militant African Americans led by A. Philip Randolph, the head of the all-black Brotherhood of Sleeping Car Porters. Twenty-two years later, Randolph would be in the front ranks of the march for jobs and freedom led by Martin Luther King Jr., and the following year Congress would enact the most significant civil rights law since the Civil War.

Much earlier than that, it had become apparent to realistic observers that Micheaux's proposed solution for America's racial dilemma—taking up agricultural land in the Northwest—was a chimera. More relevant was his denunciation of racial violence, segregation, and other modes of oppression. Booker T. Washington's quietistic approach, by itself, would not have brought the kind of progress that was achieved by judicial petition, demonstrations, and legislative action as they evolved during the 1950s and '60s. Clearly, however, much remains left today to accomplish before full racial equality is achieved.

Micheaux's intuition that geography would play a major role in ameliorating racial injustice strikes us today as more sensible than it probably seemed to most people in his own time. Historically, blacks had been prisoners of a socioeconomic system that held them hostage in the rural South both before and after the Civil War. Real progress began to be made only when they moved in massive numbers first of all into urban areas in the South and then north across the Mason-Dixon Line and the Ohio River and west across the Mississippi River. Only a small number of them, such as the Exodusters of 1879 and others who established rural agricultural colonies in places like Oklahoma, Kansas, and South Dakota, followed Micheaux's advice to stay on the land. A few wound up in small towns in the North, the Middle West, and the West. The vast majority of them, however, established residence in larger towns and cities.

Carver retained more of an interest in and connection to his Missouri roots than Micheaux did to his beginnings in southern Illinois. Carver returned once or twice to the area around Diamond to visit and reminisce, but no record exists of Micheaux visiting his former home ground in Metropolis.[70] For Micheaux, the questions of where and how to live, including the relative desirability of small towns and big cities, were of central importance both in his life and in his art. He escaped what he considered to be the boredom and constrictions of small-town Illinois as quickly as he could, but he soon discovered that the initial allure of Chicago was mostly false. He wound up homesteading in South Dakota, where a thousand people made for a very large town. Several of his books digressed from their central plots to discuss the development of town life in the Dakotas—a subject that apparently fascinated him. They went into some detail about land sales and values, the significance of railroads in opening up an area, the roles played by town leaders and entrepreneurs, and the ubiquitous battles fought between towns aspiring to acquire county-seat status. Similar stories were passed on about frontier development in every state in the Midwest.

In urging his fellow blacks to follow his example and take out homesteads in the great Northwest, Micheaux was obviously being overly romantic, and though he continued to praise the region's virtues, by his actions he betrayed them.[71] As book author and salesman, he wound up living in Sioux City, Iowa, and as film producer and marketing agent, he operated out of headquarters located in Chicago and New York—the nation's two largest cities at the time. There seemed to be no escaping the drift to the city that artistic and financial success presumably demanded.

But throughout his career, Micheaux kept his finger on the pulse of his people, traveling extensively in the South and elsewhere, through large cities and small towns. He remained essentially ambivalent about urban America, on the one hand deprecating its crudeness, materialism, amorality, and lack of community, while on the other admiring its vitality, creativity, energy, and stimulation. Likewise, he maintained a bifocal view of small towns, seemingly content to wax nostalgic about them and their rural environs but preferring to live in them in memory, not actuality.

In that, he was not unlike most of his fellow small-town boys. The ones who remained behind generally lived out their lives in relative obscurity— happy or discontented, successful or mediocre, influential or mundane. The ones anybody ever heard of outside of their hometowns generally had to leave home to make their marks. Black Americans shared in this condition. Life might have been different in many ways for them, but in this they found themselves to be in the same situation as their white counterparts.

■

Embattled Small Towns during Prosperity, Depression, and War, 1920–1945

Introduction to Section II

The 1920s proved to be a pivotal decade in the way Americans perceived and felt about their small towns. In the aftermath of the Great War that had rent Europe asunder and had drawn the United States into its vortex, people began to think more subtly and profoundly about themselves, their habits and values, and their ways of living than most of them had been used to in the past. Change seemed to accelerate far more than ever previously experienced, and traditional practices and institutions came into question and sometimes under sustained attack in ways requiring direct response. Historians classify the decade as a modernizing one, citing trends in art and architecture; intellectual breakthroughs in philosophy, psychology, and other fields; and an explosion of interest in popular culture. Automobile ownership rapidly increased; movies played to much larger audiences, contributing to a rising cult of celebrity; radio listening, nonexistent at the beginning of the decade, had become a widespread pastime by the end of it; and participation and spectatorship in sports proliferated.

Most of these changes originated in and were concentrated in cities and urban areas. By the 1920s, many small towns were beginning to lose population. The revelation by the director of the census after the count in 1920 that the United States had passed into a new era—the urban population (counting places with more than 2,500 population) now amounting to 51.2 percent of the total—stimulated considerable discussion and debate.

In many ways, small-town residents and the farm population felt themselves to be on the losing end of things, even beleaguered. Modernizing tendencies and the rising trends of urbanization, industrialization, bureaucratization, and corporate expansion all posed significant challenges—indeed, threats—to rural America. In response, a counterthrust emerged in defense of small-town traditions and habits, which manifested itself in a variety of ways, including the revival of old-time music and dancing, historical preservation efforts, and the growth of organizations such as the Ku Klux Klan.

Nothing did more to shift Americans' thinking about their small towns than the appearance in 1920 of Sinclair Lewis's novel *Main Street,* one of the most sensational publishing events of the twentieth century. Other writers, from Mark Twain and Hamlin Garland to Sherwood Anderson and Edgar Lee Masters, had poked fun at and criticized American village life, but no one else did it with so much verve, detail, and just plain wit. With its droll depictions of the stultifying conformism and the mindless complacency that characterized small-town living, the book became the defining document of the literary "revolt from the village" that flowered during the 1920s. Lewis soon followed this with *Babbitt,* a similar exposé of life in medium-sized cities, a book hardly less successful and packing a strong punch in its own right.

Lewis, who had grown up as a bright but maladjusted youth in the sleepy town of Sauk Centre, Minnesota, during the 1890s, had reason to strike back at the people who had laughed at and teased him while he was a student there. The general assumption of his readers and literary critics was that he must have hated small-town residents in general. But his feelings were more complicated than that. He no doubt exaggerated his indictment because of the hurt that still lingered when he published the book at the age of thirty-five, and he realized that a full-scale attack would sell more books than any half-baked treatment. Most evident in readers' minds was the satirical bent of his depictions of small-town folkways, practices, and ambitions. But Lewis also possessed the soul of a reporter, intent on describing in minute detail, much as a journalist or a sociologist might, all the goings-on that constituted the lives of the residents of the community. It was Sauk Centre that he remembered, but in the novel he called the town Gopher Prairie and he noted that its Main Street was "the continuation of Main Streets everywhere." This could have been a story set in any state of the Union; its lessons were universal.

What almost everyone failed to realize was just how conflicted the author was about his subject—both the story that he told through the eyes of his protagonist, Carol Kennicott, and the remembered Minnesota town he had grown up in before making his escape and heading off to Yale. When invited to write something for the town's high school yearbook in 1931, when he was in his mid-forties, he observed that if he had cast aspersions on prairie villages, he had been equally critical of cities like New York and Paris, as well as of other institutions. He was probably not being disingenuous when he recalled with some degree of fondness the fun he had experienced as a kid in Minnesota swimming, fishing, picnicking, and listening to orators in the GAR Hall. It had been, he averred with no trace of irony, a good place for him to grow up. Lewis criticized the nation's small towns in large part because he was capable of imagining how much better they could be. His ambivalence toward them mirrored that harbored by Americans then and now. In any case, another of his observations resonated deeply with many readers: "It is extraordinary how deep is the impression made by the place of one's birth and rearing, and how long lasting are its memories."[1]

Like most of the other successful small-town and farm lads from the Middle West discussed in this book, Carl Sandburg left home and rose to prominence in a big city, in his case Chicago. His work as a newspaperman provided him an opportunity to move into other literary lines—poetry, children's stories, biography, and memoir. After two decades of living in Chicago, he settled down for the last three and a half decades of his life in the small towns of Harbert, Michigan, and Flat Rock, North Carolina. He would be called the "Voice of the Midwest" and would especially be associated in the public mind with the central-midwestern metropolis at the lower tip of Lake Michigan. During the 1920s, his poetry reading, ballad singing, and restless ways carried him down many byways—both urban and rural—across the United States. In the end, he became the voice not only of Chicago and the Midwest but, in a real sense, of all America and even mankind.

As he worked on his massive biography of Lincoln and on his sprawling work of poetry *The People, Yes,* which was made up of stories, proverbs, myths, and folklore, he emerged as the quintessential democratic voice in the United States. In the six large volumes of his Lincoln biography, he enacted the role of prairie poet while he was writing the life of the prairie politician. In his poetical works he painted a dense and variegated tapestry of wheat fields and country lanes, factories and streetcars, Fourth of July celebrations and schoolyard games—in sum, a pageant of Americana that defined a people in all their splendor and variety. Sandburg was nothing if not eclectic; everything seemed to come within his purview. Small towns and farmsteads stood out as no more important in his telling than city streets, clamorous and full of life. But neither were they any less important.

Stories from his boyhood contained in two volumes of memoirs—a brief one, *Prairie-Town Boy*, aimed at a younger audience, and a longer one, *Always the Young Strangers*, carrying his life up to age twenty—revealed the affection and nostalgia that Sandburg retained throughout life for the days of his youth in Illinois. Galesburg, a railroad hub and a manufacturing and commercial center, grew from a little over 10,000 people to almost twice that size during the two decades that he spent growing up there during the 1880s and 1890s. The values and habits he developed in the community carried over into adulthood and shone through in his writing. He was the second child and eldest son in a growing brood of seven children of Swedish immigrant parents. His father, who toiled ten hours a day, six days a week for fourteen cents an hour as a railroad shopman and blacksmith's helper, was a practical man who questioned the value of his son's interest in books. His mother was more understanding. She encouraged him to read and explore. Like many other boys, he dreamed of playing big-league baseball.

His adult memoir describes all-day marathons of playing the game and engaging in other childhood pastimes. But as it happened, it took a stroke of luck to get him out of Galesburg and on track to a literary career. Brief service in the Spanish-American War made him eligible for a scholarship to Lombard College in Galesburg. With the assistance and inspiration of his teachers there, this small-town boy, who had never spent a day in high school, constructed one of the most impressive literary careers of twentieth-century America.

Whereas Sandburg's writing had the effect of pointing his readers' attention out beyond the confines of the local and into the regional and national arenas, the popular painting style of the three major midwestern regionalist artists of the 1930s had the effect of redirecting their audiences' attention back to the section of the country they most closely identified with. Grant Wood, perhaps most often identified as the spokesman for the group, hailed from little Anamosa, Iowa, 25 miles northeast of Cedar Rapids in the east-central part of the state. Even more prolific, both as an artist and as a writer elucidating the philosophy and intent of the group, Thomas Hart Benton was the grandnephew of his namesake, the famous antebellum U.S. senator from Missouri, and the son of a four-term congressman from Neosho, in the southwestern corner of the state. John Steuart Curry grew up on a farm near the little town of Dunavant in northeastern Kansas; after much traveling about, he wound up as artist in residence at the University of Wisconsin.

As Benton wittily described their roles within the lively trio, Curry was the typical Kansas farmer, Wood represented the small-town stalwart, and he, Benton, was just an Ozark hillbilly. Although all three had studied in Paris and possessed cosmopolitan outlooks, they also retained strong ties to and affection for the places of their birth and upbringing. Wood traveled the least distance to carve out a career for himself, moving from Cedar Rapids to Iowa City in his forties to teach art at the state university there. Benton spent two decades in New York City before moving back to Missouri, locating in Kansas City at age forty-six. Curry ventured out to Madison, Wisconsin, after working for a number of years in Connecticut and New York. All three of these moves occurred in 1935 and 1936, just as the three were attaining national prominence for their American Scene painting.

The 1930s were a decade of ferment in the art world, just as they were in business, politics, and other arenas of American life. The convergence of these three artists and the simultaneous rise of their careers were largely coincidental, but the trio felt a personal attraction to each other as well as an intellectual and professional affinity that encouraged them to interact cordially and to allow themselves to be associated with each other in the public mind. Curry, excellent artist that he was, was the least loquacious of the three and largely allowed Wood and Benton to articulate the case for regionalism, which was most famously made by Wood in his 1935 article "Revolt against the City." In it, he emphasized that he was not a "booster" for any particular region of the country (many critics, friendly and unfriendly, identified the trio as advocates for the Midwest); rather, he wanted a rich form of regionalism to evolve that would describe and interpret the special characteristics of each region in turn. For the most part, this was also the position of Benton, who sometimes caused trouble for himself and his compatriots with his outspoken off-the-cuff pronouncements and exaggerations.

Each artist had his own peculiar style of painting. They possessed wildly varying personalities and political viewpoints. Likewise, they approached their work and their relationships with the public and the art community in different fashions. Yet they all clearly were strongly affected by their remembered boyhoods, retained a strong attachment to place, and constructed their work around their shared sense that art should be meaningful, constructive, and relevant to people's everyday lives. To their way of thinking, this meant that it should be representational. For a brief period during the 1930s, this made them the quintessential artistic exemplars of American democratic values and culture. With the coming of World War II and the unfortunately premature deaths of Wood in 1942 and Curry in 1946, their standing in the art world quickly diminished, as the New York art scene was taken over by abstract expression and action painting during the late 1940s and into the 1950s. It was left to Benton to carry on preaching the gospel of regionalism as he continued to paint, write, and propagate the vision until the day he died at the age of eighty-five in 1975.

After he left home in 1918 to attend the state university in Bloomington, Ernie Pyle's hometown of Dana, Indiana, retained no unusual fascination for him. He did visit it frequently in subsequent years—not to wax nostalgic over old haunts and times but rather to visit a few friends and relatives. Nor did he harbor any special affection for the Middle West. While traveling the United States from coast to coast during the second half of the 1930s as a special-feature newspaper columnist, the region that interested him most was the Southwest. He and his wife built a house in Albuquerque in 1940, but he never found much time to enjoy it. His work, first as a roving correspondent in the United States and then as a war correspondent on World War II's fighting fronts, rendered him homeless, in effect, and he seemed to thrive on it, despite (or perhaps because of) the numerous personal demons that afflicted him.

What growing up during the early 1900s on a small farm near the Indiana-Illinois border and going to school in the town of Dana did for him was nurture a set of qualities that made him seem to millions of Americans in and out of military uniform the prototypical midwestern small-town boy. In practical terms, that meant he was curious, unassuming, straightforward, and honest. People were willing to talk to him and tell him things they might not have divulged to others, because he was a good listener and they trusted him to use the information in a frank and respectful fashion. Pyle possessed a highly developed capacity for understanding and communicating the normal thoughts and feelings of ordinary people in their everyday activities and of the soldiers on the fighting fronts.

Six days a week, 1,000 words a day, his columns regularly reached 13 million readers by the end of World War II. His six and a half years on the road in the United States (with forays into Canada and South America), beginning in 1935, had honed his skills as an interviewer and biographical profiler to a sharp edge. His genuine curiosity about and empathy for his subjects enabled him to convert the mundane doings of people's daily lives into something that touched the hearts of his readers. In the process of personalizing the war for his readers, he made it, in effect, "Ernie Pyle's war." His untimely death in the Pacific in 1945, shortly before the Japanese surrender, left a huge number of his readers and admirers personally bereft. He was a new kind of war correspondent, and his background as a small-town boy from the Midwest deserves much of the credit for his ability to connect with people, ask the right questions, and translate their answers into prose that was gripping and reassuring to his readers. In the process, he managed to reinforce the image that large numbers of Americans had of themselves as people who came from identifiable places and communities where individual effort, in tune with cooperative teamwork, still mattered even as large corporations and bureaucratic organizations increasingly extended their influence in society.

CHAPTER FIVE

Sinclair Lewis: The Man from Main Street

What would these sober professors say if they knew that I'm just a young fellow from the middle west—Red Lewis of Sauk Centre, as different from everything they're saying as any human being can be?

—Sinclair Lewis, on winning the Nobel Prize, 1930

The publication of Sinclair Lewis's *Main Street* in October 1920 hit the American literary scene with the force of an explosion. It was, in the words of his biographer Mark Schorer, "the most sensational event in twentieth-century American publishing history."[1] Sales were strong from the start, boosted in part by favorable reviews but even more by word of mouth. Within six months, 180,000 copies had been sold; by the end of a year, close to 300,000. Lewis's publisher, Alfred Harcourt, recalled, "It was a mad scramble all that spring to keep the stores supplied." The best-selling novel not only of 1921 but for the entire period from 1900 to 1925, *Main Street* quickly established the reputation of its thirty-five-year-old author, turning him into a household word and launching him on the path that, by the end of the decade, would make him the first American to receive the Nobel Prize in literature.[2]

Even greater than its consequences for the author's reputation was the impact the book had on people's thinking about its primary subject—the American small town. *Main Street* was not the first, but it certainly was the most successful novel to take direct aim at the honeyed vision of village life then prevailing, which pictured small towns as places where moral, enterprising, well-intentioned people went about their daily lives industriously and harmoniously, leaving them satisfied, content, and confident of their future progress. Never again would Americans be able to view themselves and their small towns in the same smug and assured manner. *Main Street* forced people to reconsider their assumptions about the places that had dominated life in the United States from the earliest European settlements.

The 1920s—a modernizing decade that witnessed the birth of radio, the widespread ownership of automobiles, the growing popularity of the cinema and the introduction of sound to movies, and the proliferation of electrical appliances and other gadgets—were also associated with a literary "revolt from the village." No one was more closely connected in the popular mind with this movement than Sinclair Lewis, but he was not its creator. Writers as far back as Mark Twain had poked fun at some of the less pleasant and less desirable facets of small-town living. During the final two decades of the nineteenth century, E. W. Howe's *The Story of a Country Town* (1884) and Hamlin Garland's *Main-Travelled Roads* (1891) were among the more realistic depictions of the grim realities of rural life. By the time of World War I, acerbic versions of the small-town scene were becoming increasingly prevalent. Edgar Lee Masters's *Spoon River Anthology* (1915) and Sherwood Anderson's *Winesburg, Ohio* (1919) served as primary examples in Carl Van Doren's 1921 article in the *Nation*, "The Revolt from the Village," that gave the literary movement its name.[3]

None of these volumes compared to *Main Street*, however, in the popularity they achieved or the debates they provoked. With its publication, according to Anthony Hilfer, "the revolt from the village became official, public, almost institutional." *Main Street* was, Lewis remarked when he won the Nobel Prize, his first novel "to rouse the embattled peasantry," owing much to its being "a success of scandal. One of the most treasured

American myths had been that all American villages were peculiarly noble and happy, and here an American attacked that myth. Scandalous! Some hundreds of thousands read the book with the same masochistic pleasure that one has in sucking an aching tooth."[4] As early as 1905, when he was back home in Sauk Centre, Minnesota, on his summer vacation from attending college at Yale, Lewis had begun thinking about a novel that would illuminate the darker aspects of small-town life. His central conception at the time—and the title he had in mind for the book—was "The Village Virus," embodying all the stultifying, conformity-inducing, repressive features of village living as he had observed them as a boy growing up in Sauk Centre. Not for another decade, however, did the idea begin to jell in his mind. When it did, it was because he had matured and his thinking had grown more sophisticated and because he was now able to look at the town from a new perspective, that of his wife Grace, whom he married in 1914. In 1916, they spent several months in Sauk Centre while he was working on his third novel, *The Job,* and he began looking at the town through her eyes—those of an intelligent, well-educated easterner who, like him, had been involved in the publishing business. That summer, he began thinking seriously about setting, characterization, and plot for the book that emerged four years later as *Main Street.*[5]

In the meantime, he published two more novels and became firmly established as a slick-magazine short-story writer. Lewis was nothing if not prolific. Story ideas flooded from his fertile imagination. Before being able to benefit much financially from his own writing, he sold a number of unused story plots to fellow author Jack London. When fully in harness, he was capable of turning out 3,000 to 5,000 words a day. Working eight or more hours a day, sometimes seven days a week, he developed astonishing speed as a two-fingered typist. By the time he sat down in late 1919 to write *Main Street*—first in Mankato, Minnesota, and then in Washington, D.C.—he had his vision of the book firmly in mind and cranked out pages of manuscript at a feverish pace, all the while enormously enjoying the process of writing. He anticipated the book's selling well and making a major impact. He believed, he wrote his publisher, that it would be "the real beginning of my writing. No book and no number of short stories I've ever done have ever meant a quarter of what this does to me."[6]

In portraying a single small town within a midwestern setting, Sinclair Lewis's purpose was to describe small towns in general. "This is America— a town of a few thousand, in a region of wheat and corn and dairies and little groves" began his famous preface to the book. "The town is, in our tale, called 'Gopher Prairie, Minnesota.' But its Main Street is the continuation of Main Streets everywhere. The story would be the same in Ohio or Montana, in Kansas or Kentucky or Illinois, and not very differently would it be told Up York State or in the Carolina hills."[7] Lewis's narrative is one of types and caricatures, for the most part. Some space is left for individuality in a few of his characters, including the protagonist, Carol Kennicott, and her husband, Will, the town doctor.

Carol is an idealist who views the town through the eyes of an outsider and attempts to beautify and reform it, but she is rebuffed by the narrow-minded, hypocritical residents of Gopher Prairie. Though outwardly friendly, they are devoid of vision and self-awareness, fearing to challenge the ways things have always been done in town. Even Will Kennicott, a competent and caring physician and a man of honesty and integrity, possesses little understanding of or sympathy for his wife's quixotic behavior. For the most part, he adheres to the standards and expectations of the townspeople, retrograde and commonplace as they are. After several inconclusive rebellions, Carol temporarily leaves her husband, working for a time in Washington, D.C., but she soon discovers that people there exhibit the same kinds of myopia and lack of individualism as they do in small towns. In the end, she returns to her husband, more appreciative of his virtues and of those of their neighbors, reconciled to living there with them, but still determined to make some modest changes in their lifestyles.

Carol's thirty-two-minute walk down Main Street at the beginning of *Main Street* sets the tone for what is to come. What she saw was not a pretty sight. "Oozing out from every drab wall, she felt a forbidding spirit which she could never conquer," Lewis wrote. Adjective piles on adjective to convey Carol's disillusionment and desperation: besides oozing, the places and things she observed were muddy, dismal, shabby, fly-specked, rickety, greasy, sleazy, broken, raw, forbidding, curdled, and pawed-over. Conversely, she also noticed things that were pleasant, new, neat, clean, shiny, pure, even exquisite. The overwhelming impression, however, favored the former over the latter. No wonder that when her tour was done she stood on the corner of Main Street and Washington Avenue and despaired.[8] The remainder of the book extends the grim discussion from the physical surroundings of Gopher Prairie to the people, the practices, and the institutions that ordered their lives, all of which were found profoundly wanting.

What made *Main Street* so extraordinarily successful, granting it preeminence in the "revolt from the village" of the 1920s? Certainly important was the timing of its appearance, just two years after the end of World War I in the midst of deep public disillusionment. Huge hopes and expectations about fighting a "war to end all wars" and transforming social relations in the process were shattered by the treaty conference and other postwar developments. Many Americans were in a surly, scolding mood in 1920, receptive to the critical observations of the small town served up in *Main Street*. Beyond that, small towns and American civilization in general were on the cusp of portentous change at that precise moment. The transition from a rural, agrarian society to an urban, industrial one had been proceeding for two generations. The census of 1890 had announced the "end of the frontier." Thirty years later, after the 1920 census, it was reported that for the first time most Americans resided in urban areas (defined as places of 2,500 or more). The 1920s became a decade of particularly rapid modernization, but they also spawned major efforts to reclaim traditional values and to remember the past. Historical memory and nostalgia coexisted uneasily with progress and modernity throughout the decade.[9]

Also contributing to the success of Lewis's blockbuster novel was the growing shelf of books paving the way for critical thinking about America's small towns. None of them captured people's imaginations as thoroughly as *Main Street*, however. The style and substance of the book set it apart from anything that had gone before. Exaggerated and unfair as it tended to be in places, its description of small-town narrowness and provincialism demanded that people take a stand with it or against it. For every reader willing to admit the general accuracy of the portrait, another could be found ready to vociferously deny it. Although many of the kinds of background circumstances, characters, and themes that infused *Main Street* had surfaced in Lewis's previous books, they had never been bundled together with such overwhelming force and with such attitude.

Lewis's sensitive understanding of the mass audience was a significant factor in the sales of his books. Not to be underestimated in attempting to explain the enthusiastic critical reception of *Main Street* was the influence of an increasingly powerful coterie of eastern literary critics and intellectuals, such as Van Wyck Brooks, Carl Van Doren, and Alfred Kazin, who promoted the notion of "the revolt from the village." Generally unacquainted with thought patterns in the interior, they welcomed the Minnesota native's assault on what they perceived as the bogus pieties and small-town provincialism of the region. Lewis, for his part, as an author with his eye fixed firmly on the marketplace, understood that scandal sells. In addition, according to biographer Richard Lingeman, the book sold well because it "meshed with the postwar mood of cynicism among the intelligentsia and the young." This attitude was welcomed and promoted by the critics of the small town, who tended to overlook the divisions, ambivalences, and contradictions that characterized many of the authors—including Lewis, Sherwood Anderson, and Edgar Lee Masters—who were counted as being within the "revolting" group. The Midwest thus became a convenient whipping boy for intellectuals intent on gaining assent for their viewpoint and concerned about their own professional advancement, and all too often, later commentators and historians accepted their assessments as received truth.[10]

The book had the effect of a steamroller. Lewis employed every trick in his bag to create a crushingly complacent, dull, narrow, bigoted, and mindless town. In Gopher Prairie, the "village virus" ruled everything. Other books had suggested the negative qualities of small towns or had placed them in context. Lewis described them in such overwhelming detail and with such verisimilitude that readers open to his viewpoint found themselves constantly nodding in agreement. Lewis's townspeople included an array of recognizable American types: the cruelly sanctimonious widow (Mrs. Bogart), the radical village atheist (Miles Bjornstam), the sentimental yearner (Raymie Wutherspoon), the practical idealist (Vida Sherwin), the vociferous booster (Jim Blausser), and the complacent, commonsensical husband (Will Kennicott). These characters were as real to many readers as were the stores on Main Street described in Carol Kennicott's walk through town.

Many readers identified with Carol's critical point of view because they shared her romantic yearning for something better. They harbored similar vague feelings that something, somehow was desperately wrong with current circumstances. In that context, Lewis's choice of a female protagonist was propitious. Women made up the preponderance of novel readers in 1920, just as they always had, and they were more likely to identify with Carol Kennicott than they would have with a male character. Originally, Lewis had intended to install the lawyer Guy Pollock in the role. But the author's visit to Sauk Centre with his wife in 1916 caused him to change his mind. Now, viewing his boyhood haunts as much through his wife's eyes as through his own, he began to perceive them in an entirely different way. Putting Pollock, a victim of the village virus who was crushed by its overwhelming power to induce conformity, at the center of the story would certainly have been one way to tell it. But by replacing him with Carol Kennicott, an idealistic dreamer who gets beaten down but never gives up hoping to effect real change in the community, Lewis created a more likable main character and one easier for the majority of his readers to identify with.

No one better epitomized the kinds of cultural assumptions and attitudes about American small towns that Carol Kennicott (and Lewis) was rebelling against than America's beloved "Hoosier Poet," James Whitcomb Riley, who died four years before *Main Street* appeared. In Riley's words, as presented in paraphrase in Lewis's book, the common view of the time was that the American village "remains the one sure abode of friendship, honesty, and clean sweet marriageable girls." Carol, however, believed that small-town culture reflected "the contentment of the quiet dead" and "the prohibition of happiness." In sum, she thought, "It is slavery self-taught and self-defended. It is dullness made God." Without mentioning Riley by name, Lewis stuck a dagger in the heart of the Hoosier Poet's already waning reputation by describing a social evening when Miss Ella Stowbody gave a reading of "An Old Sweetheart of Mine." Carol would hear the poem recited nine more times before the end of the winter. It was one of Riley's most popular offerings.[11]

Lewis's popularity as a critic of small towns derived both from his satirical treatment of them and from his reportorial realism in depicting them. His two-pronged approach reflected his ambivalence toward his subject matter. Many readers and critics at the time and since have focused their attention on the satirical element, reacting with either appreciation or dismay. As a satirist, Lewis challenged the cheerful assumptions and comfortable traditions of small-town America. Few targets remained unscathed; the family, education, religion, business, architecture, entertainment, and organizational life were all subjected to his critical gaze. This part of his method depended heavily on careful selection and exaggeration. His treatments, although often arresting and humorous, were not always fair.

Satire, however, did not exhaust Lewis's bag of tricks. His writing was also heavily sociological. Whatever his tone at any particular moment, he presented readers with highly detailed descriptions of people, places, and events. A masterful mimic, he skillfully reproduced people's speech habits. Realism and satire coexisted in his writing, though not always easily; nor could readers always be sure of the author's intent. Was he simply describing things as they were, or was he poking fun at them? Referring to Lewis's keen powers of description, E. M. Forster commented, "Photography is a great gift, whether or not we rank it as an art. If we have not been to Gopher Prairie we cry, 'So that's it!' on seeing the snap. If we have been we either cry: 'How like it!' or 'How perfectly disgraceful, not the least like it!' and in all three cases our vehemence shows that we are in the presence of something alive."[12]

Other reviewers of *Main Street* emphasized its photographic realism, not its satirical intent. Many of Lewis's friends and readers commended him for drawing so intricate a portrait and one that so accurately represented its subject. C. M. Flandrau congratulated him on producing a wonderful book: "In writing about Gopher Prairie, you have written about the country—not perhaps the *last* word, but a great many magically true ones. 'A nation of villagers' as Shaw called us." F. Scott Fitzgerald chimed in with, "I want to tell you that *Main Street* has displaced Theron Ware in my favor as the best American novel. The amount of sheer data in it is amazing! As a writer and a Minnesotan let me swell the chorus—after a third reading."[13]

Main Street relied heavily on Lewis's childhood memories of Sauk Centre and on subsequent observations of small-town residents in the scores of places where he had lived or passed through during his travels around the country. His next novel systematized his methodology, establishing a model for much of his later writing. Even before *Main Street* appeared, Lewis went to work on *Babbitt*, intending it to do for the medium-sized American city what he had just done for the nation's small towns. This time he intended to tell the story of the "Tired Business Man," who, beset on all sides by the forces of conformity and accommodation, discovers that he wants more out of life than he has obtained thus far. Like Carol Kennicott, George Follansbee Babbitt (Lewis settled on the name after considering others, such as "Pumphrey" and "Fitch") is trapped in a stultifying environment and yearns for escape. In Lewis's telling, "He is all of us Americans at 46, prosperous but worried, wanting—passionately—to seize something more than motor cars and a house *before it's too late.*"[14] Whereas Carol Kennicott's quest was partly successful, however, Babbitt's turned out to be mostly a failure.

Responsive to critics who complained that his small-town novel had failed to probe deeply into the psyches of its characters, Lewis endeavored to make Babbitt a fuller, more rounded character by more intensely exploring his inner life and psychological motivations. Simultaneously, he set out to produce a work that would provide an even more detailed examination of social life and institutions than his previous book had done. The task this time presented more of a challenge, because Zenith, his medium-sized city, exceeded Gopher Prairie in size by a factor of a hundred. Zenith was intended to stand for the typical American city of between 80,000 and 1 million population. Lewis thought of these places as "transitional metropolises" or "overgrown towns," and in choosing to write about them he was attempting to establish continuity between the two novels. This time, a short walk up and down Main Street by his protagonist would not have sufficed to describe the physical layout of the place, nor would a few references to clubs and organizational activities have been able to encompass the social life of the community. To adequately describe Babbitt's environment, Lewis thought it necessary, in preparation for writing the novel, to draw large, intricate maps of the city and sketch layouts of the interiors of selected buildings and homes. He fashioned detailed biographies of all his major characters, filled notebooks with observations and ideas, and wrote up an extensive plan of the book before drafting a single page of it. He went on a research trip to visit cities in Ohio, Michigan, Illinois, and Wisconsin, spending most of his time in Cincinnati.[15]

Lewis, who had journalism in his background and who had briefly considered going for a Ph.D. degree in English and becoming a literary scholar, packed his books with observations and information of the kinds that interest sociologists, anthropologists, and historians.[16] For him, context was as important as character, as the former played a crucial role in shaping the latter. His novels had the aura of field studies or case histories about them. After *Babbitt*, he would write books about religious charlatans (*Elmer Gantry*), science and medicine (*Arrowsmith*), social work (*Ann Vickers*), organized philanthropy (*Gideon Planish*), domestic fascism (*It Can't Happen Here*), the theater (*Bethel Meriday*), and race relations (*Kingsblood Royal*), among others. The city of Zenith is the subject of *Babbitt* as much as are Babbitt himself, his family, and the people with whom he comes into daily contact, just as the subject of its precursor is Gopher Prairie as much as it is Carol Kennicott, her husband, and the rest of the townspeople.

But even if *Main Street* remains the most famous novel ever written about an American small town, it is still not entirely clear what attitude Sinclair Lewis harbored toward it. That may sound strange in light of the controversy surrounding the book's publication. Some readers expressed shock and anger, believing the author had engaged in cheap fun at the expense of decent men and women.[17] Even Sherwood Anderson, whose own criticisms of village life established him as a key figure in the "revolt from the village," considered Lewis's treatment lopsided and unfair. Certainly, Anderson admitted, many of Lewis's descriptions were apt and skillfully done, but too much had been left out of the portrait of Gopher Prairie. He belonged with writers who falsely manipulated readers' emotions, Anderson believed, writers who "have made for us towns in which no grass ever grows. Grapes and apples never ripen there. There are no spring rains. They are towns to which no ball teams ever come, no circus parade." Anderson attributed much of his counterpart's success to the tone he had assumed in the book—one that aroused people's contempt. "There is that streak in all of us," he observed. "We all adore hating something, having contempt for something. It makes us feel big and superior."[18] Anderson, who had grown up in Clyde, Ohio, averred that on the whole he had liked the small-town people he had known. He liked lounging around county court houses, fishing in the spring, and hunting in the fall. He enjoyed county fairs and Fourth of July celebrations. He rejected the viewpoint "that sees nothing in the small town but Rotarians and boosters" and "that does not see people as people," guessing that Lewis had obtained his impressions from the small town where he had grown up. "He must have seen his home town as an ugly place and so all towns became ugly to him."[19]

Though Anderson's logic was plausible, his premises were not entirely accurate. He certainly was correct in his observation that Lewis had omitted many things from *Main Street*—aspects of life that would have provided a more balanced and accurate view of small-town life. But assuming that the author of *Main Street* possessed an unrelievedly gloomy attitude regarding small towns and extrapolating from this that he had probably derived such a stance from his own sorry childhood was going too far. In fact, Lewis retained more positive feelings about his hometown than many people realized, and these colored his portrait of it. Like millions of his fellow Americans, Lewis found the changes overtaking America vast and bewildering, leaving him uncertain about how to respond to them. His ambivalence toward small towns and the forces impinging on them found expression in *Main Street* and in his other writings.

The man from Sauk Centre had good reason to feel ungrateful and resentful toward the town where he had lived from his birth in 1885 until boarding a train for New Haven to attend Yale College in 1903 (he had previously spent six months at Oberlin Academy in Ohio preparing for the Yale entrance exams). Thin, gawky, dreamy, childish, whimsical, bookish, and impractical, the doctor's son had few friends and little sense of accomplishment as a child. Resentful toward but also respectful of his stern, dignified father and feeling unable to match the exploits of his accomplished and popular older brother, Claude (Lewis in his fifties said he had spent his entire life trying to impress his sibling), young Harry (also called Hal or Red, because of his copper-colored hair) Lewis at least had the encouragement and love of his stepmother, Isabel Warner Lewis, whom his father married in 1892, a year after the death of his first wife. When Claude and his chums were not tying up Hal's clothes after he shed them to go swimming or instructing him to "go chase himself" when he tried to join their games, the unlucky boy found himself being laughed at and scorned by his classmates.

Mark Schorer begins his heavily researched but negative and one-sided 814-page biography of the author with the sentence "He was a queer boy, always an outsider, lonely," concluding with the judgment that his subject was "one of the worst writers in modern American literature," although "without his writing one cannot imagine modern American literature."[20] This biography, which relegated Lewis to a minor position in American letters and helped dampen scholarly interest in him for a generation, drew a picture of a man crippled by a friendless and unhappy childhood, possessed of scant literary talent but tons of nervous energy and ambition, and troubled by alcoholism and an inability to mature gracefully. But even if Lewis's boyhood was not exactly idyllic, we should not conclude that it was an unrelieved nightmare.

In an article published in 1937, Lewis admitted that his attempts at literary expression as a student may have in part been motivated by a desire to get even with his schoolmates, "who could outfight, outswim, outlove, and in general outdo him." But that could not entirely explain his bookish interests, he said, for he "was neither a cripple nor a Sensitive Soul." His stepmother had read to him more than was the custom, and his father's library further nourished his impulse to read. Later, there were shelves of books in the town library to be devoured and vacation work at the *Sauk Centre Herald* setting type, working the handpress, and sometimes writing local paragraphs on goings-on about town.[21] We should hesitate to take

Lewis completely at his word (in a 1927 self-portrait) that his boyhood had been "utterly commonplace" apart from a love of reading that was unusual in such a small town.[22] But neither do we need to accept the opposite contention that it was almost entirely friendless, joyless, and depressing. The truth lay somewhere in between.

Lately, scholars and writers such as Richard Lingeman have increasingly rejected Schorer's judgments with regard to both Lewis's literary abilities and his childhood.[23] They are more inclined to acknowledge the sincerity of the author's declaration in the 1931 edition of the high school yearbook, *O-Sa-Ge,* that growing up in Sauk Centre had been a good experience for him. Could he possibly have meant it? Probably as much as many of the pronouncements he so easily offered. Like many other people, he often had a difficult time making up his mind about things. In the fiftieth anniversary issue of *O-Sa-Ge,* which had solicited a contribution from him, he defended himself against people who had interpreted *Main Street* as an indictment of small-town life:

> If I seem to have criticized prairie villages, I have certainly criticized
> them no more than I have New York, or Paris, or the great universities.
> I am quite certain that I could have been born and reared no place in
> the world where I would have had more friendliness. Indeed, as I look
> at these sons of rich men in New England with their motor cars and
> their travel, it seems to me that they are not having one-tenth the fun
> which I had as a kid, swimming and fishing in Sauk Lake, or cruising
> its perilous depths on a raft (probably made of stolen logs), tramping
> out to Fairy Lake for a picnic, tramping ten miles on end, with a
> shotgun, in October; sliding on Hoboken Hill, stealing melons, or
> listening to the wonders of an elocutionist at the G.A.R. Hall. It was a
> good time, a good place, and a good preparation for life.[24]

How seriously should these words be taken, coming from a forty-six-year-old former resident, America's best-selling author, newly vested with the Nobel Prize, given an assignment with no monetary reward attached to it—only the impact it would have on his reputation in his hometown? He could have knocked out the 500 words on his typewriter in a few minutes. Did he stop long enough to think much about his boyhood? "It is extraordinary how deep is the impression made by the place of one's birth and rearing, and how lasting are its memories," he wrote.[25] They were as vivid in his mind as if he had left just the day before, he noted. Lewis may well have meant every word as he was writing, but in another venue—a court of law, for instance—he might have had difficulty providing evidence of their veracity.

A significant clue lies in *Main Street*. There are hardly any children there. This may have been accidental, or it may have been a deliberate plot device. Could it have been because his childhood was so unpleasant that he chose not to remember it or subconsciously repressed it?[26] Or might it have been because young Red Lewis spent so much time with his nose in a book that he could not remember in much detail how normal children lived? Their absence, at least, is highly unusual and thought-provoking. Abraham Lincoln had stories to tell about his boyhood. Mark Twain's readers loved him for his youthful tales of Huckleberry Finn and Tom Sawyer. James Whitcomb Riley's world was filled with swimming holes and fishing poles and boy adventures in town. If little boys had fun in Gopher Prairie, we would need someone besides Red Lewis to tell us about it.

Yet it will not do to think of Lewis simply as the man who exposed the dark side of village life to public scrutiny. For if he played the roles of diagnostician and satirist, he was also something else—a quester. In him, the ideal coexisted side by side with the real. Never satisfied with the world as he perceived it, he always yearned for something better. It was, to use the literary critic Martin Light's word, the "quixotic" spirit in him that shone through, not only in many of his writings but also in his behavior.[27] As a student, he had been fascinated with medieval knights and ladies, and many of the poems and short stories that he published in the Yale literary magazine were set during the days when knighthood was in flower. Lewis recognized this tendency in himself. In a magazine essay in 1935 commenting on the changes that had occurred during the half century since his birth, he focused not on the amazing technological developments that had emerged but rather on the quality of spirit that characterized the period—the sense of questing and daring that had inspired momentous achievements and improvements. The era had been one, he asserted, when "there was romance everywhere, and life, instead of being a dusty routine, was exciting with hope and courage and adventure in utterly new lands. Handsome young men in helmets rode the fastest steeds that ever had been known." All in all, he wrote, it was "a golden age, a romantic age, a passionate age."[28]

In Lewis, illusion and reality constantly warred with each other. The romantic streak in him shone through in his behavior and in his writings. His emotions were marked by wild mood swings and manifested themselves in strangely unpredictable behavior. People, to accept him, had to understand what lay behind his exuberant outbursts, flamboyant performances, angry rantings, drunken binges, and moments of contrition. Strangers might be enthralled by his monologues and his mimicry, but when he held forth for an hour or two, refusing to let anyone contradict him or take away the spotlight, they were not sure what to make of him.[29]

The heroes of Lewis's books were often yearners and rebels, quixotic like himself. That made him, in addition to being a realist and a satirist, a fabulist.[30] Asked whether he saw part of himself in the figure he had drawn of Carol Kennicott, he admitted that he did. She was a person, like him, who was "always groping for something, . . . intolerant of her surroundings and yet lacking any clearly defined vision of what she really wants."[31] Lewis was often accused of being simply negative, of being a constant critic of things without having a clear idea of what he wanted to put in their place. Although the charge rings true in some respects, nothing requires a novelist to outline a reform agenda, and Lewis had a great deal of company in failing to articulate a detailed plan for social improvement. In *Main Street*, Carol Kennicott expresses her inchoate vision to another yearner, the lawyer Guy Pollock:

> I believe all of us want the same things—we're all together, the industrial workers and the women and the farmers and the Negro race and the Asiatic colonies, and even a few of the Respectables. It's all the same revolt, in all the classes that have waited and taken advice. I think perhaps we want a more conscious life. We're tired of drudging and sleeping and dying. We're tired of seeing just a few people able to be individualists. We're tired of always deferring hope till the next generation. . . . We want our Utopia *now*—and we're going to try our hands at it. All we want is—everything for all of us![32]

This, as much as anything, expressed Sinclair Lewis's own vision of a better life. Mark Schorer lists the values that Lewis suggested would save Zenith and Babbitt: love, friendship, kindness, tolerance, justice, integrity, beauty, intellect. In the words of another critic, Sheldon Grebstein, Lewis "simply wants people to be better." Similarly, Richard Lingeman concludes his biography of the man with, "*He really cared.*"[33]

Whereas Lewis's early commentators judged him deficient in his ability to articulate an alternative vision, recent ones have begun to speak more admiringly of the integrity and decency that marked his views. It was admirable to have identified himself with embattled workers and farmers during the prosperity decade, with women when patriarchy prevailed, with Jews when anti-Semitism flourished, with blacks when racism ruled, and with quixotic dreamers when cynical realism militated against them. Though he could be as blind to political realities as anyone else, his basic instincts were noble. During a time when many of his fellow writers and artists were hoodwinked by the Communists, he understood them for what they were and bluntly marshaled the case against them. Shucking off the romantic socialistic views he had acquired as a student and young man, his political views, when he admitted to having any, remained somewhat left of center during his maturity.

Lewis's identification was not only with Carol Kennicott but also with her husband Will—the staid, resolute physician, devoted to his task of healing and seldom bothered by ideas and notions that might elevate him from dull daily routine. Alongside Carol, the yearner, lay Will, the plodder. Sinclair Lewis could never be conceived of as a plodder, except, perhaps, in his amazing ability to turn out, in rapid succession, a stream of novels over the course of his career, twenty-two in all. But this son of Gopher Prairie found much to admire in the competence, steadiness, and simplicity of people like Dr. Will Kennicott, who was modeled, in part, on Lewis's father. Lewis ultimately identified as much with the virtues of the husband as he did with the aspirations of his wife. Granville Hicks captured this in an essay written in the middle of the Depression in which he noted Lewis's careful steering away from communism and radicalism. His life neatly illustrated middle-class contradictions. "The side of him that secretly sympathizes with Will Kennicott and George Babbitt lends authority to his portraits, and the side of him that damns them gives his books their salt," Hicks wrote.[34] Lewis would never have joined Rotary or the Union League Club and was incapable of behaving like a typical bourgeois, but if he identified with anybody, it was with the middle class.

In the end, Lewis, like a famous politician who flourished simultaneously with him—Huey Long—was sui generis. He was like nobody else, and could not be. Whether it was his genetic endowment that facilitated him, his childhood that had damaged him, his father who had stifled him, his occupation that had isolated him, his ego that was boundless, his insecurities that paralyzed him, his drinking that wounded him, his failures that haunted him, or his aspirations that escaped him, Lewis could never behave like an average human being.

Besides his bouts with liquor and his monomaniacal performances at parties and on other occasions, this condition manifested itself primarily in his constant moving from place to place. Once he deemed himself financially able to quit his publishing job and devote himself full-time to writing when he was in his early thirties, he never stayed in one place more than a few months at a time. His constant urge to move on to new venues contributed to the breakdown of both his marriages and undermined most of the friendships he ever had. His first move had been away from home to go to school. A trip to England working on a cattleboat during a summer vacation from Yale was the first of scores of trips that took him all over the United States and to much of Europe and Latin America in later years. These travels became the basis for many of his novels and short stories, but Lewis denied that he intended them for that purpose. The explanation for this compulsive behavior, he wrote of himself in 1927, was that "he is afflicted with Wanderlust, which is the most devouring of diseases."[35]

Here, Lewis recognized the phenomenon as a disease, and at other times he noted the problems deriving from his peripatetic ways. In a piece published in the *Yale Literary Magazine* in 1906, he pinpointed "The Fallacy of Elsewhere," which led people to look outside New Haven for information and adventure when much of interest and significance could be found right there. And in a whimsical self-composed obituary published as a magazine piece in 1941, he made reference to "the chronic wanderer's discovery that he is everywhere such an Outsider that no one will listen to him even when he kicks about the taxes and the beer."[36]

Lewis bought five houses or apartments during the last decade and a half of his life, but no place could hold him for long. He frequently talked about settling down but never managed to do it. His compulsive travels may have been tied to his habit of reading, because both activities made him an observer, an outsider, a person of vicarious experience.[37] According to his first wife, the early years of their marriage were "the only time in his life when he sincerely cherished the idea of home, or roots, no matter how many houses he was to buy later." Especially after their son Wells was born, Grace hoped that her husband would be willing to settle down, but he coldly squelched the idea: "I thought you said a baby wouldn't make any difference to our wandering. Are you both trying to chain me up so soon? I don't want a home." He wanted something else, he said. "I want to travel, to see, to feel—."[38]

For Lewis, travel represented freedom; a settled home, chains. Being married, though congenial in the beginning both times he tried it, was not something he seemed really committed to. As a father, he was an abject failure, as testified to by both Grace Lewis and Dorothy Thompson, his second wife.[39] He made friends quickly and energetically, but he cast them aside just as easily. With some exceptions, such as H. L. Mencken and Carl Van Doren, few of his friends stayed close to him for long periods of time. When the end came, in a lonely hospital in Rome in January 1951, no friends at all were by his side, only an Italian travel agent who had befriended him and taken care of him during his final days, probably for the money.[40]

Yet at the end, he wanted to come home; he had instructed that his ashes be buried in Sauk Centre beside his father. His brother Claude expressed surprise when he heard it, concluding, "He must have loved the old town." And there are indications that he did, including his essay for the 1931 high school annual; his various returns home to visit the town (the last time in 1947); his several residences in the Midwest in Minneapolis, Duluth, and Madison, where he struck up a friendship with midwestern regionalist painter John Steuart Curry; his praise for midwestern regionalist writers such as Ruth Suckow; and his use of midwestern locales for many of his novels. He even created a fictional midwestern state—Winnemac—as a setting for some of them. Despite all the barbs he directed against his hometown and home region, he continued to direct his authorial gaze at it and essentially "never graduated from the Midwest," according to the literary critic Ronald Weber.[41]

But even though he loved his hometown and his home region, that longing was colored by a huge amount of ambivalence, and he never would have dreamed of actually returning to live there permanently. His departure in 1903 was unregretted and final. Just as with the rest of his life, Sauk Centre remained, in the end, more vision than reality, more fancy than fact. Sinclair Lewis, satirist and realist that he was, was ultimately a dreamer, a yearner, a visionary, a quixote. He once told Dorothy Thompson that he lived mostly above the neck. He had a place called home, but it was not a physical place; it could not be located on a map. It could only be inhabited by someone with a highly active imagination.

His ashes were flown home in January 1951, in the dead of winter. A memorial program was held in Sauk Centre's high school auditorium. The organist played a Viennese waltz called "Olden Days." Someone read a brief biography, and then Lewis's sentimental high school yearbook piece about his boyhood as "a good time, a good place, and a good preparation for life" was read. The young author Frederick Manfred, whom Lewis had befriended, gave the eulogy, and then the mourners went out to the cemetery to bury the ashes.[42]

No wonder Red Lewis had fled to Italy. There was no blue in the Minnesota sky that day and it was bitterly cold, 22 degrees below zero. A hole about 2 feet square had been dug in the frozen ground, but when the urn was tilted to pour out the ashes, a gust of hot air quickly puffed up and, blown by a light wind, drifted off slowly to the east. "Well, they tried to bring Red home, but at the last second there he still got away," Manfred playfully noted.[43] His spirit hovers still over our conceptions of small-town America. His true home lies in the hearts and minds of his readers. If he criticized the small town, it was only because he imagined the many ways it could have been so much better. If we remain ambivalent about small towns today, it is only because we share in the yearnings and questionings that he and so many other American writers and artists brought to their portrayals of small-town life.

CHAPTER SIX

■

Carl Sandburg: The Eternal Seeker and People's Poet

To write [Lincoln] down anew, after scores of men had tried to catch his portrait, Carl Sandburg had merely to put himself back into his own boyhood on the Illinois prairie lands and in little sleepy inland towns, and to search his heart for the joy, hope and sadness that life had put here. And knowing this he was able to understand Lincoln. . . . [The Prairie Years] lives with its character. It moves with him through the experiences of the little frontier hamlet, through the life of the inland town, through the development of the nation.

—Harry Hansen, review of *Abraham Lincoln: The Prairie Years*

Carl Sandburg wore many hats during his lifetime. When he was fifty, he observed, "There was puzzlement as to whether I was a poet, a biographer, a wandering troubadour with a guitar, a Midwest Hans Christian Andersen, or a historian of current events."[1] In fact, he was all of these and more. At the time, he had yet to publish the last four volumes of his monumental biography of Abraham Lincoln. His autobiography and his 1,000-page foray into novel writing, *Remembrance Rock*, still lay far in the future. Never content to stick to one or even several genres, he consistently transcended the boundaries of the usual and the expected in literature. In the end, his public persona embodied all the roles that collectively composed his multifaceted personality. He projected a larger-than-life presence, making him a widely beloved, but somewhat controversial, cultural presence on the American scene. Carl Sandburg was, in a word, a "character."

He first achieved public notice with the appearance of "Chicago" and eight other poems in the March 1914 issue of *Poetry* magazine, published in Chicago by Harriet Monroe, a pioneer in the new modernist literary trends of the early 1900s. Two years later, these poems, collected with other early work and published by Henry Holt as *Chicago Poems*, established his reputation as a poet of the city. He always remained connected in the public mind with Chicago, where he lived between 1912 and 1932. But this avatar of the city was originally a small-town boy. He had grown up 160 miles to the west in Galesburg, Illinois, a vibrant manufacturing and commercial center and transportation hub, whose population grew briskly from 11,437 in 1880, two years after he was born, to 18,607 twenty years later. The values and assumptions he absorbed there during the final two decades of the nineteenth century guided his life and wound their way through his writings. *Prairie-Town Boy* was the title he tacked onto a brief memoir, aimed at a younger audience, that traced the trajectory of those years. Sandburg's second volume of poetry, *Cornhuskers*, concentrated on life in the rural Midwest and its ubiquitous small towns. As early as 1926, Rebecca West had dubbed Sandburg "the voice of the Middle West."[2] That was another role he would play during his career. Having established himself as a poet of the city and of the small town, this Illinois native son emerged as the poet of all America in *The People, Yes*, written in the midst of the Great Depression. By 1955, when he collaborated with his brother-in-law Edward Steichen on *The Family of Man* photography exhibition at New York's Museum of Modern Art, he had strengthened his claim to being the poet of the entire human race.

Contradictions marked the man and his work. This small-town boy who discovered his voice and vocation in the big city never lost his gratitude and affection for his small-town roots. He happily returned home to visit from time to time, but he harbored no desire to live there permanently. This man who devoted most of the period between the world wars to researching and writing his massive Lincoln biography managed, in the meantime, to become a student of folklore and folk songs. He published his findings in 1927 in *The American Songbag*. But Sandburg, who spent so much time rummaging through history, frequently voiced his disdain for the past. Among his most frequently quoted lines was "The past is a bucket of ashes."[3] He wanted people to focus their attention on the present and the future, not the past. Traditions were meant to be broken, and old assumptions needed to be scrutinized, in his way of thinking. He enjoyed quoting Lincoln's "We must think anew, we must act anew, we must disenthrall ourselves," but he was also a man who used the past to help people overcome it.

Ironies abounded in Sandburg's life. He was a man of action who spent most of his time in the realm of words and thoughts. He was a gregarious loner who preached the virtues of "creative solitude." Restlessness overcame him whenever he stayed in one place too long. As a teenager, he succumbed to the urge to roam. He remained the "eternal hobo"—always seeking new experiences, new ideas and viewpoints, new friends, and new materials for his poetry, writing, and song.[4] Unlike Sinclair Lewis, who shared his restlessness and love of the open road, Sandburg also possessed a strong nesting instinct, becoming heavily dependent on having a solid home base where he could collect his research materials, think, and write. Also, unlike Lewis, he managed to sustain a marriage with a supportive woman who understood his problems and idiosyncrasies. Lilian Steichen totally devoted herself to him and willingly tolerated his frequent absences and the sometimes exorbitant demands of his literary career. Abandoning her own ambition to be a teacher and subordinating herself to his needs and demands, this intelligent and feisty woman raised their three daughters, shushed them while he was trying to write, managed their household finances, took care of much of their correspondence, and served as his helpmate and "buddy" for almost six decades. After twenty years in Chicago, they lived for more than a decade in Harbert, Michigan, on the eastern shore of Lake Michigan, before removing to Flat Rock, North Carolina, south of Asheville, where Sandburg spent his last two decades.

Before firmly establishing his reputation as a writer, Sandburg alternated between moods of supreme self-confidence and nagging doubts about his work.[5] Even later, after winning many prizes and receiving unmatched public adulation, he continued to worry about how he and his work would be received. He had some reason for doing so, for criticism was never lacking. He frequently ventured into uncharted territory, almost daring the critics to pounce. In his poetry, Sandburg celebrated life, but he also explored its darker sides, chronicling people's doubts, defeats, and despairs.[6] As time went by, the celebratory aspects of his work increasingly outweighed the critical ones. But his capacity to stimulate outrage did not diminish, as can be witnessed in the pained reactions of some readers to his reference in a 1956 ceremony to the "fat-dripping prosperity" that he saw as pervasive in the Eisenhower 1950s.[7]

Sandburg's political trajectory associated him with men like Thomas Hart Benton and Sinclair Lewis who moved from a youthful enthusiasm for left-wing causes and programs to a more mainstream brand of liberalism in middle age. They retained a sense of outrage at injustice and inequality along with a continuing optimism that well-intentioned reform efforts could improve society.[8]

Sandburg's poetry was simultaneously rugged and delicate. In reviewing his first book, Harriet Monroe referred to him as "Chicago Granite." He possessed, she thought, "the unassailable and immovable earthbound strength of a great granite rock," as reflected in his salutation of Chicago as "stormy, husky, brawling." But, inspired by softer imagery, "the poet's touch becomes exquisitely delicate. Indeed, there is orchestral richness in his music; he plays diverse instruments."[9] Sandburg, contradictory in so many ways, also projected those contradictions onto his hero, Abraham Lincoln. Clearly, he was describing himself as well as his subject when he spoke before a joint session of Congress on Lincoln's birthday in 1959: "Not often in the story of mankind does a man arrive on earth who is both steel and velvet, who is as hard as rock and soft as drifting fog, who holds in his heart and mind the paradox of terrible storm and peace unspeakable and perfect."[10] The words he used to describe Lincoln constituted stock items in his poetic repertoire: "steel" represented triumphant, technology-driven industrialism and urbanism; "fog" stood, in contrast, for nature, rurality, and the soft (as opposed to the hard), the muted (as opposed to the loud), and the delicate (as opposed to the rugged).[11]

Sandburg built his literary reputation by fashioning striking and memorable images of the city, the prairie, and the people who inhabited them. Later, in biographical form, he enshrined Lincoln, and in two volumes of autobiography he memorialized his hometown of Galesburg and its residents. His images were colorful and powerful, but his achievement lay as much in the complexity of his vision as in the clarity of it. His ability to perceive and render artistically the contradictions in Lincoln's character and in American life explain much of his books' popularity and their continuing value. As an interpreter of the profound changes that occurred in American life during the century after the Civil War, he captured much of its flavor and vitality. Hugely contradictory himself, he tuned naturally into the contradictions that lay all around him.

Much influenced by and often identified with the Brooklynite poet Walt Whitman, Sandburg, in the estimate of his friend Harry Golden, was closer to Mark Twain than to Whitman.[12] Born and raised in the small-town Midwest, Twain and Sandburg both developed early a footloose urge to venture out and see the places where their fellow Americans worked and played. They both had a natural affinity for people and were able to understand and communicate with them because, in large part, they were so much like them, and in their own lifetimes they were among America's most loved and most read writers.

Who could have predicted that Carl August Sandburg, the second child and the eldest son of August and Clara Sandberg's brood of seven, would eventually earn fame as a writer? His parents were Swedish immigrants who arrived by separate paths in the United States and settled in Galesburg after getting married. They were part of the immigrant flood that swept across the United States during the years after the Civil War, modifying the nation's character forever. Carl's father, like most Swedes, possessed a common surname—Johnson or perhaps Danielson (it is not entirely certain which).[13] Possessing first and last names in common with several other men in the community and growing frustrated when his mail and paychecks wound up in the wrong hands, he took the practical step of changing his last name to Sandberg. (His son went a step further and changed the spelling.) Such a shift was easy enough to make, but trying to build an economic stake for himself and his family in rapidly industrializing America turned out to be a much more difficult task.

For thirty-five years, August Sandberg worked as a blacksmith's helper and shopman for the Chicago, Burlington, and Quincy Railroad. He labored for fourteen cents an hour, ten hours a day, six days a week, with Sundays off and three holidays a year. As an immigrant with minimal formal education (he had learned to read but not to write), his chances of rising up the economic ladder were limited. Within the confines of his circumstances, he worked extremely hard, continuing his labors at home far into the evening, working in his garden, fixing up his house, and doing odd jobs around the neighborhood to supplement his income. Highly frugal and constantly concerned about money, he was a responsible but not very affectionate parent. Carl Sandburg regretted that his father's life had been dictated so much by fear of want and dread of "the rainy day." For all their penury, absence of luxuries, and dependence on the continued health of the man of the house, however, the family came close to having a middle-class lifestyle. The houses they moved into became increasingly commodious as time went by. Although he reacted against his father's dourness, practical-mindedness, and lack of curiosity, young Carl absorbed his penchant for hard work, his earnestness, and his dogged sense of responsibility.[14]

Clara Sandberg's cheerful and compassionate nature inspired like qualities in her son; from her, he learned to dream and to hope and to enjoy life. "She had ten smiles for us to one from our father," Sandburg later recalled. She had worked as a hotel maid before meeting her husband. Her work in the household was no less tiring than his. Starting at six in the morning, she cooked, cleaned, washed, sewed, and did the housework for a growing family of nine. She provided most of the emotional warmth that made it a happy and enjoyable household rather than a dull and gloomy one. She understood Carl in a way that her husband could not, and she encouraged his budding sensitivity and curiosity. Because of her, he developed aspirations far exceeding the mundane, practical goals that her husband had in mind for him. The father complained, "Sholly, you read too much in de books— what good iss it?" But the mother, without her husband's consent, purchased books for her children from traveling salesmen, and then defended her purchases to her skeptical husband. Young Charlie (as Sandburg started calling himself when he entered school, perhaps to discourage people from thinking he was the son of immigrants) spent much of his time reading and soon came to enjoy it. He especially treasured history books, such as J. T. Headley's *Napoleon and His Marshals* and *Washington and His Generals*. Best of all was Charles Carleton Coffin's *The Boys of '76*, which allowed him to imagine himself a boy during the days of the Revolution. He later claimed to have read the book three or four times. *Tom Sawyer* and *Huckleberry Finn* possessed less appeal for him.[15]

Despite his penchant for books, even the most prescient observer could hardly have predicted a distinguished literary career for the boy. His interests and ambitions seemed typical of the time. With his friends in the neighborhood, he played mumblety-peg, baseball, shinny, and two-old-cat. In the summertime, the boys excitedly awaited the arrival of the circus train and walked four and a half miles over dusty roads to take in the Knox County Fair. Traveling road shows frequently visited the community, which was located on a major east-west rail line extending from Chicago, and Carl, when he could, attended many plays, minstrel shows, and more refined entertainments. He was impressed by a diorama of the Battle of Gettysburg, and he took in productions of *Hamlet* and *Uncle Tom's Cabin*. He got to hear big-name lecturers, such as religious skeptic Robert Ingersoll; John Peter Altgeld, a controversial Illinois governor; Henry M. Stanley, the African explorer; pugilists James J. Corbett and John L. Sullivan; Robert Todd Lincoln, son of the president; and the redoubtable William Jennings Bryan. In fact, he got to hear Bryan twice, because he and some of his friends rode the cowcatcher of a train 16 miles down the line to listen to him orate in Monmouth. For a time, Bryan was his hero.[16]

It was a boyhood later recalled with nostalgia in *Always the Young Strangers*, which recounted his life up through his service, at the age of twenty, in the Spanish-American War. While he was growing up, his thoughts and dreams were typical of the times. Possessing natural athletic ability, he aspired for a while to glory on the baseball diamond. Some summer days, he and his friends would start playing ball at eight in the morning, run home at noon for a quick meal, continue till six o'clock, grab another bite to eat, and then play until dark. "What is this fascination about making a hickory stick connect with a thrown ball and sending the ball as a high fly or a hot grounder for a safe hit?" he asked himself half a century later. "What is this fascination about picking up a hot grounder and throwing it to first for a putout—or running for a fly and leaping in the air for a one-handed catch and a putout?" These questions had captivated untold numbers of boys like himself, he realized. Whenever one of his friends managed to obtain a new ball, the boys played with it in the realization that it was the same kind that Amos Rusie—the "Hoosier Thunderbolt"—was flinging for the New York Giants. Carl could read about the exploits of the fireballing pitcher and other major leaguers in the papers he delivered to homes in Galesburg, and for several years he confidently rattled off statistics of every team and all their players. Sometimes, his head seemed empty of anything but baseball names and figures. In time, he came to realize that he would never make it to the major leagues but would have to make a living at some more mundane occupation.[17]

Small towns like Galesburg were wonderfully suited for young men willing to work, unskilled jobs of all kinds being readily available. Better-paying ones and those requiring further education generally lay beyond the reach of a boy like Carl, but he never had any difficulty obtaining the first kind. Despite an admirable record as a student, he was forced to quit school after eighth grade to help supplement the family's income. At the time, only a tiny minority of children attended high school, but dropping out reduced Carl's chances of getting a better, higher-paying job. A couple of years later, in 1893, economic depression descended on the United States. Industrial armies, groups of unemployed and destitute workers who marched to demonstrate for government action, roamed the country, and the young man's prospects appeared to be more limited than ever. While still in school, he had taken a job sweeping out a real estate office. Later he delivered newspapers, drove a milk wagon, and worked as a barbershop attendant, a tinner, a potter's turner, an ice cutter, and a bottle washer; he also apprenticed himself to a plumber, a carpenter, and a house painter.[18]

It was not an unhappy boyhood, but neither was it a fully satisfying one. In *Always the Young Strangers*, Sandburg described many of the town's people and places in considerable detail and with much affection, although he was also quick to note some of the town's seamier aspects. Settled a half century earlier by pious New Englanders, Galesburg expanded rapidly after the arrival in 1854 of the Burlington Railroad, which designated it as a division point and established shops and yards there.[19] By the 1880s, when Sandburg was growing up, it had increased to approximately 15,000 people, elevating it to the largest town in a 40-mile radius. Its rapid expansion provided it an opportunity to wrest the county seat away from neighboring Knoxville, which unleashed further potential for growth. The town had specifically been founded for the purpose of establishing a denominational school, and Knox College emerged as one of the best of its kind in the Midwest, contributing further to the attractiveness of the community. With the addition of Brown's Business College and Universalist-run Lombard College, Galesburg acquired the nickname of "College City." Further invigorating the town's economy were several manufacturing enterprises, although Galesburg never became a major industrial city. It was widely known for producing agricultural implements, and the squeal of train wheels could be heard every hour of the day and night. A steady influx of immigrants during the decades after the Civil War transformed the initial makeup of the town, adding contingents of English, Irish, Scotch,

Germans, and Italians, as well as a fair number of blacks and a smattering of Jews and Chinese. Swedes made up about one-sixth of Galesburg's population while Sandburg was growing up, providing a significant support group for him and his family but also ensuring that his Swedish background would be a significant factor in his life during his youth.

Galesburg and the surrounding area provided enough attractions to hold the allegiance of Carl's brothers and sisters and most of his friends. His older sister Mary taught school nearby for a while, later becoming a nurse and marrying a Galesburg man. Mart, who was Carl's only remaining brother after Emil and Fred died of diphtheria on succeeding days in 1892, took a position at the Burlington depot and held a variety of other jobs in Galesburg over the years. Their sister Martha married a man from Galesburg and remained there the rest of her life; Esther also lived a long time in her hometown after marrying a local man, later moving to another community in Illinois and then to California during their retirement.[20]

Carl might have stayed home, too, had it not been for the Spanish-American War, which became the crucial turning point in his life. Galesburg had begun to feel too small for him, too restrictive, too confining. He had little direct chance to know what lay beyond it, but he learned enough from experience and observation to realize that his ambitions were larger than the town was capable of delivering. He could read books and newspapers, attend lectures at the opera house, listen to conversations in the barbershop, and observe traveling men coming and going daily through the Burlington depot. There was a bigger world beyond Galesburg, he understood, and he wanted to see it and experience it.

In 1894, when he was sixteen, he persuaded his father to get him a railroad pass so he could visit the state fair in Peoria, 50 miles to the southeast. Even more exciting, he obtained another pass two years later and went on a three-day excursion to Chicago. It was an eye-opening experience. Carrying only $1.50 in his pocket, he made the most of the opportunity, walking for miles through the downtown business district and along the lakeshore, visiting and observing State Street department stores, elevated train lines, the Board of Trade, offices of the newspapers he delivered in Galesburg, and dozens of other places. The trip was exhilarating. "From that time on he was never content in one place for too long," biographer Penelope Niven writes.[21]

Back home, he chafed at a succession of dead-end jobs and could only anticipate more of them in the future. He grew increasingly restless, searching for direction. Shyness and penury made it difficult for him to approach girls. He admitted later that he had briefly contemplated suicide. But the notion quickly faded; it was out of character for him. What came over him during these years, he later wrote, "wouldn't be easy to tell. I hated my home town and yet I loved it. And I hated and loved myself about the same as I did the town and the people." Galesburg itself, he understood, "was a pretty good home town to grow up in." He realized that his trouble lay less in the town and its people than in himself.[22]

In the summer of 1897, Carl decided to ride the rails west to work in the harvest fields of Kansas. The journey lasted three and a half months and affected him profoundly, leaving him infatuated with the lives of hoboes and desirous of getting around and seeing more of the country. On the way to Kansas, he waited tables in Iowa, worked on a railroad section gang in Missouri, and washed dishes in Kansas City. He walked past William Allen White's newspaper office in Emporia, Kansas, too timid to walk in and ask to see the famous newspaper editor. He slept in hobo jungles, rubbed shoulders with thieves and panhandlers, worked for meals and sometimes received free ones, and fell asleep while riding the bumpers on a train, almost killing himself in the process. After working with the threshing crews, he detoured west to the Rocky Mountains before returning home. The trip changed him, removing some of his shyness, inspiring confidence and hope, and elevating his expectations. It opened his eyes to the world that lay beyond the Illinois prairie and to some of the social problems confronting the nation.[23]

What would have happened to the young man had not the war in Cuba erupted in 1898 is difficult to say. Perhaps another trip or two would have landed him a job or put him in a school where his career would have developed along lines similar to what actually happened. One thing is certain: his enlistment in Company C of the Sixth Illinois Infantry Regiment opened a career path that had been blocked. The war ended quickly and victoriously, Sandburg's unit never seeing combat. Back home in Galesburg, he discovered that Lombard College would waive tuition for a year for war veterans. Having never attended high school, he first had to enroll in the preparatory department, although he was allowed to take some college classes at the same time. With the help of a friend, he obtained a job as a call man at the Prairie Street Fire Department to earn money to pay for his other expenses.[24]

Charles Sandburg—as he continued to refer to himself—would leave

Lombard before acquiring the necessary credits for graduation, but the three and a half years that he spent there further transformed his life. Several years older than most of the other students and still somewhat shy and awkward, he quickly established himself as a serious and popular student. With 175 students and a faculty of nineteen, the college allowed—indeed, basically required—a lot of participation in student activities, and everyone knew each other by face and by name. Sandburg became a star on the basketball team, a member of the debating society, the editor of the student literary journal, and a coeditor of the yearbook. In his second try, he won the Swan Oratorical Contest. In his classes, he obtained a deeper understanding of history, literature, and other subjects, and he began to think of writing as a possible vocation.[25]

The most important single influence on him was the inspiration and role model provided by a remarkable young professor on the staff, Philip Green Wright. Later a professor of economics at Harvard, the versatile Wright conducted classes in mathematics, astronomy, and English, as well as economics, at tiny Lombard. In his Daily Themes class, Sandburg learned how to analyze and improve his own writing as well as that of others. At informal Sunday evening get-togethers in Wright's home adjoining the campus, students read aloud selections from a wide variety of authors, such as Rudyard Kipling, Ivan Turgenev, and Twain. During Sandburg's senior year, Wright organized a Poor Writer's Club, placing himself in the same classification with his students in attendance. Wright was a disciple of British social reformer William Morris, and his socialistic political views rubbed off on Sandburg. More important, he provided his young charge encouragement and a model of what a literary life could be.

The notion that he could make a vocation of writing appealed to Sandburg, but exactly what direction he should follow did not make itself immediately apparent. Leaving school without a degree at the age of twenty-four in the spring of 1902, he needed to find a way to support himself until the answer appeared. Talented and resourceful, he had no trouble finding jobs, but it would be more than two decades before he finally worked out a practical routine that allowed him all the time he needed for his writing. Before leaving college, he had worked summers traveling through Illinois and nearby states going house to house selling stereographic photographs and viewers. Now he discovered it was possible, if he lived frugally, to earn enough money to live on by selling the viewers and cards two or three days a week. This allowed him time to read and write the rest of the week. Meanwhile, he was adding to his store of experiences while he was experimenting with his writing.[26]

On a little handpress in the basement of his home, Philip Green Wright printed several booklets of Sandburg's poetry and prose during the first several years after he left Lombard, making him a published author. But editions of a few hundred copies provided only a small taste of the kind of recognition Sandburg hoped eventually to achieve. During his late twenties, he continued to drift, selling stereographs, writing poems, billing himself as an orator, even going on the vaudeville stage temporarily. His act (a Swedish humor routine) went over well enough with audiences, but Sandburg quickly lost interest in comedy. As a college student he had discovered and come to admire the works of Walt Whitman, and his favorite lecture was one he developed about that author of *Leaves of Grass*. Along with Wright, Whitman became a role model for him.

Sandburg was seeking his vocation. He continued to give lectures when he was able to obtain bookings, toiled in a series of editorial jobs, wrote advertising copy, traveled Wisconsin as an organizer for the Social-Democratic Party, served as private secretary for Milwaukee's Socialist mayor Emil Seidel, wrote for several business publications, and continued to experiment with poetry. His politics were leftist, influenced by Wright, Eugene Debs and his fellow Socialists, Robert La Follette and other progressive politicians, and his wide and continuing program of reading. Sandburg empathized with and took the side of ordinary people—the kind he had grown up with in Galesburg and with whom he interacted on a daily basis. Sandburg's life among hoboes and tramps while riding the rails reinforced his natural sympathy for poor people and down-and-outers. His poems reflected his understanding of the kinds of trials and obstacles they faced every day.

In addition to searching for a vocation, Sandburg during his twenties and thirties was seeking to fashion his own unique personality. Inspired by Whitman, Twain, Ralph Waldo Emerson, and others, he was determined to become an "ideal soul," capable of creating great art. On the lecture circuit, he followed in the steps of Lincoln, Twain, James Whitcomb Riley, and other great platform performers who successfully projected personas capable of capturing the attention and approval of their audiences. The publicity photographs advertising his lectures presented him in dramatic poses. In his reading, writing, and lecturing and in his interactions with the public, he was fashioning an identity for himself as an artist who captivated his audience. In the words of his biographer, "Sandburg was becoming an artist whose primary creation was himself."[27]

He moved to Chicago in 1912 and became identified with that city for the next twenty years. Four years earlier, he had successfully ended his quest for the "ideal woman," having found her in Lilian Steichen, the sister of the famous photographer Edward Steichen. He met her while she was working for the Social-Democrats in Milwaukee. Now, as he worked on the staffs of the *Chicago Day Book,* the *Chicago Daily News,* and other publications in the city, she bore the responsibility for the care of their three daughters and served as his editor, inspiration, and encourager. Sandburg always mentioned her, along with her brother and Wright, as the three most important influences on his life.[28]

During the early decades of the century, Chicago was a center of political progressivism and radicalism, muckraking journalism, new art, and literary renaissance. Apart from New York City, perhaps, it was the most exciting place in the United States for an artist or intellectual to be. Working at the *Daily News* most of the time between 1917 and 1932, Sandburg drew inspiration from his colleagues there—people like Ben Hecht, Lloyd Lewis, Harry Hansen, and managing editor Henry Justin Smith. For a time, he wrote editorials and was given free reign to work on stories about almost anything that struck his fancy, including the big 1919 race riots in the city. Then, for seven years during the 1920s, he reviewed movies. He got into the practice of watching five or six movies over a weekend and quickly working up their reviews, leaving the rest of the week available to pursue his personal writing projects. During this period, he completed the first two volumes of his Lincoln biography.[29]

Lloyd Lewis related a poignant story about a dinner party given in Chicago in 1925 for novelist Sinclair Lewis. The author was just back from Europe, riding high on a tide of applause for *Main Street* and *Babbitt.* That evening, Ben Hecht jokingly referred to the red-haired Lewis as "Sir Red," since rumors were circulating that he had recently turned down a British baronetcy. The atmosphere in the room grew somewhat heated, however, when the pugnacious novelist and some of his friends began attacking one of the assemblage for critical remarks he had made in a review of *Main Street.* Sandburg, puffing quietly away on his cigar, kept fairly quiet through all of it until Morris Fishbein, who had organized the dinner, asked him if he would be willing to sing for the group. As Lloyd Lewis described the scene, a hush fell over the room as the poet began strumming a guitar and, in that "soft, don't-give-a-damn way of his," sang "The Buffalo Skinners." Sandburg, a self-trained singer and guitarist, could play only a few simple chords, but his mellow baritone voice was capable of transfixing audiences. The old ballad, which had been uncovered by Texas folklorist John Lomax, was a particularly touching one, sounding "like a funeral song to the America that has gone." When Sandburg was done, Sinclair Lewis, tears streaking his face, murmured, "That's the America I came home to. That's it."[30]

It was during the 1920s that Sandburg started taking a guitar along with him on the road and integrating folk songs into his poetry readings. Audiences loved it. The songs contributed a new dimension to his performances. In his forties, Sandburg emerged as a consummate stage performer. Prematurely gray, he looked older than his years; the flap of hair that constantly skittered down over his eyes added to his already distinctive appearance. His unmodulated but expressive voice captured audiences' attention.

Working on his biography of Lincoln, Sandburg subtly changed his public image of himself, while at the same time reorienting his writing career by taking on the roles of historian and biographer. In the process, he was finally able to establish financial independence for his family, allowing him to concentrate full time on his own writing. He stopped doing movie reviews but did not finally sever his connection with the newspaper until Depression-induced salary cuts there led to his resignation in 1932. Sandburg received $21,600 for the magazine serialization of *The Prairie Years* before it ever hit the bookstore shelves, and he earned thousands more in royalties when the two-volume edition became a best seller.[31]

Despite its popularity with readers and the approval of most reviewers, some critics questioned whether the Lincoln work legitimately deserved to be called either biography or history. Sandburg had been collecting information on Lincoln for years. Now he toiled energetically to locate documents and other materials housed in libraries, archives, and private collections all over the country. No one doubted either his sincerity or his industry in his research, but many critics wondered about his competence and his judgment in sifting the facts, since he possessed no professional training as a historian and seemed unconcerned about arguing for his conclusions. The volumes contained no footnotes or other standard scholarly paraphernalia; furthermore, their author frequently inserted words in his characters' mouths and placed thoughts in their heads, created scenes out of whole cloth, and in general applied his poetic imagination to his subject. This was especially true with regard to Lincoln's early years, for which documentation was scanty. As the future president matured, facts about him become more readily available, and for the later volumes on the war years, Sandburg's narrative became much more standard in form and reliable.

Despite the author's unconventional techniques, even most professional historians were quick to praise the work, although some placed it in the category of imaginative literature rather than conventional history or biography. Historian James Truslow Adams, writing in the *New York Sun*, deemed it "a remarkable book from several standpoints," one of which was that it was "alive with a warm humanity." The book's "extraordinary vitality" impressed the *New York Times*'s reviewer. A "masterpiece" that "suits its subject" was the judgment of the *New Statesman*. It was "a beautiful monumental prose story of Abraham Lincoln," said William Allen White. The *St. Louis Post-Dispatch*'s reviewer cast aside caution and proclaimed it "the greatest book produced thus far in the twentieth century and in the English tongue."[32]

But criticism would not die. Lincoln expert William E. Barton, although admiring the book's "atmosphere and fine flavor" and quick to acknowledge the author's industriousness in going about his research, discovered almost no significant new material in it and found it marred by numerous inaccuracies. Like many other knowledgeable readers, he concluded of the author that he was more a poet than a historian. Mark Van Doren, in a similar vein, found the book to be "amply and profoundly beautiful," not because of but in spite of "some rather obvious 'poetry' stuck in here and there." He was especially impressed that Sandburg had visited and talked to people who had known Lincoln in many towns in Kentucky, Indiana, and Illinois.[33]

James Truslow Adams was one of many reviewers commenting on Sandburg's unique suitability for the task he had undertaken: "Sandburg knows his West. As a poet he knows also the hidden springs of a man's heart. The book, which relates Lincoln's life only while in the West and up to his taking office as President, reveals the union of these two elements."[34] Sandburg, like Lincoln, was prairie-born, and like Lincoln, he was a small-town boy who intuitively understood the thoughts, the aspirations, and the dreams of the kinds of people who inhabited small towns. "I was born on the prairie," the poet wrote in "Cornhuskers," "and the milk of its wheat, the red of its clover, the eyes of its women, gave me a song and a slogan."[35] Galesburg lay in Lincoln country, less than 100 miles from New Salem and Springfield. Growing up there, Sandburg became acquainted with many people who had personally known Lincoln.[36] Countless times, he had walked past the east entrance of the Old Main building at Knox College, where Lincoln and Stephen A. Douglas had held their fifth debate in 1858, and as an adult he frequently recited the words of Lincoln memorialized on a plaque there: "He is blowing out the moral lights around us when he contends that whoever wants slaves has a right to hold them."[37] Reminders of Lincoln's presence were ubiquitous in the community. The *Galesburg Republican-Register* frequently printed fillers with information and gossip about Lincoln. As a boy, Sandburg read these stories; as an adult, he remembered them. The two lives strangely paralleled each other. Financial hardship limited the early education of both. Finding a vocation and molding a character to fit it likewise occupied each. Lincoln's mother and Sandburg's father could not write their names; as boys, Lincoln wrote letters for his mother and their neighbors in Indiana, and Sandburg did the same for his father and their neighbors in Illinois. Lincoln was twenty-three when the Black Hawk War broke out; Sandburg was twenty when he participated in the Spanish-American War. In both cases, the experiences turned out to be crucial turning points in their lives.[38]

Sandburg's *Abraham Lincoln,* similarly, was written at a crucial moment in his life. In Joseph Epstein's somewhat jaundiced judgment, it "was, from the standpoint of his reputation, a beautiful stroke. The great prairie poet writing the life of the great prairie politician—it was a match made, if not in heaven, then in the publicity office."[39] Too much should not be made of the calculated nature of Sandburg's decision to take on Lincoln as a subject. He had grown up in the proximity of the great folk hero, been fascinated with him as a youth, collected extensive materials on him as he grew older, and written poems about him. It was at the suggestion of his editor, Alfred Harcourt, that he had undertaken in 1922 a 400-page biography of Lincoln for young readers.[40] In quick order, the task grew beyond its original scope. By the time he finished the project, Sandburg had compiled a six-volume, 4,500-page monument to Lincoln's myth, which, at 1,175,000 words, outweighed both Shakespeare (1,025,000 words) and the Bible (925,000 words, with the Apocrypha included).[41]

The literary critic Edmund Wilson quipped that at times a reader was tempted to feel that falling into Sandburg's hands had been "the cruelest thing that has happened to Lincoln since he was shot by Booth."[42] But that was not the common viewpoint. The biography, in the process of humanizing Lincoln, burnished his reputation and at the same time rendered Sandburg a large presence on the American literary scene. The four volumes on the war years, published thirteen years after the volumes on the prairie years came out, confirmed and further enhanced his standing. The Pulitzer Prize committee selected *Abraham Lincoln: The War Years* for the 1940 history award, since the rules precluded works on George Washington and Abraham Lincoln from being considered in the biography category. Sandburg benefited from the 1930s' heightened fascination with history, an interest explained by John Dos Passos: "In times of change and danger, when there is a quicksand of fear under men's reasoning, a sense of continuity with generations gone before can stretch like a lifeline across the scary present."[43]

Whether Carl Sandburg had successfully uncovered the mainsprings of Lincoln's identity in his biography of him engendered considerable debate, but, in the process, he fixed his own identity. While writing Lincoln, he had, in a sense, become Lincoln. The same qualities of thoughtfulness, compassion, commitment, perseverance, and humor that he attributed to the prairie statesman could be seen in him. Just as Lincoln stood out as the people's politician, Sandburg stood out as the people's poet. As early as 1906, he had written about Lincoln as a champion of the average man.[44] His poetry and other writings always had common people at their center, and during the 1930s, as he continued working on the biography, Sandburg took time out to write his classic celebration of ordinary people in poetic form.

The People, Yes is a book-length encomium to the industriousness, suffering, perseverance, hopefulness, and optimism of Americans and, indeed, of the whole human race. The population of the United States was part of "the Family of Man," and both became Sandburg's subject. Often blundering and bewildered, wrongheaded and mean, as well as intelligent and kind, the people of whom Sandburg wrote with such great passion and tenderness were the same ones that Lincoln had eulogized in the Gettysburg Address when he spoke of government "of the people, by the people, and for the people." During a decade when dictators strode unchecked across Europe and Asia, threatening the peace of the world, Sandburg invested his energies in a great poetic saga memorializing common, everyday people as "the last best hope of earth." With the eye of a reporter and the ear of a musician, he wove a tapestry of cornfields and silos, band concerts and ice cream parlors, stockyards and streetcars—everything the American people represented. The people could be duped and slow to understand, but ultimately they would respond and assert themselves. He once referred to *The People, Yes* as "my footnote to the last words of the Gettysburg Address."[45]

He called it his favorite poem. It was poetry with a purpose, poetry as therapy. It was, he said, "the best memorandum I could file for the present stress."[46] As with many of his previous efforts, critics stepped forward to deny that it was poetry at all or that more than a small fraction of it was. In 107 sections, the work integrated within its sprawling format an amalgam of stories, anecdotes, adages, proverbs, myths, slang, popular beliefs, jokes, and folklore. It articulated the hopes and dreams of people in their own, often vulgar language. In it, Sandburg distilled from everything he had seen, experienced, and studied a portrait of the people who were yet asleep, but who would eventually awaken. Only a person as widely traveled and as hungry for experience as Sandburg was could have written the long poem. Encompassing a kaleidoscope of moods and impressions, *The People, Yes* ultimately affirmed the worth and dignity of the American people and of the family of man. Like himself, the people he wrote about were seekers, questers, and dreamers; in the end, they would prevail.

Ever a realist, Sandburg was always, in an even more profound sense, a dreamer. He imagined life better, fairer, more generous, and just. Sandburg never jettisoned his radical instincts. *The People, Yes* contained much indignation about poverty, inequality, indignities perpetuated on workers, and the struggles of the masses. But by now Sandburg's focus had shifted. The rough edges of his politics and his poetry had been smoothed over, and his manner had become more mainstream. Eugene Debs was dead, and socialism was no longer an option for Sandburg. During a decade when many famous writers and novelists committed themselves to communism and other radical isms, Sandburg identified with Franklin Roosevelt and the New Deal, campaigning actively for the president during the critical election year of 1940. Ironically, Sandburg's popularity was so great and his political views veiled enough that some Republican politicos seriously thought of him as a possible choice as their party's nominee for the presidency that year. Roosevelt, in the meantime, wanted him to consider running for Congress as a Democrat.[47]

By the 1940s, Sandburg had become something of a public treasure, one who, in large measure, transcended partisan squabbles and narrow interests. Like General Dwight D. Eisenhower, whom he extolled as a great hero during the late 1940s but of whom he quickly became critical when the former soldier emerged as the 1952 Republican presidential nominee, Sandburg stood above politics, a grand old man of democratic tastes and popular acclaim. He enjoyed the kind of fame as a literary man that Eisenhower had earned as a soldier. Awards and honors showered down on him, and he became, in the public mind, the representative man of American democracy. He enjoyed literary fame whose magnitude was perhaps only ever equaled by that of Mark Twain and Ernest Hemingway. No other American writer was simultaneously so widely read and heard.[48] A second Pulitzer Prize came to him in 1951, this time the poetry award, for his *Complete Poems.* A Nobel Prize for him was considered but never conferred. He quipped that he felt honored anyway, because Hemingway, on receiving the Nobel Prize in 1954, told reporters that Sandburg was the one who deserved it. (John Steinbeck reacted similarly five years later.)[49] Honorary degrees descended on him, a man who had never spent a day in high school. Harvard and Yale feted him on successive days, *Time* and *Newsweek* featured him on their covers, Edward R. Murrow invited him to appear on *Hear It Now* and *See It Now,* and he became a popular guest performer on television programs ranging from *Today* and *The Tonight Show* to those hosted by Milton Berle, Howard K. Smith, and Ed Sullivan.[50] Two dozen schools and a Chicago housing development were named for him, and Lyndon B. Johnson awarded him the Presidential Medal of Freedom in 1964. More unusually, he published six new poems in *Playboy* magazine and was photographed in New York and Hollywood dancing and discussing poetry with Marilyn Monroe.[51] He presided as the country's unofficial poet laureate, and his public performances packed enthusiastic audiences into auditoriums all over America.

Public adulation for Sandburg carried little weight with the critics, however, and may have even worked against him. Although he remained popular with ordinary reviewers and general audiences, academic critics and his poetic peers remained ambivalent about, even downright hostile toward, his work. William Carlos Williams's fusillade in the September 1951 issue of *Poetry* magazine set the tone for later criticism: the poet's work, he asserted, was shapeless and formless, lacked a motivating spirit to control it, and demonstrated no development over time. Sandburg's first, brilliantly successful poems about Chicago should have been his last, in Williams's view.[52] As time went by, Sandburg suffered not so much from criticism as from neglect. John Ciardi, on a visit to Knox College in 1959, expressed disdain for the hometown hero's work, predicting, "Nobody will know about Sandburg 100 years from now." Listing William Butler Yeats, Robert Frost, and T. S. Eliot as the three greatest American poets at mid-century, Ciardi sniffed, "In this company Carl Sandburg doesn't even exist."[53] After Sandburg's death, in fact, his literary reputation plummeted.

Though he tried to laugh such criticism off, Sandburg was surely hurt by it, and he demonstrated his disdain for ivory-tower intellectuals by referring to them as the "Abracadabra Boys," who locked themselves up in library stacks and cloisters, spinning jargon and arguing over piffles while separating themselves from real life and real people.[54] Sandburg aggressively struck back at "obscurantists," who, in his opinion, elevated form over substance in literature, even making insinuations about their masculinity. At his grand seventy-fifth birthday celebration in January 1953, with more than 500 guests gathered to pay homage to him at Chicago's Blackstone Hotel, he lit into contemporary writers, the ones he called "new criticists," whose work was unintelligible to the average reader. "You've got to have a code, or imagine you have a code, to imagine you know what the hell they're writing about," he complained. "They are proud that the average truck driver on Wabash Avenue can't understand them."[55] "I say to hell with the new poetry," he told reporters later at a press conference. "They don't want poetry to say what it means. They have symbols and abstractions and a code amongst themselves—sometimes I think it's a series of ear wigglings."[56]

But mostly his birthday bash was awash in nostalgia and good spirits. Edward Steichen paraphrased poet James Whitcomb Riley in saluting his brother-in-law: "When God made Carl, he didn't do nothing else that day but just sit around and feel good."[57] That is how most people felt about Sandburg during his waning years. They paid little attention to his radical past and unconventional ideas; they did not worry about poetic form. They just enjoyed reading his work, liked him as a person, and enjoyed him as a performer. Let the critics be contemptuous; they would honor the people's poet. Let the Westbrook Peglers caricature him as a shrewd vulgarian who capitalized on "the winsome forelock flopping down over his eyes" to win over the hoi polloi to his "homespun school of doggerel and affectation."[58] Sandburg remained the poet of the people, and the people loved him.

When he died on July 22, 1967, Detroit was going up in flames and

American society was imploding over the issues of race and Vietnam. By then, Sandburg seemed like a voice from another era, but the words and thoughts of America's bard were not irrelevant to the times. The small-town boy from Galesburg—the poet, the dreamer, and the seeker, both a perpetual optimist and a wide-eyed realist—contained within himself contradictions and fissures that have run through American society from the beginning. His words still speak to us today. To those who would assert, "The people is a myth, an abstraction," he would reply simply:

> And what myth would you put in place of the people?
> And what abstraction would you exchange for this one?
> And when has creative man not toiled deep in myth?[59]

In America's democratic poet, the people obtained a myth fit for the size of their dreams and aspirations and relevant to their conflicts and contradictions.

CHAPTER SEVEN

Thomas Hart Benton, Grant Wood, and John Steuart Curry: Painting the American Scene

So many of the leaders in the arts were born in small towns and on farms that in the comments and conversation of many who have "gone East" there is today a noticeable homesickness for the scenes of their childhood.

—Grant Wood

I believe in subject matter. The artist ought to paint people doing things. . . . The use of life as an excuse for clever arrangements of color or other pictorial elements ends where it begins.

—John Steuart Curry

Grant Wood is dead and John Curry is dead. They were closer to me in basic attitude of mind, in their social and aesthetic philosophies, than all other artists. Together we stood for things which most artists do not much believe in. We stood for an art whose forms and meanings would have direct and easily comprehended relevance to the American culture of which we were by blood and daily life a part. . . . We hoped to build our "universals" out of the particularities of our own times and our own places, out of the substances of our actual lives as most of the great artists of the world's past have done.

—Thomas Hart Benton

During the Depression decade of the 1930s, the regional triumvirate of American Scene painters from the Midwest—Grant Wood, Thomas Hart Benton, and John Steuart Curry—struck a nerve. Among critics, connoisseurs, and their fellow artists, as well as among the general public, these three men, from Iowa, Missouri, and Kansas, respectively, stimulated ardent respect and admiration, on the one hand, and vituperative criticism and denigration, on the other. In 1983 and 1989, after decades of neglect had seemingly left them in art world limbo, retrospective exhibitions of Wood's and Benton's works reignited the debates. Half a century after their heyday, these midwestern artists retained their power to entertain, astonish, and upset their audiences. Why all the fuss?

The 1983 Grant Wood retrospective at the Whitney Museum of American Art in New York City was the first major showing of his work since 1942, the year he died. Robert Hughes, *Time* magazine's curmudgeonly art critic, perceived a connection between the Iowa native's revival and the cultural climate of the Reagan years. Nostalgic, conservative, vulgar, and provincial—earlier critics' assessments of Wood's art were all true, Hughes believed. Since midcentury, he asserted, the Iowa native's audience had consisted of two groups: on the one side, a small band of loyalists from the heartland who venerated his paintings as truthful renderings of America; on the other side, unimpressed viewers who considered him a "provincial cornball," worthy of less than a footnote in American art history. Hughes left no doubt about which group he identified with, although he allowed that Wood represented "some deep-struck hopes and illusions" in the public sphere and therefore deserved understanding.[1]

Grace Glueck commented in the *New York Times* that within respectable art circles Wood's name elicited only snickers. Received opinion classified him, along with painters such as Maxfield Parrish and Norman Rockwell, as "superficial cutesifiers of American life." Glueck labeled the painter "essentially an illustrator-decorator with a moralist's program."[2] At *Newsweek,* John Ashbery saw in the Whitney exhibition evidence that Wood's work "must remain a dead letter, a cluster of prettily made baubles that inspired no imitators and whose thinly veiled regionalist-chauvinist principles seem not only quaint but slightly distasteful today." Wondering what Wood might have accomplished had he lived on into the postwar period, Ashbery pronounced him "a minor artist saddled with an inflated popular reputation."[3] Some reviews were kinder and more understanding, but it seemed unlikely that the Iowa scene painter would be admitted back into the pantheon of first-rank artists.[4]

Whatever the art establishment might have had to say about Wood and his fellow regionalists, these three midwestern painters have always retained an appreciative popular audience. Critics were never of one mind about them, nor was the public, but popular enthusiasm for their work manifested itself in many ways. Large crowds attended the Wood retrospective, as it worked its way from New York to showings in Minneapolis, Chicago, and San Francisco. The phenomenon repeated itself six years later, when a major retrospective was mounted in Kansas City, Missouri, on the centenary of Thomas Hart Benton's birth. The show attracted large crowds and generated more publicity than any other event in the history of the Nelson-Atkins Museum.[5] Benton retained an uncanny ability to spark controversy and debate 100 years after his birth and 50 years after his career peaked. Opinion about him tended to polarize; few observers were content to strike a balanced judgment. His detractors continued to display a kind of rancor that few contemporary artists were capable of stimulating.

Hughes, who had thought it necessary to try, at least, to understand Wood, accorded no such courtesy to his sidekick—"the Michelangelo of Neosho, Mo.," as he called him. In the estimate of *Time*'s opinionated reviewer, "He was flat-out, lapel-grabbing vulgar, incapable of touching a pictorial sensation without pumping and tarting it up to the point where the eye wants to cry uncle." Exhibiting his low estimate of popular taste, Hughes predicted success for the show, "because Benton was a dreadful artist most of the time." Hughes readily admitted Benton's likability and "his lack of cant, his indomitable energy, his cussedness and independence," but none of these characteristics necessarily made him a great artist. Hughes pronounced that Benton, like his friend Wood, practiced an art of "idealization and propaganda." Worse, the Missourian seemed to have been inspired by racism, Hughes asserted, in his treatment of blacks, although his depictions of white hayseeds and politicos admittedly were equally harsh.[6] *Newsweek* rated Benton higher as a verbal duelist than as a painter of the American scene. In *Newsweek*'s view, although Benton had succeeded in capturing part of mainstream America, his work did not measure up to Walker Evans's photography or Edward Hopper's paintings. More to the point, his sentimentality was comparable to Walt Disney's and his bombast to that of P. T. Barnum. And although Benton could draw, in his own cartoonish manner, and could color, in simplistic fashion, he was incapable of painting.[7]

More notable yet in the uncompromising one-sidedness of their opinions were Roger Kimball of the *New Criterion* and Hilton Kramer, editor of the *New Criterion* and former *New York Times* art critic. Kimball called a large number of the paintings in the exhibition "astoundingly bad." Many were "painfully vapid" and "drenched in sugary nostalgia." Kramer judged Benton's work to be "awful—an unrelieved panorama of pictorial clichés which seem to have been derived from old Hollywood movies." Benton, in his view, was "a failed artist," and he went so far as to call for the resignation of the director of the Whitney Museum for staging the show in New York because it was proof of a lack of standards at the institution. No one was more strident in his condemnation than *Kansas City Star* art critic Donald Hoffman. "Benton's mature paintings demonstrate everything that art ought not to be: contrived, overblown, strident, garish, clumsy, lifeless and thoroughly unconvincing," he wrote. In a word, the exhibition organizers had assembled "the largest concentration of bad painting" Hoffman had ever encountered in forty years of museum-going.[8]

Benton did have his defenders, however. The art historian Henry Adams, who curated the exhibition and arranged for a ninety-minute PBS documentary to accompany it, wrote an excellent book connecting the painter's life with his art. While acknowledging many of Benton's foibles and failings, Adams struck a middle ground, judging the Missourian to have created significant art. He had been perhaps America's most famous painter during the Depression decade and was "an interesting historical figure who captured the spirit of the 1930s." Responding to Hoffman's trashing of the hometown celebrity, Kyle MacMillan of the *Omaha World-Herald* opted for a more balanced view, one that could account for the complexity of the man and his art. "Benton believed deeply in the region he painted and especially in the people he painted," he noted. "The sincerity and honesty of his feelings come through in the paintings and give them much of their appeal, especially to the public at large." When the show got to Detroit, *Detroit News* art critic Joy Hakanson Colby found it to be "great fun." True, the paintings were "vulgar, cranky, strident, and bombastic," but they turned into something positive when combined with "personal vision, high energy, and strong commitment." As the retrospective proceeded from Kansas City to Detroit to New York and eventually to Los Angeles, evaluations of it ranged from one extreme to the other. Some judged Benton's work to be among the most important of the twentieth century; others scorned it as awkward, kitschy, cartoonish, retrograde, and insignificant.[9]

John Steuart Curry, who during the heyday of regionalism in the 1930s had been less in the limelight and was not as controversial as Benton or Wood, did not get a retrospective exhibition until 1998, in a show curated by the Elvehjem Museum of Art at the University of Wisconsin. The exhibit later traveled to San Francisco and Kansas City.[10] Although some considered Curry the best painter of the three, his style was much less idiosyncratic and more straightforward than those of the other two. His paintings stimulated less controversy and discord.

As a group, Benton, Wood, and Curry established regionalism as the most popular and important development in American art during the 1930s.[11] Having risen quickly in public esteem, the movement swiftly went into decline during the following decade and by midcentury had become little more than a historical curiosity on the American art scene. Meanwhile, Jackson Pollock, a onetime student of Benton's, emerged as the leader of the newly dominant school of abstract expressionism, or "action painting." Despite seeming to be totally different from his mentor's work, with its adherence to a representational style that was narrative in intent and attached to particular places, Pollock's drip paintings, in all their abstraction and dislocatedness, drew directly on compositional principles to which Benton had introduced him during the 1920s and '30s. In their devotion to the requirements of form composition and in their desire to make their art a device to promote freedom, Benton and Pollock were in agreement; on almost everything else, they differed.[12]

The new generation of painters, centered in New York City, made abstraction their god. The value of a work of art lay in the technique of its making, in the painting itself, rather than in the references it made to the outside world. All of this had been anathema to the regionalists—the very thing against which they fought so hard during the 1930s. Their goal was to champion a meaningful art that would be understandable to the average person and would carry social and moral significance. Despite the label they worked under and despite their backgrounds in the Midwest, their work was geographic only incidentally. In the words of Grant Wood, "They were simply observing the old truth that in general the artist interprets most effectively the experience he knows best and feels most profoundly, and that his best material is apt to lie close at hand."[13]

Although each of the three arrived at regionalism by his own particular route, all were influenced—as were other American Scene painters, such as Charles Burchfield, Edward Hopper, and Ben Shahn—by demands for an indigenous American art that were heard in the wake of World War I. The devastating and unsettling experience of war did much to undermine old traditions and values, while at the same time it stimulated a longing for a return to order, security, and simple virtues. Beginning in the 1920s and continuing into the 1930s, American writers, artists, and intellectuals launched a search for "a usable past," becoming more historically minded at the same time that they sought to come to grips with the new technologies and forms of organization that were rapidly modernizing American society.[14]

Just as they were attacked by their enemies during their heyday for being too provincial and isolationist, the regionalists were also accused of being backward looking—desirous of escaping from the problems and dilemmas of modern society. Looked at in a more positive light, they were said to be engaged in a self-conscious attempt to identify with a rapidly disappearing way of life. They were reproached for being antiurban, antiSemitic, racist, reactionary, isolationist, and conservative, and even for being fascistic and friendly to National Socialism.[15] Most of these charges were absolutely false and scurrilous; others were, at least, exaggerated.

But the regionalists bore responsibility themselves for some of the disputes they found themselves in. At times, in the heat of polemical battles, they spoke loosely or for effect and let their emotions get the best of them. In preparing to leave New York City to relocate in Kansas City in 1935, for instance, Benton sounded off on all the frustrations that had been building inside him during his contentious battles with Communists and other leftists living in New York, on the New York art establishment, and on everyone else who was unprepared to accept his calls for a new kind of representational art. He regularly characterized his opponents as "the professors, the critics, and the museum boys." Loosely mixing his revulsion for homosexuals and left-wing ideologues with his growing discomfort in the big city, Benton informed reporters that he was sick of living in New York. It had lost its dynamic quality, he asserted; it had grown feeble, querulous, and touchy. "The place has lost its masculinity," he contended. Even the burlesque shows had become tame. The atmosphere had become far too "scholastic—monkish and medieval." He said he was moving to the Midwest, which was not so wrapped up in verbal logic, where action was more important, and where he might be able to escape "verbal stupidities."[16]

Six years later, Benton managed to get himself fired as a teacher at the Kansas City Art Institute for even more-indiscreet remarks. America's museums, he asserted at that time, were "full of ballet dancers, retired businessmen, and boys from the Fogg Institute at Harvard," and the typical museum was run "by a pretty boy with delicate wrists and a swing in his gait." If he had his way, he would get rid of museums, he said, since nobody went to them anyway. He preferred to sell his paintings to "saloons, bawdyhouses, Kiwanis and Rotary clubs, and Chambers of Commerce—even women's clubs." Statements like this made it hard to know when Benton was being serious and when he was not, and he admitted afterward that sometimes he talked loudly and embellished his words with "linguistic flourishes not generally associated with serious intentions." His objections to museums, he said, were serious, but the language he had used had been hyperbolic.[17]

Unlike Grant Wood, who was likewise capable of pushing his arguments so hard that respondents could misinterpret his thinking, Benton usually did not identify artists with particular regions. (Wood sometimes assumed the role of advocate for the Midwest as a special or superior region.) The Missourian traveled frequently through New England, the South, and the West, making sketches along the way and drawing on them for the murals and easel paintings he did back in his studio. Yet, at about the time he left New York, he uncharacteristically did so in a forum published in the leftist journal *Art Front*. Benton was asked by Stuart Davis, an outspoken political antagonist, whether he believed that the future of American art lay in the Middle West. Benton answered, "Yes." The reasons he put forward were not very convincing (for example, that the Middle

West was, on the whole, the least provincial area in America) and could only be explained by his overwhelming frustration with the art scene in New York at the time.[18] But statements like these by Benton (and Wood) gave some substance to their critics' assertions during the 1930s that they were provincial and isolationist.

A problem with the regionalist label was that it was vague and contradictory and therefore also often misleading. It was often used as a rallying cry for its supporters or as a term of opprobrium by its critics rather than as an expression conveying specific meaning. The first examples of regionalist paintings are usually dated to the late 1920s. Curry's *Baptism in Kansas* won him instant recognition when it was exhibited at the Corcoran Gallery of Art in Washington, D.C., in the fall of 1928.[19] A single painting likewise cast the spotlight on Wood when *American Gothic* won a bronze medal at the 1930 annual exhibition of the Chicago Art Institute. The curiously quaint portrait of a farmer and his daughter (or was it husband and wife?) gazing enigmatically at the viewer was popular with the public and attracted critical notice beyond Chicago in Boston and New York.[20] Benton, meanwhile, had become fairly well-known as a watercolorist, oil painter, art teacher, and muralist in New York City during the 1920s, especially for the mural series *The American Historical Epic*. But it was *America Today*, his first commissioned mural, which he executed for no pay in 1930 at New York's New School for Social Research, that garnered his first critical acclaim and elicited further mural assignments during the next several years, bringing him into increasing prominence.[21]

Curry met Wood in 1933 at the latter's art colony at Stone City, Iowa, close by his boyhood home of Anamosa, and served on the teaching staff there that summer. Benton met Curry in 1926 at a National Academy of Design exhibition, but not until 1934, when Benton and his wife began inviting Curry to spaghetti dinners in their New York apartment, did they really get acquainted. Benton and Wood had a brief encounter when the latter visited New York in October 1934. It was three months later, when Benton gave a lecture in Iowa City, that the two were able to sit down and talk, initiating a warm and lasting friendship. The three artists discovered that in addition to holding similar ideas about the need for a representational art based on a close relationship to the people and the land, they were congenial spirits who got along well together. None tried to upstage another, and all expressed their full, if sometimes critical, support for the work their colleagues were doing.[22]

But it was not until *Time* magazine ran a famous cover story on the subject in December 1934 that regionalism became widely recognized as a discrete phenomenon in the United States. Interestingly, the article never once used the word itself, referring instead to a new school of painters who were "bent on portraying the U.S. scene."[23] Twenty-six new painters were mentioned in the article, with separate paragraphs on Chicago, Detroit, Boston, California, and Taos, New Mexico. Charles Burchfield was identified as a pioneer of the movement, Reginald Marsh also merited a paragraph, and each had an example of his paintings reproduced in an extensive color section of the magazine. The three artists singled out for special attention, however, were Benton, Wood, and Curry. They would remain the ones most closely associated with the regionalist label and, in some accounts, they were the only regionalist painters. Wood, who received four paragraphs in the article, and Curry, with two, were pictured together wearing bib overalls at Wood's Stone City art retreat. *Time* reproduced two of Wood's paintings: *Dinner for Threshers* and—taking up an entire page—his instantly famous *American Gothic*. Curry was represented by his striking work *The Tornado*. Benton rated five paragraphs in the article, and not only were two of his works displayed—*Cotton Town* and *The Jealous Lover of Lone Green Valley*—but his 1925 self-portrait also graced the cover, making him the first artist so honored by the magazine.[24]

Although the three midwesterners had been steadily gaining recognition for their work, the *Time* article catapulted them into the public consciousness, and for a time they became the glamour boys of American art. The tone of the article was entirely positive. Though the articulate and outspoken Benton might just as well have been accorded the laurel, *Time* identified Wood as the "chief philosopher and greatest teacher" of the new trend in representational art. Wood taught at his art colony at Stone City in 1932 and 1933 and, beginning in 1934, at the University of Iowa. In 1935 he published "Revolt against the City," the best-known and most widely read piece on the purposes and motivations behind regionalism. That article, however, although expressing Wood's views and using statements and writings of his, had been ghostwritten, or at least put together, by his friend and colleague Frank Luther Mott of the university's journalism department.[25] As a lecturer, interview subject, and author of books and articles, Benton was much more prolific—and bombastic—than Wood. His autobiographical accounts—*An Artist in America* (1937, with later additions) and *An American in Art* (1969)—sparked enthusiastic responses from readers and reviewers, even among outspoken critics of his painting style. Wood, meanwhile, who talked for several years about working on his own autobiography, managed only to produce a manuscript carrying his life up to the age of ten, which was never published. Curry, meanwhile, preferred to work rather than talk or write, relying on his colleagues for the most part to speak for the movement, to the degree that it actually was one.

For all his loquacity about his art and about what he and his friends Wood and Curry were doing, Benton never felt comfortable with the regionalist label. In 1943, by which time the phenomenon was in rapid decline, Benton told an interviewer that he did not characterize his art by any ism. He had been called an advocate of regionalism, he allowed, but it was merely a word, one "without much meaning, a typical art critic's refuge which saves him (or her) the bother of thinking." His art, Benton pointed out, had dealt with the whole of American culture and in so doing ran "from coast to coast, a pretty big region."[26] Back in 1924, when he had returned home to Missouri to be with his dying father, Benton had rediscovered the pleasures and the wonder of places and people in America's hinterland. In meeting and talking to his father's old political cronies and other Ozarks dwellers, Benton was moved by a great desire to learn more about the America he had glimpsed there and "to pick up again the threads of my childhood."[27] Beginning the following year, he made a practice of taking his sketch pad and going off for several weeks or months every year to trail through the country—the South, the Ozarks, the West, and elsewhere—to connect with the people there and bring back material that he could use in his paintings. Eventually, he made contact with almost every part of the country.[28]

Wood, whose work was more localized in the Midwest, particularly around the area where he lived and had grown up, in northeast and east-central Iowa, felt more comfortable with the regionalist label than did Benton. In "Revolt against the City" the Iowan emphasized that he was not a booster for any particular section of the country; rather, he called for establishing regional art centers where painters and writers could describe and interpret the special characteristics of each region. Out of the resultant ferment, "a rich American culture" would grow in somewhat the same fashion that Gothic architecture had emerged from competition among different French towns to construct the largest and finest cathedrals.[29]

Wood promoted regionalism through his painting, his writing, and his teaching as well as by serving briefly as state director of the Public Works of Art Project, funded by the federal government as a relief measure. Both his colleagues also involved themselves in teaching, but Curry had the distinction of becoming the first university artist in residence in the country when the College of Agriculture at the University of Wisconsin persuaded a donor to fund the project in 1936. Curry's arrival in Madison the following spring was widely noted in the press and hailed as a new approach to art education and bringing art to the public. Like Benton, whose travels frequently took him to the far corners of the United States, but unlike Wood, who except for several trips to Paris tended to stay closer to home, Curry had led a peripatetic life, growing up in Kansas, studying art in Kansas City and Chicago, attending college in Pennsylvania, living in New Jersey and New York City, making a pilgrimage to Paris, and living in the affluent art colony of Westport, Connecticut, before moving to Madison. No rustic rube was he. Yet on establishing himself in Wisconsin, he quickly formed warm relationships with neighbors and colleagues at the university as well as with farmers, Main Street citizens, and art students who came to him for advice. An editorial written at the time of his death extolled his common touch: "He was not content in the artist's attic. He was a stranger to the ivory tower. He knew what art means in its deeper significance and he toiled to show it to others, to inspire an appreciation and an active interest in it for thousands of people to whom it had been something a million miles away from their own lives."[30] Curry's work at the University of Wisconsin allowed him to implement in practice his long-held theory that art should be made directly relevant to rural people's daily lives.[31]

As Benton once described the roles that he and his congenial colleagues played out, Curry was cast as the typical Kansas farmer, Wood became the standard Iowa small-towner, and he was just an Ozark hillbilly. "We accepted our roles," Benton observed, adding, "Actually the three of us were pretty well educated, pretty widely read, had had European training, knew what was occurring in French art circles, and were tied in one way or another to the main traditions of western painting."[32] Herein lies a clue to understanding regionalism. It was a real enough phenomenon, discussed and analyzed by art critics, acknowledged by at least some of its practitioners, and applauded by the public. But there was always an element of staginess about the whole thing, a certain wink that came along with the delivery. Being identified as regionalist was good for the artists; they were able to sell more of their paintings, and at higher prices. It was good for the art establishment; it gave them a way to categorize people and provided them with something to discuss. It was good for the public; it provided them a sense of understanding what it was all about. It was even good for those who were left out of or were even opposed to regionalism; it gave them something to rail and fulminate against.

Regionalism was useful also to future students of history, for it provided them a window through which to peek into the culture of the 1930s and a means by which to better understand various developments and issues. Regionalism, in the first place, tells us something about the social and cultural crisis of the 1930s and about how aesthetic issues became bound up in it. It also obviously was involved in the history of American art, emerging as the most significant development in painting during the decade. Beyond that, its rise and fall illuminated the system of art patronage and the way reputations were made and broken. Again, as with many other things during the 1930s, regionalism reflected a continuing concern about and dedication to the concepts of "the people" and democracy, and it reenacted a special relationship that came to exist between artists, writers, performers, politicians, and others, on the one hand, and the general public, on the other.[33] Beyond that, regionalists exhibited an ambivalence toward their lives and the culture in general, which can be seen time and again in many places and forms. Also, regionalism was controversial, in large part, because of the political overtones that accompanied it, and therefore it contributed a useful perspective on American politics during a highly politicized decade. Finally, the movement and its outstanding representatives—Benton, Wood, and Curry—provided a helpful way of understanding midwestern culture, which shaped their mentality and art, and its small towns, from which they all derived.

The stock market crash of 1929 occurred in the midst of the regionalists' emergence to public recognition at the end of the prosperity decade. The full effects of the Depression took awhile to make themselves felt, but for the rest of the 1930s, the economic crisis facing the nation became the dominant fact in people's lives. No one escaped its impact. Regionalism arose and declined within this context. It was not an economic crisis alone; the effects of factory closings, rising unemployment, farm destitution, and the widening circle of poverty manifested themselves across society, politics, and culture generally. Capitalism found itself under siege. Radical political forces gained strength. The fate of democracy itself was called into question. In all areas of American life, it was a time of questions, doubts, fears, and unravelings. But it was also a time of opportunity—for the expression of new ideas and assumptions, new ways of looking at things, and new options, hopes, and dreams.

The Depression cannot be understood without connecting it to the immense changes that culture and society had been undergoing for the better part of a century. Central to these developments was the transformation of the United States after the Civil War from a rural, agrarian society to an urban, industrial one. Historians, philosophers, social critics, and intellectuals in general attempted to understand and explain this phenomenon and to formulate prescriptions for coping with it. Frederick Jackson Turner, Thorstein Veblen, William James, John Dewey, Charles Beard, and Lewis Mumford were a tiny handful among scores of commentators who addressed the challenge of modernity.

Artistic expression responded, too. The New York Armory Show of 1913, which introduced Americans to new styles and trends in European art, was an eye-opener and a shock. Benton, who had studied for three years in Paris, spent the decade experimenting with modernism, going through phases of impressionism, neo-impressionism, Cézannism, synchronism, and constructivism.[34] Wood got to Paris to study three times during the 1920s. Both his and Benton's mature styles were heavily influenced by the modern art they came into contact with in their journeys and studies.[35] Curry made a pilgrimage to Paris, too, but he paid little attention to the new forms of art developing there, and his painting style remained unaffected by them.[36]

By the 1930s, a whole succession of European trends had come and gone in the United States, some with more lasting impact than others. Benton and Wood believed that the eastern art establishment had become thoroughly dominated by Parisian influences. Their particular nemesis was abstraction, which both had experimented with but then abandoned during the 1920s. Although they probably exaggerated the extent to which artists, critics, and museums were in the thrall of Paris, they were correct in noting the division that existed between those who focused on artworks as formal and technical problems to be solved and who found their meaning in the canvases and the paint themselves, on the one hand, and those who sought a social context for their art and discovered their meaning in the interaction between the artist and the "real world," on the other. In part then, the cultural crisis of the 1930s constituted a crisis of meaning, relating to the function of art and artists—a crisis that would have occurred regardless of the country's economic condition.

The cultural crisis of the 1930s was bound up in the implications of the new urban-industrial order, a phenomenon exacerbated by the economic problems facing the country. What was the future of capitalism, industry, urban America, and rural areas left behind? Who would address the problems unleashed by uncontrolled economic forces? How would issues of power, wealth, inequality, and social disorder be resolved? What role could ordinary citizens play in a system dominated by oligarchic forces? What function did art perform in depicting the realities of this new order, in understanding the forces that were operating, and in working to solve social problems? American artists seldom thought about these issues before the turn of the century. The ashcan school of art of the early 1900s moved in the direction of a more realistic depiction of society. During the late teens and early 1920s, Benton moved in radical circles in New York City that advocated the making of a "social art" that could bring about revolutionary change. But he tired of the interminable wrangling, grew impatient with the heated polemics, found new ways to connect with ordinary people after he took to the road with his sketchbook in 1925, and by 1930 found himself on the other side of the divide from the Marxists and Communists with whom he had earlier consorted.[37]

The revelation of the 1920 census that, for the first time, more than half the U.S. population lived in urban areas (put another way, less than half lived in rural areas) caused considerable comment and discussion during the ensuing decade. In the 1930s, which witnessed a back-to-the-land movement because of the hard economic times, the long urbanization trend was temporarily reversed, but Americans were made aware in many ways of the declining importance and influence of small towns and rural areas. The 1920s had witnessed a "revolt from the village," as writers such as Sinclair Lewis and H. L. Mencken pummeled small-town backwardness and provincialism, but the decade also gave birth to a reaction in the form of a new regard for history, a new interest in folk songs and folklore, efforts to resuscitate old-time fiddlers' contests and old-fashioned dancing, and a push to restore traditional American values. Such nostalgia and history-mindedness were manifested by Henry Ford's historical re-creation, Greenfield Village; their downside could be seen in movements like Prohibition and the Ku Klux Klan. In a society where success was measured largely by progress, change, and forward movement, efforts to recall the past or to preserve it bucked prevailing winds.[38]

Regionalism, in one sense, reflected an effort by artists, writers, intellectuals, planners, and others to maintain a sense of tradition, of balance and order, of closeness to the land and identification with place, of face-to-face connections with other people, civility, and mutual help. But to argue that the work of Benton, Wood, and Curry in the main glorified rural people and rural places, displaying a nostalgic glow and evading political questions, would be misleading. Benton, especially, did not limit his subject matter to small towns and farms. His early murals *America Today* and *The Arts of Life in America* pulsated with the sights and sounds of the city, and his later ones depicting the social histories of Indiana and Missouri gave considerable attention to industrial progress and business activity in places like Kansas City and St. Louis. As a child in Neosho, he had been captivated by railroads and machines, a fascination that never left him. They appeared prominently in his work during the 1920s and '30s. He observed, "An artist must be alive to what is going on. Ours is a mechanical age and we all live in an atmosphere of machines and vast building activities." Gadding about America, he observed and sketched many different kinds of industrial activities. Writing about his travels during the late 1920s in *An Artist in America*, he noted, "I got into the great steel mills, shipbuilding plants, and other industrial concerns of the country. I made hundreds of drawings—of furnaces, converters, cranes, drills, dredges and compressors, rigs and pumps, rakes, tractors, combines, and oldfashioned threshing machines. I stuck my nose into everything."[39]

Grant Wood, it should be acknowledged, largely shunned depicting modern machinery and devices in his landscapes and scenes of rural and small-town Iowa. The nostalgic glow of his vision of a bygone rural age no doubt contributed to the popularity of his work. Nor could one find many motorized vehicles and machines in Curry's work, but the mural he executed for the Bedford Junior High School in Westport reflected his interest in modern popular culture, with its references to Popeye and Olive Oyl, Mickey Mouse, Charlie Chaplin, Will Rogers, and other cultural icons. Benton, like Wood and Curry, turned his attention increasingly away from the city and toward the country as the 1930s wore on, which can be interpreted as an evasion of the realities and trends encompassing American society.

But what the regionalists chose to paint can be seen in another light. They did not presume that they could depict all of America; it was too vast, too complex, too contradictory. Benton, on his energetic journeys around the country, exhibited an unlimited appetite for new experiences and new subjects, but even he had his limits. What the regionalists preached was that artists could represent best what they had personally experienced and what they understood best. This meant being rooted in place and establishing close connections with the people among whom they lived. That explains why Wood worked so hard to encourage Benton to return home to the Midwest in 1935, and why he pushed the University of Wisconsin to invite Curry to be an artist in residence the following year.[40]

Midwesterners, of all people, were especially concerned during the 1930s about the future of the rural and small-town culture that had evolved there over the previous century. During the 1920s, with the rapid increase in automobile use and the expansion of the road network, the introduction of radio and the maturation of the movie industry, the increasing availability of electricity and the proliferation of electrical appliances, the beginning of the chain-store movement, and a variety of other modernizing developments, midwesterners were able to enjoy and appreciate improvements occurring in their lives, if they could afford them. But they were also worried about the implications of these changes for their small towns and farms. Automobiles made it easier to bypass the closest town and drive further to bigger centers to shop. Trucks began to replace railroads for transporting agricultural products to market, and buses hauled increasing numbers of passengers. Many small towns witnessed population losses for the first time during the 1920s, and the hard times that followed only added to their problems.

Forty years earlier the historian Frederick Jackson Turner had suggested a reason for concern in enunciating his famous frontier thesis of American history. Turner, who had gone on from the University of Wisconsin to a professorship at Harvard, died in 1932, but his ideas never seemed more relevant. Politicians from the La Follettes of Wisconsin to Franklin Roosevelt in Washington invoked Turner's thesis in their efforts to explain the Depression.[41] Benton had read Turner during the late 1920s, although he denied that the historian's ideas had significantly influenced him. "I did not at any time think of Turner's thesis as affording pictorial material," he later wrote the art historian Matthew Baigell. "Turner's 'Frontierism' lent support, however, to my own more paintable conceptions of the development of our American culture—development through 'action of the people' as they moved west with the advancing frontier."[42]

Whatever influence Turner's ideas may have had on the regionalist painters, the notions that the end of the frontier had been reached and that the United States needed to come to grips with problems unleashed by the new urban-industrial order formed the backdrop for their work during the 1930s. Explicitly or implicitly, Benton, Wood, and Curry painted pictures arguing for the significance of rural, small-town America. Without denying the importance and even dominance of urban society, they wanted people to recognize and acknowledge their existence. Cities had a tendency to distance people from each other, from social institutions, and from the technologies that increasingly shaped their lives. In the country, people could be closer to nature, to other people, and to the truths that gave meaning to their lives.

Regionalists understood that, beyond the social, political, and economic crises confronting Americans during the 1930s, people were facing a crisis of meaning in their lives. The direction in which American art was heading was too much dictated by alien influences, with understanding and significance being lost in the process, they believed. Benton and Wood had been much affected by modernism and continued to utilize elements of it in their work during the 1930s, but they parted company with it when it became wholly abstract. In their opinion, abstraction divorced art from the people and places that infused it with meaning. Regionalism, at its heart, was an effort to redirect American painting back toward a representational mode and to reconnect the artist to the human sources that lay at the foundation of all significant art.

Although work done by the regionalists grew increasingly popular with the public and also won the plaudits of many art critics, Benton believed that the art establishment in the United States was dominated by muddle-minded aesthetes who were in the grip of foreign ideas. Among their supporters, the regionalists were championed as heroes leading art back to its basis in real life, returning it to the people, and rooting it in experience. Unlike abstractionists, who thought of art in purely formal terms with no relation to reality, and unlike the Communists, who viewed it simply as propaganda, Benton and his colleagues were, according to Benton, "more interested in things than in ideas."[43] In this, they took their cue from John Dewey and early twentieth-century pragmatists, who emphasized facts and practical results and called for an art rooted in everyday experience. In *Art as Experience,* published in 1934, Dewey urged the connection "of aesthetic experience with normal processes of living."[44] Learning from his experiments in modernism that design is important, Benton parted company with modernists in their excessive attention to form. He was interested in things, he said—in "faces, tree trunks, old shoes." He traveled the country in search of them and worked them into his finished easel paintings and murals. He liked painting murals, he told someone, "because I can include more stuff in them. I'm interested in American life. I would like to enclose it all."[45]

Ironically, regionalism's greatest publicist among art critics was Kansas-born Thomas Craven, who had been one of the earliest promoters of modernism in the United States. During the second decade of the twentieth century, while Benton was trying to establish himself in New York City, he and Craven had become good friends, even rooming together at times, and Benton had helped the aspiring writer think through and write some of his early critical essays. By the early 1930s, having changed his mind and become an outspoken critic of modern art, Craven had established a considerable reputation for himself as a commentator. His enthusiastic pleading for Benton and the regionalists was highly beneficial to them, but his increasing reputation within the art community as a narrow-minded, extreme, and even anti-Semitic chauvinist later backfired against the triumvirate and led their enemies to associate them with his shortcomings.[46]

Many of the more objective critics likewise recognized the value of regionalism's contribution to American art during the 1930s. In his 1939 survey, *Modern American Painting*, Peyton Boswell Jr., editor of *Art Digest*, deemed the rise of American Scene painting to be "the most healthy development in the entire three hundred years of American art history." The artist, he believed, was retreating from foreign isms and returning to the soil for subject matter, stepping "down from his ivory tower and out into the fields, the streets and the factories." Increasing numbers were discovering "paintable America through realistic observation of the everyday life about them." The return to the soil not only became the dominant trend of the 1930s but, overall, was a salutary one, in Boswell's estimation. "A new, tingling sense of participation has come to the public—to the workers in the factories, to the cowhands in the West, to those who love the land on which they live and the people with whom they mingle. This mutual affection for America and things American has brought a greater communion between artist and public."[47]

Whereas Benton blamed Parisian influences and pressures for the shift toward nonrepresentational art, Wood understood the phenomenon more as an aspect of regional "colonialism," in which too much deference was paid to eastern cities, and felt the chance for an independent art was being squandered in the process. He contended, "Our fight in art is not with French influences, but with that older and more basic colonial idea. I feel that the break will come in the West rather than in the East where the colonial tradition has a stranglehold."[48]

Regionalism's mid-1930s dominance in the American art world proved short-lived. The U.S. entry into World War II shifted people's focus from internal problems to the international scene. The regionalists got lumped by many observers with the America First movement and with reactionaries who resisted international involvement. This was unfair. Benton, especially, supported President Roosevelt's foreign policies. After Pearl Harbor, he painted a series of garish propaganda posters to stimulate public backing for the war effort. Tragically, Wood died of liver cancer in 1942, two hours shy of his fifty-first birthday, and Curry succumbed to heart disease at the age of forty-eight four years later. What chance the regionalists had for making a comeback and further developing their art was lost with these men's premature deaths. Benton persisted, continuing to work until the day he died in 1975, at the age of eighty-five. He had much good work left in him, including a mural for the Truman Presidential Library, but for the most part, his interests turned toward nature and scenes in the West, and the controversies and attention-grabbing canvases that had brought him so much notoriety during the 1930s became a thing of the past. In the vacuum created by regionalism's demise, abstract expressionism and the New York art scene rose to a position of absolute dominance by midcentury, leaving regionalism seemingly in the dustbin of history. Did the regionalists deserve more than a footnote in that narrative?

There is a twofold problem with the scenario just sketched. In the first place, greater continuity existed between regionalism and abstract expressionism than this account implies. In the second, regionalism deserves far more attention and respect than those who would relegate it to a temporary aberration from a steady march toward abstraction are willing to confer on it. Although largely counterintuitive, significant connections can be drawn between the midwestern American Scene painters and their abstract successors. Although very different in most respects and certainly not united in method or purpose, the two movements were linked concretely by the mentoring relationship that existed between Thomas Hart Benton and his student Jackson Pollock, who emerged as the most prominent practitioner of abstraction during the late 1940s and 1950s. Somewhat like his teacher, who had begun as an abstractionist and then repudiated it for a representational form of art, Pollock began painting in Benton's style, later switching over to his drip method of painting. Although he was the student most strongly influenced by Benton's theories and teaching, Pollock deprecated what he had learned from him, saying, "My work with Benton was very important as something against which to react very strongly, later on; in this, it was better to have worked with him than with a less resistant personality."[49]

Benton's influence on Pollock operated through his theories of form and design. Although Pollock expressed his designs abstractly rather than representationally, a clear similarity can be perceived in the methods each used to construct the relationships among the separate elements in their works. Benton's continuing emphasis on form and design provides a clue to the second way in which regionalism and abstract expressionism were connected: Contrary to much naive discussion of Benton's and Wood's work, the two artists never painted scenes directly from life, attempting to render as close a likeness as they could. Both worked meticulously and laboriously to re-create the images they observed with their own eyes and to render them artistically in a way that would have a dramatic effect on the viewer.[50]

Benton, Wood, and Curry were masters of self-publicity, even if they were unable to convince everyone of their worth. Curry was the most straightforward and least flamboyant of the three. He won the praise and admiration of people by his simple, unpretentious approach to his work and by his congenial personality. A shy, private man, he disliked speaking to formal groups, but his gentle, soft-spoken demeanor won him friends.[51] For someone who had lived so long in the eastern metropolis and who had moved easily in sophisticated society, counseling farmers and small-town people on how to produce better art, of necessity, required a certain amount of posturing. But Curry never was much for acting or putting himself on display, and, of the three, he remained least in the public eye.

Wood seemed to change the most as he progressed with his career. In high school, it was said, he was so bashful that he barely could look a person in the eye. He retained a curious habit of weaving from side to side as he talked, and his speaking style was very slow and deliberate.[52] Though he once built a house for himself and his mother and was a good craftsman, he always gave an air of impracticality. He didn't like to be bothered with ordinary details. One could never be sure if he would make a train connection, and matters concerning money seemed to constitute a foreign language to him. But cherubic-faced Wood was not quite the innocent rube that those who were unacquainted with him might have surmised. Very likable and possessed of a gentle humor, he easily captured the affection of people and made them want to protect him. His assistant Park Rinard called him "essentially a simple man."[53] But Wood proved masterful in managing his career, once he got rolling, painting pictures year by year during the 1930s that combined just the right amount of satirical humor and idealized description to make the critics and the public try to anticipate what his next move was going to be. The fun he poked at the ladies of the Daughters of the American Revolution (DAR) in *Daughters of Revolution* (1932) elicited considerable backlash. Wood admitted his purpose, observing, "I'd rather have people rant and rave against my painting than pass it up with 'Isn't that a pretty picture?'"[54]

Benton was the master showman of the group. Never shy, never reticent, he hankered after the limelight, beginning in childhood, and much of the time he found himself bathed in it. His father, Congressman Maecenas E. Benton, had groomed his firstborn to follow him into law and politics, but young Tom had rebelled, searching after attention in other arenas. Loud and boastful as a lad, he was so enamored of the first-person pronoun that his father began calling him "the Big I." Never doubting his own genius and his special destiny as a young man, he weathered long years of apprenticeship before garnering public acclaim during the early 1930s. After that, his talkativeness could not be curbed. Although his father had failed to mold his attitudes and ambitions, much of the elder Benton's combativeness and style rubbed off on young Tom. "He was in politics all his life," his son, Thomas, remarked of him, adding, "He promoted himself as an artist as if he were running for Congress. He had political abilities for winning friends and influencing people. That he inherited. It was congenital."[55]

Both his words and his art reflected Benton's urge to flamboyance. His friend Curry observed in 1943, "Tom enjoys a good fight and he has carried enough weight to make his ideas stick. I don't mean to infer that Benton goes out of his way to quarrel, but neither will he hold his tongue in deference to the feelings of those people who can 'dish it out,' but, notoriously, 'can't take it.'" A not-too-friendly Reginald Marsh put a different twist on it: "Benton is a colorful, scrappy, uncouth person, with a demonic energy and a strong tendency to publicize himself."[56] That Benton relished the limelight is clear from his own writings. In *An Artist in America* he described the unprecedented prominence that had come to him as an artist as a result of his provocative murals, the myriad controversies he became embroiled in, and the prominent display of his work in the picture weeklies. "As is well known," he wrote, "I found no difficulty in accepting this new situation. For nearly ten years I lived in a generally continuous glare of spotlights. Like movie stars, baseball players and loquacious senators, I was soon a figure recognizable in Pullman cars, hotel lobbies and night clubs. I became a regular public character. I signed my name for armies of autograph hunters."[57]

Benton's detractors suspected that he and his art were merely an act—that he was no more than a cartoonist and a con artist. Toward the end of Benton's life, Mike Wallace of *60 Minutes* quoted a critic who had referred to him as "cornball" and asked whether it was true. Benton shot back, "Probably. What of it?"[58] Clement Greenberg, whose critical outlook veered 180 degrees from Benton's, said he thought of the painter as an actor, no more than a source of hot air.[59] No doubt Benton had a tendency to lead people on and enjoyed acting out his self-appointed role as the Peck's Bad Boy of the art world, but even when he was having fun, a serious intent usually lurked behind it. He admitted that he sometimes talked too loud and resorted to "linguistic flourishes" to make his points.[60] But Lewis Mumford, acknowledging Benton's tendency to strut and shout, reminded people, "Benton is a complex man, and his real talents as a painter begin at the point where its ballyhoo gestures and his sentimental rhetoric leave off."[61]

Had they lacked talent, Benton, Wood, and Curry would have been unable to successfully assert themselves during the 1930s and would be unremembered today. Added to their talent and to their ability to speak to the times, they had the ability to connect with the public and to take advantage of the resources available to them, thereby making a major impact. They were uniquely qualified and situated to pursue a democratic art during a decade that witnessed a flowering of the democratic spirit.[62] In the nation's capital, Roosevelt was constructing his New Deal around the need to protect and assist "the forgotten man." He and his liberal cohorts aimed their rhetorical fusillades against the "economic royalists" and the "money-changers in the temple." Middle-brow culture burgeoned, appealing as it did to a continually expanding audience, with offerings like *March of Time* newsreels (1935), new picture magazines (*Life* in 1936 and *Look* in 1937), and musical offerings like *Porgy and Bess* (1935). During the decade, Mr. Smith went to Washington, Huey Long was already there, and Father Charles Coughlin hoped to join them. Sinclair Lewis warned Americans that if the wrong people got into power, "it could happen here," but Carl Sandburg expressed an unbounded faith in Americans in *The People, Yes*. Will Rogers, who obtained his information from reading the newspapers, was America's favorite political philosopher; Dr. Francis Townsend, its most popular medical doctor. Popular culture blossomed with radio programs like *Amos 'n' Andy*, movie musicals like *Gold Diggers of 1933*, and the rise of jazz and swing. Shirley Temple was America's sweetheart. The St. Louis Cardinals "Gashouse Gang" endeared themselves to baseball fans. Mickey Mouse emerged as a huge culture hero, prompting the historian Warren Susman to observe that although political historians might characterize the period as the age of Roosevelt, cultural historians would most probably classify it as the age of Mickey Mouse.[63]

The ambivalence that characterized the regionalists' paintings of heartland scenes reflected the uncertainty of their feelings about their own origins in the region. They, like their fellow midwesterners, remained attached to their birthplaces even though, at the same time, they often seized the first opportunity to escape. Benton finished high school at a military academy in Alton, Illinois, before heading off to art school in Chicago, later furthering his studies in Paris before settling in New York. Curry left home at eighteen to study at the Kansas City Art Institute and then at the Art Institute of Chicago and Geneva College in Pennsylvania. Wood, who left for art school in Minneapolis on the day of his high school graduation, returned to Cedar Rapids and remained there until he was forty-four, when he moved 25 miles south to Iowa City to teach art at the University of Iowa.

Cedar Rapids, home to a growing population of more than 25,000 people during the early 1900s, was really a small city rather than a small town. Wood had lived his first ten years as a typical farmer's child on a farm 3 miles east of Anamosa, a town of 2,000 people 25 miles northeast of Cedar Rapids. Educated in a one-room school, largely insulated from the outside world, Wood displayed an early interest in and talent for drawing, something his mother, Hattie, encouraged but his father, Maryville, an educated and progressive man in his own way, considered impractical. Wood's unfinished ghostwritten autobiography, which ends with his father's premature death when the boy was only ten years old, depicts his father as a stern, rather aloof man who was incapable of granting his son the full approval and affection that he sought. One can perceive the authoritarian Maryville in the stern images of men that Wood later depicted in paintings like *American Gothic* and *Parson Weems' Fable*.[64] If Wood was a latent or closeted homosexual, as writers such as M. Tripp Evans have suggested, his relationship with his assertively manly father may have been a significant part of the psychosexual dynamics that help explain his sometimes childlike behavior. Hattie, in contrast, was an understanding and affectionate person who lived with her son until she died in 1935, and Wood was always perceived as a mama's boy. Her presence can be felt in Wood's painting *Woman with Plants*; in *The Midnight Ride of Paul Revere*, a story she told her children when they were young; and in his lush Iowa landscapes, exuding health, vitality, and abundance.[65]

Whatever differences Wood may have had with his father, he later relied heavily on memories of childhood when painting scenes of rural, small-town Iowa. Like his truncated memoir, which left out most of the miseries and hardships of farm life, Wood's paintings generally invoked a cheerful, mythical image of life on the farm and of goings-on in Iowa's small towns. Paintings such as *Spring in Town*, which depicted a neat, orderly, and comfortably prosperous townscape with people engaged in a variety of tasks under the protective watch of a steepled church, and *The Birthplace of Herbert Hoover*, which pictured the president's hometown of West Branch, Iowa, as a quiet, peaceful, and contented community, untroubled by any obvious threats or dangers, typified Wood's output during the 1930s. That the painter actually harbored more complex feelings about small-town life than most of his paintings suggested can be seen in the nine drawings he executed for a special illustrated reprint of Sinclair Lewis's *Main Street*, published in 1937 by the Limited Editions Club. Wood was an admirer of Lewis's work and did not find it difficult to get into the spirit of the novel by satirizing characters such as Mrs. Bogart (*The Good Influence*), Jim Blausser (*The Booster*), and even the book's main protagonist, Carol Kennicott (*The Perfectionist*). That Wood shared many of his friend Benton's objections to class divisions and privilege in American society can be inferred from the two drawings he made of buildings, contrasting images in *Main Street Mansion* and *Village Slums*.[66] Wood's *Main Street* drawings suggest an artist holding a more critical view of the small town than he generally chose to depict. Hints of it could also be discerned in the satirical works he did during the early 1930s. Wood generally denied any satirical intent in his work (except for *Daughters of Revolution*), but it is clear that he harbored ambivalent attitudes, and this ambivalence shone through in a number of his paintings, adding to their appeal and popularity.

Curry's Kansas scenes, from *Baptism in Kansas* and *The Tornado* to his capitol mural in Topeka, likewise reflected a profound division in his own mind about his subject. They invited multiple interpretations and viewers were often confused regarding his true intent. The work he did later in Wisconsin was generally more obviously positive and approving of its subjects. Curry, like Wood, grew up on a farm. His parents, unconventional enough to have gone on a European honeymoon, operated a more prosperous farm than the Woods' had been in Iowa, and everything was up to date. Progressive in many ways, they were also old-fashioned in their devotion to hard work and old-style religion. Curry liked to say that he had been brought up on hard work and the short catechism. T. Smith Curry did not overtly stand in the way of his son's artistic interests, which were encouraged by his mother, Margaret, but he thought it strange that a husky twelve-year-old boy would be drawing pictures when there was farmwork to be done. Like Benton, and unlike Wood, who had had to scrape for every nickel he could save, Curry grew up in a family that was able and willing to support his training in art school. As with many other budding artists of the day, he wound up at the Chicago Art Institute, later learning the craft of magazine illustration in Harvey Dunn's New Jersey studio.[67]

By the time Curry got back to Kansas in 1929, having recently won recognition for his painting, his hometown of Dunavant, in northeastern Kansas, was fast becoming a ghost town. Earlier, it had been a typical railroad boomtown on the prairie—a commercial hub boasting four trains a day transporting grain and livestock to markets in Kansas City, 60 miles away, and hauling back hardware, clothing, and manufactured items for sale in Main Street stores. By the late 1930s, the railroad tracks had been removed, the schoolhouse was gone, and the town where Curry had attended school had virtually disappeared.[68] Its disappearance may help explain why the midwestern scenes he painted were set almost entirely in the countryside and almost never in town. Of his own hometown, he had little to rely on but memories.

Benton did not return to Neosho for half a century after departing it for Chicago, Paris, and, finally in 1912, New York. He received a rousing homecoming from townsfolk there in 1962 when he brought former president Harry Truman along with him on the train from Kansas City. But

Benton retained memories of the town, recollections reinforced on tours through countless small towns in almost every section of the country over many years. In 1972 he accepted a commission from Joplin, Missouri, where he had worked as a newspaper artist when he was seventeen years old, to execute a mural of the town on the occasion of its 100th anniversary celebration. In between times, Benton had traveled small-town America incessantly, watching it disappear before his eyes. "My early childhood," Benton began his autobiography, "was passed in a country radically different in atmosphere and flavor from that known to boys today."[69]

His birthplace of Neosho was a railroad town and the seat of Newton County in the southwest Missouri Ozarks. Benton remembered it as an old-fashioned and isolated community, but a pretty one, where old Civil War soldiers lounged about the livery stables or in the shade of store awnings and everybody moved at the unhurried pace of horse-drawn transportation. Celebrations of all kinds enlivened the town many times during the year, and band concerts on the square were a regular feature every Saturday night during spring, summer, and autumn. The Benton home was often not a particularly happy place, as the incompatible parents frequently bickered and fought. It was considerably livelier than most, however, for Maecenas Benton was a politician of wide acquaintance, and prominent lawmakers, from Champ Clark to William Jennings Bryan, dined at the family table. As was the case with many of his fellow small-town boys, his mother, Elizabeth, encouraged his creative and idiosyncratic tendencies, while his father resisted them and fumed.[70]

Benton's childhood recollections of Missouri called up "a very rustic and backwoods atmosphere. The country was isolated, self-sufficient. Corn and wheat were readily grown in the bottoms. Game and fish were plentiful. Life was easy and, although perfectly secure, had very much of a pioneer flavor."[71] Young Tom Benton hardly lived "a Huck Finn childhood," as some stories later claimed. After his father's election to Congress in 1896, the family moved back and forth between homes in Washington and Neosho for the next eight years. But he was strongly affected by his Missouri boyhood, writing later that life in the nation's capital could not compare with it. Most of his boyhood memories centered on southwestern Missouri. During the 1930s and 1940s, he eagerly accepted commissions to illustrate editions of Mark Twain's *Tom Sawyer* and *Huckleberry Finn* and his memoir *Life on the Mississippi*. He told a reporter that he reread the two novels every year, usually in February. In 1939, while working on drawings to illustrate *Tom Sawyer,* Benton noticed the changes that were overtaking the Missouri countryside. "Things are different back in the hills," he observed:

> Ten years ago I'd start out with a pencil and a notebook and a harmonica. I'd head for the country roads, cut across pastures and fallow fields, working along the way. Along about dark I'd stop at a farmhouse, ask for a meal and a night's lodging and even pay for it sometimes with my harmonica playing. We'd all sit around the parlor and play and talk. When I left, the whole family would stand on the front porch waving and calling to me to come back sometime.
>
>   You can't travel like that now. After the hazards of the depression too many persons are bitter and suspicious. So many families are on relief you're likely to be taken for a WPA snooper sent out by the government to see if the families deserve their $23 a month.[72]

World War II and rapid economic expansion in the 1950s changed things even more in rural America. Benton, of course, was getting older, but the country was undergoing profound transformation, too. Automobiles, television, new technology and gadgets, and a whole panoply of changes were combining to render the kinds of lives Curry, Wood, and Benton had known in Anamosa, Dunavant, and Neosho little more than nostalgic reverie. Small towns struggled on, but they lost their authority as the locus of American society. Cities housed most of the people now, and city ways dominated their behaviors. "The manners of the city had become the models for all manners," noted Benton in his eighties. "The question is whether this development—urbanization—is good or bad. I don't know. I know the country is a damn sight less interesting." Maybe the problem lay in himself, Benton speculated; maybe he had become less interesting. When he was young, he had had no trouble butting into conversations in the saloons and hotels where men ordinarily gathered. "Now they whiz by in fast cars on the way to the city. Try to talk to somebody and I get a look that says, 'What's that old goat after?'"[73]

By 1970, when Benton said that, small towns were clearly on the downswing and on the defensive. Back in the 1930s, when the regionalist painters featured small towns and the rural Midwest in their works, they had captured public attention with their vision. The basis of that appeal lay in the emotions that their images evoked in the public. Generally ambivalent, sometimes nostalgic, but always interesting, they ascended to the top of the art world for a short time. When World War II and postwar developments turned Americans' attention elsewhere, regionalism went into swift decline, but a strong undercurrent of support and enthusiasm for their art always remained. For people who understand the underlying value and interest of small towns, the regionalists remain a cultural treasure.

CHAPTER EIGHT

Ernie Pyle: Hoosier Vagabond and GIs' Friend

Throughout the war he would insist that a goodly number of the men he wrote about derived their strength of purpose from an upbringing close to nature or from the ties of a small community. His fondest profiles would be of men fresh from the country or small towns, unsullied by the fractiousness and wise-guy posturing of the big cities. . . . One of Pyle's biggest gripes was that from what his contemporaries read in the newspapers or heard on the radio, they could easily get the idea that American life centered in New York and Washington and sometimes Los Angeles—that nothing in between mattered. At great cost to himself, Pyle worked hard arguing for the specificity of person and place as an important part of our American past and present.

—David Nichols

For Ernie Pyle, the much-loved chronicler of the World War II GI, life became a series of escapes: first, from the farm where he grew up and from his hometown of Dana, Indiana; then, from his home state; later, from a desk job at the *Washington (D.C.) Daily News*; and after that, from a roving reporter assignment that carried him all over the United States, Canada, and Latin America during the late 1930s. Finally, he escaped from life itself, which had become for him—unbeknownst to his multitude of adoring fans—a frustrating series of encounters with alcoholism, depression, impotence, marital discord, and a nagging suspicion that life was meaningless. To the 13 million readers of his six-times-a-week column, which by the end was appearing in almost 400 daily and 300 weekly newspapers around the United States, Pyle stood for the prototypical small-town midwesterner, and he possessed an extraordinary capacity to understand and communicate the thoughts, feelings, and aspirations of the average soldier. In the public mind, he emerged as the quintessential Everyman, and in the process of writing about the great global conflagration he made it "Ernie Pyle's War."[1]

John Steinbeck, who like countless others became Pyle's friend instantly on meeting him, observed that World War II was actually two wars. The first was that of George C. Marshall, U.S. Army chief of staff, who presided over a huge logistical effort, putting 12 million men into the field against the armies of Tojo, Hitler, and Mussolini. An immensely complex and sophisticated operation arose to furnish the soldiers, sailors, marines, and airmen with weapons and equipment needed to keep them going against the enemy. Only about one in ten men in uniform actually engaged in combat at the fighting fronts. It was this huge organizational mechanism and the industrial might of the United States that—along with the skill, grit, determination, and sacrifice of the men (and women) in uniform—finally overwhelmed the aggressors, ensuring victory. The other war, in Steinbeck's telling, consisted of the day-to-day struggles and terrors experienced by the "grunts" in the field—fighting men imbued with ordinary hopes, dreams, and fears. They might have had a girl or wife back home, perhaps a kid or two, parents, neighbors, and friends in the community, all concerned about their safety and welfare and wishing for their safe return. These were real people, with real faces, names, and addresses. It was Ernie Pyle's special talent to be able to capture them in their particular, individualized humanity for his readers back home.[2]

Pyle was not unaware of and sometimes referred in his column to the first conflict—the one consisting of industrialized, mechanized, bureaucratized armies, navies, and air forces, wreaking havoc and wholesale destruction on each other and on civilians who happened to get in their way. But it was the second, more intimate war—the one involving individual combatants in their daily struggles with boredom, fear, danger, and death—that the famous war reporter was especially attuned to and uniquely qualified to write about. In a sense, he had been training all his life for the task. Growing up as an energetic but insecure youth on a small farm in west-central Indiana, he developed qualities that later served him well as a journalist: unassuming friendliness, broad curiosity, a tendency to listen more than to speak, and an unusual ability to look deep into people and establish empathy with them. As a practicing journalist, he paid keen attention to words and learned the intricacies of his craft. Six and a half years of traveling around North America as a roving correspondent during the 1930s had taught him how to live out of a suitcase and to search out human-interest stories virtually anywhere, almost by instinct. By the time the United States entered World War II, little adjustment was required on his part to transfer the skills and practices that had made him one of America's most popular regular newspaper columnists during the Depression to his new role as the reporter who made famous "the story of G.I. Joe."[3]

In the process, Pyle embodied, as few Americans ever have, the democratic spirit with which the United States engaged in its colossal wartime struggle to define the future of the world. In an environment transformed by industry, technology, and bureaucracy, this diminutive man from Indiana reminded people of their own roots in small-scale communities, conjuring up images of individual heroism and tenacity, even as historical processes were making it more difficult for those qualities to be observed. Instinctively a rebel and an outsider, Pyle championed and celebrated the average soldier. Ever committed to individualism and freedom of action, he lauded community involvement and civic responsibility and rendered meaningful the ultimate form of obligation—sacrificing one's life for one's country. In attempting to come to grips with his own newly won fame, Pyle acted out a democratic script, confronting the messy demands of popular acclaim and his own principles and standards.

For Pyle World War II, in a sense, arrived just in time. The conflict that caused so much death and destruction and that in the end took his life also provided him with a sense of purpose and personal satisfaction that had long eluded him. The man who appeared so down-to-earth and commonplace, so evidently secure and satisfied with what life had dealt him, was in fact a bundle of contradictions. Born on a farm a mile and a half south of the little town of Dana, on August 3, 1900, Ernest Taylor Pyle was the only child of Will and Maria Pyle, whose ancestry traced back to England and Scotland. Pyles had established themselves along the Indiana-Illinois border long before the town of Dana emerged in 1869. Ernie's grandfather Samuel Pyle had been brought as an infant to Helt Township from Chillicothe, Ohio, and his father, born in 1867, seldom ventured far from home. His mother, Maria Taylor, born three years later across the state line in Illinois, provided him with his middle name. The family, including his mother's older sister Mary, always referred to him as "Ernest," not "Ernie."

Growing up as an only child on a modest, moderately successful midwestern farm cultivated independence in the boy, but it also engendered loneliness. His feelings of awkwardness in the presence of town kids came through in a column he wrote during the 1930s. Dana, with its 850 or so residents, had been a pretty little town, he allowed, and its residents considered it a "medium-good town." In spite of that, "I have never felt completely at ease in Dana," he wrote. "I suppose it is an inferiority hangover from childhood. For I was a farm boy, and town kids can make you feel awfully backward when you're young and a farm boy."[4]

Ernie's mother was the biggest influence on him as he was growing up. Known for her frankness and tenacity, Maria Pyle was the emotional center of the family. She was a practical woman and had a temper that she sometimes expressed forcefully, but she was also tender-minded, thoughtful, and possessed of a lively sense of humor. She looked out for neighbors and friends and enjoyed visiting and caring for people when they were sick or needed assistance. Always a hard worker, she played the violin and attended neighborhood square dances to provide needed diversion. A devout Methodist and an advocate of prohibition, she nevertheless cast her vote for Al Smith in 1928 because he seemed to her to be the better man. Her son considered her the broadest-minded, most liberal woman in their neighborhood. He could not remember her ever telling him that he could not do something. She always indicated what she thought was right and wrong but left him to decide for himself. She never tried to hold him back but, rather, encouraged him to make something of himself. Many of Pyle's adult personality traits were modeled on his mother's.[5]

His father was quiet, never one to show much emotion. The son of a farmer, he became one himself but seemed happiest after World War I,

CHAPTER EIGHT

when he was able to rent out his acres and work as a carpenter and handyman. He was "a wizard with tools," according to his son, and really "a carpenter at heart." He earned respect among his neighbors for his talents and occupied a number of minor leadership roles, serving as worthy patron for the Eastern Star lodge and running a losing race as a Democratic candidate for township trustee in 1932. "He has never said a great deal to me all his life," Pyle reminisced about his father in one of his columns, "and yet I feel we have been very good friends." One thing he accomplished: putting his son behind a plow at the age of nine eradicated any desire the boy might have had to carry on the family tradition of farming.[6]

Although Ernie acquired an early distaste for farm labor and sometimes felt ostracized by kids in town, his childhood was a normal and generally happy one. He attended Sunday school regularly at a little rural Methodist church several miles away. His dog Shep was his constant companion. He liked to fish and sometimes hunted rabbits and trapped muskrats. Although as an only child he was allowed to roam by himself more than most of his peers, he had playmates in the neighborhood, including several cousins and Thad Hooker, his best friend, who was a year older.[7]

Though Thad encouraged him to try sports, Ernie's slight stature and awkwardness convinced him that he was no good at physical games, so he avoided them. He was, however, an inveterate prankster and practical joker. He found escape in reading and in dreaming of worlds that existed beyond Vermillion County and Indiana. When Ernie was fourteen or fifteen, Will Pyle bought an Overland automobile and taught him how to drive it. In 1916 Ernie got his own Model T and began to dream of becoming a race-car driver. Dana, right off U.S. Highway 36, was only 70 miles west of Indianapolis, the home of the Indianapolis 500, and Ernie festooned his room with sketches of sleek cars careening around its famous "brickyard." As an adult he confessed, "I would rather win that 500-mile race than anything in this world."[8]

Once he became a journalist, Pyle returned home frequently, but he came back to visit his parents, his Aunt Mary, and a few close friends, not to see the town. These visits provided an opportunity to write about his mother or father and to reminisce about his childhood or about the town itself. His regular readers came to identify and understand Ernie Pyle as a small-town boy from Dana, Indiana. Though some of his memories of the Midwest evoked melancholy, others recalled happier, carefree times that Pyle generally felt were lacking in the cities that he became acquainted with as an adult. In March 1937, after his mother suffered a stroke, he described the outpouring of love and generosity the misfortune elicited from neighbors and friends in the community. Food, flowers, help with chores, and other kindnesses were evident in abundance. "We who live in cities have almost forgotten what a good neighbor is," Pyle wrote afterward. "But the country people know. It's the same thing it was thirty years ago, and maybe even a hundred years ago. Let me tell you."[9]

It is ironic that Ernie Pyle, the boy who left home as soon as he was able to and who never succeeded in establishing a permanent home for himself, used his newspaper columns to depict an America where home remained the central anchor of people's lives and where small towns and farms reigned as ideal places for people to live. Undoubtedly, his prolonged absence from the farm and from Dana gave him a more favorable and forgiving attitude toward them than would have been the case had he actually been living there. But the sense of neighborliness that had surrounded him as a youth remained strongly ingrained in him; throughout his career, he would be careful to identify his subjects by name and by the place where they lived so that his readers would be able to picture them both as individuals and as products of their unique environments.

There was no question about Ernie's leaving home once he completed high school. He wanted to enlist in the service when the United States entered World War I in 1917, but he was too young. After graduating the following spring, he managed to get into the Navy Reserve, but it was too late for him to see any action. The following year, he enrolled in Indiana University, uncertain of his future but full of energy and ambition. Only 80 miles separated Bloomington from his hometown, but emotionally they were worlds apart.

At the university the young man blossomed. Shucking off some of his shyness and feelings of inferiority, he emerged by his senior year as a big man on campus. He pledged Sigma Alpha Epsilon fraternity, got introduced to hard drinking, and made a number of lifelong friends. One of them, Paige Cavanaugh, according to an often-told story, steered him in the direction of his future career by suggesting that he sign up for a journalism course because it was reputed to be a snap. Pyle, who took his major in economics, would probably have turned in that direction anyway. He poured most of his energies as a collegian into working on the student newspaper, rising to city editor and doing a stint as editor in chief. One of his colleagues on the *Indiana Daily Student* later recalled, "He was a shy boy but worked hard and made friends quickly."[10] During his junior year, demonstrating a wanderlust that never left him, he and three of his fraternity brothers accompanied Indiana University's baseball team on a Japanese tour, paying for their passage by working as cabin boys on the ship.[11]

He also fell madly in love. The object of his affection was a pretty redhead from Bloomington named Harriet Davidson. But when he dropped out of school during the spring of his senior year to take a job on the *Daily Herald* in La Porte in northern Indiana, they were separated by distance, and her ardor soon flagged. When she started dating someone else and returned his pin, Ernie was heartbroken and resolved to leave the state. For years thereafter, he studiously avoided returning to Bloomington, the hurt apparently being too much to bear.[12]

Luck was with him, however, as he received an offer soon from the *Washington Daily News* at a starting salary of thirty dollars a week. The paper, just a year and a half old, was an energetic one-cent tabloid, eager to attract readers away from the capital's four other dailies. Part of the Scripps Howard organization, it ran on aggressive reporting and smart writing.[13] The young man from Dana seemed somewhat out of place in the paper's newsroom. Thin and fragile-looking, bashful and unimposing in demeanor, he seldom impressed people at first glance. But his gift with words and his ability to concoct snappy headlines soon prompted his bosses to transfer him from his reporter's beat to the copyediting desk. Those were happy, heady days on a neophyte newspaper with a young staff, full of ambition and energy. They were not making much money, fellow newsman Lee Miller later recalled, but they were sure having fun.[14]

Having escaped the farm and Indiana, Pyle soon grew impatient with his desk job in Washington and with the general tone of American life during the prosperity decade. In Geraldine Siebolds, a vivacious, free-spirited civil service clerk from Minnesota, whom he met in the fall of 1923, he discovered a kindred spirit. Almost identical in age, they had similar outlooks on life. Both were rebellious; both displayed impatience with convention, rules, and boring people; and both were open to new experiences and new adventures. Attractive and witty, Jerry, as everyone called her, complemented Ernie's low-key diffidence. Her unconventionality extended to an aversion to the institution of marriage, but his background and deference to his parents' wishes would not permit him to live with her without an exchange of vows, so the couple compromised by getting married while pretending to their friends that they weren't wedded. She abjured wearing a ring and failed to observe their wedding anniversaries. The two began married life together in the summer of 1925, a happy and unconventional pair ready to take on the world.[15]

As Ernie's desk job became increasingly tiresome, he grew impatient to get away and travel. So the following spring, he and Jerry both quit their jobs, purchased a Model T Ford and a tent, and set off on a three-month swing around the rim of the United States. Afterward, following short intervals working for New York's *Evening World* and *Evening Post,* Pyle landed back at the *Washington Daily News,* and for the next four years he wrote a pioneering aviation column, which was carried by a number of other papers in the Scripps Howard stable. He began to develop the techniques of interviewing and writing personal profiles that he later honed to perfection as a roving reporter and as a war correspondent. Not content to focus merely on technological and organizational developments in the industry, he included many human-interest stories in his column. The Pyles' apartment in Washington became a sort of informal headquarters for anyone connected with the nascent aviation industry. Both Ernie and Jerry enjoyed mingling with the interesting characters that made it up. This was probably the happiest time of Pyle's life.[16]

When Ernie was asked to come back to a desk job, he reluctantly assented. For the next three years, he threw himself into the task of managing editor, doing an excellent job but hating it all the while. Being saddled with the responsibility of making the whole operation work smoothly left him little time for his own writing. His approach to the news as an editor foreshadowed his later practice as a traveling correspondent: something does not have to be significant to be newsworthy, but it does have to be interesting. To find interesting things to write about, reporters need to be interested themselves, he noted in a memo to his staff. "Always look for the story—for the unexpected human emotion in the story," he counseled. "You don't have to be smart-alecky or pseudo funny. Be human. Try to write like people talk."[17]

Effective and efficient as he was, no one anticipated his later emergence as a standout in the field. It would take a different venue—a pioneering one at that—to bring that about. Pyle's desk job continued to bore him even as his relationship with Jerry steadily unraveled. He wanted to have a child, but she resisted the idea. Once she got an abortion, disturbing him deeply. He told a friend that he had failed to achieve his ambitions. "In fact my life the last few years has gone in such a routine and deadening way that I am not sure any more just what my ambitions are."[18] A decade earlier, when he was just starting out at the *Daily News* and the future had looked full of possibility, he had told a colleague, "You know, my idea of a good newspaper job would be to travel around wherever you'd want to without any assignment except to write a story every day about what you'd seen."[19]

Remarkably, the opportunity to do just that opened up in early 1935. On doctor's advice, when he failed to shake the lingering effects of a bout of influenza, he obtained a three-month leave of absence to take an automobile trip through the South and Southwest. Then, when Heywood Broun, a popular *Daily News* columnist, went on vacation, Pyle filled his slot with eleven whimsical columns about his and Jerry's experiences on the road. Among those in Washington impressed by them was George "Deac" Parker, Scripps Howard's editor in chief, who perceived "a sort of Mark Twain quality" in them.[20] Pyle took advantage of the situation to press for an opportunity to have a trial run at the roving reporter column he had described earlier. Although nobody had ever done such a thing before, his bosses saw no harm in letting him try. The *Daily News* agreed to carry the column six days a week, and other papers in the chain were invited to run it as often as they wished. No restrictions were imposed on him; he was free to go wherever he liked and write about whatever struck his fancy. The fate of the column would be in his readers' hands. So, one day before his thirty-fifth birthday, Ernie and Jerry drove out of Washington on a journey that, with some interruptions and many adventures, would end only after he became a full-time war correspondent in Europe six and a half years later.[21]

His first column, about the Lindbergh baby kidnap-murder case, was datelined August 8, 1935, from Flemington, New Jersey, site of Bruno Hauptman's trial. With Jerry usually at his side, at least during the early years, Pyle crisscrossed the continent thirty-five times and made it to every state in the Union at least three times. Along the way, he wore out three cars and three typewriters. He enjoyed driving. Seldom pushing his speed over 50 miles per hour after several early close calls, he took advantage of his time behind the wheel to think through his columns before committing them to paper. Living out of a suitcase, he kept his wardrobe simple, owning just one suit, one sport jacket, and an extra pair of pants or two. Socks came in a single color—white—and he felt no need to own more than three ties.[22]

Pyle's friendly, unassuming demeanor opened doors for him wherever he went. People were happy to talk to him about their personal lives and the small towns and cities in which they lived. They often said, "Ernie talks our language." That, along with readers' vicarious thrill of traveling around the country with him as he tracked down material for his daily pieces, was the key to the column's success, thought Lee Hills, editor of the *Oklahoma News*. "It's folksy, human and as unsophisticated as nine out of ten readers," he admiringly wrote the roving reporter.[23] Pyle, for his part, had difficulty convincing people that what he was doing required intense concentration and industry on his part. "The thing is so damned hard," he wrote Lee Miller, "because people can't realize that I actually have to work; they feel that I'm practically on vacation; they don't realize that I work at reporting all day and must have the nights for writing."[24]

He toted around a little wooden box containing cards with names, addresses, and story ideas that he jotted down as they occurred to him. He also carried along an old German-made camera, and sometimes the *Daily News* featured one of his photographs along with his column. He pecked out his stories with respectable speed on an Underwood portable typewriter, corrected them himself, and then either retyped them or got Jerry to do it for him before mailing them in to Washington. The Post Office Department never lost a single one. Sometimes, after researching his stories during the day, he would write them up in his hotel room at night. More often, he would wait several days, accumulating impressions and information, and then hole up someplace for a day or two to churn out a week's worth of columns, each a thousand words, all at the same time. As the columnist Westbrook Pegler described the process, "Ernie Pyle writes his way along, keeps out of New York and other big cities that are overcovered by other reporters and writers, knows more small-town and dirt-road Americans than Jim Farley, and is better informed on the condition—or anyway the feeling—of the small people than Mrs. Roosevelt herself."[25] Altogether, the more than six years' worth of columns that he compiled constituted the equivalent of twenty-two full-length books.[26]

In search of material, he talked to literally thousands of people, making devoted friends of many of them, while constantly expanding his readership. It took a while for the column to catch on. Pyle's focus on ordinary people who sometimes did extraordinary things appealed to readers who were uninterested in or oversaturated with commentaries on politics, economics, and other important matters. Providing an escape from the serious business of the day, his columns were seductive in their attention to the doings of everyday life, rendering their author an insightful anthropologist of contemporary culture. In them, people could read about a town crier in Provincetown, Massachusetts; Detroit's municipal diver; a letter-writing farmer from West Jefferson, Ohio, who made state legislators sit up and listen; a sheepherder from Castle Rock, South Dakota; a Caterpillar driver in the California redwoods; a man who lived in a dump in Memphis; a train engineer from Virginia who played tunes on the whistle of his locomotive; a sponge fisherman in Florida; the mayor of a Seattle Hooverville; and, in Evansville, Indiana, the champion soda jerker of the United States. He set people firmly in their specific locales—small-town, country, or city—and in the process he threw light both on the people and on the places they derived from, as well as on the connections between them. During a decade that witnessed the rise of the documentary impulse, Pyle exemplified its powerful appeal.[27]

It was a rootless existence, all this traveling about. Once a year or so, he got back to Washington to touch home base. He also returned to Dana periodically to visit his parents. What most people did not realize was how enervating this rootlessness was for him—mentally, physically, and emotionally. Folks tended to assume that his wanderings were one long vacation, allowing him to go wherever he wanted and do whatever he pleased, writing up his experiences whenever the spirit moved. But digging out stories day after day, week after week, was incredibly hard work. Locating new subjects, conducting interviews, researching facts, looking for hooks on which to hang his columns, and finally writing everything up made for a constant daily grind. It may have appeared easy to outsiders, because Pyle seldom took any notes besides observing the spelling of people's names or jotting down addresses or a few facts and figures that would be difficult to recall. Out of these seemingly casual conversations came his columns. Larger cities and towns sometimes occupied him for several days, in rare cases a week or two. Most of the smaller places were in the spotlight for only a day. Always, there were new places to head for, to see what the morrow would bring.

Driving back to Washington in January 1937, after being on the road for seven months, Ernie found himself experiencing some weird emotions. As he and Jerry approached closer and closer to home, he became more and more anxious about the reception he would receive from the people he ran into. Once back in town among his friends and colleagues, however, his fears quickly dissipated. The episode was a reminder that ever since leaving Washington he had not had a place to call home. In one sense, his situation was interesting and exciting, but it could also be disconcerting. His columns, which were so geared to place and community and so emphatic about the importance of environment and circumstances in people's lives, contrasted starkly with his own lack of an anchor. "I am probably the only solvent person in America," he wrote in 1940, "who literally has no home, no place to hang his hat, no base to go back to and start away from." Two years earlier, while considering why he answered in the negative when people asked whether he was getting tired of traveling, he observed,

> I've tried to figure out myself why we haven't tired of it. And my conclusion is that our travel is an escape. In the end it sums up to the cowardly fact that we don't have to stay and face anything out. If we don't like a place, we can move on. If something happens that isn't pleasant, we can leave, and settle it later by letter, or just let it go forever. Stability cloaks you with a thousand little personal responsibilities, and we have been able to flee from them.[28]

Pyle's feelings on the subject remained ambivalent, and they varied over time. He loved the freedom, excitement, and lack of obligation that the open road offered. The actual writing of the columns was a difficult, even painful task, but the satisfaction they engendered in him made them worth all the effort. His favorite time was when he and Jerry were packed and ready to move on to a new town. But the constant, grueling pace exacted a heavy toll in mental and physical exhaustion, an inability to cultivate lasting relationships with people, and the pressures it imposed on their marriage. Too often, Ernie and Jerry compensated by excessive drinking, and she compounded the problem by getting hooked on drugs. Seductively appealing during the early years of their marriage, their bohemian lifestyle eventually palled, leaving Jerry more and more withdrawn as she lapsed into bouts of mental illness. She harbored mixed feelings about her husband's increasing success, resenting the way his editors and readers were displacing her in his life. He, in turn, disappointed that they were childless, suffered from impotence and grew weary of her manic unpredictability and suicidal impulses.[29]

A home of sorts eventually emerged in Albuquerque, where they built a house in 1940. Among all the places that Ernie especially enjoyed, including Seattle and Santa Fe, Albuquerque stood out. The Southwest was also his favorite region of the country, partly because of its amiable climate. His native Midwest, interestingly, held no special allure for him. Ernie and Jerry figured that by acquiring a home base for themselves they might be able to establish a semblance of the stability she yearned for, providing her some contentment and respite from the demons and sense of futility that were increasingly enveloping her.[30]

Now, however, foreign events began to move too fast to let them settle down in New Mexico and try to make it their home. Before the house was finished, Pyle was off to London for his first look at the increasingly critical military situation there. Even after World War II had broken out in September 1939, Ernie, like many of his fellow Americans, had been reluctant to pay much attention to it. By November 1940, however, with England alone remaining to hold out against Hitler, world events had become too compelling to ignore. His vivid descriptions of the London blitz and of the bravery of the British citizenry under fire garnered more attention than anything he had previously written. After several months of reporting from England, however, he headed back to the States, planning to continue his by now well-established routine of wandering around the country in search of human-interest profiles and offbeat stories.

Nothing could be routine again between him and Jerry, however, as her erratic behavior escalated and her roller-coaster moods veered ever more violently. Her drinking binges only added to her troubles, which were rooted in some sort of fundamental personality disorder. Her husband, unable to change her despite his best efforts, discovered some solace in liaisons with at least two other women, but these were begun only out of desperation in a vain search for the kind of intimacy that had eluded him in his marriage. The only thing he could have done that might have extricated her from her funk was to quit his travels and find a place where they could live a more settled life. But this might not have changed anything, and in any case, he was unwilling to give up his job. In a desperate move in April 1942, the two decided to get a divorce, figuring that the move might provide an emotional jolt that would lead Jerry to take control of her life. Ernie made it clear that he was ready to remarry her as soon as she made a real turnaround in her thinking and behavior, and in fact, they did get remarried later, by proxy, in March 1943 while he was reporting from North Africa. The divorce, however, worked no permanent change in her. Tragically, she would die of complications from influenza only seven months after he was killed in 1945.[31]

In the face of Pyle's multiple efforts to rescue his wife from the effects of mental illness, becoming a war reporter proved, in many ways, to be an excellent therapeutic move for him. In England and North Africa, and later in Italy, France, and the Pacific, he discovered a cause outside himself that was capable of absorbing all his energies and that engaged his moral sensibility. In the war that eventually took his life, he ironically found something that made life worth living. This, despite the fact that he hated war and all the death, destruction, and heartbreak it entailed. If truth be told, the man who became the most acclaimed reporter of World War II was a pacifist. Time and again, he found himself plaintively wondering, "What on earth are we doing here?"[32]

Though lauded by the soldiers he chronicled and by his admiring readers as some kind of saint, Pyle remained a complicated character. A colleague of his in a position to observe him closely, Don Whitehead of the Associated Press, told Lee Miller, "The Ernie Pyle of the column was a rather meek little guy who always is sort of shoved to one side by the bigger, tougher guys, who was beset by all kinds and sorts of ailments and misfortunes and a country boy trying to do the best he could." But there was another side of Ernie: "He was a tough, candid, experienced newspaperman who knew all the angles and how to take care of himself in any league." Whitehead added, "Along with his gentleness and understanding and kindness, Ernie was a hard drinking, hard working, hard cussing reporter."[33]

Twice, mental and psychological fatigue forced him to leave the battlefront and return to the United States for a respite, first after the Sicilian campaign and again after the liberation of Paris. "I have had all I can take for a while," he wrote in a valedictory column from Europe.

> I do hate terribly to leave right now, but I have given out. I've been immersed in it too long. My spirit is wobbly and my mind is confused. The hurt has finally become too great. All of a sudden it seemed to me that if I heard one more shot or saw one more dead man, I would go off my nut. And if I had to write one more column I'd collapse. So I'm on my way.[34]

What rendered the war meaningful for Pyle was the dignity and sacrifice of the individual soldiers he met and memorialized in his columns—not grand strategy, not the big picture, not even high ideals and principles. Large abstractions occupied little place in his thinking and found almost no expression in his writing. The war he wrote about was the one experienced by the individual man in uniform—"hardly ever bigger than a hundred yards on each side of him." It was "perpetual dust choking you, the hard ground wracking your muscles, the snatched food sitting ill on your stomach . . . heat and flies . . . the go, go, night and day . . . [the] emotional tapestry of one dull, dead pattern—yesterday is tomorrow . . . and when will we ever stop, and God, I'm so tired."[35]

Pyle made ordinary GIs the heroes of his column; in the process, he became their hero. In their minds, he was the reporter who best understood what was happening to them and what was going through their minds. Like Bill Mauldin's cartoon characters, Willie and Joe, Pyle's soldiers were weary, solemn, dirty, and drooping. There was nothing glorious about the war they were fighting; their main goal was to get back home without being killed, and their main obligation was to their buddies, who in turn looked out for them. In Tunisia, during the North African campaign in 1943, Pyle for the first time fully recognized the contribution of the infantrymen, to whom he gave his ultimate accolade—the "mud-rain-frost-and-wind boys," as he referred to them. "They have no comforts, and they even learn to live without the necessities. And in the end they are the guys that wars cannot be won without."[36]

They were "just guys from Broadway and Main Street," the normal sorts of fellows that everybody knew back home. The reporter generally took care to mention the hometowns of the servicemen he wrote about. "Ernie Pyle has known too many towns not to honor the individuality of each," wrote Charles Fisher in his book *The Columnists.*[37] Pyle was sorry about what war did to soldiers. He realized that people back in the states would never fully grasp what it was like to be a soldier at the front, but he did his best to describe it for them. He was determined to write with objective detachment and to tell the truth about the cold, discomfort, fear, and loneliness that enveloped them. When the terror of shells and bullets abated, the monotony and dreary sameness of the days wore on them. The frontline soldier he wrote about "lived for months like an animal, and was a veteran in the fierce world of death. Everything was abnormal and unstable in his life."[38] Pyle was fascinated—and horrified—by the conversion of men into killers, individuals who, for their own survival and for that of their comrades, were forced to make a profession of killing.

Few of them were able to articulate very well what it was they were fighting for, besides each other. But they realized that their job had to be done, so they did it.[39] Nor did Pyle make much of an attempt to define the war in abstract terms that might justify the killing and mayhem. As always, he looked at the world through facts and particulars. The same techniques and mind-set that had guided him earlier along the highways of America worked effectively now for him on the wartime battlefronts. At a wiry 5'8" and 115 pounds, he would have been able to blend almost invisibly into the background as he moved from point to point on the battlegrounds of Europe and Asia had he not been such a celebrity to the men he was writing about. "One reason that Ernie Pyle has been able to report this little man's war so successfully," noted *Time* magazine, "is that he loves people and, for all his quirks and foibles, is at base a very average little man himself."[40]

Of necessity, he traveled light, his portable typewriter being his main encumbrance. As was his habit, he seldom took notes, besides jotting down the names and addresses of the soldiers he talked to. As had been true back in the States as he crisscrossed the country during the 1930s, it was difficult for those who did not understand how he worked to tell whether he was actually on the job. In fact, however, he was always on the job; anything he observed or heard became possible grist for his mill. He spent enough time at the front under fire to understand fully the nature of combat soldiering. Many of the soldiers who revered him for it did not realize that most of the time he operated further back from the front lines, observing and writing about the support troops who constituted the bulk of those in uniform. He did stories on laundrymen, artillerymen, tank-retrieval crews, medics, pilots, grave diggers, bakers, public relations specialists, aircraft-carrier crews, and people in many other specialties. Almost always, he provided some of the names of the men he talked to and often their addresses. In so doing, he made them real for his readers. "Overnight, as it were, the skinny guy of the column has become known to millions of Americans," wrote Frederick C. Painton in the *Saturday Evening Post*. "As the cheerful, droll character in the column he has lived in foxholes with the advanced infantry, with the gunners of the big 155's, in the desert with the bomber commands, swapped gossip with soldiers from one end of North Africa to the other. Always Ernie Pyle, the Midwest farm boy, darting around a battlefield like a curious bird. That's the character you meet in the column."[41]

Pyle's attention focused almost entirely on the lower-ranking enlisted men. Seldom did he write about anybody above the rank of captain, although he did turn out several effusive pieces on General Omar Bradley. In making ordinary GIs the heroes of his pieces, Pyle reenacted well-established democratic rituals, which were especially treasured in his native Midwest. Traveling around the country during the 1930s, he had expressed little interest in the large events that were shaping the times and had adopted an easygoing, democratic manner that effortlessly carried over into his role as a war correspondent. "He was a new kind of war correspondent—democracy's perfect symbol in a democratic war," wrote John Mason Brown in *Saturday Review.* "What was exceptional about him was his *seeming* averageness; his ability to enclose every man's war within the parentheses of his own personality. Scores of correspondents have had his courage, but none has had his heart. Ernie remained the small-town boy in a big-time war. He was one Little Man writing about all the others in this Little Man's war."[42]

In this massive global encounter, "everything depends on teamwork," Pyle observed. "The lone dashing hero in this war is certain to be a dead hero within a week. Sticking with the team and playing it all together is the only guarantee of safety for everybody."[43] While emphasizing the importance of teamwork in the drive for victory, the Indiana native provided his subjects with individual identities, which people could take hold of and empathize with. Men in uniform such as Sergeant Frank Eversole, Private First Class Tommy Clayton, and Captain Arthur Waskow won immortality in his columns. His piece on the captain's death during the Italian campaign became an instant classic. It commanded the entire front page of the *Washington Daily News* on January 10, 1944, and was reprinted in countless publications.[44] Waskow, translated into a Christlike figure by Pyle, represented the ultimate example of the suffering-servant image of the GI that Pyle painted in his column. In so doing, he discovered atonement for the way in which the war had transformed so many small-town (and big-city) boys into efficient killers. "The human spirit is an astounding thing," Pyle observed, and that realization provided a glimmer of hope for when the war would finally be over.[45]

Pyle's 1,000 words a day, six times a week, from the battlefronts and rear echelons of the war reinforced an image of Americans in which individual contributions still mattered and where teamwork still counted. His was not the world, by and large, of the huge, bureaucratic organizations that were increasingly coming to dominate American society. Instead, it was a world hearkening back to his youth in Indiana, when farmers and small-town storekeepers and child-caring mothers constituted the core of society. Pyle was not unaware of the tremendous logistical and organizational efforts that lay behind the individual soldiers' war-making on the battlefronts, and sometimes he wrote about these massive achievements in his columns. He described the "machinelike precision" of night convoys in North Africa, the "gigantic thing" that the air war had become, the multifaceted organization of the Normandy invasion, and the huge supply lines that extended across the Pacific. Indeed, it had become as much an engineer's war as an infantryman's one. "War makes strange giant creatures out of us little routine men who inhabit the earth," he observed.[46] Managing the war was, in many respects, "like running a big business," and Pyle respected efficient managers such as Dwight Eisenhower and Omar Bradley who made the whole thing operate effectively.[47]

But although he acknowledged the crucial importance of organization and bureaucracy, he devoted most of his attention to—and his heart remained with—the GIs in the foxholes and the support troops in the rear, the men who did most of the dirty work, the suffering, and the dying. Pyle himself met death on the battlefield, taking a bullet through his helmet while under fire on the island of Ie Shima on April 18, 1945, less than four months before the war ended in the Pacific. His premonitions of death had turned out to be prescient.

After Vietnam, some critics would judge his attempts at truth to be less than totally honest, for he, like all his colleagues, maintained a clear set of boundaries around his writing. Although none of his readers could doubt the horror and misery of the lives of the soldiers in the field, they were spared its most gruesome depictions. Naysayers might rightly accuse Pyle of sugarcoating the darker realities of the war, but within the context of the times he certainly deserved the acclaim he received for his work, including the 1943 Pulitzer Prize for correspondence. By letting other reporters cover grand strategy and the day-to-day progress of battles and maneuvers in the field, he was able to concentrate his attention on small-focus glimpses of people and places, just as he always had. In the process, he reinforced Americans' image of themselves as a nation of people from identifiable places and communities where individual effort and teamwork still counted and where huge organizations provided the backdrop for individual will and initiative.

Frederick Jackson Turner (seated, second from right) with his University of Wisconsin history seminar, circa 1893. Courtesy of the Wisconsin Historical Society.

William Jennings Bryan as a college student orator. Courtesy of the Nebraska State Historical Society.

William McKinley speaking to a crowd from the front porch of his home in Canton, Ohio, during the presidential election of 1896. Courtesy of the Ohio Historical Society.

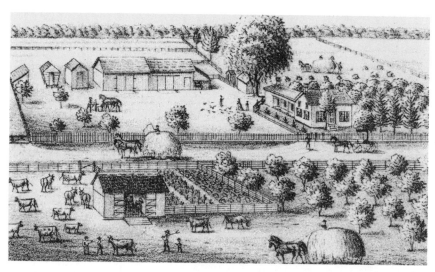

An idealized view of the farm near Dearborn, Michigan, on which Henry Ford was born and where he grew up. From *Illustrated Historical Atlas of Wayne County, 1876*.

George Washington Carver and his friend Henry Ford at the new Carver Nutrition Laboratory in Dearborn, Michigan, 1942. From the Collections of The Henry Ford (THF73362).

Filmmaker Oscar Micheaux (in black hat, to right of camera) on one of his movie sets.
Courtesy Jerry Wilske, Oscar Micheaux Center, Gregory, South Dakota.

Thomas Hart Benton, back home from studying art in Paris, out for a walk with
friends in Neosho, Missouri, circa 1912. Courtesy of Larry James.

Carl Sandburg (first row, far left) with his Swedish Lutheran confirmation class in Galesburg, Illinois. Courtesy of the Rare Book and Manuscript Library, University of Illinois at Urbana-Champaign.

Main Street of Sauk Centre, Minnesota (circa 1925), which inspired Sinclair Lewis's best-selling book *Main Street*. Courtesy of the Minnesota Historical Society.

Grant Wood as a young artist in Cedar Rapids, Iowa. Courtesy of the Cedar Rapids Museum of Art Archives.

Ernie Pyle's high school graduation photo, 1918. Courtesy of the Lilly Library, Indiana University, Bloomington.

University of Wisconsin artist in residence John Steuart Curry discusses an artwork with interested onlookers. Courtesy of the University of Wisconsin Archives (#S10017).

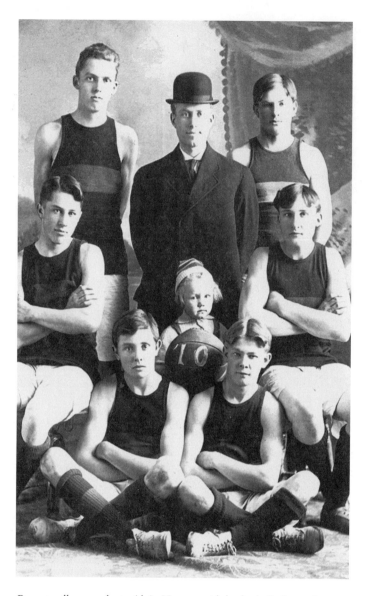

Recent college graduate Alvin Hansen with basketball players he coached and taught at Lake Preston (South Dakota) High School, circa 1910. Courtesy of South Dakota Magazine.

James Dean, a star basketball player at Fairmount (Indiana) High School, was voted the best senior athlete in 1949. Courtesy of the Fairmount Historical Museum.

Teenage pitching sensation Bob Feller (center) stands with his father, Bill, and mother, Lena.

Meredith Willson poses, piccolo in hand (front row, fourth from right), with the Mason City (Iowa) Boy Scout Band. Courtesy of the Mason City Public Library Archives.

Kansas Street, the main street of Marceline, Missouri, during the early 1900s, inspiration for Main Street U.S.A. at Disneyland. Courtesy State Historical Society of Missouri.

A young Lawrence Welk would take his accordion a long way in the musical world from his hometown of Strasburg, North Dakota. Courtesy of the Welk Archives, Los Angeles.

Johnny Carson practicing card tricks as a teenager in Norfolk, Nebraska. Courtesy of the Elkhorn Valley Museum and Research Center.

After employing his Pyramid of Success to motivate his high school and college basketball players and English students, John Wooden used it to illustrate his views on personal self-improvement. Courtesy of UCLA Athletics.

Ronald Reagan saved an estimated seventy-seven lives as a lifeguard during seven summers in Dixon, Illinois. Courtesy of the Ronald Reagan Library.

As student body president, star athlete, thespian, and scholar, Sam Walton merited a full page in 1936 in the Cresset, the yearbook of Hickman High School in Columbia, Missouri. Courtesy of the State Historical Society of Missouri.

■

Reverberations of the Small-Town Myth, 1945–1965

◼

Introduction to Section III

The rapid economic expansion unleashed by U.S. participation in World War II finally brought an end to the Great Depression. Growth continued at a healthy, though more moderate, pace for nearly three decades after 1945. Not only did production and consumption thrive, but population growth proceeded at unprecedented rates in absolute numbers, providing much of the impetus propelling economic growth. Closely tied to these developments was a remarkable movement of population out to the suburbs, as the percentage of the population living in suburban areas grew from 15.3 percent in 1940 to 23.3 percent in 1950, 30.9 percent in 1960, and 37.6 percent in 1970. In the meantime, the proportion of the workforce engaged in agriculture dropped by three-quarters, from 16 percent to 4 percent.

Many small towns, meanwhile, saw their population numbers drift steadily downward, the smallest towns experiencing the greatest decline. Bigger towns fared better, overall, as the sorting-out process accelerated, resulting in retail trade, services, and amenities being increasingly concentrated in larger places. Smaller towns stagnated and declined. This process had been going on since at least the 1920s. Now, with better roads being built, as the new Interstate Highway System set the pace, with schools and churches rapidly consolidating, with fast-food franchises anchoring expanding strips along routes leading into and out of towns, and with new malls and discount stores taking over an ever-larger segment of the retail trade, small towns found themselves not so much under attack as simply forgotten and increasingly invisible. As they came to be home to a smaller and smaller proportion of the total population, they also found their status and influence rapidly draining away. When Americans thought about them now, it was more in terms of what they once had been than what they had become. The small-town myth seemed more potent than the reality.

One person retaining happy memories of and strong affection for his rural and small-town upbringing was Alvin Hansen of Viborg, South Dakota. He had grown up on a farm near the little town within a heavily Danish rural settlement. As in many other families, he, along with an older sister and two older brothers, had to learn English at school, because his parents' native tongue was still spoken at home. The boy, a curious and precocious lad, was the first person from the area to go beyond eighth grade and the first to continue on to college. After obtaining a PhD degree in economics at the University of Wisconsin, he rose rapidly in the field, winding up at Harvard for the last nineteen years of his teaching career.

He arrived in Cambridge, Massachusetts, in 1937, just a year after the publication of the British economist John Maynard Keynes's pathbreaking treatise calling for active government intervention in the economy in order to prevent or, if necessary, bring about recovery from depressions. Hansen emerged during the late 1930s and 1940s as the foremost American advocate of the controversial Brit's ideas, and he did more than anybody else to introduce and bring about the acceptance of modern macroeconomic theory in the United States. As the author of numerous books and countless academic and popular articles on the subject, he was called on frequently to testify before Congress and to serve on panels and advisory councils in Washington. The unprepossessing, unpretentious intellectual had come a long way from home. The very ordinariness of his appearance, the plain-spokenness of his address, and his friendly folksy personality that obtained a hearing for him owed much to his upbringing in South Dakota. His ideas and policy proposals were instrumental in passing the historic Employment Act of 1946 and later in inspiring the enactment of the Kennedy-Johnson stimulatory tax cut of 1964. In many eyes, he had become the most influential economist in the United States, and his former students carried his ideas into college classrooms from coast to coast and filled important positions in many government agencies.

It is ironic that this former farm boy from the Dakotas would devote most of his academic efforts to proposing solutions for problems focused in America's cities, although he never neglected agricultural questions and problems of the rural countryside. Whenever he returned home to Viborg to visit, which was often, he would always search out farmers to ask about current conditions on the farm. As his two daughters moved through their school years, the family set aside many Sunday nights for Daddy to fondly relate stories about his growing-up years in South Dakota (it had still been part of the Dakota Territory for the first three years of his life). Hansen never forgot his local roots, but the frugal habits instilled in him as a youth, he realized, were not necessarily what a dynamic, expanding economy required. Fostering economic growth demanded that people loosen their wallets and spend money; consumption drove the economy. When that failed and business investment lagged, the government needed to step in with compensatory spending, à la Keynes, in order to revive business activity. In this fashion, Hansen did his part to hold on to old habits and values while at the same time he worked to redefine economic prescriptions for a new era.

Baseball, which had emerged as the national game in the United States before the Civil War, continued to grow in popularity during the decades leading up to World War II. No player arrived on the sporting scene with such ballyhoo and panache as a hard-throwing, right-handed pitcher from Van Meter, Iowa, a country boy named Bob Feller. Only seventeen years old in 1936 and still a year away from high school graduation, the schoolboy phenom was so good that the team that signed him, the Cleveland Indians, decided to put him into a big league uniform that summer and let him pitch in relief out of the bullpen. Given a chance to start a game against the St. Louis Browns, he struck out fifteen batters, and several games later he struck out seventeen to set a new American League record for whiffs and tie the major-league mark. Soon, newspapers were running the serialized life story of the "Heater from Van Meter," whom they also referred to as the "Iowa Farm Boy."

When Feller came up to the big leagues, ball players were still often identified with their hometown or home state. Ty Cobb, the "Georgia Peach"; Lou Gehrig, the "Columbia University Slugger"; Stan Musial, the "Donora [Pennsylvania] Flash"; and "Country" Enos Slaughter were among the many major leaguers who were known by fans all over the country for their local or regional origins. By the 1950s and '60s, though a few players like Wilmer "Vinegar Bend" (for his hometown in Alabama) Mizell and Mickey Mantle, the "Commerce [Oklahoma] Comet," still carried on the tradition, the practice was rapidly dying out. By then, the majority of players were coming out of cities and comparatively characterless suburbs that tended to duplicate each other and lacked the distinctive features that had set small towns apart. But Feller would always be associated in people's minds with his origins in rural Iowa.

When he was thirteen, he helped his father, Bill, who had groomed him for the big leagues from the day he was born, carve out a baseball diamond on their farm outside Van Meter. They put up an outfield fence, some bleachers for the fans to sit on, and a scoreboard. Bill Feller bought uniforms, recruited a team called the Oakviews (named after the oak trees surrounding the field), installed his teenage son as shortstop and pitcher, and challenged nearby teams to try to beat them. It was, people around Van Meter point out to this day, a "field of dreams" before the book and the movie about it were ever made.

The precocious youth had more than a strong right arm to carry him through, phenomenal though that was. The farm boy from Van Meter displayed confidence and maturity beyond his years, winning 107 games by the age of twenty-three, when he became the first major-league baseball player to enlist in the military, just two days after Pearl Harbor. Back from the Navy at the end of 1945, he picked up right where he had left off and soon began displaying new sides to his creativity. In 1946 and 1947, he recruited a group of fellow major-league all-stars to play a month of exhibition games after the end of the regular season against a group of their African American counterparts led by the legendary pitcher Satchel Paige. Several of Feller's recruits actually earned more money playing one month for him than they had during the entire season playing for their regular teams. He demonstrated his creativity and entrepreneurialism in a variety of ways, being one of the first ballplayers to follow a regimen of stretching and strengthening exercises, learning to fly his own plane, cooperating in a ghosted autobiography, lining up a string of endorsements for various products, and becoming baseball's first incorporated participant. His fellow athletes voted him the American League player representative for talks with the owners, and he later served as president of the newly organized Major League Baseball Players Association and became a member of the Major League Pension Committee.

Long after he moved to a Cleveland suburb, Feller maintained strong ties to his hometown of Van Meter, and he returned a number of times in his eighties to sign autographs to help fund the building and maintenance of a small museum that was built in his honor. Although Feller remained attached to his small-town beginnings in Iowa, he demonstrated a deft ability to negotiate the many changes that came about in American society during a career lasting from 1936 to 1956 and during the decades thereafter.

The last thing many people would think of when hearing the name James Dean would be "small-town boy from the Midwest." More likely, they would think of mindless rebellion, juvenile delinquency in the 1950s, the younger generation, Hollywood, and youthful excess. Dean's image—piercing blue eyes, carelessly combed blond hair, insouciant expression, perhaps a cigarette dangling from his lips—came to stand as the iconic emblem of the restless "rebel without a cause" (the name of his second and most famous movie) that emerged along with television, space flight, interstate highways, and tail-finned cars during the first full decade after World War II.

Dean's neighbors, friends, and classmates in Fairmount, Indiana, 50 miles northeast of Indianapolis, where he graduated from high school in 1949, remembered him as a mischievous and somewhat rebellious teenager, but for all that a normal, happy-go-lucky, all-American kid. The many stories out of Manhattan and Hollywood about his weird, uncontrollable, antitaboo behavior did not ring true with them. They thought of him as a boy who liked to ride his motorcycle, engage in horseplay with his friends, and compete in interscholastic sports—baseball, track, and basketball—which he was very good at.

If Jimmy's behavior was sometimes a bit odd, that could be attributed to the fact that his mother had died when he was nine and that, for all intents and purposes, his father had left him to be raised from then until he graduated from high school by his aunt and uncle, Marcus and Ortense Winslow, who lived on a farm 2 miles north of Fairmount. They treated him like their own son, but Jimmy, not surprisingly, had to fight demons telling him that he had been abandoned. For the most part, he was able to keep them in check, and he found his greatest release in sports, forensics competition, and acting in school plays. The vague dream he harbored of becoming an actor drove him to leave town immediately after graduation to look for opportunities to break into the field.

That path would lead him through Los Angeles, New York City, and finally back to Hollywood. He only had six and a half years of his short life remaining before an ill-fated car wreck took his life when he was only twenty-four in 1955. Receiving no help from his father, who had relocated to the Los Angeles area, he had to depend on his own talent, wit, and ability to fend for himself and to ingratiate himself with people who could be of help to him. And despite growing up among Quakers in Fairmount, he seems to have left behind any scruples or moral imperatives from his youth. He wasn't necessarily a bad kid, but as he proceeded from the West Coast to the East and back again, he seemed willing to break any strictures or taboos that society might have tried to impose on him.

A shy boy before leaving home, he soon discovered the kind of seductive appeal he had for individuals of both sexes, and he felt no compunctions about using his gifts for his own immediate pleasure or for personal advancement. Mostly, though, he just seemed intent on trying everything, experiencing everything, and sucking the marrow of life. Aspiring actor that he was, he seemed fully capable of acting normally offstage or out of sight of a camera, but as time went by, he became more and more addicted to playing out a variety of roles whenever he was in the company of more than one or two friends. That attraction to role-playing helps explain some of his extremely bizarre behaviors while acting in television in New York, and then for the last few months of his life in Hollywood.

Still, he felt a clear nostalgia for his former life in Fairmount, returning to visit it half a dozen times to reestablish ties with his aunt and uncle, former friends, teachers, and townspeople. How Dean would have lived out his life had he survived a normal threescore years and ten rather than a mere twenty-four is impossible to know. Suffice it to say, he never quite progressed much beyond adolescence in his personal development, and both in his screen roles and in his personal life he projected an image of a rebellious young man; he took a youthful generation just emerging in the 1950s by storm and inspired a host of imitators and admirers in later years.

None of the figures discussed in this book probably had a closer and more affectionate relationship with his hometown than Meredith Willson, the piccolo player, songwriter, composer, music director, radio and television personality, and playwright from Mason City, Iowa. He reminisced about the prairie town in northeastern Iowa on his NBC radio programs and in private conversations with so much warmth and obvious fondness that a musical friend of his finally challenged him to write a musical play about the town. To our good fortune, he did.

The show we know as *The Music Man* (its original working title was "The Silver Triangle") went through as many as forty revisions before it finally hit the Broadway stage in December 1957, but the night it did, there was no holding it back. At the end of the performance, the audience spontaneously stood up and started clapping in rhythm to the tune of "Seventy-Six Trombones." *The Music Man* quickly became the hardest ticket to obtain in Manhattan, playing to standing-room-only audiences for 1,375 performances. It was the biggest hit of the year during a year of major hits, edging *West Side Story* out for best play and best musical. Four years later, it was made into a movie, and it remains hugely popular to this day in revivals in summer repertory theaters and on high school and college stages. A half dozen of its songs have become standard tunes in America's popular song bag.

In writing the book for the musical as well as the lyrics and tunes for all its songs, Willson assumed roles that were usually distributed among three or four different individuals in creating a musical play. It was his first attempt at the genre, although he was experienced at composing popular songs and writing lyrics, directing orchestras, and performing the functions of a musical director in various media. Doing *The Music Man* was obviously a labor of love for Willson and a completely natural thing for him to do as a small-town boy from a community whose population had expanded to more than 12,000 at the time of the imagined events in his musical (1912).

The mythical River City, however, was a sleepy little town of 2,212 people as Willson described it, not like Mason City, a bustling, midsize, progressive, and rapidly growing railroad, commercial, and industrial center that dominated an area 100 miles in diameter in northeastern Iowa. No one would have guessed from watching the musical that Mason City manufactured portland cement and automobiles and was the largest producer of clay drain tiles in the world. No one should view *The Music Man* as a detailed and fully accurate portrait of the town that Willson hailed from. In the tone he adopted toward his tribute to his hometown and in the general picture he drew of its inhabitants, he certainly was acting truthfully and sincerely, however. For Willson was a true believer in the virtues and benefits of growing up in a small town.

The heedful reader will have noted that the young man wasted no time in leaving town after graduating from high school, heading straight for New York City's Institute of Musical Art (later the Juilliard School of Music). He quickly rose to a position as a flutist in John Philip Sousa's touring band, then to first chair in the flute section of the New York Philharmonic Orchestra, and after that to a succession of increasingly responsible musical assignments. We know now, thanks to recent biographies of Willson, that, contrary to the consistent impression he gave of his family in later years, it had in fact been a quite dysfunctional one. Shortly after he left home his father left his mother to marry a younger woman half his age. Growing up in the household must have been a heavy, even miserable, burden. But none of this detracted from the perpetually sunny, enthusiastic outlook on life that Willson always displayed to his friends, fellow musicians, and reporters. Sometimes, what you see is not actually what is going on behind the scenes.

Whatever the nature of life in his family as he was growing up, we can be certain that Willson's enthusiasm for the town of Mason City, its people, and his life in it was the genuine article. He would be called on in later years to write fight songs and publicity tunes for his high school, the University of Iowa, Iowa State University, the state of Iowa, President John F. Kennedy's physical fitness program, and President Gerald Ford's anti-inflation program. In each case, he delivered the goods with enthusiasm. *The Music Man* should be understood as one of a genre of booster productions, akin to James Whitcomb Riley's poems about small towns, toothpaste and car ads, and patriotic songs about the nation. They were not necessarily untruthful, although they certainly were selective in emphasis and shamelessly exaggerated, and they insistently accentuated the positive. In Willson's memory and thinking, the small-town way of life was the ideal one, and he was never reluctant to say so. He may have gotten out of town as quickly as he could, but he returned enthusiastically to visit many times over the course of his life, and he could never get his hometown out of his system. His was the classic musical evocation of what small towns sometimes were and, in their admirers' imagination, always could be.

Much as Willson's nostalgic memories of Mason City inspired *The Music Man,* a Missouri boy's idealized recollections of the brief period he spent on a small farm while growing up in the north-central part of the state gave rise to Disneyland. It was the first theme park of its kind and may well have been the most successful entertainment venture of all time. Walt Disney had lived the first four years of his life in the Midwest's largest metropolis, Chicago, and he spent his teenage years in another rapidly growing urban center—Kansas City, Missouri. But for four and a half years, before he reached the age of ten, he and his parents lived on a 48-acre farm a quarter mile north of Marceline, Missouri. Walt remembered little about Chicago, and the daily chore of delivering hundreds of newspapers both morning and afternoon in Kansas City was something akin to slavery, which put a damper on the experience. But life in the woods and fields around Marceline and frequent forays into the up-and-coming railroad town marked an idyll he never forgot and would always cherish.

The ferment, the excitement, and the practical opportunities that accompanied being in Kansas City, however, made possible his start in the cartoon business. He was a young man with energy, ambition, and seemingly endless creativity, allowing him to flourish, first there and then later in Hollywood, during the 1920s. As with many of the other individuals described in this book, Disney benefited enormously from good timing, getting involved in the film industry just a few years after it began. Walt Disney Studios played a leading role in sound technology, 3-D picture-making, storyboards, and other innovations in the manufacture of cartoons. With the making of *Snow White and the Seven Dwarfs* in 1937, he produced the first feature-length cartoon, ushering in a whole new genre in the field.

By the late 1940s and early 1950s, however, he grew increasingly restless and spent most of his time and energy planning and then building the first substantial theme park in the United States. The opening of Disneyland in July 1955 ushered in a new era in American entertainment, transforming the Disney organization, which simultaneously branched out into television production, into a hugely profitable operation. Los Angeles in the 1950s epitomized postwar suburban sprawl and consumer culture. Disney responded brilliantly to the new kind of American society that was emerging: youth-obsessed; structured around the automobile; focused on the one-eyed monster, television; and dedicated to consumption, leisure, pleasure, and economic growth. Meanwhile, Los Angeles and Southern

California retained a substantial flavor of the Middle West. Many of its inhabitants had only recently migrated from the region, first pushed out by the Dirty Thirties and then attracted to manufacturing jobs in the state during the economic boom stimulated by World War II.

Disneyland was its creator's baby—his fondest accomplishment and, in his mind, "the happiest place on earth." In short order, it emerged as a prime symbol of American culture, drawing visitors from all over the world. Disney encircled his theme park with a railroad emanating from his recollections of his hometown. The first place visitors enter when coming into the Magic Kingdom is Main Street, consciously modeled on the Missouri boy's recollections of Marceline, which he had enjoyed so much as a child. In Disneyland, dream and reality intermingled, much to the advantage of the former, and memories of the small-town Midwest insinuated themselves into the American psyche, mostly unconsciously but no less powerfully, even as contrasting images of fantasy, frontier adventure, and the future commingled with nostalgia and reverie.

CHAPTER NINE

Alvin Hansen: South Dakota Farm Boy Turned Keynesian Prophet

Alvin in his later years would refer to himself as "just a simple farm boy," suggesting wonderment at where his good fortune had taken him, no less than pride in his early community's values, the importance of work, and the directness of tasks that had to be met, if the farm or, for that matter, the U.S. economy was to thrive.

—Richard A. Musgrave

Alvin Hansen was not a likely candidate for a revolutionary. Plainspoken and unpretentious in manner, balding and stocky in appearance, courteous and obliging in conversation, he scarcely seemed to pose a threat to the existing order. But during the late 1930s and 1940s, this farm-bred boy from South Dakota became the point man for an intellectual transformation in the United States that rewrote the economics textbooks, recast public policy, and set the terms for political debate for the next quarter century.

During the years after the appearance in 1936 of British economist John Maynard Keynes's pathbreaking treatise *The General Theory of Employment, Interest and Money*, the South Dakota native emerged as Keynesianism's leading interpreter and advocate in the United States.[1] From Hansen's position in the Economics Department at Harvard, his influence radiated outward among fellow economists and academicians, government officials, and the general public. Keynes's theoretical defense of government intervention and spending and tax policy to stabilize the economy and stimulate economic growth challenged reigning economic orthodoxy. But within three decades of its appearance it had established itself as the dominant paradigm in the profession and garnered much of the credit for the record-breaking economic expansion of the 1960s.[2]

Hansen played the central role in bringing the Keynesian revolution to the United States. Paul McCracken, a former student of Hansen's, wrote him at the time of his eightieth birthday celebration, "It is certainly a statement of fact that you have influenced the nation's thinking about economic policy more profoundly than any other economist in this century."[3] Gerhart Colm, another former student, wrote him, "You can look back on a life of great accomplishment but the greatest accomplishment was that you always stirred up things and thereby became a great teacher not only of students of economics but of a whole generation of thinking laymen."[4] The citation on Hansen's Francis A. Walker Medal, the highest award granted by the American Economic Association, called the South Dakota economist

> a gentle revolutionary who has lived to see his cause triumphant and his heresies orthodox, an untiring scholar whose example and influence have fruitfully changed the directions of his science, a political economist who has reformed policies and institutions in his own country and elsewhere without any power save the force of his ideas. From his boyhood on the South Dakota prairie, Alvin Hansen has believed that knowledge can improve the condition of man. In the integrity of that faith he has had the courage never to close his mind and to seek and speak the truth wherever it might lead.[5]

Hansen was born on August 23, 1887, on a farm three miles south of the brand-new town of Viborg when the area was still Dakota Territory.

Surrounded by fellow Danish immigrants, Hansen's family, which included two older brothers and an older sister, continued to speak the ancestral language in the household as long as he remained at home. This countryside, described by the novelist Ole Rölvaag in *Giants in the Earth*, was characterized by expansive fields of corn, wheat, and other crops, extending to the horizon under an immense sky. The environment was inspiring and beckoning to many but was capable of driving others mad. Hansen's upbringing in a pious Baptist household, where both parents played active roles in the local congregation, was more conducive to striving and hopefulness than to madness and dementia.[6] He never forgot his local roots, putting a nostalgic gloss on the community feeling that centered around the Baptist church his family attended and on what he referred to as the "sturdy simplicity" of the Danish "peasants" among whom he grew up. Not enamored of the "social snobbery" and "petty aristocracy" frequently characteristic of small-town life, he observed as a young man, "I'm glad I was raised close enough to the soil to value the worth of the common man—that's all I claim to be myself."[7]

Alvin performed his chores dutifully, but he longed for the day when he could escape his surroundings and venture out into something more adventurous. He liked to read and to study, a bent encouraged by his grandfather, a well-read retired minister, and his mother, who understood the boy's urge to learn and to explore the world around him. After graduating from eighth grade at the local rural one-room school, he enrolled in an academy in Sioux Falls, 35 miles to the northeast for his secondary education, and then entered Yankton College, 40 miles to the southwest on the Missouri River. Alvin was one of the first two students in the Viborg area to attend high school and the first to go on to college. At Yankton College, a small Congregational school carrying on the New England tradition of learning, the aspiring student majored in English and studied Shakespeare. He also edited the student newspaper, took part in plays, and served as president of the campus YMCA when he was not earning money for his schooling by milking cows, waiting on tables, and attending to other jobs. At Yankton, he also met Mabel Lewis, his future wife.[8]

Like a number of other young men who grew up on the South Dakota prairie, including the economist Theodore Schultz, the physicist Ernest O. Lawrence, the historian John King Fairbank, and the historian-turned-politician George McGovern, Hansen was determined to pursue his scholarly bent. With money earned during three years of teaching, coaching, and serving as principal and then superintendent at Lake Preston High School, he enrolled in graduate school at the University of Wisconsin in 1913 to pursue a PhD degree in economics. There he came into contact with pathbreaking scholars such as John R. Commons and Richard T. Ely, who were pioneering in institutional economics and sociology—emphasizing the influence of institutions such as business, labor unions, and government agencies on the economy and society. Wisconsin was the home of La Follette progressivism, a spearhead in the movement to improve American society and politics through gradual, practical-minded reform. Although inclined by his upbringing, religion, and education to favor melioristic change, young Hansen adopted a basically conservative brand of economics. He was suspicious of excessive government intervention and supportive of market-based decisions as a rule, a stance placing him in the mainstream of the profession at the time.[9]

The evolution of economic thinking in the United States during the middle decades of the twentieth century constitutes one of the more characteristic intellectual odysseys in U.S. history. Aside from the Civil War, no event posed a greater challenge to the country's future—indeed its survival—than the economic upheaval of the 1930s. Out of the fears and traumas unleashed by the business collapse and subsequent bloating of unemployment rolls, businessmen, economists, politicians, and serious thinkers—along with quacks and charlatans of every variety—weighed in with ideas on what might be done to remedy the collapse. In the midst of all this, in 1936, Keynes's epochal book appeared, seeming to refute the central foundation of classical economics. Rejecting the notion embodied in an economic principle known as Say's law (named after economist Jean-Baptiste Say), that supply creates its own demand, Keynes contended that capitalism contains within it inherent tendencies toward stagnation. Therefore, when private consumption and business investment flag, the role of government should be to step in and fill the gap by engaging in compensatory spending (or in complementary tax reductions) to get the economy back on track. Conversely, should the economy become overheated and inflationary tendencies start to appear, government should respond with appropriate fiscal policies of a different sort—raising taxes, reducing spending, or both.[10] Hansen, like his colleagues in the profession, was forced to grapple with the intellectual challenge posed by Keynes's theory.

Had the South Dakotan not been offered a job at Harvard in the fall of 1937, a year after the publication of Keynes's thought-provoking *General*

Theory, his influence on American economic thought would probably not have been nearly as great. The mantle of being Keynes's leading American apostle might have fallen on somebody else. "Like Keynes in Cambridge, [England]," writes the historian Peter Clarke, "Hansen, once established in the other Cambridge, was in a position to put a prestigious institutional imprimatur upon notions that might otherwise have been dismissed as populist heresies, peddled only by cranks."[11]

The road to Harvard had been a long one. After completing his PhD studies at the University of Wisconsin and teaching for three years at Brown University, Hansen taught at the University of Minnesota from 1919 to 1937. His reputation there was so glowing that his dean worried continually that some higher bidder might approach him with a job offer and lure him away. Harvard's offer of the newly endowed Littauer Chair of Political Economy carried with it a $10,000 salary. That was more than half again as much as the $6,510 Hansen was making at Minnesota, where he was already one of the highest paid professors on the roster.[12] "If you were leaving us to go anywhere else we should all be very cross with you; but it would be virtually impossible to resist a Harvard call, and Harvard badly needs a big tonic," wrote Herbert Heaton, a colleague in the History Department. "I hope you will find abundant opportunities for fruitful work, many worthwhile students and not too much carping tradition to vex your mid-western spirit."[13]

At Minnesota, Hansen had established a solid reputation, publishing a steady output of books and articles and positioning himself to be elected president of the American Economic Association at the beginning of 1938. Harvard provided him with a much more visible platform from which to expound his views, spread his influence within the profession, and make an impact on public policy. There, he and his colleagues had easier entrée to the corridors of political power. Graduate students under his supervision would populate government agencies and assume positions of influence. Anything Hansen said or wrote would be attended to with greater deterence and respect. Harvard was clearly a step up for him, and during the next nineteen years, until his retirement in 1956, Hansen emerged as the single most read and listened to economic policy adviser in the country. For a decade after that, he continued to speak, write, and testify before congressional committees, and students of his rose to the highest policy-making positions in the federal bureaucracy.[14]

Hansen was more of an integrator, developer, and popularizer than a pure theorist, but he did make some significant contributions at the theoretical level, too. His *A Guide to Keynes* carefully summarized the basic premises and arguments of Keynes's masterwork and may have done as much to educate Americans about the British economist's ideas as did Keynes's writings themselves. In the process of extending and elaborating Keynesian theory, Hansen opened up new pathways for American economists to follow. In building on the analytical apparatus of British economist John R. Hicks, he developed the so-called IS-LM framework, which soon became a standard feature in economics textbooks. This model explained the relationships linking interest rates, savings, investment, demand for money, and income. Even more important, Hansen encased his theoretical arguments within a solid historical dimension, making sure that statistics and mathematical formulas did not overwhelm sound thinking about the economy "on the ground," so to speak. His background in farming naturally grounded him in an understanding of real things—the land, the natural environment, the weather, technology, plants and animals, agricultural markets, and so forth. His brand of economics—whether at the practical level or at the theoretical—would be no less grounded in reality, and historical context was fundamental to proper thinking about economic processes.[15]

None of this would have been possible had not Hansen possessed an unusual array of useful qualities and skills, enabling him to convert what in the minds of many was rankest economic heresy into something more palatable for academic and public consumption. This is not to suggest that Keynesianism would not have taken root in the United States in due time. It presumably would have, but its triumph probably would have come a little more slowly and carried less impact than it did, in fact, under the guiding influence of Alvin Hansen.

To have suggested in 1936, at the time Keynes's treatise was published, that Hansen would emerge as America's leading expositor and advocate of the controversial economist's theories would have generated considerable skepticism in the profession. Hansen's initial reaction to *The General Theory*, like that of most economists, was hesitant at best, hostile at worst. "The book is more a symptom of economic trends than a foundation stone upon which a science can be built," he wrote in a review.[16] Having studied business cycles during the 1920s and written *Economic Stabilization in an Unbalanced World* in 1932, at the low point of the Depression, Hansen believed that much of the world's economic instability had been caused by misguided government policies and other forms of social control. There was a necessary trade-off between security and progress. Too much government intervention, in the name of security, necessarily cut into growth and slowed progress. Many elements of the economy were too complex to be amenable to effective social control, he believed.[17]

During the two years after publication of *The General Theory*, however, the Harvard economist underwent an about-face in his thinking. His student Paul Samuelson later half-jokingly remarked, "On the train from Minnesota, so to speak, Hansen must have seen the light."[18] His arrival at Harvard in 1937 coincided with a drastic dip in the economy that was quickly labeled the Roosevelt Recession. Just turning fifty when he moved to Cambridge, Hansen soon found himself engaged in lively conversations and debates with graduate students and younger colleagues who, unlike most professors his own age, were intrigued by Keynes's novel arguments. Hansen's presence "brought a breath of fresh air to Harvard economics," in the words of one of his graduate students, Walter Salant.[19] His intellectual curiosity and his confident sense of self were reflected in his willingness to engage in a search for answers rather than remaining satisfied to pass on accepted doctrine. "When I say that I learned so much from [my students], I am simply telling the naked truth," he wrote Salant after he retired. "And I think you will agree that I was never afraid to display my own ignorance. The great thing about that year was the fact that we were all students trying to find our way about."[20]

Hansen may have been a convert to Keynesianism, but he was no unquestioning disciple. He pointed out mistakes he perceived in Keynes's reasoning and exposition, and he sought to clarify the British economist's notions about the use of tax and spending policies as tools for stabilizing the economy. He was able to give a more practical operational meaning to the general presentation Keynes had made in his book, which was sometimes confusing and could have stood a heavier editorial hand. Another divergence revolved around the issues of interest rates and monetary policy, in which Hansen believed his British counterpart placed too much faith.[21]

The way Hansen operated the fiscal policy seminar he conducted jointly with Professor John H. Williams, whose specialty was money and banking, tells much about the man. The two were, in many ways, opposites: Williams, conservative and reserved in his opinions about new and untested ideas; Hansen, liberal, enthusiastic, and ready to put new ideas to the test. "Students used to say that Hansen gave them lovely views of our society, and that I poked holes in them," Williams later recalled. "But, notwithstanding our differences," he added, "I shall always think of Alvin as the closest friend I have ever had."[22] Government officials and business executives often dropped in on their seminar to say hello or to engage in the ongoing conversation. "Visitors from the Washington firing lines mixed with local students and faculty," recalled a student, James Tobin. "I had the feeling that history was being made in that room." (In 1981, Tobin won the Nobel Memorial Prize in Economic Sciences.)[23] The fatherly relationship Hansen developed with many of his students broke down barriers and encouraged them to their best work.[24]

The feedback Hansen received from his colleagues and students and their openness to his inquiries and ideas fed his creativity, but the intellectual challenges posed by the recession of 1937–1938 forced him to rethink some of his fundamental premises.[25] Now for a time, worried by declining population growth rates, the shutoff of territorial expansion, and an apparent slowdown in technological innovation, he began to warn about what he called "secular stagnation." This notion received its fullest statement in Hansen's presidential address to the American Economic Association in December 1938. Echoing Frederick Jackson Turner's comments in Chicago forty-five years earlier about the end of the frontier, Hansen observed, "We are passing, so to speak, over a divide which separates the great era of growth and expansion of the nineteenth century from an era which no man, unwilling to embark on pure conjecture, can as yet characterize with clarity or precision."[26]

Such pessimism, however, soon gave way to pervasive optimism, based on the ability of the economy to grow if correct government policies were followed. Hansen became firmly committed to the Keynesian notion of governmental fiscal stimulus as a means of keeping the economy expanding on an even keel. The nation's major goal now, he attested, should be full employment. (Unemployment in the United States was 17.2 percent as late in the Great Depression as 1939.) That was a purpose around which a wide variety of economists, policy advisers, and politicians were able to coalesce during the years of World War II. The big question defining the parameters of political debate then and later was what role the government should play in order to achieve full employment.[27]

Conservatives continued to look to business for leadership in their effort to minimize the role of government. Liberals agreed on the need for larger government responsibility but disagreed on what specific approach to take.

Hansen emerged as the leading spokesman for a form of moderate Keynesianism. It should be, in his opinion, flexible in approach and inclined to experiment but committed to assigning a major role to the federal government and to the use of fiscal (and monetary) policy in promoting full employment and economic growth. Following the lead of Hansen and others, Keynesians persuaded an increasing fraction of the economics profession of the wisdom of their views, moved into important government positions, and continued to expand their influence with the general public. For several years during the early 1940s, Hansen commuted weekly by train from Cambridge to Washington to serve as an adviser to the Federal Reserve Board and the National Resources Planning Board.[28] Indirectly, his influence radiated during subsequent years through the activities of his former seminar students. They included, among others, one chairman and three other members of the President's Council of Economic Advisers, four members of the board of governors of the Federal Reserve System, two undersecretaries of the Treasury, and two assistant secretaries of state for economic affairs. Other seminar members took positions as secretary of defense and undersecretary of health, education, and welfare, and as directors of many bureaus and agencies of the federal government.[29]

Hansen's greatest policy legacy, although he did not actually participate in writing the legislation, was the passage of the Employment Act of 1946, recognizing a federal responsibility for promoting maximum employment, production, and purchasing power. Though substantially watered down by conservatives in Congress, the act embodied the Keynesian philosophy of using government fiscal policy to promote the growth and stability of the economy.[30] In developing specific proposals for government stimulus of economic growth after the war, Hansen, along with others, outlined a liberal political agenda for the next generation, culminating in John F. Kennedy's New Frontier and Lyndon B. Johnson's Great Society. Hansen stated his views in numerous articles in scholarly journals and popular magazines, interviews, testimony before congressional committees, and classroom lectures and seminars. He believed the federal government could involve itself in urban housing, river-valley and regional development, transportation modernization, soil conservation, reforestation, rural electrification, social security, medical care, child welfare, assistance to the elderly, foreign aid, and a variety of other programs.[31]

Though not victorious immediately, the ideas and proposals advanced by Hansen and his colleagues helped set the terms for economic debate in succeeding years. They framed them as elements of a "mixed economy" or "middle way" rather than simply as implementations of liberal principles. Many of the policy ideas he advanced during the 1940s were written into law during the next quarter century. By 1964, when Johnson pushed through the stimulatory tax cut introduced by his predecessor, Kennedy, Hansen could take satisfaction that Keynesian economic theory was finally driving national economic policy. Two of the three members of Kennedy's Council of Economic Advisers (James Tobin and Kermit Gordon) had been participants in Hansen's Harvard seminar, and the third member of the council, the chairman, Walter Heller, was a self-proclaimed "intellectual godchild" of Hansen's.[32] Another major adviser to the administration at the time was Paul Samuelson, Hansen's former student and one of the most influential economists of the twentieth century.

What had seemed to some observers to be radical and outlandish only a few years earlier had achieved widespread acceptance by the 1960s. Although the drift toward greater government intervention in the economy was, in large measure, probable in the wake of the traumas of the Great Depression and World War II, Hansen's participation in the process helped accelerate it and make it go down easier with Congress and the public. The characteristics he had acquired as a small-town boy growing up in the Midwest rendered many of his controversial proposals more palatable. His rural origins and the persona he projected, that of a stolid, commonsensical, practical midwesterner, increased his credibility and authority when it came to persuading members of Congress, fellow academics, and the general public to accept his views.

Hansen's public image was the opposite of that of a wild-eyed, radical professor. Standing 5'6" tall, bespectacled, stocky and with a bit of a middle-aged droop, and frequently sporting a green eyeshade to protect his overly sensitive eyes, he looked more like an accountant or a Main Street businessman.[33] But appearances can be deceiving. Richard Lee Strout wrote in the *New Republic,* "Behind the mildest and most reasonable of exteriors he sometimes offers comments which are simply political dynamite."[34] Hansen's presentation of himself on the public stage did much to defuse the outrage and objections that might otherwise have attended his economic advice.

Hansen's rhetorical techniques and moderate ideology likewise enhanced his influence. Always plainspoken and direct, he was careful not to sound too extreme. He knew how to package radical ideas in unthreaten-

CHAPTER NINE

ing terms. For example, he preferred the term "compensatory spending" to "deficit spending."[35] His tone always remained reasonable, temperate, and measured. As he built fact on fact, example on example, and argument on argument, he changed people's minds. His conclusions, even when they challenged conventional wisdom, often took on the appearance of logical inevitability. Rather than emphasizing government's role as regulator or intervener in the economy, he liked to use the metaphor of government as a "balance wheel."[36]

The goals Hansen proposed were achievable, and the means he advocated were pragmatic. His ultimate aim was not to abolish capitalism or to fundamentally transform it but, rather, to modify it incrementally as a way of helping it operate more effectively. He sought to promote "a mixed system in which economic decisions are widely diffused—a system in which production is mainly by private enterprise, but in which the state, by adequately supplying those needs which it alone can serve, is able to act as a balance wheel to the economy." The result would not be socialism or communism or any other kind of foreign ism but rather "a better-functioning market economy."[37]

Though couched in the rhetoric of moderation and reasonableness, the implications of Hansen's ideas were far-reaching and profound. This midwestern farm boy, for whom the simple, rural way of life never lost its appeal, understood the significant sea change that American society was going through. He realized that never again would the rural, small-town way of life dominate its activities. Born on the edge of the agricultural frontier, just as it was terminating, Hansen understood that the landed frontier in America had disappeared and that for economic growth to continue new frontiers would have to be discovered.[38] During the 1930s, Governor Philip F. La Follette of Wisconsin had called for new "vertical frontiers" of economic growth to rejuvenate and stabilize the economy.[39] Three decades later, John F. Kennedy would attach the phrase "New Frontier" to his administration. Writing in 1946, Alvin Hansen observed, "We now need to develop a new frontier so to speak, in our own back yard and thereby open new outlets for private investment."[40]

As a professor at Minnesota and Harvard, Hansen made frequent visits back to Viborg, where he enjoyed visiting relatives and friends, going out on drives and attending picnics, and just relaxing with his wife and children.[41] While the girls were growing up, Sunday nights were always looked forward to as a special treat, as the family sat around eating popcorn and listening to Daddy "tell stories about his childhood and describe what growing up in Viborg meant to him," daughter Marian recalled. "His family and his community were important to him."[42]

While recognizing the vital importance of farmers within the system, Hansen knew that as a percentage of the total workforce they were destined to continue to decline. "The plain fact," he wrote at the end of World War II, "is that all advanced individual nations have moved very far away from the atomistic individualism of the mid-nineteenth century. Then economic opportunity meant essentially a chance to operate your own farm or small business. Today economic opportunity means largely a chance to get a job. Then the bulk of the population lived in the country—on farms or in small villages. Today they live in great urban centers." It was this shift away from the conditions Hansen had experienced while growing up in South Dakota that necessitated the kinds of organized social control and government intervention that Keynesian economic principles were a part of. The great challenge of modern life was to find a way to reconcile individual rights and freedoms with the necessity for group and community action. That was the problem democracy would have to resolve in the decades ahead.[43]

Beyond acknowledging that the center of gravity in the United States had shifted from agriculture to industry and from rural precincts to city streets, Hansen also understood that a whole new psychology had emerged since he was a boy. At home in Viborg he had been instructed in and imbued with traditional Judeo-Christian virtues of industry, frugality, punctuality, integrity, and responsibility. These principles in many ways retained their relevance. But the twentieth century had also introduced a new set of values revolving around the activity of consumption. No longer, it seemed, was the producer king; into that place had stepped the consumer. With origins reaching far back into the nineteenth century, the accelerating rise of a consumption society during Hansen's lifetime significantly altered relationships between production and consumption, between work and leisure, and within social groups. These shifts, in turn, exposed what the sociologist Daniel Bell labeled the "cultural contradictions of capitalism."[44]

For someone like Hansen, who had grown up on a farm and known the rigors of farmwork but who had left for the city and a life in academia, the implications were profound. The professor never abandoned the industrious habits he had acquired as a youth. The dozens of books and articles that rolled off his typewriter testified to his strenuous work ethic. The energy he expended in promoting his ideas and beliefs in the political arena gave evidence of his sense of civic duty. The affability and cooperativeness he displayed with friend and critic alike bespoke his broad-mindedness and humanity. "I saw a lot of Alvin Hansen outside the classroom," recalled Paul Samuelson, "but I never heard him utter a critical word about a colleague."[45] Hansen's colleague John Williams noted that he gave more time to his students outside the classroom than any other professor Williams had ever known.[46]

Although Hansen was highly consistent in his own personality and actions, the Keynesian economic theory that he endorsed imposed new requirements on people that often contradicted the values he had grown up with. The challenge of the new economic world of the twentieth century, Keynes argued, was not so much to spur production as it was to maintain adequate levels of consumption. While seeing the need for growing levels of purchasing power within a rising standard of living, however, Hansen worried about the implications of mindless consumption. Like his Harvard colleague John Kenneth Galbraith, he criticized frivolous private expenditure while public needs were sorely neglected. The roads were filled with 300-horsepower cars, while schools, hospitals, roads, and other public services languished. "Never before has there been so great a waste of productive resources on things that have little or no inherent value," he lamented in 1961.[47] The major potential source of growth and the greatest challenge for directing future economic expansion lay in America's cities, Hansen, the country boy, believed. Public funds should be directed toward schools, hospitals, low-cost housing, urban transportation, juvenile delinquency programs, and other similar arenas.[48]

Ultimately, Hansen remained an optimist. For more than a decade after retiring from Harvard at the age of sixty-eight, he continued to be active as a teacher, scholar, and writer. He filled temporary teaching positions at Smith, Haverford, Yale, Michigan, and California as well as lectureships in India, Japan, and Sweden. Always a family man, he and his wife, Mabel, had raised two daughters, and after retirement he was able to spend more time with his grandchildren.[49] The Nobel Prize in Economics, which had been inaugurated too late for him to be carefully considered for it, was awarded to several of his former students and students of theirs. The Keynesian revolution that he had promoted in the United States became routine. As Hansen's former student James Tobin recalled, "Alvin Hansen was never close to Presidents or politicians, and he never held a major government office. Yet no American economist was more important for the historic redirection of United States macroeconomic policy from 1935 to 1965. As the principal intellectual leader of the Keynesian conquest, Hansen deserves major credit for the 'fiscal revolution in America.'"[50] The fruits of his teaching and writing were incorporated in economics textbooks. By the time of Hansen's death in 1975, what one magazine writer had written about him thirty years earlier remained true: "An ex–farm boy has come a long way."[51]

CHAPTER TEN

Bob Feller: Iowa Farm Boy on the "Field of Dreams"

Home is where your youth is, where your family is, and where you grow up. My home in Iowa was three miles northeast of the town of Van Meter, and I'm proud that I grew up on that farm, in that state, and with my parents. I enjoyed life in Van Meter, and I knew everyone in town—the barber, the grocery man, and the druggist at the pharmacy where I purchased milkshakes in the late 1920s and early 1930s. . . . My classmates and teammates still live in Van Meter, and I'm proud of my roots there.

—Bob Feller

The realm of baseball consists as much of myth and dreams as it does of reality. From Abner Doubleday and "Casey at the Bat" to Babe Ruth, Roy Hobbs, and *Field of Dreams*, it has been difficult to disentangle fact from fantasy. Countless generations of young boys have aspired to be big-league ballplayers and to hear the roar of the crowd. Having one's image reproduced in living color on little pieces of cardboard has held far more appeal to millions of youngsters than the possibility of becoming president of the United States. If baseball is a game of dreams, the dream of many young players has been to get a ticket out of town or away from the farm and take a trip to a city of bright lights and roaring crowds.

The early history of baseball in America is closely associated with the development of the game in New York and in other city settings.[1] Its rapid spread across the United States after the Civil War took it into every corner of the rural countryside. "From the standpoint of participation," wrote Ken Smith in his 1947 history of the National Baseball Hall of Fame, "baseball is essentially a small-town game. Big-city attendance enables the sport to operate as a big business, but a preponderance of those players first see the light of day in country villages."[2] What once may have been true no longer holds, for suburban and metropolitan America now serve as the primary breeding grounds for future major leaguers. For much of its early history, however, baseball remained to a considerable degree a small-town game. Most towns, whatever their size, fielded a team—sometimes two or more—and their residents took pride in their boys' accomplishments. Local newspapers provided detailed accounts of contests against rival communities, establishing bragging rights in the process. Main Street businessmen often hired ringers from other towns to improve the home team's chances. With the rise of major-league baseball, small-town heroes began to dream of the day when they would be playing for St. Louis, Chicago, or Philadelphia. A young man's prowess at hitting, throwing, and catching a baseball outranked his ability to parse a sentence or figure a sum. There was no need, if one were so blessed, to walk behind a plow, work an assembly line, or sit at a desk.

In a world of rapid and bewildering change, as the United States evolved from a rural, agricultural society into an urban, industrial one, baseball furnished both a method of accommodating change and a means of transcending it. As a recreational outlet available to farmers and small-town dwellers, as well as to city folks, it offered escape from drudgery and routine. Though its rules had been worked out by New York City enthusiasts during the 1840s, a legend arose about the sport's birth in upstate New York, in Cooperstown, a legend created by a future Civil War general named Abner Doubleday. No truth attached to the story, but the tidy village at the foot of a picturesque lake in the east-central part of the state successfully capitalized on it, and the Baseball Hall of Fame was dedicated in the little town in 1939.[3]

Baseball supplied a physical and emotional outlet for people ensconced in the new urban-industrial order. Games, after all, were played on "fields" of dirt and grass. In the country, baseball diamonds theoretically could extend indefinitely, until they ran into barriers like cemeteries and hillsides. Sometimes balls hit between the outfielders disappeared into creeks or cornfields. City parks, on the contrary, sported fences separating the playing area from surrounding sidewalks and streets. In either case, the greenness of the grass kindled images of rurality, the outdoors, freedom, and the past. Baseball, thought of in this way, provided an escape from urban concrete and steel. More than other American games, such as basketball and modern football, its rules scarcely varied from decade to decade, the nature of the game remaining remarkably stable.

"Baseball," according to poet Donald Hall, "because of its continuity over the space of America and the time of America, is a place where memory gathers."[4] Reverie links past to present; baseball fans typically exhibit more nostalgia than other sports aficionados. It is difficult to contemplate the exploits of Albert Pujols, Miguel Cabrera, or Justin Verlander without comparing them to Babe Ruth, Ted Williams, or Dizzy Dean. But players and fans are as concerned about the future as they are about the past. They want to know what their teams and players are going to do tomorrow and next week, and they rest their hopes and dreams on the probable likelihood of success or failure. Baseball, like other games, introduces contingency into our lives—something at once exhilarating and frightful. Without the risk of failure, little gratification exists in success. But without the possibility of success, life remains sterile and dull.

The dream world of baseball is plentifully supplied with real and imaginary phenoms—brilliant young athletes who burst suddenly onto the scene and take our breath away with their extraordinary skills and potential. For every bright prospect who succeeds in the major leagues—a Stan Musial, a Willie Mays, or a Sandy Koufax—there are countless others whose star shines brightly for a moment, then flickers out—a Steve Dalkowski, a Clint Hartung, or a David Clyde. One of the most awe-inspiring prospects to reach the big time during the middle decades of the twentieth century was a farm boy from Iowa who seemed to epitomize the virtues and strengths of the rural, small-town way of life. Bob Feller came up with the Cleveland

Indians in 1936 and pitched for them until 1956, losing the better part of four years to military service during World War II.

The young man was born to play ball. His father, who had harbored aspirations of his own to play the game, groomed his son from an early age to be a big-league ballplayer. His 360-acre farm three miles northeast of Van Meter was typical of the era. At a time when ballplayers were routinely connected in people's minds with the hometowns from which they derived, Van Meter, Iowa, a typical farm service center of around 500 population, was a great little town to have come from. Feller retained strong ties to Van Meter after leaving home, was honored frequently by it during his early days as a ballplayer, and in later years returned to visit it from time to time, especially after the community erected a small museum in his honor.[5]

The farm boy displayed athletic precocity early. As commonly happens with talented athletes who can hit and throw, he alternated between pitching and playing shortstop before settling down on the mound. Feller was only seventeen, with a year left to go in high school, when he made his first appearance in a Cleveland uniform during the summer of 1936. He was fortunate in having a manager, Steve O'Neill, who took a special interest in him and who attempted to protect him from the pressures bound to descend on him. Unfortunately, O'Neill lasted only two more seasons with the team before getting the ax.

The fireballing hurler never played a game in the minors; his astounding performances in an exhibition game against the St. Louis Cardinals and in his first two starts against American League teams made him an instant sensation. Observers searched for metaphors to describe what they were seeing. He took on legendary status, seeming to travel as much in the realm of myth as in the world of reality. The blazing speed and movement on Feller's fastball stimulated instant comparisons with Walter Johnson and every other hard thrower who had ever played the game. Throughout his career, people would argue about whether Feller was faster than the "Big Train" (as Johnson was known), Amos Rusie, Van Lingle Mungo, or any of the other fireballers they may have seen. Later the discussion would shift to Sandy Koufax, Nolan Ryan, and Stephen Strasburg. Feller's arm seemed like magic, something he and his father accepted matter-of-factly, and they focused on protecting it. They began referring to the youngster's strong right arm as "It." In 1934, Feller's mother sewed an arm warmer out of discarded long johns for him to wear in the dugout between innings to protect the valuable appendage. He took the homemade contraption along with him to the big leagues and continued to use it for years. Cleveland's trainers examined Feller's arm, stretched it, rubbed it, and kneaded it, protecting it as if it were the crown jewels. A magazine article reported that he always reached for doorknobs, light switches, and other objects with his left hand, careful to save his right one for pitching.[6]

The strikeouts, no-hitters, and victories that Feller's right arm racked up over the years invited endless celebration and analysis. Even his wildness, resulting in a high ratio of walks, was a tangible asset, since batters hesitated to dig in against him. Although many ballplayers accumulate impressive numbers over the course of their careers, few manage to inspire an entirely new statistical measure of prowess. Endless debates over Feller's velocity and its comparison to that of his predecessors spurred several ingenious tests designed to measure the velocity of his pitches. In one, a speeding motorcycle shot down a road, and Feller released a pitch just as the rider passed by, with ball and rider moving parallel to each other toward a fixed target. More sophisticated devices emerged later. In August 1946, a U.S. Army lumiline chronograph, proclaimed to be accurate within 1/10,000th of a second, clocked one of his fast balls at 98.6 miles per hour, faster than anyone else who was tested by it. In later years, Feller and others estimated that he could throw the ball 104 or 105 miles per hour when he was humming.[7]

No rookie ever registered as immediate an impact on the majors as Feller did in the summer of 1936, and few continued to live up to their potential over a long career as completely as he did. Superlatives were the order of the day that summer, as writers strained for labels to describe him. "Miracle Kid," "Wonder Boy," "Boy Wizard," "the Babe Ruth of the mound," "the schoolboy of baseball," and "the Cinderella boy of baseball" were among the many nicknames attached to him. "Iowa farm boy" was among the favorites, and some writers were still calling him that during the 1948 World Series, when he was almost thirty years old. Rogers Hornsby, who had been his idol, took one look at Feller and proclaimed, "The boy's a natural."[8] Over the years, the moniker that stuck was "Rapid Robert." Speed was always the attribute uniquely associated with Feller, even after he had lost most of it.

Feller may have been the most ballyhooed rookie of all time. Future Hall of Famer "Big Ed" Walsh, a forty-game winner in 1908, called him the greatest prospect ever to enter the game. "He has as much stuff as any pitcher who ever threw the horsehide," he observed.[9] After calling one of his games, the legendary umpire Bill Klem commented, "Feller showed me stuff the like of which I've never seen in all my life."[10] Soon credible observers were predicting that he was capable of winning 400 or 500 games, surpassing Walter Johnson's and Cy Young's victory totals. Nothing seemed impossible.

Fiction blended easily with fact in countless anecdotes told about him. Did Dick Bartell of the Giants strike out thirteen of the sixteen times he faced Feller in spring training after asserting that Van Lingle Mungo could throw harder than the kid? (Yes.) Did Feller strike out every St. Louis Cardinal he faced in a three-inning exhibition stint against them, the first time he ever pitched against major leaguers, as Grantland Rice recalled in at least two different columns? (No. But eight of the nine outs he recorded were strikeouts, and the Cardinals managed only two hits against him.) A photographer asked the great Dizzy Dean if he would object to having his picture taken with the fuzzy-cheeked fireballer. "Me object?" drawled the great hurler. "After what I seen today, I reckon you'd a better ask him if he objects to posing with me."[11] Did Yankee hurler Lefty Gomez actually light a match once when he stepped up to the plate against Feller while dusk was gathering over Yankee Stadium? "Whazzamatter?" asked the ump. "Can't you see the plate?" "Certainly," Gomez replied. "I just want to make sure that Feller can see it, too." (Probably. With "Goofy" Gomez, almost anything was bound to happen.)[12]

Much of baseball's appeal derives from its stories, ranging from the solidly verifiable to the clearly preposterous. What made Feller so special was that in his case the verifiable and the fantastic blended in such large proportions. What nobody believed possible was demonstrable on the basis of box scores and movie reels. The boy took his exploits in stride. Almost from the time he started playing team ball as a young teenager, his goal was to play in the major leagues. The question in his mind and his father's was not "if?" but "when?" Once established in the big leagues, he readily admitted his ambition to become the greatest pitcher of all time.[13] During his prime, he was the biggest draw in the league, and he had a unique incentive clause inserted in his contract linking his compensation to attendance figures. His salary from the start outstripped almost every other player's at similar stages in their careers. He was the highest-paid rookie ever (after his spectacular sixty-two-inning stint as a high schooler in 1936), and he kept getting sizable increases after that, eventually making him the highest-salaried pitcher during the 1940s and one of the three best-paid players in the game, along with Joe DiMaggio and Ted Williams. Fans wanted to see Feller whether he won or lost, because the potential was always present for a no-hitter or a new strikeout record. In 1938 he broke his own single game mark by striking out eighteen Detroit Tigers, and in 1946 he set a new single season whiff standard with 348. His three no-hitters and twelve one-hitters remained a record for low-hit games until Nolan Ryan broke it in 1989.[14]

But Feller's records and accomplishments, as impressive as they were, did not account entirely for the excitement and attention that his presence engendered on the field, at least before inevitable decline set in. There was an aura about him that set him apart—not exactly cockiness, but confidence in his own ability and certainty regarding his destiny. His spectacular debut as a seventeen-year-old stirred huge expectations, and his growing confidence and ability, year by year, reinforced them. From the beginning, he possessed a stride that seemed to project arrogance as he ambled to and from the mound, but friendly observers said it merely reflected the peculiarities of his bone structure. On the pitching rubber itself, he always seemed in control, confident of his ability to fool any batter or blow the ball by him. He never showed surprise at any of his exploits; whatever new records were set or milestones reached, it was all part of a plan that he and his father had worked out long before, when he was a kid. Just as impressive as his on-the-field accomplishments were his off-the-field activities, which, in their own way, were as innovative and surprising as his playing record.

Bob Feller's story was not a simple script of unalloyed success. It also had its share of disappointment, failure, and heartbreak. Feller had to struggle with his first wife's descent into addiction to prescription drugs. For baseball fans, the big question about his career was what he might have accomplished had the United States not entered World War II just when he was at the height of his pitching powers. Two days after Pearl Harbor, he became the first major leaguer to enlist in the military when he signed up as a chief boatswain's mate in the navy's physical training program. Lieutenant Commander Gene Tunney, former heavyweight boxing champion, was commander of the unit.[15] Feller, a physical fitness buff who regularly worked out with weights and pursued a complicated routine of stretching and strength exercises long before most of his fellow ballplayers ever gave them a thought, soon hungered for more action, so he volunteered for gunnery school. By the spring of 1943, he had risen to become chief of a twenty-four-man antiaircraft crew on the 35,000-ton U.S.S. *Alabama,* doing patrol duty in the Atlantic. Its 2,900-member crew was five times larger than the population of Van Meter. In August, it was reassigned to the Pacific theater, and during the next two years the ship accumulated eight battle stars in engagements in the Marshalls, Saipan, the Marianas, New Guinea, Tarawa, Bougainville, Guam, and the Philippines.[16]

Although he managed to play a little baseball in the navy—first before action heated up in the Pacific and then after returning to the States in 1945, when he replaced major-league catcher Mickey Cochrane as manager of the Great Lakes Naval Training Station team—Feller spent most of his tour on regular duty, much of it in heavy combat. Many major leaguers lost only a year or two to military service. Feller was out almost four full years. He was released from active duty in 1945 in time to get into nine games with the Indians, compiling a 5–3 record. Feller gracefully accepted this hiatus in his career and never complained about the lost time. He was proud of his war service, considering it his patriotic duty. Returning from the war, he realized that he would probably never challenge the records for career victories and strikeouts, but he still hoped to establish himself as the best pitcher who ever played the game.

Such ambitions were not necessarily pretentious for someone who, from the time he began to play the game competitively, had always outshone his competitors. Baseball was in the blood in the Feller household. Both Bob's father, Bill, and his maternal grandfather, Edward Forret, had aspired to play big-league ball, but neither possessed the requisite skills. Instead, Bill Feller projected his own dreams and aspirations on his firstborn and only son (he had a sister, ten years younger), hoping that his boy might succeed where he and his father-in-law had failed. Bill was never excessively pushy with his son about the game, preferring to let him decide on his own how much he wanted to play and practice it. "Contrary to what may have been written," Bob reminded people, "my dad never forced baseball on me."[17] Clearly, however, there was more going on than simple encouragement. As an infant, he received balls, rather than rattles, to play with. Growing up, he and his father played catch with each other, practiced hitting, and studied books on the science of the game. They picked up broadcasts of Chicago Cubs games on the radio. For a while during the early 1930s, a young man named Ronald Reagan broadcasted the play-by-play accounts of Cubs games over Des Moines radio station WHO.[18]

One day when Bob was nine, his father came home with a Rogers Hornsby fielder's glove and a Ray Schalk catcher's mitt along with a striped uniform and a pair of spikes. Now the lad could look like a real big-league ballplayer when the two were playing catch. After dark, they would turn on a light to illuminate the yard. When the weather turned bad, they would transfer into the barn. Supper often cooled on the table while father and son continued to play after chores. "It's still amazing to me how firmly my father believed that I couldn't miss becoming a big leaguer," Feller recounted in his ghosted 1947 autobiography, *Strikeout Story.* "He wasn't a braggart, but it was one subject upon which he was always outspoken in town. Everybody knew Bill Feller and his dream. They kidded him about it in an affectionate way."[19]

After Bob made it to the majors, stories datelined Van Meter noted that Bill Feller had altered his farming methods to accommodate his project to make his son into a big-league ballplayer. He had allegedly switched over to exclusively planting wheat, which required less care than corn, allowing more time for baseball. In fact, in the tradition of two generations of Fellers on the land in Iowa, Bill Feller was a progressive and highly successful farmer who switched out of corn when commodity prices plunged during the late 1920s. He subsequently bought a state-of-the-art Caterpillar tractor and combine to harvest wheat, which proved to be a more profitable crop for him. The innovative and well-researched decisions that he made to become a successful farmer found their counterpart in his son's later creativity in striking out in new directions and enhancing his earning power as an athlete and businessman. Both men likewise demonstrated a high degree of skill in constructing narratives of their own activities and successes that, while based substantially on real accomplishments, also tended to enhance and exaggerate their virtues and achievements.[20]

Nor was it true that the young Bob Feller was excused from farmwork to concentrate on the game. In helping his dad with the plowing, cultivating, and harvesting and in the process of milking, hauling water, shoveling wheat and oats, and all the other chores that needed to be done, Bob was building up muscles that provided him a ticket away from the farm. His parents carefully watched his diet and monitored his schedule. While friends were out having fun, Bob was already in bed asleep, earning him a reputation as a "papa's boy."[21]

Bob entered the world of organized baseball in 1931, at the age of twelve, playing for the American Legion team at Adel, a nearby town three times as large as Van Meter. Till then, Rogers Hornsby, the great St. Louis Cardinals second baseman, had been his idol, and hitting had been his favorite part of the game. But Bill Feller was beginning to think that his son's strong right arm was probably his greatest asset and would provide his best chance for a ticket to the majors. As he climbed the rungs of youth baseball, the boy continued to alternate between shortstop and the pitching mound. Though he still loved to take his cuts at the plate, it was his mound skills that captured people's attention.[22]

In 1932, Bob and his father constructed a baseball diamond in their own backyard, so to speak, a quarter mile east of the barn. They put in several rows of seats; installed a scoreboard, a backstop, and a chicken-wire fence from first base around to third to protect the spectators; and erected outhouses and a soda pop stand along the right-field line. They named the field Oakview Park, referring to a stand of oak trees between it and the Raccoon River, a mile away. Bill Feller organized a team called the Oakviews, bought team uniforms, and became its manager. Several hundred people would turn out for games on Sunday afternoons to watch Bob and his teammates play the opponent of the week. In 1989, when the movie *Field of Dreams* came out, people around Van Meter observed that an actual "field of dreams" had existed half a century earlier in central Iowa.[23]

Word of Bob's prowess got around; by the time he was sixteen, major-league clubs started taking note. Unfortunately for the others, Cy Slapnicka, who scouted the region for the Cleveland Indians, got there first, signing the phenom up for a song the summer after his sophomore year in high school. Elements of fable surrounded the actual circumstances of this signing: the Cleveland scout showed up in a wheat field where father and son were combining to find out when their next game was scheduled, the contract was handwritten on the back of a piece of hotel stationery, and the Indians violated a rule against signing a player directly off the sandlots without going through a minor-league club. Adjudicating the case two years later, baseball commissioner Kenesaw Mountain Landis almost stripped the Indians of their rights.[24]

Everything about the Feller lad seemed outsized. At sixteen, while pitching for the Des Moines Farmers' Union team, he averaged nineteen strike-outs per game. He was so fast and so wild that opposing batters were afraid to stand in to swing against him. Jimmy Ahern, one of Bob's catchers, remembered that the first time he took warm-up pitches from him the ball went sailing over the backstop. "Every batter that got up there knew he was taking a chance," Ahern recalled.[25] Bob's pitches were tough to catch in any case, and passed balls sometimes allowed hitters who had struck out to reach base safely.

Feller hoopla carried on the following summer, when the Indians planned to keep him under wraps on the roster of a local semipro team in Cleveland. But after the eight strikeouts he recorded against the powerful Cardinals lineup in a three-inning exhibition stint in July, the Indians hurriedly elevated him to their regular roster and began working him as a relief pitcher. In his first starting assignment against the St. Louis Browns, Feller struck out fifteen batters, one shy of the American League record. In his fifth start a few weeks later, the farm boy amazed everybody when he broke the twenty-eight-year-old American League record by whiffing seventeen Philadelphia Athletics. The performance also tied Dizzy Dean's three-year-old major-league record. The enthusiastic Slapnicka predicted that his discovery would some day strike out twenty batters in a game. "If he had said twenty-seven, the possible maximum in a nine-inning game, no one would have argued," raved one Cleveland sportswriter. "You can't put a limit on a miracle."[26]

One thing that makes baseball so interesting to observers is the element of contingency it injects into everyday life. The inability to predict—or plan for—the future added a roller-coaster element to Feller's first several years in the big leagues. A sore arm plagued him in 1937, causing some people to wonder whether he had merely been a flash in the pan. He finished the year with a modest 9–7 record. In his third season, he improved to 17–11, but a mediocre 4.08 earned run average kept him from the ranks of the best pitchers in the league. During the next three years, however, he set a blistering pace, establishing himself as one of the most consistently overpowering pitchers ever to play the game, as he averaged 25 victories and over 250 strikeouts a year. The big hole left in his record by the war must remain a matter of speculation, but considering how well he did when he came back in 1946 and 1947, it is reasonable to assume that during those years he would have established one of the best career pitching records in the history of the game. His first full year after the war, when he toted up 26 victories, along with the 348 whiffs and an impressive 2.18 earned run average, was his best.

Had he been able to continue at that pace for several more years, it would have gone far toward making up for the gap caused by his war service. Unfortunately, a freak accident on the pitching mound in June 1947 seriously injured his arm, and he was never quite the same again. Losing his footing as he strode forward on a curveball, he tripped and performed a complete somersault, landing awkwardly on his back. In the process, he tore a muscle behind his right shoulder blade and also hurt his knee.[27] He still managed to compile an excellent 20–11 record that year and had one more outstanding season left in him, but never again would his fastball carry the same zip. He would have to rely primarily on guile and experience, locating his pitches more carefully and mixing his curves and sliders with a now merely so-so fastball. But as his career unfolded, he continued to make a unique—and much different kind of—impress on the game.

For a farm kid from Iowa with only a high school education, Feller possessed an impressive flair for the dramatic gesture and frequently challenged accepted ways. A ghosted autobiography of his childhood, *My Own Story,* syndicated in newspapers during the spring of 1937, signaled his willingness to exploit opportunities opened up by his mound mastery. By 1940, as his salary approached $30,000, making him already, at the age of twenty-one, one of the highest-paid pitchers in baseball, Feller built a dream home for his family on their farm. A fashionable two-story English-style brick house consisting of ten rooms and costing $25,000 to build, it was fitted out with all the latest gadgets and furnishings. In rural Iowa, where electricity was only beginning to penetrate, the house boasted a modern heating system, air-conditioning, an electric garage-door opener, and, in the kitchen, an electric dishwasher and automatic sewage disposal. Bob, who for several years continued to return home during the off-season, had a welter of electric outlets installed in his room, although his thirteen-year-old sister Marguerite's room was bigger than his. The young man's penchant for speed behind the wheel also attracted press attention. His quick decision to enlist in the military after Pearl Harbor typified his nature. In many ways still a kid, and one remaining close to his family, he quickly acquired a reputation for innovation and the grand gesture and evinced an unusual ability to translate his baseball skills into personal advancement.

Returning from the war in 1945 as a decorated veteran and symbol of valor (he was the first major-league baseball player to volunteer for service after Pearl Harbor), he was still only twenty-six and determined to make up for lost time. During the late 1940s, Feller emerged as an established star, even as his pitching skills began to decline and he first experienced

CHAPTER TEN

more than scattered boos in the stands and criticism from sportswriters. This period proved to be a time of troubles for him even as he continued to generally shine on the field. More than his fellow players, he found ways to increase his income by exploiting his name and the popularity of the game. While corporate America was rapidly expanding its power and influence and the "organization man" epitomized the character traits it demanded of its employees, Feller stood out from his counterparts in his ability to transform himself into a marketable commodity and to enhance his income.

In 1946, Feller persuaded baseball commissioner Happy Chandler to extend the postseason barnstorming period in October from ten days to thirty to compensate for a spring training camp for military veterans he had set up. His further contention that he and other veterans who had foregone considerable amounts of money while defending their country deserved a chance to recoup some of their losses was hard to refute. Beyond that, in 1946 a wealthy businessman named Jorge Pasquel inaugurated the Mexican League to compete with the American game and succeeded in wooing a number of established major leaguers, including Sal Maglie, Max Lanier, and Mickey Owen, who quit their clubs and signed large contracts with teams in his new operation. Stan Musial reportedly almost jumped the Cardinals, and Feller turned down a multiyear offer of $100,000 a season.[28]

Team owners were justifiably nervous. After the World Series that fall, Feller and a group of major league all-stars that he had recruited played thirty-five games in thirty days, mostly against a group of black all-stars captained by the legendary pitcher Satchel Paige. They appeared before approximately 250,000 paying customers in cities extending from New York to Los Angeles, as well as several in Canada and Hawaii. It was the most ambitious such enterprise since Charles Comiskey and John McGraw had organized a round-the-world tour in 1913. For his efforts, Musial received $6,000. Lesser-known players such as Mickey Vernon, Johnny Sain, and Charlie Keller rated smaller paychecks, but for some of them it was as much as they had earned from their teams during the entire regular season. The players he had recruited were happy with the results, and Feller himself could not have been more pleased. He estimated that he cleared $80,000, after expenses, from the venture. The tour was a pathbreaker in several ways—in its unprecedented use of airplanes for transportation, in its bringing top-level baseball to the Pacific coast and thereby promoting the possibility of major-league expansion into the area, and in its helping pave the way for Jackie Robinson's breaking in with the Brooklyn Dodgers the following season.[29]

Feller's imaginative entrepreneurialism impressed many people; sportswriters spilled quantities of ink assessing its implications. Some onlookers expressed concern that players would tire themselves out playing the extra games, which would reduce their value to their teams during the regular season. Washington Senators owner Clark Griffith complained that Musial, his own Vernon, and Feller himself suffered subpar years in 1947 because of overexertion the previous year. Fearing just that possibility, along with the danger of injury or accident, the Boston Red Sox paid Ted Williams and the Detroit Tigers gave Hal Newhouser $10,000 *not* to go along on the tour. The owners, enjoying neither the idea of their players unnecessarily risking injury nor the competition to themselves of Feller's operation, were anything but pleased with his shenanigans. They especially shuddered at the notion of their stars flying together in the leased plane that transported them from site to site.[30]

After the 1947 season, Feller ran another successful barnstorming tour and intended to conduct one again the following year. But midway through the 1948 season, his arm rebelled and his record was stuck at a mediocre 9–12, stimulating considerable concern, speculation, and criticism among fans and sportswriters both in and outside of Cleveland. Feller himself grew increasingly worried that he might be losing his stuff, although he expected that his arm would eventually come around, as it had in the past. The boo-birds, always a distinct minority in the Cleveland stands, became increasingly vocal. Fans in Cleveland and in other cities around the league blamed Feller not only for having worn out his arm barnstorming (pitching two to five innings almost every day for an entire month) but also for what they perceived as the underlying greed that lay behind it. Stories about Feller now often concentrated less on his athletic prowess than on his various efforts to make a buck and on his executive skills in managing his own career. What with product endorsements, an autobiography on bookstore shelves, recorded broadcasts piped out over forty-five radio stations, and a number of other entrepreneurial ventures, Feller was, according to *Washington Post* sportswriter Shirley Povich, "cleaning up very nicely. By 1948, with contractual bonuses linked to attendance figures driving his salary up over $80,000, his total income probably doubled that figure when counting his outside sources of revenue.[31]

The kid from Van Meter obviously was doing all right for himself, but was he doing right by his team and his fans? Midway through the 1948 season, he announced that he would forego barnstorming that fall. He planned to concentrate entirely on capturing the pennant and on winning the World Series. His popularity with fans and sportswriters had nosedived when he opted out of playing in the All-Star Game for the second year in a row. In 1947, his bad back had provided a valid excuse, but his argument the following year, that he was having a lousy season and did not deserve inclusion on the team, fell flat. Critics asserted that he was just looking out for himself, shunning his responsibility to the pastime, and collaborating with the Cleveland Indians' management in resting him up for the pennant race.[32] If that was his intention, it apparently worked, because he came on strong in the second half of the season, finishing with a rush by winning nine of his last ten games.[33] The Indians triumphed over the Boston Braves in a six-games World Series that October, but the series was disappointing for Feller personally. Although he pitched well in the opener against Johnny Sain, he got burned by a bad call in the eighth inning on a pickoff play at second base on Phil Masi. When the Boston catcher subsequently scored, Feller absorbed the loss in a heartbreaking 1–0 decision. He pitched poorly in the fifth game, but the Indians came back the next day to win it all, so his two defeats had no effect on the final outcome of the series.

In the fall of 1948, Joe King of the *New York World-Telegram* reflected on Feller as a rising young executive in the baseball business: "The capitalistic ventures of the farm boy embarrassed him this year because he measured the size of the dollar sign more scientifically than any in the history of his trade. He never went to college, but he is a slide-rule engineer on a treasury note."[34] Living in a luxurious home in a Cleveland suburb, Feller now piloted his own airplane, hobnobbed with business executives, and saved time by shaving in his car while driving to the ballpark. As Ro-Fel, Inc., he became baseball's first incorporated athlete. "The simple Iowa farm boy," observed the *Saturday Evening Post*, "has grown up to be a business smoothie—one of the smartest ballplayers, from a financial standpoint, who ever picked up a fountain pen."[35] On the one hand, people were startled and impressed by Feller's success in his business ventures; on the other, some worried that all his outside activities were detracting from his performance on the diamond.

In 1955, with his baseball skills rapidly eroding and his career winding down, Feller took on the job of American League player representative in negotiations with the owners. Still only in his midthirties, he was regarded by his fellow ballplayers as something of a financial wizard, and his long experience in the game and reputation for speaking directly and honestly and for standing up to the owners made him—along with some others, such as Stan Musial, Ted Williams, and Robin Roberts—one of the most respected and influential players in the game. During the next several years, both before and after his retirement at the end of the 1956 season, he spoke out forcefully for solidifying the players' pension fund and for utilizing revenues from radio and television rights to World Series and All-Star games to build it up. Required to quit as player representative when he retired, he continued to voice his concerns first as president of the newly formed Major League Baseball Players Association and then as a member of the Major League Pension Committee.[36] Feller had been ahead of his time during the 1930s and 1940s in capitalizing on his celebrity status to augment his own income. Now he participated on the ground floor of the players' movement in demanding more rights for themselves and in seeking to force the owners to transfer more of the rewards of the business to the men in the field. Statements Feller made about the owners during the late 1950s upset not only them but some traditionalist writers who thought that players and ex-players like Feller were becoming too mercenary and business-minded.

Feller missed the game after retiring but quickly discovered plenty of things to keep busy with. He had his own insurance agency and involved himself in a variety of other business ventures. For a couple of years, he toured the country as a self-appointed ambassador for baseball, putting on pitching exhibitions for youngsters,[37] talking up the game, and encouraging baseball executives to change with the times and meet the demands and expectations of a new kind of fan that was emerging in postwar, tail-finned, jet-age, television-addicted America. Feller was as comfortable in a business suit as he had been in uniform on the pitching mound. He had always lived cleanly, had never been a smoker and was not a drinker. He had been a physical fitness buff before it became fashionable, and he continued to demonstrate his pitching form into his eighties. Baseball had been good to him, and he never regretted living out his father's dream to make him into a major-league baseball player. As the Baseball Writers Association of America prepared to vote him into the Baseball Hall of Fame in 1962, Jimmy Cannon explained why he would vote for the Cleveland ace: "After a while a guy in my business has to be cautious about the myths that famous athletes inhabit. But the myth of Bob Feller is true and wonderful. It is one of the great legends of sport and this country. His life is a boy's version of manhood and it has endured without defacement."[38] He had arrived on the scene during the Depression-ridden 1930s when ballplayers like himself were still frequently identified with their hometowns. After retiring from the game, he found himself living in a world dominated by suburbs and metropolitan areas—a homogenized order in which one's rural roots were submerged in a culture increasingly governed by the mind-set and goals of mass fashion, the mass media, and the mass mind. Only when Latino players and then athletes from Japan began signing contracts in large numbers did place and one's origins again become major identifying marks for baseball's heroes of the diamond.

■

James Dean: The Indiana Rebel without a Cause

[James Dean was] a small-town boy rocketed to success without warning, without preparation—an average young American still confused by a new life, not yet adjusted to fame, fortune and fan mania.

—William Mellor, cinematographer

Reports of James Dean's death at the age of twenty-four in an automobile accident on September 30, 1955, stunned his friends and acquaintances, along with a rapidly growing coterie of fans and followers of the young actor's career. Christine White, who had successfully auditioned with him for Actors Studio in New York, gasped and dropped the phone on hearing the news. "There was no way I could think of this guy who was moving all the time as being dead. It was just impossible," she said later. For others, the news, though painful, came as no surprise. Former girlfriend Barbara Glenn commented, "I knew it was imminent. I knew some day he was never coming back." Film director Elia Kazan, whose *East of Eden* had less than a year earlier catapulted Dean onto the list of Hollywood's rising young stars, sighed, "That figures." Humphrey Bogart commented sardonically, "He died at just the right time. He left behind a legend. If he lived, he'd never have been able to live up to his publicity."[1]

Not since Rudolph Valentino's premature death at thirty-one in 1926 had the movie industry witnessed anything like the outpouring of emotion stimulated by the young actor's passing. "In sixteen months of acting, he left a more lasting impression on the public than many stars do in thirty years," noted the producer Henry Ginsberg.[2] Dean's demise did nothing to diminish the moviegoing public's fascination with him. Within days of the crash, the release of *Rebel without a Cause,* his second feature film and the one that did most to fix his public image, further enhanced the small-town Hoosier's reputation as an unusually gifted actor, converting him into a fifties icon. His image was that of the rebellious, questioning, emotionally starved teenager who calls down on the older generation a torrent of criticism and complaint. Though perhaps less technically adroit and satisfying than Kazan's *East of Eden,* Nicholas Ray's *Rebel,* which was made in close collaboration with his young star, directed attention toward emotions and feelings that reverberated meaningfully with a generation of young Americans growing up after World War II who were just beginning to view themselves as a coherent entity.

Something in Dean's film persona and offscreen behavior connected with youthful audiences in a way that had never been experienced before. Within nine months of his death, more than 400 fan clubs were perpetuating his memory in the United States, Canada, South America, and Europe. Warner Brothers reported receiving 5,000 to 8,000 letters a week, many of them addressed directly to their former star, and three years later Dean was still getting as many as 2,000 letters a week, more than any living actor.[3] Many of the letter writers refused to accept that Dean was dead. Rumors circulated that he had been horribly disfigured in the crash and was hidden away somewhere in a sanitarium or a monastery or was living on an obscure desert island.

Like medieval religious enthusiasts seeking relics of the saints, eager Dean worshippers searched out photographs, pieces of clothing, locks of his hair, chips from his tombstone—anything that might help them feel a personal closeness to the hero of their imagination. His tombstone (inscribed simply "James Dean, 1931–1955") disappeared more than once from the graveyard in his hometown of Fairmount, Indiana, until one replacement, anchored so securely in the ground that only a formidable piece of machinery could have dislodged it, foiled future vandals. The crumpled frame of the Porsche Spyder that Dean had been driving on the day of the accident was purchased by an enterprising couple who charged people twenty-five cents apiece to view it and twice that to actually sit in the death seat and touch the twisted, broken steering wheel.[4] Almost 200 magazine articles about Dean—his movie roles, love life, racing career, friendships, odd behavior, dreams, and fantasies—appeared during the two years after his death. Readers could not seem to get enough of stories with titles such as "James Dean's Last Ride," "I Almost Married Jimmy Dean," "Jimmy Dean's Hidden Heartbreak," and "How Jimmy Dean Still Works Miracles for Others." The iconic image of Dean, one of the most photographed figures of his time, pervaded the culture. His visage, reproduced in books, magazines, paintings, posters, T-shirts, movies, postage stamps, and other formats, became one of the most recognizable and memorable cultural artifacts of the time, not only in the United States but around the world.

We can only speculate about the way Dean's image would have survived and evolved had a college student named Donald Turnipseed not swerved his Ford automobile directly into the path of Dean's speeding race car that hazy, sun-spattered afternoon and had Dean naturally aged and proceeded through the kinds of transmutations that contemporaries such as Elizabeth Taylor and Marlon Brando navigated. Contradicting those who assume that he must have harbored a death wish, the young actor's thoughts on the day he died were clearly on a future in which he would be racing automobiles, playing new movie roles, perhaps marrying and starting a family, widening his range of experiences, expanding his intellectual horizons, and—most compelling to him—eventually forsaking acting and taking up directing.[5] In dying young, after completing only three movies, Dean etched forever the screen image of himself as the exemplar of sensitive, misunderstood, and alienated youth, longing for meaning and respect in a society distorted by excessive materialism, antiquated tradition, and narrow-minded provincialism.

Public reaction to him probably would not have been as intense and long-lasting had he emerged on the scene much earlier or later. The social and economic developments transforming the United States at the time paralleled similar changes occurring elsewhere around the globe during the early post–World War II era. In 1951, Spanish film director Luis Buñuel carried off the prize at the Cannes Film Festival with *Los Olvidados,* a story depicting juvenile delinquency in Mexico City's shantytown suburbs. That year also marked the appearance of J. D. Salinger's *Catcher in the Rye,* a story of adolescent angst and alienation. *Blackboard Jungle* brought juvenile delinquency in the United States to the big screen in 1955. Marlon Brando, who had earlier made his mark as a movie actor in *A Streetcar Named Desire* and *On the Waterfront,* established the popular image of the leather-jacketed, motorcycle-riding juvenile hoodlum in the 1954 production *The Wild One,* when he replied to the question, "What're you rebelling against, Johnny?" with "Whaddya got?" Rebelliousness in the 1950s originating in specific grievances directed against concrete obstacles and burdens easily morphed into free-floating whining and unfocused resistance to whatever stood in the way of adolescent desires and fantasies. Thus, Dean's screen roles embodied, according to the cultural critic Diana West, "the giant tantrum that was starting to roil the larger culture, a brave, new emotional world where perpetual adolescents would live on in churning opposition not just to adults, but to the idea of adulthood itself."[6]

The Indiana native's major roles were all of a piece: first in *East of Eden* as Cal Trask, a perplexed youth who rebels against a highly moralistic, tightly controlling father; then in *Rebel without a Cause* as Jim Stark, a confused and troubled high school senior who resents the bickering between his weak, henpecked father and domineering, interfering mother and who can never figure out how to fit in with his peers; and finally in *Giant* as Jett Rink, the penniless cowhand as antihero who, after striking oil on inherited land, becomes a victim of his own uncontrollable thirst for revenge for having been belittled and spat on all his life. Some observers questioned whether Dean was acting at all when he played those roles, for he seemed naturally cast in all of them. Elia Kazan, describing his introduction of the then unknown actor to *East of Eden*'s author, John Steinbeck, recalled, "I took Dean up there, and John liked him right away for the part. He said, 'Jesus Christ, he is Cal!' which is pretty close to the truth—he was."[7]

The gap between actor and role narrowed even further in *Rebel,* the quintessential Dean film, in which he was cast as Jim Stark—the first name drawn from his own and the last being an anagram of "Trask," the name of the character he had played in his first film. Many who were acquainted with him would have endorsed the assessment of photographer Dennis Stock, a member of the movie's production team: "When you saw 'Rebel Without a Cause,' that was Jimmy you were seeing up there on the screen." The role of Jett Rink in *Giant* posed more difficult challenges, requiring the young actor to age more than two decades during the course of the action, but the screen persona and the actor playing it shared similar iconoclastic tendencies and traits of alienation, insecurity, and ambition. Much later, Leonard Rosenman, a sometime intellectual mentor for Dean, said, "I really think Jimmy had no idea in the world who or what he was. Obviously he identified with the three movie roles he had, but I think they were given to him because he was those roles, or in some ways they were created for him—and it all had to do with confusion!"[8]

Residents of Dean's hometown of Fairmount refused to buy that interpretation, then or later.[9] To them, he remained the same old Jimmy they had always known: mischievous and a tad rebellious, to be sure, but fun-loving, gregarious, unspoiled, and basically an all-American boy—in a word, normal. They detested, and some still do, characterizations of him as a rebel, a loner, a crude fellow, a sulker, or a smart aleck. Especially offensive to them are witnesses who say that he was homosexual or bisexual. They claim never to have perceived any of that in the boy while he was growing up in Fairmount.[10] Although some townspeople resented or envied Dean's developing fame as an actor, most evinced considerable pride in his accomplishments. At the time of the release of his first movie, 3,000 residents of Grant County put their signatures of congratulation on a 7-foot scroll and sent it to him.[11]

The eastern Indiana town of 2,600 where Dean had grown up was a typical midwestern farming community where his relatives—Deans and Winslows—had been active participants in community affairs for several generations. According to local town boosters, the quiet, simple railroad stop, 50 miles northeast of Indianapolis, boasted a much higher percentage of *Who's Who* entries (fourteen times the national average, according to one piece of booster literature) than most places.[12] Although James Dean is today its most illustrious product, the town is also proud of being the boyhood home of Jim Davis, creator of the cartoon feature *Garfield,* and CBS newscaster Phil Jones, as well as of a number of authors, scientists, artists, inventors, and several college presidents. Its most distinguishing feature lies in its origins as a Quaker town, largely populated in the beginning by members of that religious persuasion, including Deans and Winslows. Young Jimmy Dean regularly attended Back Creek Friends Church with his family while he was growing up there.

Publicity churned out by Hollywood flacks and stories printed in newspapers and magazines frequently took note of Dean's beginnings as a small-town boy from rural Indiana. "Only a few years ago James Dean was a farm boy in Fairmount, Indiana," his first bio from Warner Brothers studio began.[13] In interviews with fan magazines and reporters, Dean sometimes referred to his boyhood days in Indiana, and during the six and a half years he lived after graduating from high school, he returned to Fairmount to visit relatives and friends at least five times and was planning another trip between the filming of *Rebel* and *Giant,* until the former ran eleven days over schedule, forcing him to revise his plans.[14] Dean's ambivalent attitude toward Fairmount shone through in a not-very-good poem he wrote about it while living in New York City several years after leaving home. Against its presumed virtues, which included religiousness, diligence, attention to daily newspaper reading, and sweetness, he cataloged several defects, including diffidence, idolatry, "industrial impotence," and bigotry (examples being anti-Catholicism and anti-Semitism). The poem's final line, "My town is not what I am, I am here," suggested that by the time he composed it he had moved beyond the orbit of the community. In fact, his behavior and trend of thought reflected that the ways and attitudes of the small town he had grown up in had quickly lost most of any influence they may ever have had on him.[15]

Yet Fairmount retained a deep nostalgic hold on him. Whenever he was back home in Indiana, he seemed to revert to the simple, fun-loving boy that friends and relatives remembered him as being. In October 1952, while waiting for a chance to audition for a Broadway role, he hitchhiked out to Indiana with roommates Bill Bast and Liz Sheridan when his father Winton, a dental technician, offered to travel all the way from California to fashion a new plate for his two missing front teeth. Back in familiar surroundings, among kin and friends, Dean flashed a side of himself seldom in evidence in New York City, becoming more open, relaxed, and natural than usual. Tramping around his Uncle Marcus and Aunt Ortense Winslow's farmstead, where he had grown up after his mother's death, from age nine to eighteen, he gave his friends a personal tour of his childhood haunts. They had fun skipping stones on the farm pond, swinging on a rope in the hayloft (where he had lost his two front teeth while attempting a difficult trapeze stunt), target-shooting with a BB gun, and shooting baskets at a hoop in the barn, where he and his buddies had spent many enjoyable hours as high schoolers. "After all the years of seeing Jimmy alone and without a family," Bast observed, "it was a wonderful thing to watch him touch again the gentle roots of his early years. He was back in his element and he loved it."[16]

Next day, they drove into Fairmount, a typical midwestern agricultural service center replete with gas station, feed store, hardware store, barber shop, drugstore with ice-cream parlor, high school, and several churches. Liz Sheridan was curious how someone like her friend, who had grown up in such a seemingly simple place, could have turned out so complicated. Tipped off that her star pupil was back in town, Adeline Brookshire, Dean's former speech teacher and drama coach, invited him and his friends to drop by and talk to her high school class. Eagerly responding to the bait, he strode dramatically to the front of the room like a bullfighter—one of his favorite poses—and startled the class by shouting, "MY NAME IS JAMES DEAN AND I AM AN ACTOR!" He followed that with a series of readings illustrating different feelings and approaches to acting—laughing hysterically, rolling on the floor, leaping in the air, spinning in circles, even sobbing. Having hugely enjoyed himself and his antics, he quickly reverted to normal demeanor, thanked the class, and paid tribute to his former teacher, calling her the best one he had ever had.[17]

Summoned back to New York several days later to audition for *See the Jaguar,* the Broadway play that lifted him from obscurity and set him on the road to fame, Dean continued to act out daily the myriad roles he had grown accustomed to after leaving his native Midwest. He seemed continuously to be "on," his personal life turning into a series of spontaneous performances. "He was always doing a number," observed actor and friend Bill Gunn. Unless people interacted with him on a one-to-one basis, they could not really know him, Bill Bast noted. "Because in a group or in a social situation it was impossible for Jimmy to relate. More than one person and you would see a personality instead of a person. You got a show."[18]

By the time of his last visit to Fairmount in the spring of 1955, after *East of Eden* had launched him on the road to film stardom and right before shooting commenced on *Rebel,* it had become virtually impossible for people to separate the "real" James Dean from the many masks he adopted to divert people's attention. "Later I came to understand that his notorious 'strangeness' was just an act," concluded Karen Sharpe, who had known him when he was just starting out. "But he played that part so long, maybe he became the act."[19] Shortly after filming *East of Eden*, he teamed up with Dennis Stock to do a photo essay for *Life* magazine intended to depict the environmental influences that had shaped him in rural Indiana and New York City. Dean, who loved being photographed, cooperated enthusiastically in the project, suggesting locations and props and posing in a variety of staged scenes that as much disguised who he was as revealed it.

For Dean, that trip to Indiana during the first week of February 1955 was a journey back to his roots. An emerging star, he intuited that the world of his origins in Fairmount and the one of his future in Hollywood were incompatible. The *Life* piece contained four photographs of him in Fairmount—one of him listening to grandfather Charlie Dean's stories and three hammy poses burlesquing his agricultural roots: standing stone-faced beside a 700-pound hog, reminiscent of Grant Wood's *American Gothic*; sitting on the ground with a goofy grin amid a group of calves; and sitting cross-legged in the hayloft of the barn, suit-clad, reading a book. These pictures, purportedly reflective of the environmental influences that had molded him, were, in fact, more camp than reality. For an image of him standing in the driveway of his aunt and uncle's farm gazing wistfully into the distance, he proposed the caption "You can't go home again." That shot did not make it into the photo essay, nor did ones taken by the bemused Stock in Hunt's Funeral Parlor, where his eccentric subject impulsively jumped into a coffin and invited the photographer to click away.[20]

Dean's ambivalent feelings regarding Fairmount cropped up repeatedly during the week that the two young men spent there. Having rigged up a hidden microphone in his sleeve, he surreptitiously recorded interviews with his grandparents and aunt and uncle about family history. As Jimmy pulled out a copy of the collected poems of his favorite Hoosier poet, James Whitcomb Riley, nostalgia overcame him as he read "We Must Get Home" to the folks gathered around the kitchen table. Irony abounded as the young actor, whose driving ambition to succeed was limitless, reverently read Riley's piquant critique of fame and ambition. The hometown boy who had escaped Fairmount immediately after high school, landing first in Los Angeles, then in New York, and then trailing back to Hollywood, reverently read the poet's lines about homesickness and the need to get back home again.[21]

Whatever nostalgia Dean harbored toward his hometown, he had already severed his ties to the place. "It was a strange time for Jimmy," Stock commented afterward. "I think that as much as he loved the farm and the earth around it, he realized he had outgrown his past, and Indiana could never really be home for him again." Several of the pictures that did not make it into the magazine article reflected this even more than the ones that did. Sitting alone in a high school classroom, staring blankly at the camera in the Winslows' attic, grinning incongruously from a coffin—he appeared strangely out of place in the haunts of his childhood.[22]

The noisy, crowded streets of Manhattan by this time had become more of a home for him than the place in which he had grown up, a site of refuge from the glitter of Hollywood—so important to him in his race for recognition and success but so alien to him as a place in which to live. The four pictures of him in New York that made it into the *Life* article were no more indicative of his true self than the ones taken in Indiana. In one iconic pose, he trudged alone in a drizzle in Times Square, slouched over, with both hands in his pockets, a cigarette dangling from his lips, and wearing an old chief petty officer's coat that he had picked up in an army surplus shop. Impulsively, Dean asked Stock to shoot him sitting motionless in a furniture display window near Rockefeller Center. "He was very playful, and I was very playful. What we had in common was the sense of the surreal," the photographer later recalled.[23] The article included images of him sitting backstage at the Cort Theatre talking to actress Geraldine Page, with whom he had played in *The Immoralist,* and of him, feet propped on desk, going over his finances with an accountant. Manhattan now held more familiar associations for him than Fairmount, but the caption for the picture of him strolling through Times Square suggested something else: "His top floor garret on Manhattan's West Side is no more home to him, he says, than the farm in Indiana. But he feels that his continuing attempt to find out just where he belongs is the source of his strength as an actor."[24]

Central to the story of Dean's rise from Indiana farm youth to Hollywood idol was his continuing search for identity. Cinematographer William Mellor, who struck up an acquaintance with Dean on the set of *Giant,* pegged him as "a small-town boy rocketed to success without warning, without preparation—an average young American still confused by a new life, not yet adjusted to fame, fortune and fan mania."[25] The photogenic young actor's obsessive snapping of roll after roll of close-ups of his face in the mirror reflected not only his intense narcissism but also his compulsive search for his true self.[26] Photographer Roy Schatt, who taught Dean some of the craft's basic skills and who took several of our most fa-

CHAPTER ELEVEN

miliar images of him, came to the conclusion that "he could never be a real person himself—he was always hiding behind someone else's persona."[27] In escaping Indiana, Dean figuratively reconstructed himself, borrowing aspects from other people's visages and personalities, their expressions, gestures, and verbal patterns. Spending hours closely observing friends and fellow actors and mimicking aspects of their speech and behavior, Dean gained a realization of his own personality as pastiche. "I don't really know who I am, but it doesn't matter," he wrote an old friend in Fairmount.[28] Trying to discover the "authentic" James Dean, therefore, becomes a futile quest. He would have admitted himself that trying to peel back the layers of his personality presented an unending task.

Any attempt to account for Dean's rise to stardom and to explain his frequently bizarre behavior must begin with the double shock inflicted on him by his mother's death when he was nine years old, immediately followed by his father's virtual abandonment of him. By all accounts, the pair possessed exactly opposite personalities. His father, Winton Dean, was a slender, taciturn dental technician who had grown up in Fairmount and moved to the nearby town of Marion after landing a job there at the Veterans Administration hospital. Handsome and protective, he could turn women's heads but was not a warm or demonstrative person and lacked intellectual curiosity. The woman he married, Mildred Marie Wilson of Gas City, located midway between Fairmount and Marion, exhibited entirely different kinds of traits. Lively, vivacious, curious, and playful, she enjoyed music, possessed a quick sense of humor, and loved mimicking people. Interested onlookers may have wondered where the attraction lay between the two, but the arrival of a son they named James Byron Dean on February 8, 1931, little more than six months after the wedding, provides a clue. Mildred's unplanned pregnancy had stimulated a hasty marriage, and Winton never seemed able to accept or to cope with the son that he almost certainly never wanted in the first place.

Winton's remote, humorless demeanor and his failure to connect emotionally with his child left the two of them in separate boxes, incapable of communicating or interacting with each other in any meaningful way. He tried playing ball with the boy and endeavored to "make him a man," but father and son seem never to have emotionally bonded. "Jim and I," the elder Dean explained to a reporter for a movie magazine years later, "we've never had that closeness. It's nobody's fault really. Just circumstances." From the other side, Jimmy, who tried hard at connecting, seemed incapable of pleasing his father. "I never understood him," he would say as a young adult. "I never understood what he was after, what sort of person he'd been, because he never tried to get on my side of the fence, or to try to see things the way I saw them when I was little. I was always with mom and we were very close."[29]

Deprived of a close bond with his father, Jimmy emerged as a classic mama's boy. Mildred loved him and spoiled him. More important, she cultivated his natural proclivities for making things, learning, performing, and expressing himself in a variety of ways. She was a nurturing woman; nothing was too much for her to give to her son. She read to him, played games with him, even enrolled him in tap-dancing lessons when he was three. After living in several places in and around Marion and Fairmount until Jimmy was five, the family moved to California in 1936, when Winton Dean accepted a transfer to the Veterans Administration hospital in Santa Monica. There, while attending kindergarten and grades one through three, the boy experienced difficulty making friends, and the bond between mother and son grew even stronger. Violin lessons were added to the tap-dancing. Mildred and Jimmy played endless games of make-believe, and she constructed a little cardboard theater, which they used for making up plays and stories. Through her son, Mildred Dean found a way to act out the artistic dreams she harbored for herself.

Then, almost before anyone understood what was happening, she was diagnosed with uterine cancer. Within months during the summer of 1940, at age twenty-nine, Mildred Dean passed away, leaving her only child motherless. It was a blow from which Jimmy Dean never fully recovered.[30] On top of it, the family decided to send the boy back to Fairmount to live with Winton's sister, Ortense Winslow, and her husband, Marcus, on their farm 2 miles north of Fairmount. The explanation family members tendered over the years as to why Jimmy was so precipitately separated from his father was that in the wake of Mildred's illness, family finances had dictated the decision. Furthermore, it was noted, the move was intended to be only a temporary solution until Winton could get on his feet economically. But three years later he was drafted into the army, and during the nine years that Jimmy was growing up in Fairmount, until he graduated from high school, the two hardly ever saw each other. It seems in retrospect that convenience, rather than necessity, dictated the decision to separate father from son. For young Jimmy, it was bound to appear that his father had abandoned him in the wake of his mother's death.

CHAPTER ELEVEN

What mixture of bewilderment, guilt, remorse, and resentment must have troubled his young mind is difficult to fathom, but that the event was traumatic for him cannot be doubted. "It seemed to me worse than dying itself," Dean later said of the experience.[31] Though in most respects he appeared to be an ordinary enough boy while continuing through the elementary grades in Fairmount and then on to high school, memories of his mother frequently haunted him and, at least for a while, elicited tears and outbursts in the classroom. Sometimes when teachers asked what was bothering him, he would blurt out, "I miss my mother." Talking to a magazine interviewer years later, he said, "My mother died on me when I was nine years old. What did she expect me to do? Do it all by myself?"[32]

At their rural home, the Winslows, who also had a fourteen-year-old daughter of their own, welcomed Jimmy into their family as if he were their own son and made things as comfortable and supportive for him as they could. When the boy expressed his liking for their bedroom furniture, they gladly moved it into his room. Their willingness to cater to his needs and whims, following on his mother's indulgence of him, contributed to his feelings of entitlement and of being special. Everyone who was acquainted with Jimmy during his adolescence testified to his energy, drive, and independence and to his unwillingness to take no for an answer. He knew how to get what he wanted, and he would persist until he succeeded, utilizing a blend of whining, pleading, and cajoling, always outlasting the opposition. Though often giving the impression of being shy, he liked being the center of attention and enjoyed shocking people, while at the same time he sought their approval. "He just did things his own way," remarked a neighbor. "He was—well, a little different."[33]

Jimmy gravitated toward the kinds of games and activities that boys his age liked to engage in—baseball, basketball, horseplay, motorbikes. The pond out back of the barn provided a fine place for swimming, and when frozen over in winter, it became the site for games of ice hockey with friends from town and nearby farms. His uncle tacked up a basketball hoop in the barn, where the boys often gathered to play pickup games. In 4-H, he raised chicks and grew a garden and won a grand prize for a bull he entered in the county fair.[34] But unlike most of his peers, he took even greater interest in artistic pursuits, especially in performing before audiences. He learned to play the clarinet and was a drummer in the high school band. He enjoyed drawing and painting and grew quite good at them. His first efforts on the stage were recitations and parts in tableaux for his aunt's chapter of the Women's Christian Temperance Union, and in high school he made something of a local name for himself with his many performances in church skits, class plays, and other productions. Crucial improvements in his technique and a boost to his confidence came from Adeline Brookshire, who perceived unusual talent in the boy and encouraged him to push it as far as he could.[35]

Always determined to prove himself, Jimmy played on the baseball squad and captured a slew of ribbons on Fairmount High's track team as a hurdler, shot-putter, broad-jumper, and pole-vaulter. His best sport was basketball, and the forty points he accumulated in three play-off games at the end of the season, including fifteen against Marion in the sectional finals, helped earn him the class medal for best senior athlete. That he broke more than a dozen pairs of glasses on the hardwood court bespoke his tenacity and competitiveness. He also walked off with school medals for being best art and forensics student, the latter based on his work in debate and declam. His rendition of Charles Dickens's "A Madman's Manuscript" from *The Pickwick Papers* captured first place at the Indiana state tournament in Peru and then took sixth-place honors at the national tournament held in Longmont, Colorado. That feat got headline coverage in the *Fairmount News* and a picture on the front page. He was not an exceptional student overall; his grades as a senior were all Bs except for As in art and music, ranking him twentieth out of forty-seven graduates in the class of 1949.[36]

That young Jimmy Dean possessed special talent and the potential to make something of himself was obvious. More important to his eventual success, however, was his determination to follow his dream and the intensity with which he pursued it. His frequent visits with Rev. James De-Weerd, who had served as an army chaplain during World War II, reinforced his sense of himself as someone who could go places. The Wesleyan minister, who was well educated and a man of many interests, introduced his young protégé to yoga, bullfighting, and automobile racing and helped broaden his horizons in art, poetry, philosophy, and, some say, sex.[37]

By the time Jimmy graduated from high school, he was fixed on a career in acting. Confident in his ability, he never wavered in his desire to make it big. Highly revealing is an essay he composed for Fairmount High School's new principal, Roland DuBois, who invited students to write about themselves to help him get to know them better. In "My Case Study," Jimmy matter-of-factly noted, "I had always lived such a talented life," in reference to his violin playing, tap-dancing, theatrical activities, and art. "I think my life will be devoted to Art and Dramatics," he continued. "I got it and I know if I better myself, that there will be no match. A fellow must have confidence." Speaking of his involvement in athletics, he wrote, "As one strives to make a goal in a game there should be a goal in this crazy world for each of us. I hope I know where mine is, anyway, I'm after it."[38]

Although his ultimate destination remained vague in the spring of 1949, Dean's determination to get out of Fairmount and make a mark for himself was evident. At the National Forensic League Tournament in Longmont, he struck up a friendship with a student from New York City named Jim McCarthy. Jimmy told him, "Man, the minute I get out of school I'm heading west. California."[39] After graduation, he intended to move to Los Angeles and study acting at UCLA with help from his father, who lived in nearby Santa Monica with his second wife. Though willing to help his son get started in college, Winton Dean insisted that Jimmy enroll in Santa Monica City College (SMCC) and major in something more practical than acting. During his freshman year at the 1,600-student school, Jim registered in the prelaw program, toyed with his regular classes, joined the Jazz Club, did some announcing for the college radio station, dated the homecoming queen, and was a third-string guard on the basketball team, while channeling most of his energy into two drama courses and extracurricular theater activities. For a summer theater production in which he also served as stage manager, he billed himself on the program as Byron James, an indication that he was already thinking seriously about a show-business career.[40]

Both at SMCC and later at the much larger UCLA, where he transferred for his sophomore year, Jim Dean stepped up the kinds of social and intellectual climbing that he had begun to exhibit in Fairmount with his acting and art and in sessions with Reverend DeWeerd. He obtained the role of Malcolm in a production of *Macbeth*, but his notices were not very good. He hung out with athletes and wrote letters home to the Winslows inflating his accomplishments. But he got kicked out of Sigma Nu fraternity for flouting their rules and procedures. No diligent student, he eventually quit attending classes altogether and dropped out of school before spring graduation. By then, he was spending most of his time hanging around Hollywood and Burbank, on the lookout for parts in movies and television commercials. He even lined up an agent, with help from a fraternity brother, but mostly he had a miserable time because the jobs that he managed to snag were infrequent and paid a pittance. Generally broke and frequently in debt, he learned how to exist on shredded wheat and jam a good part of the time.

A sign of better things to come, however, could be found in the $150 he received in March 1951 for his television performance in *Hill Number One,* a religious drama in which he played the Apostle John. Despite his small role, involving only a few lines, he got his first fan club out of it when students at a nearby Catholic girls school who had been assigned to watch the program invited him to visit them. Dean was already demonstrating an unusual ability to break through to audiences in a way that few actors could. Mostly, the girls thought he was cute.[41]

In October, frustrated with his general lack of success, Dean acted on advice from actor James Whitmore, who had recently moved to California. He decided to change scenery and go to New York to hone his acting skills in television productions and live theater. Later, after exploding into public prominence in Hollywood, Dean would attribute his success to hard work and devotion to his craft, failing to credit several people who played crucial roles in helping him rise up the ladder. His agent in New York, Jane Deacy, almost a mother figure to him, recognized his potential. She encouraged and prodded him and found roles for him that allowed his talent to shine through.[42]

No less important, but more hidden, was the help of Rogers Brackett, whom Dean had met in California. The thirty-five-year-old advertising executive introduced him to people in the industry and channeled him into some minor roles in radio dramas and movies and even one in a radio commercial for Toni home permanents. Brackett also facilitated Dean's move to New York, loaning him money and contacting friends to welcome him and help him get set up in the city. Some commentators have gone so far as to say that Brackett was the key to Dean's career. One can surmise why the young actor never talked about him to the media, however, because Brackett was a homosexual, and Dean did not want to admit that he had traded sexual favors for help in pushing along his career.[43]

During the years after his death, revelations continued to filter out about Dean's sexual involvement with a number of men and myriad women. The boy who had been too shy to date much in high school turned out to be prolific once he got the hang of it, although many of his former lovers testified that sex was never a high priority with him. Formidable evidence points to his bisexual proclivities.[44] One of the subliminal appeals of *Rebel* was that director Nicholas Ray sensed the three-way sexual attraction among his central actors—Dean, Natalie Wood, and Sal Mineo—on the set and made the situation work for him in ways audiences probably only dimly understood. "Sal and Natalie were both seduced by Dean's charisma, mystery, and sexual ambiguity," writes Mineo's biographer. "An undercurrent of desire boils beneath the surface between all three characters that is startling and as groundbreaking as Ray had imagined."[45] In this area, Dean responded to his determination to burst through cultural constraints and to live life as he pleased. He would let nothing stand in his way in the pursuit of his goals and of living his life.

In New York, Dean continued to behave as he had in California, only more so. Totally unpredictable, he could be sweet and sunny one minute, morose and uncommunicative the next. "Impulsive," "creative," "inspiring," "patient," "kind," "gentle": these were words people used to describe him. But so were "neurotic," "mixed-up," "frustrated," "disconnected," "irresponsible," "immature," and "self-centered." "Mercurial" was the one perhaps applied most frequently. Not surprisingly, a few people suggested that he might have been bipolar. One who did was author Kenneth Anger. "Dean was withdrawn, compulsively promiscuous, but friendless, suspicious, moody, uncooperative, boorish and rude," he observed. "He could, on occasion, be charming; on most occasions he was annoyingly nuts. He betrayed a psychopathic personality with fits of despondency that alternated with fits of wild jubilation. A classic manic-depressive."[46] As countless observers noted, he was as many different people as those who described him. He put on different fronts for different people, and his was an instantly changeable personality.

Movie magazines ran stories with titles like "Who Is the *Real* James Dean?" Dean understood that he did not know himself who he was, intuiting that this somehow contributed to his success as an actor.[47] Playing Cal Trask in *East of Eden* he cried out, "Talk to me father. I gotta know who I am. I gotta know what I'm like." No less compelling were his pleading lines as Jim Stark in *Rebel without a Cause* when he told a social worker, "If I just had one day when I didn't feel so confused." The movie's director, Nicholas Ray, viewed his star as the living embodiment of the recurring American conflict between fathers and sons. "The drama of his life," Ray observed, "was the drama of desiring to belong and of fearing to belong (so was Jim Stark's). It was a conflict of violent eagerness and mistrust created very young. . . . The intensity of his desires, his fears, could make the search at times arrogant, egocentric; but behind it was such a desperate vulnerability that one was moved, even frightened."[48]

Lacking a solid core of personal conviction and values on which he could depend to guide him through his personal miseries and dilemmas, Dean frequently felt lost and alienated. Though raised as a Quaker, he had no use for organized religion after leaving home. To him, Jesus was a champion. "Any guy who would do all that has got guts and balls," he told actress Chris White. "*That's* what I like. All that theological, ideological ritual crap is nothing but boring."[49] His willingness to become a Catholic if that was what it would take to get actress Pier Angeli to marry him only underlined the fact that he did not care about creeds and doctrines. Nor did organized politics hold any allure for him. He paid no attention to the Eisenhower-Stevenson presidential campaign in 1952; any mention of it turned him off. One would have to examine his statements with a fine-tooth comb to find anything of political import in them.

Although he was basically apolitical, countercultural radicals during the following decade would cite him as inspiration for their views. Dean thought of himself as an explorer, searching for knowledge but reaching no fixed conclusions. He refused to be confined by limits set by others. His determination to know and experience everything guided him as an actor. "An actor must interpret life and in order to do so must be willing to accept all experiences that life has to offer," he said. "In the short span of his lifetime an actor must learn all there is to know, experience all there is to experience, or approach that state as closely as possible."[50] He was always inclined to push toward extremes, to test limits, and to see how far he could go before he was reined in. Partly because it was his nature, partly because he wanted to show off, partly because he had a thirst for love and a compulsion to test the depth of people's devotion, and partly because he believed that outrageous behavior would attract attention and advance his career, Dean gravitated toward extreme behavior, which alienated some people and appealed to others.

What most Americans knew about him at the time of his death and a year later, after the release of his final two films, was the image they witnessed on the screen and the stories and photos they were exposed to in the popular press. Tabbed by some as a Marlon Brando clone (Dean, in fact, was obsessed with Brando and Montgomery Clift, sometimes playfully signing letters "James Brando/Clift Dean"),[51] hailed by others as a charismatic young actor, worshipped by many as a symbol of rebellion, adored by others for his good looks, Dean lived on in a public persona vague enough that moviegoers of many different types and interests could project onto him their own personal feelings, fantasies, and wishes. During the early 1950s, he and Brando popularized a new character type on the American scene—one linked with vulnerability, authenticity, and antiauthoritarianism rather than cockiness, cynicism, and hedonism.[52]

In dying young, he ensured that myth, more than reality, would guide people's understanding of him. His period of stardom lasted less than a year before he met his violent end. During the half century since then, he has remained an icon capable of meaning just about anything people want it to. Identified by cultural commentators as a symbol of alienated youth during the affluent 1950s, he continues to resonate with admirers in a manner unmatched by any other actor of his time. His image transcends time. Many factors account for this: his vulnerability, confusion, rebelliousness, androgyny, style, flair, hopefulness, ambition, insouciance. James Dean was the progenitor of "cool." In his wake, the youth culture was born. Predecessors such as Frank Sinatra and Marlon Brando had already pointed the way. But with the Indianan's elevation to stardom, the young took their place as cultural arbiters in American society. He died too young to become an Elvis Presley fan, but the Memphis truck driver idolized him, watching his favorite film, *Rebel without a Cause,* countless times and memorizing all of Dean's lines. The popular singer romanced Natalie Wood and Ursula Andress, knowing that both had been paired with Dean.[53]

Presley, a small-town boy from Mississippi, and a generation of teen idols following in his wake carried their rebellions several steps beyond anything Dean had ever contemplated during the early 1950s. What the farm kid from Indiana had only suggested or implied, his successors acted out more explicitly and extensively. Something momentous, however, happened around 1954 and 1955 during the brief period of time that Dean was making his movies in Hollywood. Those years gave rise to a new take on life, one that left behind small-town pieties, hypocrisies, strictures, and traditions that had managed to hold up until then, opting for a free-floating sensibility that was open to all possibilities, bathed in an environment dominated by the mass media and mass culture. Historians suggest that every period is a time of transition, but if one were to look for the moment when small-town America finally lost its grip on the mentality and sensibilities of the American population, they could do worse than to inspect mid-'50s Hollywood and the career of a small-town boy from Fairmount, Indiana—James Dean.

CHAPTER TWELVE

■

Meredith Willson: The Music Man from Mason City

I've thought and puzzled over why Iowa sticks with me. I can still hear the back screen door closing. I can see the grass in the back yard. I can hear the sound of the cold air register at the entrance of the First Congregational Church as we kids ran across it with snow on our shoes.

—Meredith Willson

New York City in the 1950s was the world's most populous city and, by many reckonings, its greatest. The metropolis was in its heyday. Everything about it spoke size, wealth, and power, as well as vitality, energy, and creativity. Not only the center of U.S. industry and finance, it also reigned preeminent in publishing, journalism, entertainment, and the arts. Almost 8 million New Yorkers occupied its five boroughs, covering an expanse of

320 square miles. Most of the action, however, centered in Manhattan, an island 2 and a quarter miles wide and 13 miles long, extending across 23 square miles and home to 2 million people.

Central Manhattan, the cultural capital of the United States, was renowned for its neighborhoods. Here the nation's major book firms, magazine publishers, radio and television studios, art galleries, and theaters were concentrated in an area of 5 or 6 square miles. One could get around town relatively easily on foot or in a cab. In terms of space, central Manhattan was hardly larger than a good-sized American town. If a person could have mentally erased the row after row of skyscrapers and the deep canyons cutting through them, along with the several million people who lived and worked there, it would have been possible to imagine Manhattan as a small town whose connecting links were marked by the places one frequented and the people to whom one was connected.

Live theater, for example, had gradually moved uptown decade by decade and was clustered now in an area 5 blocks long and 2 blocks wide, from Forty-Fourth to Forty-Ninth Streets between Eighth Avenue and Broadway. Having begun to concentrate around Union Square during the last quarter of the nineteenth century, the "Great White Way," as people called the theater district, had moved north by the early 1900s to the area around Long Acre Square (later renamed Times Square). The 1920s saw theater activity peak, with 264 shows opening in seventy-six Broadway theaters during the 1927–1928 season. The advent of sound movies that year and the impact of the Depression cut seriously into the profits of legitimate theater, and the industry would experience its ups and downs during the next three decades.[1]

By midcentury, theaters were disappearing regularly, and the number of plays staged on Broadway was down by about two-thirds from its peak thirty years earlier. Serious concerns arose about the viability of live theater; Broadway, in the minds of many, was a sick community. But musicals, which had entered a new era of sophistication and professionalism with the 1943 production of *Oklahoma!*, reached unprecedented levels of popularity during the late 1950s, exemplified by the arrival of *My Fair Lady* in 1956, *West Side Story* in 1957, and *The Sound of Music* in 1959. It was not unusual for a dozen or more musicals to light up Broadway's marquees during a typical season, despite the high cost of staging them. The average musical cost around $150,000 to produce, with ticket prices ranging around $7. Middle-class theatergoers, most of them in their thirties and forties, attended at least five times a year, and many could be heard humming or whistling tunes from the latest hits.[2]

Broadway in the 1950s still connoted bright lights, glitz, glamour, and excitement. Theatergoing meant dressing up; people went out to see and to be seen. Broadway remained a national institution. Taking in a show or two constituted a necessary part of out-of-towners' itineraries. Approximately 20,000 people were connected in one way or other with the theater community, half of them actors, the rest made up of everyone from stagehands, set designers, and ticket takers to choreographers, directors, and producers.[3] They had their own restaurants and hangouts where they would gather: Sardi's and the Blue Ribbon Restaurant on Forty-Fourth Street, Hanson's Drug Store on Fifty-First and Broadway, Dinty Moore's, "21," and the Four Seasons. "After the curtains went up," recalled the theatrical advertiser Fred Golden, "the managers and press agents would come out and walk through Shubert Alley to Sardi's and have a drink at the bar. I could do all of my business that way."[4] On opening night, show people gathered there and elsewhere to celebrate and await the first reviews. The *New York Times* offices were just around the corner, and depending on the write-ups of Brooks Atkinson and other critics, the place would either light up in hugs and toasts or empty out quickly. There was a pecking order that sorted people out. The Russian Tea Room and the Algonquin Hotel were high-class places that attracted the literary set. Jazz joints up on Fifty-Second Street appealed to some, and other restaurants, bars, and nightclubs were sprinkled throughout the district.[5]

A newcomer to the New York theater crowd in the 1950s, and one who entered it with a bit of trepidation, was a small-town boy, born in 1902, from Mason City, Iowa. He was well acquainted with the geography of the town as a result of a musical career that had landed him in downtown Manhattan fresh out of high school three decades earlier. Meredith Willson, just turned seventeen in 1919, had gotten out of his hometown as fast as he could after graduation, enrolling in New York's Institute of Musical Art (renamed the Juilliard School of Music in 1946), where he studied flute with Henry Hadley and Georges Barrère.[6] Musically precocious as a youngster, the boy had started taking piano lessons from his mother, Rosalie, at around age seven, later taking up the snare drums, banjo, mandolin, and ukulele. When he was ten, his mother sent off for a mail-order flute, because she thought he would have a better chance of gaining distinction with it than on the piano and because her father had played the instrument. Meredith's father, who was also musically inclined, had played a cornet in the Notre Dame band. While still in high school, the youth earned the unusual distinction of being allowed to play in Mason City's municipal band; he also enjoyed singing tenor in the school's glee club and in his church's choir.[7]

Going the musical route proved to be an excellent choice for the lad, who was not athletically inclined. The youngest of three children, in high school Meredith participated in the orchestra, band, and chorus, as well as in the glee club, and had roles in an opera during his junior year and in a minstrel show during his senior year. When he was a junior, the school's football team, whose record was marred by a single tie, racked up 529 points to its opponents' 7 during a ten-game season, including victories by lopsided scores of 133–0, 123–0, and 68–0. Music offered a student like Meredith more of a chance to shine than competition on the gridiron would have. His school's orchestra consisted of eleven violins, three cornets, two flutes, two pianos, one clarinet, one horn, and one trombone. He was one of the flutists.[8]

During his senior year, the high school yearbook, *The Masonian*, took note of his rendition of "Good-Bye Alexander" in the annual minstrel show and included this class prophecy about him: "I always expected him to become famous—but no, he only plays the banjo in a small dance orchestra in New York City, making a meager living for himself and happy wife."[9] In 1920, Willson married his high school sweetheart, Elizabeth Wilson (with one *l*), and for the next quarter century theirs would be regarded as one of show business's more ideal pairings.[10] Willson's stature as a musician escalated rapidly during the 1920s. In 1921, learning of an opening for a flutist in John Philip Sousa's band, he applied for the job and won it, rising quickly to principal of the section. After three years of touring the country with Sousa, he took over as first flutist in the New York Philharmonic Orchestra, playing with it for the next five years under such distinguished conductors as Wilhelm Furtwängler and Arturo Toscanini. In the meantime, he began composing; his first major composition, "Parade Fantastique," was performed in 1924. He also began conducting, being invited in 1928 to lead the Seattle Symphony in an outdoor concert series, and he soon found himself working in movies and radio.[11]

After composing film scores for Hollywood in 1929, he signed on as musical director for radio station KFRC in San Francisco. Three years later, he took over the same position at NBC's western division. By the late

1930s and throughout the following decade, with time out for World War II, he was in charge of the musical portion of several radio variety shows under the sponsorship of Maxwell House Coffee. Willson got to work with Frank Morgan and Fanny Brice, George Burns and Gracie Allen, and a variety of other stars on these programs. In 1941, "You and I," the theme song he wrote for the Maxwell House program, was number one on *Your Hit Parade* for nineteen consecutive weeks. Earlier, Willson had created the program that was the precursor of the *Hit Parade*. Possessed of a seemingly boundless supply of energy, he found time to compose two symphonies— *San Francisco* in 1936 and *The Missions of California* in 1940—and was frequently invited to conduct the Los Angeles, San Francisco, and Seattle symphony orchestras. He also collaborated on the score of Charlie Chaplin's movie *The Great Dictator* (1940) and wrote the score for the movie version of *The Little Foxes* (1941). During the war, he took a commission as a major in the army and headed the musical division of the Armed Forces Radio Service.[12]

By the late 1940s, with television looming insistently on the horizon as a major new challenge to the radio industry, Willson, like many other people in the business, found himself caught in the middle of the transition. In 1949, he tried unsuccessfully to translate his popularity as a radio performer to the new medium when he briefly hosted a pilot television program, *The Meredith Willson Show*. Then, from 1950 to 1952, he served as musical director for *The Big Show*, presided over by deep-voiced actress Tallulah Bankhead. The hour-and-a-half variety show was radio's last major effort to compete head-to-head with the new one-eyed monster. Willson produced another hit with the theme song he wrote for it, "May the Good Lord Bless and Keep You," using the words his mother had said back in Mason City every week in sending her students home from her Sunday school classes. When the show folded, he took over as disk jockey of a classical music program, *Meredith Willson's Music Room*, and he continued working sporadically on several other radio programs during the early 1950s.[13] As he entered his fifties, it appeared possible that the Iowa musician's main achievements now lay behind him.

Throughout his career, whenever he had a chance, Willson interjected happy reminiscences about his boyhood in Mason City both in his banter on the air and in offstage conversations. His friends became familiar over the years with Mama's Sunday school classes, the sound of train whistles, the old swimming hole, and the clink of billiard balls at the local pool hall.

Mostly, his memories were nostalgic and full of affection for his hometown and native state. Willson referred to himself as a "small-town kid," obviously considering himself to be a better person for having been one.[14]

"We were awfully proud of being from Mason City," he wrote in a 1950 magazine article. "We always were very excited about the population figures." When the number was still 14,000 or 15,000, people would brag that it had grown to "nearly 20,000." Willson remembered Vance's music store, where he and his friends had hung out listening to records and thumbing through sheet music and where they bought instruments out of a catalog from Chicago. Every October, the *Mason City Globe-Gazette* would put up a display in its front window to record the progress of World Series baseball games as results came in over the ticker. He remembered Willow Creek and the bridge where he dangled under the iron girders. Also Central School, the Carnegie library, and the First Congregational church, where his mother taught Sunday school. Once, she got the Humane Society to erect a fountain and a drinking trough for horses across the street from the church—the first ones in that part of town.[15]

Mason City was a dry town, and while it was growing in population and industry, it still moved largely to the rhythms of a horse-drawn society. Boys liked to jump on wagons for a free ride, being especially partial to the Wells Fargo ones. Willson noted,

> The man who designed Wells-Fargo trucks did almost as much to spatter the memories of millions of kids with high thrills and bug-eyed joy as Santa Claus himself. Good solid runners, front and back, high enough so you could slither right on to them with one foot, as easy and smooth as the brakeman grabbing on to the caboose steps. And the sides were just slightly over waist-high so you could hang on all day if you wanted to.[16]

Willson was "Mason City's greatest booster in Hollywood and on the radio networks," the *Globe-Gazette* proudly observed in 1946. He "has never forgotten his home town and friends while climbing the ladder of fame to a unique position in the world of music," the paper noted.[17] Willson returned to Iowa frequently to visit family and friends, and whenever people back home called on him to do something musical to boost their interests, which was not infrequent, Willson generously obliged. In 1944, he wrote "Iowa." Bing Crosby sang it over the radio and recorded it on a platter, and two years later, it was adopted as the state centennial song.[18] The piece ended with "It's a promise for tomorrow and a mem'ry of long, long ago; I-o-wa, what a beautiful name when you say it like we say it back home." The words were heartfelt, and no trace of irony lingered in them. No wonder Willson was given titles like "Iowa's Super-Salesman" and "One-man Mason City Chamber of Commerce."[19] In 1950, Willson wrote a new fight song for the University of Iowa to replace the older "Iowa Corn Song," which one Mason City resident characterized as "rickey-tickey." Three years later, he did the same for Iowa State University and for his hometown high school.[20]

Willson somehow found time to write four books over the course of a dozen years between the late 1940s and the late 1950s—an autobiography, a novel, an anecdotal account of his career in show business, and the story of his first musical play, *The Music Man*. These books afforded him another opportunity to reminisce about his boyhood in Iowa. In his autobiography, *And There I Stood with My Piccolo,* published in 1948, Wilson recalled his mother playing songs like "Jerusalem the Golden," "Jesus Wants Me for a Sunbeam," and "The Church in the Wildwood" on Sunday mornings on the family's upright piano in the parlor. He remembered well his first ice-cream cone and first street carnival, his first moving picture and first kaleidoscope. He wrote about magic-lantern slide shows, learning to swim, and his first kiss.[21] His novel, *Who Did What to Fedalia?,* concerned a small-town Iowan—a girl from Fort Madison—who, like him, set out alone to go to New York City to make a career in music. Where Willson succeeded, however, the fictional Fedalia failed, and she wound up going back home.[22]

On a wall over his desk in his music room, Willson hung a picture of Mason City's first high school band, with him holding a piccolo. In *"But He Doesn't Know the Territory,"* Willson recalled that the picture had been taken in 1912, but his memory must have been faulty on the point since he would have only been ten years old at the time. He figured he had been a freshman when the picture was taken, which would have been in 1915 or 1916.[23] Childhood memories featured so prominently in the stories he told his friends that some of them began urging him to do something more with them. His wife Rini, a French-Russian opera singer whom he married in 1948 after his first marriage fell apart, due in large part to the long absences from home that his career necessitated, encouraged him to write a musical about his hometown.[24] It was apparently one of his showbiz friends, however, who set Willson to seriously thinking about the idea.

Frank Loesser, a native New Yorker eight years Willson's junior, was a versatile composer who worked both in Hollywood and on Broadway, turning out memorable tunes such as "On a Slow Boat to China" and "Baby, It's Cold Outside" and writing lyrics and music for such shows as *Where's Charley?* and *Guys and Dolls.*[25] One day in 1949, after listening to one more story about Mason City, Loesser exclaimed, "What an idea! Why don't you write a musical about it?" He suggested that his friend make the fire chief the leader of the town band, install a real brass band in the pit, and have a narrator who could tell stories about the town as Willson remembered it.[26]

The idea of writing a musical play about his boyhood in Mason City intrigued Willson, but several years passed before he seriously put his mind to it. His continuing work in radio and his abortive efforts with television prevented him from devoting much time to it. He auditioned in New York for a role as emcee of *The Big Surprise,* an NBC quiz show, but that fell through. But with the demise of *The Big Show* and with his daily obligations as a classical disk jockey not being too time consuming, he finally had more time to devote to his musical. His sister, Dixie, a successful writer herself, helped get his creative juices flowing by suggesting that he build his story around a music professor teaching young boys how to play their instruments. His early working title for the play was "The Silver Triangle."[27]

Willson's résumé as a composer and writer was impressive, but writing a musical comedy turned out to be a daunting task. He discovered that playwriting possessed its own unique imperatives and that, even as closely connected as he was to the music and theater worlds, his previous experience could carry him only so far. Writing the songs was the easiest part. Establishing a story line, inventing dialogue, and matching music to the story turned out to be the most difficult assignments. Willson did not lack for material; he was full of ideas. In preparation for the task, he wrote thirty or so "priming essays" describing his Iowa boyhood, along with approximately twenty songs about typical residents and activities in a small Iowa town. Normal procedure in writing a musical would have been to collaborate with three or four people, divvying up responsibilities for the music, the lyrics, and the book. Willson, a complete neophyte at creating a musical, decided instead to do everything himself. It would not be easy, but if he could pull it off, going it alone would enhance the unity of the final product.[28]

Willson's first protagonist was not the town fire chief, as Loesser had suggested, but a kindly music teacher, easily conjured up from his childhood music lessons. He later switched the role to a likable con artist who sold musical instruments to gullible parents of would-be band boys but always managed to skip town before the time came to teach them to play.[29] The basic narrative line allowed Willson to develop themes that he had often included in his stories about Mason City over the years. It took nearly five years and as many as forty rewrites before his script was shaped into final form. Right up to the end, he struggled constantly to cut it down to manageable size.[30]

Just as important as establishing the characters and honing the plot was discovering the right tone for the play. It was to be a musical comedy based on memories of Willson's hometown. If the production came off as too trite and sentimental, the theater crowd would dismiss it as childish and corny. The Iowa native was, in fact, sentimental in his approach, but he was also ambivalent about small towns, well aware of their negative as well as their positive qualities. He recognized small-town dwellers' nosiness, prudery, stubbornness, pettiness, and love of gossip—and he wrote all these peccadilloes into the play. "Iowa Stubborn," the opening number sung by the townspeople when Professor Harold Hill arrives in River City, establishes their dual character—both friendly and stubborn. They welcome the professor to join them at a picnic and they are willing to offer him, if necessary, the shirts off their backs, but they admit that they also could be as "cold as our falling thermometers in December" and so stubborn that they could stand touching noses "and never see eye to eye."[31] Willson later admitted that he had experienced a few qualms while writing the opening lines of "Iowa Stubborn," but he reasoned, "That's the way we are."[32] By including such realistic observations in the play and by injecting a high degree of energy and excitement to balance the nostalgia and homespun feeling that shone through in it, Willson managed to maintain an even tone, which prevented the production from being drowned in smarmy sentimentalism.

As he plugged through the writing of the play, draft after draft, Willson alternated between high hopes and blank despair.[33] Toward the end of summer 1956, a chance meeting with playwright and script doctor Franklin Lacey provided him with the vital assistance he needed to shorten the script and get it to flow more smoothly. The two worked on further polishing the dialogue and songs, incorporated the "Ya Got Trouble" speak-song in the first act, and made several other major revisions. By early November, after a number of failed efforts, Willson finally found someone to produce the show—Kermit Bloomgarden, one of New York's hottest producers.[34] That just led to a host of new questions: who to direct and choreograph it, whom to cast in it, what theater to do it in, and a dozen other, smaller decisions. The book and the songs needed further refinement, Bloomgarden noted, and Willson attacked these issues again, certain now that his efforts would soon pay off.

Considering the hugely positive popular and critical response the play received when it debuted on Broadway in December 1957, one year to the day after the Willsons auditioned it before Bloomgarden and his staff, it is instructive to observe how many difficulties beset the production process and how many theater dopesters predicted that it would fall flat on its face. By Broadway standards, *The Music Man* was too corny, too simpleminded, and too unsophisticated to go very far.[35]

Finding a director for the play proved more difficult than expected. Moss Hart, who lived in the same apartment building as Bloomgarden, was the first prospect to be approached. His only comments after listening to the Willsons audition it for him were, "You sang very prettily" (to Rini), "Phone you in the morning" (to Bloomgarden), and "Good night" (to Meredith). He didn't like it.[36] But in Morton Da Costa, who agreed to direct it, they discovered a wonderful collaborator who cooperated effectively with Bloomgarden, Willson, and everyone else involved in working the last kinks out of the show. Willson, who had moved with his wife into an apartment near the St. Moritz Hotel on Central Park South, frequently walked the twenty-three blocks separating their place from Da Costa's apartment on Central Park West, where the two hammered out the final revisions. Willson was able to think better while walking. What he was doing now was not so different from what he had done as a kid back in Mason City or in Hollywood. He worked over the words and the music in his head as he pounded the pavement or cut through Central Park on the way to Da Costa's. He could just as well have been walking the streets of Mason City.[37]

One of the first things they decided to do was eliminate the spastic boy subplot from the play, which Willson had resisted doing, having grown quite attached to the boy in his wheelchair. They created a substitute they thought would work better and significantly reduce the length of the play—a lisping kid. Picking Onna White as choreographer involved a bit of a risk, since she had never been employed in more than an assistant capacity before. But her dance routines turned out to be one of the highlights of the show.[38]

The toughest decision, and ultimately one of their best ones, revolved around the question of whom to cast in the lead role of Harold Hill. Milton Berle wanted the assignment. Danny Kaye and Gene Kelly were not interested. Half a dozen other big names, including Art Carney and Ray Bolger, were considered. The inspired choice was to go with Robert Preston, a forty-year-old stage and screen actor who had never sung or danced professionally in his life. Preston filled the role brilliantly, his zest and energy captivating audiences and infecting the rest of the cast with his enthusiasm. Casting the other roles was less difficult but posed one especially interesting challenge—who to play the lisping boy. Eddie Hodges got the part of Winthrop Paroo after Rini chanced to see him on a television program, *Name That Tune*. The barbershop quartet that Willson wrote into the plot was a Broadway first, and many observers thought it would not go over, but casting a real singing group, the Buffalo Bills, in the role was perfect.[39]

Finding the $300,000 necessary to launch the show was made especially difficult by a business recession and shaky stock market. The stake had to be put together by pooling the resources of a number of small investors, who would profit handsomely from their risk taking. Nor, interestingly enough, was it easy to identify a recording company willing to cut the original cast album. Four major companies usually bid for the opportunity, but Columbia, Victor, and Decca all preferred to pass on this one, leaving it to Capitol to reap the profits. During rehearsals in October and early November, the cast got acquainted with one another, establishing something like the kind of camaraderie that Willson had known as a boy in small-town Iowa. Expectations began to build for the show as the Manhattan rumor mill swung into high gear. Doubters remained, however, and a tune-up month in Philadelphia turned out to be less than overwhelming, leaving everyone wondering how people would react when the curtain went up in New York.[40]

They need not have worried. The capacity audience at the first performance at the Majestic Theater on December 19, 1957, broke into spontaneous applause at the end of the performance, clapping in rhythm to the tune of "Seventy-Six Trombones." It continued like that every evening thereafter. Newspaper reviewers echoed audience enthusiasm, virtually unanimous in their praise for the spectacle. "A marvelous show," Brooks Atkinson called it in the *Times,* adding, "If Mark Twain could have collaborated with Vachel Lindsay, they might have devised a rhythmic lark like 'The Music Man,' which is as American as apple pie and a Fourth of July oration." The *Herald Tribune*'s Walter Kerr called it "a wow. A nice wow." To the *World-Telegram and Sun,* it was "a knockout."[41] A few discordant voices registered their dissents, but they were in a distinct minority.[42]

Willson's musical bouquet to his hometown of Mason City became the biggest hit in a year of major hits, beating out *West Side Story* for best play and best musical awards. *Variety* reported that not in recent memory had audiences been so carried away with a performance. *Life* magazine ran a big spread on the show, *Time* put it on the cover, and other publications jumped on the bandwagon. For many weeks, *The Music Man* was the hardest ticket to get in Manhattan; every night it was standing room only, keeping the show going for 1,375 performances.[43]

Mason Citians were prouder than ever of their native son. Now Willson, who had spoken so often and so affectionately about them on his radio programs, had memorialized them for all time in his musical play. "I didn't have to make anything up for 'The Music Man,'" he told a reporter for *Time* magazine. "All I had to do was remember."[44] But memory is a tricky thing, and a play running only a bit over two hours requires ruthless selectivity as to what to include and what to leave out. Many of Willson's characters' names came straight out of his memory. He recalled classmates named Tofflemeier and Eulalie, he had an aunt and a grandmother named Lida, and his mother's name was Rosalie. A Mr. Washburn was a photographer in town, and Constable Locke had been the chief of police. There was a Dunlop family, there were Shinns and two Marcelluses, and his sister had married a Squires.[45]

A number of his characters were inspired by people he had known in Mason City, although he emphasized that all of them were composite figures, none a copy of a real person. Charley Haverdegraine had lisped. The MacNider family was prominent in town, responsible for the town's new library, several parks, and other benefactions, echoing the contributions of Miser Madison. Marian the Librarian had been inspired both by an English teacher of his and by a longtime librarian in the community, but after he had written her into the story, Willson realized that she derived mainly

CHAPTER TWELVE

from his mother, who had also given piano lessons and who had lived her life by the same kinds of precepts and ideals that the fictional Marian held to. The Music Man himself had a counterpart in a character who once came through Mason City, although he had not been a con artist like Harold Hill. The fellow had actually known something about music, but, as remembered by one of Willson's classmates, "he sure did promote a scheme to get the townspeople to buy band instruments and the uniforms."[46]

Willson had played in his high school orchestra and in the town band, and one summer he had played the piccolo with an orchestra at Lake Okoboji, Iowa. In 1914, a boys' band was organized in Mason City under the direction of J. H. Jeffers. It put on performances in the Cecil Theater, on the roof garden of the Knights of Columbus Hall, and at the North Iowa Fair.[47] After school, Willson sometimes joined his friends sneaking into one of the pool halls downtown, but they often got thrown out because no one under eighteen was allowed inside. Harley Ransom, a classmate whose father ran a billiard parlor (as he preferred to call it), recalled of Willson, "He wasn't much of a pool player. His talents were in a different direction."[48] In writing *The Music Man,* Willson relied on his memories of Willow Creek, which ran nearby his house, and the footbridge across it, a few blocks further down.[49] He also had the Rusty Hinge Barbershop Quartet, fireworks and Fourth of July celebrations, and Indian dances as memories to draw on.[50]

In June 1958, Willson returned to Mason City with several of the cast members of the play for the big North Iowa Band Festival. During the parade, great ham that he was, he had a lark jumping out of the convertible in which he was riding to lead the Mason City High School Band part of the way along the parade route. Waving his baton, prancing, strutting, and wisecracking, Willson delighted 20,000 enthusiastic onlookers, who cheered and applauded. Four years later, four or five times as many people lined the streets when he returned with several cast members of the movie version of *The Music Man* to again participate in the band festival and parade.[51]

But the Mason City that Willson remembered—at least the town that he memorialized in *The Music Man*—bore little resemblance to the actual Mason City as it existed in 1912, the year in which the musical play was set. By that time, the town had already emerged as Iowa's fifteenth-largest population center, was home to a wide variety of industries, and was going through its most rapid growth spurt in history. First settled by Europeans seeking land during the 1850s, after the Indian tribes previously living in the area had been pushed out, Mason City originated as a typical agricultural trade center, catering to farm families who were rapidly moving into the region. Masonic lodge members spearheaded the settlement, first naming it Shibboleth, modifying that later to Masonic Grove and Masonville, and finally settling on Mason City (after the Post Office Department informed them that a Masonville post office already existed in the state).[52]

The acquisition of the county seat in 1858, after a spirited contest for the designation with nearby Clear Lake, and the arrival of the Milwaukee Railroad in 1869 (four more rail lines would later establish connections) provided Mason City a leg up on potential rivals. Eventually, the town's trade area extended 40–60 miles in every direction. Its advantageous location was part of the explanation for its emergence as the largest trading community in the northeastern part of the state. The town also benefited from being home to a variety of dynamic, creative individuals, some of them nationally famous. Carrie Chapman Catt served as superintendent of schools before going on to become a leader in the national fight for women's suffrage, Herbert Quick was principal of the Garfield School before emerging as a well-known novelist, and Hanford MacNider, whose family was heavily involved in banking and industry, became the second most highly decorated U.S. soldier in World War I, national commander of the American Legion, assistant secretary of war in Calvin Coolidge's administration, a leader of the isolationist forces standing against foreign policy adventures during the 1930s, and the first American general to be wounded during World War II.[53]

Mason City was a progressive town. In 1883, the first light plant went in; two years later, a municipal water system was installed. In 1896, an electric rail line linked Mason City with its neighbor to the west, Clear Lake. In 1899, a new county courthouse was built. A major building boom occurred downtown between 1900 and 1912. President William McKinley laid the cornerstone for one of the new business buildings while visiting in 1900. Between 1908 and 1910, the town became the site of one of Frank Lloyd Wright's prairie homes as well as two downtown buildings he designed—the City National Bank and the Park Inn Hotel. Wright's partner, Walter Burley Griffin, drew up the plans for half a dozen other houses that went in on the east side of town during the 1910s. Other major new buildings constructed between 1910 and 1912 included the Elks Block, the First

National Bank building, a new hotel, the Fifth Street Fire Station, and a new Knights of Columbus Building. Mason City's skyline extended upward during these years; several of the buildings rose to six or seven stories, though most remained only two or three stories tall.[54]

Between 1911 and 1915, the downtown streets were paved, and street signs were ordered by the city council in 1915. In 1913, the first traffic laws went into effect, and that same year the town instituted a new commission form of government. Contracts for a $32,000 sewage plant were let in 1911, and at the opening of the new $60,000 National Guard Armory in 1915, the general in charge of the Iowa Military Department judged it to be the finest one in the state. The five-year period between 1910 and 1915 marked the most rapid growth in Mason City's history, as measured by the federal and state censuses, with population jumping from 11,230 to 17,152. A 1912 ballot initiative to enlarge the boundaries of the city passed easily, 859–412. The town's budget that year was one of the largest in many years.[55]

Situated at the confluence of Willow Creek and the Winnebago River, the site had already been a transportation hub during Indian days. A 1680 map showed a double line, marking the Chemin des Voyageurs, connecting Prairie du Chien, Wisconsin, and the Missouri River. The Chemin des Voyageurs, used by the Sauk Indians, was a fur trading route and passed right through the future location of the town. In 1855, the Iowa legislature designated it as State Road 1.[56] By 1906, the *Mason City Globe-Gazette* was already noting the presence of a considerable number of automobiles in and around Mason City, enough to induce the city council to set a speed limit of 10 miles per hour, under penalty of fine. Good attendance was reported at the town's first auto show, held in 1915. During the decade after 1910, Mason City became a crossroads for both the Atlantic-Yellowstone-Pacific (AYP) Highway, a major east-west road, and the Jefferson Highway, connecting New Orleans and Winnipeg. At first, these "highways" were merely dirt or, in a few cases, gravel roads. Soon, however, calls for paving the roads began to be heard, and the first mile of rural paving in Iowa was done as an experiment in 1913, beginning a mile west of Mason City's city limits. Two years later, another mile was laid, connecting "the first mile" with the town. Both were later incorporated into U.S. Highway 18. Meanwhile, air travel began to interest Mason Citians, with aviation meets and exhibitions beginning in 1911 and 1912.[57]

Culturally, too, the town was up to date. A $25,000 Carnegie library opened its doors in 1905. The Bijou Theatre, constructed the following year, offered the first silent movies. Under summer Chautauqua tents a short train ride away at Clear Lake, Mason Citians could find inspiration in oratory from the likes of Billy Sunday, Carry Nation, William Jennings Bryan, and other spellbinders. When the Wilson Opera House, whose boards had featured many famous actors, ranging from Sarah Bernhardt to John Drew, burned down in 1911, it was quickly replaced by the beautiful new Cecil Theater.[58]

What primarily set Mason City apart from most other towns like it, however, was its vigorous growth as a site of industrial manufacturing. In 1911 and 1912, several new factories came on line. An estimated $8 million in capital investment occurred in the community during the five years after 1910. Benefiting from large lime and clay deposits in the area, it became a center for the production of portland cement and for a while was the largest manufacturer of clay drain tiles in the world. Surrounded by corn and hogs, it emerged as a major meatpacker and also as a processor of sugar beets and other products. No wonder the Iowa Manufacturers Association decided to hold their twelfth annual convention in Mason City in 1914. In 1916, the Safety Vulcanizing Company, which produced devices for patching auto tires, went into operation. For a time, the town even got involved in automobile manufacturing. The Colby Motor Company opened a new $1 million factory in 1910, doing well enough to expand its facilities two years later. The experiment was short-lived, however, as the company went out of business several years later.[59]

Theatergoers received scarcely a hint of any of this activity when they saw *The Music Man* on the Broadway stage. Willson's mythical River City bore some resemblance to the town in which he had grown up. Many of the characters, places, and activities described in the play were derived, at least to some extent, from actual experience. But River City was a dream town, not a real one, and therein lay its tremendous appeal. Although the play evoked some of the realities of early twentieth-century midwestern small towns and was appealing as an exercise that called to mind some of their positive and negative qualities, it scarcely represented the historical reality of the actual town that Willson had grown up in. Mason City in 1912 was a relatively large and rapidly growing center of trade and commerce and home to an unusually vigorous manufacturing sector. Not only were trains and automobiles commonplace, but airplanes were beginning to dot the horizon. It was not a sleepy little town of 2,212 people, as Willson described it, but a rapidly growing one five or six times larger.

Willson, in translating Mason City, circa 1912, into theatrical entertainment did not enlarge the town in real terms. He did enlarge it, however, in mythological terms. The small band and orchestra that he had played in became "seventy-six trombones . . . with a hundred and ten cornets" in *The Music Man*. The framed portrait of Iowa citizens (intended to evoke an image of Grant Wood's *American Gothic*) that appears at the beginning of the play and in the movie provided a clue to Willson's intentions. It was a dream world, not reality, that he served up in his play.

Even if *The Music Man* did not go very far in accurately describing the real Mason City or every little tank town along the railroad during the early 1900s, it nevertheless went a long way toward expressing the elemental emotions and attitudes that small-towners like Meredith Willson retained and continued to cherish as they grew older. It evoked memories of a less populous, slower society in which face-to-face relationships predominated and people cared for and looked out for each other. They may have gossiped too much and sometimes fought among themselves over petty issues, but they also lived life on a human scale. In that world, dreams did not always translate into reality, but at least they conjured up images of how lives could be better lived. Wishing on the evening star provided hope, and fantasies about librarians and brass bands provided incentive and morale. Willson was one of many small-town boys who got out of town as quickly as they could, but he could never get his hometown out of his system. He became America's beloved music man, and his *The Music Man* became a classic evocation of what America's small towns could be and, to a lesser degree, of what they sometimes actually were.

CHAPTER THIRTEEN

■

Walt Disney: Memories of Marceline and Dreams of an Ideal Tomorrow

@ Disney

Marceline . . . did not seem the sort of place to inspire a sense of magic and fantasy. But it did precisely that to Walt Disney. As a matter of fact, this rather unremarkable town held a key to the boundless creativity that fueled the enormous Disney cultural enterprise. . . . As an adult, he often talked about his love of rural life and spun tales about his Marceline days. . . . In later years, Walt liked to portray himself as a self-effacing farmboy from the Midwest.

—Steven Watts

In the eventful decades after World War II, a time of dramatic social, economic, and cultural change in the United States, many observers looked to Los Angeles as the place where the future would be defined. Over the course of four centuries of growth and development, Americans had seen the locus of power and influence shift constantly westward, from Jamestown and Boston at the outset, to New York and Philadelphia, then to St. Louis and Chicago, and finally, at the edge of the continent, to Los Angeles and its sister urban aggregations on the West Coast. Between mid-century and 2000, the population of Los Angeles almost doubled, from 2.0 to 3.7 million, while the county's numbers more than doubled, from 4.1 to 9.5 million. By the 1960s and 1970s, demographers were heralding the dramatic rise of the Sunbelt and the Southern Rim, of which Los Angeles was the dominant anchor.

To a significant degree, however, the metropolitan region's cultural texture retained the flavor of the small-town Midwest, because so many of its inhabitants hailed from that region of the country. Every year, a number of communities around the area held Illinois, Iowa, and South Dakota picnics for families that retained happy memories of and affection for the farms and small towns they had left behind them in the Midwest. No wonder social commentators could refer to the City of Angels as "the child of Hollywood out of Kansas" or "a prairie city transplanted to a luxuriant subtropical setting" or the "Middle-Westerner's Nirvana, his reward for years of toil, economy, or shrewdness." This pleasant fairyland, "an amalgam of the Middle West and the movies," in the words of cultural historian Neil Harris, "was the land of the happy ending, bereft, critics charged, of critical intelligence, a traditional class structure, good taste, and a willingness to face unpleasant facts."[1] It is not altogether surprising, therefore (although it was completely unplanned when I began my research for this book), that of the twenty-two midwestern natives highlighted here, eight would wind up in Los Angeles—Frederick Jackson Turner, James Dean, Meredith Willson, Walt Disney, Lawrence Welk, Johnny Carson, John Wooden, and Ronald Reagan.

None of these men harbored greater affection for his midwestern origins than Walt Disney,[2] who on July 17, 1955, a hot summer Sunday afternoon, enthusiastically opened Disneyland in Anaheim, 27 miles southeast of downtown Los Angeles, dubbing it "the happiest place on earth." The site had been carefully chosen by an expert consulting firm on the basis of prevailing weather and climate conditions, population growth trends, emerging traffic patterns (the new Santa Ana Freeway was located close by), economic factors, and consumer surveys. But the Disney team had not counted on the heat melting newly poured asphalt walkways, gobbling up women's high heels; plumbers striking, preventing the completion of the water fountains (in a choice between them and toilets, the latter won out, but long lines queued up to use them, too); eating places running out of food and drink; or eager visitors often having to wait hours for the few rides that were up and running.[3]

The park was still only partially completed, the first shovel of earth having been turned only a year earlier. But rather than delay the grand opening, as many had urged him to do, Disney had plunged forward, as he generally did, determined to keep things on schedule. Many reports emphasized the disorder that resulted when upwards of 30,000 visitors showed up; only a fraction of that number of tickets had been printed (they were easily duplicated). The unfinished park would have had trouble accommodating even the anticipated number of visitors. Traffic jams tied up vehicles along major routes leading to Disneyland and on the side streets surrounding the park. A young park employee ran up alongside Walt's brother Roy when he drove up in his Cadillac. "A lot of these people have been stuck in traffic for hours," the young man breathlessly reported, "and the kids need to go to the bathroom. Now they're peeing all over the lot."

"God bless 'em," Roy replied, smiling broadly. "Let 'em pee."[4]

People watching the 90-minute ABC-TV special hosted by Art Linkletter, Bob Cummings, and Ronald Reagan remained unaware of how chaotic things actually were as the announcers circulated through the park, describing exhibits and rides, interviewing celebrities and happy Disney fans, and expounding on the event's historical significance. Walt himself was largely unaware of the myriad problems of the moment, as he was whisked about from point to point for the television cameras. Twelve-year-old Sharon Baird, one of the Mouseketeers on the new television program linked to the park, was standing next to him in his personal apartment above the Main Street fire station when the gates opened. "When I looked up at him," she said later, "he had his hands behind his back, a grin from ear to ear, and I could see a lump in his throat and a tear streaming down his cheek. He had realized his dream."[5]

Disneyland was Walt's baby, the culmination of years of fantasizing, planning, organizing, and going counter to the advice of almost everyone who mattered to him—his wife, his brother and business partner Roy, and fellow Disney executives and employees, as well as bankers, businessmen, and other theme-park owners. It seemed as if hardly anyone thought his idea would work or was even able to imagine what exactly he had in mind. In the end, however, Disneyland turned out to be his greatest coup. After years of innovating in areas that others hesitated to venture into—sound and color cartoons, feature-length animated films, and televised kiddie shows—Walt Disney was not inclined to let other people tell him what he could or could not do. He seemed, in fact, to welcome the skepticism of the naysayers, and in short order, vindication came. Within two months' time, a million visitors had passed through Disneyland's turnstiles, spending 30 percent more than company bean counters had predicted. The number of visitors mounted to 3.6 million during the first year of operation, and it took less than two and a half years for it to reach 10 million, making the park a bigger draw than the Grand Canyon, Yellowstone, or Yosemite. Within a decade, Disneyland became the largest visitor attraction in the country, drawing one-quarter of the U.S. population through its gates, making it "one of the wonders of the modern world."[6]

Most important from the standpoint of the Disney enterprise, the success of the park marked a historic turn in the company's financial fortunes. Until 1955, despite all the awards and honors accumulated by Disney, the company had always teetered on the financial abyss. Frequently in debt to the tune of millions of dollars, Walt kept pushing the creative envelope, eagerly venturing into new domains and spending huge amounts of money in the process in search of artistic perfection, while Roy kept sweating over the financial balances and trying to restrain his younger brother's enthusiasm. Never was the company able to achieve full financial security and feel comfortable in its success—not, that is, until Disneyland and the accompanying television contracts started pouring millions into its coffers. Disney's gross revenues jumped from $11 million in 1954 to $24.5 million the following year, when Disneyland opened. By the end of the decade, the figure had risen to $70 million. The company, which had gone public in 1940, saw its stock earnings leap from $0.35 a share in 1952 to $2.44 in 1957.[7]

Disneyland, popular from the start, quickly grew into a cultural icon. From the moment it opened, the architectural curator Nicholas Olsberg has observed, it became "a key symbol of contemporary American culture, celebrated and attacked as the ultimate embodiment of the consumer society, of simulation and pastiche, of the blurring of distinctions between reality and imagery."[8] The "Magic Kingdom" constituted the ultimate Rorschach test, inviting both extravagant praise and vituperative denunciation. Intellectuals and the art critics mainly accounted for the latter; the former derived heavily from a broad spectrum of the public.

Disneyland was immensely appealing to a wide variety of people. The rides and attractions were the most technologically advanced available. In addition, the many features based on Disney characters, such as Mickey Mouse, Snow White, and Dumbo, made the park quite entertaining, especially to children. The fantasy quotient was high at every turn, as visitors proceeded through Adventureland, with its Jungle Cruise; Frontierland, with its triple-decker steamboat plying the Rivers of America; Fantasyland, with scenes from Disney movies such as *Peter Pan, Alice in Wonderland,* and *Snow White and the Seven Dwarfs*; and Tomorrowland, with its monorail and Rocket-to-the-Moon ride. The facility, as befitted Disney's own personality, was sparkling clean. The psychological atmosphere was relentlessly optimistic, and everything about the place was sentimental and dreamy. In truth, Disneyland was the physical embodiment of its creator's dreamworld.[9]

Disneyland embodied a plethora of relentlessly positive meanings for millions of Americans and others around the world, but it held special personal significance for Walt Disney, who spoke of the place with a lover's passion. "That place is my baby," he told a *Look* magazine writer in 1964, "and I would prostitute myself for it."[10] For the better part of a decade before it opened, as he converted vague dreams and yearnings into concrete plans and then reality on the ground, he poured all his imaginative resources into the venture. During this period, he gradually withdrew from other projects to devote most of his time and energy to it. "Like a shiny, challenging new toy presented to a precocious kid, Disneyland became a wonderful outlet for Walt's enthusiasm, sense of wonder, and intense work ethic," writes biographer Steven Watts. "Dammit, I love it here," Walt remarked to a collaborator on the project. The work was relaxing and fulfilling, especially during a period in the late 1940s and early 1950s when things were not going well at the studio. When someone suggested that as popular as he was, he could be president if he chose to run, he quipped, "Why would I want to be president of the United States? I'm the king of Disneyland."[11]

Many things attracted him to the concept of a theme park. Some writers have traced its origins to his visits to amusement parks and carnivals in Kansas City, Missouri, during the early 1920s before he moved to Hollywood. He himself often noted how frustrated he became with dirty, sleazy rides and attractions at the parks that he took his daughters to after Sunday school during the 1930s and 1940s. As the Disney studio in Burbank, California, became a more popular place for enthusiastic fans to visit during the latter decade, Walt began to think about creating displays and attractions that might entertain them on the studio lot.

What really hooked him on the idea, however, was his growing interest in trains, which served a highly useful recreational function for a workaholic who needed a diversion to take his mind away from his work after an injury playing polo in 1935 largely limited more vigorous forms of exercise. Beyond that, railroads spoke to a growing sense of history and nostalgia for the past that people observed in him during the 1940s, as he progressed through his forties. By the 1940s Walt was turning his thoughts more and more to the period in his life from 1906 to 1911, between the ages of four and nine. His father, Elias Disney, had bought and moved his family of five children to a 48-acre farm just a quarter mile north of Marceline, Missouri. Walt (born in Chicago on December 5, 1901, the fourth child and youngest of the four boys in the family) had enjoyed living on the farm, and the Atchison, Topeka, and Santa Fe Railway had run nearby. As Walt's enthusiasm for constructing a new kind of theme park blossomed and ideas for how to do it began to jell in his mind during the late 1940s and early 1950s, Marceline and the farm he had lived on were uppermost in his mind. It was not exactly a midlife crisis he was going through, but memories of his childhood wove their way through his thinking. His work as an artist had always been aimed largely at children, and many people close to him thought that he was pretty close to being an overgrown kid himself.

It may sound somewhat strange to learn that a place where Disney had lived for only four and a half years before he was ten years of age should have exerted such a powerful influence on him. But leaving Chicago at such a young age left him with few concrete memories of it. Moreover, Walt's later experience in Kansas City between ages nine and seventeen was one that, in many respects, he would have gladly forgotten. There had been many happy times and ordinary activities in Kansas City. He enjoyed playing and hanging out with a neighbor kid, Walt Pfeiffer, whose household served as a sort of surrogate family for him. The two boys palled around and staged little performances for anyone willing to watch. Disney, who never displayed much interest in schoolwork, had a flair for drawing, and it became a compulsion with him. He reveled in the art classes his parents allowed him to enroll in at the Kansas City Art Institute and began to think about making a career in art. But drawing was also an escape from the drudgery his father imposed on him when the family moved to Kansas City.

Elias Disney's efforts to make an economic go of it on his tiny farm out-side Marceline had failed, and a bout of diphtheria and declining economic fortunes had induced him to move his family once again in 1911. He bought a newspaper distributorship in Kansas City and put his two boys remaining at home to work delivering the *Kansas City Times* in the morning and the *Kansas City Star* in the afternoon to approximately 700 sub-scribers on each route. Roy opted out of the situation after a year, but Walt continued to have to get up at 4:30 (or earlier) every morning to deliver the papers before heading off to school and then left classes early in the after-noon to go through the process all over again. Sometimes he got so tired he would fall asleep in an apartment hallway or doze off in class. If Walt for-got a customer or if a paper blew away in the wind and his father received an annoyed phone call to report the problem, the boy would get cuffed or switched or worse. Elias, a decent man and a devout Congregational church member, constantly read his Bible, was a hard worker, and was well-intentioned in many ways. But he was essentially humorless, was little attuned to the needs and desires of young children, and exhibited a tightly controlling personality. Fortunately for Walt, his even-tempered mother provided emotional ballast and support, softening her husband's sternness and bringing a note of gaiety to the house.

Looking back later at his childhood, Walt not surprisingly focused ea-gerly on his carefree years in Marceline as a sort of Edenic experience. Nat-urally, there was work for him to do as a youngster there, but it was not very onerous. Most of the time, he was free to roam the woods around the house, observe animals and wildlife, fish, skinny-dip, and watch trains go by on the railroad tracks that passed near the farm. The town of Marceline possessed its own allures. Established as a division point on the Santa Fe line connecting Chicago and Kansas City (which lay about 125 miles to the southwest), it was less than twenty years old when the family moved there—an up-and-coming, progressive place. Influenced by the trends of the times, it had grown to about 4,000 residents by the time the Disneys arrived and was in the process of paving its streets, installing electricity, and building a new school, a new waterworks, and a new power plant. Walt was especially impressed by the new 600-seat theater that showed movies and presented performances by traveling troupes of entertainers. Typical of midwestern small towns at the turn of the century, Marceline sported a railroad depot, a city park, and the usual contingent of stores and businesses, ranging from a dry-goods emporium, a meat market, an implement dealer, and a creamery to department stores, an ice company, hardware and jewelry stores, and a barber shop. Besides seeing Maude Adams play Peter Pan in a touring road show, Walt attended his first circus and his first Chautauqua meeting in Marceline. There was a gazebo where the band played in Ripley Square. The town was a hotbed of support for William Jennings Bryan.[12]

These experiences and impressions churned around in Disney's memory as time went by, reworking themselves in his imagination and fantasy life. He idealized the town in attempting to recall it. "Everything connected with Marceline was a thrill to us," he reminisced with affection.[13] "All who knew Walt agree that though it was brief, the most significant time in his life was the few years, ages five to nine, he lived in Marceline, Missouri. His life's work—drawing, animation, film, trains, Main Street at Disneyland, and more—all have roots deep in those green Missouri hills," write Amy Boothe Green and Howard E. Green.[14] "Although they stayed only a few years while the father tried his hand at farming, this period had an impact on the young boy's psyche and values that lingered for a lifetime," observes biographer Steven Watts. "As an adult, he often talked about his love of rural life and spun tales about his Marceline days. Such sentiments were not only for public consumption. In late middle age, rich and famous as a Hollywood filmmaker, Disney built a small barn behind his house near Beverly Hills to serve as a workshop. It was an exact replica of the one he remembered from the Marceline farm."[15]

Ironically, those years in Marceline were the only period in his life that Disney did not live in a large and growing city, except for a year after World War I when he was working as a Red Cross ambulance driver in France, and then much of his time was spent in and around Paris. Home from France after the war, Walt looked for a position as a newspaper cartoonist in Kansas City. Unsuccessful in that, he obtained a job as a commercial artist and quickly ventured into the brand-new field of animated cartoons, only several years after New York City artists had begun producing them. He was only eighteen years old. The experience established a pattern that the young man would adhere to for the rest of his life: precocity in his actions and timeliness in getting in on the ground floor of new ventures.

After getting started and floundering for three years in Kansas City, making what he called "Laugh-O-Grams" and then cartoon shorts featuring a four-year-old actress named Virginia Davis (called the "Alice" comedies), Disney packed up in 1923, at age twenty-one, and moved to Hollywood. Once there, he enticed his brother Roy to team up with him and act as financial and business manager while he took care of the creative side of the business. The partnership, though often strained and tempestuous, proved to be an excellent and highly productive match. It continued until Walt's death in 1966, after which Roy took over the company himself until he passed away in 1981.

The 1920s were a decade of trial, error, and ultimate success, as Walt Disney Studios (originally called Disney Brothers) progressed from the "Alice" cartoons through the highly successful "Oswald the Lucky Rabbit" series to, finally in 1928, their first major breakthrough—the cartoons featuring Mickey Mouse. As the staff expanded from about a dozen in the early 1920s to twice that in 1927 and nearly 200 by 1934, Walt turned over the actual drawing of the cartoon figures (which, despite his enthusiasm for it, he was never very good at) to hired hands and devoted himself to presiding over the entire creative process. By 1926, the brothers felt confident enough to build a new studio on Hyperion Avenue in Hollywood, where they would remain until the late 1930s.

The Depression decade would be remembered as golden years at Disney for all their innovations; for the awards—both monetary and critical—the studio garnered; for the huge popularity they achieved with the public; and for the rare sense of creativity, camaraderie, and mission that the happy band of animators enjoyed. Walt was a hard-driving and hugely demanding—but also friendly, collegial, and encouraging—boss, and his coworkers believed that they were contributing to something new and significant in the culture. With the appearance of the first cartoon featuring their new hero ("Plane Crazy," a takeoff on Charles Lindbergh's famous flight), Mickey Mouse emerged as an instant sensation in May 1928. Six months later, Disney introduced sound in animated cartoons in his third Mickey short ("Steamboat Willie"), and in 1932 he pioneered in color cartoons with "Flowers and Trees." No less important, his animators injected personality into their cartoon characters in a way that had never been done before, and the use of storyboards to plan out every sequence of a film before going into actual production—a process developed by Disney—was soon established as an industry standard. Always quick to adopt new technologies, Disney had his staff develop and put into use a new multiplane camera for producing 3-D effects in *Snow White and the Seven Dwarfs* (1937), which itself was a major innovation as the first feature-length animated cartoon. Meanwhile, the studio had moved quickly during the early 1930s to market spin-offs of its cartoon characters (whose repertoire was expanded during the decade to include figures such as Pluto, Goofy, Dumbo, and Donald Duck). Sales of ancillary products leapt from $20 million in 1934 to $100 million a decade later.[16] With the huge success of *Snow White*, Walt Disney's image grew larger than life. He was featured on the cover of *Time* magazine in December 1937, and the following year Harvard, Yale, and the University of Southern California all conferred honorary degrees on him. *Snow White* received a special Academy Award for its groundbreaking production techniques and general excellence, and the cartoon shorts that the studio kept grinding out captured Oscars almost every year during the decade.

The 1940s turned out to be something else again—a challenging, frustrating, and often-maddening decade for Disney. Walt, who had expected to be loved and showered with gratitude from his employees for the large, expensive, state-of-the-art facilities the studio moved into in Burbank in 1939, heard grumbling and reproach instead. They were, some people said, too antiseptic, too anonymous, too dehumanizing. A four-month-long strike in 1941, which was understandable at a time when the labor force at the studio had expanded to over 1,200 and unionizing activities were going on in many industries around the country, caught him by surprise and ultimately embittered him. The war itself had contradictory impacts on the studio. On a positive note, it provided continued work and a reliable flow of cash (though only enough to break even, and a large accumulated debt hung over the enterprise throughout the early 1940s). At the war's peak, around 90 percent of the studio's efforts were engaged in war work—training and propaganda films mostly. The negative result was that almost any opportunity for creativity was forgone. In any case, animated films were hardly profitable to produce any more. Walt desperately began to search for new outlets for the studio's energies, but few prospects appeared on the horizon. He thought of focusing on educational films or industrial films, but opportunities proved limited in both areas.

After the war, as he continued to turn out short animated films in smaller numbers and to make a few feature-length ones (*Cinderella* came out in 1950, and others followed, such as *Peter Pan* and *Sleeping Beauty*), Disney started moving into live-action films, nature documentaries, and, most important, television. The last proved to be the studio's salvation and the key that made possible Walt's new hobbyhorse and the thing that by the late 1940s had begun to dominate most of his waking hours—building a new kind of theme park. Several factors led Walt to start thinking along these lines, but frustrations with the situation at the studio and a distancing of himself from his workers and the work he had been doing for almost three decades were of major importance. Most significant, in many ways, was the impulse he felt to look back on his own life and especially on his happy, small-town boyhood in Marceline. Never one to confide much in others and possessing few close friends, perhaps none, he appeared by the late 1940s not only to be a loner but, more important, to be a lonely man, even in the midst of large crews of employees and associates. Interacting with dozens of people on a daily basis, he became increasingly cranky, aloof, and often cruel, although he remained perfectly capable of turning on the charm when he chose to do so.

The thing people noticed about him in those days was a new and pronounced fascination with trains. He seemed to be reverting to childhood when he purchased a Lionel model train set for himself in 1947, explaining that he had never been able to have one as a boy. Soon he decided, much to his wife's frustration, to construct a one-eighth-scale train on the two-and-a-half-acre lot on which he was building a new house for them in the Holmby Hills, near Beverly Hills. They moved into the house in 1950, and eventually the track extended half a mile, twisting and turning around the property. Meanwhile, in August 1948 he invited Disney employee and train enthusiast Ward Kimball, who had relocated a *full-scale* train locomotive and tracks onto the property around his house, to go along with him to a railroad fair celebrating a century of railroading in Chicago. Once there, the two men reveled in examining and learning about all the historic trains and locomotives on display. On their long train ride to Chicago, Walt reminisced at length about his boyhood. After hugely amusing themselves for several days at the fair and detouring to Detroit to visit Henry Ford's historic Greenfield Village, Walt regaled his railroad buddy all the way home with his plans for what he was now calling "Disneyland."[17]

Meanwhile, he had developed a passion for constructing miniature set pieces of old-time historic scenes. He spent a good deal of time scouring antique papers and ads as well as actually collecting miniature versions of historic houses, buildings, and scenes. In 1952 at the California Festival of Living, an exhibition held at the Pan-Pacific Auditorium in Los Angeles, he displayed a miniature scene he had constructed, entitled "Granny's Cabin," which reproduced a set from the 1949 Disney movie *So Dear to*

CHAPTER THIRTEEN

My Heart. The film was a highly nostalgic story set on a midwestern farm in 1903 (three years before the Disney family moved to Marceline).[18] "'So Dear' was especially close to me," he told a reporter interviewing him. "Why that's the life my brother and I grew up with as kids out in Missouri."[19] As Walt thought more intensively about Disneyland and commissioned drawings depicting what such a theme park might entail, a small railroad town always looking very much like Marceline was emerging in his imagination.

At planning sessions with artists and designers such as Harper Goff and Marvin Davis, he entertained them by the hour with stories based on fond memories of Marceline. He described to them various buildings in the town that could serve as templates for structures to be laid out in the new theme park. From the beginning, the group planned to make Main Street the common point of entry in Disneyland—a place that every visitor would pass through on the way to the park's other attractions. Also, a railroad would encircle the park, with a depot reminiscent of the one in Walt's little Missouri town. Although Disney's vision inspired the development of Disneyland, the theme park's courthouse and some of the other buildings resembled ones in Goff's hometown, Fort Collins, Colorado. In other words, on this project, as on all the others done at the Disney Studio, work was collaborative. Although Walt's input was most important, other people's ideas got thrown into the mix, too. The railroad was given a prominent place because Walt had installed a similar model railroad in his own backyard, notes the historian Karal Ann Marling. Disneyland, in effect, she observes, was "the autobiography of the little boy who heard the whistle calling, took the long journey to California, and made the movies that define the lands adjacent to the hub. All of Disneyland is Walt Disney but the most personal, idiosyncratic part of the autobiography written there in buildings, streets, and sidewalks is Main Street, U.S.A."[20]

Thus, Disneyland, with all its high-tech rides and features and with Tomorrowland being one of the four main attractions radiating out from the Cinderella Castle at the center, was somewhat schizophrenic in its focus on both the past and the future. The only time period omitted from the mix, it has been pointed out, was the present. A high berm encircled the park, blocking out any view of what existed outside this self-enclosed place of wonder and delight and ensuring that people inside would remain focused on fantasy and imagination. The same would be true later of Walt Disney World in Orlando, Florida, which was announced at a press conference in

1965, a little more than a year before Disney died. It would open in October 1971. Although Walt was not one for repeating himself and for a while denied any intention of building a second Disneyland, by the early 1960s he had begun to devote most of his energies to the project. This time, however, he was scarcely interested in the amusement park itself, which in most regards would duplicate the original Disneyland on a larger scale.[21] Rather, he became obsessed with building a planned city nearby for the people who worked in the park and with making it an experimental laboratory for addressing the urban ills he perceived to be afflicting the United States.

Four decades of driving around Los Angeles had soured him on freeway traffic and urban sprawl, and he had grown increasingly concerned about such urban blights as crime, pollution, overcrowding, and disorder. By 1960, he had been so successful at so many things and had received so much praise for his achievements that he had come to believe that nothing was impossible if he simply set his mind to it and was able to obtain adequate financial backing and expert advice. He began to imagine a small city of 20,000 people in which automobiles would be banished to the periphery; residential, service, commercial, and industrial functions would be integrated in rational fashion; and such issues as employment, preschool education, home environment, adolescent development, and aging would be addressed by experts using scientific methods. He began reading and carrying around books like architect and mall designer Victor Gruen's *The Heart of Our Cities* (1964) and British visionary Ebenezer Howard's *Garden Cities of To-morrow* (1902, reissued in 1965). In a sense, turning his attention toward urban planning was a logical extension of his earlier work as a cartoonist, in which as an animator he had been able to totally control the behavior of his imaginary characters, and of his success in channeling and controlling the movements and behavior of millions of tourists visiting Disneyland every year. In his work at the studio and in his own personal life, Disney had demonstrated an insatiable need to control everything down to the last detail, growing more obsessive about it as time went by. By now, he brooked virtually no dissent from his decrees. Extending his control to urban residents and thereby creating a more ideal society—not in people's temporary experience in a theme park but in actual life—may have come to seem altogether possible to him.

Alas, it was not to be. The man who was such a workaholic and such a personally self-controlled person that he felt the need to impose his control on his own workers and staff had not been able to manage his own compulsion to smoke. Once his health began to fail rapidly in 1966, the end came swiftly. After having his cancerous left lung removed in November, he was soon forced to return to the hospital. To almost everyone's surprise and probably also his own, he passed away quickly on December 15. The day before, while lying in his bed in the hospital, he was still mentally manipulating elements of his planned EPCOT (Experimental Prototype Community of Tomorrow) on the ceiling tiles above his bed. He remained working right up to the very end—dreaming, planning, and scheming. He was ready to try to remake human behavior in American cities in the same way he had reconstructed people's imaginations and fantasies in his cartoons, movies, and amusement parks. This small-town boy from Marceline, Missouri, embodied in his own contradictions and strivings the many fault lines and dreams that continued to animate the American people.[22]

SECTION FOUR

The Lingering Presence of the Small Town, 1965 to the Present

Introduction to Section IV

People living through the 1960s sensed that history was being made in front of their eyes, what with all the drama, conflict, and, sometimes, violence that characterized the period. Looking back across the decades, what stands out now in many minds are the protests, the demonstrations, and the confrontations over so many different issues—the Vietnam War, civil rights, family relations, crime, inequality, the environment, and a dozen other things. Authority, tradition, the Establishment—they were all under siege, and the only question seemed to be, What institution would be challenged next?

Not so easily observable at the time and not much remarked on in retrospect were significant demographic shifts that accelerated during the period, shifts that placed unprecedented stress on America's small towns and remoter regions. For decades, such places had been undergoing transition; the specter of outmigration from farm areas and small towns had become a worrisome and chronic challenge, causing much hand-wringing and concern. By the 1960s, the situation seemed to have reached a tipping point. The July 8, 1963, cover story of *Newsweek* magazine, "Smalltown, U.S.A.," captured the mood. Using the southeastern Iowa town of Keosauqua (population 1,023) as a case study, its authors observed, "All across the U.S. map, the agricultural town is dying, and Keosauquans are haunted by the statistics." It and small towns like it tottered tragically "on the edge of darkness." But hope continued to persist, and many small-town dwellers, as well as their urban counterparts, retained "the sociologically unprovable but instinctive American feeling that the little town and the countryside are the source of civic energy for the nation." On the other side of the equation, the article quoted sociologist Philip Hauser, who noted, "What the small town may have contributed in the past is one side of the coin; the other side is urbanism and the greatest opportunity in the history of man for him to reach his full potential. Where the small town kept him prisoner, urbanism gives him freedom of choice—choice of education, choice of profession, choice of marriage. If the small town is passing, we can't bemoan it."[1]

Demographic trends followed something of a roller-coaster course for the rest of the century, with rural areas and small towns regaining ground for a time in the 1970s, falling back in the 1980s, and then enjoying a brief revival again in the 1990s before leveling off. The long-term direction of change, however, was apparent to clear-sighted observers: small towns were more and more sidelined from the mainstream of the nation's forward progress. The causal forces that were operating were plain enough: throughout history, urban places emerged to serve mainly economic functions but also social, cultural, and governmental ones. During the nineteenth and early twentieth centuries, midwestern small towns had risen up almost automatically to provide services for farmers and nearby residents as transportation routes and migration patterns pushed constantly westward across the continent. During the decades after World War I, as agriculture decreased in relative importance in the economy and as rural areas depopulated, the small towns that had emerged to serve them lost momentum, too. For a time, manufacturing and commerce were able to fill the gap in at least some places, but these proved a shaky reed on which to rely, as mammoth corporations and globalizing forces centralized power and control in fewer and fewer hands and as big-box retailers shoved aside mom-and-pop stores on Main Street. Stripped of their historical economic functions, small towns increasingly found themselves depending on tourist traffic, post offices, schools, medical facilities, Social Security checks, and government services to keep them going. The most dependable role remaining for most of them to play was to serve as bedroom communities for the larger towns and cities that did have operating major manufacturing and commercial concerns. Even as their economic functions disappeared or were pared down, however, the social and cultural functions that these towns performed continued to operate. Meanwhile, large numbers of Americans continued to profess a preference for the small-town way of life, even if they chose or were compelled by circumstances to live in metropolitan areas.

Johnny Carson and Lawrence Welk are seldom discussed in connection with each other, but they possessed a number of things in common, including their similar origins in rural/small-town America on the edge of the midwestern prairie. Though born a little more than two decades apart, both first obtained national audiences on television in the 1950s, both wound up in the Los Angeles area after some years of moving about (Welk much more than Carson), both became hugely popular by determining what their audiences desired and then providing it, and both achieved unusual success and mountains of money from what they did.

Both men also took pride in their midwestern backgrounds and returned a number of times (again, Welk more frequently than Carson) to visit their hometowns in Strasburg, North Dakota, and Norfolk, Nebraska. The former, a tiny burg near the Missouri River in the south-central part of the state, honored Welk by erecting a sign on the edge of town, placing a picture of the Champagne Music Maker in the post office, and naming its swimming pool and city park after him. The North Dakota Hall of Fame chose him as one of its ten original inductees in 1967. Carson, for his part, had a theater named after him at the University of Nebraska, and a hospital in his hometown in northeastern Nebraska was named for his parents, after he made large donations to both.

The Lawrence Welk Show, although appealing strongly to Southern Californians and television viewers all over the United States, derived much of its popularity from the nostalgic reveries and small-town aura it evoked in its weekly airings. Its youngish, well-scrubbed, and telegenic singers, musicians, and dancers all stirred wistful memories of an America that seemed to be rapidly fading. It was no wonder that his weekly audiences tended toward lots of gray-haired oldsters or that young folks tended to view it as corny and superannuated. Carson emerged as the most lucrative and powerful performer in the medium by creating an atmosphere on his *Tonight Show,* which, in a sense, re-created gatherings around the old-time stove and cracker barrel in small-town general stores, ubiquitous all over the Middle West. The guests on his program tended to be showbiz personalities, entertainers, and popular-culture figures, interspersed with animal trainers, offbeat figures plucked from the news, and others who might elicit from his audiences chuckles or raised eyebrows. Both programs worked amazingly well within the parameters their stars established for them.

Juxtaposing Welk and Carson reminds us that small-town boys from the Midwest, similar as they were in some respects, could vary immensely in their mind-sets, interests, values, and approaches. Welk always projected a whiff of naïveté along with his friendly, open, sincere demeanor. Carson, in contrast, came across as a modern, "with-it" sort of guy—knowing, cool, ironic, and insouciant. Yet, just like Welk, whose every performance and utterance sounded like a tribute to his stolid, midwestern origins, Carson could go weepily sentimental when reminded of his boyhood days in Norfolk. The affectionate feelings he retained for his Nebraska roots came through clearly in the production of a 90-minute TV special for NBC aired in 1982. This was a program he had wanted to do for a long time, and he even wrote a good part of it. Going back home to drive country roads in the family's old Chrysler sedan, stopping by the barber shop on Main Street, visiting with former classmates at a high school reunion, hanging from the girders of the railroad bridge outside town where he and his buddies had congregated, Carson relived the days of his childhood and became suddenly wistful. When the spectators at a football game serenaded him on his birthday, he joked that they were blowing his image as a cold, aloof loner. Those charges obviously stung the man who never quite overcame his childhood shyness and felt a need to maintain distance between himself and strangers. Welk and Carson both had obviously been strongly affected by their respective childhoods on the farm and in midwestern small towns, but the outcomes in their cases had been quite different.

No collegiate basketball coach, and probably no coach in any sport, was more successful than John Wooden of the UCLA Bruins, who captured ten national championships during his last twelve years at the helm at the Westwood campus. But Los Angeles was not a natural fit for this reluctant emigrant from the rural Midwest. After moving there in 1948, while he was in his late thirties, from Indiana State Teachers College, he found the press of people, freeway traffic, high cost of living, and new lifestyles disconcerting. To supplement his salary, he took a part-time summer job at a dairy for several years. Had a Big Ten team come along at the right time with a job offer, he would have readily moved back to home territory in the Midwest. But after several years in Southern California, he and his wife and two children settled in and made it their new home, even if the coach himself never felt entirely comfortable in his new environment.

Wooden's upbringing in a frugal, pious Christian farm family living 35 miles southwest of Indianapolis instilled in him a set of strict habits and principles for living that became only more ingrained as the years and decades passed by. Like all three of his brothers, he became a teacher, and that is the way he always thought of himself—as a teacher more than as a coach. In fact, during his first eleven years after graduating from college, he continued to teach English in the classroom in addition to performing his coaching and other administrative duties. He even continued to do that during his two years in Terre Haute before moving to UCLA. When he was in his nineties, he could still recite long passages from James Whitcomb Riley and others of his favorite poets. Even if he was not the typical intellectual one might conjure up when thinking of a college professor, Wooden remained a committed reader, thought deeply about subjects that were important to him, and frequently felt moved to pass along life lessons to his student athletes and, as time went by, to anybody else who was willing to listen.

The 620–147 record he compiled at UCLA as a coach and all the other awards and honors he compiled over the course of a long lifetime earned him a large audience for his views, but in the end he believed that his most important tasks were to promote character education and to impart his principles and advice about living one's life. As early as 1934, during his second year of high school teaching, he began to develop his famous Pyramid of Success, encapsulating fifteen major virtues or habits he thought crucial for winning athletic contests and for living successfully. These virtues included friendship, loyalty, cooperation, industriousness, enthusiasm, self-control, and initiative, supplemented by a number of complementary characteristics, such as adaptability, resourcefulness, and reliability. He liberally distributed copies of his pyramid to anybody who displayed interest in it, as well as wallet cards containing words of advice presented to him by his father when he graduated from eighth grade. The latter included counsel such as "Be true to yourself," "Make each day your masterpiece," and "Make friendship a fine art."

Although the coach was a long way from home, in his ways of thinking and living he had not traveled far. A country boy at heart, he had loved his life on the farm and in small-town Indiana, and in crucial respects he always remained true to those beginnings. He returned to Martinsville, where he had been a three-time all-state basketball player, a number of times and was grateful for the various ways in which his hometown had honored him. For Wooden, as for many small-town boys from the Middle West, home was where the heart was.

Like many successful politicians, Ronald Reagan was a masterful myth-maker, skilled at fashioning powerful political imagery. Naturally he leaned heavily on his midwestern small-town origins in crafting a narrative for himself that would go down well with the voters. In many ways, the stories he told about his school days in Dixon, Illinois, his gridiron and life-saving exploits, and his thespian ambitions rang true. As in all such self-serving accounts, there were slippages, exaggerations, and sizable gaps. But the affection and nostalgia he maintained for Dixon and the several other northern Illinois towns he grew up in were real. Even more, he genuinely loved Eureka College, and he went back to visit his alma mater no less than twelve times after graduating in 1932. Small-town schools like the ones he attended in Dixon and small colleges like Eureka provided opportunities for their charges to participate and shine. Students could gain the confidence they needed to step out into the world and accomplish the things they had only imagined they might be able to do.

Reagan was the quintessential dreamer, and with considerable talent, a lot of chutzpah, a willingness to work, and a certain amount of luck, he was able to fulfill his wildest ambitions as he progressively moved from radio announcer to movie star, president of the actors' union, state governor, and president of the United States. In the last position, he was, as one of his biographers noted, assuming the largest role of his life. Through it all, the essential person enacting the various roles he successively assumed remained somewhat elusive. Hailing from the small-town heartland did not guarantee that everyone he met would be able to penetrate the surface to perceive the core of his identity. His opaqueness bewildered even his closest friends and associates, his children, and his beloved wife, Nancy, who knew him best.

As a kid, according to his own testimony, he had lived in an imaginary world—a world of pretend. As he moved through adulthood, it was sometimes difficult for observers to determine where imagination left off and reality set in. As grateful and indebted as he was toward his small-town beginnings, he readily forsook the Middle West when the opportunity arose in 1937 to go to Hollywood, and he never looked back. For the rest of his life he felt quite comfortable playing the role of a westerner as an adoptive son of Southern California. He genuinely loved to ride horses, hankered after western roles on-screen, and looked really good in denim and cowboy hats. That is the way he is depicted in the larger-than-life-size statue of him that greets visitors at his presidential library in Simi Valley, and that is the way people remember him—as an urban cowboy who glided effortlessly through a life that saw him evolve from a lower-middle-class, small-town kid in the Midwest into, for eight years, the most powerful man in the world. It should be noted, however, that although he calculatedly employed small-town imagery in order to get elected, once in office he seldom paid attention to the way his policies might specifically affect—either positively or negatively—the kinds of small towns from which he derived.

None of the individuals discussed in this book has been more intimately involved with small towns than Sam Walton, founder of Wal-Mart stores. Born in Oklahoma, he grew up in several small towns in Missouri before locating his first five-and-ten-cent store in Newport, Arkansas, a town of 7,000 in the Mississippi River Delta. Despite his rural origins, after a stint in the military during World War II, Walton was prepared to go into the department store business in St. Louis, Missouri, with a former college roommate until his wife intervened and insisted that they had to raise their family in a small town (which she defined as a place with fewer than 10,000 people). So instead of becoming a metropolitan retailer, Walton spent his first three decades in business operating in small towns, which in many ways was a distinct advantage during the initial rapid expansion of what ultimately became the Wal-Mart empire.

During the 1960s and 1970s, after establishing his first Wal-Mart franchise in Rogers, Arkansas, in 1962, he was able to develop an efficient and effective business model while largely flying under the radar of his competitors and Wall Street. He liked it that way. His first stores were strictly made-on-the-run operations. He would drive to nearby states to pick up trailer loads of cheap discount items direct from manufacturers and set them out on tables and racks for customers to browse. With thirty-two stores in operation in 1970 and 276 in 1980, he began to penetrate the largest towns and metropolitan areas during the 1980s. The story of Wal-Mart's growth from a single store in the Arkansas Ozarks to the largest company in the world by the early 2000s was a remarkable tale marked by ambition, creativity, inspired enthusiasm, and attention to detail, as well as by single-mindedness, ruthlessness, tight-fisted control, and exploitation. Whether Sam Walton would have recognized, had he lived longer, the ultimate results of what he had originated—let alone have approved of them— is open to speculation.

During the early years, he and his company benefited from his intuitive understanding both of his customers and of the available workforce in the Ozark region of northwest Arkansas, southwest Missouri, and eastern Oklahoma and Kansas. He realized that farm women and those living in declining small towns in the area would be willing to work for less than the minimum wage as the region was undergoing wrenching social and economic change. The young men without college educations whom he was able to recruit as managers to run his stores were relatively easy to train and mold because they looked at the world the way he did. In a variety of ways, the rural/small-town origins of the company dictated how it developed and in turn made possible the implementation of Walton's unique hands-on managerial style. During the last decade of his life, as Wal-Mart grew beyond anything he had originally remotely imagined, the operation was able to keep duplicating and expanding its original format and begin functioning like the major national and international business enterprise it had rapidly morphed into.

Through all this, Walton kept driving around town in his beat-up old Ford pickup truck with his bird dogs in the box, happily playing out his role as the rural rube who had pulled a fast one on the big boys on Wall Street. He converted his original Walton's dime store on the square in Bentonville, Arkansas, into a museum that told the story of his and his brainchild's success. By 2010, the town, which had numbered 2,900 residents when his young family had moved there in 1950, had exploded to over 30,000 people, and manufacturers' representatives from all over the United States and all over the world had built offices in town where they could show their wares and try to convince Wal-Mart buyers to sell their stuff on their shelves. Meanwhile, the thousands of small-town retailers that Wal-Mart had driven out of business provided a visible reminder that just because someone grows up in a small town does not mean that he or she will feel any obligation to preserve the old ways of doing things in them.

◼

CHAPTER FOURTEEN

Lawrence Welk and Johnny Carson: Dancing and Talking the Night Away

One of the greatest things about this country is that there is a lot of influence exerted on all of us by small towns. There is an honesty and faith about people from rural areas that has had an effect on the entire country, including the cities. Many of the people who live in the cities came from small towns.

—Lawrence Welk

A guy from the Midwest—that's who I was, that's who I am. I grew up in Norfolk, Nebraska, after living in other small towns. . . . I think there's a great advantage to growing up in a community where you feel comfortable. There was a closeness, a security there I still miss. I had a typical small-town Midwestern boyhood in Norfolk.

—Johnny Carson

Outside the reputations they built for themselves over many decades as two of the country's most popular entertainers, most people would not be inclined to speak of Lawrence Welk and Johnny Carson in the same breath. Welk, the North Dakota farm boy with the heavy German accent, represented traditional values, simple tastes, and schmaltzy entertainment. Carson, the Nebraska small-town kid who commanded the deference of a god in Hollywood, was the perennial Peck's Bad Boy—irreverent, ironic, sophisticated, and with-it. The former never strayed far from his midwestern roots; the aroma of the barnyard never quite left him, and his performances evoked visions of church picnics, country dances, and ice-cream socials. The latter seemed perfectly molded for the new television era emergent in postwar America. A comedian who delighted viewers with his quick wit and who ironized Welk's kind of people, the genial TV host possessed an unsurpassed capacity for milking laughs out of his audiences. He looked at the world and thumbed his nose at it, persuading people to laugh along with him.

Closer consideration, however, reveals many commonalities between these seemingly disparate figures. Both grew up on the edge of the prairie, and both wound up where so many other former midwesterners did—Los Angeles, the "City of Dreams." Both went through Omaha. It became Welk's temporary base of operations during the late 1930s, and it was Carson's starting point in a radio and television career after graduating from the University of Nebraska in 1949. Both men followed circuitous paths to stardom. Welk experienced an enjoyable decade in Chicago before moving to California, and Carson spent a little more than a decade and a half in New York between two runs in Los Angeles.

Both men were proud of their midwestern backgrounds, referring frequently to their small-town roots long after they had left them behind. The older they got, the readier they became to reflect on the meaning of their childhood experiences. As teenagers, both were drawn to performing in front of audiences, instinctively understanding what it took to please people. As adults, they benefited from fortunate timing, taking advantage of the rise of radio and television. Both established a magic rapport with their audiences. Their operating rule was simple: find out what the audience wants and give it to them.

Although in different ways, both Welk and Carson understood that there were boundaries of taste and decorum limiting what they could do and say on stage. The former took every opportunity to elucidate the principles and values he lived by, discussing them with fans, media people, and anyone within earshot. Carson, whose wisecracking humor gently challenged social norms and standards, retained strong opinions about what was proper and improper. In some ways, the Nebraskan and the North Dakotan were not so far apart in their thinking.

The two entertainers' paths seldom crossed, but the two were in Los Angeles together during the early 1950s, boosting their careers. It was in front of a television audience waiting to watch *The Lawrence Welk Show* that Carson auditioned for the slot of host of *Who Do You Trust?*, and later, when Welk appeared on *The Tonight Show*, Carson gamely made an awkward attempt at dancing the polka.[1] Welk (born in 1903, twenty-two years before Carson) achieved success on national television first. *The Lawrence Welk Show* quickly established itself as a hit, somewhat to the pundits' surprise, as a summer replacement on the ABC network in 1955 and garnered consistently high ratings thereafter. From time to time it managed to wrest the number-one spot away from *Gunsmoke*, engendering media watchers' curiosity. What was the source of Welk's appeal? His band gained a reputation as a "meatgrinder," capable of driving one rival after another off the air, none of them able to compete with the lively, cheerful menu of musical entertainment Welk served up for one hour every Saturday evening. His victims included Jimmy Durante, Robert Montgomery, Herb Shriner, and Janis Paige.[2] To the consternation of media sophisticates, even Sid Caesar, the wacky comic genius who kept viewing audiences in hysterics for six years, succumbed to Welk's competition, leading one reviewer to call the North Dakota bandleader "the man who killed Caesar."[3]

With television's assist, Welk's Champagne Music Makers reigned as America's most popular band during the late 1950s. Few other big bands remained, the rest having been killed off, in large part, by the flickering gray images on the television screen. Ironically, the phenomenon largely responsible for declining interest in bands like those of Guy Lombardo, Ray Anthony, Paul Whiteman, and the Dorsey Brothers was also what helped transform Welk's regional reputation into a national one.

Welk's chance to go coast-to-coast emerged after he had built up a large and enthusiastic following in Southern California with his broadcasts over KTLA-TV in Los Angeles. There was nothing fancy about the program in the beginning—just shots of the band members playing their instruments and pans around the dance floor as dancers swayed and whirled under the revolving chandelier of the Aragon Ballroom in Santa Monica, California.

The management had booked Welk there for a four-week engagement in mid-1951. KTLA, having promised to air just one of his shows, took notice of the public's enthusiastic response to the first program and quickly extended the run. The Aragon, which had seemed on the verge of shutting down before Welk's arrival, took on new life. Dancers crowded onto the dance floor. The good time they were having was no accident. Welk and his entourage established a happy, party-like atmosphere that came across forcefully on the TV screen. Welk later noted in his autobiography, "Inside that big, vaulted barn-like interior at the Aragon, the mood was just like that of a Strasburg wedding dance magnified a hundred times, a thousand times." Just as he had done back in the Midwest, Welk strolled through the crowd with his accordion, chatting with people, and taking their requests.[4] In Los Angeles, the destination of tens of thousands of midwestern migrants during the depressed 1930s and war-torn 1940s, Welk discovered an audience he could easily relate to. Now he pioneered a whole new way of communicating with it through the new medium coming across the airwaves. He was able to capture and hold on to that audience, not by depending on innovative technology or gimmicks but simply by serving up the kind of music that he had always liked to play and just by being himself.

The Southern California Dodge Dealers Association had been looking for a program to sponsor. Now, it chose Welk's band over two other popular contenders. The peppy bandleader, intuitively understanding television's potential for expanding his audience, did not limit his activities for the association to his weekly broadcasts. He drove the company's automobiles, spoke its praises glowingly, and went out of his way to visit as many area dealers as he could and to cultivate their friendship. He appeared frequently, either by himself or with some of the band members, in auto showrooms and attended events and benefits sponsored by local Lions and Kiwanis clubs and other groups on behalf of his sponsor.[5] Many viewers took his advice to mention his name when they visited Dodge showrooms. Meanwhile, the band continued nightly performances at the Aragon, drawing large and enthusiastic audiences.

Welk wanted national exposure; it did not take long to arrive. Producer Don Fedderson from Beresford, South Dakota, who was responsible for boosting Liberace's television career, persuaded Dodge to sponsor Welk as a thirteen-week summer replacement, beginning in July 1955.[6] Many industry insiders snorted on hearing the news. Some predicted he would not last six weeks. One veteran orchestra leader groused, "Who is this square? He stumbles all over the stage and his band plays corny arrangements that we threw away fifteen years ago." TV critic John Crosby grumbled, "The Welk style is about as subtle as a metronome."[7]

By now, though, Welk possessed the experience and confidence he needed to stand up to the moguls who wanted to liven up his show with comedians and chorus lines. He emphatically vetoed such notions, saying he would rather drop the series than abandon the formula he had relied on in the past. No risqué jokes or scantily clad choristers would besmirch his show. Welk warned, "This mother who is watching us—the first time a comedian cracks a joke with a double meaning, or she feels something is not quite right—she will just get up and turn the program right off. You have lost her—and may I say, she's not very apt to go out and buy a Dodge car, either!"[8]

He would do it his way or not at all, he insisted, demanding complete control over program content. Two things moved him: idealism and practicality. At age fifty-two, Welk, a staunch Catholic, possessed strong moral beliefs and well-considered ideas about how they applied in the world of entertainment; nothing morally questionable would be allowed on his program. He had developed a natural rapport with his audiences, and he concluded that they thought the same way he did and would not stand for anything that he did not hold to. At times in the past when he had delegated to others the choice of what songs to play or decisions about how to run his show, things had turned out badly. Morality, in this case, reinforced commercial success and vice versa.

The moral issue is arguable, but there is no gainsaying Welk's ability to size up his audience. Television viewers loved the show. Its Nielsen ratings catapulted from 7.1, early on, to 32.5. An estimated 30 million viewers tuned in each week.[9] Nothing too loud, too frenzied, or too spectacular ever occurred on the show. It emphasized the same sorts of things that had worked well for him in Chicago, Pittsburgh, and other stops along the way. Welk had a ready answer for people who wondered why his program was so popular with the public: "In order to be successful on TV, you have to play what people understand. Our music is always handled crisply. It's rhythmic and has a light beat all the time. Our notes are cut up so they sparkle. And, against the sparkle, we have an undercurrent of smoothness in violin, organ and accordion."[10]

Welk's formula for success, stated differently at different times, boiled down to this: give people what they are familiar and comfortable with; keep listening and asking them what they want; play sweet, melodic music capable of being whistled or hummed; play tunes people can dance to; and finally, keep it simple. The formula served him exceptionally well during the 1950s. In 1956, ABC added a second Welk program to its lineup, *Lawrence Welk's Top Tunes and New Talent Show,* aimed at young listeners. At a time when rock and roll was taking over the popular culture, the traditional bandleader continually attempted to reach out to a younger audience. Nevertheless, he expressed relief three years later when the new show was canceled, allowing him once again to concentrate his attention on the main program. Remarkable energy was required (reporters noted that he worked twelve- to eighteen-hour days) to do everything that needed to be done with the television show, performances five nights a week at the Aragon Ballroom, the production of new singles and albums, the continual search for new talent, and oversight of his entire, increasingly complex operation.

Welk was bewildered by stories about him and his band that emphasized their alleged fast rise to fame or rapid emergence from obscurity during the late 1950s. What did people think he had been doing for the past thirty years? Welk and his bandsmen had indeed paid their dues many times over, perfecting their routines in a thousand drafty barns, bandstands, gymnasiums, theaters, opera houses, radio studios, and dance halls. They had played in big towns, little towns, county fairs, magnificent ballrooms, and drafty, shabby venues. They had performed in major cities from Chicago and Milwaukee to Pittsburgh and New York and in Podunk towns all across the United States. Even today, old-timers in the Dakotas and surrounding states can remember the night (or nights) that Lawrence Welk and his band came to town. By the 1950s, he was hardly a Johnny-come-lately to the musical scene; he had been bouncing around the Middle West and other parts of the country for more than a quarter of a century.[11]

In fact, we can date the beginning of his wanderings precisely. On March 11, 1924, the day of his twenty-first birthday, Larry Welk woke up early, got dressed, counted his money (three one-dollar bills, which he pinned inside his coat pocket), said his good-byes to his family, and hopped on a train headed for Aberdeen, South Dakota, 100 miles southeast of Strasburg.[12] The town he could not wait to get away from as a youth later drew him back almost every year to visit relatives and friends after he made it big in show business. Lying 20 miles east of the Missouri River and

15 miles from the South Dakota border, Strasburg was a town whose founders and 90 percent of its residents were German-speaking. Most of them were German Russians: Germans who had settled in Russia to escape German military service and to be able to worship freely, staying there until freedoms that had been granted them (notably, exemption from military service) were abolished in the 1870s, forcing them to move once again, this time across the ocean to the United States.

Lawrence Welk's parents, Ludwig and Christina, had been born in Alsace-Lorraine. As children, they moved with their parents as part of a larger group migrating to Odessa in the Ukraine in southern Russia. In 1892, the young people joined a contingent of German Russians who settled near Strasburg, homesteading a claim 3 miles from the town. Lawrence, who arrived on the scene eleven years later, was the sixth child in a family of eight (four boys and four girls) and did the same kinds of things that every other frontier farm child did at the time—mainly work. Being strong Catholics, the family attended mass every Sunday, even in the coldest of weather, and said their prayers before every meal. Piety was strong and discipline strict in the home, but it was also full of love and respect. There was time for play and relaxation in the evening and during the cold winter months that gave the Dakotas their reputation for blizzards and unpredictable weather.

Among the few things that Ludwig and Christina Welk had been able to bring with them on their ocean voyage were an accordion and several leather-bound Catholic missals. Ludwig enjoyed taking out his music box in the evening and gathering the family around to listen and sing. He also was able to earn a little extra money occasionally playing for dances, weddings, and other occasions. Young Lawrence's earliest clear memory as a child was of crawling across the floor of the family's sod farmhouse toward his smiling father as he played his accordion. He could remember his huge pleasure as a child in being allowed to press the keys and elicit a few wavering sounds from the instrument.[13]

Welk also remembered how skinny, shy, and sickly he had been as a youth. When the time came, he started attending parochial school in Strasburg, which was run by Ursuline nuns who had immigrated from Germany. Although the nuns were able to speak English, classes were taught in German. German likewise was the common mode of communication at home as well as in stores in town and at the Church of St. Peter and St. Paul, where they attended. Until his twenty-first birthday, Lawrence hardly ever heard English spoken. His distinct accent greatly embarrassed him, often leaving him tongue-tied.

Little outwardly distinguished the boy while he was growing up. Had it not been for a near-tragic occurrence when he was eleven years old, he might have become a farmer, like most of his playmates, or perhaps a storekeeper or a schoolteacher or a mechanic. Music was his great joy, and he practiced on the family's pump organ for hours on end, just about driving everyone else crazy. But except for a ruptured appendix and peritonitis that set in in 1914, almost killing him, the young music lover might have proceeded no further with his boyhood interest than to become a church choir director or to make music his hobby. Having to remain in the hospital for seven weeks and after that spending the better part of a year recovering from the illness provided the boy with plenty of time to sit and dream—and to practice music. When he regained his strength and was able to get out of bed, he spent many hours daily playing the family's pump organ and his father's accordion. Gradually, an overpowering thought began to build in him. He loved music so much that maybe—just maybe—he could avoid becoming a farmer and make his living as a musician instead.[14]

After his year-long absence from school, Lawrence convinced his parents to let him drop out rather than go back into a class with children a year younger than he. Assuming that he would become a farmer and not need more than a fourth-grade education, Lawrence's parents reluctantly agreed, and his schooldays were over. During the next several years, as the boy's body turned into a man's, he got better on his father's accordion, playing it occasionally at barn dances and other functions. By trapping muskrats, skunks, and squirrels, he scraped together fifteen dollars and sent off for a mail-order accordion of his own. It was so cheaply made, however, that it quickly fell apart, as did a second one, but Lawrence was not a boy who easily gave up.

He came up with a creative solution to his problem and persuaded his father to go along with it. At the age of seventeen, he audaciously proposed that the elder Welk buy him a $400 accordion, which he could play at barn dances and socials for money. He promised to stay and work on the farm for the next four years, handing over every nickel he earned from his playing to repay the loan. When he turned twenty-one, he would strike out on his own and live on what he could earn as a musician. More surprising still, after carefully weighing the idea, Ludwig Welk agreed and sent off for the precious musical instrument. No doubt he assumed that the boy would outgrow his craze for music and settle down as a farmer, just like his brothers and the other boys in the neighborhood. Much to his parents' chagrin, however, Lawrence went ahead and left home to follow his dream, and unlike most who did so, he ultimately succeeded.

Welk's path up the musical ladder was neither easy nor straight. Along the way occurred setbacks and detours, but persistence finally won out. Several years of playing in other leaders' bands were instructive, but his association with veteran vaudeville trooper George T. Kelly changed his life. Kelly, his most important mentor, convinced him of the need not only to cater to his audience's wishes but also to develop his own character and to take a positive outlook on life. Many of Welk's later habits and practices derived from Kelly's example and advice, and he frequently acknowledged his indebtedness to his old friend and employer, telling TV columnist Hank Grant in 1962, "What success I've achieved I owe to this fine gentleman."[15] Kelly served as sort of a father figure for him; later, Welk himself played a similar role for many of the "boys and girls" in his own entertainment "family."

The former North Dakota farm boy benefited from several big breaks during his career. It was fortuitous that he and his four-piece band happened to be in Yankton, South Dakota, in 1927 on the day radio station WNAX went on the air under new ownership. He and his group had been heading south, lining up band dates and hoping to escape unseasonable spring snowstorms in the Dakotas. Eager to grasp opportunities as they presented themselves, Welk asked the station manager for an audition. Passing the test, the band immediately went on the air. Audience response was so positive that WNAX made Welk (who quickly added a couple of players to his little group) one of its regular morning features.[16]

It was the twenty-four-year-old bandleader's first big break, and it turned him and his sidekicks into regional celebrities. With a listening radius of several hundred miles around Yankton, the station publicized the group in a four state area, helping them line up a steady stream of dance dates. For the next six years, Welk and his band did some hard traveling; they played the morning show regularly and drove to and from engagements in the afternoon and the early hours of the morning. To make things easier on himself and his boys, he bought a bus equipped with beds so they could sleep as they traveled. The constant moving around sapped a person's energies, frequently requiring Welk to find replacements for members who dropped out.[17]

Traveling bands are not conducive to a happy home life, but having grown up in a tight-knit family, the young bandleader wanted both a career and a family. In 1931, he persuaded a local nurse whom he had met at one of his broadcasting sessions to forgo her own career, marry him, and raise their children. Fern Renner was a bright, attractive young woman with ambitions of her own, and the prospect did not immediately appeal to her. Lawrence persisted, however, and at five-thirty in the morning on April 19, 1931 (Welk had just returned from a gig in Norfolk, Nebraska, the previous day), the couple was married in a Catholic ceremony in Sacred Heart Cathedral in Sioux City, Iowa. The early hour was because the band had to make a quick getaway that morning for an engagement in Albany, New York. It portended the kind of life the young couple would lead for the next decade.

Not only did both newlyweds hail from North Dakota (Fern's home town was St. Anthony), but both also traced their ancestry back to Alsace-Lorraine, both came from large families (eight children in each), both were devout Catholics, and both had grown up longing to get away from home and strike out on their own.[18] Subordinating themselves to their husbands was a choice most women made in the 1930s, but it was often a hard life for Fern, raising three children largely on her own while her husband was out on the road most of the time.

Starting out in the Great Depression meant there were no guarantees of success. Money remained scarce, and merely surviving was an accomplishment. In 1936, Welk decided to move his base of operations to Omaha. The band's first big move into a larger venue than the one-night stands in small towns it had been accustomed to was an engagement at the St. Paul Hotel in 1937. The following year brought a breakthrough of another sort. At the William Penn Hotel in Pittsburgh, the band played its first extended run of national broadcasts over the Mutual Broadcasting Network.[19] It was in Steel City that the term "champagne music" first got attached to the Welk crew. When WCAE announcer Phil David informed the bandsman of all the letters coming in to the station using the words "sparkling," "light," "bubbly," and "effervescent" to describe the music they were hearing, Welk decided to adopt the nickname of "Champagne Music Makers." It sounded classier than other monikers that had been attached to them over the years—"America's Biggest Little Band," the "Hotsy Totsy Boys," and the "Honolulu Fruit Gum Orchestra." Now the band began to earn a reputation for itself nationally, converting it from a $150-a-night orchestra into a $2,500-a-week attraction.[20]

Into his late thirties, Welk remained so timid and self-conscious about his accent that he refused to say much on the bandstand, preferring to blend in with his fellow musicians and play his accordion. Now and then he got up the nerve to introduce a piece, but usually he hired someone else to do the announcing. An engagement at the elegant Edgewater Beach Hotel in Chicago in 1939 changed all that. The hotel manager insisted that Welk introduce his own numbers and chat with the audience between songs. While the prospect unnerved him and he flubbed a lot of his lines, he discovered that he was capable of doing it. The Chicago gig helped establish the band among the big-name groups touring the country and, perhaps more important, got Welk talking.[21]

Soon he engineered a deal with the Trianon Ballroom, giving him a permanent home in Chicago for a decade. The band sometimes went out on tour and also played dates at the Trianon's sister ballroom across town, the Aragon. Welk emerged as a fixture in the Windy City during the 1940s, providing greater stability for his growing family (two girls and a boy). Fern appreciated having her husband at home on a regular basis. In Chicago, Welk refined the techniques that would serve him well for the rest of his career. He grew more confident fronting the band, chatted amiably with his audiences, and went out of his way to be friendly, happily signing autographs for people when requested to do so. The band's female vocalist came to be called the Champagne Lady, after the bubbly, melodic, danceable music that became the group's identifying mark. Welk, who had experimented with different kinds of music and arrangements during the 1930s, now was convinced that most people wanted simple, danceable music like he had played touring the cities and small towns of the Midwest and the East. Remaining close to his audiences, he was certain that success would follow as long as he gave people what they desired to hear.[22]

Eventually, however, he grew dissatisfied in Chicago and reached out for new opportunities. Just as programs on WNAX had spread his name throughout the region around Yankton, broadcasts over WGN in Chicago had made him famous all around the Middle West. But his earnings were not increasing in conjunction with the band's reputation. Finally, an extended engagement at the St. Francis Hotel in San Francisco introduced the band to a West Coast audience, opening up an opportunity to settle permanently in Los Angeles in 1951. Building on that base, Welk's band developed first a regional television audience in Southern California and then a national one, emerging as the number-one big band in the country by the mid-1950s.

Never during all of this did Welk forget his rural roots. Friends and reporters marveled that as his fame and fortune increased, the North Dakotan remained his same humble self. A touch of naïveté clung to him. Friendly, open, talkative, and solicitous, he treated everyone alike, going out of his way to please people. The word that came quickly to mind on meeting Welk was "sincerity." Although some skeptics remained, even those who approached him warily and suspiciously were usually quick to grant the man's honesty and openness.

Female admirers mailed him cakes, cookies, and fudge and knitted socks for him. At concerts and dances and on his weekly television shows, they lined up eagerly to dance with him. It was they who sent him most of the 5,000 fan letters that arrived every week, keeping half a dozen secretaries busy answering them and tabulating their comments. Welk liked to say, "The mothers of America are my biggest fans."[23] In analyzing his audience, Welk began with the mothers, then noted their husbands, tacked on the older set, and admitted that teenagers and young adults were least likely to tune in. (His Saturday-night time slot went far to explain this, he believed; teenagers seldom stayed home on Saturday night.) Always catering to a family audience, Welk devoted considerable time and energy to the question of how to broaden his audience and extend his appeal to "the younger set." During the late 1950s and on into the 1960s, he evinced strong ambivalence about the rise of rock and roll. Welk always thumbed his nose at "progressive jazz," but he blew hot and cold on the new teen music, at times trying to tame and domesticate it in his repertoire, at other times criticizing it as vulgar, immoral, and unmusical. FBI boss J. Edgar Hoover and former ambassador Joseph P. Kennedy were confirmed Welk devotees, and men constituted a significant part of his fan profile, but Welk's strongest appeal was to middle-aged women, who, according to Arthur Sasso, perceived in him "a reincarnation of something deliciously reminiscent of their summer years."[24]

Social class also factored into the equation. Multimillionaire Joe Kennedy was an enthusiast, but Welk's audiences, as he himself noted, were more likely to eat steak and hamburger than caviar. George T. Kelly had taught him that common folks outnumbered ritzy ones. Geography played a role, too. Welk noted, "It's so wonderful to have lived in a small town." His largest and most enthusiastic following lived in rural America. "We're really just country people at heart," he said. "And we find the Midwest a good mirror of the country's taste in music and entertainment." Having grown up in the Midwest and spent most of his first quarter century as a performer there, wherever he played, he aimed his music at his fellow midwesterners. He told *Time* magazine in 1956, "There seem to be a lot of Midwesterners everywhere." One TV critic cracked, "Lawrence Welk has the only orchestra around that can give a Middle West flavor to a tango."[25]

To his fans, Welk's loyalty to his midwestern, small-town roots was admirable; to critics, it helped explain his mediocrity. "If ever there was a rube, Larry baby is it. He even starts the band with 'a one and a two' stuff that went out with the A&P gypsies," a *Television-Radio Age* writer guffawed in 1967. "They remind one of a talented amateur Rotary Club band in Indiana. They might win the state contest but they'll never make the big time."[26] What critics classified as "corn," "schmaltz," and "mediocrity," however, his multitude of admirers lapped up enthusiastically. They liked his melodies, their danceable beat, the cheery fresh-scrubbed singers and bandsmen, the enthusiasm, the positive feel-good atmosphere, and the wholesomeness of it all. When John Crosby called Welk's output "the squarest music this side of Euclid," irate readers rose up in defense of their hero. "You have the nerve to criticize one of the best TV entertainers," wrote one. "At a time when young people are becoming noticeably more delinquent, Welk offers the teenagers an opportunity to express their talent and wholesomeness." Another chided, "Your comments on Lawrence Welk are disgusting and without foundation in any way," adding, "There are thousands of us who think the show is the finest on the air."[27]

Age, gender, class, and geography provided revealing insights into Welk's audience appeal, but the most significant identifiers lay elsewhere—in people's hearts. Welk's fans were highly committed. They not only liked him; they loved him. They appreciated him for what he was and for what he represented. His personality won them over. "When he gets up in front of the mike, there's something of the shy, sincere farm boy in him still," a *Chicago Tribune* writer observed in 1957. "He stammers a little and he has that accent. That accent may be one of his greatest assets. It pegs him as an ordinary, average guy. Millions of people can identify themselves with him. They're happy to see a homespun Dakota man strike it rich. It gives them vicarious satisfaction."[28]

His "musical family," too, largely fit the profile of his audience. Performers desiring more freedom to sing or play their own songs or to "do their own thing" rather than fitting into the maestro's highly structured sense of what was appropriate and popular soon left the program. The rest were comfortable with and willing to follow Welk's four basic rules: be prepared, no drinking on the job, do not put on weight, and be on time.[29] Other requirements were implicit: deference to the boss, no profanity, cooperative demeanor, and "niceness."

What Welk stood for reinforced who he was. He represented stability in a rapidly changing world. He promoted familiar values when morality seemed to be disintegrating. He was a patriot while flag-burners garnered the publicity. He was devoutly religious in an increasingly secular world. More and more during the 1970s and 1980s, Welk preached a vision of simple core values, to which he attributed his success and which he thought could extricate America from its moral morass. He had begun doing this during the 1950s by publishing small booklets such as *Sweet Notes of Friendship* and writing articles for *Guideposts* magazine and other publications. Over time, his television shows became more overtly patriotic and reflective of conservative values, and he published several books, including *My America, Your America*, in which he eulogized values such as work, responsibility, self-control, independence, and freedom from government intrusion.

An editorial in the *Tuscaloosa (Ala.) Graphic* during the tense year of 1968 captured the spirit of Welk's admirers. Taking off on a statement by novelist John O'Hara that "the Lawrence Welk people" were the kind who kept the nation going, the editorial writer observed that they "liked the old and familiar tunes of the family-style orchestra." They were the "solid citizens." They did not make headlines, were not glamorous, did not appear in society columns. Instead, they were "the workers and the doers." They did not complain; they were too busy to take to the streets to protest and demonstrate. They went to church and sent their children to Sunday school. They flew flags on Veterans Day and on the Fourth of July. They worked at the YMCA and participated in Community Fund drives. When called on, they were always ready to do their part. "They may be squares and 'uncool,'" the editorialist concluded, "but democracy would go down the drain without them."[30]

These were the people with whom Welk identified and whom he saw as his audience. They were the kind of people he had grown up with in Strasburg, the ones he had played for at dances throughout the Midwest and who remained the core of his following into the 1980s. He liked to say he was "a farm boy in the music business," and he attributed his success to the values and habits ingrained in him as a child. His hometown remembered him by erecting a sign at the edge of the community identifying it as the "Birthplace of Lawrence Welk," by hanging his picture in the post office beside that of the president, and by naming its swimming pool and city park after him. North Dakota State University granted him an honorary doctorate in 1965, and two years later he became one of ten original inductees into the North Dakota Hall of Fame. Obviously, a mutual love affair existed between Welk and his hometown and his home state. His hardcore admirers, mostly the over-fifty crowd, continued to watch reruns of his shows on Public Television during the years after his death in 1992. Welk's life and career epitomized one kind of Middle West and small-town environment and mind-set. It was one that had dominated the country while he was growing up, and it retains a hold today on a substantial segment of midwesterners themselves as well as people outside the region.

Norfolk, Nebraska, is located 350 miles south and a little bit east of Strasburg, North Dakota. Both towns lie on the border where the Midwest meets the Great Plains. The social and cultural environments in which young John Carson grew up during the 1930s and early 1940s differed greatly from those of Lawrence Welk two decades earlier, but significant similarities marked the two communities, too. They were primarily agricultural market towns, geared to providing services for the farmers in the surrounding area. Both had first been settled by religious groups searching for a spot to raise their families as they saw fit and to pursue economic opportunity—mostly German Russian Catholics in Strasburg, predominantly German Lutherans in Norfolk. Both depended on the railroad to ship their grain and livestock to market and to connect them to the rest of the country. Both were heavily Republican politically and conservative culturally.

But Strasburg, like most of the scores of little farm communities in the region, never expanded its commercial reach beyond the farms in its immediate area. Its population of 273 in 1910 rose over time, peaking at 944 in 1940. Norfolk, in contrast, benefiting from three rail lines, managed to develop a sizable industrial base and rose to become the dominant commercial hub of northeastern Nebraska. When the family of Homer "Kit" Carson arrived there in 1933 from Avoca, Iowa, a town one-tenth the size, Norfolk's population was pushing 11,000, ranking it sixth in the state. Eight-year-old John was awed by the buzz of activity in the downtown business district. "I thought it was the biggest city I ever saw," he later recalled. "It was like moving from Omaha to New York. I remember staying at first in a hotel on Main Street, on the fourth floor, and looking out the window and thinking that was the biggest traffic jam I ever saw."[31]

More than size and the passage of time separated Norfolk in the 1930s from Strasburg two decades earlier. The bustling town in which John Carson grew up came under the heavy influence of the modernizing trends characterizing America in the 1920s. By then, most families living in town took electricity for granted, many had radios, high schoolers had access to parents' cars, and talking movies, which appeared by the end of the decade at Norfolk's Granada Theater, included plots and language that would have shocked the Welks. The town supported a minor-league baseball team (the Norfolk Elks of the Nebraska State League) and boasted a radio station (WJAG, one of the first in the country). It was the Dirty Thirties, to be sure, and the Great Depression registered its presence here as everywhere else, but Homer Carson was the district manager of the Iowa-Nebraska Electric Light and Power Company, and the family could afford to buy John a shiny new Schwinn bicycle in 1937 for $38.75, minus $10.00 for a trade-in. As a high schooler, he was permitted to drive the family's 1939 Chrysler Royal to take girls on dates.[32]

During the years Carson grew up in Norfolk, from age eight to eighteen, the United States weathered and survived the Great Depression, witnessed the emergence of swing and the big-band sound, saw color added to movies and streamlining to cars, underwent a protracted debate over whether to enter World War II, and had the question resolved by the bombing of Pearl Harbor on December 7, 1941. John (he began to call himself "Johnny" later, when he went to work in radio and TV) was a junior in high school and working as an usher at the Grenada Theatre that fateful afternoon. Showing that weekend was *Nothing but the Truth*, starring Bob Hope and Paulette Goddard. Learning of the Japanese attack during the showing of the film, John passed the news on to people as they filed out of the theater.[33]

One's teen years are times to experiment, dream, try on new identities, and attempt to overcome one's fears and insecurities. Growing up in a comfortable, middle-class household on the right side of the tracks, Carson was spared the worries and financial insecurities many young people had to endure.[34] Along with ushering at the Grenada (an especially prized job in the summertime, being about the only air-conditioned place in town), his work in a variety of different jobs—delivering furniture, driving trucks, and jerking sodas—taught him responsibility and the value of a dollar. There was also plenty of time for fun and play. Sandwiched in between an older sister, Catherine, and a younger brother, Dick, he displayed many of the fun-loving, adventuresome qualities of a middle child. He liked to bicycle and hike out into the country and especially enjoyed hanging out with his buddies at Black Bridge, along the railroad tracks a couple of miles west of town, where they liked to loaf, fish, and skinny-dip.

Never very industrious as a student (he graduated 54th in a class of 141 from Norfolk High School in 1943), he did well enough in his classes when he applied himself. But Carson always seemed more interested in having fun and playing pranks. Although somewhat shy, he did not lack for friends. He was too small to play football. His one tryout for the high school team ended quickly when his 140-pound frame collided with a pair of 240-pound linemen. Norfolk was a football powerhouse at the time, racking up an eight-and-two record his senior year. He also failed to make the cheerleading squad, so he gravitated toward dramatics and journalism, joining the Thespians, acting and being part of the crew for several plays, and writing for the student newspaper and yearbook. When he was a senior, several pages of the *Milestone* yearbook were devoted to a humorous spoof he wrote about the month-by-month happenings of the previous year. Sample:

FEBRUARY—Month of Washington's birthday. If Washington (who never told a lie) could hear some of the excuses the kids hand Mr. Gerdes every morning, he would turn over in his grave and get up and run for a third term—and probably say, "What, Roosevelt still in?"

Everyone was getting his date for the Junior-Senior banquet. For the benefit of the sophomores, I will explain in detail how to get a date. The first thing to do is to call up the best looking girl in school and ask her. After that, call up someone who will go with you! I was turned down so many times, I felt like a bed spread!

Not to mention the Valentine verse I received from my draft board which went like this: Upon this February morn the draft board wishes to inform, we love you much, and all that stew, but never mind, we'll wait for you![35]

Not being an athlete or a student government leader, Carson established himself as a wit and a prankster. When someone concocted an odiferous brew in the chemistry lab and dispersed it through the ventilation system, causing classes to be dismissed for a day, suspicion flowed in his direction. Once, unbeknownst to the principal, he commandeered the school's public-address system to announce an assembly, where he proceeded to entertain his fellow students with magic tricks. In his schemes and merry pranks, John proved bold and ingenious. A teacher recalled that he was not so much rowdy as full of life.[36] Much of his youthful energy went into worthwhile causes. Students took the initiative in the wartime scrap drives, incentive swelled by competition between the junior and senior classes over who could accumulate the largest tonnage. Carson and his crew outdid everyone else, collecting every item of surplus metal and rubber available (and, it is safe to say, some things not actually intended for the scrap heap). Their major accomplishment was borrowing a storekeeper's old truck to transport their junk. Afterward, the vehicle mysteriously disappeared, leading many to suspect that the boys had dismantled it to add to their pile of junk.[37]

The boy's driving impulse from the age of twelve onward was magic and comedy. One of his friends obtained a deck of marked cards from a magician's supply house in Chicago. John ordered a magic kit and a copy of *Hoffmann's Book of Magic* from the company's catalog and quickly became hooked. Magic became his passion; he spent endless hours practicing card tricks and sleight of hand. His father bought a movie camera, and in the films for the next six Christmases in a row, there was John in the background shuffling his deck of cards. His constant invitation to people to "pick a card, *any* card" became a family joke. His mother vividly remembered sitting in the bathroom one day and having him barge in, asking her to pick a card.[38]

Magic became his identity, setting him apart from the other boys. His first professional experience occurred at the age of fourteen in front of the local Rotary Club, earning him three dollars. He billed himself as "The Great Carsoni." His mother sewed a green cape for him with the name on it and a black shirt with a white rabbit on the back that he wore for performances. His schoolmates got to see him do his tricks at assemblies; he put on his act for local clubs, in church basements, and friends' houses; and he even went along to other communities with representatives from the local Chamber of Commerce to be a booster for Norfolk and its businesses. Through magic, Carson overcame his hesitancy in front of crowds, and obtaining laughs and calling attention to himself gave him a great feeling. Magic blended perfectly with his natural tendency to see the humorous and the absurd in everything. He accompanied his acts with a constant patter. "I've been kidding the pants off people, places, and things since I was twelve," he told an interviewer in 1965. "Once I discovered an audience I was absolutely hooked. That applause is the sweetest thing this side of anywhere."[39]

Carson's passion for magic and Lawrence Welk's love for the accordion emerged in the boys at about the same age. Both ultimately transformed their passion for performing into hugely successful careers. Carson's path to entertainment superstardom, while in some ways more difficult and personally consuming, was faster and more direct than Welk's. It led him to Los Angeles not once but twice, by way of New York. Carson managed to bypass all the small towns—and larger cities—that Welk became well-acquainted with during the 1920s and 1930s. Like his North Dakota counterpart, he started out in radio, but he spent most of his career in television, and indeed he was the ultimate creature of the new medium. The pressures of performing in front of the camera day after day exacted a heavy toll. They contributed to his drinking problem and led him to neglect his family. He went through three divorces and had difficulties with his three boys from his first marriage.

Welk expended enormous energy on his music and left the raising of their three children largely to his wife while he was out on the road with his band, but he nevertheless managed to successfully combine a career with family life. Most of the credit belongs to Fern, who discarded her own career ambitions to devote herself to the children. Carson, in effect, married his career, which became the dominant thing in his life in a way that Welk's never was. After graduating from Norfolk High School in 1943 and serving a three-year stint in the navy during World War II, Carson enrolled in the University of Nebraska under the GI Bill, graduating with a bachelor's degree in radio and speech in the spring of 1949. An indifferent student, as always, he concentrated on the things that interested him most, which were performing and working for radio station KFAB in Lincoln, where he helped write scripts for a western comedy program called *Eddie Sosby and the Radio Rangers*. He had two goals now: to obtain a radio show of his own and to succeed as a magician. He put together a tape, *How to Write Comedy Jokes*, consisting of examples of comedians' jokes along with his own commentary on how they were made to work. It became his undergraduate thesis. He finished his studies in three years and then took a job at Nebraska's number-one radio station, Omaha's WOW, which was just on the verge of going into television. It was a propitious moment. Simultaneously, his future sidekick, Ed McMahon, was getting started in Philadelphia with his first program, soon earning the title of "Mr. Television" in that city.[40]

Getting in on the ground floor of television proved to be both a liability and an advantage. Although few precedents were available to lean on and most things needed to be created from scratch, audience expectations were low in the beginning, great leeway for experimentation existed, and creativity and boldness found their reward. Quick advancement was possible for the able. Like Welk, Carson harbored high ambitions and was not satisfied to remain a big personality in Omaha, even if it was Nebraska's premier city. Starting broadcasting in August 1949, WOW was the first television station in the surrounding five-state region. Carson, only twenty-three years old and fresh out of college, was already hosting his own morning radio program, *The Johnny Carson Show*. He quickly persuaded management to let him try a fifteen-minute television program called *The Squirrel's Nest*. On it, he told jokes, conducted humorous interviews, and aired just about anything he thought might attract viewers. He began fashioning an on-camera personality as a casual, spontaneous, witty, charming, and unconventional character with a devil-may-care attitude.[41]

Meanwhile, his new wife, Jody, who in college had been his assistant in his magic performances, started having babies. Johnny (which is what people began calling him now), however, made his job his top priority, and during the coming decade, as his career began to blossom, things at home gradually deteriorated. The marriage culminated in divorce in 1962. The pattern repeated itself during the next two decades, as he married and divorced twice again. (Graphing the ages of his wives results in a rather smooth curve: wife number one was two years younger than he; number two, seven; number three, sixteen; and number four, twenty-five.) Carson later accepted blame for his first three failures at marriage, observing, "If I had given as much to marriage as I gave to the *Tonight* show, I'd probably have a hell of a marriage. But the fact is I haven't given that, and there you have the simple reason for the failure of my marriages. I put the energy into the show."[42]

In 1951, Carson put together a half-hour audition film and spent his two-week vacation in California, trying to interest television stations in San Francisco and Los Angeles in hiring him. Rebuffed almost everywhere, he was totally disheartened by the experience. But in Los Angeles at KNXT-TV, a CBS affiliate, he chanced to run into Bill Brennan, a boyhood chum from Avoca, who went to bat for him at the station. Several months later, Brennan called to offer Carson an announcer's job, which would actually be a step down for him. But it would give him a chance to get into a bigger market, and there would undoubtedly be opportunities to move up the ladder, so Johnny took it.[43] Not far away, Lawrence Welk was beginning his rise to television stardom with ABC.

Many things converged in California during the early 1950s: the coaxial cable was linking the country from coast to coast, opening the way for simultaneous national broadcasts; the three networks were beginning to perceive Los Angeles as a rival to New York as a production site; and the nation was in the midst of a huge demographic shift that would soon make California the most populous state in the Union and bring into prominence terms such as "Sunbelt" and "Southern Rim." Huge numbers of Kansans, Nebraskans, and Dakotans had followed the Okie trek west to California of the 1930s, and the midwestern influence remained strong there during the 1950s and later.

Carson's climb to stardom was neither smooth nor without setbacks, but compared to others, it was one of the more meteoric success stories in the entertainment industry. Hosting several local shows in the Los Angeles area built up his confidence and honed his on-air skills. His big break occurred in August 1954, when Red Skelton, for whom he was working as a writer, injured himself during preshow rehearsals. In desperation, the producers called Johnny two hours before the live telecast went on the air, asking him to fill in. His coolheaded impromptu performance, including a hilarious comedy routine, impressed both viewers and CBS execs, who started keeping a close eye on the young comedian. The failure of a new *Johnny Carson Show*, which debuted in June 1955 (at the same time that *The Lawrence Welk Show* was beginning its national run) and folded after thirty-nine weeks, proved not to be a fatal blow. The program taught him an important lesson: not to let the "experts" and network spokesmen dictate what he did. Seven different directors and eight writers arrived and departed before the show mercifully expired.[44]

Carson's first success on national television came as host of *Who Do You Trust?* between 1957 and 1962. Doing it required moving to New York, which became home for him for a decade and a half. The game part of the show was far less important than the humor of the host's jokes, ad-libs, and general zaniness. As quick and inventive as Carson was, however, he could not possibly generate enough fresh material to keep his audiences laughing five days a week, month after month, without help. While quick with repartee and ad-libs, he relied heavily on material generated by a staff of writers. He possessed an unusual ability to take their words and ideas and make them his own, leading audiences to think that everything was springing spontaneously out of his own fertile imagination.[45]

Who Do You Trust? established Carson as one of the brightest, most talented young comedians in the business and served as wonderful training for his later hosting of *The Tonight Show.* It also linked him up with Ed McMahon, whose career had taken off in Philadelphia during the 1950s and who would stay on as Carson's announcer and sidekick to the end. Although born only two years earlier, McMahon looked and acted much older than Carson, whose puckish brand of humor was reminiscent of his school days back in Nebraska. The bond between them, although suffering through some rocky patches over the years, proved a lasting one. McMahon, having once resolved to play second fiddle as a straight man, tied his career to Carson's, making himself rich and famous in the process. *Who Do You Trust?* also gave Carson a producer, Art Stark, with whom he was comfortable and in whom he put complete confidence. Like McMahon, Stark later followed Carson over to *The Tonight Show.*[46]

By 1962, when Jack Paar abruptly announced he was leaving *The Tonight Show,* Carson's name figured prominently on a short list of potential replacements. His quick wit, audience rapport, and cool command of every situation were all impressive. On the other hand, he was only thirty-seven and relatively untried with a national audience. NBC approached and was turned down by several other stars, such as Bob Newhart, Jackie Gleason, Joey Bishop, and Groucho Marx, before offering the slot to the Nebraskan. His first impulse was to turn it down. Although he had guest-hosted the program for a total of three weeks, Carson doubted his ability, night after night, to step into the shoes of Paar, who had developed an ardent following and had made the talk show the largest grosser on the network. However, after considering the unique opportunity the job afforded him to do the kind of "nutty, experimental, low-key thing" he liked to do and hearing out the arguments of his manager, Al Bruno, who had lobbied hard with NBC to get him the job, he took it. Since his contract with ABC had another six months to run, guest hosts filled in during the interim, making it easier for him when he took over in October.[47]

The story of Johnny Carson's thirty-year reign as host of *The Tonight Show* constitutes one of show business's all-time success stories. He quickly recast the program in his own image, veering sharply away from Paar's highly charged, excitable style in favor of a more whimsical, ironic approach. Where Paar had been hot, Carson was cool. Where he had been involved, Carson remained detached. Paar had frequently talked about and even brought his family and their activities into his monologues and patter, no doubt sometimes to the embarrassment of his teenage daughter, Randy. Carson virtually never discussed his family on air or let his own personal problems or activities intrude, except when he was making jokes about one of his ex-wives or reminiscing about some of his alleged youthful adventures in Norfolk. Critics quickly noted the contrast.[48]

Carson also made it clear that he would not imitate his predecessor in conducting in-depth discussions of social or economic issues. He had no desire to compete with Paar or Mike Wallace in attacking America's social problems, solving its political quandaries, or tripping people up. Time only further convinced him that his only goal on the show was to entertain his audience. He left it to others to inform, educate, uplift, and improve them. When people complained that his performances were intellectually vacuous and challenged him and his producer to name guests who were not show business figures or who had contributed something to society, they trotted out a stock list of prominent individuals who had appeared at one time or other on the program to discuss issues of substance. In his famous *New Yorker* profile of Carson, Kenneth Tynan heard the same names—Paul Ehrlich, Carl Sagan, Gore Vidal, Shana Alexander, and Margaret Mead—mentioned so often that he soon found it amusing.[49]

Carson described his goal quite simply: "It's comedy oriented. It's entertainment."[50] He fully understood that maintaining the show's appeal over a long period of time required scaling down audience expectations. His low-key approach coincided with Marshall McLuhan's theory that television was a "cool medium" and was right in line with the early 1960s—an era that also put on stage such real and fictional embodiments of cool as John F. Kennedy and Ian Fleming's Agent 007, James Bond. Carson, as an interviewer, understood the importance of not outshining his guests. While relegating Ed McMahon, bandleaders Skitch Henderson and later Doc Severinsen, and other performers on the program to straight-man status, *The Tonight Show* host himself resolutely acted out his own role as straight man for his guests. When they looked good, he looked good, so he did everything he possibly could to make them shine. Conversely, he seldom did anything to challenge or embarrass the people he brought onto the show. The downside was that they were expected to perform, and they had better do a good job of it or they would not be invited back for another visit.

Accolades for Carson were quick in coming. Ratings started out high (Paar had bequeathed to him the top-ranked late-night program) and remained strong, year after year. When competitors rose to challenge him, he steamrolled them, outlasting them all. A list of talk-show hosts who came and went during his long tenure includes Merv Griffin, Joey Bishop, Dick Cavett, David Frost, David Brenner, and Joan Rivers. NBC, well aware of and appreciative of the revenues flowing into their coffers from the program (at its height, *Tonight* brought in 17 percent of network revenues), rewarded him handsomely, tearing up his contract several times before it expired to increase his pay and perks. Starting out at $100,000 a year in 1962, Carson's salary reportedly rose to $700,000 by 1967, $2.5 million in 1979, and $25 million by 1990. Somebody calculated that by then he was making $2,380 every minute he was on the air. Meanwhile, the program shrank in length from an hour and forty-five minutes in 1962 to one and a half hours in 1967 and one hour in 1980. Meanwhile, Carson's vacation period was extended to fifteen weeks, while his work weeks were reduced to three days (guest hosts or reruns filled in the other days).

In the process, Carson's influence in the industry soared, first in New York and later in California, after the show moved there in 1972. A *Newsweek* cover story asserted that he had accumulated "as much personal power as any other television performer in history." In 1981, *People* magazine called him "perhaps the most powerful man in U.S. entertainment." Eight years later, in a special issue on the top twenty-five stars in the entertainment industry, *People* installed Carson at the head of the list, delivering this encomium: "He is Mr. Television. Titan of talk, minister of celebrity, night watchman of the global village, comedian laureate of a nation that loves to laugh itself to sleep."[51]

Carson's unique audience appeal caused many to speculate about its sources. Had a simple answer been available, competing networks might have looked for someone like him to go head-to-head with the *Tonight Show* host. But Carson's magic was not easily fathomed or duplicated. When asked to explain his style of humor, Carson feigned ignorance. "I can't tell you," he told one magazine writer. "I really can't. I guess I do it by instinct and by editing. I suppose there is a certain irreverence to my humor. But when somebody asks 'How do you work?' or 'How do you describe yourself?', I find it impossible to do a self-analysis on it. Most comedians do what they do without trying to think it out. Analysis gets in the way."[52] That may have been disingenuous coming from one whose college thesis analyzed in detail a variety of comedic types. A superb mimic, swift ad-libber, and physically dexterous, he certainly understood what he was doing in front of the camera and willingly acknowledged his debt to others regarding many of his techniques—Jack Benny, Fred Allen, Oliver Hardy, and Bob Hope among them.[53] Carson had grown up in the heyday of radio. He had spent hours sprawled on the living-room rug in Norfolk listening to programs. Jack Benny especially impressed him. "I think you steal a little from everybody—particularly when you are starting," he admitted. "You pick it up here and there, and ultimately you have your own style, and people start stealing from you."[54]

Carson's signatures were the quick double take, the forlorn stare into the camera with eyebrows slyly raised, the breakup into laughter at a particularly funny story, the nervous touching of his forehead or nose, the tapping of his pencil, and other gestures that made him a staple for impersonators doing their own comedy routines. "I'm a reaction performer," was his description of what he did. "I react off a situation."[55] His introductory monologues largely revolved around comments on the news of the day. The show possessed an unpredictable quality about it; spontaneity seemed to reign. Yet while Carson and McMahon sometimes took off on flights of whimsy and improvisation, the show was tightly scripted and under the complete control of Carson and his producer, who communicated with each other through eye contact and hand signals.

Carson's innocent, boyish appearance allowed him to make irreverent and sex-laden comments without seeming to be threatening or offensive. Carrying on in the direction he had established as host of *Who Do You Trust?*, he became known for frequent double entendres and challenges to the network censors with risqué language and jokes. But he denied that he was raunchy and was defensive about his double meanings, blaming criticisms directed at him on the narrow-mindedness of his accusers. "If you can't say a few sophisticated things at twelve o'clock at night without being called dirty, we're in trouble," he protested.[56] His antennae were sensitive to what audiences would or would not tolerate. "Along with freedom comes a certain responsibility," he observed. "You've got to self-edit yourself as newspapers do."[57] In 1975, when NBC started broadcasting *Saturday Night Live,* with its young cast and satirical style, Carson thought the show went over the line, offending his sense of decency. He drew that line at different places, depending on the circumstances, setting it at one point for *Tonight,* extending it a little further when he played arenas from Waco to Seattle, and pushing it a little beyond that in his Las Vegas nightclub acts. Always, however, he recognized that a line needed to be drawn somewhere. In that respect, he and Lawrence Welk were in complete agreement, although they drew the lines in different places.

Carson carried on with the *Tonight Show* formula that had been established by his predecessors, Steve Allen and Jack Paar, elaborating on it and refining it over the years but never scrapping it. The two primary elements—the opening monologue and several interviews—provided the model for every other nighttime talk show that arose to compete with it. Carson's greatest strength as an interviewer was the close attention and deference he paid to his interviewees. "The principal thing is he listens," observed McMahon. "That's the secret of the show."[58] Although Carson sometimes demonstrated impatience with boring or nonperforming guests by stifling a yawn or staring, glassy-eyed, at the camera and could emit strings of expletives off camera about ones who annoyed him, his attitude on the air was almost always one of easy camaraderie and genuine interest in what was being said. Getting booked on *The Tonight Show* was never about money; it was about exposure. It is also well to remember that guests were not brought on the set to improve, enlighten, or educate the audience; their only goal was to perform and to entertain. That is why the great preponderance of them were singers, actors, comedians, and other showbiz personalities, punctuated occasionally by athletes, people with unusual skills—such as bird-calling or snake-charming—individuals in the news, and even some serious thinkers.

Carson seldom talked to his guests before they came on camera. "If they talked to me beforehand," he explained, "they might leave their fight in the gymnasium."[59] Nor did he hang around after the lights dimmed to talk to guests or to people in the audience. It could be an eerie experience for a guest to arrive, do an eight-minute interview, and be gone without ever really getting a chance to meet the star. The talk-show host who appeared so warm and welcoming on camera developed a reputation for being cold and aloof off the air. Essentially a shy and private person, he told his sidekick McMahon, "I'm good with ten million, lousy with ten."[60]

Carson's pride and joy, and what he considered his main legacy as a performer, was the monologue, which usually ran six to ten minutes at the beginning of the program. It was what he missed most when he retired.[61] Most of the jokes were written by a stable of writers, many of whom arrived and departed in short order. They were well paid, but job insecurity and constant pressure to produce were the price exacted. Carson picked and chose from the individual scripts that were submitted to him every afternoon, modified and rearranged the material, sometimes added creations of his own, and stamped the whole with his own personal signature. He was often at his best when his material was worst. One of his most frequently mentioned skills was an uncanny ability to recover from failed jokes. He had so many prepared comebacks for jokes that died that sometimes it must have seemed as if he actually preferred telling bad ones so he could deliver a new one.

In his takeoffs on the news of the day and barbs at politicians and other figures, Carson seldom revealed his own political viewpoint. He realized that the platform NBC provided him, though it could be used for partisan or parochial purposes, depended in the long run on his ability to hew to a safe middle course, eschewing political controversies and divisions. Privately, he adhered to a mildly liberal stance on political issues, but he realized that he had everything to lose by expressing his opinions in public, telling Barbara Walters, when she put him on the interviewee's couch, "I'm not dumb enough to express political opinions on the air."[62] Both the Right and the Left, Republicans and Democrats, became targets of his zingers. When Carson started telling denigrating jokes about someone or something, people said, it was a signal that the target had become fair game. Although a variety of explanations existed for Richard Nixon's resignation in 1974, one prominent view held that when Carson started telling Watergate jokes, the end was predictable. In spite of his aversion to partisan appeals, or perhaps because of it, Carson became a fairly accurate barometer of the public mood during his tenure on *The Tonight Show*. The *New York Times* once referred to him as the "comic consciousness" of the United States. A writer for *TV Guide* speculated, "I believe he reflects the great American majority, its values, its myths. He is the American Dream personified: the typical middle-aged boy next door, who has come out of Nebraska (he frequently reminds us of this) and become a self-made millionaire."[63] Utilizing the same format, the same setting, and similar program content for several decades, Carson provided his viewers with a comfortable sense of stability. Meanwhile, he evinced an uncanny ability to keep pace with the enormous social changes that occurred between the early 1960s and the early 1990s. That quality set him apart from people, like Lawrence Welk, who clung tenaciously to the values and ways of living they had grown up with decades earlier.

It rankled Carson to be compared unfavorably to his friend Dick Cavett, who established a reputation for himself as an intellectual talk-show host. The person on the street, when questioned, might say that TV was full of pap and that the networks should provide more news, information, and culture, Carson noted. "But he *watches* the pap. Sure, there's a lot of garbage on TV, but most people's tastes are fairly plebian. Put 'Gilligan's Island' on next to the Bolshoi Ballet and who do you think is going to get the ratings? Bolshoi? No way. No *way*."[64] Like Welk, Carson responded to his audiences. He discovered what people wanted and gave it to them. Both of them possessed an intuitive understanding of what the public preferred, but neither was willing to rely on instinct alone. Nielsen ratings guided Carson and the television moguls, and every night he could infer from audience reaction what was working and what was not. Similar to Welk, Carson went on tour periodically with his comedy routine, providing him another perspective on people's thinking. Other talk-show hosts had the same methods at their disposal but never succeeded in dethroning the "King of the Night."

Underlying it all—the monologue, the interviews, the comedy skits—the foundation supporting *Tonight* and making it work was the shimmering personality of Johnny Carson. It is possible to describe his actions and to characterize him with a string of adjectives. Ultimately, however, his magic remained elusive. Like Lawrence Welk, he projected intimacy and established close empathy with his audience. One of his predecessors on the show, Steve Allen, observed that Carson "just doesn't look like show biz. He's got that just-folks, Kansas City–Oklahoma City look about him."[65] With McMahon like a steady older brother at his side and with bandleader Severinsen in his outrageous outfits kidding around with him and the audience, Carson established something of a family feeling on the show—a place where people could return night after night and expect to be comfortable while at the same time anticipating a few surprises. Although he increasingly turned into one as time went by, the witty, affable host did not come on as a big star. "Low-key" was his middle name.

Carson frequently made reference to his midwestern antecedents and to his growing-up years in Nebraska. "A guy from the Midwest—that's who I was, that's who I am," he was quoted as saying in a 1988 story in *Cosmopolitan* magazine describing the childhoods of various media personalities. He believed that while growing up he had derived a great deal from the closeness, the sense of security, and the feeling of comfort that came from what he described as "a typical small-town Midwestern boyhood in Norfolk."[66] Nielsen ratings revealed that *The Tonight Show* dominated in the region west of Illinois all the way to the Rocky Mountains.[67] "If the heartland had a body and a voice, they'd have no choice but to name it Johnny Carson," *Newsweek* magazine observed at the time of his retirement.[68]

But Carson's relationship with his origins, as with his audience, remained ambiguous. He returned home to Norfolk to visit a number of times. In 1964, he went back over Labor Day weekend with Chris, his oldest son, to search for a can of keepsakes and treasures he had buried by the side of the family's garage when he was a kid. In 1976, he accepted an invitation to be the commencement speaker at the Norfolk High School graduation ceremony. Later, he returned to dedicate a wing of the local hospital as the Carson Regional Radiation Center, named in honor of his parents, and he donated $650,000 for its construction. In later years, he contributed more than $12 million to a wide variety of organizations and charities in Norfolk and elsewhere in Nebraska and Iowa.[69]

Carson obviously continued to feel the pull of his hometown and home state and harbored considerable nostalgia for them. Shortly before marrying his fourth wife, Alex Maas, in 1987, he also made an unannounced and apparently spur-of-the-moment visit to Avoca, where he had lived from the ages of five through eight.[70] When his boyhood friend Bill Brennan, who had helped him land his first job in Los Angeles in 1951, died in 1992, Carson contributed $3,000 as a memorial in his honor to the Avoca Public Library. As he grew older, his thoughts frequently turned back to the towns he had grown up in. Earlier, he had often tried to brush off inquiries about them. "Do we have to?" was his response when Nora Ephron, who was writing a book about him, raised such a question. "It's another era." Going back to Nebraska, he told her, was a depressing experience for him.[71] But back in Norfolk to dedicate the radiation center in 1988, Carson said that he was honored to have hailed from the Midwest. "People out here are decent, good people," he noted. "I hope I will always have a place to come back here and say hello as often as I can."[72] Did that mean that Norfolk was merely a nice place to visit and reminisce about but not a place where he would want to live?

Nebraska may still have been a good place to visit, and Carson retained friends there, corresponding from time to time with former teachers, classmates, and neighbors, but who could believe that the biggest figure in American show business really had much in common with his old friends? A most interesting episode was the making of a ninety-minute television documentary titled *Johnny Goes Home,* which ran on NBC in 1982. This was something Carson had wanted to do for a long time, and he wrote most of the script himself. The program contained some wonderful scenes: dust trailing his dad's 1939 Chrysler as Johnny drove along country roads outside Norfolk, a tour of the family's home on Thirteenth Street, a high school football game, a bicycle ride, a scene in a barber shop, people smiling and laughing on Main Street, and a reunion of Carson's 1943 graduating class.[73] All stirred up memories of previous times and an older way of life. Carson remained visibly wistful about it, even as he lived in Malibu in his $8 million mansion with private tennis court. Carson said that in making the film he wanted to recapture the "innocent era" of his childhood. "You felt like you were part of the town or community," he commented during a break in the filming. "It was comfortable, secure. You knew most of the people in town or they knew you." He told one reporter, "Everyone, once in a while, gets homesick," adding, "I've never been a big-city person."[74] It was an interesting remark coming from someone who had spent his previous forty years in Omaha, New York, and Los Angeles.

The program impressed several reviewers. Columnist Kay Gardella of the *New York Daily News* noted that she rarely gushed over television programs, "but I loved every minute of this one." She observed that in putting the program together, Carson was treading delicate ground where even the slightest hint of exploitation would spoil the effect. "But he has such good taste, and obviously has been raised with the right sense of values, that he never tips the scale." Carson's friends and former classmates enjoyed the program, too. Chuck Howser thought that it was "well done" and that "John was very sincere in his efforts."[75] Back in Los Angeles, Carson got together with fellow Nebraskan Dick Cavett to talk about his recent experience in his home state. "He'd been very moved by the trip and he wanted to talk to someone about it," Cavett related. "We ended up chatting about everything from adolescent sexual experiences to our old high-school teachers." Cavett wished people who considered Carson cold and uncommunicative could have seen him at that moment.[76]

Carson's pilgrimage to Norfolk in 1981 obviously moved him, provoking tears more than once. What else it meant to him is hard to say. It did, after all, revolve around a TV special, which was the whole occasion for the film and the class reunion (Carson's class normally would not have re-assembled for another two years). He flew in six of his former classmates for one of the scenes (chosen because they had been captured on film by his father shortly before they went into the navy), and it cost $25,000 to rent a train for a scene by Black Bridge west of town, where Johnny hung on to the girders as train cars passed overhead, the way they had done it when he was a teenager. A clue to Carson's thoughts lay in his obvious satisfaction with the positive reception hometowners gave him. When the crowd at the Norfolk-Columbus football game joined in singing "Happy Birthday" to him at halftime, he cracked, "You're blowing my image here. I'm cruel and aloof, don't you know that?"[77]

His reputation for remoteness clearly bothered him, and he endeavored to correct it from time to time, but not to the degree of changing his behavior very much. The paradox of Johnny Carson lay in the distance that separated his public persona from his private behavior. Genial, relaxed, and outgoing on TV, he was reputedly distant, isolated, and even hostile in private. Joan Rivers, who had reason to be biased after Carson completely cut her off because he did not like the way she had quit as his permanent guest host and tried to start her own talk show, insisted that television lies. "Don't give me this nonsense that television tells the truth. Excuse me. Look at Johnny. He's totally isolated but he has great charm, boyishness, on the air."[78] Unlike Welk, Carson studiously avoided strangers and auto-graph seekers, seldom went out to eat or to take in concerts, attended parties infrequently, and in general built up a wall of protection around himself. The suspicion grew that he had no real friends, although he played tennis regularly with buddies such as Steve Lawrence and George Segal.

Several explanations for his remote behavior vied for acceptance, each one containing part of the truth. Like many comedians, people said, Carson was actually very shy and compensated for it by developing a public persona considerably at odds with his private behavior. Carson's aloofness was largely self-protective. Especially after taking over *Tonight,* he was hounded mercilessly for autographs by total strangers and sometimes pursued by stalkers, requiring him to isolate himself to remain safe and retain some measure of privacy. Some observers suggested that Carson's parents and their strict Methodist rules had permanently harmed their son, that his mother, especially, had been cold and domineering, damaging his psyche and making it difficult for him to relate meaningfully to women. His brother Dick once said about the family, "Put it this way—we're not Italian. Nobody in our family ever says what they really think or feel to anyone else."[79] McMahon, who got rich playing second fiddle to him, once explained, "Johnny is not overly outgoing or affectionate. He doesn't give friendship easily or need it. He packs a tight suitcase."[80] Especially during the late 1950s, Carson's heavy drinking adversely affected his behavior, something he willingly admitted and regretted.

Another explanation is possible. Carson himself preferred to believe that people were simply misjudging him and failed to understand him. Being tagged as a "loner" and a "cold fish" constantly annoyed him. Realizing that he was withdrawn and self-conscious in group settings, he tried to avoid them. Going to parties was usually frustrating, because people fawned all over him, repeated stale jokes, and acted weird. There was nothing very complicated about him, he believed, nothing requiring deep analysis. To a *Life* magazine reporter working on a cover story headlined "Johnny Carson: The Lonesome Hero of Middle America," he fretted, "The word that's always applied to me is aloof, or private, or any combination of those two. That's me. I didn't invent it." He said that he had been that way in high school, and he was not likely to change. "You can't run your life to please everybody; it just doesn't work. But I don't play a ruse, an attitude. I am what I am."[81]

The seemingly uncomplicated, glint-eyed Nebraska boy turned out to be not so simple after all. Carson's reputation, influence, and significance emanated from his public persona, not his private life. He was the ultimate product of television. The shadow world of the medium was his natural habitat. Within the parameters of the *Tonight Show* stage and images of it borne over the air to millions of late-night viewers, he helped establish the tone of the culture. When the tube turned dark, he reverted to being just an ordinary citizen, and by most accounts, not one to attract special notice. The man who retained considerable affection and nostalgia for his Nebraska small-town roots had grown about as far away from them as it was possible to get.

CHAPTER FIFTEEN

John Wooden: Small-Town Values on the Hardwood Court

I was a farm boy at heart, and our whole family had loved small-town life in Indiana.

—John Wooden

The first thing attracting our notice and compelling us to pay attention to John Wooden is the amazing statistics he compiled over his career as a basketball player and as a coach. Playing guard on the Martinsville, Indiana, high school team, Wooden earned all-state honors during his sophomore, junior, and senior seasons, leading his teammates to the state championship game all three years. At Purdue University, he only got better, being chosen as a consensus all-American[1] all three years he played, leading the Boilermakers to two Big Ten Conference titles and one national championship, and being selected as the national player of the year in his final season. The award he was proudest of, however, was the Big Ten medal he received as a senior for scholarship and athletic prowess, as he compiled the highest grades of any player in the conference.

In forty years as a high school and college coach, he experienced only

367

one losing season—his first, at Dayton (Kentucky) High School. During two years there and nine at South Bend (Indiana) Central High School, he accumulated 218 wins against 42 losses. His two-year record at Indiana State Teachers College was 47–14, and over the course of twenty-seven years at UCLA he was 620–147. His ten national titles in twelve years at UCLA earned him the Naismith Award as the college basketball coach of the century and made him arguably the best coach ever in any intercollegiate sport. His 335–22 record over the course of those last twelve years included a record 88-game regular-season victory streak, a 38-game National Collegiate Athletic Association (NCAA) postseason tournament victory streak, and a mark of 149 wins against only 2 losses at home in Pauley Pavilion after it opened in 1965. Only two other coaches, Kentucky's Adolph Rupp and Duke's Mike Krzyzewski, won as many as four NCAA championships. Wooden was NCAA basketball coach of the year seven times, *Sports Illustrated*'s Sportsman of the Year in 1972, and one of America's forty outstanding sports figures after midcentury in the estimate of that magazine on its fortieth anniversary in 1993.[2]

Proud as he was of these accomplishments, Wooden obtained even greater pleasure from being named, in 1969 by the Disciples of Christ (the denomination he belonged to), the outstanding basketball coach in the United States for services rendered to the sport and to humankind, and from having a statue of him erected and a street named after him in his hometown of Martinsville.[3] Wooden returned to his hometown a number of times to receive awards or just to visit, and he retained a strong affection for it. Interestingly, the man who may well have been the winningest coach of all time never emphasized the importance of winning to his players and thought of himself not primarily as a coach, but as a teacher.[4]

High school coaches—and many college coaches—during the 1930s also taught regular subjects in the classroom. Wooden's high school contracts and his first college coaching job at Indiana State required him to teach English, a subject he truly enjoyed. His yen for poetry stimulated him not only to memorize large chunks of it but also to try his hand at writing it. With a master's degree in the subject, some work completed toward a PhD degree, and a principal's certificate to go along with it, Wooden might have made a career of teaching high school English and coaching basketball on the side had not World War II come along to upset the status quo and create new alternatives and opportunities.[5]

It was in connection with his role as a teacher that the fledgling coach developed his famous Pyramid of Success, which played such a central role later in his coaching and in the philosophy that he developed for living in general. Disturbed that his high school students and their parents became upset when the students failed to receive As or Bs on their work, he cast about for a way of explaining to them that success as a student could not always be measured by receiving the highest grades. What was important, instead, was that the student had tried his or her best to learn the material. A lower grade in that case would not be a mark of failure but would simply reflect different students' varying abilities, backgrounds, and conditions of the moment. Wooden started thinking seriously about the things he had learned from his father, his coaches, and his teachers and began molding those lessons into a scheme that would be useful for motivating students to do their best. Out of this emerged his famous pyramid, which he refined and elaborated over the years.[6]

"I began searching," Wooden later explained, "for some way that would not only make me a better teacher but give the youngsters under my supervision something to aspire to that was more productive, more fair, and more rewarding." His thoughts took him back to what his father had frequently emphasized to him and his brothers when they were living on their farm in Indiana. They should not worry about being better than anybody else; instead, they should strive to be the best they could possibly be, because that was something they could control. By 1934, two years out of college, Wooden had set down his own definition of success as "peace of mind that is the direct result of self-satisfaction in knowing that you did your best to become the best that you are capable of becoming."[7]

Starting from that assumption, scores, trophies, championships, fame, and monetary rewards all become mere by-products of success rather than the thing itself. Inspired by an illustration he came across showing a ladder of achievement with five rungs representing necessary components to get to the top, he came up with the idea of a pyramid and began thinking about what to put into its constitutive blocks. Ultimately, there would be fifteen blocks. He tinkered with the idea for years, hanging a version of it on his office wall and handing out copies by the thousands to players, coaches, students, friends, and anyone who expressed an interest.

The virtues or habits he chose to represent overlapped considerably with the kinds of things that frequently appear in self-help books, motivational speeches, and ethical guides, but they also reflected his own well-thought-out philosophy of life. The cornerstones of the pyramid, anchoring the base of five blocks along the bottom row, were industriousness and enthusiasm. The necessity of working hard had been instilled in him as a youngster; it was the crucial component of the Horatio Alger myth and virtually every other model of the self-made man. Enthusiasm was a worthy complement to hard work. Remembering his father's words—do not whine, complain, or criticize—Wooden latched onto a component that could serve to motivate people to the tasks at hand, making them enjoyable and satisfying rather than merely dull and obligatory. In the center row, taking his cue from his much-admired coach at Purdue, Ward "Piggy" Lambert, he placed the qualities of conditioning, skill, and team spirit. Focusing on these goals would guide his approach as a coach throughout his career. The other qualities to strive for—friendship, loyalty, cooperation, self-control, alertness, initiative, intentness, poise, and confidence—all led to the ultimate goal at the top of the pyramid: competitive greatness. Ten other virtues were positioned along the sides of the pyramid, as a sort of mortar to hold the blocks firmly in place: ambition, adaptability, resourcefulness, fight, faith, patience, integrity, reliability, honesty, and sincerity. Success in this scheme relied on one's own effort and will to excel, not on mere hopes or dreams. "I have dreams," Wooden would say later. But dreams alone were not enough, in his estimation. "If you're relying on dreams and think the pyramid will make your dreams come true, you're going to be sadly disappointed," he cautioned.[8]

Wooden's development of his Pyramid of Success characterized his approach to teaching, coaching, and life in general. He constantly preached to his basketball players that becoming a great athlete required being a good person first.[9] To many first-time observers, this was pure corn, or pure hypocrisy. The coach, in their mind, was a throwback. Listening to his homilies and aphorisms, wrote Joe Jares in *Sports Illustrated*, "a visitor begins to think it is all just a giant put-on. Nobody could be that square. But Wooden is real all right," the sportswriter was quick to note.[10] There was seldom a trace of irony in his conversation. When people thought about John Wooden, they immediately associated him with UCLA and Los Angeles, the "City of Dreams," that great urban complex dependent on five-lane freeways, home of surfers and starlets and Tinseltown, enveloped in a haze of smog or smiled on by sunshine and expanses of blue sky. Los Angeles was urban America carried to its logical extreme, and John Wooden became a part of it when he moved there from Indiana.

But though he lived *in* Los Angeles, he was hardly *of* it. People might think of him as an LA person, but he still remained at heart a small-town boy from Indiana. As Andy Hill, one of his players, noted, "Coach is still a Hoosier, despite the fact that he's lived in Los Angeles since 1948."[11] The lessons, values, attitudes, drives, and ambitions that he had incorporated into his thinking as a youth remained his guides and motivations through more than half a century in the sunny climes of California. His intense competitiveness as well as his religiousness were learned amid the corn rows and on the basketball courts of Indiana. The shyness that never quite left him, along with the fiery leadership that molded headstrong, balky young men into smoothly functioning team players, derived from his heartland origins.

Wooden was born in 1910, the second of four boys (two sisters died in infancy), in the small village of Hall, Indiana, 25 miles southwest of Indianapolis. His family moved several years later and he grew up mainly on a 60-acre farm near Centerton, a town of fifty people a few miles east of Hall. They never had very much monetarily, but that placed them in the same category as most of their neighbors. The house contained two small bedrooms for the six of them and had no electricity or running water. Like farm women everywhere, Wooden's mother, Roxie, worked constantly—cooking, canning, churning, washing, ironing, mending, and performing all the other chores that farm life entailed in the early 1900s. Water came from a pump on the back porch. Wooden hardly remembered his mother ever having a store-bought dress. She made her own clothes, and she sewed overalls and shirts for her menfolk.[12]

Though deeply admiring his mother and the work that she did, as a boy he was more deeply influenced by the example and teaching of his father, Joshua Hugh Wooden, who never accumulated much in a material way but was a man of deep faith and conviction. He had exhibited some skill as a baseball pitcher and enjoyed playing the game enough to carve a baseball diamond out of a field that otherwise grew corn, wheat, and alfalfa. The family also raised cows, pigs, and chickens and tended a large garden. It was Joshua who cut the bottom out of a tomato basket and nailed it to the wall of the barn for a basketball goal for his boys and later forged a hoop out of iron for them to shoot at. It was not his father's interest in athletics, however, that impressed young John so much as the habits he modeled and the wisdom he imparted in the processes of ordinary living. Wooden considered the four most profound personal influences on his life to have been three of his basketball coaches, and his father. "Both my philosophy of life and of coaching come largely from him," he wrote in his autobiography.[13]

Joshua Wooden believed in work, and his sons imbibed that work ethic, toiling in the fields and performing their chores. More important, he was a deeply religious man and read the Bible daily to his family. He also loved to read poetry to them at night, and John learned his love of poetry and of reading from him. Their father's love of literature led all four boys to major or minor in English in college and become schoolteachers. His behavior, as much as his intellect, impressed John, who remembered him as a gentle man, one who could get a mule to perform by the soothing sound of his voice. He never used profanity, and his son later became famous for the repetition of his strongest epithet—"Goodness gracious sakes alive!"[14]

Less than a mile from their farm, Centerton contained two stores, a grain elevator, a post office, a church, a grade school, and not over eight or ten houses. When he graduated from eighth grade, John received as a present from his father a sheet of paper on which he had written a creed that he suggested the boy try to live by. Its seven points: "1. Be true to yourself. 2. Make each day your masterpiece. 3. Help others. 4. Drink deeply from good books, especially the Bible. 5. Make friendship a fine art. 6. Build a shelter against a rainy day. 7. Pray for guidance, count and give thanks for your blessings every day." John folded and kept the handwritten original in his wallet for many years until it began to fall apart, then had copies made of it and continued to carry one with him. "I wish I could say that I have always lived by that creed," he later wrote. "I can't, but I have tried."[15]

As a kid, John loved baseball even more than basketball. He later included Earl Warriner, the grade school's combined principal, teacher, and coach, one of the four most important influences in his life. Once during a basketball game when John was being recalcitrant, the coach sat his high scorer on the bench the rest of the day, as the team went down to defeat. "After it was over," Wooden later related, "he put an arm on my shoulder and said, 'Johnny, we could have won with you in there, but winning just isn't that important.'"[16]

The Wooden family fell victim to the difficult economic times that settled across the Farm Belt during the 1920s. A batch of cholera vaccine turned out to be bad; instead of warding off the disease, it infected their hogs, killing them all. Later they put money in an investment company that turned out to be a fraud. Unable to pay off their mortgage debt, the family was forced to give up their farm in 1924 and moved to Martinsville, 10 miles to the south. Joshua took a job working in a bathhouse and giving massages at one of the half dozen sanatoriums that had established themselves in town. The community had become a popular resort because of its artesian wells and baths. The job was a step down from being an independent farmer, but he made the best of it and did not complain.[17]

During his freshman year of high school, John had commuted to Martinsville on the interurban train. Living right in town made life a lot more convenient for him. Martinsville was a sizable community of around 5,000 people and the seat of Morgan County. In a state fanatically devoted to basketball, Martinsville stood out in its ardor for the game. (Martinsville over the years became known as a hotbed of Ku Klux Klan support in a state whose Klan activity was among the highest in the nation.) "You'd have to be brought up in Martinsville to know the crazyness of high school basketball," Wooden told me when I visited him in 2001.[18] The team had won the state title two years earlier (about 740 schools of every size were lumped together in a single division for the tournament), and that same year the team had moved into a big new brick gymnasium whose seating capacity was larger than the population of the town. For a bright, but shy, young man who loved to compete, attending school in a place like Martinsville was an ideal way to make his mark.

Like many outstanding athletes, John was used to playing with boys several years older than he. Without a school baseball or football team to play on, he concentrated his energies on basketball. As he progressed through his last three years of high school, he became the leader of one of the state's outstanding teams. The large Martinsville gym filled for every game. With John capturing all-state honors each year as a speedy, sure-handed guard, the Martinsville Artesians lost in the championship game in 1926 to Marion by a score of 30–23, defeated Muncie Central, 26–23, the following year, and lost a heartbreaker to the same team in his senior season by a score of 13–12. During the final seconds of that game, as Wooden recalled it, Muncie's center, Charlie Secrist, tipped the ball back to himself on a center jump, whirled, and flung it underhanded from midcourt toward the basket in a wild, sweeping motion that lifted the ball up through the rafters and down through the basket, hardly rippling the net as it swished through it.[19] But although his team won only one state championship, Wooden's heroics were highly appreciated. "He was the king, the idol of every kid who had a basketball," recalled Tom Harmon, the Michigan football great. "And in Indiana, that was every kid."[20]

The budding athlete had the good fortune in high school of playing under the guidance of Glenn Curtis, who later preceded him as coach at Indiana State and then went on to coach for Detroit in the pros. Curtis had already won a state championship at Lebanon, in 1918, and he captured three more at Martinsville, in 1924, 1927, and 1933. His emphasis on fundamentals became an integral part of Wooden's own coaching philosophy. "He was a brilliant psychologist and handler of young men," his avid pupil noted later. "He had a tremendous talent for inspiring individuals and teams to rise to great heights. He demanded perfection in the execution of fundamentals and was a master strategist."[21]

Courted by Stanford, Kansas, Notre Dame, and several Big Ten schools, Wooden decided on Purdue in his home state because of its reputation as an engineering school. He later dropped out of the program, however, because he had to work summers to pay his way through college and was unable to attend the summer engineering camp that was required of students for graduation. Full-ride athletic scholarships were not common at the time. Wooden earned money to pay his bills by waiting on tables, taping ankles and taking care of athletic equipment, hawking football programs, and working other jobs. During his senior year, the 5'10½" dynamo broke the conference scoring record with 154 points in twelve games and was named College Player of the Year.[22] Wooden's frenetic, all-out style of play landed him in the bleachers and down on the floor scrambling for loose balls so often that he earned the nickname "India (or Indiana) Rubber Man" for his ability to bounce right back up every time. He was widely regarded as the best basketball player the state produced until Oscar Robertson played for Crispus Attucks High School and the University of Cincinnati during the late 1950s and early 1960s. Even today Wooden is commonly regarded, along with Robertson and Larry Bird, to have been one of Indiana's three greatest basketball products.

Coach Lambert at Purdue became the fourth great influence on Wooden's life, along with his father, Earl Warriner, and Glenn Curtis. Lambert had been a fine athlete himself, playing quarterback at Wabash College and, for a time, professional baseball. Dynamic and fiery and a master psychologist, he was also a careful student of the game and taught Wooden much about its technical aspects. He was a pioneer in emphasizing conditioning, drilling on fundamentals, pressing on defense, and running the fast break, all of which Wooden later incorporated into his own coaching style. Like Lambert, Wooden tried to exploit the particular strengths of each individual on his teams and build a controlled offense that allowed players options and individual initiative. As a player at Purdue, Wooden began keeping a notebook on the game and started thinking about the possibility of becoming a coach himself after graduation.[23]

Although he was offered $5,000 a year to turn professional, Wooden decided to put his education to work and become a teacher. His first job after graduation was at Dayton (Kentucky) High School, an institution of about 300 students just across the Ohio River from Cincinnati. There, he took on duties as athletic director, supervisor of the entire elementary and secondary physical education curriculum, and English teacher, in addition to being head basketball, football, baseball, and track coach. Leading his basketball team to a 6–11 record during his first year on the job, he was able to better it to 15–3 the next time around. Wooden moved on to South Bend Central High, a school ten times larger, in the fall of 1934. There he was hardly less busy, serving as the school's comptroller and director of athletics, along with teaching English and coaching basketball, baseball, and tennis. In nine years in South Bend, he racked up 197 victories against 28 defeats, establishing himself as one of the most successful basketball coaches in a state where the sport was king. His teams were often ranked first, second, or third in the state, but they never managed to get to the championship finals or win it all. On weekends throughout the 1930s, he earned $50 a game playing for Frank Kautsky's Wholesale Grocers and other semipro teams, once sinking 134 consecutive free throws during a string of games. One of his teammates was University of Illinois star and future Cleveland Indian baseball great Lou Boudreau. Playing against teams coming from towns ranging from Fort Wayne, Indiana, and Toledo, Ohio, to Sheboygan and Oshkosh, Wisconsin, he would often drive all night to get to the games and then return home in time to teach his classes on Monday morning.[24] He and his wife, Nellie, his high school sweetheart, also had a growing family to raise—a boy and a girl. Nellie was the love of his life—she was totally devoted to him and he to her. Wooden frequently mentioned the close bond between them and the central importance of family in his life, a carryover from his boyhood days.[25]

During those busy years Wooden developed a philosophy of coaching that he integrated into a total outlook on life that incorporated strong religious principles and the values associated with his Pyramid of Success. As a coach, he was a strict disciplinarian. But also, in ways, he was a buddy to his players, as when he took them along to Indianapolis to watch him play in the semipro league. He often joined in scrimmages with his players, directly indicating to them exactly how he wanted things to be done. Having been able to outhustle his opponents as a player because of superior conditioning, he drove his teams to get into the best possible condition.[26] It was a formula he never abandoned. There was always more to learn, and Wooden was learning, day by day, year by year.

Had World War II not intervened, the coach wrote in his autobiography, he might well have spent the rest of his career teaching at Central High. "We weren't getting wealthy, but we had a wonderful life, a fine school, great associates, and I always felt I was cut out for the high school level. I loved to teach, and I lived for it."[27] Like most in his generation, however, Wooden responded to duty's call, serving three years in the navy, mostly spending his time getting combat flyers into physical shape. Returning home after the war, having lost his house because his military salary did not allow him to keep up on house payments and upset with the way his school was treating some of his fellow veterans, Wooden decided to make a switch and take a collegiate coaching job.

With an enrollment of around 2,500 students, Indiana State Teachers College in Terre Haute was actually smaller than Central High, and Wooden's duties there as athletic director, head basketball and baseball coach, and part-time English instructor made comparable demands on his time. His predecessor there was Glenn Curtis, his former high school coach, who had taken a job with the professional Detroit Falcons. Wooden refused an invitation to the postseason tournament of the National Association of Intercollegiate Basketball the first year because they would have barred the team's only black player from participating. When the contingent (including the black student) was invited back the following year, they advanced all the way to the championship game before losing.[28]

Now major universities began knocking on his door. In 1948, Wooden received offers from both Minnesota and UCLA. He preferred the former, in part because of its location in his familiar Midwest. However, when an unexpected snowstorm tied up telephone lines that spring and Minnesota's call could not get through until an hour after the agreed-upon deadline, Wooden verbally committed to UCLA and felt obligated to honor his word to them. By this quirk of fate, he and his family found themselves established on the West Coast that fall, living in a university-owned home in Culver City, near the MGM movie studios and a long way from the Middle West, where he and Nellie had grown up and had been raising their children. Los Angeles, with a metropolitan area containing about 4 million people, was about as far away from Martinsville, geographically and culturally, as a person could get. But the area harbored large numbers of migrants from the Midwest, an encouraging fact, and the minister of the church they joined in Santa Monica was Wales Smith, who had been a fellow student with Wooden back in Martinsville. In addition, their doctor, Ralph Irwin, had once performed an emergency appendectomy on him in Iowa City.[29]

Despite some friendly faces and reassuring markers around him, Wooden discovered living in Los Angeles to be a difficult adjustment and was not very happy his first couple of years there. The freeways, the sheer size of the place, people's lifestyles, and the high cost of living all seemed foreign to him and his wife. "I was not at ease in Southern California," Wooden admitted a quarter of a century later. "Frankly, I came from the farm—small communities—and Los Angeles was frightening for me. I didn't fit in." Not a social drinker, Wooden frequently felt uncomfortable in the laid-back environment surrounding him. Some people wondered just how square he was.[30] Driving the Pasadena Freeway almost scared him to death. "We'd never seen a freeway before," Nell recalled. Once, all upset by the rush of traffic, John blurted out, "What are we doing here, anyway?"[31]

In its effort to woo the Indianan to accept the position, UCLA officials had indicated that a new basketball gymnasium would be available for his team within three years—the length of the contract he had insisted on before agreeing to come. The school's old Men's Gym, though architecturally pleasing and not really all that old (it had been built in 1932), was not a good venue for playing. With a seating capacity of only 2,450 when the bleachers were pulled out and accessible only by several small doors on either end, the poorly lit, badly ventilated gymnasium on the third floor of the building was a fire trap, which finally led fire marshals to reduce the number of spectators allowed in for games to 1,000. That is why during the decade preceding the dedication of 12,800-seat Pauley Pavilion in 1965, UCLA did not even have a home basketball court to play on. Their home games were scheduled in a variety of auditoriums, including those of Venice High School, Long Beach City College, Pan Pacific Auditorium, Los

Angeles Sports Arena, Santa Monica City College, Long Beach Arena, and Bakersfield Junior College.[32]

The decades after World War II were a period of explosive growth in higher education, and UCLA was a part of it. Established a year after the end of World War I as a liberal arts institution grafted onto a state teachers college, "Southern Campus," as it was called at the outset, was a poor sibling to the state's flagship institution, the University of California at Berkeley. But the populations of Southern California and particularly Los Angeles were burgeoning. Enrollment at the new campus in Westwood, which sprang up during the 1920s on a hillside in what was then the middle of nowhere, multiplied along with the population once the Depression dissipated and World War II was won. Having held steadily at around 5,000 from the early 1930s to 1944, UCLA's enrollment almost tripled in six years' time, to over 14,000 by 1950. It continued upward, approximately doubling during the following two decades, reaching 29,000 by 1968. Such expansion both necessitated and was further reinforced by a major building boom extending all through the late 1940s and 1950s and continuing into the following decade and beyond. Between 1944 and 1950, $38 million in new buildings went up. California's educational system emerged during these years as the largest in the United States as UCLA established itself as one of the nation's premier educational institutions. During the 1940s and 1950s, all this meant that the basketball program had to bide its time waiting for its new gymnasium.[33]

Meanwhile, Wooden's teams were succeeding wildly beyond the expectations of almost everybody except, perhaps, himself. Basketball at UCLA before his arrival had definitely been a second-class sport, especially in comparison with football. Even before the arrival in 1949 of coach Red Sanders, football had firmly established itself on campus. Sanders carried the team to new heights of achievement during the 1950s until a heart attack struck him down in 1958. His successor, Tommy Prothro, continued the building of the Bruins into a football powerhouse during his reign from 1965 to 1970. But in the twenty-one years after conference play began in 1927, the UCLA basketball team's conference record had consisted of only three winning seasons, sixteen losing ones, and two in which they broke even. With no returning starters on the team, forecasters had the Bruins finishing last for the coming season when John Wooden arrived in the fall of 1948.[34] Wooden's recruiting allowance amounted to a miserly several hundred dollars a year. When the team went on the road, he and the

CHAPTER FIFTEEN

trainer had to scout around to find the cheapest restaurants for the team to eat at.[35] The coach's beginning salary of $6,500 (at his retirement, it remained a modest $32,500, with an additional $8,000 from postgame radio appearances) was so low that to afford a down payment on a house he took a part-time job their first four summers in town, working in a nearby dairy.[36]

But all that would change. In the 1948–1949 season, the team that sportswriters had picked to finish last in the conference instead wound up on top of the Southern Division (which also included Stanford, Cal-Berkeley, and crosstown rival Southern Cal) with a 10–2 record, compiling a fine overall mark of 22–7. It lost a three-game play-off to Oregon State for the Pacific Coast Conference championship. Wooden would always say that this was his most satisfying year of coaching.[37] People's expectations were still low, and they were very happy to be winning at all. Having launched the "big turnaround," during the next dozen years, the new coach not only established respectability for UCLA basketball but made the program one to pay attention to nationally. In his first eight years in Los Angeles, Wooden's teams captured the Southern Division crown in all but two of them, going on to win the postseason play-off for the conference championship three times.

Two years after taking over in Westwood, Wooden was invited back to coach at his alma mater, Purdue. By then he was homesick for Indiana and his native Midwest. He would have loved to take the job and even asked UCLA's athletic director, former coach Wilbur Johns, for permission to move, but Johns and the school's president reminded him that he had been the one who had insisted on a three-year contract and that although they were willing to let him break the agreement, they thought he should honor it. A person less devoted to principle than Wooden might have left, but conscience nagged, so he stayed. A year later, with his contract having expired, he would have gone back to the Middle West if any attractive offer had come from a Big Ten school, but none was forthcoming at the time (many would be made in succeeding years), so Los Angeles became his permanent home.[38] After several years there, John and Nell began getting used to their new environment, enlarged their circle of friends, and settled in. Their children liked it, too, and thoughts of moving back to the Midwest faded with time. The family found a church home at the First Christian Church in Santa Monica, where John served as a deacon, and the fellowship of the congregation became an important part of their lives.[39]

The mid- to late-1950s, however, turned out to be years of frustration for him. His teams did well enough, continuing to compile winning records, but between 1956 (when the team temporarily rose to fifth place in the national rankings) and 1962 there would be no more conference championships (divisional play discontinued after the 1953–1954 season), and UCLA's win-loss record leveled off somewhat from what it had been during the earlier part of the decade. With the exception of Willie Naulls, who would go on to play professional basketball, Wooden lacked truly outstanding big men to compete with the likes of Bill Russell at the University of San Francisco or Wilt Chamberlain at Kansas. Never enjoying recruiting, he left most of that task to his assistants while he concentrated on working with the material at hand. On arrival in 1948, he had installed an up-tempo, pressuring, fast-break style of play that wore other teams down and won games, and for a while that strategy had worked successfully. But competition on the West Coast stiffened during the mid-1950s as, first, the University of San Francisco, led by Russell, emerged as the best team in the region, and, then, during the latter part of the decade, Cal-Berkeley, coached by Pete Newell, dominated conference play.[40]

Wooden's teams always featured controlled, fast-break offenses and relentless pressure on defense. He emphasized three things: "Get the players in the best of condition. Teach them to execute the fundamentals quickly. Drill them to play as a team."[41] Wooden considered himself primarily a practice coach; it was what he most enjoyed doing and it was what he thought he was best at. By the time the players were ready to take the court, they were prepared for any situation and knew what to do.

Sometimes it took the man they called "Coach" more time to plan out his practice routines than it took his players to run through them. He was completely methodical in his approach, writing down each exercise and how much time to devote to it on 3-inch-by-5-inch cards, which he followed religiously. "His cards," muttered one player. "He drives me crazy with his damn cards."[42] The sessions, seldom running more than two hours, were designed to accomplish several things: teach and reinforce the fundamentals of passing, dribbling, screening, shooting, and playing defense and making responses automatic; instill the attitude of team play; build up the players' stamina and get them into the best of condition; and serve as a schoolroom for learning the principles the coach wanted to impart. Wooden seldom held team meetings or did blackboard drills. His coaching took place almost entirely on the court during his intense practice sessions. By the end of two hours of constant movement, moving from one drill to the next, with little or no rest in between, most players would be exhausted. After that, playing a game could almost seem easy.

In practice, Coach was constantly teaching. "Wooden's practice gym was a sort of one-room schoolhouse transported from the Indiana plains," observed Alexander Wolff. "For two hours in the afternoon his pupils listened to material that seemed to have emerged from a time warp."[43] The schoolteacher was full of simple words of wisdom. "Be quick, but don't hurry" was his most repeated admonition. "Failing to prepare is preparing to fail" was another. And "Don't mistake activity for achievement."[44] All these principles were based on years of experience as a player and coach. "You will play like you practice," he told his players, so he demanded perfection. Like the teacher that he was, he applied the four laws of learning that had proven their effectiveness to him over time: explanation, demonstration, correction, and repetition. He broke every skill and activity down into their essential components, repeating them over and over again.[45]

Both before and after he started winning national championships, Wooden was so successful and his personal authority was so great that most of his players were willing to endure the rigors of practice and to accept the highly controlled environment they discovered when joining the UCLA program. Some athletes, however, rebelled, and some observers criticized the system, likening Wooden to an athletic Henry Ford, who dominated his minions through organization, discipline, and threats.[46] When one of his players quit the squad, complaining that the team was run "like a machine," the coach acknowledged the fact. "He was right," Wooden observed. "I try to make it like a well-oiled machine. I put each player into his niche. He loses individuality."[47] Wooden's obsession with detail and perfection and his insistence on maintaining control extended as far as his famous lessons on the first day of practice on how to put on socks (without any wrinkles, to prevent blisters) and how to lace shoes (tied securely over the top of the eyehole for a tighter lace, to prevent the strings from coming undone during a game).[48] Where sensible preparation ended and control for its own sake began was a line players and observers might disagree on.

The strange paradox, however, is that for all Wooden's minute instructions and insistence on doing things his way, his teams were capable of extraordinary creativity and freedom on the court. One LA sportswriter characterized the coach as "an unexciting intellectual whose teams play wildly exciting basketball."[49] He seldom scouted other teams, nor did he rely on set plays. Instead, having thoroughly coached his players in the fundamentals and having trained them in how to react to a variety of situations, they were free to be creative—dribbling, passing, driving, or shooting the ball as circumstances dictated. Thorough preparation and constant repetition of fundamentals, practiced in a highly disciplined fashion, opened up possibilities for freedom and creativity in a way that directly seeking those ends, without the methodical preparation that occurred, could never have achieved.

By the early 1960s, conditions were present for taking UCLA up to the next level. During the 1960s and '70s, the overall quality of players UCLA was able to recruit improved dramatically. The 1962 contingent, led by sophomore guard Walt Hazzard, a ball-handling and playmaking whiz out of Philadelphia, made it clear that UCLA was ready to bid for national prominence. That team went all the way to the final four in the NCAA tourney before losing in the semifinals, on a shot at the buzzer, to the eventual national champion, Cincinnati.

It appeared that the team desperately needed to come up with some kind of tactical weapon that could dramatically turn games to its advantage. During the 1963–1964 season, Assistant Coach Jerry Norman, who had played forward on the team during the early 1950s, urged his boss to consider installing a full-court zone press as a way of forcing opponents to turn the ball over and take them out of their rhythm. Wooden had played the press at Purdue and used it frequently at UCLA. But he thought that building his entire game strategy around a full-court zone press was a risky move. It took Norman's enthusiasm for the idea and exceptional persuasiveness to convince him to try it. What that year's team lacked in height (none of the starters was over 6'5"), it made up for in speed and athleticism, making it a perfect fit for a pressing defense. Led by starting guards Hazzard, now a senior, and Gail Goodrich, forwards Keith Erickson and Jack Hirsch, and center Fred Slaughter (the first three of whom went on to star in the pros), and backed up by superb substitutes Kenny Washington and Doug McIntosh, the 1963–1964 squad was the first UCLA quintet to go all the way to a national championship. It completed a perfect 30–0 season with a 98–83 victory over Duke, a powerhouse most of the experts had predicted UCLA could not beat.[50]

Looking back on the run afterward, nine more championships during the following eleven years might have seemed inevitable to some observers; in fact, they were anything but. The following year's team lost three starters, but Goodrich and Erickson were well supported by new replacements drilled in the Wooden system. The arrival of Lew Alcindor (later Kareem Abdul-Jabbar) on campus in 1965 (freshmen were ineligible to play varsity ball at the time) probably would not have been possible if UCLA had not captured its first championship or if the new gymnasium had not been built, which was expedited by the first two titles. Seven more championships would follow in succession, then a missed opportunity in 1974, when the (Bill) "Walton Gang" failed during their senior year to duplicate Alcindor's three-peat, and one final title in 1975. At the final four in San Diego that year, Wooden announced his retirement right after the team's semifinal victory over Louisville, which was coached by his former player and assistant coach, Denny Crum.

The string of victories built during the late 1960s and early 1970s constituted a remarkable achievement. The question of how Wooden managed to pull it off continually arose. Some attributed his success to his big men, Abdul-Jabbar and Walton (which, at the most, could have explained only five of the ten titles). Others assumed that he must have benefited from recruiting violations. The role played by Sam Gilbert, a millionaire building contractor who befriended many UCLA players and who some said lavished gifts and money on them, ignited considerable speculation.[51] Wooden's ability to obtain preferential treatment from officials was also sometimes put forward as a reason for his success. None of these factors, to the degree that any of them were remotely true, went very far in explaining the UCLA phenomenon, however. Critics also complained that he rode referees too hard and even shouted obscenities at opposing players. Wooden sheepishly admitted that he sometimes yelled things at players, but convincingly denied that he had used bad language. Also, as time went by, he became calmer on the bench and was subtler in talking to the referees and opposing teams. Some of his counterparts accused him of hypocrisy, referring to him as "St. John" behind his back. Though many of them envied his acclaim and questioned some of his tactics, most respected his ability. His record of accomplishment was an undeniable fact.[52]

More disturbing to Wooden were criticisms voiced by some of his players. He admitted to treating starters and reserves differently, but he insisted that he did what circumstances demanded, was fair about it, and always did what was required for the good of the team. Since he usually played just seven or eight men until games were clearly decided, it was always a chore to convince the benchwarmers, most of whom had starred on their high school squads, that their roles on the team were important. Occasionally, a player had enough temerity to challenge the coach openly. Most frequently, the confrontation was over hair length or dress codes on the road, but the most publicized episode occurred at the traditional postseason banquet in May 1970, when graduating reserve forward Bill Seibert, a psychology major, instead of saying what a wonderful time he had had at UCLA, voiced some of his frustrations in playing for a coach who, in some minds at least, had become almost a god. By the time he finished complaining about the unequal treatment meted out to starters and reserves and the lack of communication that existed between coaches and players, people in the audience were shouting for him to sit down and his mother was crying.[53]

Seibert wasn't the only player to criticize Coach, only the boldest in his manner of expressing it. Edgar Lacey quit the team in 1968 after the famous matchup between UCLA and a University of Houston contingent led by Elvin Hayes in the Houston Astrodome. After a subpar first half, Lacey had been benched during the second half and never got back into play. On departing, he was quoted as saying, "I have never enjoyed playing for that man." He blamed Wooden for everything from not really listening to him to trying to change his shooting style. The senior forward, who was being touted as a top pro prospect, said, "I'm glad I'm getting out now while I still have some of my pride, my sanity, and my self-esteem left."[54] There were other, less celebrated cases, too. The charge most often leveled against Wooden was that he did not "relate" well to his players, at least to some of them. In their minds, he was insensitive and failed to try to understand them.

There is no question that Wooden never tried to buddy up to his players, as he sometimes had done as a high school coach. He was always open to talking with them and discussing whatever was on their mind, but he usually let them take the initiative and did not go out of his way to involve himself in their personal relationships.[55] Part of this, no doubt, reflected his traditional Hoosier reserve and holdover shyness. Partly, also, it stemmed from his realization that his own personal standard of conduct was much more conservative than that of the new generation coming to maturity in the 1960s and 1970s. In this regard, he was in a double bind: some would criticize him for intruding too much in players' lives and trying to control their behavior, while others felt that he did not care about what they did off the court and wanted him to behave more like a father figure to them. The years of UCLA's greatest success, between 1963 and 1975, were also a period of great social and political upheaval in America. Wooden, whose own personal moral standards and sense of propriety had been established in Indiana during the early decades of the century, continued to adhere to a stern moral code, but he was pragmatic enough to bend with the times during this turbulent era. At the same time that he was mellowing in his own behavior toward the referees and rival players and coaches, he was relaxing some of his rules on things like hair length, dress codes, and curfews. Bill Sweek, who sometimes clashed with Coach while playing guard on the 1966–1969 teams, looked back later on the period and observed, "I can see now that he did change and try to adjust to the times."[56]

Like many of Wooden's players who had not always seen eye-to-eye with him when they played for him, Sweek came later to admire and revere him. Wooden's refusal to bend to the demands and desires of his players and the distance that he maintained between himself and them were motivated in part by his effort to maintain control and authority but also flowed from his sense of self as a man committed to well-considered principles and beliefs. Failure to ingratiate himself with players in the short run often brought deeper admiration and respect over time. In subsequent years, dozens of former players would maintain close relationships with Coach and express their profound feelings of love and admiration for him. Andy Hill, who had starred on his high school basketball team and as a freshman at UCLA, greatly resented being forced to the bench and being allowed only a small amount of playing time during his three years on the varsity, and he blamed Wooden for it at the time. Twenty-five years later, however, he suddenly realized that "virtually everything I believed in and used in my professional life" was derived from lessons he had learned from Coach. Hill reestablished contact with Wooden and collaborated with him on a book incorporating the lessons he had taught about life and about the game.[57]

Kareem Abdul-Jabbar, who was named college basketball's player of the century at the same time that Wooden was honored as coach of the century, found adjusting to conditions in California difficult, after growing up in New York City. Blocked from talking to the press during his first year on the varsity, he later voiced discontent with his coach and the program in a much-discussed three-part interview published in *Sports Illustrated*.[58] Like many others, however, as the years went by he appreciated more and more what Wooden had been doing. In many ways, the two could hardly have been more different: a white and a black; an under-six-foot, fleet-footed guard and an over-seven-foot giant of a center; a small-town boy who enjoyed Lawrence Welk, adhered to traditional values and habits, and gave the appearance of being a square and a city boy who grooved on jazz, bebop, and metropolitan life and exuded cool; a man shaped by the experiences of the Jazz Age, the Depression, and World War II and one who was molded by the 1960s, the era of rock and roll, Vietnam, and Watergate. Yet in other ways their lives overlapped: both very intelligent, they were highly articulate and loved to read and learn; they were intense competitors and perfectionists in what they did; for different reasons, they felt out of tune with the society around them; and they both possessed a serious philosophical and religious bent. Wooden adhered to the religion of his childhood; Abdul-Jabbar, having been reared a Catholic, converted to Islam and changed his name. In his memoir of his last season as a pro player, Abdul-Jabbar indicated that coach and player had startled each other at first. Yet despite their differences and a thirty-seven-year age difference, "there was an immediate simpatico between our temperaments and a kind of pragmatic idealism that we shared, although I couldn't have put that into words back then. I just knew I was drawn to whatever he had and that the plainness of his demeanor was deceptive." Abdul-Jabbar did not know why fate had placed him in the older man's hands, but he was grateful for it.[59]

No one was a bigger Wooden booster than Bill Walton, his "bad boy" of the 1971–1974 teams, who tested Coach's hair-length policies, got arrested in an antiwar demonstration, and used his position as a UCLA star to express his many strongly held opinions about the Vietnam War and American life in general. Despite their widely varying views on politics and lifestyles, however, Wooden had a special affection for his outspoken, wildly exciting center. He later said that Abdul-Jabbar had been his most valuable player, in the sense of his impact on a game, but that Walton had been his most highly skilled player, in terms of how he would have been graded on the various elements of his play on the court. After his retirement from the pro game, Walton stayed in close touch with his former coach, talking to him frequently on the phone and singing his praises to anyone who would listen. From the perspective of a quarter century after his playing days at UCLA, Walton would say, "John Wooden was hired at UCLA to coach basketball, but what he really taught during his twenty-seven years at Westwood was life." His talk was not about strategy or statistics but about people and character. "And he constantly reminds us that once we become good people, we then have the chance to become good basketball players—or whatever else we may want to be in life."[60]

Wooden always conceived his role to be that of a teacher more than that of a coach. As a teacher, he was a moralist and a molder of young men. He was a competitor who played hard to win, but to him winning was less important than preparing the utmost to win and giving one's best effort in the process. Lessons on the basketball court were translatable to everyday life. In a real sense, he was a philosopher. "It was as if John Wooden had read Musashi, the great seventeenth-century samurai mystic," observed Abdul-Jabbar. "Musashi wrote about the need to be determined through calm, to cultivate a level mind, to be neither insufficiently spirited nor overspirited, an elevated spirit and a low spirit being equally weak."[61] Wooden would no doubt have chosen his sources differently, quoting from his beloved Abraham Lincoln or Mother Teresa, referring to one of the many poems he could quote by heart or other literary references, or pulling a quotation from his well-used Bible. But in recounting the lessons he learned as a farm lad and small-town boy growing up in the Midwest, Wooden was also drawing on wisdom whose provenance extended beyond the boundaries of a geographic region. To the degree that they are valuable and life-changing, the lessons learned in a small-town environment are not exclusive to place or time.

CHAPTER SIXTEEN

Ronald Reagan: Small-Town Dreamer on the Stage of History

All of us have to have a place we go back to; Dixon is that place for me. There was the life that has shaped my body and mind for all the years to come after. . . . It was a good life. I never have asked for anything more, then or now.

—Ronald Reagan, *Where's the Rest of Me?*

One of Ronald Reagan's favorite rhetorical gambits was to assert that while there are no easy answers to difficult problems, there are, indeed, simple ones.[1] Many people mistakenly assumed that Reagan himself was a simple man possessed of an undifferentiated personality—either heroic or retrograde, depending on one's own particular point of view—and that his thinking was all of a piece, simplistic to the extreme. More than for most politicians who have risen to the presidency, his seemingly transparent image belied complexities and contradictions not apparent to all, and his opaqueness left even close associates baffled and uncomprehending.[2] "He's not an easy man, although he seems easy," his wife Nancy, who knew him best, told Reagan biographer Lou Cannon in 1989. "To everybody he seems very easy, but he is more complex than people think."[3] Admiring conservative chronicler Steven F. Hayward agreed: "He is a paradox, a seemingly simple man whose simplicity masks great complexity, making him a far more complicated character than many of his obviously intricate Oval Office peers."[4]

A fiercely conservative critic of government, Ronald Reagan spent his early years as an ardent admirer of Franklin Roosevelt and the New Deal and frequently quoted him as president. A vigorous defender of the family ideal, the divorced Reagan in practice proved a distant father, leaving him alienated at times from all four of his children. He championed traditional values but made a career in Hollywood, which often appeared to denigrate them. A devout believer who unself-consciously witnessed his faith, he sometimes acted in ways that cast doubt on the depth of his conviction. Often intellectually lazy, uninterested in vigorous give-and-take debate, and habituated to delegating details and lesser decisions to staffers, Reagan appeared to many observers to be unengaged and ill equipped to lead. Other onlookers, however, knew him as a wide-ranging reader allegedly possessed of a photographic memory, author of his own radio scripts and large parts of his own speeches, and in command of difficult issues and policy questions, both foreign and domestic. Once an outspoken critic of government deficits, Reagan seemed to be unconcerned about his own administration's rapid accumulation of red ink once he was in Washington. Aggressively scathing in his critique of liberals, he often found it expedient to compromise with them when circumstances dictated. A dedicated anti-Communist who memorably characterized the Soviet Union as an "evil empire," he quickly warmed to Mikhail Gorbachev after the latter's accession to power there and, remarkably, appeared ready to abolish all nuclear weapons at their second summit in Reykjavik, Iceland, in 1986.

It should not be too surprising that this small-town boy from the Midwest professed an abiding affection for his home town of Dixon, Illinois, and relished nostalgic visits back to the state. But Reagan, like most of his fellow small-town luminaries, had fled home as soon as he could. He wound up in Southern California, where he fit comfortably into a moviemaking culture that simultaneously affirmed and undermined traditional village customs and mores. Throughout his rise from regional radio announcer to B-movie actor, actors' union president, General Electric (GE) corporate spokesman, California governor, national radio commentator, newspaper columnist, and ultimately president of the United States, Reagan burnished an iconic image of himself congenial to the sort of people among whom he had grown up and to those who came to admire and identify with him. He also exhibited an unusual capacity for adjusting to the circumstances in which he found himself at any given moment, while exhibiting a sure-footed ability to navigate the treacherous shoals of a rapidly changing culture.

Reagan became one of the twentieth century's most successful politicians by intuitively understanding politics as salient symbol and powerful metaphor. "Myths and metaphors permit men to live in a world in which the causes are simple and neat and the remedies are apparent," writes political scientist Murray Edelman. "In place of a complicated empirical world, men hold to a relatively few, simple, archetypal myths, of which the conspiratorial enemy and the omnicompetent hero-savior are the central ones."[5] Reagan became a masterful purveyor of appealing imagery and resonant rhetoric. He always played himself off against imagined conspiratorial enemies and implicitly presented himself as a hero-savior riding to the rescue. His sunnily optimistic demeanor, determined and reassuring tone of voice, and skillful manipulation of language and imagery consistently won over enough voters to give him large electoral margins in two runs for governor and two for president. (He also narrowly failed to win the nomination in 1976, after making a last-minute, symbolic challenge in 1968.) Although he generated intense adulation among a loyal segment of enthusiastic admirers, his popularity in the polls gyrated more widely than most of his admirers are inclined to recall. His average approval rating of 53 percent placed him in the middle of the pack among his contemporaries, ahead of Richard Nixon, Jimmy Carter, Harry Truman, and Gerald Ford, and behind FDR, John Kennedy, Dwight Eisenhower, Lyndon Johnson, George H. W. Bush, and Bill Clinton. On the other hand, Reagan's standing with the public steadily increased after he left office. In recent years, they have ranked him second only to Kennedy among presidents since 1960.[6]

People responded unusually strongly—both positively and negatively—to the persona Reagan projected on the public stage. Often these reactions were only loosely related to the particular policy stances he took. Rather, his magnetic personality, rhetorical appeal, and leadership style created an aura generating powerful responses in many people. Much of the explanation for this was related to his origins in the Midwest and what that background meant for him. He liked to remind his audiences that as a small-town boy from Illinois, he had grasped at opportunities offered in America to launch a successful movie career and eventually become president of the United States. He implied that if he could do it, anybody could. "On his foreign trips, as in so many of his movie roles," writes Cannon, "he portrayed the wholesome hometown boy who had made good." He especially liked the campaign ads put together for his reelection effort in 1984 because they made him and his fellow viewers feel good about themselves. Cannon, who understood him as well as anyone, observes, "He was a powerful and sentimental spokesman who understood that the magic of his presidency was linked to his ability to embody the values of mythic America. When he saw himself on the screen, he saw America."[7]

As with so much else about him, there was nothing simple about Reagan's relationship with the small towns in which he grew to maturity. At once nostalgic about them and grateful for the advantages they had conferred on him, he harbored no desire to live in one permanently, being satisfied to make an occasional sentimental journey back. He had deliberately chosen a new life for himself in sunny California, specifically Hollywood, the dream factory of the nation. There he was able to pursue his visions of stardom and riches; at the same time, his visage on the silver screen fed the fantasies of countless watchers, who projected their own hopes and aspirations onto the stories and personages they witnessed weekly in the darkness of their local movie theaters.

With acting techniques honed in the industry, political savvy and leadership skills acquired as a union activist, and forensic expertise obtained as a radio announcer, traveling General Electric representative, and television host, Reagan parlayed his special talents into a significant advantage over political rivals. What many of them learned to their regret was that he also possessed considerable knowledge and firmly held convictions about public policy and had a knack for discerning people's thoughts and concerns about political matters. In tending to fit what he heard and read into a rigidly ideological framework and in readily discarding information contradicting his preconceived opinions, he was only aping a large portion of his contemporaries. What particularly stood out about him was his ability to dramatically and forcefully articulate his beliefs, the constancy with which he adhered to them, and his canny willingness to deny whatever contradictions and inconsistencies existed in them and between them and his actions. Almost never did he admit mistakes. Also, like most successful politicians, he benefited heavily from good luck, fortunate timing, rivals' underestimation of him, and public forgetfulness. There was nothing inevitable about Reagan's rise to the presidency, but throughout his life he benefited from a happy sense of timing, possessed a canny ability to perceive opportunities when they presented themselves, and had a rare instinct and willingness to take advantage of them.

Journalists and authors often noted Reagan's proclivity to dwell in dreams. Garry Wills observed that Reagan and some of his Iowa friends who had followed him to California during the late 1930s "had come to the land of America's dreams because they were dreamers themselves."[8] John Patrick Diggins pictured a Reagan who "stood for freedom, peace, disarmament, self-reliance, earthly happiness, the dreams of the imagination and the desires of the heart."[9] Sean Wilentz and Jon Meacham called him simply "the American dreamer."[10] Though some were charmed by this tendency, others found it disturbing or even downright scary. It was both Reagan's greatest strength and his most characteristic weakness. "Reagan already lived in a world of illusion when he arrived in Hollywood," Lou Cannon observed. "Later, he would invent an America that never was and share with his fellow citizens a bright, shining vision of our nation's greatness founded on an imagined version of the past. . . . Even in old age, he clung to his youthful dreams." Political scientist Benjamin Barber observed of the president in 1985, "He dreams. He is drawn to other dreamers, like John Kennedy and Franklin Roosevelt. He wants to help make *your* dreams come true." The problem with Hollywood dreamers like Reagan, Barber argued, is that they tend to emphasize individual aspirations exclusively, not collective ones. "They are dreams of, by, and for solitaries: John Waynes and Horatio Algers, prospectors and entrepreneurs," whereas true emancipation historically has been a matter of community achievement.[11]

Dreaming was woven into the fabric of Reagan's speeches and commentaries from beginning to end. From his 1964 speech for Barry Goldwater in the latter's run for the presidency, which launched Reagan in politics, throughout his later career, Reagan's rhetoric was peppered with references to dreams: In his 1983 celebration of the bicentennial of air and space flight, he said, "God gave angels wings. He gave mankind dreams. And with His help, there's no limit to what can be accomplished." In his second inaugural address, he declared, "We believed then and now: There are no limits to growth and human progress when men and women are free to follow their dreams." And on his last day in office, in a Presidential Medal of Freedom ceremony, he asserted, "While other countries cling to the stale past, here in America we breathe life into dreams."[12] The very last words he addressed to the American people likewise bespoke this tendency. His 1994 handwritten open letter informing them of his oncoming Alzheimer's ended with these touching words: "I now begin the journey that will lead me into the sunset of my life. I know that for America there will always be a bright dream ahead. Thank you my friends. May God always bless you."[13]

The bright-eyed dreamer who had begun life as a small-town boy in the Middle West had made many stops along the way on his journey to becoming the most powerful man in the world. As a boy he had dreamed of being a football star, of winning a girl, then of going to college, and later of becoming an actor. Tempering his ambitions with a dose of reality, he stated his hope of becoming a radio announcer. After he made it to Hollywood, he dreamed of bigger roles, larger paydays, and playing in westerns. As time went by, he imagined corralling Communists, rolling back bloated government, and perhaps playing a role like his friend Jimmy Stewart in *Mr. Smith Goes to Washington*. When the opportunity arose to step onto the political stage, he eagerly seized it. Later, he offered little resistance to wealthy friends who suggested that he, whose only political experience had been as a Hollywood union leader, run for the governorship of the largest state in the Union. Even before starting on that quest, his eye was on the White House, which, on the third try, he achieved. In Washington, he dreamed of slashing taxes, cutting back government spending and regulations, squashing the Soviet Union, building an impregnable antimissile space shield, and eventually eliminating all nuclear weaponry. His reach always exceeded his grasp, but what he did accomplish was considerable, more than many had expected. Those who underestimated him—and the list was extensive—often learned to their regret that he possessed uncommon talents and tenacity, which became obvious only in retrospect. Being human, he also harbored a healthy quantity of faults and shortcomings.

Reagan's identity needs to be understood as a continual work in progress, for he was never a single thing—never simply a small-town boy from Dixon or a fire-eating anti-Communist crusader, not just a B-movie actor or TV pitchman, not merely a naive liberal do-gooder or right-wing ideologue, not simply a pragmatic politico or courageous political leader, not just a practiced reader of lines or Superman-type hero. His was a constructed identity, generally fashioned unconsciously, molded by circumstances, and channeling itself into paths of least resistance and biggest payoffs. Reagan was a protean American seeker—ambitious, resourceful, idealistic when practically able, and corner-cutting when necessary. His boyish good looks, boy-next-door demeanor, enthusiasm, unpretentiousness, and malleable behavior helped him fit in wherever he went. His mask of amiability concealed a core of intensity and tenacity that many failed to appreciate. His adult personality emerged originally out of his childhood tendencies, hopes, hurts, and dreams, but it did not progress predictably or in a straight line.

Reagan's boyhood in small-town Illinois did much to shape his adult personality. But it was only one of many influences operating on him, and it worked in contradictory ways. Before Dixon, he had called three other small towns in northern Illinois home, with a brief detour through Chicago. The disorienting experience of attending four different schools in four years at one point left him somewhat shy and withdrawn, inclined to play by himself, immerse himself in nature, and indulge in fantasy and books. Having learned to read with the help of his mother at the age of five before going off to school, he regularly checked two books a week out of the town library, establishing a lifelong habit of reading. But he was never a bookworm or an intellectual. Growing up during the golden age of sports in the 1920s, his ambitions hinged more on glory on the gridiron.[14]

Reagan was nine, going on ten, when his family arrived in Dixon, a town of around 8,000 people, in December 1920, a few months after Sinclair Lewis published *Main Street*. Often described as a typical farm market town, Dixon was more than that. It was a generally blue-collar, lower-middle-class community with considerable industry, including a large milk-condensing plant and a plow factory. It was also the county seat and home to a teachers college. Its signature landmark was a large arch extending across the town's major thoroughfare with the letters *D-I-X-O-N* emblazoned on it, erected in honor of World War I veterans. Young "Dutch," as he preferred to be called, his parents, and his brother Neil (called "Moon"), two and a half years older, moved into a rented two-story frame house on the south side of Rock River, which bisected the community. Although today the house stands as a historical site commemorating the fortieth president, the family had not stopped its moving around and lived in several other places in town before Ronald graduated from high school.[15]

His father, Jack Reagan, was an Irish Catholic shoe salesman, a driven and restless man whose large ambitions were continually frustrated. He had not finished grade school, but he dreamed of owning the largest shoe store in Illinois outside of Chicago, though he never seemed to catch a break. Tall, handsome, and possessed of dramatic flair, he was a captivating storyteller and was called by his younger son "the best raconteur I ever heard." In his post-presidential autobiography, *An American Life*, Reagan would write, "I learned from my father the value of hard work and ambition, and maybe a little bit about telling a story." He also learned about racial tolerance and common decency, for Jack Reagan was a fierce critic of the Ku Klux Klan and was notably outspoken in his advocacy of racial tolerance and general good will toward his fellow human beings. He was also "a sentimental Democrat," a proclivity reinforced by his experience during the Great Depression, when he became chief New Deal relief administrator for Dixon. What reinforced his lifelong devotion to his party also kindled in his son strong admiration for Franklin Roosevelt and the New Deal. But that would undergo partial change as time went by.[16]

Charismatic when sober, Jack Reagan suffered from a weakness for the bottle. While he was capable of abstaining for months, his wife and sons always lived in fear of the time when he would fall off the wagon and go on a spree. Never violent, he could nevertheless be mean and surly when that happened. Reagan often told the story of returning home one evening at age eleven to discover his father lying drunk on the front porch and of managing to get him into the house and put him to bed. His first inclination had been to pretend that his father was not there, but instead he accepted his duty and helped him. Studies show that many children of alcoholics suffer from low self-esteem and find it difficult to form intimate relationships, and they are often prone to denying reality, to creating fantasy worlds for themselves, and to withdrawing from society. Neil was extroverted, ran around with a gang of rowdy boys, and developed a reputation as a great promoter; his younger brother turned out quiet, modest, and self-conscious as an early elementary school student. "As a kid I lived in a world of pretend," Reagan later told a Hollywood magazine writer, "I had a great imagination . . . and I used to love to make up plays and act in them myself . . . but I soon got self-conscious."[17]

Young Ronald's penchant for playacting probably served as compensation for anxieties triggered by his father's affliction. It also drew him closer to his mother, Nelle, the parent most influential on his developing personality. That he would later refer to his wife Nancy, the only person he felt comfortable confiding in, as "Mommy" is highly suggestive. Reagan was a mama's boy. Nelle Reagan was in many ways the opposite of her husband. A devout member of the Disciples of Christ and fiercely opposed to drink, she drilled it into her boys that their father was a sick man, not a bad one. A do-gooder to her core, she constantly engaged in benevolent projects, teaching Bible classes, leading songs at church, and assisting neighbors more poverty-stricken than she. She instilled in Ronald the conviction that God makes everything happen for a purpose, and from her he obtained his spiritual outlook, ingrained optimism, and cheerfulness.[18]

Beyond her devotion to the church and good works, she possessed two other passions. One was for the stage, and this, too, she passed on to her son. She got him started early performing in skits and doing readings for dramatic recitals that she organized, and he quickly discovered that he enjoyed it. She also was a firm believer in education, although she, like her husband, had not progressed beyond elementary school. So while Ronald never became an outstanding student, he did understand the importance of education. He would say, "From my mother, I learned the value of prayer, how to have dreams and believe I could make them come true."[19]

The dreams that ran through schoolboy Reagan's mind as he proceeded through elementary school and on into high school revolved largely around four things: football, swimming, girls, and acting. Ronald was never much good at baseball, he discovered later, because he was very nearsighted and could not see a pitched ball as much more than a blur. Learning at around age thirteen of his condition and that corrective lenses could bring the world around him into focus was a revelation. His difficulties trying to hit a baseball turned his passion toward football; he hoped to become a star. Because he had skipped a year in grade school, he was small as a freshman, and his diminutive size (5'3" and 108 pounds) barred him from fulfilling his dreams of glory on the field. But he blossomed as a junior and managed to make the starting team partway through the year. He played guard and end during his senior year on a losing team, but he never became a star.

He was an exceptionally good swimmer, however, and put the skill to good use as a lifeguard at Lowell Park on Rock River during the summertime. He took great pride in the hard work and long hours he put in during seven summers while he was in high school and college. More important, he assumed an identity as a "rescuer" by notching seventy-seven life-saving rescues during that period. Ronald never studied hard enough to become an outstanding student, but his exceptional memory enabled him to slide by in his classes without exerting much effort. Instead, he poured his energies into a variety of extracurricular activities, starting in high school, including Hi-Y, a YMCA affiliate for teenage boys, and work on the school yearbook, culminating in his election as student body president. Of greater significance for him was participating in school plays. The formerly shy fellow also obtained a girlfriend, the daughter of the pastor of the Christian church he attended, and he went along with her to college, too. Her name was Margaret Cleaver, and during the six years they went together, they both assumed they would eventually get married. When she broke off the relationship after graduation, he was devastated.[20]

College turned out to be more of the same, but better. At a time when only about four out of ten young people graduated from high school and one in fifteen graduated from college, Reagan was determined to enroll, although it required hard work and determined saving during the summer, some fancy financial footwork, and a bit of luck to accomplish it. He loved Eureka College and would remember this period between 1928 and 1932, during which the country slid into deep economic depression, as the happiest time of his life. In later years he returned a dozen times to Eureka to deliver speeches, receive awards, and reminisce about the good times he had experienced there. There was Margaret (they were still in love), there was football (he was a starting guard on the team in his final two and a half years), there was swimming (he was both the star and the coach, for a time, of the team), there were even more extracurricular activities than in high school (including the presidency of the Booster Club and of the student council), and, most of all, there was dramatics. Little if any time was left for studying. He chose to major in economics apparently because the professor was a notoriously lax grader. Lou Cannon notes that neither in his interviews with Reagan nor in Reagan's autobiography was there a single story about his classroom experience at Eureka. It was a small institution of fewer than 250 students; everything the students did was considerably magnified in scale, providing room for many to shine. The town itself, located 90 miles southeast of Dixon, was only about one-fifth the size of his hometown. "Oh, it was a small town, a small school, with small doings," Reagan would later write. It was here that he exhibited his first feats of political oratory, and he also gave an indication of a budding interest in politics.[21]

In a place with hardly more than a hundred male students, he was able to play a significant, even though not distinguished, role on the gridiron, but on stage he could be a star. Acting in seven plays during the four years he was there, he usually played the lead roles. In a one-act play contest at Northwestern University during his junior year, the cast captured second place in the competition, and Reagan received a special award for his acting. The director of the Northwestern program suggested that he might want to consider acting as a career. From then on, without letting anyone know for fear they might think him delusional, he cultivated the dream of becoming an actor. Playing football and acting were fostering in him "a personality schizo-split between sports and the stage," he would write. "The fact was, I suppose, that I just like showing off."[22]

In 1932, straight out of college, the brand-new graduate started looking for a job during the worst economic climate in the nation's history. Displaying the kind of resourcefulness—and luck—that would characterize him throughout his career, he landed a job as an announcer at Davenport, Iowa, radio station WOC. They soon transferred him to their partner outlet, WHO in Des Moines, which recently had been elevated to a 50,000-watt, clear-channel station whose reach extended to six states around. Not yet ready to make an assault on Hollywood, he considered radio to be a useful launching pad toward his ultimate goal of becoming an actor. He quickly emerged as a popular personality on the air, with a distinctive and appealing voice that made him well-known throughout much of the Middle West. During five years in Des Moines, a small city of about 140,000 people, he broadcast about 45 football games from most of the major press boxes in the region and nearly 600 major-league baseball games, as well as numerous track and swim meets. In addition, he interviewed celebrity guests, including evangelist Aimee Semple McPherson, filled in as a general announcer for the station, and wrote a weekly sports column for the *Des Moines Dispatch*.[23]

He was best known for announcing home games of the Chicago Cubs and White Sox, taking brief summaries of the action off a ticker and translating and embellishing them into full-blown, play-by-play descriptions of the action. He became expert at filling in information about the weather, the fans in the stands, and the actions of the players on the field. All of this was almost entirely made up, so it required a lively imagination and a glib tongue as well as quick thinking and steady nerves to make it all believable. Reagan never tired of telling the story about the day the tape went

dead on him just as Billy Jurges was at bat and how in waiting for it to re-
activate he described the Cubs infielder fouling off seventeen pitches (or
was it a few more or less?). Sometimes the batter turned into Augie Galan.
But no matter, he would chuckle, it was all good fun. Thus, even in telling
the story, he would make up facts and numbers so convincingly that he
would keep his listeners smiling and on the edge of their seats.[24] What his
years between twenty-two and twenty-six provided were experience, self-
confidence, a bit of financial stability, and extended practice at maintaining
a patter and calling on his imagination to create fanciful pictures of reality.
Dutch Reagan's audience for the broadcasts beamed out from Des Moines
was predominantly small-town midwesterners living in Iowa and nearby
states. In the process he gained valuable experience in communicating with
ordinary Americans who one day would go into the voting booths to cast
their ballots for or against him. As a popular speaker who received invitations to address scores of Kiwanis, Lions, and Rotary Clubs, he became a
practiced platform speaker and stage performer.

The dream of launching an acting career persisted. In the spring of 1937
he did something about it when he convinced the Cubs to send him to
spring training with the team on Catalina island, near Los Angeles, so he
could better get to know the players he was describing on air. They agreed
to the idea, and, without informing them, he took several days off to visit
Los Angeles. There he looked up Joy Hodges, whom he had met earlier in
Des Moines and who was now an aspiring actress doing some work at the
studios. She put him in contact with her agent, who arranged a screen test
for Reagan. In quick order, the twenty-six-year-old radio announcer from
Des Moines was offered a seven-year contract by Warner Brothers at $200
a month. The studio could opt out of the deal if Reagan proved a dud, but
he did not. Within a week after arriving on the movie lot, he was acting in
his first screen role in a B-film, *Love Is in the Air*, playing, not surprisingly,
a radio announcer.[25]

Until 1942, when he entered the wartime army, most of his roles remained relatively undemanding, consisting almost entirely of two types—
friendly boy-next-door characters, on the one hand, and government
agents and action heroes, on the other. Several times he was cast as a sports
announcer. Jack Warner perceived star potential in him, but studio execs
estimated that only one in ten contract players ever rose to top billing in A-
grade features. Reagan climbed the ladder more quickly than most, although never fast enough to match his expansive ambitions. He was aided

by his steady habits, willingness to follow direction, ability to memorize lines, and strong work ethic. It did not hurt that Hollywood celebrity journalist Louella Parsons, who also hailed from Dixon, quickly became his champion. What he lacked, unfortunately, despite his good looks and pleasing screen personality, was that distinctive spark or killer appeal that translated directly into box office hits.[26]

Before World War II came along, Reagan continued to hope that he could move up into regular starring roles in A films. His biggest on-screen successes were a brief but impressive portrayal of Notre Dame running back George Gipp in *Knute Rockne—All American*, a role that he had lobbied vigorously to obtain, and the role of Drake McHugh in *Kings Row*, Warner's biggest hit of 1942. The latter turned out to be Reagan's most impressive performance in his fifty-four-movie career. It led to a tripling of his salary when his agent, Lew Wasserman, was able to obtain for him the first million-dollar contract in Hollywood history (stretched out over seven years). After a three-year wartime hiatus, however, Reagan grew increasingly frustrated as his movie career steadily slid downhill just as his first wife, Jane Wyman, was moving into Oscar-winning territory.[27]

The late 1940s and early 1950s were a challenging period for the actor, a period during which he watched his career steadily decline and his marriage disintegrate. Meanwhile, his interest in politics blossomed, and he gained useful experience in the practical side of it and in organizational leadership while serving five one-year stints as president of the Screen Actors Guild (SAG). These were the years of the Communist controversy in Hollywood as well as in Washington, D.C., and Reagan began a slow, difficult transition from being a self-proclaimed "hemophiliac liberal" to an unreconstructed right-wing conservative. In addition to battling Communists in Hollywood—he was important enough as an in-house spy for the FBI that it assigned him a personal identification number ("T-10")—several other things pushed Reagan rightward. These included frustrations in dealing with the military bureaucracy during World War II; the pain caused when his new contract and elevated wartime tax rates pushed him into the 91 percent marginal tax bracket; conversations with the archconservative father-in-law he acquired by marrying actress Nancy Davis; and finally, his experience working as a corporate representative in connection with the *General Electric Theater* television program between 1954 and 1962. From being associated during the 1940s with several liberal and left-wing organizations, from Americans for Democratic Action and the American

Veterans Committee to the Hollywood Independent Citizens Committee of the Arts, Sciences and Professions, Reagan by the end of the 1950s was cozying up to the newly organized John Birch Society and to Fred Schwarz's Christian Anti-Communist Crusade. What his Hollywood experience did for him, in sum, was to further hone his speaking and communication skills, stimulate him to read extensively and educate himself about government and politics, and develop his negotiating skills through his stint as head of the actors' union. (He quipped that after presiding over the Screen Actors Guild, dealing with Soviet leader Gorbachev was a snap.)[28]

During the early 1950s, as he moved into his forties and as competition from television was forcing major changes in the film industry, Reagan received fewer and fewer film roles to his liking and made little progress in convincing the studios to let him act in westerns (Wasserman had renegotiated his contract with Warner's, allowing him to freelance). After completing a demeaning emcee gig in Las Vegas and vowing never to do anything like that again, in 1954 he grabbed at an opportunity to host the new *General Electric Theater*, which paid a lucrative $125,000 a year (soon raised to $150,000). Two years earlier, as president of SAG, Reagan had signed a blanket waiver allowing Wasserman's Music Corporation of America (MCA) to enter TV production in addition to representing actors, which had been its original purpose, an action that afterward "haunted Reagan's reputation in Hollywood," according to Lou Cannon. Generating little publicity at the time, the deal, which granted MCA a partial monopoly over recruitment and production in the movie capital, came under increasing scrutiny in subsequent years, and in 1962 Attorney General Robert F. Kennedy's Justice Department investigated it for possible antitrust violations. Called in to testify, Reagan attempted to justify SAG's favoritism toward MCA, denying any conflict of interest. At many points in the questioning he indicated that he could not remember the details of the agreement. Although his explanations often appeared evasive and contradictory, the Justice Department failed to bring an indictment. Soon afterward, General Electric canceled *General Electric Theater*, abruptly severing its eight-year relationship with Reagan. Many figured the break was because the program was losing in the ratings to the new hit western *Bonanza*, but some suspected that it had more to do with the MCA investigation.[29]

The eight years that Reagan spent working for GE were among the most formative of his career, for they provided him, in effect, with an apprenticeship in politics. In his own words, the period constituted "almost a postgraduate course in political science" for him.[30] During this time he developed and solidified his political views, completed his migration from liberalism to conservatism, nurtured a growing desire to step onto the political stage, and cultivated friendships with potential supporters around the country. He grew especially close to a group of wealthy Californians who would come to be known as his "kitchen cabinet." The deal Wasserman had negotiated for him in 1954 called for Reagan to host the half-hour program weekly and to act in several episodes each year. The show, airing at nine on Sunday evenings, soon shot up in the ratings to number one in its time slot and was one of the most popular and profitable offerings on the air. More important for Reagan, however, were the additional duties he was assigned to represent the company as a goodwill ambassador, visiting all 139 GE plants in forty states and speaking to its quarter million employees in an effort to link them more closely to company management. Touring the country, he was in a sense returning to his roots, because the types of people he met and talked to daily in the factories and on the podium were, as he described them to one person, "very different people than the people Hollywood was talking about. I was seeing the same people that I grew up with in Dixon, Illinois. I realized I was living in a tinsel factory. And this exposure brought me back."[31] The tours also tied him much more closely to business opinion and attitudes. More specifically, they reinforced his sympathies for the military-industrial complex, of which General Electric was a crucial member.[32]

In effect an eight-year seminar in business's way of thinking and operating, the GE years had two lasting results. In the first place, his close relationships with company president Ralph Cordiner, one of the country's most influential CEOs, and, even more important, with Lemuel Boulware, vice president in charge of personnel, public, and community relations, bolstered his knowledge and awareness of business and economic practices and conditions. They helped transform, fix, and further articulate his economic and political views. Boulware's well-thought-out theories of labor-management relations and of the ways business could get its message across to its own workers, to political leaders, and to the general public influenced a whole generation of business managers and corporate consultants.

"Boulwarism," a term coined by a *Fortune* magazine writer that became popular during the 1950s, referred both to a pro-business ideology that stated a vision of what America should be and to a methodology by which that goal could be achieved. Boulware denied that he was antiunion but argued that many of the goals that organized labor was trying to achieve were linked to an insidious program of socialism that itself was dangerously close to communism. The GE executive viewed himself as a teacher determined to enlighten people about the conspicuous benefits of free-market capitalism, the virtues of competition and entrepreneurship, and the hazards of constricting government regulations and excessive taxes. His program at GE involved a variety of in-house publications, public speaking by himself and others, the formation of alliances with other business leaders, and collaboration with politicians and government officials to reduce the size of government. Boulware's famous speech "Salvation Is Not Free," delivered to a group of graduating students and alumni at the Harvard Business School in June 1949, laid out the message that he would preach over and over again in a variety of forums during the following decade—the years that Reagan would be associated with the company. In many ways, the speech served as an inspiration and model for the speech that the former actor would gradually develop during those years and use to launch his political career in October 1964.[33]

The second, more visible result of Reagan's eight years with GE was his budding talent on the speaking platform. Early on, his talks to local service organizations and informal chats with company employees, often consisting primarily of insider anecdotes and stories about life in Hollywood, impressed company officials, who had not fully realized his speaking talents. The bigwigs supported and encouraged their new company spokesman as he increasingly turned his attention to excessive government taxation and intrusion in the marketplace, the Communist menace, and the virtues of patriotism and freedom. By the late 1950s and early 1960s, Reagan emerged as one of the most sought after convention speakers in the country, and GE benefited from the spillover of his popularity. As he traveled by train around the country three months every year, he read constantly, clipping articles and statistics from newspapers and magazines such as *Human Events, National Review,* and *Reader's Digest*. He integrated the information into his talks, all of which were variations on the same themes and which eventually became known simply as "The Speech." By the time he left General Electric in 1962, hundreds, perhaps thousands, of audiences had heard it in one of its many variations.[34]

Two years after departing the company, while serving as cochair of the

Goldwater presidential campaign in California, Reagan was primed and ready when a group of wealthy California business friends arranged for him to present "The Speech" at a GOP fund-raiser in Los Angeles. The performance was such a smash hit that they convinced the Republican National Committee to purchase coast-to-coast television time so the entire nation could listen to their man's pitch for Arizona's Senator Goldwater. Besides raising $8 million for the party's coffers, Reagan's half-hour address, entitled "A Time for Choosing," instantly established him as a national political star and led directly to his candidacy for the California governorship two years later.[35]

Reagan's million-vote trouncing of two-term incumbent Pat Brown in November 1966 could be interpreted as the result of one unique individual's impressive charisma, policy stances, and campaign skills. The former movie actor certainly did demonstrate formidable political talent. But the conservative takeover of the state that year also depended on a host of converging variables, setting the stage for Reagan's equally successful run for the presidency fourteen years later, when a similar alignment of favorable trends worked to the advantage of the Republicans. Reagan's win in 1966 was especially ironic considering the huge drubbing dealt Barry Goldwater by Lyndon Johnson two years earlier, after which many respectable pundits seriously discussed whether the Republicans would survive as a viable political party. By 1966, however, growing public disaffection with Johnson's war policies, civil rights legislation, Great Society expenditures, and governmental expansion was occasioning considerable voter backlash. While many youthful protestors and some of their older confederates were drifting toward a "new politics," large segments of the population were beginning to react against unfamiliar lifestyles, a burgeoning drug culture, evolving sexual mores, and, in some minds, anarchy.[36]

Reagan played on those fears and concerns while running for governor in 1966, focusing especially on student protestors at the Berkeley campus of the University of California and making reference to sexual "orgies" and other unconventional behaviors and criminal activities. Just as Richard Nixon would campaign for the presidency two years later by appealing to what he called the "silent majority," Reagan in 1966 reached out to those he referred to as "forgotten Americans." Later, in campaigning for the White House, he would benefit substantially from a whole new political infrastructure of conservative think tanks, magazines, journals, political action committees, academic organizations, political columnists, and talk-radio hosts. By 1966, at least some of this array was beginning to come into place. Most important, perhaps, William F. Buckley's *National Review* magazine had been in operation for a little more than a decade as a rallying point for conservatives of all stripes. Reagan also profited from splits in the California Democratic Party and from the public's weariness with Governor Pat Brown and concern about the financial strains that were beginning to become apparent in the state's budget.[37]

Beyond that, candidate Reagan enjoyed the financial backing of a group of wealthy friends, some of whom he had known for a quarter of a century. He and Justin Dart, a multimillionaire drugstore magnate, had been acquainted since 1940. Others in his emerging kitchen cabinet of advisers, whom he would heavily rely on for staffing his administration, financing his campaigns, and developing his legislative programs, included Holmes Tuttle, a Ford dealer he had known since buying a car from him in 1946; oil developer Henry Salvatori; and Cy Rubel, chairman of Union Oil. Also included were publisher Walter Annenberg, Diners Club founder Alfred Bloomingdale, and nursing home millionaire Charles Wick. Many of these men and their wives were part of a cozy little circle of friends who met frequently in each others' homes, including the Reagans', for meals, conversation, and entertainment. In addition to money and friendship, they extended him advice, encouragement, and a healthy push in their effort to achieve the conservative, free-market goals they hoped to incorporate at both the state and national levels. Like the man they were backing, they had their eyes more on Washington than on Sacramento from the very beginning. The "citizen-politician" who proclaimed himself to be a "populist" governor was in fact much more oriented toward the ideas and goals of a small clique of extremely wealthy businessmen without whom he would have had much greater difficulty in obtaining high office.[38]

They arranged to bring in the highly talented Spencer-Roberts political management firm, which had previously orchestrated liberal Republican Nelson Rockefeller's presidential nomination campaign. They also hired a couple of behavioral psychologists to retool the candidate. Just as he would be during his eight years as governor and eight years in the White House, Reagan was very much a manufactured and managed candidate who was provided with briefing papers, scripts, talking points, and other advice to help keep him on the right track and in the right psychological mood. "Despite his cosmopolitan surroundings in Hollywood, he was still parochial in his views and tastes," writes Garry Wills. That was the challenge they all faced in grooming him for the campaign trail. "He lived in a small world he had carried with him from Dixon and Eureka, Davenport and Des Moines. He knew only part of America, and practically nothing of the rest of the world. But he was sure his part of America was the best part of the world's best people."[39]

But if the newly minted politician remained in some ways in thrall to his small-town midwestern past, he continued to grow and evolve in the governorship and later during his presidency, just as he had always done. Change marked his life, along with continuity. Though the small-town imprint never left him, the Hollywood experience, in many ways, became his primary point of reference. In truth, during the years after arriving in Hollywood in 1937, he became more of a westerner in habit and attitude than a midwesterner. Riding horses, which he had learned to do in Des Moines, became his primary form of relaxation and recreation. He eventually bought four different ranches in the Los Angeles area, and while president he spent 345 days at his beloved Rancho del Cielo (Ranch in the Sky) northwest of Santa Barbara.[40]

He had lobbied hard for western roles as an actor; he envied John Wayne's image. Aside from presidential pinstripes, the outfit most people associated with him consisted of chaps and a slouch hat or cowboy hat. He intuited what Henry Kissinger once observed: "Americans like the cowboy who leads the wagon train by riding ahead alone on his horse, the cowboy who rides alone into the town, the village, with his horse and nothing else."[41] Fittingly, the entrance to his presidential library in Simi Valley would later feature a larger-than-life-size statue of him in cowboy regalia. The western persona, constructed though it was, proved comfortable and natural for him. It fit observers' image of him as a crusader for freedom, self-determination, and law and order.[42]

In moving to California, Reagan adapted completely to the new way of life he found there. Though he waxed nostalgic at times about boyhood days in Illinois and though in his memoirs he emphasized the impact of his hometown on his psyche, in his actions Reagan gave little indication that they really mattered very much to him as an adult. He had become an adoptive Californian, with all that term implies. "Reagan evidenced no sense of geographical identity or family tradition," writes Haynes Johnson. "He was western, not eastern, in thought and impulse and action."[43] The western imagery he adopted for himself coincided with a major postwar historical shift that occurred in the United States after World War II and was one of the most potent factors in Reagan's political success—the rise of the Sunbelt or Southern Rim.[44] In the meantime, as his native Midwest's population growth slackened and the region lost political representation in Congress, its industrial economy faltered, earning it the name "Rust Belt," and its cultural cachet declined in relation to the two coasts.

Reagan ran both for governor and for president as a change maker and even as a revolutionary, bringing controversy and conflict along with him as a result. Upwards of a thousand books have been written about him, the people around him, and the movement he championed. It would take far more space than is available here to trace his political record and leadership style in any detail. He, like every other person discussed in this book, was able to make a major impact on his chosen field of endeavor, but he had to operate, in large part, within prescribed channels and under significant constraints. The man who ran for governor to slash taxes, curtail government regulations, and transform culture wound up as a much more pragmatic administrator in practice than he had sounded like as a candidate. Facing a huge inherited budget crunch during his first year in Sacramento, he found himself pushing through the largest tax increase in the state's (or any state's) history during his first term of office in his attempt to balance the budget. Afterward, he continued to try to reduce taxes and expenditures. After calling for and obtaining the resignation of University of California president Clark Kerr, Reagan wound up providing substantially increased subsidies for the university system. While continuing to push his conservative agenda along many fronts, he also completed his second term in office with actions much applauded by environmentalists and tax and welfare reformers. His governorship proved to be a time of learning, and his rhetoric turned out to be far more radical than his practice. What Reagan was, it is clear, was a master of political symbolism. In saying that, I am not implying anything different about him than what can be said about most other politicians in this day and age.[45]

In the White House, he ramped up the symbolic offensive, honed the rhetoric, and paraded his ideology in aggressive terms. Once again, he proved to be more moderate and practical in his actions than he seemed to promise in his speeches. Of course, many of his policy positions and actions stimulated huge controversy. The tax cuts of 1981 (followed by several large tax increases in subsequent years), the massive defense buildup, the stripping down of government regulatory activity, not always successful efforts to roll back spending in many areas, the escalation of covert and overt military activities around the globe—these made news and riled up enemies. Despite the stridency and seeming single-mindedness of his antigovernment rhetoric, his critical contribution was less in the realm of concrete achievement in cutting back governmental functions than in changing the terms of the political debate. Ultimately, his primary legacy will probably be his willingness to engage in dialogue with Gorbachev and the subsequent ending of the Cold War and collapse of the Soviet Union. Did Reagan deserve major credit for that outcome, or were broader historical forces operating at the time primarily responsible for it? Historians will debate the matter for decades.[46]

Reagan continued to be underestimated in Washington just as he had been all along the way. In recent years, liberal historians such as Sean Wilentz and John Patrick Diggins, despite deep reservations about many of his actions and policies, have joined their conservative counterparts in elevating Reagan to the level of Lincoln and the second Roosevelt in the pantheon of American presidents. The historical profession as a whole still has not come around to that high estimate.[47]

Reagan, the small-town boy from the Midwest, owed much of his success to his regional origins, less because of the attributes and qualities of character that his background in the heartland nurtured in him than because of the opportunity it provided him to apply the lessons of public relations and mythmaking he had absorbed in his new home, Hollywood. The viewing public found it easy to transfer their identification with the sunny, optimistic roles he generally played on screen and his seemingly straightforward midwestern personality to the president who told them it was "morning in America" as he campaigned for office. "America, at least for a season," observes Sidney Blumenthal, "became a small town where the ideology assumed human shape." The California politician had, in a sense, become the personification of home. "Home, in Reaganite mythology," writes Wilentz, "was a re-created bygone place of close-knit families and neighbors," whether it came in the form of a small town like Bedford Falls in Frank Capra's *It's a Wonderful Life,* a big-city ethnic neighborhood, or Laura Ingalls Wilder's *Little Town on the Prairie.*[48]

But while the public's attraction to small-town imagery and mythology helped get Reagan installed in the White House, his memories of growing up in Dixon and several other little towns in Illinois did little to concretely shape his thinking or to affect his policies once in office. Like other presidents of his era, he tended to focus his attention on global issues, foreign crises, economic growth, budgetary policy, and urban problems. Small towns remained a low priority, when they were thought of at all. More to the point, his policies of tax cuts for the affluent, corporate deregulation, and privatization of governmental functions often worked to the detriment of rural towns and contributed to a declining sense of community around the United States, which has been noted by many observers.[49] Eight or nine decades earlier, it had still been possible for a presidential candidate, such as William Jennings Bryan, to run for the highest office in the land as a champion of rural/small-town America. By the late twentieth century, such a campaign was hardly conceivable due to the precipitate falloff in the nation's rural population and to the relative decline in the status of its small towns.

■

CHAPTER SEVENTEEN

Sam Walton: Main Street Shopkeeper Turned Global Behemoth

Sam Walton will be remembered, or should be, as the Henry Ford of mass merchandising. . . . Between them, they changed the way we live, for better or for worse. Under the heading of Unintended Consequences comes the irony that Sam and his imitators have probably done more than anything since Henry and his imitators to destroy the small-town America both revolutionists loved. Henry re-created his love in Dearborn. Sam lived his in Bentonville. . . . No use whining about it, I suppose. It's the American Way, isn't it? Progress and all that.

—*Columbia Missourian* editorial, 1992

The story of Sam Walton and Wal-Mart[1]—one of the most extraordinary, compelling, and conflicted odysseys in the history of American business— has "small town" written all over it. Beginning in 1962 with a single store in a small town in the Ozark Mountains of northwestern Arkansas, the chain of discount outlets expanded exponentially to 32 stores by the end of the decade, 276 in 1980, 1,528 in 1990, 3,985 worldwide in 2000, and 8,416 worldwide in 2010 (4,304 of them in the United States). By then, it had moved beyond the small towns that had been its almost exclusive habitat during its first two decades of existence to conquer many of the nation's cities and was operating stores in all fifty states and in fifteen foreign countries.

By the end of the first decade of the twenty-first century, on annual sales of $405 billion, netting profits of more than $14 billion, the company contributed approximately 2.7 percent of the U.S. gross domestic product. The behemoth that is Wal-Mart emerged as the global economy's largest company, its 2.1 million employees worldwide (1.4 million in the United States) making it by far the world's largest private employer, and it had become perhaps the world's most powerful agent of economic change.[2] It was the pacesetter for a retail revolution that, in the words of one analyst, has "transformed the nature of U.S. employment, sent U.S. manufacturing abroad, and redefined the very meaning of globalization." It now stands, some have said, as the template for twenty-first-century capitalism.[3]

Its founder, creative genius, and indefatigable leader, until his death from bone cancer at the age of seventy-four in 1992, was Sam Walton—better known to his fellow company executives, Wal-Mart "associates" (the name he gave his employees), and the world at large as "Mr. Sam." Born in a small town in central Oklahoma, he grew up in a series of Missouri towns and continued to live in similar places all his life. For several decades, he deliberately located his stores in small towns that other discounters avoided and sought out managers with small-town backgrounds similar to his own. Visionary, expansive, innovative, and inspirational, he was also hard-headed, demanding, relentless, and often ruthless in his drive to make his brainchild the most efficient, effective, and smooth-running business machine possible. From a start as a regional discount retailer, he built Wal-Mart into one of the largest firms in the United States by the time of his death and witnessed the beginnings of its expansion overseas. In the process, his company unintentionally did more to undermine the economic underpinnings of small-town Main Streets than any other single force in the second half of the twentieth century. Smiling guilelessly all the while, genial, grandfatherly Mr. Sam vehemently denied that he and Wal-Mart bore any responsibility for the transformation they were bringing to rural America.

The key to Walton's early success as a seller of general merchandise was his initial bold—some said foolhardy—decision to plant his stores in rural towns that rivals like Kmart and Target disdained because of their presumed dearth of purchasing power. Later on, he became recognized as a merchandising genius for observing that there was "much, much more business out there in small-town America than anybody, including me, had ever dreamed of."[4] Had the choice of where to locate been his alone at the outset, he would have invested his energies in an urban setting, not a rural one. His wife Helen had different ideas, however. Returning to civilian life after World War II, the twenty-seven-year-old Missourian was all set to enter into a partnership with a former college roommate to start a Federated Department Store in St. Louis, Missouri, when Helen intervened. She told her husband that she wanted them to remain independent and not be tied down with a partner in the business. More to the point, she refused to live in a "big city," insisting that they look for a place that had less than 10,000 people. Respecting her wishes, Sam went searching for a location in northern Arkansas, settling on Newport, a cotton town and county seat of about 7,000 population in the Mississippi River Delta, 80 miles northeast of Little Rock and situated on the edge of the Ozarks. Forgoing his chance to become an urban entrepreneur, Sam Walton pursued his dream of business success in the kinds of small towns that he had become intimately familiar with while growing up in central Missouri.[5]

Throughout his life, people associated Walton with the small-town way of life, and he, too, was quick to identify himself as a small-towner. Living in Bentonville, Arkansas, after 1950, he made a point of driving old cars and beat-up pickups—often with bird dogs yelping in the rear—reinforcing an image he constructed for himself as a regular, unpretentious fellow, unaffected by wealth and power. He cultivated a persona as an unsophisticated, small-town rustic and delighted in surprising eastern reporters and business representatives with his down-home ways and modest lifestyle. Insisting also on a frugal, no-frills mode of operation for his company, he was ostentatiously unostentatious in paring costs to the bone in his stores and at his Bentonville company headquarters. He made this commitment to cheapness a core principle of Wal-Mart's corporate culture. "Some of this culture grew naturally out of our small-town beginnings," he noted in his autobiography, written shortly before he died.[6] Walton's values became the company's values. Don Soderquist, who rose through Wal-Mart's ranks to become vice chairman and chief operating officer, wrote in The Wal-

Mart Way of his and his fellow executives' efforts to maintain those small-town values.[7] More than any other high-profile businessman in the twentieth century, Walton reveled in his identity as a small-town boy. "Sam Walton's personality was very much small-town, and though he became the wealthiest man in America he clung tenaciously to his country roots, preferring to live more like a commoner than a king," observes business writer Robert Slater.[8]

Although Samuel Moore Walton was born in the tiny town of Kingfisher, Oklahoma, 30 miles northwest of Oklahoma City, on March 29, 1918, he was really more of a Missouri boy than an Oklahoman. The Walton family, originally from Virginia, arrived in Missouri in 1838, when William P. Walton began farming in the central part of the state. His son Samuel W.—Sam Walton's grandfather—opened a small general store there before moving to Webster County, east of Springfield, Missouri, where he also served as local postmaster and engaged in the fruit and lumber businesses, along with running a general store. (Webster County lies directly west of Wright County, where Laura Ingalls Wilder—famed depicter of frontier, small-town America—lived the last sixty-three years of her life.) His entrepreneurial spirit carried over to his grandson. When Samuel W. Walton and his second wife, Clara, died within a few months of each other in the fall of 1894, their third and youngest child, Thomas, was just over a year old. Several years later, Thomas's older half-sister, Mollie, brought him and his two older brothers to Oklahoma and helped put them through school. There, his uncle J. W. Walton, who was involved in the farm-loan and real estate business, took young Tom under his wing and put him to work in his farm-mortgage business. In 1917, Tom married a local farmer's daughter, Nancy Lee Lawrence, and decided to try his hand at farming. During the next four years, two sons expanded the family, but the farming did not go so well. By 1923, when Sam was five years old, Tom gave it up and moved his young family to Springfield, where he went back into the farm-mortgage business, this time working for his older half-brother, Jesse.[9]

In his autobiography, Sam Walton said he remembered nothing of his family's early experience in Oklahoma. He started first grade in Springfield, but the family soon moved on to Marshall, halfway between Kansas City and Columbia. He continued through the seventh grade there. The family spent two years after that in Shelbina, 35 miles west of Hannibal, before moving to Columbia in 1933, just as Sam was beginning his sophomore year in high school.

The 1920s were generally hard times for farmers in the region, making for a less-than-lucrative business for Tom Walton. He briefly switched direction and spent several years selling insurance and real estate before returning to farm-mortgage brokering. With the 1929 stock market crash, things got worse. The Walton family never lacked for food and necessities, and they were much better off than many of their neighbors, but money was never plentiful. They never rose above lower-middle-class status. Sam Walton's famous frugality no doubt had its inception here, as he adhered to the penny-pinching habits instilled in him by his parents. "No question about it," he would say later, "a lot of my attitude toward money stems from growing up during a pretty hardscrabble time in our country's history: the Great Depression." Tom Walton influenced his son in many ways. Like him, Sammy, as the lad was known as a schoolboy, was an early riser and a compulsively hard worker. He obtained a reputation for honesty and integrity, adopted a conservative political outlook, and was known as something of a character. In Tom Walton's work as an appraiser and mortgage lender, which during the 1930s, especially, involved numerous foreclosures on defaulted loans, he necessarily had to take a realistic, hardheaded, and often hard-edged approach to his business. His work involved a lot of travel and risk-taking as well as wheeling and dealing. Sam remembered his father as loving to trade and deal for just about anything—farms, houses, cars, cattle, horses, and mules. He was "the best negotiator I ever ran into," Wal-Mart's future founder would say, although he claimed that, unlike his father, "I lack the ability to squeeze that last dollar."[10]

If many of Sam Walton's business skills and mature personality traits resembled those of his father, he was equally influenced by his mother, Nan. She had quit college after a year to get married, but she never let go of her high regard for or desire to acquire education. She was extremely ambitious for Sam and his younger (by two and a half years) brother, Bud. She insisted that Sam attend college and make something of himself, and it was she, apparently, who was responsible for having the family move to a college town. In addition to two women's colleges, Columbia, a community of 30,000 people, was the home of the University of Missouri. Nan believed it would be easier for her boys to attend there if the family lived in town. Sam Walton later attributed his extreme drive and ambition to her. "I took her seriously when she told me I should always try to be the best I could at whatever I took on," he wrote. "So, I have always pursued everything I was interested in with a true passion—some would say obsession—to win."[11]

That obsession began to show itself when he was a grade school student in Marshall. He got engaged in competitive sports, despite being comparatively small, and he served as a class officer for several years. He bet several of his friends that he would be first in the group to make Eagle Scout, but not until the family moved to Shelbina was he able to complete all the requirements. There, at age thirteen, he became the youngest Eagle Scout in Missouri up until that time. He also lettered as an offensive back at Shelbina High School as a 130-pound freshman. Meanwhile, he took on a variety of jobs—running a paper route, selling magazine subscriptions, milking cows and delivering the milk, raising and selling rabbits and pigeons, and doing odd jobs.[12]

There was something compulsive about the boy's constant busyness and application to tasks. A major reason no doubt was a desire to escape his parents' constant bickering. While Sammy undoubtedly admired and loved them both, he could not stand their seeming necessity to quarrel over every little thing. In 1940, the year he graduated from college, his parents separated, although they never divorced. The son swore that should he ever marry he would never expose his children to the kind of squabbling he had endured while growing up.[13]

At Hickman High School, which with 650 students was much larger than his previous two schools, Sammy Walton really came into his own. Hobbled by a broken leg suffered playing baseball before he arrived in Columbia as a sophomore, he had to wait until his junior year to take up football again. As a senior, he quarterbacked the undefeated state champion Fighting Kewpies and followed that by playing guard on the school's undefeated state-champion basketball team. He continued to be a diligent and successful—though not brilliant—honor-roll student. He also competed on the track team and played a starring role in the senior class play, *Growing Pains*. Involved in and often serving as president or officer of many clubs and organizations—from the Forensic Club, Magic Club, and Scroll Club to the Library Club and Student Council—he was also vice president of the junior class and student body president as a senior. Selected as the school's "most versatile boy" that year, he commanded a full page in Hickman High's 1936 yearbook. In his spare time, he delivered newspapers, worked part-time at a local five-and-dime, and did various odd jobs. People noted his affability and lack of pretense. With a smile for everyone and an optimistic outlook on life, he felt that everybody he met was a friend, and they probably were. Still modest and somewhat reserved, he had largely overcome the shyness he had displayed in the earlier grades. His high school years revealed a young man mature beyond his years, an able organizer, highly motivated and goal-oriented, and one who had learned how to deal with and get along with people.[14]

Enrolling in the University of Missouri in the fall of 1936 proved an easy transition for him. Too small to compete in collegiate sports, Sam participated in intramural athletics with his Beta Theta Pi fraternity brothers. He worked his way through college, waiting tables, lifeguarding during the summer, and handling an extensive newspaper route in which he managed several other carriers. Again, he proved to be a joiner par excellence, operating as president of the largest Sunday school class in the nation, rising to cadet captain of his Reserve Officers' Training Corps unit, serving as a student senator, and getting elected president of the senior class. By now quite consciously endeavoring to make friends and win support, he resolved to speak to everyone he met on the sidewalk before the other addressed him and estimated, probably accurately, that he was acquainted with more students than anyone else on campus. His selection for the exclusive honor society QEBH clearly marked him as a big man on campus. The seed of ambition that his mother had planted and that had grown over the years now had no limits, but his goals remained unfocused. Even the presidency of the United States seemed reachable to the optimistic young man.[15]

After all this success, however, as he graduated with a degree in economics in 1940, Walton remained uncertain about his future. The insurance-salesman father of one of his girlfriends had planted in him the idea of selling insurance, but his inability to finance graduate study at the Wharton School of Finance, which he considered essential to pursue that route, ruled that notion out. Instead, he interviewed with Sears Roebuck and J. C. Penney, planning to become a management trainee. Representatives for the latter impressed him more, and soon he was off to Des Moines at seventy-five dollars a month to learn the retail trade.[16]

He soon concluded that he had made the right choice. "Maybe I was born to be a merchant, maybe it was fate, I don't know about that kind of stuff," Walton wrote in his autobiography. "But I know this for sure: I loved retail from the very beginning, and I still love it today. Not that it went all that smooth right off the bat."[17] Walton enjoyed selling, but he was neither much good at nor very interested in paperwork and details.

That remained more or less true for the next fifty years. There was much to learn, and the newly minted college graduate displayed great aptitude for the field. James Cash Penney himself visited the store one day and personally demonstrated how to tie a neat and well-presented package with a minimum of string and paper. Frugality, efficiency, and customer service, all preached by Penney, later became watchwords at Wal-Mart. "Serving the public" was one of the seven key principles Penney preached. Walton later adopted it as one of his own "ten commandments of retailing." The primary strength of Penney's stores was in small towns and smaller cities, just as Wal-Mart's would be. Walton would later allow store managers to buy small stakes in their stores, as Penney did, and he adopted Penney's practice of "management by walking around." Walton would wait almost a decade after launching Wal-Mart, however, before beginning to refer to his employees as "associates," as Penney did.[18]

There would be no quick opportunity for Walton to implement what he learned during the year and a half he spent in Des Moines. People who are inclined to read history backward and are tempted to infer that Wal-Mart's success was somehow foreordained would do well to consider the series of accidents and unpredictable developments that helped shape Sam Walton's destiny early on. His mother's determination to get him a college education can be seen in retrospect as a major factor in his future course. The lack of finances that kept him from attending Wharton may have deprived the insurance industry of a major overhaul, but it freed a young man fired by ambition and a wealth of ideas to transform discount merchandising. Then again, Walton could easily have been killed or permanently disabled in World War II, as hundreds of thousands of others were. But his army physical declared him ineligible for combat duty, confining him to stateside duty. He spent three relatively uneventful years supervising security at prisoner-of-war camps and aircraft factories in California and Utah. In the meantime, he met his future wife in Claremore, Oklahoma, after taking a job in a munitions plant in the nearby town of Pryor while waiting to be inducted into the military. He had left Des Moines in part to distance himself from a young woman who thought he was going to marry her. The housing shortage in Pryor forced him to look for a place to live in Claremore, 19 miles away.[19]

There he ran across an athletic, attractive young woman named Helen Robson at a bowling alley. Unhesitatingly, he approached her, introduced himself, and the two quickly fell in love. She had the advantages of being highly intelligent (valedictorian of her high school class), well-educated (having recently graduated from the University of Oklahoma with a degree in economics), goal-oriented, and rich. Her father, L. S. Robson, was a highly successful lawyer, banker, and landowner who was reputedly the wealthiest man in northeastern Oklahoma. That proved to be a distinct advantage to the young couple after the war, when Walton wanted to get started in business. Their marriage on Valentine's Day in 1943 was the social event of the decade in Claremore, as reported in the *Tulsa World* as well as in the local papers. After decreeing in 1945 that wherever they located, it would have to be in a small town, Helen swung a $20,000 loan from her father to supplement $5,000 saved from Sam's army pay to purchase their first store, a Ben Franklin franchise in Newport, Arkansas.[20]

At 50 feet wide and 100 feet deep, the 5,000-square-foot Ben Franklin store in Newport would easily fit into a small corner of a modern 200,000-square-foot Wal-Mart Supercenter. But it was well located on a busy corner, right across from its major competitor, a Sterling Store, which was turning over approximately twice as much merchandise annually as the Ben Franklin store was. The latter had rung up $72,000 in sales the year before the Waltons arrived. The ambitious, hard-charging, and creative new owner quickly sped past his rival. In five years' time, he more than tripled the store's volume, making it the largest variety store in Arkansas and the number-one Ben Franklin store in sales and profits in a six-state region.[21]

Drawing on his education and training and seeking to learn something new every day through constant observation, experimentation, and experience, Walton in Newport established a pattern of success that he would build on over time. The home company's management team provided clear operating instructions for running its stores, and for a while Walton went by the book. But it did not take long for him to question accepted ways and to begin freelancing on his own. He noted in his autobiography that while he was generally pretty conservative when it came to family, religion, and politics, he was driven in business "to buck the system, to innovate, to take things beyond where they've been."[22] In Newport, that meant buying popcorn and ice-cream machines to entice customers into the store and driving to Tennessee to pick up items directly from manufacturers more cheaply than he could obtain them wholesale from Ben Franklin. He engaged in a wide variety of promotions and other come-ons to move the merchandise from the shelves. He demonstrated astute retailing skills early on, possessing, in his own words, "the personality of a promoter," à la P. T. Barnum, and "the soul of an operator."[23]

The energetic war veteran remained able to segregate business from his home life and community involvement; work did not yet occupy almost every waking hour. By the end of their five years in Newport, the Waltons had four lively kids (three boys and a girl) scampering around the house, mostly under Helen's supervision but also under Sam's watchful eye. She, a highly intelligent, gregarious, and civic-minded woman in her own right, discovered outlets for her considerable energies both within the household and in the larger community. Newport presented a fairly lively social scene, which the Waltons quickly became part of. The family joined the local Presbyterian church. Sam, who had grown up Methodist, readily made the switch and wound up on the board of deacons. His wife dragged him out to bridge parties, and he took the family camping and hiking, enjoying the outdoors. She assumed the presidency of the local chapter of PEO (Philanthropic Educational Organization), a social service club, and became involved with a coterie of young housewives like herself. As president of the Chamber of Commerce, Sam surveyed opportunities for attracting new industries into town. He also served on the county levee board and on the city council's public affairs board. When he was able to find the time, he went quail hunting, which soon became a passion.[24]

One wonders how the family might have fared had there not occurred what at the time seemed a disaster. Walton had failed to check for a renewal clause in his store lease, which expired in 1950. When the owner of the building observed how profitable the business was, he opted not to renew the lease. Instead, he negotiated the purchase of Walton's franchise so he could turn it over to his son. Somewhat embittered by the experience, Walton began scouting for a new location. Once again, L. S. Robson played a major role in assisting his daughter and son-in-law when he offered to help them find a site, preferably in the northwestern part of the state, bringing them closer to him and his wife. A Ben Franklin franchise in Siloam Springs, on the Oklahoma border, was available, but the owner held out for $65,000, just $5,000 more than the budding entrepreneur was willing to offer. That small difference led Walton to choose Bentonville, a town of around 3,000 and 20 miles to the northeast. That sleepy burg would eventually become world famous as the headquarters of the largest business in the world, leaving Siloam Springs as just another ordinary small town. Thrilled that Helen and Sam would be living closer to him,

Robson negotiated a ninety-nine-year lease on the barbershop next door to the Ben Franklin store on the square, which allowed Sam to double the store's size. Again, he provided the young couple with financing to help get the operation up and running.[25]

As Walton progressed and began to expand in Newport, Bentonville, and then other towns, a number of practices quickly became part of his standard approach: close personal attention to his customers, most of whom he quickly learned to know by name; a concerted effort to control expenses; no-holds-barred competition with business rivals (he once bought an empty store building just to prevent his counterparts from expanding into it); and a constant compulsion to learn. Walton exhibited no embarrassment in constantly surveying rival stores' aisles to learn about their merchandising techniques, pricing policies, and promotional approaches. Over his long business career, he never became particularly known for inventing new technologies or pioneering new practices, but he was always quick to learn and adapt from others. What he did raise to a point of high principle was the idea that one can never stop learning and changing. Unlike many businessmen who are good at expounding their own personal views, Walton was instinctively curious, a person compulsively driven to ask questions and listen attentively to people who might have some answers.

Perhaps most important, the notion that lower prices and increased volume would mean higher profits in the long run became firmly set in Walton's mind. His constant search for cheaper sources of inventory reflected his intuitive sense that controlling costs was as important as maintaining prices in enhancing the bottom line. During the years after World War II, traditional merchandising continued to hold sway in most American small towns. While roads had been improving and automobile traffic had increased dramatically since Henry Ford's Model T had revolutionized motor transport, people still tended to patronize local stores. Saturday continued to be the big shopping day of the week, as farmers drove into town to conduct their business. Main Street stores obliged their customers by staying open late on Saturday, often past midnight. The iconoclastic economist Thorstein Veblen had noted in his classic 1923 analysis of the country town that store owners strove to achieve monopoly status within their local market areas, but failing that, they colluded with each other to maintain prices at artificially high levels. Prices in small towns hovered above those in cities, and the quality and variety of merchandise was seldom very high. Until it became possible for customers to drive longer distances to do their shopping, they had little alternative but to patronize their local stores. Besides, loyalty to one's own hometown and its merchants remained relatively strong. Small towns like Newport were basically sellers' markets until a new class of retailers began to come along.[26]

Walton, no worshipper of tradition, fitted into the latter category. For him, retail was aggressively competitive, just as baseball, basketball, and football had been for him as a youth. If you break a leg, you rest up and get ready to play another day. In Newport, Walton had enjoyed his first taste of business success while operating a single store. In Bentonville, he ratcheted things up dramatically. The town was less than half the size of the one they were leaving, and Helen at first found it hard to adjust to. To her, the place "was just a sad-looking little town." She soon changed her mind about it. She found the residents to be congenial and welcoming. Here she would be much closer to her parents, and Sam waxed enthusiastic about the nearby quail hunting.[27]

In Bentonville, the couple quickly got even more involved in the community than they had been in Newport, participating in church affairs, the Parent-Teacher Association, and a number of civic organizations. Sam became a church deacon and president of the local Chamber of Commerce as well as of the Rotary Club. He won election to the city council and did a stint on the hospital board. As their boys grew up, he served as scoutmaster and helped organize a Little League baseball program. He even found time to teach Sunday school.[28]

By the early 1960s, as the children progressed through high school, he reduced his community involvement and began seriously considering the possibility of greatly expanding his operations. An approach that had proven highly—but rather conventionally—successful during his first venture quickly morphed into something entirely different. Their store on the Bentonville square, directly across from the Confederate statue on the green, racked up rapidly expanding sales and profits. This time, Walton refused to remain satisfied with operating a single store. From the outset he was intent on expansion. Within two years, he had opened a second store in Fayetteville, home of the University of Arkansas, 20 miles to the south. In quick order, he added others, financed by profits from the ones already in operation. When Helen heard him say that he was thinking of a dozen stores, she almost fell out of her chair. By 1962, he had put together sixteen units—some Ben Franklin franchises and some independently operated stores—in Arkansas, Missouri, and Kansas.[29] Walton was the beneficiary of general American prosperity and rapidly shifting consumption patterns after World War II. The Ozark Mountain region was undergoing massive economic change as agriculture transformed itself, interstate highways penetrated the region, television encouraged new consumer habits, and the countryside shed some of its traditional sense of isolation.

The Ozarks—encompassing much of southern Missouri, northern Arkansas, and parts of eastern Kansas and Oklahoma—were less isolated and provincial than was claimed by some of the journalists, anthropologists, and folklorists who studied and analyzed the region.[30] Although it remained one of the most rural parts of the United States, it had undergone significant change since railroads penetrated the area during the 1880s. Subsequent transportation improvements, educational upgrades, commercial expansion, manufacturing development, and agricultural progress had brought growing segments of the populace into closer contact with the rest of the nation. The highly fertile soil and relatively flatter topography of the Springfield Plain of northwestern Arkansas made it the most diversified and prosperous agricultural region in the state. Unlike the area around Newport, which sat on the line between eastern Arkansas Ozarks and the Mississippi River Delta, northwestern Arkansas contained only a tiny percentage of blacks—around 1 percent of the population—and was as much midwestern as southern in its cultural orientation. Compared to cotton-growing regions, it had a much smaller number of migrants from Tennessee, Mississippi, Alabama, and the Southeast and more from Missouri, Kansas, Illinois, and other parts of the Midwest. It was Thomas Hart Benton country (the Kansas City artist was a grandnephew of the county's namesake, a nineteenth-century Missouri senator), populated by independent, self-reliant farmers and small-town people. They raised cattle and hogs, harvested small grains, tended apple and peach orchards, and grew strawberries, tomatoes, grapes, and other fruits and vegetables before shifting emphasis, beginning in the 1930s, toward broiler operations and milk production.[31]

The acceleration of major economic and social trends in the 1940s and 1950s rendered the Ozarks a place of flux and out-migration. Mechanization and consolidation in the agricultural sector resulted in considerable underemployment in rural Arkansas. Farmers increasingly thought it necessary that at least one family member work off the property if they were to make ends meet, and they aspired to a better style of living. The accelerating trend of women entering the labor force provided a ready supply of workers willing to work for low wages and also undergirded changing consumption patterns. Many women went to work in chicken-processing plants, which were expanding in the countryside, but many also went into retail. Although their wages were low by comparison with some other regions and other industries, they were a step up from what they had known, and the jobs allowed them to remain living in the region and to supplement family income, as well as to develop a tight-knit female culture of store clerks and workers.[32]

Walton, not surprisingly, continued to innovate and experiment with his stores, constantly on the lookout for new ways to cut costs, improve the merchandise, and make his operations run more smoothly. When he read about two Ben Franklin stores in Minnesota that had adopted self-service, he went up to inspect them personally, quickly deciding to adopt the policy himself. Throughout the decade, largely because of intense efforts to control costs, his stores remained rather ramshackle, unsightly affairs. His supply chain and distribution system continued to be haphazard, and he struggled to find store managers he could train and keep under close scrutiny and control. A major breakthrough occurred around 1957, when Walton discovered that he could keep in closer touch with every store in his growing chain by taking to the air. He learned to fly, and from then on he made a practice of spending part of every week traveling from store to store to monitor them and ensure that his instructions were being carried out.[33]

Walton read the trade journals closely, kept a constant eye on his retail competitors, and stayed abreast of evolving consumer buying habits. He sensed by the late 1950s that a major wave was about to hit retail marketing, and he was intent on catching a ride on it. Deep discounting was not an entirely new idea in the 1950s, but it was just beginning to get major traction, based on the records of small chains such as E. J. Korvette, Masters, Inc., and Vornado, Inc.[34] Having read about them in the trade papers, Walton traveled east several times to talk to company executives who could explain to him how they went about doing their business. Affecting his best "country boy" manner, he was able to get many of them to open up to him about their operations. None of them suspected that within two or three decades he would vastly surpass them and everyone else in the discount business.[35]

The year 1962 was the *annus mirabilis* in discount marketing in the United States, for in that single year Wal-Mart, Kmart, Target, and Woolco all made their debuts. The latter three were all spin-offs from much larger chains, conferring on them a huge advantage over Walton's homegrown operation, whose sixteen stores around Bentonville made him a remarkably successful regional retailer but left him completely off the charts nationally. The other three companies benefited from name recognition, buying power, management expertise, and access to capital for rapid expansion. Wal-Mart's growth was heavily constrained by having to finance new stores from profits and bank credit. For the latter, Walton depended heavily on James H. Jones, an up-and-coming Dallas banker a dozen years his junior. Jones was impressed by the Arkansas entrepreneur's success and by his ambitious plans for growth, but he also had to protect his own firm's interests and to conform to generally accepted banking practices. In 1961, with the Texan's assistance, Walton purchased the Bank of Bentonville to facilitate expansion, a move that during the following decade helped make Wal-Mart's rapid development possible.[36]

The first Wal-Mart discount store opened on July 2, 1962, 6 miles east of Bentonville in Rogers, Arkansas, a town about twice its size and better connected to transportation lines. There was nothing fancy about the store building. At 16,000 square feet, it was, like all of the new chain's early stores, relatively small, not air-conditioned, and simply furnished with tables for displaying merchandise, a few racks for hanging clothes, and cash registers for ringing up sales. (During the early years, conditions were so primitive that at some store openings cashiers had to make change out of cigar boxes until the cash registers arrived.) "Wal-Mart Discount City" announced the sign outside. Bob Bogle, the manager of Walton's Bentonville five-and-dime, had suggested the "Wal-Mart" moniker, in part, at least, because the short name would minimize signage expense. The signs also advertised prominently "We Sell for Less" and "Satisfaction Guaranteed," two operating principles that had propelled store operations from the beginning and stood at the center of the company's philosophy. The bargain-basement appearance of the stores did little to discourage customers, who were attracted to their lower prices. In the beginning, the quality of the goods played little role in the thoughts of Walton's store managers or their customers. "What we were obsessed with was keeping our prices below everybody else's," Walton wrote in his autobiography. Those low prices would remain the driving force behind Wal-Mart's remarkable expansion during most of the next half century.[37]

Keeping wages down was another element that remained constant in

Wal-Mart's operating philosophy. The imperative to minimize costs virtually demanded it. Store clerks were paid $0.50–$0.60 an hour, considerably below the $1.15 minimum wage.[38] Walton felt no compunction about the practice because other stores did the same thing, he assumed that his mostly female workforce were not their families' main source of income, and the women were willing to work for the wages he was prepared to offer. The socioeconomic changes sweeping the Ozarks at the time made available a large, pliable source of labor for the company, and the cultural patterns of the region dictated that women should gratefully and willingly accept their subordinate status. Most of them calculated that they were better off working at Wal-Mart than they would have been staying at home. All the early store managers were young men without college degrees. The status and the power they exercised over their female labor force paralleled Walton's own relationship with women. At the outset, Wal-Mart culture was implicitly patriarchal, hierarchical, and domineering—a condition comfortably attuned to the broader rural, small-town Ozarks and midwestern culture in which Walton had grown up and with which most of his employees, store managers, and early headquarters executives had no quarrel.[39]

For a decade, a corporate structure barely existed. Walton probably tried to do too much himself, but that was his nature. On the job at four-thirty or five every morning, he routinely put in fourteen- to sixteen-hour days. In the process, he cut back almost entirely on his community involvement, and Helen, who had always played the major role in raising their children, now saw less of him than ever. At first, store management consisted entirely of the personal relationships existing between Walton and his store managers. He visited them by flying weekly from town to town. The boss gave all of them considerable freedom to experiment, but he also held them personally responsible for their stores' success. He dispensed encouragement and approval as well as tough demands and unvarnished criticism with equal fervor. If someone failed to perform up to his high expectations, that person could be demoted or let go. He spent as little time as possible in his own cramped, spartan office in Bentonville, where his desk consisted of a sheet of plywood laid across two sawhorses. He kept each store's paperwork in blue binder ledger books in pigeonholes along the wall. Bud Walton helped his older brother build the operation during these birthing years, investing most of his energy in real estate transactions and the construction of new facilities.[40]

Don Whitaker, the Rogers store manager, became Walton's first assistant when he took over the role of regional manager. Walton seriously began scouting for talent to aid in managing the growing little empire. Most of his new managers were young men lured away from other retail and discount merchandisers. They all had midwestern or Ozarks roots and exhibited the same kinds of values and cultural preferences. Ferold Arend joined in 1966 to manage new store openings. He steadily assumed new responsibilities during the ensuing decade and a half. Ron Mayer came on board in 1968 as a communications technology expert. Six years later Walton would temporarily hand the reins of the company over to Mayer in a short, ill-fated first attempt to ratchet down his own activity in response to Helen's repeated entreaties. Jack Shewmaker arrived in 1970 and likewise rose rapidly through the ranks until being passed over for promotion to CEO in 1988 when the company's founder designated David Glass as his successor. Walton's sure instinct in tabbing aggressive, creative managers who could fit into his unique system of management and who were willing to devote the energy and long hours that he did to getting the job done was a major factor in his company's initial and long-term success. Wal-Mart emerged as a direct reflection of the founder's own personality, and in the process he molded its executive crew and workforce and instilled in them the same values, goals, and methods that he believed in.[41]

Success came quickly. The stores were profitable from the start, providing a steady stream of revenue that financed further expansion. Opening two new stores in 1964, one in 1965, four in 1966–1967, and five in both 1968 and 1969, Walton had eighteen Wal-Marts by the end of the decade, along with fourteen variety stores, for a total of thirty-two units. The stores varied in floor space from 11,000 to 44,000 square feet, with most containing between 30,000 and 40,000. Except for the North Little Rock, Arkansas, unit, all were located in towns of under 25,000 residents, and most had fewer than 10,000. In 1969, with around 1,000 employees, Wal-Mart netted $1.2 million profit on sales of $31 million. These were impressive figures for an operation that had opened its first discount store less than a decade earlier.[42]

Compared to Kmart, which quickly jumped to dominance in the discount wars, the boys from Bentonville remained strictly Hicksville. While Wal-Mart had risen to thirty-sixth on the list of discount operators, Kmart was number one, with sales about forty-five times larger, and it ranked fourth among all retail merchants, behind Sears, J. C. Penney, and Montgomery Ward. The Arkansas upstarts clearly were no match yet for Target and Woolco, let alone Kmart. Luckily for Walton and his crew, they remained below the radar in the jumbled world of discounting. Had they been forced to go head-to-head with the pacesetters this early in the game, they might not have survived. Walton's decision to stick to small-town markets in retrospect appears to have been a stroke of genius.[43]

By the end of the 1960s, the company's founder sensed a major transition brewing. Uncomfortable with approximately $2 million in debt and chafing at the capital shortage hampering his efforts to open new stores, he concluded that the time had come to go public. The initial public offering of 300,000 shares of Wal-Mart stock sold in October 1970 at $16.50 a share and generated $5 million for the company. After compensating seventy-eight partners, including relatives, friends, store managers, and others who had invested with him, the Walton family retained 61 percent of the firm's ownership. A second sale two years later, raising another $9 million and rendering the company eligible for listing on the New York Stock Exchange, left the family with 38 percent of the stock. (By 2000, after eleven stock splits, an initial investment of $1,650 in 100 shares would have ballooned into 204,800 shares worth approximately $11.25 million.)[44] Relieved of debt and fueled by cash from the stock sales, Walton moved quickly during the early 1970s to establish new stores. During the decade, as he converted or phased out his Ben Franklin franchises and independent variety stores, his stores multiplied to 276. Annual revenues expanded to $41 million on sales of $1.2 billion. His workforce grew from around 1,000 to twenty-one times that. The company's more than 40 percent annual compound growth rate made it the fastest-expanding regional discounter and laid the foundation for even broader market penetration later on. The impressive growth, while gratifying and financially rewarding, also posed tremendous challenges and problems. It was a constant struggle for Walton and his increasing coterie of store managers and executives to keep up.[45]

A workable expansion strategy developed over time—a natural outgrowth of Walton's original practices, refined by trial and error. By the end of the 1960s, it had become increasingly evident that a highly structured logistics system was needed to replace the rather haphazard procurement and distribution practices he had relied on up until that time. In 1969, a distribution center (DC) of 60,000 square feet was installed next to a new company headquarters building on the outskirts of Bentonville. Almost as soon as it was up and running, the structure had to be expanded. In 1975, a second one of 150,000 square feet went up. In 1978, a third DC—this one ballooning to 390,000 square feet—was located in Searcy, Arkansas, 160 miles southeast of Bentonville, launching Wal-Mart on a path that would allow it to grow, region by region, for decades to come. The concept was "to saturate a market area by spreading out, then filling in," Walton indicated. "Each store had to be within a day's drive of a distribution center. So we would go as far as we could from a warehouse and put in a store. Then we would fill in the map of that territory, state by state, county seat by county seat, until we had saturated that market area." Five different cookie-cutter building designs ranging from 30,000 to 60,000 square feet were developed by Bud Walton's crew, making it relatively simple and inexpensive to construct new stores adapted to the size of the towns and market areas in which they were being installed. During the first half of the decade, almost all the locations were in Arkansas, Missouri, Oklahoma, and Kansas. A small number spread into Kentucky, Tennessee, Mississippi, and Louisiana. During the latter part of the decade, expansion proceeded rapidly into Texas and Illinois, with some spillover into Alabama.[46] The key to Wal-Mart's extraordinary expansion and continued success was the company's decision to make logistics its central concern, conferring on it a huge advantage over rival Kmart. Both of Walton's successors as CEO, David Glass and H. Lee Scott, came up through the system in logistics as did most of the key executives working under them.[47]

All through the 1970s, company executives struggled mightily to keep up with the pace of store growth, which was a dozen times faster than it had been during the previous decade. Without thinking too hard about where this growth would lead, Walton and his gradually growing cadre of executives just kept rolling out the stores. They continued to avoid larger cities but began ringing some of them with locations in the suburbs. Tulsa, Kansas City, and Dallas were three of the early experiments along these lines.[48] By the early 1970s, discounting had emerged as the largest segment of the retail industry.[49] For the first time, Wal-Mart began to go head-to-head against Kmart and the other big discounters. They discovered that they could do it, although the company still was ringing up only about 5 percent of Kmart's business. With a shakeout in the industry, as the recession of 1974–1975 set in and inflation failed to abate, Wal-Mart began to emerge as a powerful potential rival to the pacesetters. The growth process stepped up with the first acquisition of a financially troubled chain— sixteen Mohr Value stores in Missouri and Illinois in 1978. Three years later, Walton purchased 104 Kuhn's Big-K outlets in the Southeast. As the discounting industry continued to consolidate during the 1970s, store face-lifts and upgrades were accompanied by the introduction of higher-quality, name-brand goods at Wal-Mart.[50]

The 1970s also witnessed a major change in the company's efforts to retain the loyalty of its workforce. Walton had always sought to stay closely connected with his workers. He talked to them and solicited their opinions as he visited the stores each week. He liked to think of and talk about his business, from himself and company executives down to the lowest-paid hourly workers, as a group of equals and "one big family" who were all engaged in the same project, to make Wal-Mart as customer-friendly and productive as possible. However, it became increasingly clear to outside observers that many of Walton's efforts along these lines, whether he was conscious of it or not, were attempts to substitute intangible rewards for cold, hard wage and benefit increases. Walton's own rural, small-town upbringing in Missouri during the 1920s and 1930s, the mores and customs of his home base in rural Arkansas, and the mind-set of mid-twentieth-century America all contributed to the conservative, patriarchal, and domineering way Wal-Mart treated its workers. For some, this was acceptable. For increasing numbers, however, change was in order. Walton himself somewhat sheepishly admitted in his autobiography, "In the beginning, I was so chintzy I really didn't pay my employees very well." He rationalized that he had been not "intentionally heartless" but, rather, so obsessed with the bottom line and high profit margins that he "ignored some of the basic needs of our people," adding, "and I feel bad about it."[51] Not bad enough, however, to substantially increase compensation for his employees or to soften his opposition to unions. If there was anything more sacred than low prices at Wal-Mart, it was absolute opposition to labor unions.

Failed efforts in 1970 by the Retail Clerks Union to organize stores in Clinton and Mexico, Missouri, provided a wake-up call for Walton. No longer could he take it for granted that sheer force of personality and engagement with his workers in the company culture could keep unions out. He accepted the advice of professional union buster John Tate, whom he hired during the Clinton and Mexico encounters, to reach out and communicate more effectively with his workforce. Walton launched a "We Care" campaign, which invited employees to vent their problems and concerns with managers. He began referring to them as "associates," just as J. C. Penney had done. He also extended more tangible benefits, including ex-

Sam Walton   429

panded profit sharing, a stock-purchase plan with company contributions, and bonuses for workers who met preset goals. The new approach did not include any substantial increase in wages, however. Walton did not believe that was feasible in the context of his business plan. During later organizing campaigns, he played hardball, threatening to close down units that voted a union in, and actually doing it. Wal-Mart had begun and remained relentlessly antiunion in its approach to labor relations.[52]

Also significant at this time was the company's big move into computerization and technology, a move that Walton had been reluctant to make but that he realized was inevitable and would have a major long-term payoff. Building on the foundation established by Ron Mayer, company executives Jack Shewmaker and David Glass persuaded Walton to invest a half billion dollars over a five-year period in upgrading computer and communications systems. That decision rapidly paid for itself many times over. Initially anchored by two big IBM mainframes housed in a 16,000-square-foot, air-conditioned building near company headquarters, the new outfit linked every store with headquarters as well as with the distribution centers and warehouses. Upgraded continually, it later evolved into Retail Link, which went far beyond information transmission to connect suppliers with delivery points and to automate ordering and inventory control. Now humans needed only to monitor and fine-tune operations. Computerizing the company facilitated the automation of the distribution centers and vastly increased the data that could be collected, analyzed, and digested by corporate functionaries.[53]

These developments were overshadowed by the transformations of the 1980s—the decade when Wal-Mart transformed from a large and growing regional retailer into a powerful national presence, registering forcefully on the public mind from Main Street and Wall Street to Washington, D.C., and the ivory tower. As discounting underwent profound alterations and as increasingly competitive conditions upset old hierarchies, Wal-Mart surged to dominate the industry. By the end of the decade, the company had 1,528 stores and 275,000 employees. Wal-Mart grew so furiously that figures for any year were quickly dwarfed by those in subsequent years. With annual growth averaging around 36 percent, sales and profits doubled every two or three years, and Wal-Mart appeared to be recession-proof. At Glass's accession as CEO in 1988, Wal-Mart's annual sales still trailed those of Kmart and Sears, but with a much more rapid growth rate than either of them, it was rapidly closing the gap. In 1990, it surged past both.[54]

Until store numbers rose to 400 or 500 during the early 1980s, Walton continued to visit every store at least once a year. He kept up with every real estate deal and viewed most new store sites before deciding to locate there. During the remainder of the decade, the Southeast was blanketed and major forays were launched into the Great Lakes states and the Southwest. Sixteen distribution centers were in place by the end of the 1980s. (Several stores were installed in California during the early 1990s while Walton was still alive. The Northeast and the Northwest were penetrated later that decade.) Store openings usually exceeded 100 per year and in some years topped 150. Universal product code (UPC) technology improved inventory control and ratcheted up sales efficiency. At 1.3 percent of sales, Wal-Mart's distribution costs were only half to a quarter of those of its rivals. In 1987, a new $20-million satellite communications network enhanced interactions among employees, managers, upper-level executives, suppliers, and customers, thereby increasing efficiency. It allowed company officials in Bentonville to control lighting and temperature in stores, determine employees' work schedules, and monitor sales in real time. It also reduced credit card authorization time to seven seconds and enabled Wal-Mart to accumulate the largest private database in the world. The company accelerated its expansion into larger cities during the 1980s. Typical store size increased from 47,000 square feet to over 65,000 square feet. After three abortive tries with 220,000-plus-square-foot "Hypermarts," the first "Supercenters," selling groceries and ranging between 180,000 and 210,000 square feet in size, appeared in 1988. During the following decade, new Supercenters and rapid expansion overseas would be key to Wal-Mart's growth, as the company moved increasingly into larger urban areas.[55]

Not everything Wal-Mart tried worked, however, as the Hypermart failure demonstrated. Walton's forays during the 1980s into Dot Discount Drugs, Helen's Arts and Crafts (named after his wife), and Save Mor home improvement centers were quickly abandoned. But the founder always welcomed new ideas and experiments and never lamented failures if lessons could be learned from them. An idea that proved to be a major success was Sam's Wholesale Clubs, initiated in 1983, which offered even deeper discounts to individual customers and retailers.[56]

During the 1980s, ordinary Americans began to notice what came to be called the "Wal-Mart effect." The giant of Bentonville had finally become too large to ignore. Between 1982 and 1985, *Forbes* magazine identified Sam Walton first as one of the richest and then as the richest man in America. Stories about him and his company began to pour out of the nation's press, much to Mr. Sam's consternation. For a long time, he had enjoyed being able to fly under the radar. Publicity about him and his company was mainly favorable and driven by huge curiosity. Most of it focused on how this seemingly rustic and unpretentious down-home boy could be so smart and wily as to shoot past the biggest corporate moguls in the United States. The coverage tended to be phrased in superlatives and astonishment.[57]

Walton and the company he ran started to win all sorts of awards and recognition: one of the five best-managed companies in America, according to *Dun's Business Review* (1982); the Horatio Alger Award (1984); *Financial World*'s CEO of the Year (1986); "quite likely the finest-managed company in America," according to analysts at First Boston (1988); number five on *Fortune*'s list of Most Admired Corporations (1989); in *Fortune* magazine, "America's Most Successful Merchant" (1991). In 1992 it was inducted into the National Business Hall of Fame. In April 1992, two weeks before Walton died of bone cancer, President George H. W. Bush, in an unprecedented gesture, personally traveled to Bentonville to award Walton the Presidential Medal of Freedom. Walton would be posthumously categorized along with John D. Rockefeller, Henry Ford, and Bill Gates as one of the most influential businessmen in the history of the United States.

With exploding size and success came intensive scrutiny. During the last decade of Walton's life, his company came under severe criticism for many of its business practices and its negative social and economic impact. Journalists, economists, social scientists, labor union leaders, environmentalists, feminists, small-town dwellers, and a variety of other critics increasingly expressed their concerns about Wal-Mart's labor practices, low wages, poor benefits, fierce antiunion tactics, burned-out executives, relentless pressures on suppliers, reliance on outsourcing, negative environmental impact, discrimination against women and minorities, homogenization of the culture, transformation of the landscape, stinginess in philanthropy, unfair competitive practices, elimination of mom-and-pop stores, and destruction of small-town Main Streets.[58]

In contrast, the points most often cited in favor of Wal-Mart's business model were the efficiency and productivity of the operation, resulting in low prices, and the beneficial effects these have had on consumers and on the overall inflation rate. Company spokesmen and its admirers and friends also noted the jobs it provided, the stimulus it provided to innovation and creativity, the sense of togetherness that existed among store "associates," and its growing emphasis on environmental and "green" business practices.[59]

It is highly ironic that someone who had grown up in several small midwestern towns and who had deliberately located his stores in small towns—much to the surprise of his major competitors—was now being blamed for the destruction of the very kind of small towns that he had operated in all his life. During the mid-1980s, Iowa State University extension economist Ken Stone, who had no particular ax to grind with Wal-Mart, was the first to document in detail the devastating consequences the company's stores could have on local businesses, especially in surrounding towns that did not have a Wal-Mart store. Dozens of articles began to appear with titles such as "How Wal-Mart Hits Main Street," "Arrival of Discounter Tears the Civic Fabric of Small-Town Life," and "When Wal-Mart Comes to Town." Many of these accounts came down hard on the frequently cited bullying tactics of the giant corporation in dealing with its suppliers and with local government agencies as well as on the negative consequences of its entry into small communities. "Wal-Mart has replaced the need for Main Street," a former newspaper publisher in Independence, Iowa, was quoted as saying in a 1989 article in the *New York Times Magazine*, summing up the attitudes of many. "Is it really worth saving a few bucks to virtually destroy the heart and soul of our small town business community?" wondered a journalist who had observed Wal-Mart's impact in Mountain View, Arkansas.[60]

Walton expressed bewilderment at the accusations. Taking what he considered to be a cold, realistic look at small-town America as he had known it, he observed that Main Street businesses had been going under for a long time, that small towns had been dying along with them, and that there were understandable reasons for those developments. Too many small-town merchants had become mired in their old and now obsolete ways and deserved to go under, he averred. Their prices were too high, their merchandise was obsolete and unvarying, and their customer service was deficient. Walton maintained that "any business that takes care of its customers can stay in business." What was happening "was absolutely a necessary and inevitable evolution in retailing, as inevitable as the replacement of the buggy by the car and the disappearance of the buggy whip makers," he contended. "The small stores were just destined to disappear, at least in the numbers they once existed, because the whole thing is driven by the customers, who are free to choose where to shop."[61]

Until his stores began to penetrate the largest towns and suburban and metropolitan areas during the 1980s and 1990s, at least, Sam Walton and his public relations minions continued to highlight the small-town nature of the Wal-Mart culture. Early ads emphasized the stores' local ownership and their down-home quality and friendly atmosphere. The first fifty store locations had an average population of a bit less than 9,000 and were clustered in the Ozarks of northwest Arkansas, southwest Missouri, and eastern Oklahoma. As the company expanded south, east, and west from there, small-town values, habits, and friendliness continued to dominate the mind-set and public posture of Wal-Mart officials, who strenuously sought to create an atmosphere of tradition and community in their stores, annual meetings, and advertising.[62]

Having grown up and lived in small towns all his life, Walton rejected complaints from critics who asserted that he and the behemoth he had created were undermining the small-town way of life. "Of all the notions I've heard about Wal-Mart, none has baffled me more than this idea that we are somehow the enemy of small-town America," he said. "It's almost like they want their hometown to be stuck in time, an old-fashioned place filled with old-fashioned people doing business in the old-fashioned way."[63] Nostalgia was no justification for endeavoring to transport people back to the old days, Walton reasoned. He sympathized with those who felt something had been lost. "As an old-time small-town merchant, I can tell you that nobody has more love for the heyday of the small-town retailing era than I do," he wrote. "That's one of the reasons we chose to put our little Wal-Mart museum on the square in Bentonville. It's in the old Walton's Five and Dime building, and it tries to capture a little bit of the old dime store feel."[64]

Today, people can visit that museum in Walton's original store in Bentonville, view the makeshift desk on which he conducted his early calculations and recorded his first profits, ogle at the dented pickup truck that he wheeled around town, and peruse exhibits chronicling the growth of the company over the decades. A mile or so to the southwest, on what used to be the edge of town, sits Wal-Mart's international headquarters. Computers hum nearby in huge, faceless buildings, linked by satellite to every store in the United States, Canada, Mexico, and other nations where Wal-Mart does business. Walton's successor CEOs—David Glass and Lee Scott— were both small-town boys from the same Missouri-Ozarks milieu in which he grew up. That midwestern-Ozarks heritage still resonates in Bentonville, but one gets the impression that even if the men in the austere, cramped offices inside the nondescript, windowless, brick structure were to disappear tomorrow, the behemoth that is Wal-Mart would continue unimpeded—monitored and directed by the computers whirring away in the building next door.

■

Coda: Small-Town Boys and
the American Dream

What do the lives of twenty-two small-town boys and farm youths who grew up in the Middle West have to teach us? A quick glance at their life stories and personalities suggests that as a group they displayed unusual ambition, industry, grit, perseverance, optimism, adaptability, and creativity. But even if it could be persuasively demonstrated that this relatively small group of individuals exemplified all these characteristics, the conclusion would hardly prove that midwesterners as a group possessed similar traits. The sample is too small, too highly selective, by no means random, and skewed in the direction of those very qualities because the individuals were initially chosen for inclusion in the study precisely because they embodied the kinds of success that require those kinds of attributes. I would be willing to accept the soft notion that these qualities are, everything else being equal, compatible with successful careers. But unlike the historian Frederick Jackson Turner, who during the 1890s boldly proclaimed that midwesterners as a group were democratic, nationalistic, individualistic, and a couple of dozen other generally positive things, I, like most of my fellow historians today, hesitate to make such sweeping generalizations.

Certain regularities, however, do seem to shout out at the reader in the telling of these stories. For instance, an event or epiphany around age ten or twelve in a boy's life that instills in him a drive to pursue or to excel in some particular activity or interest is hugely important. For Henry Ford it was automobiles; for George Washington Carver, nature; for William Jennings Bryan, public speaking; for Sinclair Lewis, reading; for Alvin Hansen, scholarship; for Johnny Carson, magic; for Lawrence Welk and Meredith Willson, music; for Bob Feller, baseball; for James Dean, acting; for Sam Walton, business entrepreneurship. Again and again, although not in every case, it was the mother who encouraged her son to pursue his passion, while the father passively acquiesced in or positively opposed the activity, wishing that his boy would become more "practical" and conventional in his behavior. Another defining factor that arises over and over again in these stories is the advantage that accrues to successful boys in the form of luck and good timing. From Horatio Alger and his "rags to riches" stories to Malcolm Gladwell, who in *Outliers: The Story of Success* describes the benefit derived by future hockey players from being born in January, February, or March, writers and social investigators have noted the advantages that luck and other kinds of accidents often confer on individuals in their pursuit of success.[1]

My purpose in this book, however, has not been to examine or evaluate such hypotheses but rather to illustrate as a general rule the profound importance of one's childhood origins and sense of place. I've tried to show how they have influenced the later lives and careers of an especially interesting and successful group of individuals who grew up in small towns or on farms in the Midwest over the course of approximately a century. These stories, I would suggest, collectively support the notion that place or geographic context exerts a strong impact on people's lives. Other writers and scholars, I expect, will carry out their own investigations that will further illuminate the phenomenon and either substantiate the proposition or call its validity into question. The important qualifier, however, is that the way this influence worked was quite unpredictable, that it made its impact in widely various ways, depending on the individual, the context, the times, and other factors.

Biographers, historians, social scientists, and humanities scholars would do well to attach more significance to the impact of place, especially the influence of one's childhood beginnings, on subsequent developments in people's lives. Not that this approach has not been taken to some extent in the past. But in comparison to other causal factors and influences on people's ideas and behavior, the impact of place has often received short shrift. So much weight has been given to factors such as race, class, and gender, as well as to influences such as religion, ethnicity, education, occupation, and social status, that the power of place has often been subordinated or totally neglected.

Beyond that, what impressed me time after time in writing these chapters, in ways I had not anticipated, were the frequent references to dreams and dreaming in the lives of these men, beginning in boyhood and continuing through adulthood. Americans as a people have always exhibited an affinity for dreaming. Beginning with the original Native Americans who inhabited the land, followed by wave on wave of European immigrants, the pattern repeated itself over and over again. It was the historian James Truslow Adams who coined the phrase "the American dream" in a book written in 1931, but the idea behind it had been circulating for generations, perhaps millennia. In his classic *The Liberal Imagination,* the literary critic Lionel Trilling noted, "Ours is the only nation that prides itself upon a dream and gives its name to one, 'the American Dream.'"[2]

Decade by decade, generation on generation, the dream evolved, incorporating over time groups that originally had been omitted. Martin Luther King Jr. summoned listeners of every color to action with his "I Have a Dream" speech. President Barack Obama included the notion in the titles of both his books—*Dreams of My Father* and *The Audacity of Hope: Thoughts on Reclaiming the American Dream.* "The republic is a dream. Nothing happens unless first a dream," the poet Carl Sandburg once wrote. President Ronald Reagan quoted that statement in his address to an emotional joint session of Congress during his first public appearance after recuperating from an attempted assassin's bullet during the spring of 1981, adding, "And that's what makes us, as Americans, different. We've always reached for a new spirit and aimed at a higher goal. We've been courageous and determined, unafraid and bold. Who among us wants to be the first to say we no longer have those qualities?"[3]

As boys, Reagan harbored dreams of glory on the football field and Sandburg entertained fantasies of stardom on the baseball diamond. In adulthood, they redirected their energies toward goals like world peace and literary excellence. The historian Frederick Jackson Turner enjoyed reading poems to his history classes at Wisconsin and Harvard, taking special inspiration from Rudyard Kipling's *Song of the English,* which contains the lines,

> We were dreamers, dreaming greatly, in the man-stifled town;
> We yearned beyond the sky-line where the strange roads go down.

In their political campaigns, William McKinley and William Jennings Bryan projected conflicting dreams of a better, more perfect American polity, while the scientist George Washington Carver and the novelist and filmmaker Oscar Micheaux cultivated modest hopes for simple justice and true equality for members of their own race. Businessmen such as Henry Ford and Sam Walton converted entrepreneurial visions into vast personal wealth and cornucopias of goods for their customers along with more problematic implications for their workers and the environment. In almost every case, dreams for personal advancement and success coincided with a passion to create something that would redound to the benefit of society. If that meant an inexpensive personal vehicle, a more rapidly expanding economy, or a more accurate and inspiring artistic vision of society, it might also entail happily reminiscing about one's hometown on the radio, keeping audiences laughing and dancing into the wee hours of the night, or enabling high-leaping basketball players to become good family men and responsible citizens as well as victorious athletes.

Sometimes dreams turned into nightmares, as reflected in Sinclair Lewis's critical literary take on his hometown in Minnesota, Ernie Pyle's wartime stories about death and destruction, and James Dean's on-screen depictions of youthful rebellion and juvenile delinquency. In the end, however, hopefulness, not despair, remained the dominant theme.

Ultimately, I believe, the frequent returns these small-town boys made—either literally or figuratively—to the places of their childhoods reflected a strong yearning on their part for togetherness and community, as the sense of unity and well-being they attached to the notion of home came under challenge in the increasingly urbanized and industrialized American culture that emerged during the decades after the Civil War. While most of these men discovered in the city the kinds of economic and occupational opportunities they craved, memories of home and the human connections they associated with it exerted a powerful pull on their psyches. There is nothing inherently contradictory between the highly creative and individualistic personalities of these men, on the one hand, and their search for community, on the other. But their lives and careers illustrated the continuing tension that has always existed between individual and society in American civilization.

In turning their thoughts back to boyhood rambles and adventures in the places of their origins, nostalgic reveries could sometimes lead them to misconstrue the realities they had actually experienced. The kinds of rosy

scenarios envisioned in the reminiscent songs of Meredith Willson, celebrated in the bright-hued illustrations of Grant Wood, or happily recalled
in cheerful stories spun by Ronald Reagan speak more to the needy emotions of their listeners and viewers than to a fully realistic understanding of
the past as actually lived. People's memories always play tricks on them, as
they will admit if they analyze them honestly. Beyond that, memories can
be highly misleading and deceptive when people rely on them to smooth
over contradictions and conflicts in their experience or when people turn
to them for emotional reinforcement and the bolstering of morale. If in
these pages I may seem to have fallen into this trap, it will not be for lack
of trying to avoid it. My intent, on the contrary, has been to recount as directly and honestly as possible the deeply felt emotions and attitudes that
frequently led grown men to return to the remembered days of their youth
and to illustrate how these checkered memories played out as these midwestern natives progressed through their adult years.

Men's lives—and women's, too—are many things. People live in a world
of sharp edges and unanticipated challenges. Mere survival, in some instances, stands out as a mark of success. But life also has its compensa-
tions, allures, and rewards. Awareness of reality, everything else being
equal, is generally a good thing. But people require more than warmth,
food, raiment, and shelter. They also need goals, visions, hopes, and
dreams—at least, they do if they are to be truly fulfilled. Memories of one's
childhood can constitute for some only images of horror and regret. For
others, however, they emerge as sources of sustenance, morale, inspiration,
and lessons learned. Whatever the case may be, our continuing lives are
built on foundations established in the places from which we derive. In
dreaming our dreams, we seamlessly blend past and future, fact and fantasy, cold reality and hopeful imaginings. In between, we live our lives, and
out of them history is made.

Notes

Introduction: Midwestern Small Towns and
the Experience of Place

The epigraph comes from Veblen's "The Country Town," originally published in 1923, in *The Portable Veblen*, ed. Max Lerner (New York: Penguin Books, 1976), 407.

1. Defining the term "small town" is an elusive and tricky business. The population limit for inclusion has constantly increased as the nation's population has risen. My maximum cutoff for inclusion is 25,000, a commonly used census category when dealing with size of place. Most of the men highlighted in this book came from towns much smaller than that. The U.S. census has generally classified places having more than 2,500 people as "urban," meaning that most residents of "small towns" have lived in places that are, by definition, urban, while unincorporated places or towns of less than 2,500 population are termed "rural."

2. Granville Hicks, *Small Town* (New York: Macmillan, 1947), 13; Lewis Atherton, *Main Street on the Middle Border* (Bloomington: Indiana University Press, 1954), 3.

3. Claude S. Fischer, *Made in America: A Social History of American Culture and Character* (Chicago: University of Chicago Press, 2010), 146. Currently, 93 percent of the more than 19,000 incorporated places in the United States have populations of fewer than 25,000 people. But of the 53 million people who live in these places, about 23 million live in "urban fringe" areas around larger cities and metropolitan complexes, leaving approximately 30 million people who live in self-contained small towns of less than 25,000, constituting a little less than 10 percent

of the nation's population. Robert Wuthnow, *Small-Town America: Finding Community, Shaping the Future* (Princeton: Princeton University Press, 2013), 7–8, 395n15.

4. In writing about how the American public dreams of Main Street as an ideal place, Miles Orvell observes that even as small towns as physical places have "been battered" in recent decades, "the idea of the small town lies at the heart of the American ethos, with a strong and continuing appeal for Americans." *The Death and Life of Main Street: Small Towns in American Memory, Space, and Community* (Chapel Hill: University of North Carolina Press, 2012), ix.

5. This was the opening sentence of Richard Hofstadter's Pulitzer Prize–winning *The Age of Reform: From Bryan to F.D.R.* (New York: Alfred A. Knopf, 1955), 23.

6. Robert H. Wiebe, *The Search for Order, 1877–1920* (New York: Hill and Wang, 1967), 2–4, 44.

7. Quoted in Thomas Frank, "The GOP Loves the Heartland to Death," *Wall Street Journal*, September 10, 2008.

8. Hugh Sidey, "Why Small-Town Boys Make Good," *Time*, May 24, 1976, 16.

9. Peggy Noonan, "The End of Placeness," *Wall Street Journal*, August 16, 2008.

10. Yi-Fu Tuan, *Topophilia: A Study of Environmental Perception, Attitudes, and Values* (Englewood Cliffs, N.J.: Prentice Hall, 1974), 4; Stephen C. Behrendt, "Regionalism and the Realities of Naming," in *Regionalism and the Humanities*, ed. Timothy R. Mahoney and Wendy J. Katz (Lincoln: University of Nebraska Press, 2008), 151; Tom Brokaw cites novelist Saul Bellow in quoting the aphorism in *A Long Way from Home: Growing Up in the American Heartland* (New York: Random House, 2002), 229.

11. Winifred Gallagher, *The Power of Place: How Our Surroundings Shape Our Thoughts, Emotions, and Actions* (New York: HarperPerennial, 1994), 12.

12. Becky Bradway, introduction to *In the Middle of the Middle West: Literary Nonfiction from the Heartland* (Bloomington: Indiana University Press, 2003), xii.

13. Quoted in *Home: The Blueprints of Our Lives*, ed. John Edwards with Kate Edwards and Jonathan Prince (New York: HarperCollins, 2006), 46.

14. See William Deresiewicz's review of Robinson's novels in "Homing Patterns," *Nation*, October 13, 2008, 28.

15. Susan J. Matt, *Homesickness: An American History* (New York: Oxford University Press, 2011), 4, 10, 27, 253–254.

16. James Howard Kunstler, *The Geography of Nowhere: The Rise and Decline of America's Man-Made Landscape* (New York: Simon and Schuster, 1993), 185.

17. Quoted in *Grant County (S.D.) News*, June 13, 1912.

18. Dalton Conley, *Elsewhere, U.S.A.* (New York: Pantheon Books, 2009).

19. Quoted in Bill Kauffman, *Look Homeward, America: In Search of Reactionary Radicals and Front-Porch Anarchists* (Wilmington, Del.: ISI Books, 2006), 106.

20. Harry Crews, contributor to the forum "A Stubborn Sense of Place," *Harper's*, August 1986, 39–40.

21. Evidence of reviving interest in regionalism and particularly in the history and culture of the Middle West can be found in such publications as Robert Dorman, *Hell of a Vision: Regionalism and the Modern American West* (Tucson: University of Arizona Press, 2012); James Belich, *Replenishing the Earth: The Settler Revolution and the Rise of the Angloworld, 1783–1939* (New York: Oxford University Press, 2009); David S. Brown, *Beyond the Frontier: The Midwestern Voice in American Historical Writing* (Chicago: University of Chicago Press, 2009); Nicole Etcheson, *The Emerging Midwest: Upland Southerners and the Political Culture of the Old Northwest, 1787–1861* (Bloomington: Indiana University Press, 1996); and Edward Watts, *An American Colony: Regionalism and the Roots of Midwestern Culture* (Athens: Ohio University Press, 2002). The best single-volume treatment of midwestern regionalism is Andrew R. L. Cayton and Susan E. Gray, eds., *The American Midwest: Essays on Regional History* (Bloomington: Indiana University Press, 2001). For an excellent summary of recent trends and a vigorous argument for the revival of midwestern history, see Jon K. Lauck, *The Lost Region: Toward a Revival of Midwestern History* (Iowa City: University of Iowa Press, 2013).

22. On evolving definitions of the Midwest, see James R. Shortridge, *The Middle West: Its Meaning in American Culture* (Lawrence: University Press of Kansas, 1989). For examples of books using these twelve states as their standard definition of the region, see James H. Madison, *Comparative Histories of the Midwestern States* (Bloomington: Indiana University Press, 1988); Atherton, *Main Street on the Middle Border*; and Richard Sisson, Christian Zacher, and Andrew Cayton, eds., *The American Midwest: An Interpretive Encyclopedia* (Bloomington: Indiana University Press, 2007).

23. Andrew R. L. Cayton, "The Anti-region: Place and Identity in the History of the American Midwest," in Cayton and Gray, *The American Midwest*, 141–142.

24. Andrew R. L. Cayton and Susan E. Gray, "The Story of the Midwest," in Cayton and Gray, *The American Midwest*, 17.

25. John Dewey, "The American Intellectual Frontier," *New Republic*, May 10, 1922, 303.

26. Robert Wuthnow, *Remaking the Heartland: Middle America since the 1950s* (Princeton: Princeton University Press, 2011).

27. See, for example, David J. Russo, *American Towns: An Interpretive History* (Chicago: Ivan R. Dee, 2001); Joseph A. Amato, *Rethinking Home: A Case for Writing Local History* (Berkeley: University of California Press, 2002); Richard O. Davies, *Main Street Blues: The Decline of Small-Town America* (Columbus: Ohio State University Press, 1998); Richard Lingeman, *Small Town America: A Narrative History, 1620–the Present* (New York: G. P. Putnam's Sons, 1980); Page Smith, *As a City upon a Hill: The Town in American History* (New York: Alfred A. Knopf, 1966).

28. Alexander Bloom, *Prodigal Sons: The New York Intellectuals and Their World* (New York: Oxford University Press, 1986), 306–308. On Hofstadter generally, see David S. Brown, *Richard Hofstadter: An Intellectual Biography* (Chicago: University of Chicago Press, 2006); and Arthur Schlesinger Jr., "Richard Hofstadter," in *Pastmasters: Some Essays on American Historians,* ed. Marcus Cunliffe and Robin W. Winks (New York: Harper and Row, 1969), 278–315.

29. Jack Pole, "Richard Hofstadter," in *Clio's Favorites: Leading Historians of the United States, 1945–2000,* ed. Robert Allen Rutland (Columbia: University of Missouri Press, 2000), 69.

30. Richard Hofstadter, *The Progressive Historians: Turner, Beard, Parrington* (New York: Alfred A. Knopf, 1968), 147–148; Hofstadter, *Anti-intellectualism in American Life* (New York: Alfred A. Knopf, 1963), 35–36, 42–43, 123, 129; Brown, *Richard Hofstadter,* xvi, 22, 76, 103–104, 196–198; Daniel J. Singal, "Beyond Consensus: Richard Hofstadter and American Historiography," *American Historical Review* 89 (October 1984): 980–981, 991n29.

31. Garrison Keillor, *Prairie Home Companion,* National Public Radio program from Tanglewood, Massachusetts, July 3, 2004.

32. Joyce Carol Oates, "Going Home Again," *Smithsonian,* March 2010, 74, 76.

Chapter One: Frederick Jackson Turner
The epigraph comes from Turner's letter to Constance Lindsay Skinner, March 15, 1922, quoted in Ray Allen Billington, *The Genesis of the Frontier Thesis: A Study in Historical Creativity* (San Marino, Calif.: Huntington Library, 1971), 215–216.

1. Two excellent biographies are Allan G. Bogue, *Frederick Jackson Turner: Strange Roads Going Down* (Norman: University of Oklahoma Press, 1998); and Ray Allen Billington, *Frederick Jackson Turner: Historian, Scholar, Teacher* (New York: Oxford University Press, 1973).

2. Richard Hofstadter made the sensible observation that much of Turner's thesis boiled down to the understanding "that the United States was a rural society before it became an urban one." *The Progressive Historians: Turner, Beard, Parrington* (New York: Alfred A. Knopf, 1968), 125.

3. Bogue, *Frederick Jackson Turner,* 163–166.

4. Gene Wise, *American Historical Explanations: A Strategy for Grounded Inquiry* (Minneapolis: University of Minnesota Press, 1980), 215n1.

5. Hofstadter, *The Progressive Historians,* xii.

6. Martin Ridge, "Frederick Jackson Turner, Ray Allen Billington, and American Frontier History," *Western Historical Quarterly* 19 (January 1988): 10; Ray Allen Billington, "Why Some Historians Rarely Write History: A Case Study of Frederick Jackson Turner," *Mississippi Valley Historical Review* 50 (June 1963): 9.

7. Billington, *Frederick Jackson Turner,* 127.

8. Frederick Jackson Turner, "The Significance of the Frontier in American History," in *The Frontier in American History* (New York: Henry Holt, 1920), 1.

Although Turner deserves credit for raising consciousness of the end of the frontier among historians, social scientists, and the general public, anxiety about the closing of the frontier had been rising for at least a decade. See David M. Wrobel, *The End of American Exceptionalism: Frontier Anxiety from the Old West to the New Deal* (Lawrence: University Press of Kansas, 1993), 1–68; Robert G. Athern, *The Mythic West in Twentieth-Century America* (Lawrence: University Press of Kansas, 1986), 10–22.

9. Turner, "The Significance of the Frontier in American History," 1, 30, 37.

10. Ibid., 209–214.

11. Ibid., 3.

12. Ibid., 3, 12–24.

13. Quoted in Billington, *Frederick Jackson Turner,* 83, 130.

14. Billington, *The Genesis of the Frontier Thesis,* 66–70.

15. Henry Nash Smith, *Virgin Land: The American West as Symbol and Myth* (Cambridge, Mass.: Harvard University Press, 1950), chap. 22; Billington, *The Genesis of the Frontier Thesis,* 75; David S. Brown, *Beyond the Frontier: The Midwestern Voice in American Historical Writing* (Chicago: University of Chicago Press, 2009), 40.

16. Billington, *Frederick Jackson Turner,* 5–11; Bogue, *Frederick Jackson Turner,* 3–8.

17. Andrew Jackson Turner to Frederick Jackson Turner, undated letter, box K, Turner Papers, Henry E. Huntington Library, San Marino, California.

18. Billington, *Frederick Jackson Turner,* 12.

19. Frederick Jackson Turner, three volumes of "Commonplace Books" (1881–1887), in vol. 3, numbers 1–3, Turner Papers.

20. Frederick Jackson Turner to Carl Becker, October 3, 1925, in Billington, *The Genesis of the Frontier Thesis,* 224–225. Also see Billington, *Frederick Jackson Turner,* 161, 477; Bogue, *Frederick Jackson Turner,* 343.

21. This point was mentioned by Turner in a letter to Merle Curti, August 8, 1928, in Billington, *The Genesis of the Frontier Thesis,* 259, along with the fact that at Johns Hopkins the only American history he took was a brief seminar with Albion Small focusing on the powers granted by the colonies and states to their representatives in the Continental Congresses.

22. Fulmer Mood, "The Development of Frederick Jackson Turner as a Historical Thinker," *Transactions* (Colonial Science of Massachusetts) 34 (December 1939): 288–290.

23. David B. Frankenburger, "William Francis Allen," memorial address delivered before the Wisconsin Historical Society, January 2, 1890, 81–82, box 4, William Francis Allen Papers, State Historical Society of Wisconsin, Madison; Howard R. Lamar, "Frederick Jackson Turner," in *Pastmasters: Some Essays on American Historians,* ed. Marcus Cunliffe and Robin W. Winks (New York: Harper and Row, 1969), 79.

24. Frederick Jackson Turner to Carl Becker, December 16, 1925, in Billington, *The Genesis of the Frontier Thesis*, 239.

25. Billington, *Frederick Jackson Turner*, 29–30, 38–39, 46.

26. Frederick Jackson Turner to Mae Sherwood, September 5, 1887, box B, Turner Papers.

27. For evolving conceptions and definitions of "Middle West," see James R. Shortridge, *The Middle West: Its Meaning in American Culture* (Lawrence: University Press of Kansas, 1989).

28. Billington, *Frederick Jackson Turner*, 49–50.

29. Merle Curti, "Frederick Jackson Turner," in *Wisconsin Witness to Frederick Jackson Turner: A Collection of Essays on the Historian and His Thesis*, comp. O. Lawrence Burnette Jr. (Madison: State Historical Society of Wisconsin, 1961), 182.

30. Billington, *The Genesis of the Frontier Thesis*, 30–31, 184n6.

31. Frederick Jackson Turner to William F. Allen, October 31, 1888, box 1, Turner Papers.

32. Frederick Jackson Turner to Constance Lindsay Skinner, March 15, 1922, in Billington, *The Genesis of the Frontier Thesis*, 208. On Turner's decision to champion the West and the Midwest, see Michael C. Steiner, "The Significance of Turner's Sectional Thesis," *Western Historical Quarterly* 10 (October 1979): 439–445.

33. Billington, *Frederick Jackson Turner*, 102, 104–107.

34. Steiner, "The Significance of Turner's Sectional Thesis," 443.

35. Quoted in Hofstadter, *The Progressive Historians*, 48–50.

36. Louis M. Hacker, "Sections or Classes," *Nation*, July 26, 1933, 108–110.

37. John Mack Faragher, "The Frontier Trail: Rethinking Turner and Reimagining the American West," *American Historical Review* 98 (February 1993): 107; Gerald D. Nash, *Creating the West: Historical Interpretations, 1890–1990* (Albuquerque: University of New Mexico Press, 1991), 74.

38. Frederick Jackson Turner to Arthur M. Schlesinger, May 5, 1925, in Wilbur R. Jacobs, *The Historical World of Frederick Jackson Turner* (New Haven: Yale University Press, 1968), 164.

39. Allan G. Bogue, "Frederick Jackson Turner Reconsidered," *History Teacher* 27 (February 1994): 199–201.

40. A whole industry of Turner criticism arose, tracking attacks made on his writings, responses in his defense, and efforts to find some happy medium. Good summaries of the debates can be found in George W. Pierson, "American Historians and the Frontier Hypothesis in 1941," pts. 1 and 2, *Wisconsin Magazine of History* 26, no. 1 (September 1942): 36–60; and 26, no. 2 (December 1942): 170–185; George Rogers Taylor, ed., *The Turner Thesis: Concerning the Role of the Frontier in American History* (Lexington, Mass.: D. C. Heath, 1972); Ray Allen Billington, ed., *The Frontier Thesis: Valid Interpretation of American History?* (New York: Holt, Rinehart and Winston, 1966).

41. Fred A. Shannon, "A Post Mortem on the Labor-Safety-Valve Theory," *Agricultural History* 19 (January 1945): 31–37.

42. W. N. Davis, "Will the West Survive as a Field of American History? A Survey Report," *Mississippi Valley Historical Review* 50 (March 1964): 672–685.

43. Good compendiums of new western history ideas are contained in Patricia Nelson Limerick, Clyde A. Milner II, and Charles E. Rankin, eds., *Trails: Toward a New Western History* (Lawrence: University Press of Kansas, 1991); and William Cronon, George Miles, and Jay Gitlin, eds., *Under an Open Sky: Rethinking America's Western Past* (New York: W. W. Norton, 1992).

44. William Cronon, "Revisiting the Vanishing Frontier: The Legacy of Frederick Jackson Turner," *Western Historical Quarterly* 18 (April 1987): 160. Richard Hofstadter had made a similar point two decades earlier: "Even Turner's sharpest critics have rarely failed to concede the core merit of his thesis, and wisely so. For over two hundred and fifty years the American people shaped their lives with the vast empty interior of the continent before them. Their national existence up to Turner's day had been involved with conquering, securing, occupying, and developing their continental empire." *The Progressive Historians*, 119.

45. See Ronald H. Carpenter, *The Eloquence of Frederick Jackson Turner* (San Marino, Calif.: Huntington Library, 1985).

46. See Turner's handwritten excerpt from Kipling's *Song of the English*, in file drawer 15B, Turner Papers. He used the poem to reflect the idealism of land seekers on the frontier in his "Contributions of the West to American Democracy," originally published in 1903, reprinted in *The Frontier in American History*, 262. Bogue used the second line of Turner's excerpt for the subtitle of his biography *Frederick Jackson Turner: Strange Roads Going Down*.

47. See Billington, *Frederick Jackson Turner*, 424–426; Avery Craven, "Frederick Jackson Turner: Historian," in Burnette, *Wisconsin Witness to Frederick Jackson Turner*, 110.

48. Frederick Jackson Turner to Merle Curti, June 30, 1927, box 42, Merle Curti Papers, Wisconsin Historical Society, Madison. David S. Brown also notes that Turner was influenced by German romantic historicism. *Beyond the Frontier*, 40.

49. Hofstadter, *The Progressive Historians*, 118–120.

50. George Wilson Pierson writes, "In his work with his students, Turner seems to have been modest and tentative and open-minded to a degree; but in his essays he could be and was as inclusive and sweeping as any have been since." "The Frontier and American Institutions: A Criticism of the Turner Theory," *New England Quarterly* 15 (March 1942): 248.

51. On Turner's attachment to the "method of multiple working hypotheses," see Wilbur R. Jacobs, "Turner's Methodology: Multiple Working Hypotheses or Ruling Theory?" *Journal of American History* 54 (March 1968): 853–863. Although Turner preached the idea of multiple causation, he sometimes ignored it in practice.

52. Frederick Jackson Turner to Merle Curti, August 8, 1928, in Billington, *The Genesis of the Frontier Thesis*, 257.

53. Quoted in Arthur M. Schlesinger Sr., *In Retrospect: The History of a Historian* (New York: Harcourt, Brace and World, 1963), 197–198.

54. Bogue, *Frederick Jackson Turner*, 351.

55. Ibid., 208–211, 252; Hart quoted in Billington, "Why Some Historians Rarely Write History," 21–22. According to Ellen Fitzpatrick, Turner's *Rise of the New West* "seemed the most fresh and innovative volume in the series." *History's Memory: Writing America's Past, 1880–1980* (Cambridge, Mass.: Harvard University Press, 2002), 61.

56. Quoted in Billington, "Why Some Historians Rarely Write History," 27.

57. Billington, *Frederick Jackson Turner*, 416–417; Bogue, *Frederick Jackson Turner*, 440.

58. On Turner's sectional thesis, see Billington, *Frederick Jackson Turner*, 471; Michael C. Steiner, "Frederick Jackson Turner and Western Regionalism," in *Writing Western History: Essays on Major Western Historians*, ed. Richard W. Etulain (Albuquerque: University of New Mexico Press, 1991), 103–135; Richard Jensen, "On Modernizing Frederick Jackson Turner: The Historiography of Regionalism," *Western Historical Quarterly* 11 (July 1980): 307–322; Richard White, "Frederick Jackson Turner," in *Historians of the American Frontier: A Bio-Bibliographical Sourcebook*, ed. John R. Wunder (Westport, Conn.: Greenwood Press, 1988), 660–681.

59. See Robert L. Dorman, *Revolt of the Provinces: The Regionalist Movement in America, 1920–1945* (Chapel Hill: University of North Carolina Press, 1993); Dorman, *Hell of a Vision: Regionalism and the Modern American West* (Tucson: University of Arizona Press, 2012); Merrill Jensen, ed., *Regionalism in America* (Madison: University of Wisconsin Press, 1952). In recent years, a few scholars, including Michael Steiner and William Cronon, have taken a fresh look at Turner's sectional researches and found them useful and suggestive. Steiner, "The Significance of Turner's Sectional Thesis," 437–466; Steiner, "From Frontier to Region: Frederick Jackson Turner and the New Western History," *Pacific Historical Review* 64 (November 1995): 479–501; Cronon, "Revisiting the Vanishing Frontier," 173–176.

60. Bogue, *Frederick Jackson Turner*, 37, 59.

61. Ibid., 82–83, 128–129, 131–132, 186, 188, 242–243, 333, 404–405; Frederick Jackson Turner to William F. Allen, October 31, 1888, box 1, Turner Papers.

62. Billington, *Frederick Jackson Turner*, 365, 418, 456.

63. Frederick Jackson Turner, "The Middle West," in *The Frontier in American History*, 127, 155.

64. Hofstadter, *The Progressive Historians*, 114.

65. Ibid., 77; Avery Craven, "Frederick Jackson Turner," in *Marcus W. Jernegan Essays in American Historiography*, ed. William T. Hutchinson (Chicago: Univer-

sity of Chicago Press, 1937), 269; Wise, *American Historical Explanations,* 206; Stanley Elkins and Eric McKitrick, "A Meaning for Turner's Frontier. Part I: Democracy in the Old Northwest," *Political Science Quarterly* 69 (September 1954): 330.

66. Billington, *Frederick Jackson Turner,* 238, 320, 326, 435–436, quotations at 385.

67. Lewis Mumford, *The City in History: Its Origins, Its Transformations, and Its Prospects* (New York: Harcourt, Brace and World, 1961), 5.

68. Robert N. Bellah et al., *Habits of the Heart: Individualism and Commitment in American Life* (Berkeley: University of California Press, 1985), 153–154.

69. References to urbanism in Turner's *The Rise of the New West, 1819–1829* (New York: Harper and Brothers, 1906), can be found on 36, 68, 77, 78, 82, and 105; in his *The United States, 1830–1850: The Nation and Its Sections* (New York: Henry Holt, 1935), on 15, 42, 86, 99, 154, 174–175, 259, 260, 264, 267, 273, 280, 284, 292, and 335. In *The Frontier in American History,* see 34, 42, 44, 66, 73, 78, 88, 125, 147.

70. C. Wright Mills, "The Professional Ideology of Social Pathologists," *American Journal of Sociology* 49 (September 1943): 165–180. On the rural roots and mind-sets of early twentieth-century American intellectuals, see also R. Jackson Wilson, *In Quest of Community: Social Philosophy in the United States, 1860–1920* (New York: Wiley, 1968); Jean B. Quandt, *From the Small Town to the Great Community: The Social Thought of the Progressive Intellectuals* (New Brunswick, N.J.: Rutgers University Press, 1970); and Morton White and Lucia White, *The Intellectual versus the City: From Thomas Jefferson to Frank Lloyd Wright* (Cambridge, Mass.: Harvard University Press, 1962).

71. White and White, *The Intellectual versus the City.*

72. Frederick Jackson Turner to Arthur M. Schlesinger Sr., May 5, 1927, in Jacobs, *The Historical World of Frederick Jackson Turner,* 164; Schlesinger, *In Retrospect,* 107; Schlesinger, "The City in American History," *Mississippi Valley Historical Review* 27 (June 1940): 43. See also Billington, *Frederick Jackson Turner,* 263.

73. Frederick Jackson Turner, notes for an essay on the significance of the city in American history, October 1922, file drawer 14A, Turner Papers.

74. Frederick Jackson Turner to Mae Sherwood, June 21, 24, 1889, box D, Turner Papers; Steiner, "Frederick Jackson Turner and Western Regionalism," 107–109.

75. Lewis Atherton, *Main Street on the Middle Border* (Bloomington: Indiana University Press, 1954); Elkins and McKitrick, "A Meaning for Turner's Frontier," 341; Richard C. Wade, *The Urban Frontier: The Rise of Western Cities, 1790–1830* (Cambridge, Mass.: Harvard University Press, 1959), 1.

76. See, for example, Page Smith, *As a City upon a Hill: The Town in American History* (New York: Alfred A. Knopf, 1966); Richard Lingeman, *Small Town*

America: A Narrative History, 1620–the Present (New York: G. P. Putnam's Sons, 1980); David J. Russo, *American Towns: An Interpretive History* (Chicago: Ivan R. Dee, 2001); John C. Hudson, *Plains Country Towns* (Minneapolis: University of Minnesota Press, 1985); Richard O. Davies, *Main Street Blues: The Decline of Small-Town America* (Columbus: Ohio State University Press, 1998).

Chapter Two: William McKinley and William Jennings Bryan
McKinley's epigraph quotation comes from Margaret Leech's *In the Days of McKinley* (New York: Harper and Brothers, 1959), 10; the second epigraph comes from Henry Steele Commager's *There Were Giants in the Land* (New York: Farrar and Rinehart, 1942), 101.

1. Paul W. Glad, *McKinley, Bryan, and the People* (Philadelphia: J. B. Lippincott, 1964), chap. 4.

2. H. Wayne Morgan, *William McKinley and His America* (Syracuse, N.Y.: Syracuse University Press, 1963), 222; J. Rogers Hollingsworth, *The Whirligig of Politics: The Democracy of Cleveland and Bryan* (Chicago: University of Chicago Press, 1963), 69–72; Samuel T. McSeveney, *The Politics of Depression: Political Behavior in the Northeast, 1893–1896* (New York: Oxford University Press, 1972), 181–182.

3. Roosevelt and Hay both quoted in Paolo E. Coletta, *William Jennings Bryan: Political Evangelist, 1860–1908* (Lincoln: University of Nebraska Press, 1964), 194–195.

4. Michael Kazin, *A Godly Hero: The Life of William Jennings Bryan* (New York: Alfred A. Knopf, 2006), xiii. See also clippings in folder 8, series 5, William Jennings Bryan Papers, Nebraska State Historical Society, Lincoln, Nebraska.

5. Gilbert C. Fite, "Election of 1896," in *History of American Presidential Elections, 1789–1968,* ed. Arthur M. Schlesinger Jr., 4 vols. (New York: Chelsea House, 1971), 2: 1787–1788, 1825.

6. Bryan, "Cross of Gold Speech," in *Speeches of William Jennings Bryan*, rev. and arr. himself, 2 vols. (New York: Funk and Wagnalls, 1913), 1: 248, 249.

7. Hollingsworth, *The Whirligig of Politics,* 107.

8. Unless specifically noted, most of my biographical information on McKinley comes from Morgan, *William McKinley and His America*; Leech, *In the Days of McKinley*; Lewis L. Gould, *The Presidency of William McKinley* (Lawrence: University Press of Kansas, 1980); and Kevin Phillips, *William McKinley* (New York: Times Books, 2003).

9. James Boyle, a newspaper correspondent who covered several McKinley election campaigns and later served as his private secretary while he was governor, was one of many to use the word "lovable" to describe the man. "William McKinley as I Knew Him," *Week: A Journal of Fundamental Democracy* 10 (January 23, 1915): 1.

10. For biographical information on Bryan, I have relied heavily on Coletta,

William Jennings Bryan; Louis Koenig, *Bryan: A Political Biography of William Jennings Bryan* (New York: G. P. Putnam's Sons, 1971); Paul W. Glad, *The Trumpet Soundeth: William Jennings Bryan and His Democracy, 1896–1912* (Lincoln: University of Nebraska Press, 1960); Kazin, *A Godly Hero*; and Robert W. Cherny, *A Righteous Cause: The Life of William Jennings Bryan* (Boston: Little, Brown, 1985).

11. *The Memoirs of William Jennings Bryan,* with Mary Baird Bryan (Chicago: John C. Winston, 1925), 10, 12.

12. Thomas H. Tibbets, "Bryan as a Man," in *Watson's Jeffersonian*, reprinted in *Polk County (Neb.) Democrat,* May 16, 1907.

13. Quoted in Mark Sullivan, "Bryan as He Looks Today," *New York Herald Tribune,* June 28, 1924.

14. *Denver Daily News,* August 2, 1896.

15. Bryan quoted in Glad, *McKinley, Bryan, and the People,* 130–140; R. Hal Williams, *Realigning America: McKinley, Bryan, and the Remarkable Election of 1896* (Lawrence: University Press of Kansas, 2010), 69, 76, 80–81; Stanley L. Jones, *The Presidential Election of 1896* (Madison: University of Wisconsin Press, 1964), 238–240; Koenig, *Bryan,* chap. 13.

16. On the speech, see Koenig, *Bryan,* 194–200; Coletta, *William Jennings Bryan,* 137–142; Williams, *Realigning America,* 83–86; and Kazin, *A Godly Hero,* 59–63.

17. Bryan, "Cross of Gold Speech," 241.

18. Ibid., 240–241 (my italics).

19. Quoted in Kazin, *A Godly Hero,* 61.

20. Quoted in M. R. Werner, *Bryan* (New York: Harcourt, Brace, 1929), 76.

21. The amount raised by the Republicans has long been a matter of dispute. The Republican campaign committee reported approximately $3.5 million in expenditures. See Charles G. Dawes, *A Journal of the McKinley Years,* ed. Bascom N. Timmons (Chicago: Lakeside Press, 1950), 106. But total expenditures may actually have been closer to between $10 million and $16 million. Cherny, *A Righteous Cause,* 65.

22. Jones, *The Presidential Election of 1896,* chap. 20; Leech, *In the Days of McKinley,* 86–94.

23. Kazin, *A Godly Hero,* 67–76; Glad, *McKinley, Bryan, and the People,* 176, 183–184; Coletta, *William Jennings Bryan,* 168.

24. Quoted in James A. Barnes, "Myths of the Bryan Campaign," *Mississippi Valley Historical Review* 34 (December 1947): 402.

25. Arguments on this issue work both ways. Hollingsworth, for example, contends that Bryan made a mistake in not concentrating more attention on the East because he was stronger in the region than he realized. *The Whirligig of Politics,* 87. Coletta, on the other hand, argues that Bryan should have spent more of his time in the Middle West and should have avoided "skylarking" in the East, where he did not have much of a chance. *William Jennings Bryan,* 204.

26. William Jennings Bryan, *The First Battle: A Story of the Campaign of 1896* (Chicago: W. B. Conkey, 1896), 607.

27. Jones, *The Presidential Election of 1896*, 107, 111, 277, 296; Richard Jensen, *The Winning of the Midwest: Social and Political Conflict, 1888–1896* (Chicago: University of Chicago Press, 1971), xv, 273–274; Phillips, *William McKinley*, 74–75; Cherny, *A Righteous Cause*, 65–69; Barnes, "Myths of the Bryan Campaign," 382.

28. Leech, *In the Days of McKinley*, 57, 61–62; Jensen, *The Winning of the Midwest*, 286.

29. James P. Boyd, *McKinley's Great Battles for Gold and Silver and Protection* (n.p.: James P. Boyd, 1897), 464; Murat Halstead, *Life and Distinguished Career of Hon. William McKinley and the Great Issues of 1896* (n.p.: Edgewood Publishing, 1896), 51; Richard L. McElroy, *William McKinley and Our America* (Canton, Ohio: Stark County Historical Society, 1996), 129.

30. Coletta, *William Jennings Bryan*, 165; Jones, *The Presidential Election of 1896*, 277.

31. Dawes, *A Journal of the McKinley Years*, 97.

32. Jones, *The Presidential Election of 1896*, chap. 20; Glad, *McKinley, Bryan, and the People*, chap. 8; Morgan, *William McKinley and His America*, chap. 11; Leech, *In the Days of McKinley*, 85–96; Herbert Croly, *Marcus Alonzo Hanna: His Life and Work* (New York: Macmillan, 1912), 212–218.

33. Coletta places more emphasis than most of his counterparts on the effects of bribery, intimidation, and the stuffing of ballot boxes, suggesting that a fair vote would have given Bryan the election. *William Jennings Bryan*, 192–193. Michael Kazin contends that had McKinley not enjoyed the solid support of the industrial elite, providing him with a spending edge of as much as 1,000 percent, Bryan might well have won the election. "The Other Bryan," *American Prospect* 17 (January 2006): 44.

34. Jones, *The Presidential Election of 1896*, 344.

35. Paul Kleppner, *The Cross of Culture: A Social Analysis of Midwestern Politics, 1850–1900* (New York: Free Press, 1970), 369.

36. Jensen, *The Winning of the Midwest*, 18.

37. Ibid., 164–171; Williams, *Realigning America*, 9–10, 136–139, 170–171.

38. Kazin, *A Godly Hero*, xviii–xix, 65, 123–124, 222–227, 302–305.

39. Gould, *The Presidency of William McKinley*, 231–253.

40. Leech, *In the Days of McKinley*, 144; Gould, *The Presidency of William McKinley*, 59–60, 88–90, 93, 130, 179–205.

41. Morgan, *William McKinley and His America*, 305–307; Gould, *The Presidency of William McKinley*, 92–93, 231–253; Phillips, *William McKinley*, 30, 87; McElroy, *William McKinley and Our America*, 82.

42. Gould, *The Presidency of William McKinley*, 38–39; Phillips, *William McKinley*, 143–146; Leech, *In the Days of McKinley*, 126–128.

43. Leech, *In the Days of McKinley*, 151, 389, 568; Phillips, *William McKinley*, 131.

44. Gould, *The Presidency of William McKinley*, 135–136, 207–208, 247, 250–252; Leech, *In the Days of McKinley*, 577–579.

45. Morgan, *William McKinley and His America*, 321, 323, 475; Phillips, *William McKinley*, 12. Quotations are from *Speeches and Addresses of William McKinley from March 1, 1897 to May 30, 1900* (New York: Doubleday and Mc-Clure, 1900), 1; and Leech, *In the Days of McKinley*, 10.

46. Lawrence W. Levine, *Defender of the Faith: William Jennings Bryan. The Last Decade, 1915–1925* (New York: Oxford University Press, 1965), 218.

47. *The Memoirs of William Jennings Bryan*, 9.

48. Koenig, *Bryan*, 293; Kazin, *A Godly Hero*, xix, 161–162, 277–278; LeRoy Ashby, *William Jennings Bryan: Champion of Democracy* (Boston: Twayne, 1987), 103–104; David W. Southern, *The Progressive Era and Race: Reaction and Reform, 1900–1917* (Wheeling, Ill.: Harlan Davidson, 2005), 121.

49. Richard Hofstadter, *The American Political Tradition and the Men Who Made It* (New York: Alfred A. Knopf, 1948), 193. Those who argue for Bryan's essential consistency over time include Glad, *The Trumpet Soundeth*, 58, 108; Kazin, *A Godly Hero*, 303–306; Ashby, *William Jennings Bryan*, 176–177; and Levine, *Defender of the Faith*, vii–viii, 364–365.

50. Kazin, *A Godly Hero*, 114; Glad, *The Trumpet Soundeth*, chaps. 5–6.

51. Charles E. Merriam reflected the prevailing presumption that Bryan lacked an organization and had to rely on his own charisma and oratorical skills to maintain a following. *Four American Party Leaders* (New York: Macmillan, 1926), 63. Michael Kazin notes, however, the elaborate personal network that Bryan established and maintained for the better part of three decades. *A Godly Hero*, 82, 111–112, 194–195.

52. Kazin, *A Godly Hero*, xix, 79, 148–150; Koenig, *Bryan*, 10, 356–357; Coletta, *William Jennings Bryan*, 210–211.

53. William Jennings Bryan, "The Prince of Peace," in *Speeches of William Jennings Bryan*, 2: 261.

54. Levine, *Defender of the Faith*.

55. H. L. Mencken, "In Memoriam: W. J. B.," in *Prejudices*, 5th series (New York: Alfred A. Knopf, 1926), 64, 66.

56. Michael Kammen, *Selvages and Biases: The Fabric of History in American Culture* (Ithaca, N.Y.: Cornell University Press, 1987), 25; Ashby, *William Jennings Bryan*, 70.

57. Morgan, *William McKinley and His America*, 60; Kazin, *A Godly Hero*, 4–6; Koenig, *Bryan*, 21–23.

58. "Bryan Visited Home Quite Often," *Centralia (Ill.) Sentinel*, November 3, 1996.

59. Glad, *McKinley, Bryan, and the People*, chap. 2.

60. McKinley belonged to the Grand Army of the Republic (GAR), Loyal Legion, Masons, Knights of Pythias, YMCA, Republican Party, Methodist Church (where he was superintendent of the Sunday school), a literary society, and other groups. Leech, *In the Days of McKinley,* 11. Bryan was affiliated with, among others, the Chamber of Commerce, Rotary Club, YMCA, Knights of Pythias, Elks, Odd Fellows, Masons, Moose, Royal Highlanders, Modern Woodmen, Democratic Party, Presbyterian Church (where he taught Sunday school), and a philosophical discussion group. Koenig, *Bryan,* 48–49, 56.

61. The last important thing Bryan did before his death was to prepare for publication the closing speech he had been planning for weeks but was barred from giving at the Scopes trial in Dayton. It begins with a paean to the virtues of small-town community and the rural way of life. *The Memoirs of William Jennings Bryan,* 529–530.

Chapter Three: Henry Ford

The epigraph comes from the *Chicago Tribune,* July 12, 1935.

1. Ford lived almost eighty-four years and was one of the most-written-about persons in American history. In this chapter, I rely heavily on excellent biographies by Steven Watts, *The People's Tycoon: Henry Ford and the American Century* (New York: Alfred A. Knopf, 2005); Douglas Brinkley, *Wheels for the World: Henry Ford, His Company, and a Century of Progress* (New York: Viking, 2003); and David L. Lewis, *The Public Image of Henry Ford: An American Folk Hero and His Company* (Detroit: Wayne State University Press, 1976). Every student of Ford during the last fifty years owes much to Allan Nevins's three-volume biography, with Frank Ernest Hill, *Ford* (New York: Charles Scribner's Sons, 1954, 1957, 1962).

2. Charles Merz, "The Canonization of Henry Ford," *Independent,* November 27, 1926, 618; James J. Flink, *The Car Culture* (Cambridge: MIT Press, 1975), 68; Lewis, *The Public Image of Henry Ford,* 60–62, 129, 211–214.

3. Watts, *The People's Tycoon,* 160.

4. Allan Nevins, *Expansion and Challenge, 1915–1933,* with Frank Ernest Hill, vol. 2 of Nevins, *Ford,* 113.

5. Reynold Wik, *Henry Ford and Grass-Roots America* (Ann Arbor: University of Michigan Press, 1972), 81, 212–213, quotation at 1.

6. *Cleveland Press,* April 8, 1947.

7. Nevins, *Expansion and Challenge,* 116–121.

8. Wik, *Henry Ford and Grass-Roots America,* 172–174.

9. Nevins, *Expansion and Challenge,* 603–605.

10. Neil Baldwin, *Henry Ford and the Jews: The Mass Production of Hate* (New York: Public Affairs, 2001), 82–85, 99, quotation at 185.

11. Watts, *The People's Tycoon,* 253; Reinhold Niebuhr, "How Philanthropic Is Henry Ford?" *Christian Century,* December 9, 1926, 1516.

12. Quoted in David Halberstam, "Citizen Ford," *American Heritage,* October–November 1986, 50.

13. Vincent Curcio, *Henry Ford* (New York: Oxford University Press, 2013), 270; Samuel S. Marquis, *Henry Ford: An Interpretation* (Boston: Little, Brown, 1923), 161.

14. Watts, *The People's Tycoon,* xiii.

15. Charles E. Sorensen, *My Forty Years with Ford,* with Samuel T. Williamson (New York: W. W. Norton, 1956), 6; Marquis, *Henry Ford,* 168; Hamlin Garland, *Afternoon Neighbors: Further Excerpts from a Literary Log* (New York: Macmillan, 1934), 403–404.

16. William C. Richards, *The Last Billionaire: Henry Ford* (New York: Scribner's, 1948), 9–10; Marquis, *Henry Ford,* 169; Nevins, *Expansion and Challenge,* 617.

17. Keith Sward, *The Legend of Henry Ford* (1948; repr., New York: Atheneum, 1968), 284–286; Curcio, *Henry Ford,* 220.

18. Robert Lacey, *Ford: The Men and the Machine* (Boston: Little, Brown, 1986), 235–236; Nevins, *Expansion and Challenge,* 618; Marquis, *Henry Ford,* 29–30.

19. Quoted in Brinkley, *Wheels for the World,* xv.

20. William J. Cameron, *Reminiscences,* quoted in Anne Jardim, *The First Henry Ford: A Study in Personality and Business Leadership* (Cambridge: MIT Press, 1970), 34.

21. James D. Newton, *Uncommon Friends: Life with Thomas Edison, Henry Ford, Harvey Firestone, Alexis Carrel, and Charles Lindbergh* (New York: Harcourt, Brace, 1987), 97.

22. Watts, *The People's Tycoon,* 6, 14–19; Brinkley, *Wheels for the World,* 7–10.

23. Watts, *The People's Tycoon,* 19; Brinkley, *Wheels for the World,* 10–11.

24. Watts, *The People's Tycoon,* 297–306. A good example of Henry Ford's contradictory character can be perceived in the longtime affair he carried on with Evangeline Dahlinger, an employee who was thirty years his junior. Circumstantial but persuasive evidence exists that in 1923 he fathered a child with her. Ibid., 332–340; Lewis, *The Public Image of Henry Ford,* 12; John C. Dahlinger as told to Francis Spatz Leighton, *The Secret Life of Henry Ford* (Indianapolis, Ind.: Bobbs-Merrill, 1978).

25. Watts, *The People's Tycoon,* 51–59.

26. Brinkley, *Wheels for the World,* 68–89.

27. Roger Burlingame, *Henry Ford* (1955; repr., Chicago: Quadrangle Books, 1970), 51; John B. Rae, *The American Automobile: A Brief History* (Chicago: University of Chicago Press, 1965), 58–59; Flink, *The Car Culture,* 78–79.

28. By 1926, with sales down to 1.5 million, Ford's share of the market had fallen to 34 percent, forcing the company to finally cease production temporarily the following year and design a new Model A.

29. Watts, *The People's Tycoon,* 118, 276, 344, 346; Lacey, *Ford,* 285; "Mr.

Ford Doesn't Care," *Fortune,* December 1933, 68; Brinkley, *Wheels for the World,* 60, 241.

30. John B. Rae, "Why Michigan?" *Michigan Quarterly Review* 19–20 (Fall 1980–Winter 1981): 441–444.

31. John Kenneth Galbraith, *The Liberal Hour* (Boston: Houghton Mifflin, 1960), 158.

32. Ford R. Bryan, *Henry's Lieutenants* (Detroit: Wayne State University Press, 1993).

33. Watts, *The People's Tycoon,* 115–116; Brinkley, *Wheels for the World,* 127–128; Sward, *The Legend of Henry Ford,* 24–26.

34. Burlingame, *Henry Ford,* 72.

35. Quoted in Brinkley, *Wheels for the World,* 128.

36. Quotations in Flink, *The Car Culture,* 40–41.

37. John B. Rae, ed., *Henry Ford: Great Lives Observed* (Englewood Cliffs, N.J.: Prentice Hall, 1969), 91; Wik, *Henry Ford and Grass-Roots America,* 35; Sward, *The Legend of Henry Ford,* viii.

38. Brinkley, *Wheels for the World,* 141; Allan Nevins, *The Times, the Man, the Company,* with Frank Ernest Hill, vol. 1 of Nevins, *Ford,* 466.

39. Brinkley, *Wheels for the World,* 151–156.

40. Watts, *The People's Tycoon,* chap. 10; Sward, *The Legend of Henry Ford,* 55–56.

41. Richards, *The Last Billionaire,* 402–403; Watts, *The People's Tycoon,* xii, 118–122; Wik, *Henry Ford and Grass-Roots America,* 181; Reuther quotation in Lacey, *Ford,* 130.

42. Nevins, *The Times, the Man, the Company,* 495–497, 571–573; Nevins, *Expansion and Challenge,* 613; Nevins, *Decline and Rebirth, 1933–1962,* with Frank Ernest Hill, vol. 3 of Nevins, *Ford,* 231.

43. See Baldwin, *Henry Ford and the Jews;* and Max Wallace, *The American Axis: Henry Ford, Charles Lindbergh, and the Rise of the Third Reich* (New York: St. Martin's Press, 2003).

44. Nevins, *Expansion and Challenge,* 323; Cameron, *Reminiscences,* quoted in ibid., 602.

45. Watts, *The People's Tycoon,* 312; Brinkley, *Wheels for the World,* 6–7, 510–511; Curcio, *Henry Ford,* 170–171; Peter Collier and David Horowitz, *The Fords: An American Epic* (New York: Summit Books, 1987), 107–108; Halberstam, "Citizen Ford," 50.

46. Ford's Own Page in *Dearborn Independent,* quoted in Baldwin, *Henry Ford and the Jews,* 86.

47. Henry Ford, *My Life and Work,* with Samuel Crowther (Garden City, N.Y.: Garden City Publishing, 1922), 204.

48. Ford cited in *Detroit Free Press,* July 16, 1936, and *New York American,* August 5, 1928.

49. Watts, *The People's Tycoon,* 27–28, 314–315, 486; Wik, *Henry Ford and Grass-Roots America,* chap. 5; Ford R. Bryan, *Beyond the Model T: The Other Ventures of Henry Ford* (Detroit: Wayne State University Press, 1990), chap. 1.

50. Watts, *The People's Tycoon,* 483–486; Brinkley, *Wheels for the World,* 219–220, 443–445; Wik, *Henry Ford and Grass-Roots America,* 158–159.

51. George Washington Carver to Henry Ford, March 11, 1938, August 25, 1941, March 9, 1942, Henry Ford Papers, Henry Ford Museum and Greenfield Village Research Center, Dearborn, Michigan.

52. Quoted in Arthur Van Vlissingen Jr., "The Big Idea behind Those Small Plants of Ford's," *Factory Management and Maintenance* 96 (April 1938): 46.

53. John Tobin, "Henry Ford and His Village Industries in Southeastern Michigan" (M.A. thesis, Eastern Michigan University, 1985), 54–56.

54. Ford interviewed in *Chicago Tribune,* July 12, 1935.

55. Quoted in Sward, *The Legend of Henry Ford,* 272.

56. On the village industries, see Wik, *Henry Ford and Grass-Roots America,* 189–194; Lewis, *The Public Image of Henry Ford,* 162–163; interview by Fred C. Kelly, *New York Times,* October 27, 1935; "Village Industries by Little Rivers," *Ford News,* April 1936, 63–64, 71.

57. Greg Grandin, *Fordlandia: The Rise and Fall of Henry Ford's Forgotten Jungle City* (New York: Henry Holt, 2009), 8–9, 346–347, 350.

58. "Main Street Comes Back," *Dearborn Independent,* November 6, 1926, 11.

59. Richard Hofstadter, *The Age of Reform: From Bryan to F.D.R.* (New York: Alfred A. Knopf, 1955), 12; Sward, *The Legend of Henry Ford,* 259–261; Watts, *The People's Tycoon,* 415–421; C. C. Bell to Henry Ford, January 18, 1926, Henry Ford Papers.

60. Lacey, *Ford,* 239–245; Watts, *The People's Tycoon,* 403–410.

61. Richards, *The Last Billionaire,* chaps. 12–13; Watts, *The People's Tycoon,* chap. 20.

62. Sward, *The Legend of Henry Ford,* chap. 20; William A. Simonds, *Henry Ford and Greenfield Village* (New York: Frederick A. Stokes, 1938); Henry Ford, as told to Arthur Van Vlissingen Jr., "The Idea behind Greenfield," *American Legion Monthly,* October 1932, 7–9, 50; Lewis, *The Public Image of Henry Ford,* 278.

63. S. J. Woolf, "Ford Answers Wealth-Sharers," *New York Times Magazine,* July 7, 1935, 16.

64. Watts, *The People's Tycoon,* 531–532.

Chapter Four: George Washington Carver
and Oscar Micheaux

The first epigraph comes from Carver's letter to Rackham Holt, October 13, 1941, in *George Washington Carver in His Own Words,* ed. Gary R. Kremer (Columbia: University of Missouri Press, 1987), 31; the second, from McGilligan's *Oscar*

Micheaux: The Great and Only: The Life of America's First Black Filmmaker (New York: HarperCollins, 2007), 26.

1. David Herbert Donald, "An Ambiguous Figure," *New Republic,* October 28, 1981, 35.

2. The Great Migration is discussed in Peter Gottlieb, *Making Their Own Way: Southern Blacks' Migration to Pittsburgh, 1916–30* (Urbana: University of Illinois Press, 1987); Neil Fligstein, *Going North: Migration of Blacks and Whites from the South, 1900–1950* (New York: Academic Press, 1981); James R. Grossman, *Land of Hope: Chicago, Black Southerners, and the Great Migration* (Chicago: University of Chicago Press, 1989); and Nicolas Lemann, *The Promised Land: The Great Black Migration and How It Changed America* (New York: Alfred A. Knopf, 1991).

3. James W. Loewen, *Sundown Towns: A Hidden Dimension of American Racism* (New York: New Press, 2005); Nell Irvin Painter, *Exodusters: Black Migration to Kansas after Reconstruction* (New York: Alfred A. Knopf, 1971).

4. On the conditions of black people generally after the Civil War, see Leon F. Litwack, *Been in the Storm So Long: The Aftermath of Slavery* (New York: Vintage, 1980); Frank McGlynn and Seymour Drescher, eds., *The Meaning of Freedom: Economics, Politics, and Culture after Slavery* (Pittsburgh: University of Pittsburgh Press, 1992); Jay R. Mandle, *Not Slave, Not Free: The African American Economic Experience since the Civil War* (Durham, N.C.: Duke University Press, 1992); and Eric Foner, *Nothing but Freedom: Emancipation and Its Legacy* (Baton Rouge: Louisiana State University Press, 1983).

5. C. Vann Woodward, *Origins of the New South, 1877–1913* (Baton Rouge: Louisiana State University Press, 1951), chaps. 3, 12; Woodward, *The Strange Career of Jim Crow* (New York: Oxford University Press, 1966); Rayford W. Logan, *The Negro in American Life and Thought: The Nadir, 1877–1901* (New York: Dial Press, 1954); Joel Williamson, *The Crucible of Race: Black-White Relations in the American South since Emancipation* (New York: Oxford University Press, 1984); Leon F. Litwack, *Trouble in Mind: Black Southerners in the Age of Jim Crow* (New York: Alfred A. Knopf, 1998).

6. It is understandable that Carver, who never knew either of his natural parents, witnessed a brutal lynching of a member of his own race in his teens, and was forced to take care of himself throughout most of his childhood, would have told a biographer, "There are some things that an orphan child does not want to remember." Yet on other occasions he could also "recall childhood's happy days," and he fondly remembered boyhood experiences in the country playing baseball and checkers, running, and swimming. *George Washington Carver in His Own Words,* 31, 39, 128. Micheaux, who wrote and directed several autobiographical novels and movies, always slid over the events of his childhood and seemed only to want to get out of his home town and territory as quickly as he could, which he managed to do at age sixteen.

7. On Carver's birth, kidnapping, and early childhood, see Linda O. McMurry, *George Washington Carver: Scientist and Symbol* (Oxford: Oxford University Press, 1981), 3–19. Most of the early biographies of Carver were adulatory, even hagiographic, and unreliable. McMurry's is well researched and balanced, and I have primarily relied upon it for the facts of Carver's life. Gary R. Kremer, *George Washington Carver: A Biography* (Santa Barbara, Calif.: Greenwood Press, 2011), while short and directed at high school readers, is also based on solid research and reliable; on the obscurity of Carver's birth, see pages 1–2.

8. McMurry, *George Washington Carver*, 14.

9. Ibid., 16.

10. Ibid., 22–24.

11. Ibid., 24–26.

12. Quoted in ibid., 28.

13. Quoted in ibid., 41.

14. Louis R. Harlan, *Booker T. Washington,* 2 vols. (New York: Oxford University Press, 1972, 1983), 1: 276.

15. McMurry, *George Washington Carver*, 42–51; Mark D. Hersey, *My Work Is That of Conservation: An Environmental Biography of George Washington Carver* (Athens: University of Georgia Press, 2013), 49–85.

16. McMurry, *George Washington Carver*, 52–59; Harlan, *Booker T. Washington,* 1: 272–273, 276–277, 2: 145, 207–208; Robert J. Norrell, *Up from History: The Life of Booker T. Washington* (Cambridge, Mass.: Harvard University Press, 2009), 364–366.

17. Rackham Holt, *George Washington Carver: An American Biography* (Garden City, N.Y.: Doubleday, Doran, 1943), 101–102.

18. Quoted in McMurry, *George Washington Carver,* 95. See also Norrell, *Up from History,* 153, 199.

19. McMurry, *George Washington Carver,* 167.

20. Ibid., 172–174.

21. "George Washington Carver," in *Current Biography: Who's News and Why, 1940,* ed. Maxine Block, 1st annual cumulation (New York: H. W. Wilson, 1940), 148.

22. Dewey Short, testimony in *George Washington Carver National Monument—Missouri, Joint Hearing before the Committee on Public Lands and Surveys, U.S. Senate, and the Committee on the Public Lands, House of Representatives,* 78th Cong., 1st Sess., February 5, 1943, 22.

23. Donald, "An Ambiguous Figure," 36.

24. Ibid.

25. McMurry, *George Washington Carver,* 304–313.

26. The first study, Betti Carol VanEpps-Taylor's *Oscar Micheaux: A Biography* (Rapid City, S.D.: Dakota West Books, 1999), provides a useful outline of Micheaux's life and does an especially good job of placing him within his South

Dakota context. Film historian Patrick McGilligan's *Oscar Micheaux* provides a fuller account, including a detailed filmography and discussion of the development of his literary and filmmaking careers.

27. VanEpps-Taylor, *Oscar Micheaux*, 11–14; McGilligan, *Oscar Micheaux*, 4–5; Edgar F. Raines Jr., "The Ku Klux Klan in Illinois, 1867–1875," *Illinois Historical Journal* 78, no. 1 (1985): 17–45.

28. VanEpps-Taylor, *Oscar Micheaux*, 16–17; McGilligan, *Oscar Micheaux*, 6–9; Oscar Micheaux, *The Homesteader* (1917; repr., Lincoln: University of Nebraska Press, 1994), 163–173.

29. McGilligan, *Oscar Micheaux*, 11–12.

30. Oscar Micheaux, *The Conquest: The Story of a Negro Pioneer* (1913; repr., Lincoln: University of Nebraska Press, 1994), 15–16.

31. Ibid., 13–17.

32. McGilligan, *Oscar Micheaux*, 17–18. On Chicago's black population, see St. Clair Drake and Horace R. Cayton, *Black Metropolis: A Study of Negro Life in a Northern City* (New York: Harcourt, Brace, 1945); Allan H. Spear, *Black Chicago: The Making of a Negro Ghetto, 1890–1920* (Chicago: University of Chicago Press, 1967).

33. McGilligan, *Oscar Micheaux*, 20–26.

34. Larry Tye, *Rising from the Rails: Pullman Porters and the Making of the Black Middle Class* (New York: Henry Holt, 2004), 232; Jack Santino, *Miles of Smiles, Years of Struggle: Stories of Black Pullman Porters* (Urbana: University of Illinois Press, 1989).

35. Micheaux, *The Conquest*, 43–45.

36. McGilligan, *Oscar Micheaux*, 27–34; VanEpps-Taylor, *Oscar Micheaux*, 33–37.

37. VanEpps-Taylor, *Oscar Micheaux*, 42–46; McGilligan, *Oscar Micheaux*, 40–42.

38. VanEpps-Taylor, *Oscar Micheaux*, 40–50.

39. McGilligan, *Oscar Micheaux*, 61–124.

40. Ibid., 129–131.

41. Critical interpretations emphasizing Micheaux's limitations as a filmmaker include Joseph A. Young, *Black Novelist as White Racist: The Myth of Black Inferiority in the Novels of Oscar Micheaux* (New York: Greenwood Press, 1989), 65; Donald Bogle, *Toms, Coons, Mulattoes, Mammies, and Bucks: An Interpretive History of Blacks in American Films* (1973; repr., New York: Continuum, 1997), 114–116; John Kisch and Edward Mapp, *A Separate Cinema: Fifty Years of Black-Cast Posters* (New York: Farrar, Straus and Giroux, 1992), xvii; Stephen F. Soitos, "Oscar Micheaux," in *The Oxford Companion to African American Literature*, ed. William Andrews (New York: Oxford University Press, 1997), 495. More-favorable evaluations, either noting Micheaux's talent or giving more emphasis to the difficult constraints under which he worked, include Pearl Bowser, Jane Gaines, and

Charles Musser, eds., *Oscar Micheaux and His Circle: African-American Filmmaking and Race Cinema of the Silent Era* (Bloomington: Indiana University Press, 2001), xvii, xx, xxvi; J. Ronald Green, *Straight Lick: The Cinema of Oscar Micheaux* (Bloomington: Indiana University Press, 2000), xvi, 48, 67, 231–232; Thomas Cripps, *Slow Fade to Black: The Negro in American Film, 1900–1942* (New York: Oxford University Press, 1977), 183, 186–187, 191–193; bell hooks, "Micheaux: Celebrating Blackness," *Black American Literature Forum* 25 (Summer 1991): 351–360.

42. For filmographies listing and describing Micheaux's films, see McGilligan, *Oscar Micheaux,* 352–366; Bowser, Gaines, and Musser, *Oscar Micheaux and His Circle,* 228–277.

43. McGilligan, *Oscar Micheaux,* 144, 183, 219–220, 290; Pearl Bowser and Louise Spence, *Writing Himself into History: Oscar Micheaux, His Silent Films, and His Audiences* (New Brunswick, N.J.: Rutgers University Press, 2001), 114–115.

44. McGilligan, *Oscar Micheaux,* 163.

45. J. Ronald Green, *With a Crooked Stick—The Films of Oscar Micheaux* (Bloomington: Indiana University Press, 2004), 2.

46. All quoted in McGilligan, *Oscar Micheaux,* 340–341.

47. McMurry, *George Washington Carver,* 75–76.

48. Ibid., 103, 105, 108–111; Kremer, *George Washington Carver,* 121–133.

49. McGilligan, *Oscar Micheaux,* 121–123.

50. James A. Snead, "Images of Blacks in Black Independent Films: A Brief Survey," in *Cinemas of the Black Diaspora: Diversity, Dependence, and Oppositionality,* ed. Michael T. Martin (Detroit: Wayne State University Press, 1995), 366–367.

51. Cripps, *Slow Fade to Black,* 170.

52. McGilligan, *Oscar Micheaux,* 232, 249–250.

53. Bowser and Spence, *Writing Himself into History,* 5; See also Pearl Bowser and Louise Spence, "Identity and Betrayal: 'The Symbol of the Unconquered' and Oscar Micheaux's 'Biographical Legend,'" in *The Birth of Whiteness: Race and the Emergence of U.S. Cinema,* ed. Daniel Bernardi (New Brunswick, N.J.: Rutgers University Press, 1996), 56–80.

54. On the Carver myth, see Barry Mackintosh, "George Washington Carver: The Making of a Myth," *Journal of Southern History* 42 (November 1976): 507–528; McMurry, *George Washington Carver,* vii–viii, 3–4, 155–158, 176–177, 262–289, 307–308; Kremer, *George Washington Carver,* 144–145, 180–183.

55. Quotations and figures are all from Mackintosh, "George Washington Carver," 517–518.

56. Kremer, *George Washington Carver,* 187; Latter-day historians, while downsizing the impact of Carver's scientific discoveries, have begun to suggest that his most important scientific legacy may have been as a pioneer in promoting an ecological way of thinking. See Mark D. Hersey, "Hints and Suggestions to Farmers:

George Washington Carver and Rural Conservation in the South," *Environmental History* 11 (April 2006): 239–268; Hersey, *My Work Is That of Conservation*, 1–7, 219–226.

57. Carver quoted in Mackintosh, "George Washington Carver," 521.

58. On Carver's ambivalent attitude toward race and his alternation between a sense of racial solidarity and a rejection of race as a useful category, see McMurry, *George Washington Carver*, 204. His widely publicized friendship with Henry Ford during the late 1930s and early 1940s, precipitated by their common interest in chemurgy, was a striking example of the attraction he had for many white Americans. See ibid., 232–233, 259–261, 287–288.

59. On Micheaux's affinity with Washington, see his *The Conquest*, 250–252; McGilligan, *Oscar Micheaux*, 7–8, 66, 207, 298.

60. Oscar Micheaux, *The Story of Dorothy Stanfield* (New York: Book Supply Company, 1946), 85.

61. Micheaux, *The Conquest*, 145.

62. Although Micheaux's value system coincided closely with Washington's and he vigorously allied himself with the philosophy of his hero at Tuskegee, and against that of Atlanta University's Du Bois, whom he disparagingly and transparently referred to in one of his novels as a "professor in a colored university in Georgia" who espoused "literary training," Micheaux showed himself in line with at least some of the Du Bois approach when he militantly condemned racial violence and discrimination in his work. Micheaux, *The Conquest*, 252–253.

63. Hugh M. Gloster, *Negro Voices in American Fiction* (New York: Russell and Russell, 1948), 85.

64. Dan Moos, "Reclaiming the Frontier: Oscar Micheaux as Black Turnerian," *African American Review* 36 (Fall 2002): 357–381; Oscar Micheaux, *The Wind from Nowhere* (New York: Book Supply Company, 1943), 16–17; Bowser and Spence, "Identity and Betrayal," 61.

65. Williamson, *The Crucible of Race*, 301–302.

66. Carver's close relationships with many young men have been noted, but Gary Kremer indicates that no evidence exists to support the notion that he may have harbored homosexual tendencies. *George Washington Carver in His Own Words*, 4. See also McMurry, *George Washington Carver*, 244–245.

67. Jayna Brown, "Black Patriarch on the Prairie: National Identity and Black Manhood in the Early Novels of Oscar Micheaux," in Bowser, Gaines, and Musser, *Oscar Micheaux and His Circle*, 137. M. K. Johnson agrees that Micheaux hoped to reconstitute black manhood on the South Dakota frontier but argues that he failed in the attempt. "'Stranger in a Strange Land': An African American Response to the Frontier Tradition in Oscar Micheaux's *The Conquest*: The Story of a Negro Pioneer," *Western American Literature* 33 (Fall 1998): 232.

68. References to manhood and manliness in Micheaux, *The Homesteader*, 262, 302, 347, 438, 455, 460, quotation at 528.

69. Gerald R. Butters Jr., *Black Manhood on the Silent Screen* (Lawrence: University Press of Kansas, 2002), xvii, quotation at 149.

70. McMurry, *George Washington Carver*, 50; Holt, *George Washington Carver*, 193; *George Washington Carver in His Own Words*, 39–40.

71. Patrick McGilligan observes, "Micheaux realized early on that the North was not the pure haven of freedom that he and many other descendants of slavery had imagined it to be. The stories of his films would often swing between city and country, North and South, reflecting his divided loyalties." *Oscar Micheaux*, 27.

Introduction to Section II

1. Sinclair Lewis, *The Man from Main Street: Selected Essays and Other Writings, 1904–1950*, ed. Harry E. Maule and Melville H. Cane (New York: Random House, 1953), 271.

Chapter Five: Sinclair Lewis

Lewis's statement in the epigraph is quoted from Richard Lingeman's *Sinclair Lewis: Rebel from Main Street* (New York: Random House, 2002), 352.

1. Mark Schorer, *Sinclair Lewis: An American Life* (New York: McGraw-Hill, 1961), 268.

2. Harcourt quoted in James M. Hutchisson, *The Rise of Sinclair Lewis, 1920–1930* (University Park: Pennsylvania State University Press, 1996), 42; Lingeman, *Sinclair Lewis*, 157–158. Largely coinciding with my interpretation in this chapter is Miles Orvell's "Living on Main Street: Sinclair Lewis and the Great Cultural Divide," in Orvell, *The Death and Life of Main Street: Small Towns in American Memory, Space, and Community* (Chapel Hill: University of North Carolina Press, 2012), 72–99.

3. Carl Van Doren, "The Revolt from the Village: 1920," *Nation*, October 12, 1921, 407–412.

4. Anthony Channell Hilfer, *The Revolt from the Village, 1915–1930* (Chapel Hill: University of North Carolina Press, 1969), 158; Sinclair Lewis, "Self-Portrait" (1930), in *The Man from Main Street: Selected Essays and Other Writings, 1904–1950*, ed. Harry E. Maule and Melville H. Cane (New York: Random House, 1953), 54.

5. Lingeman, *Sinclair Lewis*, 23–24, 84–86; Grace Hegger Lewis, *With Love from Gracie, Sinclair Lewis: 1912–1925* (New York: Harcourt, Brace, 1955), 97.

6. Sinclair Lewis to Alfred Harcourt, February 8, 1920, in *From Main Street to Stockholm: Letters of Sinclair Lewis, 1919–1930*, ed. Harrison Smith (New York: Harcourt, Brace, 1952), 25.

7. Sinclair Lewis, preface to *Main Street* (New York: Harcourt, Brace and World, 1920), unpaginated.

8. Lewis, *Main Street*, 36–41.

9. On modernizing tendencies during the 1920s, see William E. Leuchtenburg, *The Perils of Prosperity, 1914–1932* (Chicago: University of Chicago Press, 1993); Ellis W. Hawley, *The Great War and the Search for a Modern Order: A History of the American People and Their Institutions, 1917–1933* (New York: St. Martin's Press, 1992); and Lynn Dumenil, *The Modern Temper: American Culture and Society in the 1920's* (New York: Hill and Wang), 1995. On the symbiotic relationship between modernism and nostalgia during the decade, see Michael Kammen, *Mystic Chords of Memory: The Transformation of Tradition in American Culture* (New York: Alfred A. Knopf, 1991), 299–309.

10. Sheldon N. Grebstein, *Sinclair Lewis* (New York: Twayne, 1962), 38; Lingeman, *Sinclair Lewis,* 158. The contradictions, inconsistencies, and special pleading of the "revolt from the village" interpreters are critically examined and set in context in Jon K. Lauck's "The Myth of the Midwestern 'Revolt from the Village,'" a draft chapter in this author's possession.

11. Lewis, *Main Street,* 47, 264–265.

12. Hilfer, *The Revolt from the Village,* 158–161; E. M. Forster, "Our Photography: Sinclair Lewis," *New York Herald Tribune,* April 28, 1929.

13. Philip A. Friedman, "'Babbitt': Satiric Realism in Form and Content," in *The Merrill Studies in Babbitt,* ed. Martin Light (Columbus, Ohio: Charles E. Merrill, 1971), 64; C. M. Flandrau to Lewis, October 21, 1920, and F. Scott Fitzgerald to Lewis, January 26, 1921, Sinclair Lewis Papers, Beinecke Library, Yale University.

14. Sinclair Lewis to Alfred Harcourt, December 28, 1920, in *From Main Street to Stockholm: Letters of Sinclair Lewis,* 59.

15. Hutchisson, *The Rise of Sinclair Lewis,* 47–65; D. J. Dooley, *The Art of Sinclair Lewis* (Lincoln: University of Nebraska Press, 1967), 91–92; Helen Batchelor, "A Sinclair Lewis Portfolio of Maps: Zenith to Winnemac," *Modern Language Quarterly* 32 (December 1971): 401–408.

16. Stephen S. Conroy, "Sinclair Lewis's Sociological Imagination," *American Literature* 42 (November 1970): 348–362.

17. Daniel Aaron, "Sinclair Lewis: *Main Street,*" in *The American Novel: From James Fenimore Cooper to William Faulkner,* ed. Wallace Stegner (New York: Basic Books, 1965), 167.

18. Sherwood Anderson, "Cotton Mill," *Scribner's Magazine,* July 1930, 1–11.

19. Ibid.

20. Schorer, *Sinclair Lewis: An American Life,* 3, 813.

21. Lewis, "Breaking into Print," in *The Man from Main Street,* 71.

22. Lewis, "Self-Portrait," 49.

23. Lingeman, *Sinclair Lewis,* 552–553.

24. Sinclair Lewis, "The Long Arm of the Small Town," in *O-Sa-Gee* high school yearbook of 1931, in *The Man from Main Street,* 272.

25. Ibid., 271.

26. Schorer, *Sinclair Lewis: An American Life,* 273; James Lundquist, "The

Sauk Centre Sinclair Lewis Didn't Write About," in *Critical Essays on Sinclair Lewis*, ed. Martin Bucco (Boston: G. K. Hall, 1986), 224.

27. Martin Light, *The Quixotic Vision of Sinclair Lewis* (West Lafayette, Ind.: Purdue University Press, 1975).

28. Sinclair Lewis, "This Golden Half-Century, 1885–1935," *Good Housekeeping*, May 1935, in *The Man from Main Street*, 254.

29. Light, *The Quixotic Vision of Sinclair Lewis*, 4.

30. Ibid., 6; Constance Rourke, *American Humor: A Study of the National Character* (New York: Harcourt, Brace, 1931), 283–286.

31. "(Harry) Sinclair Lewis," in *Twentieth-Century Literary Criticism*, ed. Dennis Poupard, vol. 23 (Detroit: Gale Research, 1987), 125.

32. Lewis, *Main Street*, 201–202.

33. Mark Schorer, *Sinclair Lewis*, American Writer's Pamphlet no. 27 (Minneapolis: University of Minnesota, 1963), 14; Grebstein, *Sinclair Lewis*, 85; Lingeman, *Sinclair Lewis*, 554.

34. Granville Hicks, *The Great Tradition: An Interpretation of American Literature since the Civil War* (New York: Macmillan, 1933), 234–235. See also William L. Stidger, "Honestly—Who Is Babbitt? 'It's Me!' Says Sinclair Lewis," *Dearborn Independent*, March 6, 1926.

35. Lewis, "Self-Portrait," 50–51.

36. Sinclair Lewis, "The Fallacy of Elsewhere" (1906), in "Editor's Table" in *The Man from Main Street*, 114–115; Lewis, "The Death of Arrowsmith," *Coronet*, July 1941, in *The Man from Main Street*, 106.

37. Light, *The Quixotic Vision of Sinclair Lewis*, 11.

38. Grace Hegger Lewis, *With Love from Gracie*, 66, 112.

39. Ibid., 113, 143, 314; Dorothy Thompson, "The Boy and the Man from Sauk Centre," *Atlantic Monthly*, November 1960, 41.

40. Lingeman, *Sinclair Lewis*, 536, 539–545.

41. Ronald Weber, *The Midwestern Ascendancy in American Writing* (Bloomington: Indiana University Press, 1992), 147, 175–176.

42. Ibid., xix–xxiii.

43. Frederick Manfred, "Sinclair Lewis' Funeral," *South Dakota Review* 7 (Winter 1969–1970): 56.

Chapter Six: Carl Sandburg
The epigraph comes from Harry Hansen's review of *Abraham Lincoln: The Prairie Years*, in *New York Daily News*, February 3, 1926, 16.

1. Carl Sandburg, "Trying to Write," *Atlantic Monthly*, September 1950, 33.

2. Rebecca West, "The Voice of Chicago," *Saturday Review*, September 4, 1926, 82.

3. Carl Sandburg, "Cornhuskers," in *The Complete Poems of Carl Sandburg* (New York: Harcourt Brace Jovanovich, 1970), 85.

4. North Callahan, *Carl Sandburg: Lincoln of Our Literature* (New York: New York University Press, 1970), 219; Penelope Niven, *Carl Sandburg: A Biography* (New York: Scribner's, 1991), xvii, 69, 559, 682; Lloyd Lewis, "The Many-Sided Carl Sandburg," *Rotarian,* May 1940, 44–46.

5. Niven, *Carl Sandburg,* 92.

6. Daniel Hoffman, *"Moonlight Dries No Mittens": Carl Sandburg Reconsidered* (Washington, D.C.: Library of Congress, 1979), 37.

7. Quoted in "People," *Time,* April 30, 1956, 47.

8. Herbert Mitgang, "Carl Sandburg," *New Republic,* January 14, 1978, 24.

9. Harriet Monroe, "Chicago Granite," *Poetry,* May 1916, 90–93.

10. Carl Sandburg, "Abraham Lincoln: The Incomparable," *Vital Speeches* 25 (March 1, 1959): 293.

11. *The Complete Poems of Carl Sandburg,* 33, 151–156.

12. Harry Golden, *Carl Sandburg* (Cleveland: World Publishing, 1961), 28.

13. Niven, *Carl Sandburg,* 2.

14. Carl Sandburg, *Always the Young Strangers* (New York: Harcourt, Brace, 1953), 77.

15. Ibid., 19, 79, 89–91, 115, 117; Golden, *Carl Sandburg,* 37.

16. Sandburg, *Always the Young Strangers,* 121, 175, 189, 195–196, 270–279.

17. Ibid., 79, 182–184.

18. Niven, *Carl Sandburg,* 19–20, 25, 32; Sandburg, *Always the Young Strangers,* 209–257.

19. Ernest Elmo Calkins, *They Broke the Plains* (1937; repr., Urbana: University of Illinois Press, 1989), 215, 218.

20. George Swank, *Carl Sandburg: Galesburg and Beyond* (Galesburg, Ill.: printed by the author, 1983), 22–35.

21. Niven, *Carl Sandburg,* 30.

22. Sandburg, *Always the Young Strangers,* 375, 377.

23. Ibid., 381–400.

24. Niven, *Carl Sandburg,* 39–46.

25. Ibid., 45–49, 54–56.

26. Ibid., 59–60.

27. Ibid., 83.

28. Ibid., 129–130, 163–170; quotation on "ideal woman" at 72.

29. Ibid., 292, 332, 454–456; Harry Hansen, *Midwest Portraits: A Book of Memories and Friendships* (New York: Harcourt, Brace, 1923), 44–48. Hansen was the book editor at the *Chicago Daily News.*

30. Lloyd Lewis, "Last of the Troubadours," *Chicagoan,* August 17, 1929, 21; Niven, *Carl Sandburg,* 443–444; Mark Schorer, *Sinclair Lewis: An American Life* (New York: McGraw-Hill, 1961), 422–423.

31. Niven, *Carl Sandburg,* 18.

32. *New York Sun,* February 6, 1926; *New York Times,* February 14, 1926;

New Statesman, literary supplement, June 5, 1926, iii; *New York World,* February 7, 1926; *St. Louis Post-Dispatch,* February 6, 1926.

33. William E. Barton, "The Abraham Lincoln of the Prairies," *World's Work,* May 1926, 103, 105; Mark Van Doren, "First Glance," *Nation,* February 10, 1926, 149.

34. *New York Sun,* February 6, 1926.

35. Sandburg, "Cornhuskers," 79.

36. Carl Sandburg, introduction to *Abraham Lincoln: The Prairie Years,* 2 vols. (New York: Harcourt, Brace, 1926): 1: vii.

37. Sandburg, *Always the Young Strangers,* 242.

38. Harry Hansen, "Carl Sandburg—Poet of the Prairie," *Pictorial Review,* September 1925, 2.

39. Joseph Epstein, "The People's Poet," *Commentary,* May 1992, 51.

40. Alfred Harcourt, "Forty Years of Friendship," *Journal of the Illinois State Historical Society* 45 (Winter 1952): 396–397.

41. "Your Obt. Servt," *Time,* December 4, 1939, 84–88.

42. Edmund Wilson, *Patriotic Gore: Studies in the Literature of the American Civil War* (New York: Oxford University Press, 1962), 115.

43. Quoted in "The Theme of America," *Saturday Review,* August 6, 1949, 113.

44. Niven, *Carl Sandburg,* 525.

45. "Your Obt. Servt," 84.

46. Quoted in Niven, *Carl Sandburg,* 501.

47. Ibid., 555.

48. Gay Wilson Allen, *Carl Sandburg* (Minneapolis: University of Minnesota Press, 1972), 5.

49. Niven, *Carl Sandburg,* 489, 635.

50. "Lincoln's Man Sandburg," *Newsweek,* February 14, 1955, 49–53; "Your Obt. Servt," 84–88; Niven, *Carl Sandburg,* 602, 631–633, 638–639, 680.

51. "Tribute to Marilyn from a Friend," *Look,* September 11, 1962, 90–94.

52. William Carlos Williams, "Carl Sandburg's Complete Poems," *Poetry,* September 1951, 345–351.

53. Quoted in *Galesburg Register Mail,* April 10, 1959.

54. *The Complete Poems of Carl Sandburg,* 643.

55. "Carl Sandburg's Impromptu Speech," Blackstone Hotel, Chicago, January 6, 1953, box 26, Sandburg Papers, University of Illinois, Champaign.

56. Quoted in Niven, *Carl Sandburg,* 622–623.

57. Steichen quoted in ibid., 622.

58. Westbrook Pegler, "Sandburg and 'Lincoln Industry,'" *San Francisco Call-Bulletin,* February 25, 1959.

59. Carl Sandburg, *The People, Yes,* in *The Complete Poems of Carl Sandburg,* 456.

Wood's epigraph quotation comes from "Revolt against the City," reprinted in James M. Dennis's *Grant Wood: A Study in American Art and Culture* (New York: Viking Press, 1975), 232; Curry's, from "Curry's View," *Art Digest* 9 (September 1935), 29; and Benton's, from "Frater Ave Atque Vale" for John Steuart Curry, in Benton, *An Artist in America,* 3d ed. (Columbia: University of Missouri Press, 1968), xxii.

1. Robert Hughes, "Scooting Back to Anamosa," *Time,* June 27, 1983, 68–69. The term "provincial cornball" appears on page 68.

2. *New York Times,* June 17, 1983.

3. John Ashbery, "Beyond *American Gothic,*" *Newsweek,* June 4, 1983, 80–81.

4. For more-positive evaluations, see Karal Ann Marling, "Don't Knock Wood," *ARTnews* 82 (September 1983): 94–99; Kay Larson, "American Mythic," *New York,* July 25, 1983, 56–58.

5. Henry Adams, "Thomas Hart Benton: Bad Boy of the Art World," *USA Today,* November 1989, 43.

6. Robert Hughes, "Tarted Up Till the Eye Cries Uncle," *Time,* May 1, 1989, 80–81.

7. Peter Plagens, "A Thomas Hart Benton Bash," *Newsweek,* May 15, 1989, 81.

8. Kimball quoted in Calvin J. Goodman, "Benton's Enduring American Art," *American Artist,* December 1989, 35; Kramer article in *Kansas City Star,* August 2, 1987; Hilton Kramer, "The Lost Leader: Benton as Critical Touchstone," *Forum* (of the Kansas City Artists Coalition) 14 (June–July 1989): 2–5; Donald Hoffman in *Kansas City Star,* April 16, 1989, January 7, 1990.

9. Henry Adams, *Thomas Hart Benton: An American Original* (New York: Alfred A. Knopf, 1989), 341–343; quotation from Adams, "Thomas Hart Benton," 43; MacMillan in *Kansas City Star,* April 16, 1989; Colby in *Detroit News,* August 6, 1989; *Kansas City Star,* July 15, 1990.

10. See the catalog produced for the show edited by Patricia Junker, *John Steuart Curry: Inventing the Middle West* (New York: Hudson Hills Press, 1998).

11. Regionalist painting was part of a broader cultural realism that flourished during the decade. See Robert L. Dorman, *Revolt of the Provinces: The Regionalist Movement in America, 1920–1945* (Chapel Hill: University of North Carolina Press, 1993).

12. Erika Doss, *Benton, Pollock, and the Politics of Modernism: From Regionalism to Abstract Expressionism* (Chicago: University of Chicago Press, 1991), 320–331, 348–349, 391; Henry Adams, *Tom and Jack: The Intertwined Lives of Thomas Hart Benton and Jackson Pollock* (New York: Bloomsbury Press, 2009), 15–17, 289–291, 330–332, 355–356.

13. Grant Wood, "John Steuart Curry and the Midwest," *Demcourier* 11 (April 1941): 2–3.

14. Alfred Haworth Jones, "The Search for a Usable American Past in the New Deal Era," *American Quarterly* 23 (December 1971): 710–724; Karal Ann Marling, "A Note on New Deal Iconography: Futurology and the Historical Myth," *Prospects: An Annual of American Cultural Studies* 4 (1979): 425–431; Warren I. Susman, *Culture as History: The Transformation of American Society in the Twentieth Century* (New York: Pantheon Books, 1985), 157.

15. Steven Biel notes accusations that Wood's work resembled that done by Nazi artists during the 1930s. *American Gothic* (New York: W. W. Norton, 2005), 128, 164.

16. Quoted in *New York Sun,* April 12, 1935, in *A Thomas Hart Benton Miscellany: Selections from His Published Opinions, 1916–1960,* ed. Matthew Baigell (Lawrence: University Press of Kansas, 1971), 77–78.

17. Benton, interview in *New York World-Telegram,* excerpted in *Art Digest* 15 (April 15, 1941), in *A Thomas Hart Benton Miscellany,* 79; Benton, "Art vs. the Mellon Gallery," *Common Sense,* June 1941, in *A Thomas Hart Benton Miscellany,* 79–80.

18. Benton, interview in *Art Front* 1 (April 1935), in *A Thomas Hart Benton Miscellany,* 64–65.

19. Laurence E. Schmeckebier, *John Steuart Curry's Pageant of America* (New York: American Artists Group, 1943), 41–42, 60. See also Joseph S. Czestochowski, *John Steuart Curry and Grant Wood: A Portrait of Rural America* (Columbia: University of Missouri Press, 1981).

20. Wanda M. Corn, *Grant Wood: The Regionalist Vision* (New Haven: Yale University Press, 1983), 13. Added to the painting's inherent ambiguity, Wood's contradictory statements about its making and intent led to wildly varying interpretations from the outset. Frequently seen as ironic or satirical when it was first exhibited, by the mid-1930s the painting had come to stand for a positive brand of nationalism and celebration of pioneer virtues in the minds of many observers, while others dismissed it as nativist and provincial. Biel, *American Gothic,* 47–49, 56–61, 89–91, 111–112. See also Thomas Hoving, *American Gothic: The Biography of Grant Wood's American Masterpiece* (New York: Chamberlain Brothers, 2005).

21. Justin Wolff, *Thomas Hart Benton: A Life* (New York: Farrar, Straus and Giroux, 2012), 202–207.

22. Adams, *Thomas Hart Benton: An American Original,* 236; R. Tripp Evans, *Grant Wood: A Life* (New York: Alfred A. Knopf, 2010), 160–161.

23. "U.S. Scene," *Time,* December 24, 1934, 24.

24. Ibid., 24–27; Adams, *Thomas Hart Benton: An American Original,* 208, 216–221.

25. "U.S. Scene," 25. Evans, *Grant Wood,* 232.

26. "Thomas Hart Benton Answers Questions," *Demcourier* 13 (February 1943): 4–5.

27. Benton, *An Artist in America,* 76–77.

28. Henry Adams, *Thomas Hart Benton: Drawing from Life* (New York: Abbeville Press, 1990), 32–33, 98–99.

29. Wood, "Revolt against the City," 234.

30. Quoted in Lucy J. Mathiak, "A Stranger to the Ivory Tower: John Steuart Curry and the University of Wisconsin," in Junker, *John Steuart Curry,* 184.

31. Patricia Junker, "Twilight of Americanism's Golden Age: Curry's Wisconsin Years, 1936–46," in Junker, *John Steuart Curry,* 196.

32. Thomas Hart Benton, "American Regionalism: A Personal History of the Movement," in *An American in Art: A Professional and Technical Autobiography* (Lawrence: University Press of Kansas, 1969), 151.

33. John E. Miller, "Midwestern Regionalism during the 1930s: A Democratic Art with Continuing Appeal," *Mid-America* 83 (Summer 2001): 71–93.

34. Benton, *An American in Art,* 43.

35. Evans, *Grant Wood,* 49, 63–64.

36. Schmeckebier, *John Steuart Curry's Pageant of America,* 36–37, 40–41, 52, 71, 123.

37. Adams, *Thomas Hart Benton: An American Original,* 77–78, 88–89, 134–155.

38. Anthony Channell Hilfer, *The Revolt from the Village, 1915–1930* (Chapel Hill: University of North Carolina Press, 1969); Michael Kammen, *Mystic Chords of Memory: The Transformation of Tradition in American Culture* (New York: Alfred A. Knopf, 1991), chaps. 11–12.

39. Emily Braun, "Thomas Hart Benton and Progressive Liberalism: An Interpretation of the New School Murals," in *Thomas Hart Benton: The "America Today" Murals,* ed. Emily Braun and Thomas Branchick (Williamstown, Mass.: Williams College Museum of Art, 1985), 14; Benton, *An Artist in America,* 81; Benton, *An American in Art,* 148.

40. Adams, *Thomas Hart Benton: An American Original,* 238; M. Sue Kendall, *Rethinking Regionalism: John Steuart Curry and the Kansas Mural Controversy* (Washington, D.C.: Smithsonian Institution Press, 1986), 19–20.

41. Steven Kesselman, "The Frontier Thesis and the Great Depression," *Journal of the History of Ideas* 29 (1968): 253–268.

42. Benton to Baigell, November 22, 1967, in *A Thomas Hart Benton Miscellany,* 33.

43. Benton, interview in the *New York Times,* February 8, 1935, in *A Thomas Hart Benton Miscellany,* 75.

44. John Dewey, *Art as Experience* (New York: Minton, Balch, 1934), 10.

45. Benton, quoted in excerpt from Ruth Pickering, "Thomas Hart Benton on His Way Back to Missouri," *Arts and Decoration* 42 (February 1935), in *A Thomas Hart Benton Miscellany,* 76.

46. Adams, *Thomas Hart Benton: An American Original*, 214–216, 220, 228; Doss, *Benton, Pollock, and the Politics of Modernism*, 97–98, 122.

47. Peyton Boswell Jr., *Modern American Painting* (New York: Dodd, Mead, 1939), 78–81.

48. "The Tory Spirit," *Art Digest* 9 (October 15, 1934): 13. By mid-decade, Wood was ready to assert, "Painting has declared its independence from Europe, and is retreating from the cities to the more American village and country life." See his "Revolt against the City," 230.

49. Quoted in Doss, *Benton, Pollock, and the Politics of Modernism*, 330.

50. See chapter 6, "The Mechanics of Form Organization," in Adams, *Thomas Hart Benton: An American Original*; Adams, *Tom and Jack*, 45–48, 54–56.

51. Mathiak, "A Stranger to the Ivory Tower," 187.

52. *Des Moines Register*, December 13, 1942; Darrell Garwood, *Artist in Iowa: A Life of Grant Wood* (New York: W. W. Norton, 1944), 14–15, 30.

53. Quoted in John F. Kienitz, "Grant Wood," *Art in America* 31 (January 1943): 49.

54. Quoted in *Cedar Rapids Gazette*, September 25, 1932.

55. Quoted in Donald Hoffman, "Benton's Way with Words," *Kansas City Star*, April 2, 1989.

56. John Steuart Curry, "Tom," *Demcourier* 13 (February 1943): 6; Reginald Marsh, "Thomas Benton," *Demcourier* 13 (February 1943): 9.

57. Benton, *An Artist in America*, 277–278.

58. Benton quoted in Karal Ann Marling, *Tom Benton and His Drawings: A Biographical Essay and a Collection of His Sketches, Studies, and Mural Cartoons* (Columbia: University of Missouri Press, 1985), 1.

59. Clement Greenberg, cited in *St. Louis Post-Dispatch*, April 19, 1987.

60. Benton, "Art vs. the Mellon Gallery," 80.

61. Lewis Mumford, "The Three Bentons," *New Yorker*, April 20, 1935, 48.

62. Miller, "Midwestern Regionalism during the 1930s," 71–93.

63. Susman, *Culture as History*, 197.

64. Corn, *Grant Wood*, 3.

65. Evans, *Grant Wood*, 15–24, 78–90.

66. Lea Rosson DeLong, *Grant Wood's Main Street: Art, Literature and the American Midwest* (Ames: University Museums, Iowa State University, 2004); Corn, *Grant Wood*, 1–2, 114–117.

67. Charles C. Eldredge, "Prairie Prodigal," in Junker, *John Steuart Curry*, 90–92.

68. Kendall, *Rethinking Regionalism*, 43; Henry Adams, "Space, Weather, Myth, and Abstraction in the Art of John Steuart Curry," in Junker, *John Steuart Curry*, 118.

69. Donald Hoffmann, "From Tom Benton's Youth," *Kansas City Times*, February 4, 1973; Benton, *An Artist in America*, 3.

70. Benton, *An Artist in America*, 3–5; Wolff, *Thomas Hart Benton*, 21–31.

71. Benton, *An Artist in America*, 6.

72. Quoted in *Kansas City Times*, November 15, 1939.

73. Quoted in *Kansas City Star*, March 15, 1970.

Chapter Eight: Ernie Pyle

The epigraph comes from Nichols's introduction to *Ernie's America: The Best of Ernie Pyle's 1930s Travel Dispatches*, ed. David Nichols (New York: Random House, 1989), xliv, xlix.

1. Graham B. Hovey, "This Is Ernie Pyle's War," *New Republic*, December 11, 1944, 804; "Ernie," *Time*, April 30, 1945, 61; Randall Jarrell, "Ernie Pyle," *Nation*, May 19, 1945, 573–576; Charles Angoff, "Brave Men," *American Mercury*, February 1945, 244–246.

2. Lee G. Miller, *The Story of Ernie Pyle* (New York: Viking, 1950), 279.

3. Biographical treatments of Pyle remain surprisingly scarce. Among the best are Miller, *The Story of Ernie Pyle*; *Ernie's America*; and James Tobin, *Ernie Pyle's War: America's Eyewitness to World War II* (New York: Free Press, 1997). A popular 1945 movie, *The Story of G.I. Joe*, directed by William Wellman (United Artists), focused on his travels with the infantry in North Africa in World War II.

4. *Ernie's America*, 11.

5. Ibid., 14–15, 278, 395; Miller, *The Story of Ernie Pyle*, 68–69.

6. Columns of September 24, 1935, and May 16, 1938, in *Ernie's America*, 12–13, 279.

7. Miller, *The Story of Ernie Pyle*, 7–10.

8. Ibid., 10–11; Tobin, *Ernie Pyle's War*, 9–10, quotation on page 10; Thad Hooker to Lee Miller, December 16, 1945, Ernie Pyle Papers, Lilly Library, Indiana University, Bloomington.

9. Column of March 16, 1937, in *Ernie's America*, 187.

10. Quoted in Tobin, *Ernie Pyle's War*, 11. See also Lincoln Barnett, "Ernie Pyle," *Life*, April 2, 1945, 98.

11. Tobin, *Ernie Pyle's War*, 10–12; Miller, *The Story of Ernie Pyle*, 13–16, 21–23.

12. Miller, *The Story of Ernie Pyle*, 18–19, 24–25.

13. Tobin, *Ernie Pyle's War*, 13–14; Nelson P. Poynter to Lee Miller, November 28, 1945, Pyle Papers.

14. Miller, *The Story of Ernie Pyle*, 28–31; Lee G. Miller, *An Ernie Pyle Album: Indiana to Ie Shima* (New York: William Sloane Associates, 1946), 16–17.

15. Miller, *The Story of Ernie Pyle*, 33–35.

16. Miller, *An Ernie Pyle Album*, 18–21; Tobin, *Ernie Pyle's War*, 21–22.

17. Quoted in Tobin, *Ernie Pyle's War*, 24.

18. Quoted in Miller, *The Story of Ernie Pyle*, 50.

19. Quoted in Tobin, *Ernie Pyle's War*, 25.

20. Parker quoted in ibid.

21. Ibid., 25–26.

22. Charles Fisher, *The Columnists* (New York: Howell, Soskin, 1944), 308–309; Frederick C. Painton, "The Hoosier Letter Writer," *Saturday Evening Post,* October 2, 1943, 109.

23. Lee Hills to Pyle, May 31, 1938, Pyle Papers.

24. Pyle to Lee Miller, March 1, 1938, Pyle Papers.

25. Westbrook Pegler, quoted in "Ernie Pyle," *Current Biography: Who's News and Why, 1941,* ed. Maxine Block, 2d annual cumulation (New York: H. W. Wilson, 1941), 687.

26. Miller, *The Story of Ernie Pyle,* 60–61.

27. Pyle's columns are collected in his papers at the Lilly Library, Indiana University, Bloomington. On the documentary impulse in the 1930s, see William Stott, *Documentary Expression and Thirties America* (New York: Oxford University Press, 1973).

28. Columns of February 4, 1937, October 11, 1938, and November 16, 1940, in *Ernie's America,* 184–186, 283, 391–392.

29. Nichols, introduction to *Ernie's America,* xxxvi–xlvii.

30. Miller, *The Story of Ernie Pyle,* 132–133.

31. Tobin, *Ernie Pyle's War,* 123–124, 159–161, 219–223, 243.

32. Quoted in Paul Lancaster, "Ernie Pyle: Chronicler of the Men Who Do the Dying," *American Heritage,* February–March 1981, 34.

33. Don Whitehead to Lee G. Miller, October 26, 1945 and January 14, 1946, Pyle Papers.

34. Pyle column of September 5, 1944, in *Ernie's War: The Best of Ernie Pyle's World War II Dispatches,* ed. David Nichols (New York: Simon and Schuster, 1986), 357–358.

35. Pyle quoted in "Ernie Shared the Doughfoot's Lot, Even to Death in a Roadside Ditch," *Newsweek,* April 30, 1945, 80–81.

36. Pyle column of May 2, 1943, in *Ernie's War,* 113.

37. Fisher, *The Columnists,* 303.

38. Ernie Pyle, *Brave Men* (New York: Henry Holt, 1944), 2.

39. Ibid., 13, 123, 228.

40. "Ernie Pyle's War," *Time,* July 17, 1945, 65–66.

41. Painton, "The Hoosier Letter Writer," 17.

42. John Mason Brown, "Brave Man," *Saturday Review,* April 28, 1945, 21.

43. Pyle column of February 9, 1943, in *Ernie's War,* 75.

44. Michael S. Sweeney, "War Correspondent Ernie Pyle's 'Beloved Captain': The Life and Death of Henry T. Waskow of Belton, Texas, and the Column That Touched America," *Sound Historian: Journal of the Texas Oral History Association* 3 (1995–1996): 1–67.

45. Pyle column of January 5, 1944, in *Ernie's War,* 191.

46. Pyle columns in *Ernie's War*, 80, 154, 200, 279, 370.

47. Pyle, *Brave Men*, 224.

Chapter 9: Alvin Hansen

The epigraph comes from Musgrave's "Caring for the Real Problems," *Quarterly Journal of Economics* 90 (February 1976): 1.

1. Robert Lekachman, *The Age of Keynes* (New York: Random House, 1966), 126; William Breit and Roger L. Ransom, *The Academic Scribblers,* 3d ed. (Princeton: Princeton University Press, 1998), 81–84, 101; John Kenneth Galbraith, "How Keynes Came to America," in *Economics, Peace and Laughter* (Boston: Houghton Mifflin, 1971), 49–51.

2. Herbert Stein, *The Fiscal Revolution in America* (Chicago: University of Chicago Press, 1969). Ironically, almost as soon as Keynesianism achieved intellectual dominance, it came under assault. In 1978 a *Journal of Post Keynesian Economics* appeared on the scene and countertheories began to proliferate, especially those coming under the heading of the Austrian school of economics. In the wake of the 2008 recession, Keynesianism staged something of a comeback. See, for example, Richard A. Posner, *The Crisis of Capitalist Democracy* (Cambridge, Mass.: Harvard University Press, 2010), chap. 8; Robert Skidelsky, *Keynes: The Return of the Master* (New York: Public Affairs, 2009); and Peter Clarke, *Keynes: The Rise, Fall, and Return of the 20th Century's Most Influential Economist* (New York: Bloomsbury Press, 2009).

3. Paul W. McCracken to Hansen, August 29, 1967, Alvin H. Hansen Papers, Pusey Library, Harvard University.

4. Gerhart Colm to Hansen, August 17, 1967, Hansen Papers.

5. Citation of Alvin H. Hansen on award to him of the Francis A. Walker Medal, December 28, 1967, Hansen Papers.

6. *First Baptist Church, Viborg, South Dakota, 125 Years, 1873–1998* (Freeman, S.D.: Pine Hill Press, [1998]), 26.

7. Hansen quoted in Perry G. Mehrling, *The Money Interest and the Public Interest: American Monetary Thought, 1920–1970* (Cambridge, Mass.: Harvard University Press, 1997), 88.

8. On Hansen's early life, see "Alvin Harvey and Mabel (Lewis) Hansen Family" and "Niels and Bergitta Hansen," in Viborg History Book Committee, *Viborg, South Dakota, 1893–1993* (Viborg, S.D.: Committee, 1992), 405, 418–419; Perry G. Mehrling, "Alvin Harvey Hansen," in *American National Biography*, 24 vols. (New York: Oxford University Press, 1999), 10: 20–22; John E. Miller, "How Viborg Raised a Renowned Economist: Alvin Hansen's Journey from the Farm to Harvard," *South Dakota Magazine*, March–April 2005, 66–71.

9. Breit and Ransom, *The Academic Scribblers,* 85–88; William J. Barber, "The Career of Alvin H. Hansen in the 1920s and 1930s: A Study in Intellectual Transformation," *History of Political Economy* 19 (Summer 1987): 191, 197–199.

10. Robert Skidelsky, *John Maynard Keynes*, vol. 2, *The Economist as Saviour, 1920–1937* (New York: Penguin, 1986), 537–571. Alvin Hansen summarized Keynes's *General Theory* in *A Guide to Keynes* (New York: McGraw-Hill, 1953).

11. Clarke, *Keynes*, 164.

12. John H. Williams to Hansen, May 25, 1937, Hansen Papers; *University of Minnesota Budget for the Fiscal Year July 1, 1936 to June 30, 1937* (Minneapolis: University of Minnesota, 1936), 126.

13. Herbert Heaton to Hansen, June 27, 1937, Hansen Papers.

14. On Hansen's influence as a theorist, teacher of economic ideas, popularizer of Keynesianism, contributor to policy formation, and educator of the public, see John E. Miller, "From South Dakota Farm to Harvard Seminar: Alvin H. Hansen, America's Prophet of Keynesianism," *Historian* 64 (Spring–Summer 2002): 603–622.

15. Paul A. Samuelson, "Alvin Hansen as a Creative Economic Theorist," *Quarterly Journal of Economics* 90 (February 1976): 24–31; Hyman P. Minsky, *John Maynard Keynes* (New York: Columbia University Press, 1975), 21–38; Breit and Ransom, *The Academic Scribblers*, 91–95, 102–104; Theodore Rosenof, *Economics in the Long Run: New Deal Theorists and Their Legacies, 1933–1993* (Chapel Hill: University of North Carolina Press, 1997), 52–60.

16. Hansen book review in *Journal of Political Economy* 44 (October 1936), reprinted in *The New Economics,* ed. Seymour Harris (New York: Alfred A. Knopf, 1947), 35. See also David Laidler, *Fabricating the Keynesian Revolution: Studies of the Inter-war Literature on Money, the Cycle, and Unemployment* (Cambridge: Cambridge University Press, 1999), 294–295.

17. Alvin H. Hansen, *Economic Stabilization in an Unbalanced World* (New York: Harcourt, Brace, 1932), vii, 318–321; Joseph Dorfman, *The Economic Mind in American Civilization,* vol. 5 (New York: Viking, 1959), 723.

18. Samuelson, "Alvin Hansen as a Creative Economic Theorist," 29.

19. Walter S. Salant to Hansen, July 17, 1956, Hansen Papers.

20. Hansen to Salant, November 10, [1967], Hansen Papers.

21. Seymour E. Harris, "Hansen," in *McGraw-Hill Encyclopedia of World Biography,* vol. 5 (New York: McGraw-Hill, 1973), 89.

22. John H. Williams, "Tribute," *Quarterly Journal of Economics* 90 (February 1976): 9.

23. "James Tobin," in *Lives of the Laureates: Thirteen Nobel Economists,* ed. William Breit and Roger W. Spencer, 3d ed. (Cambridge: MIT Press, 1995), 119.

24. W. F. Stettner to Hansen, August 19, 1967, Hansen Papers.

25. Barber, "The Career of Alvin H. Hansen in the 1920s and 1930s," 200–203.

26. Alvin H. Hansen, *Full Recovery or Stagnation?* (New York: W. W. Norton, 1938), 290, 302; Hansen, "Economic Progress and Declining Population Growth," *American Economic Review* 29 (March 1939): 1–15; Rosenof, *Economics in the Long Run,* 53–65; Robert M. Collins, *The Business Response to Keynes, 1929–*

1964 (New York: Columbia University Press, 1981), 10–11, 51–52; Kenneth Weiher, *America's Search for Economic Stability: Monetary and Fiscal Policy since 1913* (New York: Twayne, 1992), 112–113.

27. Samuel Tenenbaum, "Dr. Alvin Hansen: Pioneer Economist," *American Mercury,* July 1945, 57–59; Alvin H. Hansen, *Economic Policy and Full Employment* (New York: McGraw-Hill, 1947).

28. Richard Lee Strout, "Hansen of Harvard," *New Republic,* December 29, 1941, 88; *New York Times,* January 29, 1942.

29. Walter Salant, "Alvin Hansen and the Fiscal Policy Seminar," *Quarterly Journal of Economics* 90 (February 1976): 22.

30. Stephen K. Bailey, *Congress Makes a Law: The Story behind the Employment Act of 1946* (New York: Columbia University Press, 1950), 21, 24, 45, 46, 161; Paul Samuelson, "Alvin H. Hansen, 1887–1975," *Newsweek,* June 16, 1975, 72; James Tobin, "Hansen and Public Policy," *Quarterly Journal of Economics* 90 (February 1976): 34; Stein, *The Fiscal Revolution in America,* chap. 8; Lekachman, *The Age of Keynes,* chap. 6.

31. See, for example, the following articles by Hansen: "Wanted: Ten Million Jobs," *Atlantic Monthly,* September 1943, 65–69; "Four Outlets for Investment," *Survey Graphic* 32 (May 1943): 198–200, 231–232; "A Postwar National Fiscal Program," *New Republic,* February 28, 1944, 265–271; and, with Guy Greer, "Toward Full Use of Our Resources," *Fortune,* November 1942, 130–133, 158–178.

32. "A Master Plan for the U.S. for the 1960s," *U.S. News and World Report,* February 27, 1961, 59; Breit and Spencer, *Lives of the Laureates,* 133–135; Walter Heller to Hansen, November 12, 1974, and Walter and Joanie Heller to Hansen [1967], Hansen Papers.

33. Herbert Corey, "Oh, Debt, Where Is Thy Sting!," *Nation's Business,* June 1944, 36.

34. Strout, "Hansen of Harvard," 890.

35. Corey, "Oh, Debt, Where Is Thy Sting!," 34.

36. Alvin H. Hansen, "We Can Pay the War Bill," *Atlantic Monthly,* October 1942, 63.

37. Alvin H. Hansen, "For a Stable Market Economy," *Atlantic Monthly,* August 1945, 81.

38. Samuelson, "Alvin H. Hansen, 1887–1975," 72.

39. John E. Miller, "Governor Philip F. La Follette's Shifting Priorities during the 1930's: From Redistribution to Expansion," *Mid-America* 58 (April–July 1976): 119–126.

40. Alvin H. Hansen, "Some Notes on Terborgh's 'The Bogey of Economic Maturity,'" *Review of Economic Statistics* 28 (February 1946), reprinted in Hansen, *Economic Policy and Full Employment,* 306.

41. Herb Hansen (nephew of Alvin Hansen), interview by the author, Wakonda,

South Dakota, August 23, 2000; Marian Merrifield (daughter of Alvin Hansen), "Recollections of My Father," typed notes sent to author, March 2002.

42. Marian Merrifield, "Alvin H. Hansen, 1887–1975," undated, typed manuscript, Hansen Papers.

43. Alvin H. Hansen, "Social Planning for Tomorrow," in Hansen et al., *The United States after the War* (Ithaca, N.Y.: Cornell University Press, 1945), 15–16.

44. Daniel Bell, *The Cultural Contradictions of Capitalism* (New York: Basic Books, 1976).

45. Samuelson, "Alvin Hansen as a Creative Economic Theorist," 31. In a telephone interview with the author on June 3, 2003, Samuelson said essentially the same thing about Hansen's good fellowship, his sensitivity, and his unfailing kindness to people.

46. Williams, "Tribute," 8.

47. Hansen quoted in "A Master Plan for the U.S. for the 1960s," 59.

48. Alvin H. Hansen, "Appeal for a Dual Economy," *New York Times Magazine,* March 12, 1961, 108.

49. "Alvin Harvey and Mabel (Lewis) Hansen Family," 405; "Crusader for Keynes," *Newsweek,* February 8, 1971, 12. Hansen once sat down and listed thirty different cities around the world in which he had lectured, ranging from London, Paris, and Stockholm to Rome, Calcutta, and Hong Kong. "Foreign Cities Where I Have Lectured," (handwritten list), no date, Hansen Papers.

50. Tobin, "Hansen and Public Policy," 32.

51. Corey, "Oh, Debt, Where Is Thy Sting!," 39.

Chapter Ten: Bob Feller

The epigraph comes from *Bob Feller's Little Black Book of Baseball Wisdom,* with Burton Rocks (Chicago: Contemporary Books, 2001), 3.

1. On the urban origins of baseball, see Benjamin G. Rader, *Baseball: A History of America's Game,* 3d ed. (Urbana: University of Illinois Press, 2008), 5–18; Harold Seymour, *Baseball: The Early Years* (New York: Oxford University Press, 1960), 15–40; David Q. Voigt, *American Baseball: From Gentleman's Sport to the Commissioner System* (Norman: University of Oklahoma Press, 1966), 2–9. However, John Thorne suggests that the earliest playing of the game in the United States may have been in rural New England as early as 1735 and that the game evolved its modern rules and dimensions in cities like New York before bouncing back to small towns and rural places. *Baseball in the Garden of Eden: The Secret History of the Early Game* (New York: Simon and Schuster, 2011).

2. Ken Smith, *Baseball's Hall of Fame* (New York: A. S. Barnes, 1947), 25. A growing number of baseball historians, such as John Thorne and David Vaught, have begun to refocus the argument over the game's origins by emphasizing its early roots and continuing persistence in small towns and in farm areas. See

Vaught, *The Farmers' Game: Baseball in Rural America* (Baltimore: Johns Hopkins University Press, 2013).

3. Voigt, *American Baseball*, 5, 7; Seymour, *Baseball*, 8–12; Vaught, *The Farmers' Game*, 1–34.

4. Quoted in Geoffrey C. Ward, *Baseball: An Illustrated History* (New York: Alfred A. Knopf, 1994), xviii.

5. David Vaught, "The Making of Bob Feller and the Modern American Farmer," in Vaught, *The Farmers' Game*, 76–103.

6. Jack Sher, "Bill Feller's Boy," *American Legion Magazine*, June 1947, 26. The arm warmer is on display at the Bob Feller Museum in Van Meter.

7. *New York Times*, August 21, 1946, and Los Angeles Angels Press Release, August 26, 1974, clippings files, National Baseball Hall of Fame, Cooperstown, New York. Most of the newspaper and magazine articles cited in this chapter are from these clippings files. See also *Bob Feller's Little Black Book of Baseball Wisdom*, 26–28.

8. Quoted in Sid Keener's Column, *St. Louis Star-Times*, January 19, 1937.

9. Quoted in *New York World-Telegram*, April 23, 1937.

10. Quoted in clipping, Vicksburg, Mississippi, March 28, 1937.

11. Quoted in Arthur Daley, "Exit for Rapid Robert," *New York Times*, January 7, 1957.

12. Quoted in Arthur Daley, "Blatant Electioneering," *New York Times*, January 3, 1962.

13. Howard Preston, "'Greatest Pitcher in History'—Feller's Goal," *Sporting News*, February 21, 1946, 9.

14. Statistical references in this chapter derive primarily from *The Baseball Encyclopedia: The Complete and Definitive Record of Major League Baseball*, 10th ed. (New York: Macmillan, 1996).

15. "Bob Feller First Ball Star to Enlist," *New York World-Telegram*, December 9, 1941; "Feller Is Signed by Naval Reserve," *New York Times*, December 11, 1941.

16. Bob Feller, *Strikeout Story* (New York: A. S. Barnes, 1947), 218–231; Feller, *Now Pitching, Bob Feller*, with Bill Gilbert (New York: Carol, 1990), 116–120.

17. Bob Feller, "From Rookie to Riches within 10-Year Span," *Sporting News*, December 8, 1954, 14.

18. John Sickels, *Bob Feller: Ace of the Greatest Generation* (Washington, D.C.: Brassey's, 2004), 9–19.

19. Feller, *Strikeout Story*, 11.

20. Vaught, "The Making of Bob Feller and the Modern American Farmer," 86–102.

21. Fletcher Jennings, interview by the author, Van Meter, Iowa, May 14, 1999.

22. Sickels, *Bob Feller*, 15–17.

23. Bob Feller, interview by the author, Des Moines, Iowa, May 14, 1999.

24. Sickels, *Bob Feller*, 25–27, 47–58.

25. Quoted in *Des Moines Tribune*, June 26, 1957, 18.

26. Ed McAuley, "Feller American League Strikeout King," *Cleveland News*, September 14, 1936. (Of course, if any strikeout victims reach first base on passed balls or wild pitches, there is no theoretical limit to the number of strikeouts that are achievable.)

27. Gene Schoor, *Bob Feller: Hall of Fame Strikeout Star* (Garden City, N.Y.: Doubleday, 1962), 148.

28. *New York World-Telegram*, March 7, 1946; Feller, *Strikeout Story*, 238.

29. Sickels, *Bob Feller*, 149–157, 177–181; Timothy M. Gay, *Satch, Dizzy and Rapid Robert: The Wild Saga of Interracial Baseball before Jackie Robinson* (New York: Simon and Schuster, 2010), chaps. 11–12.

30. Feller, *Now Pitching, Bob Feller*, 136–141, 151; Gay, *Satch, Dizzy and Rapid Robert*, 222.

31. Shirley Povich, This Morning, *Washington Post*, June 18, 1947.

32. Bob Feller, "When the Crowd Boos," *American Weekly*, July 6, 1952, 8.

33. Russell J. Schneider, *The Boys of the Summer of '48* (Champaign, Ill.: Sports Publishing, 1998), 61.

34. Joe King, "Rapid Robert's Stardom Undiminished by Beardon Victory—or High Finance," *New York World-Telegram*, October 6, 1948.

35. Burton Hawkins, "Bob Feller's $150,000 Pitch," *Saturday Evening Post*, April 19, 1947, 25.

36. Schoor, *Bob Feller*, 177–178, 180.

37. I was one of those youngsters when, in 1957, my father drove me, a twelve-year-old major-league aspirant, over to a Little League diamond in a northwest Chicago suburb to watch Feller, who was wearing his Cleveland uniform, put on an exhibition of how to throw fastballs, curveballs, and changeups to a large group of enthusiastic youth.

38. Jimmy Cannon, Sports Above, *New York Journal American*, January 4, 1962.

Chapter Eleven: James Dean

Mellor's epigraph quotation comes from Donald Spoto's *Rebel: The Life and Legend of James Dean* (New York: HarperCollins, 1996), 235.

1. White quoted in Joe Hyams, *James Dean: Little Boy Lost*, with Jay Hyams (New York: Warner Books, 1992), 252; Glenn and Kazan quoted in Val Holley, *James Dean: The Biography* (New York: St. Martin's Press, 1995), 277; Bogart quoted in Ezra Goodman, *The Fifty-Year Decline and Fall of Hollywood* (New York: Simon and Schuster, 1961), 292.

2. Quoted in Spoto, *Rebel*, 251.

3. Ibid., 252; Randall Riese, *The Unabridged James Dean: His Life and Legacy from A to Z* (Chicago: Contemporary Books, 1991), 2; John Howlett, *James Dean: A Biography* (London: Plexus, 1997), 150.

4. Howlett, *James Dean,* 151.

5. David Dalton, *James Dean: The Mutant King* (New York: St. Martin's Press, 1974), 273; Hyams, *James Dean,* 212.

6. Diana West, *The Death of the Grown-Up: How America's Arrested Development Is Bringing Down Western Civilization* (New York: St. Martin's Griffin, 2007), 32.

7. Quoted in David Dalton, *James Dean: American Icon,* with Ron Cayen and David Lochr (New York: St. Martin's Press, 1984), 44.

8. Stock and Rosenman both quoted in Spoto, *Rebel,* 226–227, 235.

9. In two visits to Fairmount in 2000 and 2004, I talked to half a dozen residents of the town who had known Dean. Their testimony coincides with numerous magazine and newspaper articles stating that he was a normal, well-adjusted kid, essentially no different from other boys his age. See, for example, John Dye, "James Byron Dean: The Sinister Adolescent," *Marion (Ind.) Chronicle-Tribune Magazine,* September 28, 1980, 5, 8–9; Steve Jones, "Fairmount and James Dean: Going in Search of the Legend," *Marion (Ind.) Chronicle-Tribune Magazine,* September 29, 1985, 2–3; Ed Breen, "James Dean's Indiana," *Traces of Indiana and Midwestern History* 1 (Fall 1989): 9–10.

10. Riese, *The Unabridged James Dean,* 170; Phil Ziegler, interview by the author, Fairmount, Indiana, March 11, 2004; Bob Pulley, interview, in Robert Headrick Jr., *Deanmania: The Man, the Character, the Legend* (Las Vegas: Pioneer Books, 1990), 15–17; Laura L. Castro, "Larger than Life: James Dean's Death Did a Lot for Indiana," *Wall Street Journal,* October 9, 1991; Bill Shaw, "Dead 25 Years, James Dean Is Given a Touching Hometown Tribute by Nostalgic Fans," *People,* October 13, 1980, 41. Also see the documentary movies *James Dean: Born Cool,* directed by Dennis Pietrowski (Whatantics Productions, 2000) and *The James Dean Story,* directed by Robert Altman and George W. George (Warner Brothers, 1957), which include many interviews with relatives, friends, and residents of Fairmount.

11. Riese, *The Unabridged James Dean,* 436.

12. Hyams, *James Dean,* 7.

13. Quoted in Dalton, *James Dean: The Mutant King,* 158.

14. Holley, *James Dean,* 268.

15. The ten-line poem is reprinted in Riese, *The Unabridged James Dean,* 168.

16. Liz Sheridan, *Dizzy and Jimmy: My Life with James Dean* (New York: ReganBooks, 2000), 216; Bast quoted in Ronald Martinetti, *The James Dean Story: A Myth-Shattering Biography of an Icon* (New York: Birch Lane Press, 1995), 63.

17. Sheridan, *Dizzy and Jimmy,* 223–224.

18. Quoted in Dalton, *James Dean: The Mutant King,* 143, 151.

19. Quoted in Holley, *James Dean,* 201.

20. Spoto, *Rebel,* 208; "Moody New Star: Hoosier James Dean Excites Hollywood," *Life,* March 7, 1955, 125–128.

21. Hyams, *James Dean,* 185–186; *The Complete Poetical Works of James Whitcomb Riley* (Bloomington: Indiana University Press, 1993), 219, 221.

22. Martinetti, *The James Dean Story,* 105–106.

23. Quoted in Hyams, *James Dean,* 181.

24. "Moody New Star," 125–128, quotation at 128; For Stock's photographs that did not make it into the *Life* photo-essay, see Dennis Stock, *James Dean Revisited* (San Francisco: Chronicle Books, 1987).

25. Quoted in Spoto, *Rebel,* 235.

26. Ibid., 169; Holley, *James Dean,* 207; Martinetti, *The James Dean Story,* 94.

27. Quoted in Spoto, *Rebel,* 193.

28. Dalton, *James Dean: The Mutant King,* 80–81, 94–95; Martinetti, *The James Dean Story,* 158.

29. Winton and James Dean both quoted in Spoto, *Rebel,* 16, 24.

30. Holley, *James Dean,* 18–19; Dalton, *James Dean: The Mutant King,* 6–11; Martinetti, *The James Dean Story,* 6.

31. *Jimmy Dean on Jimmy Dean,* ed. Joseph Humphreys (London: Plexus, 1990), 10.

32. Quoted in Dalton, *James Dean: The Mutant King,* 8, 32.

33. Quoted in Spoto, *Rebel,* 35.

34. Riese, *The Unabridged James Dean,* 186.

35. Spoto, *Rebel,* 35–37, 49–50.

36. Many of Dean's athletic ribbons and grade reports, his high school yearbook, and other memorabilia are on display at the Fairmount Historical Museum.

37. Dalton, *James Dean: The Mutant King,* 36–38; Martinetti, *The James Dean Story,* 12–13.

38. The handwritten "My Case Study" is on display at the Fairmount Historical Museum. It is reproduced in Riese, *The Unabridged James Dean,* 407–408.

39. Quoted in ibid., 169.

40. Holley, *James Dean,* 31–32.

41. Spoto, *Rebel,* 76–78.

42. Dalton, *James Dean: The Mutant King,* 89.

43. Spoto, *Rebel,* 87–89; Holley, *James Dean,* 6.

44. On Dean's sexual orientation, see especially John Gilmore, who argues the case for his bisexuality in *Live Fast—Die Young: Remembering the Short Life of James Dean* (New York: Thunder's Mouth Press, 1997). Paul Alexander goes farther, asserting Dean's basic homosexuality in *Boulevard of Broken Dreams: The Life, Times, and Legend of James Dean* (New York: Viking, 1994).

45. Michael Gregg Michaud, *Sal Mineo: A Biography* (New York: Crown Archetype, 2010), 46, 51.

46. Quoted in Riese, *The Unabridged James Dean,* 126.

47. Dalton, *James Dean: The Mutant King,* 195.

48. Ray quoted in Dalton, *James Dean: American Icon,* 87.

49. Quoted in Holley, *James Dean,* 145.

50. Quoted in Howlett, *James Dean,* 9.

51. Ibid., 25–26, 75; Dalton, *James Dean: American Icon,* 190–191; Barney Hoskyns, *James Dean: Shooting Star* (London: Virgin Books, 1989), 47. On the many interrelationships among Clift, Brando, and Dean, see especially Graham McCann, *Rebel Males: Clift, Brando, and Dean* (New Brunswick, N.J.: Rutgers University Press, 1993). Brando, who ran into Dean at parties, resented his rise and referred to him as "the kid." He scorned the younger man's idolatry and mimicry of him, later remembering that Dean "had an idée fixe about me. Whatever I did, he did. He was always trying to get close to me. I'd listen to him talking to the answering service, asking for me, leaving messages. But I never spoke up. I never called him back." Stefan Kanfer, *Somebody: The Reckless Life and Remarkable Career of Marlon Brando* (New York: Alfred A. Knopf, 2008), 135, 144, quotation at 133.

52. Shawn Levy, *Paul Newman: A Life* (New York: Harmony Books, 2009), 200.

53. Ibid., 332; Riese, *The Unabridged James Dean,* 408.

Chapter Twelve: Meredith Willson

Willson's epigraph quotation comes from the *Mason City Globe-Gazette,* June 6, 1958.

1. *The Encyclopedia of New York City,* ed. Kenneth T. Jackson (New Haven: Yale University Press, 1995), 1167–1171; William R. Taylor, *In Pursuit of Gotham: Culture and Commerce in New York* (New York: Oxford University Press, 1992), 96–98; Taylor, ed., *Inventing Times Square: Commerce and Culture at the Crossroads of the World* (New York: Russell Sage Foundation, 1991), 36–50, 120–130.

2. Stuart Ostrow, *A Producer's Broadway Journey* (Westport, Conn.: Praeger, 1999), 1.

3. Brooks Atkinson, *Broadway* (New York: Macmillan, 1974), 432.

4. Quoted in Myrna Katz Frommer and Harvey Frommer, *It Happened on Broadway: An Oral History of the Great White Way* (New York: Harcourt, Brace, 1998), 37. See also William R. Taylor, "Broadway: The Place That Words Built," in Taylor, *Inventing Times Square,* 214–218.

5. Frommer and Frommer, *It Happened on Broadway,* 43–45.

6. There are two biographies of Willson: Bill Oates, *Meredith Willson— America's Music Man* (Bloomington, Ind.: Author House, 2005); and John C. Skipper, *Meredith Willson: The Unsinkable Music Man* (Mason City, Iowa: Savas, 2000). Throughout his life, Willson provided few clues that his childhood had been anything other than happy and carefree, but Skipper's book revealed that bitter resentment distanced the parents from each other, driving Rosalie to divorce her husband a year after the youngest child, Meredith, graduated from high school and quickly left home. His father soon married a woman half his age. Willson himself

published a sanitized autobiography, *And There I Stood with My Piccolo* (Garden City, N.Y.: Doubleday, 1948).

7. *Mason City Globe-Gazette,* March 3, 1940; June 17, 1946; February 15, 1958; Meredith Willson, *Eggs I Have Laid* (New York: Henry Holt, 1955), 29, 33, 42, 44.

8. *The Masonian,* high school yearbook, 1918 and 1919, unpaginated.

9. Quoted in *The Masonian,* 1919.

10. Leslie Raddatz, "Grade-A Iowa Ham with Plenty of Gravy," clipping, circa 1964, in Willson Collection, Mason City Public Library.

11. Clippings in Willson Collection.

12. "Meredith Willson," in *American National Biography,* 24 vols. (New York: Oxford University Press, 1999), 23: 548–550; "Meredith Willson," in *Current Biography: Who's News and Why, 1948,* ed. Anna Rothe and Constance Ellis, 9th annual cumulation (New York: H. W. Wilson, 1949), 473–474; "Meredith Willson," in David Ewen, *American Songwriters* (New York: H. W. Wilson, 1987), 437–440.

13. Gerald Nachman, *Raised on Radio* (New York: Pantheon Books, 1998), 486–487; "Long-Hair Music Gets a Haircut," *American Magazine,* July 1953, 26–27.

14. Oates, *Meredith Willson—America's Music Man,* 60, 87, 89, 92, 97; Willson, *And There I Stood with My Piccolo,* 254.

15. Meredith Willson, "Hometown Revisited: Mason City, Iowa," *Tomorrow,* October 1950, 18–21, reprinted in *Mason City Globe-Gazette,* November 25, 1950.

16. Willson, "Hometown Revisited."

17. *Mason City Globe-Gazette,* September 30, 1946.

18. Ibid., May 10, 1946.

19. Ibid., June 12, July 8, 1953.

20. Ibid., March 22, 1951; October 6, December 14, 1953. See also John E. Miller, "Meredith Willson: Iowa's 'Music Man' and 'Ambassador to All the World,'" *Iowa Heritage Illustrated* 82 (Winter 2001): 182–191.

21. Willson, *And There I Stood with My Piccolo,* 12, 19–20, 23.

22. Meredith Willson, *Who Did What to Fedalia?* (Garden City, N.Y.: Doubleday, 1952).

23. Meredith Willson, *"But He Doesn't Know the Territory"* (New York: J. P. Putnam's Sons, 1959), 18, 21.

24. Ibid., 15.

25. Ken Bloom, *Broadway: An Encyclopedia Guide to the History, People and Places of Times Square* (New York: Facts on File, 1991), 211–212.

26. Quoted in Stanley Green, *The World of Musical Comedy* (New York: A. S. Barnes, 1968), 342–343. See also John Chapman, "The Corn Belt's Noel Coward," *New York News,* January 12, 1958; "Once Upon a Time . . . ," *Newsweek,* December 30, 1957, 41.

27. Willson, *"But He Doesn't Know the Territory,"* 23–26.

28. Ibid., 23; Mark Steyn, *Broadway Babies Say Goodnight: Musicals Then and Now* (New York: Routledge, 1999), 172, 210.

29. Green, *The World of Musical Comedy,* 344.

30. Oates, *Meredith Willson—America's Music Man,* 113–118.

31. Meredith Willson, *The Music Man* (New York: G. P. Putnam's Sons, 1958), 27–28.

32. *Mason City Globe-Gazette,* June 12, 1958.

33. Willson, *"But He Doesn't Know the Territory,"* 55.

34. Ibid., 70–77.

35. "Pied Piper of Broadway," *Time,* July 21, 1958, 42.

36. Quoted in Willson, *"But He Doesn't Know the Territory,"* 81–82.

37. Ibid., 93–94.

38. Ibid., 84–94, 107.

39. Ibid., 45, 110–114, 118–119, 129–130; "Robert Preston: Success Story of the Year," *Look,* March 4, 1958, 53–54.

40. Willson, *"But He Doesn't Know the Territory,"* 132, 136–145, 158–181.

41. *New York Times,* December 20, 1957; *New York Herald Tribune,* December 20, 1957; *New York World-Telegram and Sun,* December 20, 1957.

42. Henry Hewes, for instance, called it "a pleasant musical of no great distinction" in "The Trombone Game," *Saturday Review,* January 4, 1958, 21.

43. David Ewen, *Complete Book of the American Musical Theater* (New York: Henry Holt, 1958), 380–381; "A Happy Oom-Pah on Broadway," *Life,* January 20, 1958, 103–108; "Pied Piper of Broadway," 42–46; Gerald Bordman, *American Musical Theater: A Chronicle,* 2d ed. (New York: Oxford University Press, 1992), 606–607.

44. "New Musical in Manhattan," *Time,* December 30, 1957, 63.

45. Willson, introduction to *Eggs I Have Laid,* 33; Art Fishbeck, interview by the author, Mason City, Iowa, June 7, 1994.

46. *Mason City Globe-Gazette,* June 6, 1958; December 31, 1960; Willson, *Eggs I Have Laid,* 33; Willson, *"But He Doesn't Know the Territory,"* 175; Chapman, "The Corn Belt's Noel Coward."

47. *Mason City Globe-Gazette,* August 11, 1914; January 4, 1915.

48. Harley Ransom, interview by the author, Mason City, Iowa, June 7, 1994. See also article in the *Mason City Globe-Gazette,* November 24, 1916, headlined "Boys Must Keep Out of Billiard Establishments."

49. In 1962, the town renamed the new, larger footbridge that had been erected across the stream the Meredith Willson Footbridge. There was also some serious discussion at the time about constructing a "River Cityland" on the model of Disneyland as a way of promoting tourism and generating business and tax dollars in the city. *Mason City Globe-Gazette,* June 15, 1962. Later, a $5 million complex with a reconstruction of Main Street and other historical exhibits was erected next to the old Willson home.

50. Chapman, "The Corn Belt's Noel Coward"; *Mason City Globe-Gazette*, January 20, 1958.

51. *Mason City Globe-Gazette*, June 11, 1958; June 19–21, 1962.

52. On the history of Mason City, see R. Duane Umbarger and Ruth M. Umbarger, comps., *Memories of Old Cerro Gordo: First Person and Contemporary Tales, 1850–1890* (Mason City, Iowa: Pioneer Museum and Historical Society of North Iowa, 1990); J. H. Wheeler, ed., *History of Cerro Gordo County, Iowa*, 2 vols. (Chicago: Lewis, 1910); Mason City Public Schools Elementary Department, *The Story of Mason City, Iowa* (Mason City, Iowa: Mason City Independent School District, 1964).

53. Catt, Quick, and MacNider all have entries in *American National Biography*.

54. *Mason City Globe-Gazette*, December 27, 1900; Ronald Schmitt, *Mason City: An Architectural Heritage* (Mason City, Iowa: Department of Community Development, 1977), 23.

55. *Mason City Globe-Gazette*, October 10, 1911; April 27, May 1, 1912; May 6, September 11, November 20, 1915.

56. Mason City Public Schools Elementary Department, *The Story of Mason City, Iowa*, 113.

57. *Mason City Globe-Gazette*, June 5, September 12, 1906; July 18, 20, 1911; June 5, 1912; March 25, 1915; Mason City Public Schools Elementary Department, *The Story of Mason City, Iowa*, 114–115.

58. Arthur M. Fischbeck, R. Duane Umbarger, and James Chimbidis, eds., *Remember When . . . Mason City: A Historical Album* (Mason City, Iowa: Pioneer Federal Savings and Loan Assn., 1985), 73–84.

59. *Mason City Globe-Gazette*, September 29, December 9, 1910; August 10, 1912; September 3, 1913; May 16, 1914; May 29, 1915; February 22, 1916; August 24, 1917.

Chapter Thirteen: Walt Disney

The epigraph comes from Watts's *The Magic Kingdom: Walt Disney and the American Way of Life* (Boston: Houghton Mifflin, 1997), 4, 7.

1. For all four quotations, see Neil Harris, "Expository Expositions: Preparing for the Theme Parks," in *Designing Disney's Theme Parks: The Architecture of Reassurance,* ed. Karal Ann Marling (Paris: Flammarion, 1997), 26.

2. Disney's fascinating personality and career have stimulated a plethora of biographical and critical works about him. In sketching his boyhood and career development, I have relied especially heavily on Watts, *The Magic Kingdom*; Neal Gabler, *Walt Disney: The Triumph of the American Imagination* (New York: Vintage, 2006); and Bob Thomas, *Walt Disney: An American Original* (New York: Pocket Books, 1980). A notable departure in Disney studies occurred in 1968 with the publication of Richard Schickel's *The Disney Version: The Life, Times, Art and*

Commerce of Walt Disney, 3d ed. (Chicago: Ivan R. Dee, 1997), which is a highly interpretive study of Disney's creative approach and cultural influence and inaugurated a new era of critical examination of Disney and his art, stirring controversy and response from a variety of writers.

3. All the standard sources document the problems encountered on opening day. See also accounts in the *Los Angeles Times,* July 15–20, 1955.

4. Quoted in Bob Thomas, *Building a Company: Roy O. Disney and the Creation of an Entertainment Empire* (New York: Hyperion, 1998), 195.

5. Quoted in Amy Boothe Green and Howard E. Green, *Remembering Walt: Favorite Memories of Walt Disney* (New York: Disney Editions, 1999), 153.

6. Gabler, *Walt Disney,* 537; Thomas, *Building a Company,* 198; quotation from Margaret J. King, "Disneyland and Walt Disney World: Traditional Values in Futuristic Form," *Journal of Popular Culture* 15 (Summer 1981): 116.

7. Gabler, *Walt Disney,* 537, 562; Thomas, *Walt Disney,* 302.

8. Nicholas Olsberg, foreword to Marling, *Designing Disney's Theme Parks,* 9.

9. Watts, *The Magic Kingdom,* 388–391.

10. Quoted in Gereon Zimmerman, "Walt Disney, Giant at the Fair," *Look,* February 11, 1964, 32.

11. Watts, *The Magic Kingdom,* 402; Disney quoted in Watts, *The Magic Kingdom,* 402, 403.

12. Gabler, *Walt Disney,* 12–13.

13. Quoted in ibid., 11.

14. Green and Green, *Remembering Walt,* 2. (The family actually moved to Marceline when Walt was four.)

15. Watts, *The Magic Kingdom,* 4.

16. Ibid., 148.

17. Gabler, *Walt Disney,* 463–464, 473, 485; Michael Barrier, *The Animated Man: A Life of Walt Disney* (Berkeley: University of California Press, 2007), 211–212.

18. Barrier, *The Animated Man,* 202–203, 231.

19. Quoted in Watts, *The Magic Kingdom,* 5–6.

20. Karal Ann Marling, "Imagineering the Disney Theme Parks," in Marling, *Designing Disney's Theme Parks,* 60–62, 89–90; Miles Orvell, *The Death and Life of Main Street: Small Towns in American Memory, Space, and Community* (Chapel Hill: University of North Carolina Press, 2012), 41.

21. King, "Disneyland and Walt Disney World," 116–140; Richard V. Francaviglia, "Main Street U.S.A.: A Comparison/Contrast of Streetscapes in Disneyland and Walt Disney World," *Journal of Popular Culture* 15 (Summer 1981): 141–156.

22. There is no space here to discuss how the actual EPCOT built under Roy Disney's direction veered almost entirely away from his brother Walt's conception of it. The development nearby of Celebration, Florida, very loosely reflected some of the latter's dreams of redesigning modern urban society to bring it somewhat in

line with his romantic memories of life growing up in small-town Missouri. On Celebration, see Andrew Ross, *The Celebration Chronicles: Life, Liberty, and the Pursuit of Property Value in Disney's New Town* (New York: Ballantine Books, 1999); Douglas Frantz and Catherine Collins, *Celebration, U.S.A.: Living in Disney's Brave New Town* (New York: Henry Holt, 1999).

Introduction to Section IV

1. "Smalltown, U.S.A.," *Newsweek*, July 8, 1963, 18, 20. For similar stories, see Peter Schrag, "Is Main Street Still There?" *Saturday Review*, January 17, 1970, 20–25; Eric Pooley, "The Great Escape," *Time*, December 8, 1997, 52–64; Jeff Glasser, "A Broken Heartland," *U.S. News and World Report*, May 7, 2001, 16–22.

Chapter Fourteen: Lawrence Welk
and Johnny Carson

Welk's epigraph quotation comes from "The American Spirit—as Lawrence Welk Sees It," *U.S. News and World Report* 82 (January 24, 1977), 69; Carson's, from "Johnny Carson," *Cosmopolitan* 204 (May 1988), 273.

1. John E. Miller, "From the Great Plains to L.A.: The Intersecting Paths of Lawrence Welk and Johnny Carson," *Virginia Quarterly Review* 79 (Spring 2003): 267–268.

2. Bill Davidson, "Nobody Likes Him Except the Public," *Look*, June 25, 1957, 115–117, quotation on 116.

3. Larry Wolters, "The Man Who Killed Caesar," *Chicago Tribune Magazine*, May 5, 1957, Lawrence Welk scrapbook, North Dakota Institute for Regional Studies, Fargo, North Dakota. The dozen or so massive scrapbooks held by the institute are an invaluable source on Welk's career, and most of the newspaper and magazine article references on Welk in this chapter derive from it.

4. Lawrence Welk, *Wunnerful, Wunnerful!*, with Bernice McGeehan (New York: Bantam, 1971), 334–338.

5. "Sales Music," *Television Age*, May 1956, Welk scrapbook.

6. Welk, *Wunnerful, Wunnerful!*, 346–348.

7. Both quoted in Davidson, "Nobody Likes Him Except the Public," 116.

8. Welk, *Wunnerful, Wunnerful!*, 351–354.

9. "Champagne with Welk," *Newsweek*, May 21, 1956, 75.

10. Quoted in "The Big Corn Crop," *Time*, May 21, 1956, 89.

11. Unless otherwise noted, most of my biographical information derives from Welk, *Wunnerful, Wunnerful!*

12. Ibid., 48–53.

13. Ibid., 3–4.

14. Ibid., 16–20.

15. Quoted in Hank Grant, "Welk Will Be Back to Clobber Opposition," *Miami Herald*, April 19, 1962, Welk scrapbook.

16. Welk, *Wunnerful, Wunnerful!*, 105–113.

17. Ibid., 167–168.

18. Mrs. Lawrence Welk [Fern Renner Welk], "'Mrs. Wunnerful Wunnerful' Tells Her Own Story," *Ladies Home Journal,* July 1973, 69–70.

19. Welk, *Wunnerful, Wunnerful!*, 195–204. One of the announcers in Pittsburgh was a neophyte in the business named Jack Paar. *Pittsburgh Press TV Graphic,* April 8, 1962, Welk scrapbook.

20. Welk, *Wunnerful, Wunnerful!*, 204–205; *TV Guide* cover story, January 21, 1956, Welk scrapbook.

21. Welk, *Wunnerful, Wunnerful!*, 214–229.

22. Ibid., 233–239.

23. Quoted in Erskine Johnson, "The Lawrence Welk Story," newspaper clipping [circa 1956], in Welk scrapbook.

24. Eleanor Harris, "Bachelor Cop," *American Weekly,* April 3, 1960; Jack O'Brien, "On the Air," *New York Journal-American,* January 20, 1965; Arthur J. Sasso, "Bubbles, Bounce, and Buffoonery," *Escapade,* May 1957, all in Welk scrapbooks.

25. Harry Harris, "Welk: Clean, Maybe Corny, but Not Complacent," *Philadelphia Inquirer,* July 17, 1960; "Pepin Man Recalls Hiring Lawrence Welk," *Winona (Minn.) News,* February 1962; "Lawrence Welk—North Dakota Heritage," *Minot (N.D.) News,* September 19, 1969; Lloyd Shearer, "Lawrence Welk: The King of Musical Corn," *Parade,* November 15, 1970; Welk quoted in "The Big Corn Crop," 89; "tango" quotation in Bill Fiset, "An Evening with Lawrence Welk," *Oakland (Calif.) Tribune,* July 1962, all in Welk scrapbook.

26. Quoted in William K. Schwienher, *Lawrence Welk: An American Institution* (Chicago: Nelson-Hall, 1980), 173.

27. All quoted in *Seattle Times,* October 19, 1958, Welk scrapbook.

28. Wolters, "The Man Who Killed Caesar."

29. Former Disney Mouseketeer Bobby Burgess (longtime dancer and singer with the Welk troupe), interview by the author, Sioux Falls, South Dakota, March 9, 2001.

30. "They Keep Us Going," *Tuscaloosa (Ala.) Graphic* [circa November 1968], Welk scrapbook.

31. Quoted in Nora Ephron, *And Now . . . Here's Johnny* (New York: Avon, 1968), 53–54.

32. Johnny Carson and Robert S. Fiveson, *Johnny Goes Home,* NBC movie (Carson Productions, February 15, 1982).

33. *Norfolk Daily News,* December 6, 1941; Marilee Thorburn, interview by the author, Norfolk, Nebraska, July 14, 1999.

34. On July 14–16, 1999, I had a chance to interview a teacher of Carson's and high school football coach Fred Egley in addition to five of Carson's former school-

mates (most from the class of '43): Chuck Howser, Marilee Thorburn, Bob Bottorff, Bob Sewell, and Jerry Huse, who by then was publisher of the local newspaper.

35. Norfolk Senior High School, *Milestone*, 1944, n.p.

36. Fred Egley, quoted in *Sioux Falls (S.D.) Argus Leader,* June 17, 1992.

37. Interviews with Carson's schoolmates.

38. Ronald L. Smith, *Johnny Carson: An Unauthorized Biography* (New York: St. Martin's Press, 1987), 17–20.

39. Quoted in J. Greg Smith, "The Great Carsoni," *Nebraskaland,* February 1965, 11.

40. Paul Corkery, *Carson: The Unauthorized Biography* (Ketchum, Idaho: Randt, 1987), 35–41.

41. Laurence Leamer, *King of the Night: The Life of Johnny Carson* (New York: St. Martin's Paperbacks, 2005), 58–63.

42. Quoted in "Heeeeere's Johnny," *Time,* June 26, 1989, 66.

43. Leamer, *King of the Night,* 72–73.

44. Ibid., 91–96.

45. Ibid., 104–109, 119–122.

46. Ed McMahon, *For Laughing Out Loud: My Life and Good Times* (New York: Warner Books, 1998).

47. Edward Linn, "The Soft-Sell, Soft-Shell World of Johnny Carson," *Saturday Evening Post,* December 22, 1962, 58.

48. "Midnight Idol," *Time,* May 19, 1967, 104; "Behind the Laughter," *People,* August 19, 1991, 74.

49. Kenneth Tynan, "Fifteen Years of the Salto Mortale," *New Yorker,* February 20, 1978, 74.

50. Quoted in Pete Martin, "I Call on Johnny Carson," *Saturday Evening Post,* May–June 1979, 77.

51. "Battle of the Talk Shows," *Newsweek,* September 1, 1969, 43; "Johnny Carson: Going Home," *People,* December 7, 1981, 71; "Johnny Carson," *People,* special issue, Summer 1989, 20.

52. Quoted in Martin, "I Call on Johnny Carson," 78.

53. Jay Cocks, "The Magician of 3,328 Midnights," *Time,* October 4, 1982, 63.

54. Quoted in Cleveland Amory, "Celebrity Register," *McCall's,* March 1963, 132.

55. Quoted in "Johnny Carson: Nighthood's New Prince," *Look,* April 13, 1963, 60.

56. Quoted in Amory, "Celebrity Register," 132.

57. Quoted in Martin, "I Call on Johnny Carson," 79.

58. Quoted in "Wherrrr's Johnny?" *Newsweek,* April 17, 1967, 119.

59. Quoted in Ernest Havemann, "24 Hours in the Life of Johnny Carson," *McCall's,* March 1965, 61.

60. Quoted in Ed McMahon, *Here's Johnny* (New York: Berkley Boulevard Books, 2006), xiv, 6–7.

61. Jefferson Graham, "Tonight: Last Time to Retire with Johnny," *USA Today,* May 22, 1992.

62. Bel Kaufman, "The Carson Appeal: Why He's Lasted So Long," *TV Guide,* July 14, 1984, 27; "*Today*'s Barbara Walters Interviews *Tonight*'s Johnny Carson," *Ladies Home Journal,* October 1967, 170.

63. *New York Times* quoted in Craig Tennis, *Johnny Tonight!* (New York: Pocket Books, 1980), 29; Kaufman, "The Carson Appeal," 20.

64. Quoted in Joan Barthel, "Here's Johnny! Out There," *Life,* January 23, 1970, 52.

65. Quoted in "Midnight Idol," 106.

66. "Johnny Carson," *Cosmopolitan,* 273.

67. Corkery, *Carson,* 16.

68. Harry F. Waters, "Stranger in the Night," *Newsweek,* May 25, 1992, 95.

69. *Norfolk Daily News,* September 8, 1964; July 9; 1966; May 21, 1976; "Goodbye, Johnny," *People,* February 7, 2005, 92; *Omaha World-Herald,* January 24, 2005.

70. Ronald L. Smith, "Johnny Carson: His Private Worlds," *McCall's,* September 1987, 141–144.

71. Quoted in Ephron, *And Now . . . Here's Johnny,* 51–52.

72. Quoted in *Omaha World-Herald,* October 17, 1988.

73. *Johnny Goes Home*; "Johnny Carson: Going Home," 71–76; *Norfolk Daily News,* October 21–24, 1981.

74. Quoted in *Norfolk Daily News,* October 22, 1981.

75. Quotations in ibid., March 5, September 16, 1982.

76. Quoted in Waters, "Stranger in the Night," 98.

77. *Norfolk Daily News,* October 21, 1981; quotation in Cocks, "The Magician of 3,328 Midnights," 63.

78. Quoted in Leamer, *King of the Night,* 391.

79. Quoted in Smith, *Johnny Carson,* 16.

80. Quoted in "Midnight Idol," 111.

81. Quoted in Barthel, "Here's Johnny! Out There," 51.

Chapter Fifteen: John Wooden
The epigraph comes from Wooden's *My Personal Best: Life Lessons from an All-American Journey,* with Steve Jamison (New York: McGraw-Hill, 2004), 91.

1. There were several different all-American teams chosen at the end of the year by various organizations and press agencies. The players who were named by the largest number of these organizations became the mythical consensus team.

2. In addition to an autobiography written toward the end of his coaching career, *They Call Me Coach,* as told to Jack Tobin (Waco, Tex.: Word Books, 1972),

Wooden related his personal story many times in a number of books written with a variety of collaborators. Biographies include Dwight Chapin and Jeff Prugh, *The Wizard of Westwood: Coach John Wooden and His UCLA Bruins* (Boston: Houghton Mifflin, 1973); Steve Bisheff, *John Wooden: An American Treasure* (Nashville, Tenn.: Cumberland House, 2004); and Neville L. Johnson, *The John Wooden Pyramid of Success*, rev. 2d ed. (Los Angeles: Cool Titles, 2004).

3. UCLA–North Carolina game brochure, no date, Sports Information files, UCLA Athletic Files, Los Angeles. The UCLA Athletic Department graciously allowed me to sift through an entire file drawer of materials on Wooden when I visited in 2001, and many of the articles cited in the footnotes derive from that foray.

4. John Wooden, *Wooden on Leadership,* with Steve Jamison (New York: McGraw-Hill, 2005), xiv, 7–8, 92, 217.

5. Herbert Warren Wind, "West of the Wabash," *New Yorker,* March 22, 1969, 95; Chapin and Prugh, *The Wizard of Westwood,* 58, 66; John Wooden, interview by the author, Encino, California, June 29, 2001.

6. On the Pyramid of Success, see Johnson, *The John Wooden Pyramid of Success*; Brian D. Biro, *Beyond Success: The 15 Secrets to Effective Leadership and Life Based on Legendary Coach John Wooden's Pyramid of Success* (New York: Berkley, 1997); and John Wooden and Steve Jamison, *The Wisdom of Wooden: My Century On and Off the Court* (New York: McGraw-Hill, 2010).

7. John Wooden, *Wooden: A Lifetime of Observations and Reflections On and Off the Court,* with Steve Jamison (Chicago: Contemporary Books, 1997), 167–170; Wooden, *My Personal Best,* 4–6.

8. Quoted in *John Wooden: Values, Victory, Peace of Mind, the Pyramid of Success,* PBS documentary (Santa Fe Ventures, Steve Jamison Productions, 2003), DVD.

9. Following in the footsteps of his father, Wooden emerged more and more as a moralist, especially during his final years. See John Wooden and Jay Carty, *Coach Wooden: One on One* (Ventura, Calif.: Regal Books, 2003).

10. Joe Jares, "The Two Faces of the Rubber Man," *Sports Illustrated,* January 6, 1969, 24.

11. Andrew Hill, *Be Quick—But Don't Hurry! Finding Success in the Teachings of a Lifetime,* with John Wooden (New York: Simon and Schuster, 2001), 171.

12. Wooden interview; Wooden, *They Call Me Coach,* 21–22.

13. Wooden, *They Call Me Coach,* 23.

14. Ibid., 24.

15. Ibid.

16. Quoted in Jares, "The Two Faces of the Rubber Man," 26.

17. Wooden, *They Call Me Coach,* 29–30.

18. Wooden interview.

19. Ibid.; Jares, "The Two Faces of the Rubber Man," 34–38.

20. Quoted in Phil Hoose, "Starting Lineup," *Indianapolis Monthly*, March 2000, 183.

21. Quoted in Chapin and Prugh, *The Wizard of Westwood*, 51.

22. Wooden, *They Call Me Coach*, 42–46.

23. Ibid., 49–55.

24. Todd Gould, *Pioneers of the Hardwood: Indiana and the Birth of Professional Basketball* (Bloomington: Indiana University Press, 1998), 55–57, 78, 90, 95.

25. Chapin and Prugh, *The Wizard of Westwood*, 58–61.

26. Ibid., 44–47.

27. Wooden, *They Call Me Coach*, 60.

28. Chapin and Prugh, *The Wizard of Westwood*, 66–69.

29. Alexander Wolff, "The Coach and His Champion," *Sports Illustrated*, April 3, 1989, 106.

30. John Sandbrook and Buddy Epstein, *The 25 Wooden Years, 1948–1973* (Los Angeles: UCLA Communications Board, 1972), 9; Wooden, *My Personal Best*, 92–93.

31. Quoted in Chapin and Prugh, *The Wizard of Westwood*, 80.

32. Wooden, *Wooden: A Lifetime of Observations and Reflections On and Off the Court*, 84, 91–92.

33. "Boom at UCLA," *Newsweek*, February 9, 1953, 74; Andrew Hamilton and John B. Jackson, *UCLA on the Move during Fifty Golden Years, 1919–1969* (n.p.: Regents of the University of California, 1969). See also various issues of *Southern Campus* (yearbook of UCLA).

34. Sandbrook and Epstein, *The 25 Wooden Years*, 15.

35. Melvin Durslag, "John's Secret Was Ability," *Los Angeles Herald-Examiner*, March 31, 1975; Mark Wheeler, "Headliner: John Wooden," *Main Event*, March, 1988, 88.

36. Skip Mylenski, "Living Legend," *Chicago Tribune*, March 5, 1995; Bill Dwyre, "At the Feet of the Master," *Los Angeles Times Magazine*, March 29, 1998.

37. Wooden, *My Personal Best*, 95–96.

38. Bisheff, *John Wooden*, 30, 203.

39. Wooden, *They Call Me Coach*, 82.

40. For year-by-year team rosters and records, see Sandbrook and Epstein, *The 25 Wooden Years*.

41. Quoted in "The Wooden Style," *Time*, February 12, 1973, 66.

42. Quoted in Curry Kirkpatrick, "UCLA: Simple, Awesomely Simple," *Sports Illustrated*, November 30, 1970, 42.

43. Wolff, "The Coach and His Champion," 98, 100.

44. Wooden's basic philosophies of coaching and of teaching are summed up in the book he wrote with Steve Jamison, *Wooden: A Lifetime of Observations and Reflections On and Off the Court*. See also Hill, *Be Quick—But Don't Hurry!*

45. Wind, "West of the Wabash," 99.

46. John Capouya, "John Wooden: Zen and the Art of Basketball," *Sport,* December 1986, 51.

47. Quoted in Arnold Hano, "Winning: With Nice Guys and a Pyramid of Principles," *New York Times Magazine,* December 2, 1973, 143.

48. Scott Ostler, "When the Wizard Reached the Point of No Return," *Los Angeles Times,* April 1, 1986.

49. Sid Ziff, "Wooden, the Intellect," *Los Angeles Times,* January 10, 1964.

50. On Jerry Norman's role in installing the full-court zone press, see Bisheff, *John Wooden,* 51–56; Chapin and Prugh, *The Wizard of Westwood,* 105–111; Nick Canepa, "The Whiz behind UCLA's Wizard," *San Diego Tribune,* March 30, 1989.

51. Bisheff, *John Wooden,* 88–90.

52. The several dozen interviews contained in Johnson's *The John Wooden Pyramid of Success* delineate most of the criticisms that have been raised against Wooden, but the vast majority of respondents are highly laudatory of the coach for his actions both on and off the basketball court.

53. Kirkpatrick, "UCLA," 43; Chapin and Prugh, *The Wizard of Westwood,* 271–273.

54. Quoted in Chapin and Prugh, *The Wizard of Westwood,* 262–268.

55. Johnson, *The John Wooden Pyramid of Success,* 114.

56. Quoted in Chapin and Prugh, *The Wizard of Westwood,* 37.

57. Hill, *Be Quick—But Don't Hurry!,* 18.

58. Lew Alcindor, "My Story," with Jack Olsen, *Sports Illustrated,* October 27, November 3, 10, 1969.

59. Kareem Abdul-Jabbar, *Kareem,* with Mignon McCarthy (New York: Warner Books, 1990), 139–140, 146.

60. Bill Walton, "John Wooden: Simply the Best," *UCLA Magazine,* Summer 2000, 27.

61. Abdul-Jabbar, *Kareem,* 142.

Chapter Sixteen: Ronald Reagan

The epigraph comes from Reagan's *Where's the Rest of Me?,* with Richard G. Hubler (New York: Karz Publishers, 1981), 17, 18.

1. Peter J. Wallison, *Ronald Reagan: The Power of Conviction and the Success of His Presidency* (Boulder, Colo.: Westview Press, 2004), 45. Though this aphorism worked well for him on the stump, he quickly discovered as governor of California and was frequently reminded later as president that political issues are often quite complex and that simple solutions are frequently nowhere to be found.

2. "Frustrated by the paradoxes of Reagan's personality, some who worked with him for years have given up trying to understand him," Dinesh D'Souza observes in *Ronald Reagan: How an Ordinary Man Became an Extraordinary Leader*

(New York: Free Press, 1997), 199. Edmund Morris, who received a $3 million advance and complete access to the White House to research and write his authorized biography of the fortieth president, eventually grew so exasperated with his inability to obtain a clear grasp of his subject that he resorted to using fictionalized characters to try to capture the man's elusive essence. *Dutch: A Memoir of Ronald Reagan* (New York: Random House, 1999).

3. Quoted in Lou Cannon, *President Reagan: The Role of a Lifetime* (New York: Simon and Schuster, 1991), 32.

4. Steven F. Hayward, *The Age of Reagan: The Fall of the Old Liberal Order, 1964–1980* (Roseville, Calif.: Prima, 2001), xvii.

5. Murray Edelman, *Politics as Symbolic Action: Mass Arousal and Quiescence* (New York: Academic Press, 1971), 83.

6. On Reagan's popularity while in office, see Larry M. Schwab, *The Illusion of a Conservative Reagan Revolution* (New Brunswick, N.J.: Transaction, 1991), 7, 33–34, 36, 38; and Will Bunch, *Tear Down This Myth: How the Reagan Legacy Has Distorted Our Politics and Haunts Our Future* (New York: Free Press, 2009), 98, 112. For more recent years, see Gallup Poll results for 2006 and 2010 in "Kennedy Still Highest-Rated Modern President, Nixon Lowest," *Gallup Politics,* December 6, 2010, www.gallup.com/poll/145064/kennedy-highest-rated-modern -president-nixon-lowest.aspx.

7. Cannon, *President Reagan,* 458, 460, 513.

8. Garry Wills, *Reagan's America: Innocents at Home* (Garden City, N.Y.: Doubleday, 1987), 145.

9. John Patrick Diggins, *Ronald Reagan: Fate, Freedom, and the Making of History* (New York: W. W. Norton, 2007), xvii.

10. Sean Wilentz, *The Age of Reagan: A History, 1974–2008* (New York: HarperCollins, 2008), 208; Jon Meacham, "American Dreamer," *Newsweek,* June 14, 2004, 26–27.

11. Cannon, *President Reagan,* 230–231; Benjamin Barber, "Celluloid Vistas: What the President's Dreams Are Made Of," *Harper's,* July 1985, 75.

12. Quoted in Anne Edwards, *Early Reagan* (New York: William Morrow, 1987), 562; *Public Papers of the Presidents of the United States: Ronald Reagan* (1983), 199; ibid., (1985), 55; ibid. (1988–1989), 1752; Paul S. Boyer, ed., *Reagan as President: Contemporary Views of the Man, His Politics, and His Policies* (Chicago: Ivan R. Dee, 1990), 102.

13. Quoted in Wallison, *Ronald Reagan,* 84.

14. Ronald Reagan, *An American Life* (New York: Pocket Books, 1990), 31.

15. Lou Cannon, *Governor Reagan: His Rise to Power* (New York: Public Affairs, 2003), 17–19; Edwards, *Early Reagan,* 47–50.

16. Reagan, *An American Life,* 21–22, "I learned" quotation on 22; Reagan, *Where's the Rest of Me?,* 7–9, "best raconteur" quotation on 9.

17. Reagan, *An American Life,* 33–34; Reagan, *Where's the Rest of Me?,* 7–8;

Haynes Johnson, *Sleepwalking through History: America in the Reagan Years* (New York: W. W. Norton, 1991), 43; William Kleinknecht, *The Man Who Sold the World: Ronald Reagan and the Betrayal of Main Street America* (New York: Nation Books, 2009), 38; Reagan quoted in *Motion Picture*, November 1937, quoted in Edwards, *Early Reagan*, 62–63.

18. Cannon, *Governor Reagan*, 14–16; D'Souza, *Ronald Reagan*, 38–39; Wills, *Reagan's America*, 16–26.

19. Reagan, *An American Life*, 22.

20. Edwards, *Early Reagan*, 63–72.

21. Reagan, *Where's the Rest of Me?*, 34–38; Cannon, *Governor Reagan*, 24–33; Wills, *Reagan's America*, 36–52.

22. Reagan, *Where's the Rest of Me?*, 38.

23. Reagan, *An American Life*, 69–75; Reagan, *Where's the Rest of Me?*, 47–69.

24. Reagan, *An American Life*, 73; Reagan, *Where's the Rest of Me?*, 66; Wills, *Reagan's America*, 109.

25. Marc Eliot, *Reagan: The Hollywood Years* (New York: Harmony Books, 2008), 41–51; Stephen Vaughn, *Ronald Reagan in Hollywood: Movies and Politics* (New York: Cambridge University Press, 1994), 25–28.

26. Eliot, *Reagan*, 52–53, 62–63, 65–67; Vaughn, *Ronald Reagan in Hollywood*, 30–32, 36–38.

27. Eliot, *Reagan*, 110–118, 136–146; Wills, *Reagan's America*, 262.

28. Vaughn, *Ronald Reagan in Hollywood*; Eliot, *Reagan*.

29. Cannon, *Governor Reagan*, 103–107, 113; Wills, *Reagan's America*, 262–278, 284–285; Eliot, *Reagan*, 262–266, 305–320.

30. Reagan, *An American Life*, 129.

31. Quoted in Cannon, *Governor Reagan*, 108.

32. Reagan, *Where's the Rest of Me?*, 251–261.

33. Thomas W. Evans, *The Education of Ronald Reagan: The General Electric Years and the Untold Story of His Conversion to Conservatism* (New York: Columbia University Press, 2006), 38–56, 230–237.

34. Ibid., 57–97; Reagan, *Where's the Rest of Me?*, 263–269; Wills, *Reagan's America*, 279–288.

35. Reagan, *An American Life*, 138–143. Reagan had officially switched parties only in 1962.

36. Allen J. Matusow, *The Unraveling of America: A History of Liberalism in the 1960s* (New York: Harper and Row, 1984).

37. On the rise of the conservative movement, see, for example, Sidney Blumenthal, *The Rise of the Counter-Establishment: The Conservative Ascent to Political Power* (1986; repr., New York: Union Square Press, 2008); Lisa McGirr, *Suburban Warriors: The Origins of the New American Right* (Princeton: Princeton University Press, 2001); Mary C. Brennan, *Turning Right in the Sixties: The Conservative Capture of the GOP* (Chapel Hill: University of North Carolina Press, 1995); Kurt

Schuparra, *Triumph of the Right: The Rise of the California Conservative Movement, 1945–1966* (Armonk, N.Y.: M. E. Sharpe, 1998).

38. Kleinknecht, *The Man Who Sold the World,* 48–52; Bob Colacello, *Ronnie and Nancy: Their Path to the White House, 1911–1980* (New York: Warner Books, 2004), 325–344; Cannon, *Governor Reagan,* 132–134.

39. Cannon, *Governor Reagan,* 134–139; Wills, *Reagan's America,* 293–298.

40. Cannon, *President Reagan,* 526–528.

41. Quoted in Oriana Fallaci, *Interview with History* (Boston: Houghton Mifflin, 1976), 41.

42. "Key to the [conservative] movement's success," writes Robert A. Goldberg, "was its identification with the American West, past and present, imagined and real." "The Western Hero in Politics: Barry Goldwater, Ronald Reagan, and the Rise of the American Conservative Movement," in *The Political Culture of the New West,* ed. Jeff Roche (Lawrence: University Press of Kansas, 2008), 14. On the myth of the western hero in American culture, see William W. Savage Jr., *The Cowboy Hero: His Image in American History and Culture* (Norman: University of Oklahoma Press, 1979); and Robert G. Athern, *The Mythic West in Twentieth-Century America* (Lawrence: University Press of Kansas, 1986).

43. Johnson, *Sleepwalking through History,* 49.

44. Kirkpatrick Sale, *Power Shift: The Rise of the Southern Rim and Its Challenge to the Eastern Establishment* (New York: Random House, 1975).

45. Cannon, *Governor Reagan.*

46. Evaluations of Reagan's presidency include Boyer, *Reagan as President;* John W. Sloan, *The Reagan Effect: Economics and Presidential Leadership* (Lawrence: University Press of Kansas, 1999); W. Elliot Brownlee and Hugh Davis Graham, eds., *The Reagan Presidency: Pragmatic Conservatism and Its Legacies* (Lawrence: University Press of Kansas, 2003); and Steven F. Hayward, *The Age of Reagan: The Conservative Counterrevolution, 1980–1989* (New York: Crown Forum, 2009).

47. Wilentz, *The Age of Reagan;* Diggins, *Ronald Reagan.* With regard to polls of historians, political scientists, and other scholars and experts, surveys by the Siena College Research Institute in 1982, 1990, 1994, 2002, and 2010 produced ratings for Reagan ranging from number 16 to number 20 among the presidents who had occupied the office by the time the surveys were taken. Arthur Schlesinger Jr.'s poll of historians in 1996 ranked Reagan number 25, and a poll that same year by William J. Ridings Jr. and Stuart B. McIver placed him one slot lower. On the other hand, C-SPAN polls in 1999 and 2009 ranked him number 11 and number 9, and *Wall Street Journal* polls in 2000 and 2005 ranked him at number 8 and number 6.

48. Blumenthal, *The Rise of the Counter-Establishment,* 255; Wilentz, *The Age of Reagan,* 134–135.

49. See Kleinknecht, *The Man Who Sold the World;* and Robert Putnam, *Bowling Alone: The Collapse and Revival of American Community* (New York: Simon and Schuster, 2000).

Chapter Seventeen: Sam Walton

The epigraph comes from the *Columbia Missourian*, April 7, 1992.

1. Wal-Mart executives officially changed the spelling of the company's name to "Walmart" in 2008, but this chapter will continue to use the traditional spelling, which was used during the time span covered by this book.

2. *Walmart 2010 Annual Report*, available online at www.walmartstores.com /sites/annualreport/2010/. U.S. net sales were $258 billion in 3,708 Wal-Mart retail units. In addition, 596 Sam's Club units sold $100 billion worth, and 4,112 international units in fourteen countries had sales of $270 billion. Although the last group accounted for 49 percent of all the stores, they generated only 25 percent of all net sales.

3. Don Soderquist, *The Wal-Mart Way: The Inside Story of the Success of the World's Largest Company* (Nashville, Tenn.: Nelson Business, 2005), 10; Jerry Useem, "One Nation under Wal-Mart," *Fortune*, March 3, 2003, 64–76; "Global High Performers," *Forbes*, April 16, 2007, 143–144, 148; Nelson Lichtenstein, ed., *Wal-Mart: The Face of Twenty-First Century Capitalism* (New York: New Press, 2006), x. Quotation from Lichtenstein, *The Retail Revolution: How Wal-Mart Created a Brave New World of Business* (New York: Metropolitan Books, 2009), 4.

4. *Sam Walton, Made in America: My Story*, with John Huey (New York: Doubleday, 1992), 50.

5. Ibid., 21–22.

6. Ibid., 160.

7. Soderquist, *The Wal-Mart Way*, 28.

8. Robert Slater, *The Wal-Mart Decade: How a New Generation of Leaders Turned Sam Walton's Legacy into the World's #1 Company* (New York: Portfolio, 2003), 39.

9. Vance H. Trimble, *Sam Walton, Founder of Wal-Mart: The Inside Story of America's Richest Man* (New York: Signet, 1991), 13–20; Bob Ortega, *In Sam We Trust: The Untold Story of Sam Walton and How Wal-Mart Is Devouring America* (New York: Random House, 1998), 16–18.

10. Trimble, *Sam Walton, Founder of Wal-Mart*, 24–25; quotations from Walton, *Sam Walton, Made in America*, 3–4.

11. Walton, *Sam Walton, Made in America*, 11.

12. Ibid., 12–13; Trimble, *Sam Walton, Founder of Wal-Mart*, 25–28.

13. Walton, *Sam Walton, Made in America*, 68.

14. Hickman High School *Cresset* (1936), unpaginated; "Hickman Grads Recall Legacy of Sam Walton," *Columbia Tribune*, April 6, 1992; Austin Teutsch, *The Sam Walton Story: An Inside Look at the Man and His Empire*, rev. ed. (New York: Berkley, 1992), 32–40; Trimble, *Sam Walton, Founder of Wal-Mart*, 31–34; Walton, *Sam Walton, Made in America*, 13–14.

15. University of Missouri *Savitar* (1940), 74, 116, 124, 126, 129, 190, 266; "Sam Walton is '40 Class President," *Missouri Alumnus*, June 1940, 11; Walton, *Sam Walton, Made in America*, 14–16.

16. Walton, *Sam Walton, Made in America,* 17–18; Trimble, *Sam Walton, Founder of Wal-Mart,* 37–40.

17. Walton, *Sam Walton, Made in America,* 17.

18. Trimble, *Sam Walton, Founder of Wal-Mart,* 39–43; Ortega, *In Sam We Trust,* 22–23.

19. Trimble, *Sam Walton, Founder of Wal-Mart,* 50–51; Ortega, *In Sam We Trust,* 23–34.

20. Walton, *Sam Walton, Made in America,* 19–22; Trimble, *Sam Walton, Founder of Wal-Mart,* 51–55.

21. Walton, *Sam Walton, Made in America,* 22–28.

22. Ibid., 47.

23. Ibid., 78.

24. Trimble, *Sam Walton, Founder of Wal-Mart,* 58–61.

25. Ibid., 68–74.

26. Walton, *Sam Walton, Made in America,* 173–175; Ortega, *In Sam We Trust,* 26; Thorstein Veblen, "The Country Town" (1923) in *The Portable Veblen,* ed. Max Lerner (New York: Penguin Books, 1976), 409–416.

27. Walton, *Sam Walton, Made in America,* 32–33.

28. Trimble, *Sam Walton, Founder of Wal-Mart,* 81; Ortega, *In Sam We Trust,* 29–30.

29. Trimble, *Sam Walton, Founder of Wal-Mart,* 93–94.

30. For some excellent studies of the region, see Vance Rudolph, *The Ozarks: An American Survival of Primitive Society* (New York: Vanguard Press, 1931); and Charles Morrow Wilson, *Backwoods America* (Chapel Hill: University of North Carolina Press, 1935).

31. Brooks Blevins, "A Social History of the Arkansas Ozarks" (PhD dissertation, Auburn University, 1999), 7–11, 15, 25, 46–49, 56–58, 61–67, 142–144, 149–159; Benton County Heritage Committee, *History of Benton County, Arkansas* (Rogers, Ark.: Benton County Heritage Committee, 1991), 7–11; J. Dickson Black, *History of Benton County* (n.p.: printed by the author, 1975), 23, 53–54, 59–60, 75–78, 83; Marilyn Collins, *Rogers: The Town the Frisco Built* (Charleston, S.C.: Arcadia, 2002), 85, 91, 99; Bethany Moreton, *To Serve God and Wal-Mart: The Making of Christian Free Enterprise* (Cambridge, Mass.: Harvard University Press, 2009), 10–11.

32. Jeannie M. Whayne et al., *Arkansas: A Narrative History* (Fayetteville: University of Arkansas Press, 2002), chap. 13; Bethany E. Moreton, "It Came from Bentonville: The Agrarian Origins of Wal-Mart Culture," in Lichtenstein, *Wal-Mart,* 80; Moreton, *To Serve God and Wal-Mart,* 49–65.

33. John Dicker, *The United States of Wal-Mart* (New York: Jeremy P. Tarcher/Penguin Books, 2005), 42–43.

34. Sandra S. Vance and Roy V. Scott, *Wal-Mart: A History of Sam Walton's Retail Phenomenon* (New York: Twayne, 1994), 24–29; Franklin W. Gilchrist, "The

Discount House and Channels of Distribution," in *Changing Patterns in Retailing: Readings on Current Trends,* ed. John W. Wingate and Arnold Corbin (Homewood, Ill.: Richard D. Irwin, 1956), 113–123; Susan Strasser, "Woolworth to Wal-Mart: Mass Merchandising and the Changing Nature of Consumption," in Lichtenstein, *Wal-Mart,* 31–56.

35. Trimble, *Sam Walton, Founder of Wal-Mart,* 109–111.

36. Ibid., 112–115, 121, 148–149; J. Dickson Black, *Bentonville and Its Bank: "Growing Together for 50 Years"* (Bentonville, Ark.: Bank of Bentonville, 1981), 88–89.

37. Trimble, *Sam Walton, Founder of Wal-Mart,* 122–123; quotation in Walton, *Sam Walton, Made in America,* 50.

38. Ortega, *In Sam We Trust,* 55; Lichtenstein, *The Retail Revolution,* 88–95.

39. Moreton, "It Came from Bentonville," 80–81.

40. Walton, *Sam Walton, Made in America,* 53–66; Ortega, *In Sam We Trust,* 58–59.

41. Ortega, *In Sam We Trust,* 58–62; Trimble, *Sam Walton, Founder of Wal-Mart,* 130–155.

42. Vance and Scott, *Wal-Mart,* 46–48.

43. Soderquist, *The Wal-Mart Way,* 23; Ortega, *In Sam We Trust,* 72.

44. Charles Fishman, *The Wal-Mart Effect: How the World's Most Powerful Company Really Works—and How It's Transforming the American Economy* (New York: Penguin Books, 2006), 46.

45. Vance and Scott, *Wal-Mart,* 79–80.

46. Thomas O. Graff and Dub Ashton, "Spatial Diffusion of Wal-Mart: Contagious and Reverse Hierarchical Elements," *Professional Geographer* 46 (February 1994): 19–29; Ortega, *In Sam We Trust,* 75; quotation in Walton, *Sam Walton, Made in America,* 110.

47. Lichtenstein, *The Retail Revolution,* 36–38.

48. Walton, *Sam Walton, Made in America,* 110–111.

49. Vance and Scott, *Wal-Mart,* 58.

50. Trimble, *Sam Walton, Founder of Wal-Mart,* 236–237; "Mid-'70s Marketing Changes Put Wal-Mart on the Road to Success," *Arkansas Gazette,* March 3, 1983.

51. Walton, *Sam Walton, Made in America,* 127–128.

52. Ortega, *In Sam We Trust,* 85–93; Trimble, *Sam Walton, Founder of Wal-Mart,* chap. 22; Lichtenstein, *The Retail Revolution,* 118–148; Anthony Bianco, *The Bully of Bentonville: How the High Cost of Wal-Mart's Everyday Low Prices Is Hurting America* (New York: Doubleday, 2006), 54–57, 227–238; Cora Daniels, "Up against the Wal-Mart," *Fortune* 149 (May 17, 2004), 112–120; John Dicker, "Union Blues at Wal-Mart," *Nation* 275 (July 8, 2002), 14–18.

53. John Huey, "Wal-Mart: Will It Take Over the World?" *Fortune* 119 (January 30, 1989), 55; Trimble, *Sam Walton, Founder of Wal-Mart,* 234–236.

54. Misha Petrovic and Gary G. Hamilton, "Making Global Markets: Wal-Mart

and Its Suppliers," in Lichtenstein, *Wal-Mart*, 115; Slater, *The Wal-Mart Decade*, 86; Trimble, *Sam Walton, Founder of Wal-Mart*, 352, 372.

55. Walton, *Sam Walton, Made in America*, 110–111; Vance and Scott, *Wal-Mart*, 83–95; Dicker, *The United States of Wal-Mart*, 68–70; "20 That Made History: Sam Walton Explains the Final Frontier," *Fortune* 151 (June 27, 2005), 82.

56. See, for example, Walton, *Sam Walton, Made in America*, 198–201 and Trimble, *Sam Walton, Founder of Wal-Mart*, 252–254, 262, 357–358.

57. Fishman, *The Wal-Mart Effect*; Art Harris, "America's Richest Man Lives . . . Here?" *Washington Post*, November 17, 1985; "Family's Worth $9 Billion but He Drives an Old Pickup Truck and She Shops at Local Discount Store," *National Enquirer* 64 (November 7, 1989), 6.

58. The debate over the "Wal-Mart effect" has continued to intensify in recent years. For a sampling of criticism, see, in addition to sources already mentioned, Bill Quinn, *How Wal-Mart Is Destroying America (and the World) and What You Can Do about It* (Berkeley, Calif.: Ten Speed Press, 2000); Al Norman, *The Case against Wal-Mart* (Atlantic City, N.J.: Raphel Marketing, 2004); Gregg Spotts, *Wal-Mart: The High Cost of Low Price* (New York: Disinformation, 2005); Liza Featherstone, *Selling Women Short: The Landmark Battle for Women's Rights at Wal-Mart* (New York: Basic Books, 2004); Avis Devon Hammond Jr., *What's Wrong at Wal-Mart?* (Las Vegas: Hamco Books, 1997); Julie Pierce, *"The Walmart Way" Not Sam's Way: An Associate View from Inside* (N.p: Printed by the author, 2006).

59. In addition to sources already listed, books that take a positive view of the company's impact include Richard Vedder and Wendell Cox, *The Wal-Mart Revolution: How Big-Box Stores Benefit Consumers, Workers, and the Economy* (Washington, D.C.: American Enterprise Institute, 2006); Robert Slater, *The Wal-Mart Triumph* (New York: Penguin Books, 2003); Michael Bergdahl, *What I Learned from Sam Walton* (Hoboken, N.J.: John Wiley, 2004).

60. "How Wal-Mart Hits Main Street," *U.S. News and World Report* 106 (March 13, 1989), 53–55; Karen Blumenthal, "Arrival of Discounter Tears the Civic Fabric of Small-Town Life," *Wall Street Journal*, April 14, 1987; Geoffrey L. Moser quoted in Jon Bowermaster, "When Wal-Mart Comes to Town," *New York Times Magazine*, April 2, 1989, 28–30, 66–68; E. P. Copeland quoted in Jacalyn Carfagno, "Good or Bad, Wal-Mart's Presence Felt by Small Towns," *Arkansas Gazette*, September 3, 1989. See also Barnaby J. Feder, "Message for Mom and Pop: There's Life after Wal-Mart," *New York Times*, October 24, 1993; "MU Researcher: Wal-Mart Helps Local Economies," *Columbia Tribune*, April 27, 2004; Bianco, *The Bully of Bentonville*, 141–146; Dicker, *The United States of Wal-Mart*, 173; Fishman, *The Wal-Mart Effect*, 140–146, 153–157; Ortega, *In Sam We Trust*, 181–183; Trimble, *Sam Walton, Founder of Wal-Mart*, chap. 24.

61. Walton, *Sam Walton, Made in America*, 179.

62. Moreton, *To Serve God and Wal-Mart*, 37–38. During the year Wal-Mart

was founded, I graduated from high school in Monett, Missouri, home of store number forty-eight. Three other high schools in Monett's "Big Nine" athletic conference were located in towns hosting stores in the first fifty Wal-Mart locations.

63. Walton quoted in Mukul Pandya and Robbie Shell, *Lasting Leadership: What You Can Learn from the Top 25 Business People of Our Times* (Upper Saddle River, N.J.: Wharton School Publishers, 2005), 140–141.

64. Walton, *Sam Walton, Made in America,* 177–179. In 2004, CEO Lee Scott launched a major public relations offensive in defense of Wal-Mart's methods of operation and its impact on workers, consumers, local communities, and the economy. Andy Serwer, "Bruised in Bentonville," *Fortune,* April 18, 2005, 84–89; Robert Burner, "Can Wal-Mart Fit into a White Hat?" *Business Week,* October 3, 2005, 94–96; "Will Wal-Mart's Reforms Pay Off?," *St. Louis Post-Dispatch,* October 29, 2005. See also "Afterword: Inside the Home Office," in Fishman, *The Wal-Mart Effect,* 261–283.

Coda: Small-Town Boys and
the American Dream

1. Malcolm Gladwell, *Outliers: The Story of Success* (New York: Little, Brown, 2008), 20–33.

2. James Truslow Adams, *The Epic of America* (Boston: Little, Brown, 1931), 415–416. The evolution of the idea is traced in Jim Cullen, *The American Dream: A Short History of an Idea That Shaped a Nation* (New York: Oxford University Press, 2003); Lawrence R. Samuel, *The American Dream: A Cultural History* (Syracuse, N.Y.: Syracuse University Press, 2012); Lionel Trilling, *The Liberal Imagination: Essays on Literature and Society* (New York: Viking, 1950), 252.

3. Quoted in Richard Reeves, *President Reagan: The Triumph of Imagination* (New York: Simon and Schuster, 2005), 56.

Index

American Economic Association, 244, 247, 250
American Gothic, 178, 179, 194, 281, 309
American Historical Association, 29, 35, 36, 37
American Historical Epic, The, 178
American Indians, 8, 31, 38, 306, 307, 438
American Legion, 265, 306
American Scene painting, 172, 176, 179, 188, 189
Americans for Democratic Action, 400
American Songbag, The, 152
American Veterans Committee, 400–401
America Today, 178, 185
Ames (IA), 98
Anaheim (CA), 311
An American in Art, 179
An American Life, 395
Anamosa (IA). *See* Grant Wood
An Artist in America, 179, 185, 192
Anderson, Sherwood, 9, 126, 133, 137, 141
Andress, Ursula, 291
And There I Stood with My Piccolo, 299
Angeli, Pier, 290
Anger, Kenneth, 289
animated cartoons, 317–319, 322
Annenberg, Walter, 405
Anoka (MN), 13
Anthony, Ray, 337
anti-Catholicism, 279
anti-Communism, 393, 400, 401
anti-Semitism, 85, 146, 176, 188, 279
Aragon Ballroom (Chicago), 345
Aragon Ballroom (Santa Monica), 337–338, 340.
Arend, Ferold, 426
Arkansas, 95, 411, 412, 418, 421–422, 428, 434
Armed Forces Radio Service, 297
Army, U.S., 64, 200, 284, 286, 297, 399
Art as Experience, 187
Art Digest, 188
Art Front, 177
Arts of Life in America, The, 185

Ashbery, John, 173
Ashby, LeRoy, 70
ashcan school of art, 184
Asia, 166, 214
Asian Americans, 38
assembly line, 73, 83–84
Atherton, Lewis, 1, 46
Atkinson, Brooks, 295, 304
Atlanta (GA), 100, 109, 118
Atlantic Ocean, 54, 264
Atlantic-Yellowstone-Pacific Highway, 307
Auburn University, 111
Audacity of Hope, The, 438
Australia, 61
automobiles
    accidents, 174, 276
    advertising, 338
    and art, 185
    and community, 7
    and Detroit, 80–82
    manufacturing, 308
    and rural America, 186–188, 420
    and social change, 63, 68, 197
    and urban sprawl, 322
    See also Henry Ford; Model T Ford
Avoca (IA), 349, 355, 363
Avoca Public Library, 363

Babbitt, 139–140
Bacon, Irving, 91
Baigell, Matthew, 186
Baird, Sharon, 312
Baltimore (MD), 17, 19, 35, 36, 45, 46
Baltimore Sun, 69
Bankhead, Tallulah, 297
Bank of Bentonville, 424
Baptism in Kansas, 178, 195
Baptist church, 245
Barber, Benjamin, 392
Barker, Lester, 89
Barnum, P. T., 174, 419
Barrere, Georges, 295
Bartell, Dick, 262
Barton, William E. 164
baseball, 10, 350
    history of, 258–259